Email Security with Cisco IronPort

AF683722

Chris Porter

Cisco Press

800 East 96th Street

Indianapolis, IN 46240

Email Security with Cisco IronPort

Chris Porter

Published by:
Cisco Press
800 East 96th Street
Indianapolis, IN 46240 USA

Printed in the United States of America 1 2 3 4 5 6 7 8 9 0

First Printing April 2012

Library of Congress Cataloging-in-Publication data is on file.

ISBN-13: 978-1-58714-292-5

ISBN-10: 1-58714-292-9

Warning and Disclaimer

This book is designed to provide information about network security. Every effort has been made to make this book as complete and as accurate as possible, but no warranty or fitness is implied.

The information is provided on an "as is" basis. The author, Cisco Press, and Cisco Systems, Inc., shall have neither liability nor responsibility to any person or entity with respect to any loss or damages arising from the information contained in this book or from the use of the discs or programs that may accompany it.

The opinions expressed in this book belong to the author and are not necessarily those of Cisco Systems, Inc.

Trademark Acknowledgments

All terms mentioned in this book that are known to be trademarks or service marks have been appropriately capitalized. Cisco Press or Cisco Systems, Inc., cannot attest to the accuracy of this information. Use of a term in this book should not be regarded as affecting the validity of any trademark or service mark.

Corporate and Government Sales

The publisher offers excellent discounts on this book when ordered in quantity for bulk purchases or special sales, which may include electronic versions and/or custom covers and content particular to your business, training goals, marketing focus, and branding interests. For more information, please contact: U.S. Corporate and Government Sales 1-800-382-3419 corpsales@pearsontechgroup.com

For sales outside of the U.S., please contact: International Sales international@pearsoned.com

Feedback Information

At Cisco Press, our goal is to create in-depth technical books of the highest quality and value. Each book is crafted with care and precision, undergoing rigorous development that involves the unique expertise of members from the professional technical community.

Readers' feedback is a natural continuation of this process. If you have any comments regarding how we could improve the quality of this book, or otherwise alter it to better suit your needs, you can contact us through email at feedback@ciscopress.com. Please make sure to include the book title and ISBN in your message.

We greatly appreciate your assistance.

Publisher: Paul Boger

Associate Publisher: Dave Dusthimer

Executive Editor: Brett Bartow

Managing Editor: Sandra Schroeder

Project Editor: Mandie Frank

Editorial Assistant: Vanessa Evans

Cover Designer: Sandra Schroeder

Composition: Mark Shirar

Business Operation Manager, Cisco Press: Anand Sundaram

Manager Global Certification: Erik Ullanderson

Development Editor: Eleanor C. Bru

Copy Editor: Sheri Cain

Technical Editors: Ben Hartwell, Tim Draegen

Proofreader: Sarah Kearns

Indexer: Tim Wright

About the Author

Chris Porter was one of the first field systems engineers hired by IronPort Systems in 2003, around the time of the launch of the ESA C-series product. He has served as systems engineer, SE manager, and now technical solutions architect at Cisco, who acquired IronPort in June 2007.

Chris has been involved in planning, deploying, and configuring Email Security Appliances (ESA) at hundreds of organizations, with a chief role in both pre-sales engagements and post-sales support. His experience has made him a trusted voice in ESA product design decisions.

Chris holds a bachelor's and master's degree in Computer Science from Stevens Institute of Technology in Hoboken, NJ, and a CCNA certification. Chris is currently a technical solutions architect at Cisco, specializing in content security and the IronPort email and web-security products and services.

About the Technical Reviewers

Tim Draegen has a long history in the email space. As Agari's director of technical strategy, Tim is responsible for technical innovate and advocacy. Tim works closely with numerous financial institutions, ISPs, and enterprises to design, develop, and adopt the technologies that enable secure, authentication-based email channels. Tim chairs the OTA Email Authentication Committee and is tasked with making the value of email authentication clear to everyone—not just email gurus or security professionals. Prior to Agari, Tim spent a dozen years as a software engineer and security researcher, including a stint at Cisco/IronPort, where in late 2004, he recognized the importance of email authentication and implemented DomainKeys, setting the stage for enterprise-grade protection of email domains and PayPal's successful 2007–2008 DMARC prototype.

Benjamin Hartwell started with IronPort Systems in 2002 and remained associated with IronPort/Cisco until the fall of 2011. Ben tested, managed, or was a technical advisor for the ESA from version 2.0 to version 8.0. Ben has been involved in quality assurance for 13 years, testing both consumer and enterprise products. He is currently continuing work in the security space, focusing on web security.

Acknowledgments

I had the pleasure of working with a fantastic team of editors on this, my first technical book. The team at Pearson has been extraordinary, and has my sincerest thanks. Ellie Bru guided me through the technical-review process and provided great feedback on content and layout. Thank you to Mandie Frank, who managed this book through its iterations in final editing. Special thanks go to Brett Bartow, without whose encouragement and guidance, this book would not have even been started.

I owe a great debt to my technical editors, Ben Hartwell and Tim Draegen. Their long experience and technical expertise shaped this guide into the final product you see here. They questioned everything, asked for clarification on my statements, and suggested better examples. This book is all the better because of their work. Thank you again!

For more than eight years, I've been a part of an extraordinary team, first at IronPort Systems and now in Security at Cisco. I've never worked harder or had more fun at a job. It has been an honor serving with such an intelligent, motivated, and downright crazy group of individuals. My thanks to everyone involved with designing, building, selling, and supporting the ESA product.

Contents at a Glance

Contents

Icons Used in This Book

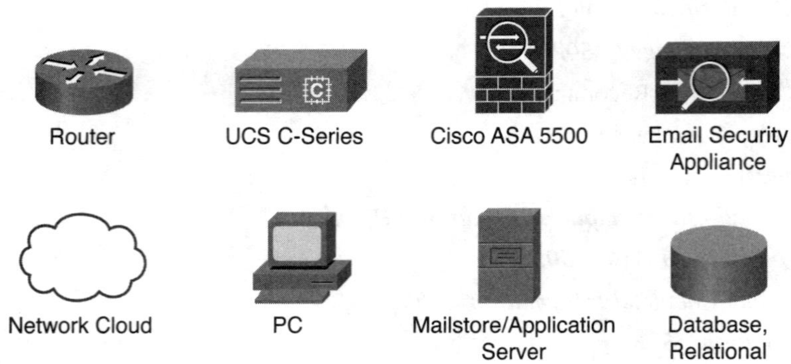

Command Syntax Conventions

The conventions used to present command syntax in this book are the same conventions used in the AsyncOS Configuration Guide. The Configuration Guide describes these conventions as follows:

- Boldface indicates commands and keywords that are entered literally, as shown. In actual configuration examples and output (not general command syntax), boldface indicates commands that are manually input by the user (such as a status command).
- Italics indicate new terms, emphasized words, and command-line variables; for command-line variables, the italicized text is a placeholder for the actual name or value.

Introduction

The Cisco IronPort Email Security Appliances (ESA) have been deployed in thousands of networks to accept, filter, and deliver email messages. The ESA is easy to deploy and its security-filtering settings are effective right out of the box. However, many organizations are looking for more from their messaging environment and have barely tapped the potential of the ESA product line.

Email on the Internet is powered by the Simple Mail Transfer Protocol (SMTP). The simplicity of the protocol is its strength and weakness. Lack of authentication and the notion that one should accept all messages, gracefully, means that it is the most abused protocol on the Internet today. Spam is the most obvious form of abuse, but other dangers lurk, like bounce storms that can force servers offline in a denial of service (DoS) attack. Many organizations struggle with having email messages rejected or dropped by overzealous filtering.

The requirements laid on SMTP have changed over the years: Most businesses consider email to be their most important communication medium, ranking above telephone. Spam volumes have increased and changed form, and legitimate message traffic is growing in size and complexity as HTML has come to be the dominant format and the use of attachments has become widespread. New standards, such as SPF and DKIM, promise to bring proper authentication to email messages.

This book introduces the challenges facing messaging environments today and offers effective solutions on the ESA. It provides a series of recipes for solving particular messaging problems, delves into obscure features, makes recommendations on improving security, and shines light on oft-ignored issues like bounce blowback. Architecture recommendations are provided for deploying multiple ESAs in a variety of organizations, with the goal of improving reliability and automatically handling failure scenarios.

Goals and Methods

The goal of this book is to contribute to a more thorough understanding of Internet email, its inherent problems, and the solutions that the ESA product provides. I intend that for every area of functionality on the ESA, I provide not only how to configure, but whether and why you should. ESA is fundamentally a security product, but also a proper foundation for a reliable email gateway environment, and I hope to prove that it's far more than just a spam filter.

My method is to tackle the biggest problems that I've seen in more than 8 years of installing and configuring the ESA, and preface it with the relevant introductory material to make it accessible. Everything you'll read here is drawn from my personal experience with the product in hundreds of organizations, from small businesses to multinational corporations, higher education, service providers, and government.

Who Should Read This Book?

This book was written with a broad audience in mind. Email administrators that are using or considering ESA will learn everything from basic setup and configuration to advanced filtering rules, deployment architectures, and integration with external systems. Network architects will learn some of the root causes of email reliability problems and how to effectively configure an environment of multiple ESAs and related services. Security teams will gain deeper understanding of email as one of the primary vectors of malware and fraud, and learn about the less-visible aspects of email security. Anyone involved in designing a new gateway email environment based on ESA, or redesigning an existing one, will find this book valuable. Messaging directors will gain insight into some of challenges presented by internal email users as well as external senders, and be able to make better decisions about filtering policy, disaster recovery architecture, and email authentication standards.

How This Book Is Organized

Although you could read this book cover-to-cover, it is designed to be flexible and allow you to easily move between chapters and sections of chapters to cover only the material you need. If you do intend to read them all, the order in which they are presented is an excellent sequence.

Chapters 1 through 15 cover the following topics:

- **Chapter 1, "Introduction to Email Security":** This chapter provides an introduction to the Cisco ESA and the AsyncOS software, their history and features, and an overview of the problems it is designed to solve. This chapter also covers the basics of SMTP and its dependency on DNS. The history and nature of SMTP abuses are explored.
- **Chapter 2, "ESA Product Basics":** This chapter gives an overview of all the ESA features and the basic connection and setup process. It reviews differences between the various hardware models. The chapter walks you through the System Setup Wizard step by step, and then reviews the configuration you'll have after completing it. After showing a simple deployment example, more complex network installations are discussed.
- **Chapter 3, "ESA Email Pipeline":** Messages accepted and delivered by the ESA pass through the filtering pipeline step by step, and this chapter covers each stage in detail. Important concepts, such as listeners and the work queue, are introduced. The configuration options for each filtering stage are discussed and best practices are presented. After reading this chapter, you should understand what happens at each stage of the pipeline, from initial connection to final delivery, and the order in which they occur.

- **Chapter 4, "ESA Web User Interface"**: This chapter covers the main administrative interface of the ESA: the web user interface. It describes how to connect to the WUI and provides an overview of all the administrative web pages. Where appropriate, it provides the equivalent CLI commands. The chapter covers other important administrative concepts, such as the commit process, user privilege levels, and centralized management through the WUI.
- **Chapter 5, "Command-Line Interface"**: This chapter discusses the command-line administrative interface. Knowing how to use the CLI is critical for power users and essential for automation. The chapter covers connecting to the CLI using common SSH clients and using public-key authentication. All available commands are described, including some hidden and undocumented commands. You learn how to investigate and troubleshoot email delivery issues with examples of CLI command usage.
- **Chapter 6, "Additional Management Services"**: This chapter covers other monitoring and information services available on the ESA. You'll learn how to enable SNMP and use the ESA MIB to query SNMP attributes and react to traps. The chapter covers the use of the ESA filesystem and how to transfer data to and from the ESA. Lastly, it covers ESA logging including descriptions of all of the log types and an in-depth analysis of the primary mail log format.
- **Chapter 7, "Directories and Policies"**: This chapter covers LDAP directories and the ESA features that make use of your directory information. You'll learn how security and performance are improved by using LDAP features and the options for tying ESA policy to directory membership attributes. It then covers basic and advanced LDAP queries, AD specifics, and troubleshooting LDAP. It ends with a series of recipes for common directory integration problems.
- **Chapter 8, "Security Filtering"**: This chapter covers anti-spam, antivirus, and Outbreak Filters, the chief security engines of the ESA. It describes the process of enabling scanning and rule updates. You'll learn the options you have for handling junk and malicious message verdicts and how to tune the settings for your organization. This chapter also covers using content filters for interaction with engine verdicts and writing filters for common security needs.
- **Chapter 9, "Automating Tasks"**: This chapter provides an understanding of how to automate administrative tasks from remote systems using the CLI and WUI. It includes descriptions of automatic configuration backups using expect and Perl, retrieving XML status data, and exporting reporting information for processing in external applications.
- **Chapter 10, "Configuration Files"**: This chapter covers the XML file format used by the ESA for saving and restoring configuration files. The structure and components of the file are discussed, and examples of configuration file manipulation are provided.

- **Chapter 11, "Message and Content Filters"**: This chapter focuses on the two custom rules engines available on the ESA: message and content filters. Every filter has one or more conditions and actions, and all of them are described here. You'll learn the difference between the two engines and when to use each. Many examples are provided, and several difficult examples are illustrated. Performance problems and other limitations are explored.
- **Chapter 12, "Advanced Networking"**: This chapter provides depth on all the possible network models you can use to deploy an individual appliance. It covers single and multihomed deployments, the virtual gateways feature, and advanced routing and DNS configurations. Other network topics, like TLS for secure connections and DSR for load balancing, are discussed.
- **Chapter 13, "Multiple Device Deployments"**: Almost every ESA deployment will involve multiple appliances, and this chapter reviews the challenges and solutions whether you have two or 20. Load balancing for reliability and performance is discussed.
- **Chapter 14, "Recommended Configuration"**: This chapter covers best practices for ESA deployment and configuration. Security options for incoming mail are reviewed. You'll learn about handling outgoing mail properly, and what it means to be a good Internet email sender. Different types of organizations and their challenges, from small and large businesses to universities and service providers, are discussed.
- **Chapter 15, "Advanced Topics"**: This chapter covers two major topics that have emerged in the last few years, and the ESA approach to the challenges they create. Two email authentication standards, SPF and DKIM, have become widespread, and we'll examine how these work and the arguments for using them. Regulatory and Data Loss Prevention (DLP) policies have put new pressures on email administrators and policy makers, and you'll learn how the ESA provides capabilities to meet these requirements.

Chapter 1

Introduction to Email Security

In this chapter, you will learn the following:

- Brief overview of the Cisco IronPort Email Security products
- A history of the AsyncOS software releases that run the Email Security Appliances
- Basic topics of Internet email, focusing on the Simple Mail Transfer Protocol
- Definition of email security and overview of the threat landscape

Overview of Cisco IronPort Email Security Appliance (ESA)

The Cisco IronPort Email Security Appliance (ESA) family was launched in 2003. IronPort Systems, then an independent security company, created ESA as a self-contained hardware and software product to provide high-performance email security. The goal was to provide a single product that accepted, filtered, and delivered Internet email messages, and to do so reliably and quickly. Initially, the ESA provided basic message features along with filtering for spam and virus messages, but subsequent releases have dramatically expanded the range of capabilities.

ESA was certainly not the first system that performed virus or spam filtering for email messages; Bulk Unsolicited Commercial Internet email (UCE, the technical term for *spam* email) has been around almost as long as Internet email itself. It was one of the first, however, to combine these features into a single product, and to do so on a purpose-built platform with extremely high performance. Prior to the introduction of messaging appliances, typical email architectures included multiple layers of filtering, either as separate products running in series or as filtering products that *plugged in* to messaging servers. These multilayer designs used either proprietary application programming interfaces (API) for moving message contents or used Simple Mail Transfer Protocol (SMTP) to deliver messages from one system to another. The all-in-one appliance form factor removes the layering complexity, lowering the cost of providing effective reliable email security. Messaging servers are freed from the role of email filtering, allowing resources to be used to serve end users.

Because of its primary goal of security filtering, the ESA does not act as a message store and does not provide end-user access protocols, like Post Office Protocol (POP) or Internet Message Access Protocol (IMAP). It does not provide a webmail client interface. To compose and read messages, your environment must have other servers for messages and end-user interfaces.

IronPort continued to deliver new security and filtering services, enhancements to the base platform features, and increased message throughput with new hardware models and software releases. Cisco Systems acquired IronPort in June 2007. The IronPort product line continues its strong history as part of the Cisco Security Technologies business unit. The ESAs are also referred to as the *C-series* line of Cisco appliances, due to most of the model numbers starting with the letter C, such as the C370 and C670. The exception is the X-series, like the X1070. Although the *X-series* models are ESAs and offer the same functionality, their high-end hardware and resulting high throughput is suitable for carriers, service providers, and extremely large enterprises. The X- moniker distinguishes the *carrier class* products. The original IronPort models—the A50 and A60—had only email acceptance and delivery capabilities, without security filtering, and have reached end-of-life status.

Note All the ESA models have the same software features and differ only in the hardware platform, with some exceptions. The chief difference between the models is CPU count and speed, and RAID disk count and RAID mode. There's no difference in the availability of software features, and this guide's configuration guidelines apply to all models. The smaller 1U hardware units (like the C150 and C160) have differences, like two physical network interface cards (NIC) instead of three, which are important in some configurations. We note these differences where they are relevant.

In this guide, we refer to all the hardware models as Email Security Appliances (ESA). The product has also been called a Message Transfer Agent (MTA) and Messaging Gateway Appliance (MGA), and sometimes incorrectly referred to as the *IronPort Spam Filter*. Because it offers far more than spam filtering, we stick with the acronym ESA.

The term MTA refers to the servers tasked with accepting and delivering messages and, in Internet SMTP architecture, is distinguished from mail delivery agents (MDA), which store messages and provide user access, and mail user agents (MUA) that allow users to retrieve, display, and compose messages. Some MTA products provide MDA capabilities directly on the same system, but the ESA does not.

AsyncOS

AsyncOS is the name given to the collected software running on the Cisco IronPort appliances. It includes the base operating system (OS), device drivers, memory management, process scheduling, and all the application and scanning software. The OS fundamentals are built on FreeBSD, with significant portions specifically altered for messaging tasks. Low-level components are written in the C programming language, while most of the application software and all the management interfaces are written in Python and use a coroutine-based model called *shrapnel*. This high-performance threading library was specifically built for the processing needs of email, allowing the ESA to handle thousands of simultaneous connections.

AsyncOS also refers to the messaging software, all the security filtering, the web-based user interface (WUI), and the command-line interface (CLI). AsyncOS versions are referred to by a *Major.Minor.Point-Build* number format, such as 7.1.0-310. Each AsyncOS software build is complete and self-contained. Upgrades from one version to another involve an entire build image, instead of individual upgrades to components. The only exception is the security engines, whose software versions are automatically independently upgraded by the system. Security engine updates are dynamic in order to provide real-time protection against the latest virus and spam variants.

Security Management Appliances (SMA)

Throughout this book, we often refer to a security management appliance (SMA) (or the *M-series* appliances). These separate Cisco IronPort appliances complement the ESA and provide centralized features, such as email reporting, message tracking, and the end-user IronPort Spam Quarantine (ISQ). It is typical to deploy one or two SMAs in conjunction with two or more ESAs to provide these centralized services for the environment. In larger deployments, of four or more ESAs, the SMA is indispensable. Despite the name, as of this writing, the SMA provides no actual configuration management for ESA devices; centralized management is done directly on the ESAs with a dedicated clustering feature.

The SMA is indispensable in ESA deployments, because it provides a single centralized interface for email reports and message tracking. The SMA consolidates the data spanning many ESAs and provides a single interface analysis or investigation. The reporting and tracking features that the SMA provides are also part of the standard ESA feature set, although limited to a single appliance when run on the ESA. Most of the reporting and tracking features we discuss are available as described in either ESA or SMA. The SMA provides much higher capacity for storage and much higher import rates for log data. The higher capacity of the SMA allows for a larger ISQ, which provides storage and user access to messages deemed to be a spam threat. Quarantine is one of the possible actions for filtered spam messages and, like the other features, is available on both the ESA and the SMA, but the SMA provides a single centralized interface and more capacity.

Another benefit of an SMA is that it offloads the processing work of tasks like message tracking and quarantine access, which are unpredictable and can place high load on an ESA when used. For this reason, in most environments, it's preferable for centralized reporting, tracking, and quarantine to be run on the SMA. Like ESA, there are different models of SMA, differing only in performance and capacity.

The SMA is built on the same code base as the ESA, and so its user interfaces, administration features, configuration options, and monitoring and reporting are similar. However, because the SMA is not intended to accept, filter, and deliver email, those portions of the configuration aren't available. Where the ESA and SMA are similar, those parts of this book are applicable to both families of appliances.

History of AsyncOS Versions

AsyncOS was first publicly available in general release with software version 2.0 for the A60 model appliance in November 2002. Versions 2.0 and 2.5 focused on high-performance message delivery and features designed to allow businesses that rely on email communications to quickly deliver email. It was quickly adopted by retail, banking, insurance, and service-provider companies that needed to manage and deliver large email campaigns.

In June 2003, version 3.0 was the first that focused on high-performance MTA features for both incoming (receiving) and outgoing (sending) SMTP mail. Table 1-1 lists the major AsyncOS releases.

Table 1-1 *History of Major AsyncOS Releases*

Version	Highlights
AsyncOS 3.0, June 2003	Public listeners and inbound mail support.
AsyncOS 3.5, December 2003	Brightmail Anti-Spam, LDAP directory integration features, and Sophos Anti-Virus.
AsyncOS 4.0, October 2004	Virus outbreak filters, dramatic WUI overhaul, including policies and content filters, policy quarantine, SMTP AUTH, HTTPS streaming upgrade.
AsyncOS 4.5, September 2005	IronPort Anti-Spam, centralized management, domain keys signing.
AsyncOS 4.7, July 2006	Bounce verification, LDAP failover features, network diagnostics, ISQ.
AsyncOS 5.0, March 2007	Enhancements to set up defaults, spam quarantines, spam filtering, LDAP settings, and notifications.
AsyncOS 5.5, October 2007	Introduction of ESA envelope encryption for email, LDAP enhancements, DKIM verification, AsyncOS reversion.

Version	Highlights
AsyncOS 6.0, March 2008	New reporting and tracking engine on ESA, introduction of the SMA features for centralized tracking. System Setup Wizard and LDAP Wizard for AD were added to simplify initial configuration.
AsyncOS 6.3, July 2008	New hardware platform support, introduction of Image Analysis engine.
AsyncOS 6.5, December 2008	External authentication and new user roles. Enhancements to destination controls, system setup, and encryption. New upgrade methods for accelerated AsyncOS upgrades.
AsyncOS 7.0, November 2009	RSA DLP engine, IPAS "marketing" verdict, intelligent multiscan, prioritized SMTP routes.
AsyncOS 7.1, April 2010	"No-auth" envelope encryption, weighted SMTP routes, TLS improvements.
AsyncOS 7.5, December 2011	Introduced SMTP "call-ahead" for recipient validation. Virus Outbreak Filters enhanced and renamed Outbreak Filters (OF). Role-based access control, password complexity, and expiration rules for user accounts. Combined text and HTML disclaimers.

Software Features

The ESA provides features for all stages of accepting, filtering, and delivering email messages with SMTP. In a typical deployment, an ESA is deployed as the first mail server for email coming from the Internet, and the last mail server on the path out to the Internet. All models of appliance provide the following features:

- **Connection controls and rate limiting:** In the past, email has the unstated assumption that anyone who wants to send mail to your organization will be allowed. Not so with the ESA, which can strictly control the connections and access of junk senders.
- **Email acceptance and delivery:** Only accept the right messages, and quickly get them to the right destination. Ensure that email delivery is reliable, highly available, and extremely high performance.
- **Security filtering:** Spam, viruses, fraud, phishing, and other kinds of unwanted messages threaten the reliability and security of your entire computing environment. ESA shuts down this infection vector and delivers clean, legitimate email.
- **Data loss prevention and encryption:** Whether through oversight or intent, users can potentially send confidential or personally identifiable information via email, in violation of company policy or state or federal regulations. ESA has filtering features to detect and stop these messages or, when the transmission is allowed but must be secure, provides means to encrypt the content in transit.

- **Custom filtering:** For other filtering challenges, ESA provides a flexible filtering engine to identify content based on the sender, recipient, subject, or body of email messages, and even within attachments in some 400 different formats.

Email Security Landscape

What does the term *email security* mean? When we think of the problems associated with Internet email, the immediate thought is usually the most visible problem: spam. Formally defined as bulk, unsolicited commercial email (UCE), spam is a clear reminder of the problems that plague email systems, aggravating administrators and users and interfering with legitimate business use of email. Although it is the most visible email problem, it's not the only threat to a company's email infrastructure.

As the single most important means of business communication, email availability is vital to any company's daily operations. It's also one of the chief means by which employees interact with the outside world. We're generally concerned with three primary tasks for email security: stopping the bad mail from coming in while allowing legitimate mail to flow unimpeded; controlling outgoing mail that might contain sensitive information, or that might be sent to unauthorized third-parties; and dealing with any unplanned situation that might cause email receipt and delivery to be stopped.

> **Note** A Cisco study conducted in 2006 showed Internet email to be approximately 75% spam; a similar analysis in May 2010 showed 85%. For the first time, however, the second half of 2010 showed a sustained decline of spam volume. Estimated average daily volume of spam was approximately 100 billion messages per day in December 2010 compared with over 300 billion messages (average) per day from May to July 2010. It remains to be seen if this is just a brief respite to be followed by another increase or a major inflection point in the business of spam.

Email Spam

Despite being simple for humans to identify, spam is difficult to define precisely and thus difficult for software to identify. Most users classify any unwanted message as spam, with a definition of unwanted that varies daily. There's a difference between messages sent in bulk by legitimate senders, such as retailers, banks, media outlets, social networking, auction sites, and the unsolicited, usually fraudulent advertising in spam messages. We can break down spam into various categories, including phishing (fraudulent messages that seek to fool recipients into revealing personal information or login credentials), advertising, advance-fee fraud, *419* scams (money-courier schemes that promise to reward recipients with a portion of the money being transferred), but it's all a problem, and it all needs to be filtered.

For this book, we use the term *spam* to refer to unsolicited email messages related to criminal activity, be it advertising fraudulent products or services or enticing users to provide information or participate in a fraud. Bulk messages sent by legitimate senders, even if unwanted, are more properly termed *marketing* or *broadcast* messages. Of course, some grey area exists here, and the conduct of legitimate senders sometimes crosses the line. Your organization may have some automated or bulk messaging, as it is an extremely effective and inexpensive means of contact with customers, partners, and vendors. (Chapter 14, "Recommended Configurations," addresses the topic of being a good bulk sender.)

In the U.S., several states and the federal government passed legislation defining and prohibiting unsolicited commercial email. In general, these laws prohibit sending email of a commercial nature without some pre-existing business relationship with the recipient and requiring messages to contain contact information and opt-out instructions. Unfortunately, as is often the case with legislation over technology, the results have been mixed. Many spam originators operate from countries with little or no technology laws, and other originators toe the line, claiming to have the pre-existing relationship with the recipient that, in practice, is nearly impossible to verify.

Viruses and Malware

Messages that contain binary attachments, whatever the source, can potentially include malicious executable software. A *virus message* is any email message that contains one or more malicious executables. We can make distinctions between different types of viral messages, like those that use social-engineering versus *Trojan horse* software that purports to have a legitimate purpose, but for us, it's all a threat that needs to be eliminated.

The world of viruses and malware has changed dramatically over the years. Viruses and worms were initially spread as a means of proving a point or gaining notoriety for their authors. Today, the motivation is almost purely criminal: to steal user credentials and personal information by means of keystroke logging and system monitoring, to establish a software foothold inside of a corporate network, and to spread the infection to other users. Email is often only one vector for infection, and the software that succeeds in bypassing security filters today is extremely sophisticated, capable of phoning home for instruction, using multiple protocols and vectors, installing new components to morph over time, and hiding from virus scanners and even the OSs themselves.

We are, of course, concerned about the email infection vector, and there, the situation has been changing. Because of the widespread deployment of email security systems, the use of broad attachment-filtering rules, improvements to mail clients and OSs, and the effectiveness of network security solutions, email has recently become less effective as a vector for distributing malware. Email-borne viruses have become more targeted, seeking out specific individuals or organizations, or exploiting social network ties and email address books to mimic communication among friends and associates.

In place of the infected email-attachment vector, more attackers have been using URLs to malicious software and messages that entice the user to click the link. The enticement takes on many different forms: Common ones are the promise of money, revealing gossip, threats of account closure, or claims of having some embarrassing information. The end goal is the same: A user clicks the link that leads to malicious software. The software-delivery methods also vary; some sites claim that the user needs updated plugins or toolbars installed, while others rely on unpatched browser software to execute a silent *drive-by* download. Whatever the message and the means, the messages represent a significant threat and a security target for the ESA.

Protecting Intellectual Property and Preventing Data Loss

Email security also means examining outgoing mail sent by local users to recipients on the Internet. This communication—to partners, contractors, suppliers, media, or the public at large—represents a public face to your organization. That public-facing nature requires the same kind of brand protection and communication policy that your organization mandates for any public communication. It also represents a serious risk, because it allows internal users with access to sensitive or confidential information a direct communication path to the Internet.

In a typical deployment, ESA is situated as the first email *hop* on the way in, and the last hop on the way out. When architected this way, the ESA is an ideal chokepoint for examining both inbound and outbound email messages and applying actions like encryption.

Protecting intellectual property in an organization is a big topic, and email is only a part of it. But, the same steps taken to identify, classify, and secure data can be applied to ESA email policies, and the rules about what can and cannot be sent to external recipients can be controlled there.

The latest emerging pressure on email environments is the introduction of legislation from state and federal governments over the transport and disclosure of certain kinds of electronic information, and email is certainly covered under these regulations. In the financial industry, these requirements have existed for years, but in other verticals, the pressure is new. The legislation is often not specific enough to dictate exact policies on electronic communication, but the ESA provides a variety of tools to allow your organization to implement the controls it deems necessary to comply.

Regulatory compliance typically focuses on a few classes of information generally encompassed under the term Personally Identifiable Information (PII): payment card numbers, bank routing numbers, and other financial account information, government ID numbers, personal names, addresses, telephone numbers, and healthcare records. The ESA's Data Loss Prevention (DLP) features provide rules for identifying these classes of data, or defining your own classes, and taking action on the messages as appropriate. A common policy is to encrypt content that contains sensitive information, when that message would otherwise be sent to an external recipient in the clear. Encrypting email content satisfies the requirement that prohibits sending personal information in the clear.

Other Email Security Threats

Aside from the obvious threats that spam and viruses pose, and the challenge of filtering outgoing mail, your organization may face a number of other email-specific problems that affect email availability:

- **Denial of service (DoS):** Almost any protocol can be compromised by DoS. In email, this can be intentional with floods of email traffic, or accidental, as with misdirected bounces or notifications. ESA provides several features to protect against these kinds of messages.
- **Fraud and impersonation:** Because of the lack of authentication in SMTP, sender addresses can be *spoofed* or impersonated. This can be an issue for both inbound and outbound traffic: Your users can be fooled into trusting message content that appears to be from reputable sources, and your own local user accounts and domains can be impersonated, potentially affecting your reputation online and potentially leading your customers or partners into fraud. This is a multifaceted problem, and there is no silver-bullet solution. However, there are some new industry efforts and technology features on the ESA that can help mitigate or eliminate this problem.
- **Online activism:** Email is an inexpensive and widely available service, and the letter-writing campaign of yesteryear lives on in email campaigns created by activists. Because of the quick spread of information and the ease of sending email addresses, anyone with a point to make can quickly do so via email and encourage or enable others to do so, too. Because it's usually easy to guess email accounts for executives or other prominent individuals in an organization, it's easy to send them a lot of email. Regardless of the message, high volumes of email can cause problems for the organization and its targeted individuals. The ESA provides filtering capabilities, allowing you to tailor a solution that fits your organization.
- **Blacklisting:** One early solution to the problem of spam, and the computers that were sending it, was to create a public listing of IP addresses that were seen sending spam. These services are known as spam black-hole lists, or blacklists. Because they typically provide their listing using Domain Name Service (DNS), they are often called DNSBLs. These have been effective as a spam-fighting mechanism, and their effectiveness has forced spammers into new techniques to avoid them. Unfortunately, some blacklists are better than others, resulting in some lists that are easy to get on and difficult to get off. When your organization is added to a public blacklist, it can affect delivery of all email to any destination that uses that blacklist, and it can be time-consuming to arrive at a root cause and get off the list. We discuss strategy and ESA features that can help you stay off of these lists in Chapter 14.

Simple Mail Transfer Protocol (SMTP)

Internet email is driven by SMTP, which is one of the most venerable Internet standards. SMTP was first formally defined by Jon Postel in RFC 821, published in August 1982. It was not the first Internet messaging protocol. SMTP evolved from experience with earlier protocols, some based on FTP, for delivering electronic messages on the ARPANET. For some time after the ARPANET transitioned into the modern Internet, SMTP was a complement to Unix-to-Unix Copy (UUCP) mail, which has since virtually disappeared. The legacy UUCP "bang path" addressing can still be found in SMTP, unfortunately only used for exploiting vulnerable systems.

The most recent specifications for SMTP and Extended SMTP (ESMTP) can be found in RFC 5321, published on October 2008. (In this book, we use the acronym SMTP in most cases, even though we are almost always referring to ESMTP. Where the distinction is important, we note it.)

Note Virtually every software, hardware, or service-based Internet email product supports ESMTP, although the ESMTP functions that are supported vary. Because it's rare to find a pure SMTP-only client or server, we make the assumption that we're always working with ESMTP-capable agents.

The RFCs for SMTP reserves destination TCP port 25 for its use. Although there are some cases for running SMTP services on ports other than 25, that's the industry standard, and the ESA defaults to port 25 in all cases. If not otherwise specified, you can assume port 25 when we're talking about SMTP. As with most application layer protocols, the TCP source port for clients is a random high number.

RFC 821 states in the first line of its introduction that the goal of SMTP is "to transfer mail reliably and efficiently." SMTP uses TCP connections for transport, although it is technically independent of transport protocol and requires only a reliable, ordered data stream. SMTP has built-in mechanisms to ensure reliable delivery. The *store-and-forward* approach that most SMTP software uses means that a message is either delivered or it's not, and the final disposition of any message should never be unknown. Transient (non-permanent) errors are a standard part of the protocol, and it is typical for clients to hold messages and attempt redelivery should a temporary error occur during an SMTP transaction.

SMTP is a plain-text protocol (technically, it was originally defined to support a 7-bit character set) and is intended to be easily human readable. In fact, messages can be transmitted manually using Telnet to an appropriate SMTP server.

I refer to an SMTP session between client and server as an *SMTP conversation*. After a TCP connection is made, roles are defined for the client, which sends commands and data, and the server, which parses the commands and responds. SMTP is fairly interactive with a back-and-forth of commands and responses between client and server. Email software that understands SMTP can act as either client, server, or both; MTAs, like ESA, routinely serve both needs. We look at the need for and use of MTAs later in this chapter.

Example 1-1 is a simple SMTP conversation example. The line numbers are not part of the session; they're here so we can refer to the commands. The client's commands are in plain text while the server's response appears in italics.

Example 1-1 *Simple SMTP Conversation Example*

```
<client connects to server esa02.cisco.com>
1   220 esa02.cisco.com ESMTP
2   HELO external-sender.com
3   250 esa02.cisco.com
4   MAIL FROM: <sender@external-sender.com>
5   250 sender <sender@external-sender.com> ok
6   RCPT TO: <chriport@cisco.com>
7   250 recipient <chriport@cisco.com> ok
8   DATA
9   354 go ahead
10  Subject: Example Message
11
12  This is the text of an example message.
13  .
14  250 ok: Message 31274 accepted
15  QUIT
16  221 esa02.cisco.com
```

Line 1 is called a banner, or greeting, that the server sends to the client. The 220 is a three-digit response code from the server, and this one indicates success, or at least, no error to this point. SMTP uses three-digit codes that RFC 5321 refers to as xyz, where x can be 2, 3, 4, or 5. Any code beginning with 2 is a *success* code, often referred to as 2yz or 200-class. The RFCs define the response codes that should be used in SMTP conversations, but in practice, the RFC definitions aren't always precisely followed. We can usually count on the first digit being accurate: 2yz for success, 3yz for success (but waiting for more data), 4yz indicating a transient (non-fatal) error, and 5yz is any permanent, fatal error. Context for the response comes from the point in the conversation where the error occurred. The second and third digits in a response code can be revealing, but because of variable interpretation by different products, you shouldn't rely on them to be perfectly accurate. Some systems respond with an error code of 550 for all mail-delivery errors and don't distinguish between causes. Table 1-2 shows some common SMTP response codes. The ESA references refer to the default configuration; many of the response codes on ESA can be customized.

Table 1-2 *Common SMTP Response Codes*

Response Code	Typical Use
220	Used as the success code for the initial SMTP server greeting.
250	Success, the command was accepted. The context of this response will determine exactly what was successful.
354	Response to an SMTP client's DATA command. It can be interpreted as *OK so far, waiting for message data.* It's the only 3yz code you'll see from an ESA.
421	Temporary failure or temporary rejection at the connection level. Usually means that the server is too busy to handle any more connections, or is deliberately rate-limiting the sender. ESA uses this to reject new connections when it reaches its global limit or has reached a policy limit for this connecting IP. Could also indicate that the service is temporarily not available (for example, if shutting down or if license key has expired).
452	Temporary failure or rejection at the message or recipient level. ESA uses this response code to reject individual recipients on a message when the sender has exceeded the limits for recipient count, or exceeded the limit for invalid recipients.
550	Permanent failure at the recipient level. This usually means that the mailbox does not exist. ESA uses this response code when a recipient address is invalid.
554	Permanent failure at the service or connection level. ESA uses this to reject SMTP connections outright, in place of a 220 banner, for low-reputation or explicitly listed hosts.

Line 2 of Example 1-1 is the first command issued by the client, HELO, and line 3 is the server response. In SMTP, a line is a string of characters terminated by a carriage return (ASCII hex character 0x0D) immediately followed by a linefeed (character 0x0A). This line termination sequence is usually indicated as <CRLF>. The "hello" is literally an introduction, and it allows the client to identify itself to the server. In practice, the use of HELO is deprecated in favor of EHLO, but the distinction isn't important in this simple example. The string that follows HELO is arbitrary, but the RFCs encourage the use of the sender's Internet domain. This is where we first encounter one of the serious limitations of SMTP: the lack of authentication. SMTP dates from a time when servers could trust clients and vice versa. There is no reliable mechanism by which we can verify that any of the information provided by the client is accurate. The HELO string can easily contain almost any value up to the maximum string length supported by the server, typically 1024 bytes. We can't trust the value contained here to always be valid or invalid and, so, it's unwise to make any filtering decisions on the basis of it. HELO/EHLO strings also come up when we discuss Transport Layer Security (TLS) for secure email delivery and Sender Policy Framework (SPF) for sender authentication.

Line 4 is the MAIL command, which tells the server that the client is beginning a new message, and it specifies the sender address. Email address literals should always be surrounded by angle brackets (< and >) and, on Internet clients and servers, should always include a fully qualified domain name (FQDN) after the @ sign. A blank sender address, specified as

```
MAIL FROM: <>
```

is valid, but is reserved for use by system messages, usually for Delivery Status Notification (DSN) messages or *bounces*. Line 5 is the response from the server. If this had been a temporary or permanent error (4yz or 5yz response code), the client would not be able to deliver this message. At that point, the client may disconnect with QUIT, use RSET to reset the connection, or simply start a new message with a new MAIL FROM command.

Line 6 begins the listing of recipients of this email message using the command RCPT TO. This example has only one recipient. Recipients specified in the SMTP RCPT command are usually referred to as envelope recipients, and they may or may not match the value in the To field you would see in your email client. This is addressed later when we discuss the difference between envelope and message body. Line 7 is the response from the server; this recipient is accepted. It's perfectly reasonable on a multirecipient message that some addresses may not be accepted. It's also reasonable for an SMTP server not to accept more than one recipient per message or to limit the number of recipients per message.

Line 8 is the DATA command, and line 9 is the 354 response. 3yz response codes translate as "OK so far, go ahead with transmit." It's not a guarantee that the server will accept the message, but up to this point, the transmission hasn't hit any reason to be rejected. After the 354 response, the sender transmits the message body line by line, which includes both the SMTP headers and what any user would identify as the "body" of the message. It would also include any attachments, which are just encoded portions of the body following the MIME specifications. (We discuss MIME in more detail later in this chapter.) This message has no attachments; it's just plain ASCII text. The message is terminated by the sequence <CRLF>.<CRLF>. That is the carriage return/linefeed combination, surrounding a period character. In hex, this combination is 0x0D0A2E0D0A. This is the only proper message-termination sequence, and sending SMTP clients must be sure never to transmit this sequence for anything but a message termination. Lines of a message body that contain nothing but a period character as typed by the sender need to be careful not to transmit it in the raw.

The blank line (line 11) indicates the break between message headers and message body. The message header is all the standard and custom headers attached to a message. This example has only one: the standard Subject header that will be displayed to the recipient in the MUA. As you can see, it's not required that the From or To headers be included, and in fact, even the Subject isn't strictly required.

Line 14 immediately follows the data termination sequence and includes the response code and text from the server. The 250 here indicates that the message was accepted.

The response provided by the server may or may not have information about the message. Often, the response is a simple variation on "message accepted, thank you," but many will systems will often return a local message identifier that can be used to trace the message as it passes from server to server. These identifiers are usually only locally significant. The ESA response in this example tells us that the message was accepted and was given the internal message ID (MID) of 31274. An administrator for this ESA could use that MID to trace it through that appliance.

SMTP Commands

Aside from the required minimal SMTP commands HELO (or EHLO), MAIL, RCPT, DATA, and QUIT, numerous other commands are defined by the RFCs. Unfortunately, many of these commands have proven to be useful to criminals in exploiting systems and stealing addresses. Because of this, the use of such commands as EXPN (Expand) or VRFY (Verify) has fallen out of favor, and ESA doesn't even implement them, although it may respond to them. The SMTP commands that the ESA responds to is listed in Table 1-3.

Table 1-3 *SMTP Commands the ESA Honors*

Command Format	Purpose
EHLO <domain>	Client greeting. Clients are required to provide an identifying domain or hostname, but this requirement is often ignored.
MAIL	Indicates the start of a new SMTP message, and the envelope sender address. Because the full command is MAIL FROM, we often refer to this address that way.
RCPT	Indicates a new envelope recipient of the message. The response from the server indicates whether that recipient is valid; a message needs at least one valid recipient, but the client can proceed even with one or more rejected recipients.
DATA	Client is ready to send message data, including both headers and body of the message. Message transmission must conclude with the SMTP termination string <CRLF>.<CRLF>.
RSET	Reset. Resets the current conversation back to a default state. All sender, recipient, and message data is discarded. Some products issue this command between messages when delivering more than one message per connection.
VRFY <email address>	Verify. Asks the receiving MTA if the email address of the recipient is valid on the destination system. Because this is easily exploited by dictionary attack to provide an address harvester with all legitimate email addresses on a system, it is not used on Internet-facing SMTP servers. The ESA does not implement this command and will respond with "252 ok" in all cases, regardless of the provided email address.

Command Format	Purpose
EXPN <email address>	Expand. For a known recipient email address, asks the receiving MTA whether this is a mailing list with multiple recipients, and if so, to return the expanded list of all members. The potential for abuse is staggering. The ESA does not implement this command and returns "500 command not recognized" in response to it.
QUIT	Terminates the SMTP conversation and closes the TCP connection.
NOOP	No operation. Self-explanatory, really. It takes no arguments and provides no function. ESA always returns "250 ok" in response. Its only purpose is as a keepalive to avoid having server timeout inactive sessions.
HELP	Help on commands. Because of security, AsyncOS strictly limits its response. There's little call for using the HELP command other than for troubleshooting, and even then, it's of marginal use.
AUTH	Provide credentials for SMTP AUTH, which, if authenticated, allows a sender to enjoy relay privileges through the ESA. Typical only in service provider and some education environments. Credentials are passed in the clear, which is a security concern unless combined with TLS.
STARTTLS	Instructs the server that the client wants to use TLS to transmit message data and to prepare for the TLS protocol negotiation. This command is only available if using ESMTP and if the ESA policy allows for the use of TLS.

ESMTP Service Extensions

When a client connects to a server and uses the EHLO greeting, in addition to identifying itself, it indicates to the server that it is ESMTP capable. Servers like the ESA then respond with a list of ESMTP *extensions* that it supports. Extensions are a way for the capabilities of SMTP clients and servers to be modified and improved without having to alter the protocol itself. Standard extensions must be registered with IANA. Vendor-specific extensions may be created, but these extensions must use names that start with X.

For example, an ESA responds to a client greeting with three standard extensions, like this:

```
EHLO cisco.com
250-mail.chrisporter.com
250-8BITMIME
250-SIZE 20971520
250 STARTTLS
```

The three extensions listed respectively tell the client that the system supports 8-bit characters in MIME messages, will accept messages up to 20 MB, and offers secure connection support using TLS. Another standard extension that ESA supports is AUTH for providing remote authentication of mail clients.

SMTP Message Headers and Body

All lines transmitted after the data command, up to the final termination sequence, can be considered the "body" of the SMTP message. The data is composed of two parts. A blank line separates the message headers and the message body proper, as we saw in line 11 of the simple SMTP example. The distinction between headers and body are important for MUAs, as the headers, with a couple of exceptions, are typically not displayed for the end user. Headers provide information about the message that's important to receiving and transmitting systems, including several that are required by RFC. RFC 5322 defines a number of standard headers, the most common of which are listed in Table 1-4.

Table 1-4 *Common RFC-Defined Headers*

Header	Purpose
From	The body sender address, distinguished from the envelope sender address. This header is for end user's benefit and is not typically examined by the ESA. Usually, the envelope sender and the body From header are the same email address, but can differ for mailing list or other automated software, for example. If this header is not present in a message received, the receiving MTA is required to create it, based on the envelope sender address. The value of the From field usually takes the form From: Firstname Lastname <user@domain.tld>, but many variants are possible.
To	The body recipient address. This "visible header" is typically displayed by the MUA and is not necessarily the same as the envelope recipients. The ESA can look at this header but, aside from some operations like masquerading, it's not normally used by the ESA other than to pass it on unchanged.
CC	Carbon copy. Indicate recipients that are not the primary recipient but are still visible in the headers of the message. Note that there is no equivalent "BCC" header; recipients that appear in the envelope but not in the To or CC are considered Blind Carbon Copied.
Subject	Obviously, the subject of the message as supplied by the sender, whether a human user or an automated system. The addition of RE: or Re: for replies and Fwd: or FW: for message forwards is purely a human and software custom, not a requirement for the Subject field.
Reply-To	A header that specifies where replies to this message should be sent. Although it can be a different address than that in the From header, it's usually the same for person-to-person messages. Messages and group email lists often make use of the Reply-To header so that replies go back to the list software and not the original author.

Header	Purpose
Received	Indicates when, how, and from where a message was received. RFCs require that all SMTP servers add a Received header to every message that it accepted, while preserving earlier Received headers. There are typically multiple copies of the Received header, and collectively, they tell the hop-by-hop history of this message. Received headers are used for message-loop determination and are extremely important for troubleshooting.
Date	A date and timestamp on a message, usually added by the sending mail client. If not present, an MTA, like the ESA, will add it.
Content-Type	Indicates the MIME type of data in the body of the message. This header can also provide additional parameter values, such as "charset" (Character Set) for text types and "boundary" for multipart types.
MIME-Version	Indicates the version of the MIME standard the message adheres to. As of this writing, only version 1.0 is defined.
Content-Transfer-Encoding	Originally, SMTP was only capable of transmitting data in 7-bit US ASCII with limited line lengths. Even today, support for 8-bit email cannot be relied on. 8-bit binary or character data must be encoded with schemes like Base64 or quoted-printable, and this header indicates which encoding was used. It can also specify that the data is unencoded, because it's already 7-bit clean or that it's unencoded 8-bit binary data.
Message-ID	Contains a single unique message ID, usually added by the originating software. If not present, an MTA like the ESA will add it. Note that although the Message-ID is recorded by the ESA, internally it uses a separate message ID called the MID to uniquely identify each message. The MID is locally significant and is not guaranteed to be unique across ESAs.

Custom headers not defined in RFCs can be added to any SMTP message. The name of these headers must start with X- and follow the RFC-defined Name: Value format and adhere to SMTP rules regarding header length and line wrapping. These are typically vendor-specific messages, although products like ESA allow organizations to add and remove headers to messages.

Message headers are extremely valuable for troubleshooting delivery and filtering issues. The standard headers provide information about the source and the intended destination and should be adequate to trace a message through multiple systems to determine an error point. They also provide enough information to the recipient so that their email client, or MUA, can compose replies and forwards.

Envelope Sender and Recipients

SMTP messages really have two sender addresses and two (or more) recipient addresses. Addresses specified during the SMTP conversation prior to DATA are the *envelope* addresses. The sender address specified during the SMTP MAIL FROM command is called the *envelope sender* address. The recipients listed in one or more RCPT TO commands are considered the *envelope recipient* addresses. These addresses are used in routing messages to their destination or sending back notifications to the sender—not the visible To: and From: fields that you see in a mail client.

This is an important distinction, because when an ESA configuration setting, table, or filter refers to sender or recipient, it is almost always referring to the envelope. In fact, the ESA rarely ever examines or alters the visible To, From, CC, or Reply-To headers unless specifically set with a filter to do so.

Transmitting Binary Data

Normally, SMTP doesn't distinguish between plain-text or other human-readable parts of the message and binary attachments. SMTP also does not natively define messages with multiple parts, such as text in different formats. Binary data and multipart messages are handled through the Multipurpose Internet Mail Extensions (MIME) standard. MIME is also used in other protocols, like HTTP, to send binary data over a plain-text protocol. The vast majority of email messages sent will be in MIME format, even very simple messages. MIME is an extensive specification covered by numerous RFCs. It's not required to be familiar with all of it, but it is important to understand how binary data is transmitted and how the ESA deals with "bodies" and "attachments" of messages.

MIME begins with a MIME-Version header that must be present in order to be considered a MIME format message. MIME-Version, of course, specifies the version number of the MIME standard that the creator of the message used. The other important header is the Content-Type header, which specifies the overall global *MIME type* of the entire message, in a format of *type/subtype* that the MIME RFCs specify. If the message is composed of just one part, this header indicates its type. A *MIME part* refers to logically grouped data: the entire message text or the entire attached file. If the message is composed of multiple parts, the global type in Content-Type will be multipart/alternative, or multipart/mixed, as this one is. The Content-Type header can also include other information about the data in the message in the form of *parameter=value* pairs. The parameters will vary depending on the type. For text types, the character set is defined in the charset parameter. For multipart types, the MIME boundary is defined in the boundary parameter. This is the ASCII text string that acts as a delimiter between parts of the message. A boundary is present even if there is only a single part to a message. Typically, the MUA generates the boundary strings, and so the format varies considerably. It must be a string that is not found anywhere else in the message other than the boundaries.

An example MIME-formatted SMTP message is shown in Example 1-2. This is the 7-bit ASCII text representation of a message, with the Base64-encoded binary data shortened for convenience—this 37 K attachment has almost 700 lines.

Example 1-2 *Example MIME-Formatted SMTP Message*

```
Received: from unknown (HELO mailstore.chrisporter.com) ([10.60.10.20])
  by mail.chrisporter.com with ESMTP; 15 Jan 2011 16:22:30 -0500
Received: by mailstore.chrisporter.com (Postfix, from userid 1001)
      id 9D52697D7F; Sat, 15 Jan 2011 16:22:28 -0500 (EST)
Received: from localhost (localhost [127.0.0.1])
      by mailstore.chrisporter.com (Postfix) with ESMTP id C98BB97D7A
      for <chriport@cisco.com>; Sat, 15 Jan 2011 16:22:27 -0500 (EST)
Date: Sat, 15 Jan 2011 16:22:27 -0500 (EST)
From: Chris Porter <cporter@chrisporter.com>
To: chriport@cisco.com
Subject: Document you requested
Message-ID: <alpine.DEB.1.10.1101151621410.24513@mailstore.chrisporter.com>
User-Agent: Alpine 1.10 (DEB 962 2008-03-14)
MIME-Version: 1.0
Content-Type: multipart/mixed; boundary="1007293450-747258728-1295126547=:24513"

  This message is in MIME format.  The first part should be readable text,
  while the remaining parts are likely unreadable without MIME-aware tools.

--1007293450-747258728-1295126547=:24513
Content-Type: TEXT/PLAIN; format=flowed; charset=US-ASCII

Chris,
      Here's that document that you requested.

Thanks
Chris

--1007293450-747258728-1295126547=:24513
Content-Type: APPLICATION/ZIP; name=credt.xlsx
Content-Transfer-Encoding: BASE64
Content-ID: <alpine.DEB.1.10.1101151622270.24513@mailstore.chrisporter.com>
Content-Description:
Content-Disposition: attachment; filename=credt.xlsx

UEsDBBQABgAIAAAAIQDdsQorbwEAAMQEAAATAM0BW0NvbnRlbnRfVHlwZXNd
LnhtbCCiyQEooAACAAAAAAAAAAAAAAAAAAAAAAAAAAAAAAAAAAAAAAAAAAAA
.
.
.
q5itppkBAAAoAwAAEAAAAAAAAAAAAAAAAAB9jwAAZG9jUHJvcHMvYXBwLnht
bFBLBQYAAAAACwALAMUCAABMkgAAAAA=

--1007293450-747258728-1295126547=:24513--
```

By using multipart/mixed, we tell the receiving MUA that there is more than one type in the message. The type of each part is defined in its MIME header, listed just after the boundary string. Each part includes its own Content-Type and, possibly, other headers. It is possible that the MIME type of a part can also be multipart/mixed, with its own *subparts*, and in fact, the nesting can continue, creating a tree structure. This example has only two levels: the root with two nodes.

The receiving MUA is free to interpret the MIME parts as it sees appropriate, but most will treat the first text/plain or text/html part (or both, if combined into a multipart/alternative) as the message body and all remaining parts as attachments. Usually, the MUA displays to the user a filename and download options for binary attachments, but it's possible to take other actions. Some email clients, upon receiving encrypted message parts, automatically decrypt parts that are encrypted with the recipient's public key (for example, assuming that the private key is available).

Note Multipart/alternative is a special multipart type that is extremely common. The root part has two or more subparts, but instead of being independent parts, the subparts all display the same information in different representations. The recipient's MUA is free to pick the representation that best fits its display. The most common multipart/alternative messages have the same message content in two parts: one in text/plain and the other in text/html. The email client picks the best version for display to the end user and ignores the other. Two different email clients might display different parts; for example, a client on a mobile device may choose the plain-text part while a desktop OS client displays the HTML.

This message has a Microsoft Excel worksheet file attached, with filename credt.xlsx. Despite that, the MIME type of this part is APPLICATION/ZIP, because the Microsoft Office formats use a compressed file type that the MUA identified as ZIP.

MIME Types

The MIME RFCs (RFCs 2045 through 2049) define not only the headers and organizational requirements of MIME messages, but also the global MIME type categories and standard subcategories, along with a procedure for defining and registering new subcategories. The five standard global categories of MIME types are listed in Table 1-5.

Table 1-5 *Top-Level Global MIME Categories*

Category	Description
`text/`	Plain-text data stored in 7-bit ASCII. text/plain refers to text data with no formatting whatsoever. Other text types include text/html and text/richtext. The most common types are text/plain and text/html.
`image/`	Any data stored in an image format that can be displayed on a monitor. Common types include image/jpeg and image/gif. Some MUAs display these images natively if they understand the image type. Text mail clients can safely ignore these types.

Category	Description
video/	Video data, covering multimedia formats that usually include both moving image and audio soundtrack data. The most common type is video/mpeg, but a type exists for almost every common format. Some MUAs can natively display multimedia, but most will only offer a way to save the data to a file on disk.
audio/	Audio-only data like music or voice recordings. Common formats are audio/mpeg for MP3 and audio/wav. Usually, the mail client launches an external player to handle these types.
application/	Any other kind of binary data that doesn't fit into the other categories. These types are typically associated with a software application, and so they are numerous. There are hundreds of different application/ types in use today. The special type application/octet-stream is used for unknown formats of binary data.

The last important MIME topic is the way that binary data is represented in the plain text SMTP protocol. In our example, the binary attachment has a header called Content-Transfer-Encoding with a value of Base64. This specifies that the binary data are represented by a set of 64 ASCII characters. *Base64* encoding is defined in RFC 2045, as is another binary-to-text encoding called *quoted-printable*. The ESA handles all these encodings transparently, and all filtering is performed on unencoded content; you don't need to convert search strings into Base64 format. ESA can even examine text content stored within binary attachments and can open compressed formats to access the files contained therein.

Note Because the Base64 algorithm encodes every three binary bytes as four text characters, they expand the data storage and transfer requirements by a third. This means that if you send a 1 MB (1024 KB) attachment in email, its size in SMTP transmission is actually about 1365 KB, plus more for MIME headers, padding, and line breaks. If you want your environment to accept 5 MB attachments, you have to set the ESA limits to 6.7 MB (6827 KB) or higher to allow for the expansion that Base64 causes.

Character Sets

SMTP was originally defined only for the 7-bit US-ASCII character set, convenient only for representing the English language. Other languages that use a Latin character set, but with diacritics like accents or tilde, can be represented, but suffer some information loss. Languages that use non-Latin characters, like those written in Greek or Cyrillic alphabets, or those that use thousands of characters in their written form, like Chinese or Korean, have to use some other format to be transmitted over SMTP. For this reason, MIME supports the transmission of data in arbitrary character sets, such as Big 5, or the ISO-8859- series, or more importantly, Unicode encodings, like UTF-8 and UTF-16. The ESA can accept and deliver messages in any character set.

The character set used by text MIME types is specified in the Content-Type header with the charset parameter. For example, 7-bit clean-text message body might use

```
Content-Type: text/plain; charset=US-ASCII
```

Where an HTML format message in Unicode might use

```
Content-Type: text/html; charset=utf-8
```

If the content is encoded with a scheme like Base64, the Content-Type character set refers to the character set of the original data, and that character set should be used for the decoded data. The MIME-encoding schemes all use US-ASCII for their encoded representation, regardless of the original source character set.

Domain Name Service (DNS) and DNS MX Records in IPv4 and IPv6

SMTP is intimately connected with the Internet Domain Name System (DNS). DNS Mail Exchanger (MX) records replaced earlier MD and MF records in RFC 973 in January 1986, some time after SMTP had been in general use. Early SMTP implementations relied on HOSTS.TXT instead of DNS.

To deliver Internet mail, any SMTP client must first determine the domain of each of the recipients of the message it is attempting to deliver. This is normally the portion of the email address after the @ sign. RFC 5321 states, unambiguously, the process for SMTP clients to follow when determining the destination host. The client must first perform a DNS MX lookup on the domain. If no MX record is found, the client must lookup an A record for the domain, and if present, treat it as it would an MX record.

An MX record is a domain-level resource record. An MX record for a domain supplies three key pieces of information: first, the Time to Live (TTL) that's common for all DNS resource records; second, one or more hostnames of servers capable of receiving email via SMTP for that domain; third, the numerical priority of each host, alternately described as MX preference, weight, or cost, of each host.

Once the list of hosts in the MX record is found, the client selects the lowest-numbered host (the lowest cost) and performs an A lookup to determine the correct destination IP. The client then makes a connection attempt on port 25 to that destination IP. Some clients, like ESA, look up all the A records for all MXs at once for efficient lookups. If there is more than one equal-cost MX, all of them are looked up and the client is free to select any at random. When a destination IP is unavailable, the client must attempt all of the equal cost hosts, before moving to the next-lowest-cost host or hosts. The process continues until the first IP that accepts connections on destination port 25 is found.

In IPv6, MX records haven't changed at all, other than the fact that the hosts they list may have both A and AAAA records, or just AAAA records. As of this writing, the number of domains publishing MX and hosts with AAAA records is fairly low, and the number of sites accepting SMTP over IPv6 is likewise low, but growing.

Message Transfer Agents (MTA)

We've used the acronym MTA repeatedly, so before we go much further, we now describe MTAs and the functions they provide. Because the ESA is, at its heart, a purpose-built MTA, it's important to know what they are and are not.

Here are the chief responsibilities of an MTA for Internet email at an organization:

- **Accepting Internet mail for local domains:** The MTA accepts connections from Internet senders for email being sent to local recipients. MTAs should not accept email for recipients in domains other than those of the local organization. Accepting mail for non-local domains means the MTA is an *open relay*, meaning that it allows any client to send email to any domain. Because this allows malicious clients to use your servers to deliver their email, your organization becomes a spam and virus source by proxy. If your servers are accidentally configured as open relays, their IP addresses will be added to the blacklists that track sources of junk email.
- **Verifying local recipient addresses:** MTAs should verify that a recipient email address exists before accepting it. This isn't required, but is strongly recommended, both for the health of your own environment and for being a better Internet citizen.
- **Queuing mail and retrying messages:** Although not strictly required, most MTAs are store-and-forward systems that operate asynchronously. That is, the transmission from client to MTA, and MTA to destination, are performed independently, at separate times and over different connections. In between acceptance and delivery, MTAs are expected to store their messages, and in the event of an unavailable destination or an error in transmissions, retry periodically until the message is delivered.
- **Directing recipients to an appropriate destination:** Local recipient mailboxes may reside across a number of different local or remote servers. MTAs typically provide features to identify recipients, look up the appropriate destination in a table or in a directory, and deliver the mail there.
- **Delivering mail from local users to the Internet:** Individual email clients and mailstores like Microsoft Exchange or Lotus Notes send all nonlocal traffic to an MTA for final delivery to an Internet destination. The MTA deals with all the vagaries of Internet email: connection reliability, DNS records, down hosts, and message queuing and retries.
- **Filtering messages:** Many MTA software packages provided basic filtering of messages, or plugin approaches to integrating external filtering, but the introduction of the ESA made junk filtering a primary task of gateway MTAs.

MTAs are one portion of email infrastructure that also typically includes a mail store or database (like Microsoft Exchange or IMAP servers) and MUAs, like Microsoft Outlook, Lotus Notes, Mozilla Thunderbird, or web-based mail clients. MTAs do not duplicate the functions of these products, and so do not provide retrieval, composition, or archiving of messages. MTAs do not typically store messages—only keeping them in memory or on disk until delivered.

It is possible to have a single server running MTA, MUA, and mailstore, although the combination of mailstore and MTA is the most common. In fact, this dual role is likely the most common experience with MTAs that administrators have.

From the basic of MTA functionality, various opensource and commercial products have expanded the scope of capabilities, transforming the traffic cop directing a few email messages an hour into a gateway security device responsible for tens or hundreds of thousands per hour.

Abuse of SMTP

Abusing the SMTP protocol is almost as old as the protocol itself. The latest RFC, 5321, deprecates certain SMTP features, or allows servers to ignore them, because of their use in exploits. SMTP was built in an era of trust and the hosts connected to the early Internet were known organizations and were trustworthy. Because SMTP requires no authentication, it's easy to forge information, and there are a number of threats related to specific SMTP tricks that the ESA can protect against.

Relaying Mail and Open Relays

Once upon a time, an SMTP server owner could trust that clients that connected would only attempt to deliver messages to recipients that were local to the server's organization. This makes perfect sense, because a client should only be aware of a given SMTP server through MX record lookup for the target organization. As a result, many SMTP servers were configured to relay mail for all destinations so that if recipients were somehow mistakenly sent to a particular server it could forward to the right destination.

This nice feature was, of course, one of the first exploits that spammers found, allowing them to deliver messages to unsuspecting legitimate servers that dutifully forwarded their junk on to a third party. Such hosts are known as open relays if they relay for all destinations. Today, all SMTP server solutions prevent relaying except by strict permission. ESA goes one step further, identifying repeated relay attempts as a sign of junk mail sources, and rate limiting or dropping these connections.

Relaying still exists today on the Internet, because many SMTP servers are configured to allow relaying by authorized clients that can successfully authenticate by using the AUTH command. This is convenient for remote users, but by having a single factor of authentication, is dangerous when publicly available. Malicious senders exert a lot of effort to steal email account credentials from users, either with social-engineering email messages, fake *password reset* websites, or keystroke loggers. Stolen credentials can be used to get a relaying "free pass" for a spam sender. Another common relay vector is web-based email open to the public Internet, protected only by username and password. Once compromised, local user accounts are used to send more junk email, using your servers and ruining their good Internet reputation.

Bounces, Bounce Storms, and Misdirected Bounces

Another standard behavior of messaging systems that assumed trustworthy senders was the Delivery Status Notification, or a *bounce* message. It's also often called a Non-Delivery Record (NDR). In technical terms, a bounce is just another SMTP message, composed by a system at some point in the delivery path back to the original envelope sender. The message usually contains information about the original message, and any information it has about why the delivery failed. Formats vary; some systems send back a copy of the entire original message and others create generic bounces with no information about the original, not even the recipient address that failed.

What happens if the sender address is forged? Well, any receiving system that accepts the message, only to have it bounce later, will send it back to the forged address. The bounce message may contain content from the original, including any malicious URLs, making this a potential threat vector for your organization. Even if the bounces don't contain malicious content, they can be confusing and aggravating to users. Additionally, although a few simple bounce messages may not be much of a threat, en masse, they represent a significant problem. If thousands of servers across the Internet each send thousands of bounces per hour to your organization, the effect is a distributed denial of service (DDoS) that can render all of your MTAs too overloaded to handle legitimate mail.

Some of these storms are intentional. If an attacker composes thousands of messages with your email address as sender and sends it to known-invalid recipients at SMTP servers that exhibit this accept first, bounce later behavior, you will get thousands of bounce messages. Figure 1-1 illustrates this problem.

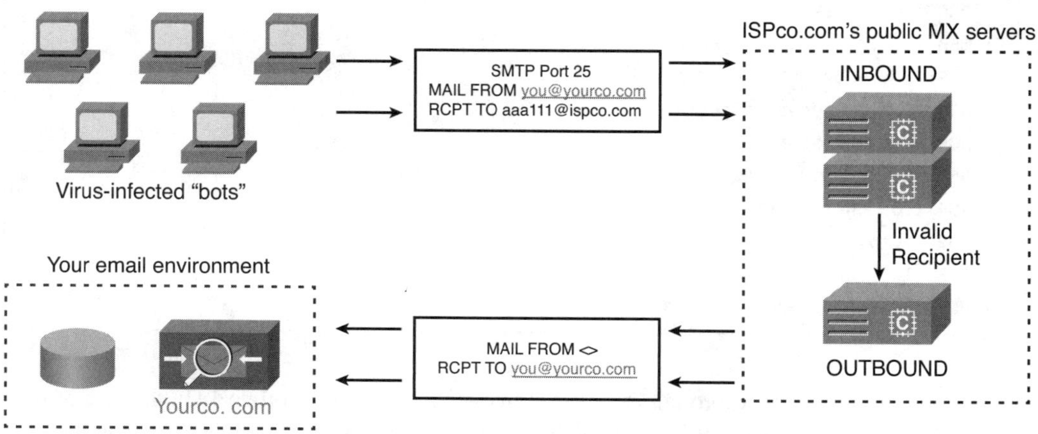

Figure 1-1 *Misdirected Bounce or Bounce Storm Problem*

The ESA provides a dedicated Bounce Verification (BV) feature to protect against this kind of attack. BV marks up messages sent by your organization, so that if they bounce, it can be recognized as having originally coming from your environment. Bounce messages lacking the markup can be discarded quickly and safely.

The other side of the problem is that you don't want to be a source of these bounces, either. The ideal solution to avoid being a source of storms is to never accept recipients that will ultimately not be delivered. This can be done by checking a table or (preferably) a directory of valid recipient addresses at SMTP connection time and providing a response code back to the sender indicating success or failure. ESA provides this through the static Recipient Access Table, via LDAP Accept queries, or a combination of both.

Directory Harvest Attacks

The directory checking and SMTP conversation-time rejection or acceptance of recipients leads to yet another problem. A system that reliably reports a recipient as valid or not can be repeatedly checked for all possible recipients. The search space of alphanumeric characters is small enough that it can be brute-force attempted in hours or minutes. From this, the attacker now has a thorough list of all the valid addresses at a given domain, and these addresses can be sold or used in spam campaigns. Example 1-3 demonstrates an SMTP harvest attack conversation.

Example 1-3 *Directory Harvest Attack*

```
220 esa02.cisco.com ESMTP
HELO external-sender.com
250 esa02.cisco.com
MAIL FROM: <sender@external-sender.com>
250 sender <sender@external-sender.com> ok
RCPT TO: chris@cisco.com
550 #5.1.0 Address rejected.
RCPT TO: cporter@cisco.com
550 #5.1.0 Address rejected.
RCPT TO: chrisporter@cisco.com
550 #5.1.0 Address rejected.
RCPT TO: chriport@cisco.com
250 recipient <chriport@cisco.com> ok
RCPT TO: chrisp@cisco.com
550 #5.1.0 Address rejected.
```

The ESA provides thorough Directory Harvest Attack Prevention (DHAP) through Mail Flow Policies. Each policy dictates the maximum number of invalid recipients per hour that are considered acceptable. Any sender that exceeds the maximum number is disconnected and cannot reconnect for a full hour, making brute-force harvests impossible. By setting the value appropriately, depending on the policy and the size of the environment, we can allow legitimate senders to be quickly and accurately notified of undeliverable mail while identifying and stopping harvesters. Example 1-4 shows an example of DHAP in use.

Example 1-4 *Directory Harvest Attack Prevention*

```
RCPT TO: <aaron@cisco.com>
550 #5.1.0 Address rejected.
RCPT TO: <abby@cisco.com>
550 #5.1.0 Address rejected.
RCPT TO: <adam@cisco.com>
550 #5.1.0 Address rejected.
RCPT TO: <alan@cisco.com>
250 recipient <alan@cisco.com> ok
RCPT TO: <alfred@cisco.com>
550 #5.1.0 Address rejected.
550 Too many invalid recipients
Connection closed by foreign host.
```

Summary

As we've seen, email security is a multifaceted problem that encompasses more than just spam and virus filtering. Cisco's ESA is designed to solve a wide variety of email delivery, reliability, and security issues, with a feature set that has evolved continually since the product's launch in 2003.

At the heart of email security and the ESA feature set is SMTP, the protocol underpinning all Internet email. SMTP is a scalable, sturdy protocol that has served its purpose well for more than 30 years, but has limitations that are important to understand. We discussed the critical parts of SMTP, DNS, and Internet email message formats.

Chapter 2

ESA Product Basics

In this chapter, you will learn the following:

- Models of appliances and their hardware features
- Running the basic system setup wizard, and the resulting configuration
- Basic networking options and recommended configurations
- Configuring and testing network access for product updates
- Configuring the security filtering features

Hardware Overview

The Cisco IronPort ESAs are 1U and 2U hardware appliances in a 19-inch rack-mount form factor. Because they're based on standard Intel platform computer server hardware, they fit in most any standard data center 19-inch racks. The appliances are supplied with sliding rails for rack mounting. Table 2-1 lists the various Email Security Appliance (ESA) models that are shipping and supported as of this writing. Earlier models included the C30, C300, C350, C60, C600, C650, X1000, and X1050 models, which are no longer available for sale.

Table 2-1 *ESA Models and Characteristics*

Platform	Form Factor	CPU and RAM	Mail Queue	RAID	Ethernet
C160	1U	One dual-core 2.4 Ghz, 4 GB RAM	10 GB	Software RAID 1 (Mirror)	Two 10/100/1000 copper
C170	1U	One dual-core 2.8 Ghz, 4 GB RAM	10 GB	Software RAID 1 (Mirror)	Two 10/100/1000 copper
C360	2U	One quad-core 2.3 Ghz, 4 GB RAM	35 GB	RAID 1 (Mirror)	Three 10/100/1000 copper
C370	2U	One quad-core 2 Ghz, 4 GB RAM	35 GB	RAID 1 (Mirror)	Three 10/100/1000 copper
C660	2U	Two quad-core 2.3 Ghz, 4 GB RAM	70 GB	RAID 1+0 (Mirrored and striped)	Three 10/100/1000 copper
C670	2U	Two quad-core 2 Ghz, 4 GB RAM	70 GB	RAID 1+0 (Mirrored and striped)	Three 10/100/1000 copper
X1060	2U	Two quad-core 2.8 Ghz, 4 GB RAM	70 GB	RAID 1+0 (Mirrored and striped)	Three 10/100/1000 copper
X1070	2U	Two quad-core 2.66 Ghz, 4 GB RAM	70 GB	RAID 1+0 (Mirrored and striped)	Three 10/100/1000 copper

2U Enterprise Models

As of this writing, the current 2U enterprise models are the C370, C670, and X1070 ESAs. All have redundant, hot-swappable power supplies, one or two quad core CPUs, 4 GB RAM, and hardware RAID, either with two drives mirrored (RAID 1) or four or six drives mirrored and striped (RAID 1+0, or RAID 10). All the disks are hot-swappable. All models have dual hot-swap replaceable AC power supplies. There are two 10/100/1000 copper network interface cards (NIC) labeled *Data 1* and *Data 2* that can be paired, and a third 10/100/1000 NIC labeled *Management*. Despite the labels, the Ethernet interfaces can be used for any supported services. Fiber-optic interfaces are available as an optional component. All models have a 9-pin serial port for console access and ship with a null modem cable.

1U Enterprise Models

The C170 is the smallest ESA and is a 1U 19-inch rack-mount appliance. It differs considerably from the larger appliances. It has a single dual-core CPU, 4 GB RAM, dual SATA drives in a software RAID 1 configuration, and two 10/100/1000 copper NICs, labeled *Data 1* and *Data 2*. It does not support NIC pairing, and it has a single AC power supply. It also provides a 9-pin serial port for console access.

Selecting a Model

The primary difference between the ESA models is performance, usually measured in terms of throughput: how many messages can be accepted, filtered, and delivered by the system in a given unit of time. Throughput is usually specified in messages per hour or messages per second, at a given average message size. Performance depends heavily on the configuration of the system, especially on the choice of security filters being run. In general, the units with more CPU cores, or faster clock CPUs, have higher throughput, as expected. In some configurations, however, the additional cores won't be used.

Another practical concern is the need for hardware redundancy. Because of hardware RAID, hot swap disk, and redundant hot-swap power supplies, the 2U models have higher Mean Time Between Failure (MTBF). Replacing drives or power supplies on the 1U models requires powering down the appliances and opening the chassis.

The 2U models also support NIC pairing, where the two physical jacks on the motherboard share the same MAC and IP address. One of the jacks is denoted as primary and is used for all network traffic until a failure occurs, and traffic is switched to the backup NIC. Cable, switch port, NIC failures, or any other problem with the physical connection triggers a failover to the backup port.

Basic Setup via the WUI System Setup Wizard

All ESA models ship in a *factory default* configuration with a single network interface preconfigured. None of the filtering engines, reporting, or even the basic Simple Mail Transfer Protocol (SMTP), is running. Logging and administrative subsystems are running at their default settings. No user accounts are available other than the superuser, *admin*. Before you do anything with the ESA, perform at least some basic setup. In this chapter, we cover the most common means of setup, using the web-based user interface (WUI) and its System Setup Wizard. Even if you're an expert, I recommend using the wizard—it's too easy to forget something doing it manually. Even after nearly 8 years installing ESAs, I start with the wizard.

Connecting to the ESA for the First Time

When you unbox the ESA, you find, along with the appliance itself, the usual accessories, like an Ethernet cable, AC power cords, and a 9-pin *null modem* cable for connecting to the ESA serial console. The Ethernet and AC power cables are just generic cables, and you're free to use your own. Save the null modem cable, even if you have no plans to use it, because a regular 9-pin serial cable will not work with the ESA console.

For the 2U models, the appliance has dual, redundant power supplies. To make use of this redundancy, you have to use the two individual AC power cords plugged into separate power sources, and not the double Y cord. The Y-cable is supplied just for convenience and isn't designed for production use.

Once plugged in, the LCD console at the front of the appliance lights up, the power supply lights turn on, and you may see network link lights on the back if you've plugged in an Ethernet cable. This doesn't mean that the appliance is powered on! In a loud data center, it can be difficult to determine if an ESA is actually up and running, and not just plugged in. If you pull down the front bezel door, a powered-on ESA will have green lights on all of the disks. To power on, just push the power button under the bezel door, or for 1U units, right on the front faceplate. The 1U units also have a small disk LED on the faceplate, which should blink periodically if the unit is powered on.

To connect to the ESA, my preferred method is to plug one end of an Ethernet cable into the ESA port labeled Management and the other end into a laptop or other PC. You have to use the Data 1 port on 1U models. A crossover cable usually isn't necessary with modern autosensing NICs. The ESA management port is preconfigured with an IP address of 192.168.42.42/24 and has SSH, HTTP, and HTTPS enabled. If you change your laptop NIC settings to a different static IP on that same network, you can connect to these management ports. Alternately, you can use a hub or switch and plug both the ESA and your laptop into it.

We are going to thoroughly address connecting to the appliance command-line interface (CLI) using SSH in Chapter 5, "Command-Line Interface." For now, launch a web browser and put the URL of https://192.168.42.42 into the address bar. Any browser that supports JavaScript should suffice. You get a certificate warning but should then be presented with the login page, as shown in Figure 2-1.

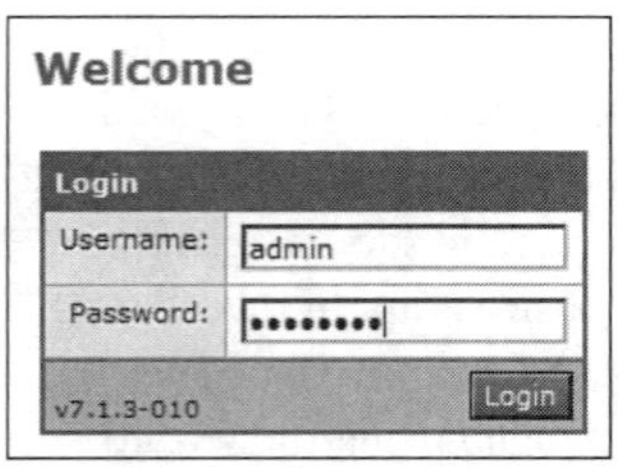

Figure 2-1 *Email Security Appliance Login Page*

Running the System Setup Wizard

From the factory, the only user account on the ESA is the Administrative account named *admin*. The default password is *ironport*. Once logged in, you should see the start of the System Setup Wizard (SSW). You must complete the entire SSW before you can see the full administrative interface. The ESA ships with a printed *Quick Start Guide* that includes blank spaces to write in the information that the SSW will ask for. It's a good idea to review this and fill it out before you start the setup process.

You don't necessarily have to run the wizard. For example, if you want only to put an ESA on a network segment to load an existing configuration file, or to join a centralized management (CM) cluster, you can do that via the command line by connecting to SSH. This topic is covered in Chapter 5, so for this chapter, we assume that you are initially installing an ESA for testing or production and want to use the wizard.

The first page of the setup wizard is the end-user license agreement, as shown in Figure 2-2. (The full text of this license agreement is available at https://support.ironport.com/license/eula.html.)

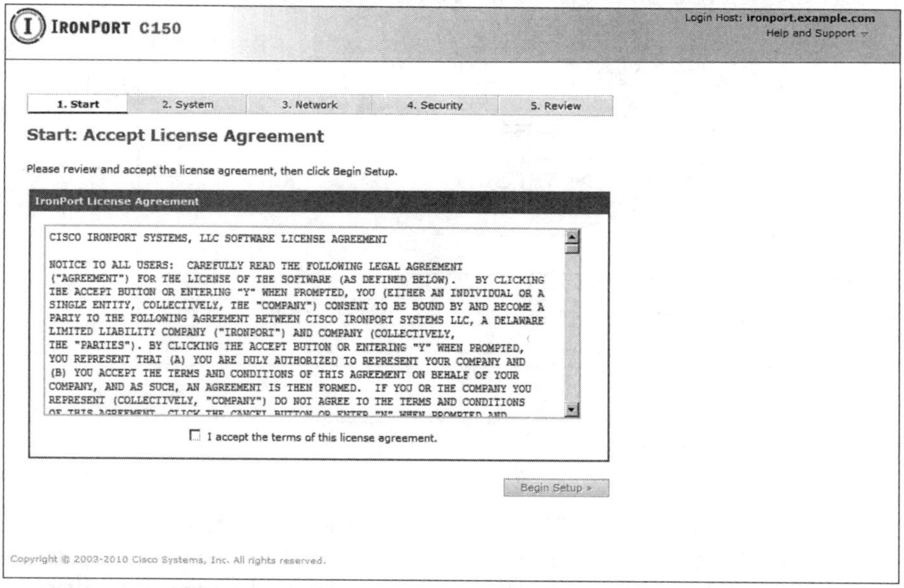

Figure 2-2 *Accept the EULA to Continue*

> **Note** If you find that you don't have a piece of information available when it's being requested by the SSW, don't sweat it. All the values you enter here can be changed later, even hostnames and IPs. So, if you're not sure of a value, put something in temporarily. Just remember to go back and correct it.
>
> Similarly, if you need to configure the ESA with a lot of data, it's often easier to import it later rather than enter it into the SSW. For example, if your company accepts email for dozens, hundreds, or thousands of domains, it's easier to put just the first one into the wizard and then later use the import features to bring it all in at once.

The second step covers global settings for the ESA. The global hostname is used for identifying the appliance and for addresses in reports and alerts. It must be a fully qualified hostname, and you must change it from the default value of *ironport.example.com*. You'll be setting the hostname on the individual IP interfaces in the next step. Figure 2-3 shows the global settings you're configuring.

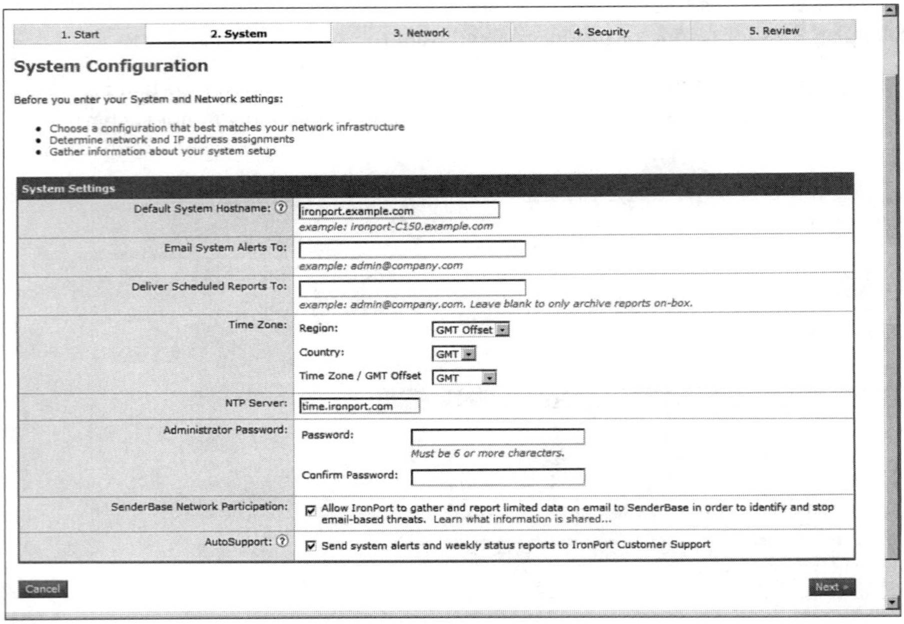

Figure 2-3 *Global System Settings*

For this example, we configure the ESA with a single IP and a single hostname, called esa02.cisco.com. We use that same hostname as the global default and for the IP interface we configure in the next step. The other settings on this page are an email address for alerts and reports. Make sure that the alert address is going to at least one real address with someone who can take action on these messages, as the alerts potentially include system health issues, like hardware failures or key expirations. Ignoring alerts can mean high-profile email outages. Time zone should be set appropriately, or to GMT offset, and if possible, an NTP server should be used. You can use the default server, time.ironport.com, provided that the ESA can get to this server on port 123/UDP.

The next boxes cover changing the password for the admin user, although the wizard will accept *ironport* if you want to keep it the same. The last two ask for two opt-in services: the SenderBase Network Participation (SBNP) and AutoSupport messages. AutoSupport is a weekly email of system-status information to IronPort Customer Support; Cisco uses it only in the event of an issue with an appliance and subsequent support calls. AutoSupport also sends you a copy every Sunday evening.

SBNP is a limited form of phone home that transmits summary information about sending IP addresses and hashed filenames of attachments to messages. The link in this box gives you a full report of the information that is shared, and Cisco provides full disclosure. The information obtained is aggregate, statistical information that helps improve all the Cisco security services. Opting-in is highly recommended, because in addition to helping Cisco improve the service, it can improve results in your environment, especially against targeted spam messages.

The next page is networking and email domain information, as shown in Figures 2-4 and 2-5. Figure 2-4 shows the gateway and Domain Name System (DNS) information.

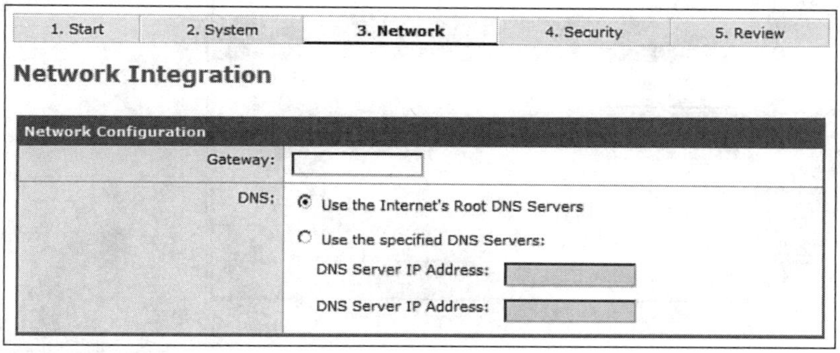

Figure 2-4 *Gateway and DNS Settings*

The default gateway must be on the same subnet as the IP interfaces we're going to configure at the bottom of this page. You can either provide a local DNS server IP address or let the ESA do its own resolution by choosing **Internet Root Servers**. If you choose the root servers, the ESA must be able to reach all Internet destinations on port 53 UDP and TCP. DNS specifies both UDP and TCP and some queries the ESA makes could require the use of TCP. I recommend that this setting be verified for accuracy and connectivity; although it can be changed later, an ESA with invalid DNS settings takes longer to allow connections while it waits for DNS timeouts.

Figure 2-5 is the bottom of the same page. We're setting up a C150 ESA model, a 1U unit, and it only has Data 1 and Data 2 interfaces. With a 2U unit, like a C360 or X1070, we would have another check box for the management interface. The diagram on the page shows a 2U unit, regardless of the model you're actually running.

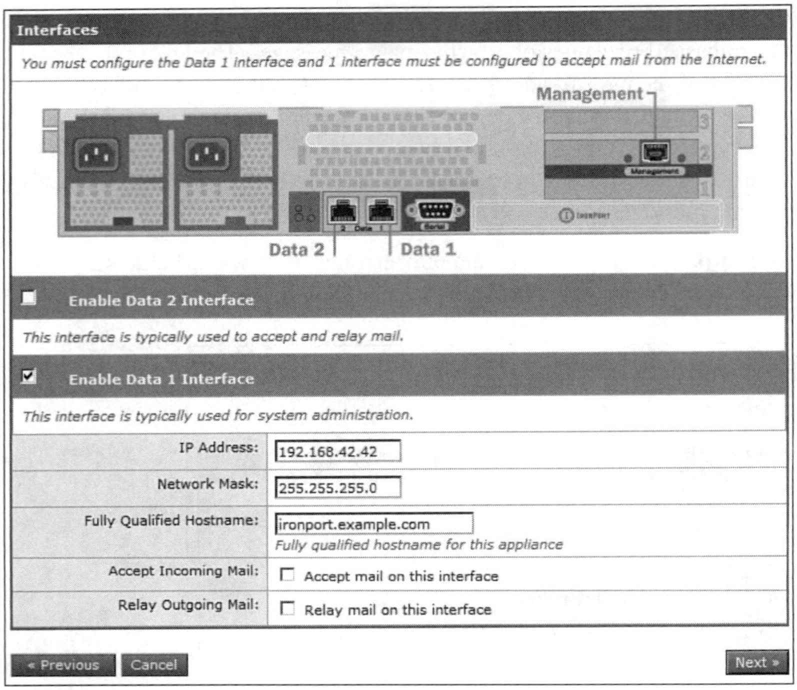

Figure 2-5 *Interface Settings*

For each physical interface, you must specify IP address, subnet mask, and hostname, and whether the ESA should accept incoming mail from the Internet and outgoing mail from internal hosts. This example setup is simple: We're just going to use Data 1, and we'll give it the same hostname as we did in the global hostname setting in the last step. At least one interface on the ESA must be on the same subnet as the default gateway.

By choosing **Accept mail on this interface**, you instruct the ESA to create a *public listener* that accepts mail for the domain or domains you list here. This means that, after the SSW finishes, the ESA will begin accepting connections on this interface on port 25. SMTP clients that connect are able to send mail to any domain that you specify here. In this case, the ESA accepts email to *<user>@cisco.com* for any user; further, the messages is delivered, after processing, to 192.168.1.60. Any messages accepted in this way are treated as incoming mail messages for policy purposes. We cover these concepts in more detail later, and in Chapter 3, "ESA Email Pipeline."

By choosing **Relay mail on this interface**, you instruct the ESA to allow the listed IPs or hosts to connect on port 25 and allow those hosts to send messages to any email address, whether at local or Internet domains. This is a high level of privilege, so this entry should be carefully considered. It should be limited to those authorized local servers that send mail outside the organization.

The next step is to set up the security engines, as shown in Figure 2-6.

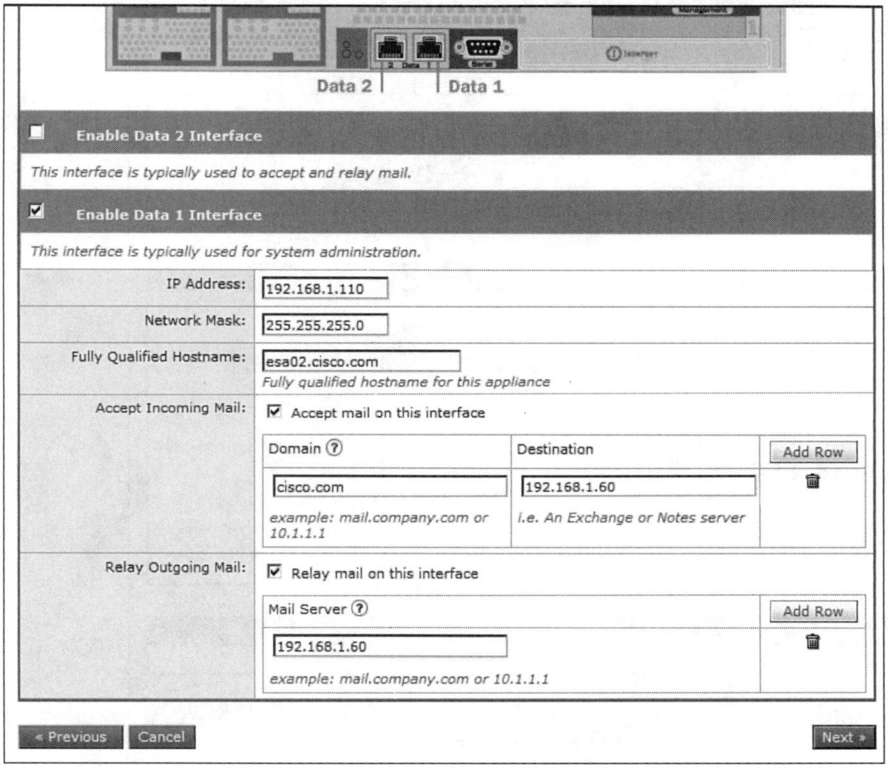

Figure 2-6 *Security Engine Setup*

This page doesn't actually require that you turn these engines on, but the radio buttons and check boxes are set by default. I don't see any reason to change these defaults right now, and we can always edit the configuration later. If you're planning to put this system into production as an Internet mail gateway, having the security engines up and running is imperative. Just click **Next** to advance to the next page, which is the last of this wizard.

The final page of the SSW is shown in Figure 2-7. It's a review page that allows you to examine all the settings you've entered so far.

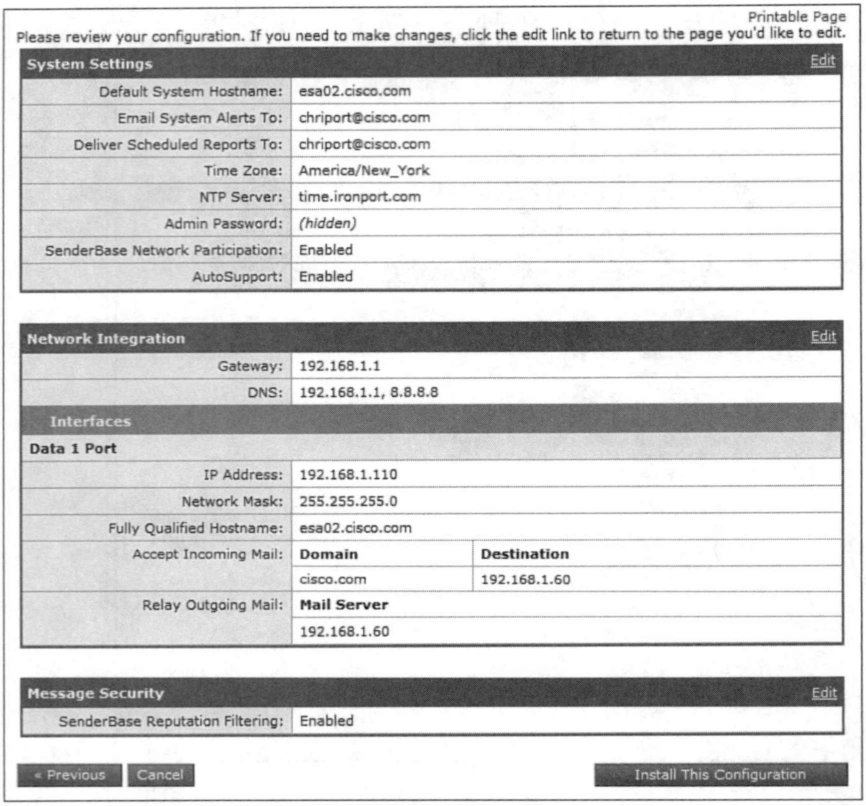

Figure 2-7 *Configuration Review Is the Last Chance to Make Changes*

On my ESA, a C150, I'm just using one physical NIC, Data 1, and I've given it an IP of 192.168.1.110. I'll have to set up a static Network Address Translation (NAT) for it to be available on the public Internet. I've set it to accept mail on this interface for cisco.com, deliver that mail to 192.168.1.60, and to accept outgoing mail from that same server.

This is a fairly typical setup for a *one-armed* configuration with a single IP address. Unless you specifically know that this configuration will not work for you, it's a model that I recommend. We discuss multiple network configurations later in this chapter and throughout this book.

Click **Install This Configuration** to make the changes effective. Because you're changing IP addresses, it's likely at this point that your browser connection will time out.

Reconnecting to the WUI

Now that the changes have been installed, your browser likely can't get back to HTTPS WUI because we changed the default 192.168.42.42 IP. At this point, you can disconnect your laptop and plug the configured port on the ESA into the proper switch port in your network. Assuming we have all the correct network information, the WUI should be available by navigating to the new IP address. In my example, that URL is https://192.168.1.110/.

Note If you can't reconnect to the WUI after setup, there are a couple of troubleshooting steps to take:

1. Verify the physical network. Check the cables and the switch port. Verify that the interface on the ESA has link and activity lights.
2. Ping the ESA from a computer on the same subnet. If the problem is a firewall, gateway, or NAT issue, you should be able to ping the ESA, and log into the WUI from the same subnet.
3. Be sure that you haven't assigned the ESA an IP that's already in use. Unplug the ESA and ping its assigned IP. This can be a difficult root cause to diagnose.

If you find that the likely cause is a misconfiguration, you have a couple of options for getting back in to an unreachable ESA:

- **Ethernet:** Reconnect the Ethernet cable directly between the ESA and another server or a laptop. Change that server or laptop's IP to one on the same subnet as the ESA. You can also plug the computer and ESA into the same switch or hub.
- **Serial:** Connect using the serial console cable supplied with the ESA, connected to a standard 9-pin serial port on a PC. Under **Windows**, start Hyperterminal and connect to COM1 with settings 9600 baud, 8 data bits, No parity, and 1 stop bit (9600-8-N-1.) From there, log in as admin and inspect the network settings with interfaceconfig and setgateway.
- **KVM:** It is possible to remove the cover over the VGA display connector, cable that to a monitor, and plug a USB keyboard into one of the two available USB ports on the back. After pressing **Enter** on the keyboard, you should get a login prompt. This is the same CLI access you would have from Serial or from SSH. This isn't supported by Cisco, however.

LDAP Wizard and Next Steps

After you reconnect, you are greeted with another setup wizard, this time for Active Directory (AD). It's your choice if you want to run this now or later. Although the SSW is not available after the initial setup, the AD Wizard is available anytime from the LDAP page of the **System Administration** tab. The configuration page of the AD Wizard is shown in Figure 2-8.

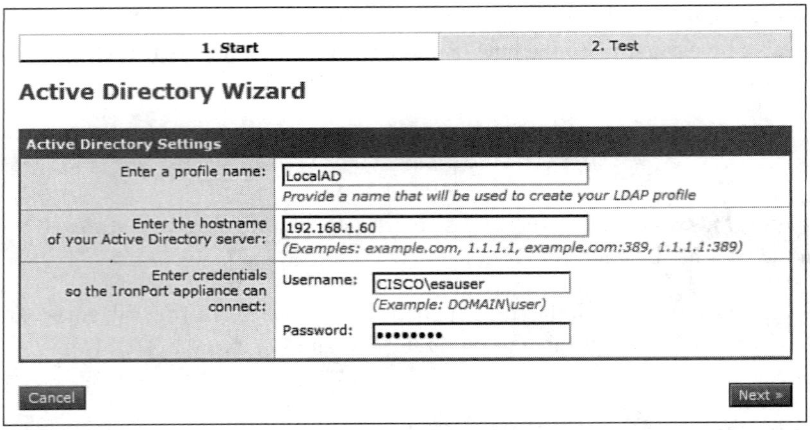

Figure 2-8 *Active Directory Wizard*

If you want to go through the AD Wizard, enter the requested information and click **Next**. For the username, I recommend using a basic AD user account whose password is not set to expire and does not need to be changed. Almost any account can be used as long as it can bind to the AD server, but I strongly recommend against using any kind of privileged account, like administrator, because the password is stored by the ESA in the clear and would be accessible to any administrator or operator user of the ESA. We are going to thoroughly cover the set up and use of LDAP and ADs in Chapter 7, "Directories and Policies." If you're not using AD or want to configure LDAP later, just click **Cancel**.

Once the test is successful, the ESA should finally present you with the full administrative web interface, with five menu tabs across the top, as shown in Figure 2-9.

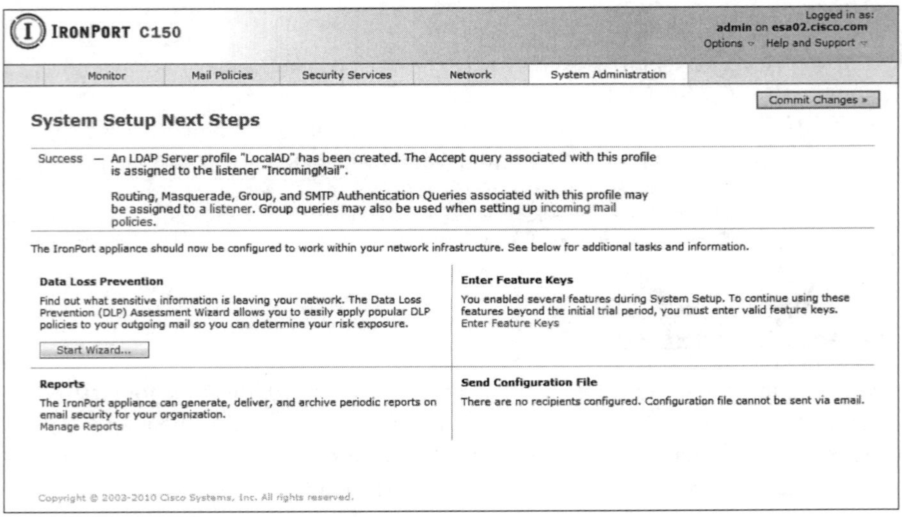

Figure 2-9 *System Setup Next Steps*

This page also provides you with some possible next steps—running the DLP wizard, creating scheduled reports, entering feature keys, and managing configuration. Because we cover all these topics in detail at other points in this book, we do not dive into them here. Note that the **Commit Changes** button is highlighted because we ran the AD Wizard. From this point on, any configuration change will not be effective until you go through the Commit process. We cover the commit process later, but it's fairly self-explanatory.

Examining the Basic Configuration

Now that the setup wizard is complete, and you've reconnected to the ESA WUI, you should see the full administrative interface of the ESA. We thoroughly examine all parts of the WUI in Chapter 4, "ESA Web User Interface." For now, however, we just look at the configuration pages for which the SSW has actually given us settings.

The most obvious are the settings for the network, which are stored in the **IP Interfaces**, **DNS**, and **Routing** entries under the **Network** menu. The IP interfaces created by the wizard should have SSH and HTTPS enabled for management. The DNS server, or servers that you entered in the wizard, all have priority 0. No static routes other than the default gateway are created.

Another important component created by the wizard for you is a listener, and two important tables that are attached to the listener: the Host Access Table (HAT) and the Recipient Access Table (RAT). These two tables are found under the **HAT Overview** and **Mail Flow Policies** items under the **Mail Policies** menu.

The settings for the physical interface ports are only available in the CLI, which is covered in Chapter 5. The **etherconfig** command, and **media** submenu, shows us the settings that the ESA chose for the ports, which is autonegotiate in all cases:

```
Ethernet interfaces:
1. Data 1 (Autoselect: <1000baseTX full-duplex>) 00:22:19:d6:0a:91
2. Data 2 (Autoselect: <link is down>)) 00:22:19:d6:0a:92
```

Cisco recommends leaving the Ethernet interfaces set to Autoselect unless you're certain you need otherwise. I agree with this setting. For gigabit (1000BASE-TX), autoselect is the only port mode supported and, even if you set it otherwise, negotiation is performed.

Next Steps

From here, a few steps are typically taken before putting the system into production. I recommend that you review the built-in **Incoming Mail Policies** in the **Mail Policies** menu to be sure that they match your expectations. If you chose to enable **IronPort Anti-Spam (IPAS)** and the **IronPort Spam Quarantine (ISQ)**, messages will be scanned for spam content, and messages flagged as such will be sent into the ISQ on this ESA. If you are running more than one ESA, with an SMA, this is probably not what you want, and you should disable the ESA ISQ and enable the **Centralized ISQ**.

It's also important to check for connectivity to other systems, first, for the ability to send and receive email over SMTP to and from the Internet, and to and from your specified internal servers. Second, the ESA needs Internet access on HTTP (TCP 80) and HTTPS (TCP 443) to be able to retrieve updates for security engines, rule updates, and AsyncOS upgrades. You can easily check the status of rule and engine updates from the appropriate item under the **Security Services** menu. IPAS and antivirus rules should have an update within the last few hours, as these engines are checking for updates every 5 minutes.

You can also check connectivity by checking for AsyncOS upgrades. This is done through the **System Upgrade** item on the **System Administration** menu. In fact, a good step before deploying a new system is to upgrade to the latest AsyncOS release, or at least to an AsyncOS version that matches the others in your environment.

Another option for testing connectivity is to use the CLI commands **ping**, **telnet**, and **traceroute**. If you can telnet to a host called downloads.ironport.com on port 80 and 443, the security engines should update without issue:

```
telnet downloads.ironport.com 80
Trying 184.84.247.65...
Connected to downloads.ironport.com.
Escape character is '^]'.
^]
telnet downloads.ironport.com 443
Trying 184.84.247.65...
Connected to downloads.ironport.com.
Escape character is '^]'.
```

Telnet on the ESA works like the same application on other operating systems, except that it defaults to port 25 if you don't specify the port.

Setup Summary

By using the SSW, you can go from unboxing an ESA to having a running configuration in just a few steps. The wizard takes care of the basics and, with a few other steps, you have a configuration that can be safely deployed as a public Internet mail gateway.

From start to finish, the process for a new ESA in factory configuration is

- **Rack, power, and connect to the ESA:** Be sure the system is turned on, and then connect a crossover or straight-through cable between the ESA's Management, or Data 1 port, and a local PC. Give the PC a static IP, like 192.168.42.41.
- **Point a browser to the ESA and run the WUI SSW:** Use the URL https://192.168.42.42 in a browser to connect. Continue past any certificate errors. Follow the SSW steps.

- **Reconnect to the ESA:** After the configuration is installed, recable the ESA to its intended production switch ports and use the newly assigned IPs to connect to the WUI again.
- **Run the AD Wizard:** If applicable, running the AD Wizard configures two important features: LDAP recipient validation and LDAP group queries. Both are covered in more depth in Chapter 7.
- **Check connectivity:** Be sure that the ESA can reach out to the public Internet on ports 80 and 443, and that port 25 in and out are available.
- **Save a copy of the configuration file:** This is a good habit to get into. Uncheck the box marked **Mask passwords** so that the file can be used to restore the unit if needed.
- **Upgrade:** Unless you have reason to be on an older release, it's advisable to upgrade to the latest generally available AsyncOS release before you do further configuration.
- **Examine the default policies:** The HAT settings from the factory follow the Cisco best practices for good spam filtering without false positives. IPAS settings are likewise configured for good spam filtering with as close to zero false positives as possible. You may choose more aggressive settings or different actions. See Chapter 8, "Security Filtering," for more on the security-filtering engines.

Networking Deployment Models

The System Setup Wizard examples earlier in this chapter used a very simple network deployment mode with a single IP address assigned to the ESA. While this approach is very simple and suitable for many organizations, there are reasons to consider configuring the ESA with multiple IP addresses.

The advantage of using multiple networks is in security and flexibility, but with additional complexity for configuration and troubleshooting.

Interfaces, Routing, and Virtual Gateways

We used the SSW to create a configuration with a single interface and hostname, or a *single-arm* configuration. I usually recommend this configuration because of its simplicity. It's far easier to deal with routing, hostnames, and delivery when we're talking about a single IP. A typical single-arm configuration with ESA on firewall DMZ interface is shown in Figure 2-10.

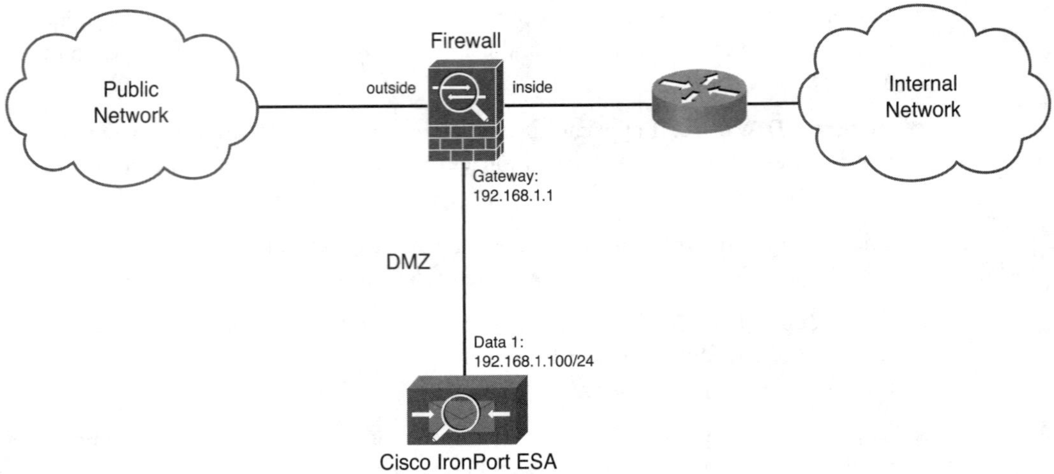

Figure 2-10 *Single-Arm ESA Configuration*

Network routing in this configuration is easy. The ESA connects to and responds to all IPs on the same subnet directly using ARP. To reach any other network, packets are sent to the default gateway. The ESA expects that the default gateway can handle traffic for both internal networks and the public Internet. In our example, we're using a private IP, so a network device like the firewall must provide a static NAT to an outside public Internet address.

With this single interface, the ESA must run all of its services here: SMTP connections for email coming from the public Internet and from inside, and management protocols like SSH and HTTP. It must also use this interface to source connections, like LDAP or syslog, to internal destinations, potentially in violation of security practices that prohibit DMZ interfaces from connecting internally. The single interface can also be assigned to a NIC pair of Data 1 and Data 2, for redundancy in case of a port failure. NIC pairing is only available on the 2U models.

Another option on single-arm configuration is to create multiple logical interfaces on the same physical NIC. Because the ESA can accept and deliver mail on these separate interfaces, Cisco calls them virtual gateways (VG). VGs aren't really a form of virtualization, but it allows you to simulate multiple SMTP servers, or clients, on the same ESA. Further, you can group together the interfaces for round-robin deliveries. You can also separate data from management by using different virtual IPs. We discuss the use of VGs and dealing with multiple delivery source interfaces in Chapter 12, "Advanced Networking."

An example of a single-arm deployment with VGs is shown in Figure 2-11. Note that the multiple private IPs we're using here would each require their own static NAT on the firewall if those IP interfaces were to be used outside.

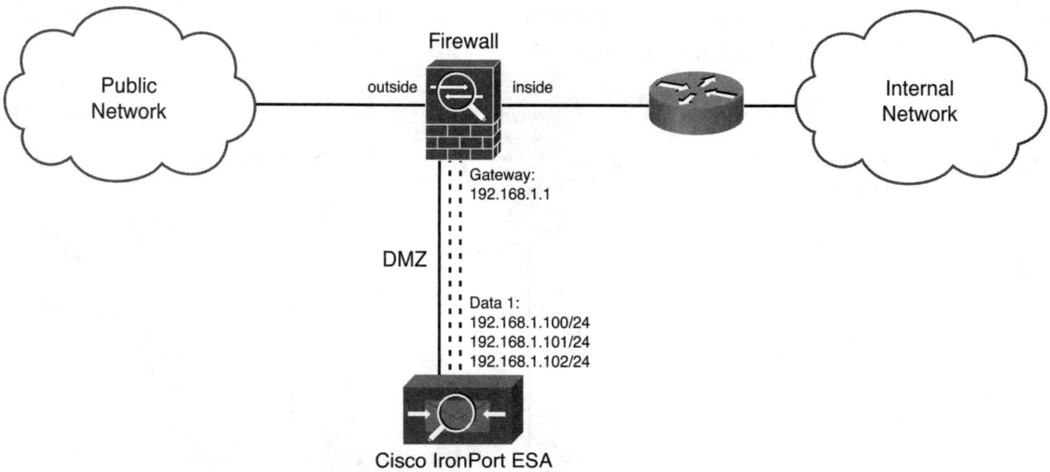

Figure 2-11 *Single Arm, Multiple Interface*

Two- and three-arm configurations are also possible. Two-arm configurations typically mean that one interface is outside and one is inside. For the 1U ESA models, Data 1 is typically the outside and Data 2 the inside, but it doesn't actually matter—these labels are just names. For the 2U models, you have a choice of using Data 1 and Data 2, one Data and Management, or even using a NIC pair of Data 1 and 2 along with Management. Such a configuration is shown in Figure 2-12.

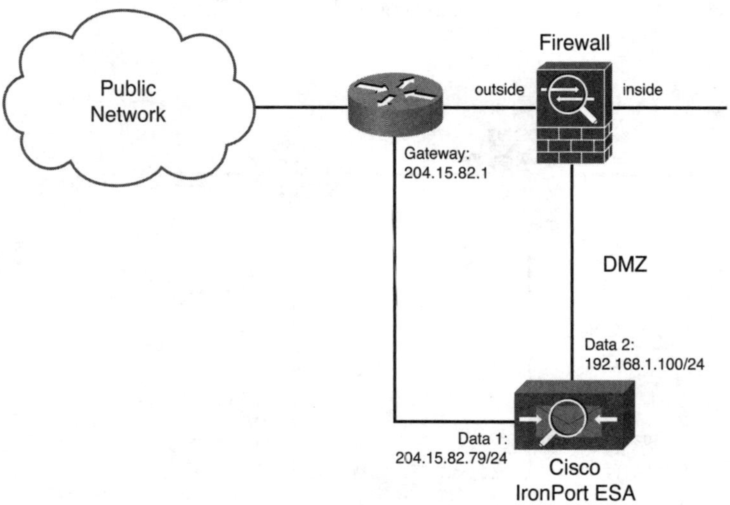

Figure 2-12 *Two-Arm Configuration, Outside and DMZ*

One condition of two- and three-arm configurations is that the two physical interfaces must be on different subnets (that is, the ESA must span networks). If you want the ESA to have two IPs on the same subnet, use the one-arm configuration with VGs, as described previously in Figure 2-10. An example of a two-armed configuration with a paired interface in the DMZ is shown in Figure 2-13. Note that this configuration is only available on the 2U units that support NIC pairing, but a similar deployment can be done with the 1U units using Data 1 and Data 2.

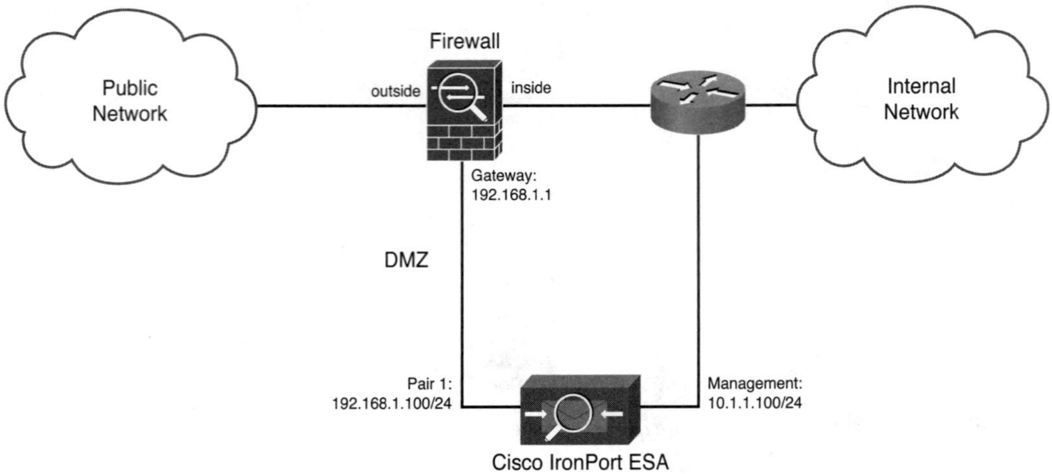

Figure 2-13 *Two-Arm Configuration, with Data 1 and Data 2 Paired*

Lastly, a three-arm configuration is shown in Figure 2-14. Use this model if you must have strict separation of Data and Management and use an out-of-band management network for all servers. Note that routing determines which interfaces are used; if the ESA needs to contact a server on the 172.16.1.0/24 network, it will use the Management interface to source that connection, even for data protocols like SMTP.

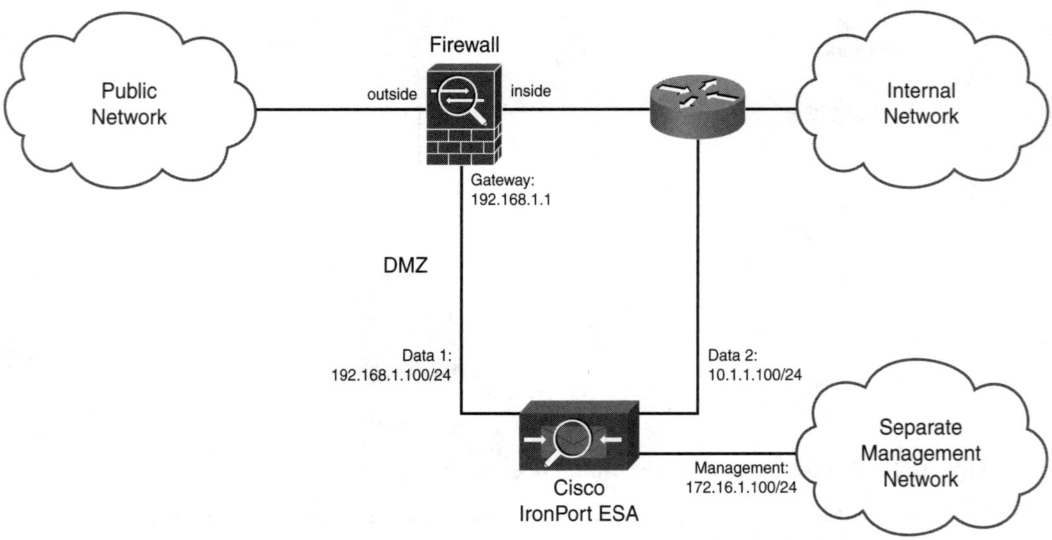

Figure 2-14 *Three-Arm Configuration with All Physical NICs on Separate Networks*

Single Versus Multinetwork Deployment

The ESAs each have two or three labeled physical NICs named Data 1, Data 2, or Management. In reality, they're all identical, and they can all be used for any purpose, not just Data or Management, as indicated by their name. On older model appliances, like the C30 and C60, the management interface supported only 10 Mb and 100 Mb, but all the current models support 1000 Mbps. The ESA does not natively restrict protocols to specific interfaces, other than what you configure. This means that you're free to use one, two, or three interfaces, and divide them up as you see fit. The difference between single and multinetwork deployments on ESA can be summarized by

- **Simplicity:** One-arm configurations don't require static routing. A single IP and hostname on ESA simplifies listeners, certificates, service updates, upgrades, and of course, network troubleshooting. There is a sort of unwritten expectation that servers have one IP and host, and only network devices like routers or firewalls have more than one.
- **Security:** One-arm configurations require all services sourcing from and going to a single interface, so we must rely on a network device like a firewall to restrict access to management interfaces. One-arm configurations with multiple interfaces can provide separation of services with little added complexity. Two-arm configurations can be locked down more thoroughly, but must span networks. Three-arm configurations can completely separate Internet, internal, and management traffic, but are more complex.
- **Performance:** Bandwidth is not really much of a factor here, but you may want to separate SMTP traffic from other data transfers, like log pushes. On Fast Ethernet and Gigabit Ethernet links, the total sum of internal, external, and management traffic will not typically approach the limits of the line bandwidth. For high volume environments, with several GBs of log transfers per day to an external system, it's ideal to move this traffic to a separate port.
- **Flexibility:** Two-arm configurations offer more flexibility, especially if listeners are created on each interface. Filter conditions that test source interface or listener of messages can be used to separate traffic types.

Features at the application layer—all the SMTP connection management, all the filtering—*are the same regardless of the deployment mode* you pick. ESA is designed to work in a variety of network environments, and you should select the model that is typical for your environment. If you have a completely blank slate and can use any model, I recommend a single-arm configuration, with one interface for everything. Simplicity wins, in my opinion. You should consider a two-arm configuration for high-volume environments that demand low latency for email messages.

If you find that the network deployment you've decided on is no longer working, or it turns out to be unsuitable for any reason, you can always change it. You can add and delete interfaces at any time. Just be careful about changing IP addresses without also considering the changes to gateway, DNS, and static routing. Although the ESA warns you, it does not stop you from deleting an interface that you're currently logged in to.

Routing on Multinetwork Deployments

The ESA is not a router. It does not support any routing protocols and has no capabilities for discovering network routes. It has only two simple rules when deciding how to send a packet, either for initiating a connection or for replying to an incoming connection:

- If the destination IP is on the same subnet as an ESA interface, use that source interface to send the packet.
- If the destination IP is not on the same subnet as any ESA interface, send the packet to the default gateway, using the interface that's on the same subnet as the gateway.

Because of this, any IP address will not be reachable at all if it is not accessible through the default gateway and not directly on the same subnet as any of the ESA's interfaces. To overcome this, we must specify static routes. For those familiar with Linux or BSD networking, this is identical to setting up routes with the *route* command.

Take, for example, this network configuration from an ESA:

```
Currently configured interfaces:
1. mgmt (172.16.1.100/24 on Management: esa02.cisco.com)
2. primary (10.60.1.10/24 on Data 1: esa02.cisco.com)
```

The default gateway is 10.60.1.1. Suppose you try to connect to the management port using a browser from a workstation with IP 172.17.23.37. TCP packets travel to the Management NIC on the ESA. To reply, however, the ESA relies only on its simple rules: Because 172.17.23.37 is not on the same subnet as any of its interfaces, it sends the packet to its default gateway, 10.60.1.1, which will probably discard it. Even if it didn't, the workstation is expecting a reply back from 172.16.1.100, and not from 10.60.1.10, and it will drop the packet. Your browser connection will time out.

To resolve this, we need to give the ESA a static route for that destination network. Route summaries are good, where possible, as they will reduce the number of static routes required in the table. For example, if the proper gateway on my management interface is 172.16.1.1, adding this route to *routeconfig*, or to Static Routes in the Network menu of the WUI, will allow the ESA to reach the 172.17/16 network:

```
Mgmt LAN Destination: 172.17.0.0/16 Gateway: 172.16.1.1
```

On the ESA, every route has a name and, in this case, it's **Mgmt LAN.** It specifies that for the destination network of 172.17.0.0/16, the ESA should use gateway 172.16.1.1. Because that gateway address is on the same subnet as one of the ESA's local interfaces, it will use that local interface to send the packet. The static route rules are based on destination network only. No other means of defining routes and gateways is possible. (Chapter 12 covers static routes in detail.)

DNS Concerns

SMTP requires proper DNS to function. Aside from using DNS to lookup MX and A records for SMTP delivery, the ESA uses DNS to lookup SBRS, PTRs, SPF and DKIM records, and even sender's email domains. Other organizations using ESAs or other products are certainly doing the same when they receive mail from or deliver mail to your ESAs. One of the key considerations for a reliable email environment is the proper setup of DNS.

Some general rules regarding deployment of new servers in your environment apply all the more strictly to email servers like the ESA:

- **All external IP addresses must have a PTR:** Any public IP address needs a PTR record in DNS to a hostname. This is not optional—most SMTP servers will simply not entertain a connection from an IP with no valid PTR and will not accept any email from such a server. If you're using NAT, the important PTR is for the outside address.
- **PTR and A records should correspond:** There should be a forward and reverse match of IP and hostname. For example, if a PTR for 204.15.82.79 returns the hostname *mail4.ironport.com*, an A record for *mail4.ironport.com* should have that IP listed. It is possible to have more than one IP for an A record. As long as one matches the PTR, you're OK.
- **The ESA's interface settings should match public DNS:** The ESA uses each interface's hostname as a greeting banner when accepting SMTP connections on the interface. This hostname should match the public hostname of the public IP. If you're using NAT, the important hostname is the one from the PTR of the outside address.

In the networking examples, we've been using a private IP in the DMZ for most deployments. If the IP of 192.168.1.100 was static NAT-ed to 204.15.82.79, this should look in DNS like this:

```
host 204.15.82.79
79.82.15.204.in-addr.arpa domain name pointer mail4.ironport.com
dig mail4.ironport.com
mail4.ironport.com. 300  IN      A       204.15.82.79
```

The network interface configuration on the ESA should then be this, gleaned from interfaceconfig:

```
Currently configured interfaces:
DMZ (192.168.1.100/24 on Data 1: mail4.ironport.com)
```

The last area of DNS concern is internal DNS inside of your environment. Unless you plan to access your appliance management interfaces by IP, it's wise to have names properly registered for the management interfaces on your ESA. For internal mail servers using the ESA as smarthosts for delivery to the Internet, it's perfectly valid to provide destination IPs, but more flexible to provide destination hosts. The ESA will not register itself with DNS servers, so A and PTR records must be created manually.

Firewall Rules

ESA depends heavily on Internet access for rule updates. The Anti-Spam and Antivirus engines will perform poorly if updates cannot be retrieved even for a short period: An hour's delay reduces spam capture rates to 70% or lower, for example. For this reason, email alerts and SNMP traps are issued if updates can't be retrieved. Constant rule updates are needed to keep up with the changing nature of spam, phishing, and viruses.

Table 2-2 illustrates the basic necessary network access that the ESA requires. It gives the destinations where applicable. The ESA also supports updates via HTTP or HTTPS proxies. If you're using a proxy server, make sure that its rules allow the ESA to retrieve content from any Internet destination web server.

Table 2-2 *Basic Network Access Required by ESA*

Protocol	Destination	Purpose
TCP/25 SMTP	All local and Internet destinations	Sending email.
TCP/25 SMTP	ESA	Receiving email.
TCP/80 HTTP	All Internet destinations	Downloading updates to security engines.
TCP/80 HTTP	ESA	WUI Management of ESA.
TCP/443 HTTPS	All Internet destinations	AsyncOS upgrades.
TCP/443 HTTPS	ESA	WUI management of ESA.
UDP/53 TCP/53 DNS	Configured DNS servers or all Internet destinations	Domain name resolution. If using local DNS servers, ESA does **not** need DNS to all destinations.
TCP 389, 636	LDAP server(s)	LDAP or Secure LDAP (LDAPS) connections to a directory server.
TCP 3268, 3269	AD domain controller(s)	LDAP or LDAPS queries to AD's global catalog port.

You will see in the *Service Updates* item in the Security Services menu the URLs that the ESA retrieves updates from. The destination downloads.ironport.com is not directly hosted by Cisco, but by a content-delivery network that uses DNS to globally distribute hosted content. As such, the IP that this host resolves to varies over time and should not be the basis of a firewall rule restricting the destination.

If it's critical to lock down the outgoing connections from the ESA to a specific network, it's possible to do so with some configuration changes. The process for moving to static service updates is fairly simple. Follow these steps, making sure that you test the connectivity between the ESA and the static servers on ports 80 and 443:

Step 1. Go to the Service Updates menu in the **Security Services** tab and click **Edit Update Settings**. The first section of this page is **Update Servers (images)**. You only need to change the settings in this section; the second section, **Update Servers (list)**, already uses a fixed set of hosts.

Step 2. In the **Update Servers (images)** section, select the radio button for **Local Update Servers**. Change the **Base URL** to http://downloads-static.ironport.com and set the port to 80.

Step 3. In the same section, change the **Host** to updates-static.ironport.com. Leave the port blank. Submit and commit the changes.

As of this writing, all the static update servers are hosted on the CIDR network range of 204.15.82.0/24, but you need to confirm these values before making firewall rule changes.

Securing Network Interfaces

The individual IP interfaces have check boxes for which management protocols are accepted (i.e., which daemons are running bound to that interface and port). When the SSW creates interfaces for you, it automatically enables certain protocols, like SSH, appropriately. When you manually add an interface through the CLI or WUI, you are given the option to enable these. New features in the ESA allow you to specify the allowed source IP ranges for these administrative protocols, rather than accepting from any source; this is covered in Chapter 4 and Chapter 5. The basic management protocols supported by the ESA are listed in Table 2-3.

Table 2-3 *Supported Management Protocols*

Protocol	Notes
FTP	File Transfer Protocol. Used for transferring configuration files, import/export files, logs, or packet captures to and from the ESA. Not secure, because credentials are passed in the clear; SCP is recommended instead. If necessary, should only be run on an inside interface or be protected by network ACL or firewall rules, or both. Note that the ESA does not support SFTP.
Telnet	Allows administrative login to the CLI. There's no reason to use this, because SSH provides a better secure option.

Protocol	Notes
SSH	The default protocol for CLI access, which is covered in Chapter 5. Also controls access to Secure Copy (SCP) for transferring files to and from the ESA file system.
HTTP	The management WUI. Credentials are sent in the clear, so it's advisable to disable this or use the option to redirect HTTP requests to HTTPS.
HTTPS	The secure HTTP management WUI that uses TLS/SSL for all communications with the ESA. Preferred over HTTP.
Spam Quarantine HTTP	The end-user interface to the IronPort Spam Quarantine (ISQ) where users examine and manage any spam messages held in quarantine. It's advisable to use the redirect option.
Spam Quarantine HTTPS	The secure interface to the ISQ. Again, this is preferred over using HTTP.

There are several other protocols that the ESA could be listening for on a particular interface. The notable one is, of course, SMTP, on port 25 or any other port, which is controlled through the listener and not the interface. An active listener on an interface opens the port, and access control is provided through the Host Access Table (HAT). Another example is SNMP, which is typically listening for requests on port 161. The SNMP daemon is not enabled by default and must be enabled through the CLI **snmp-config** command. **snmpconfig** provides access control to this port.

Security Filtering Features

If you followed this chapter closely, you now have a fully production-capable ESA configuration that can send and receive mail. You've selected a network configuration that suits your deployment model, and you've tested network connectivity and established static routes as needed. Because of the SSW, you have a basic but thorough filtering policy and proper settings for accepting and delivering email.

At this point, the product is ready for production deployment: You can create a new MX record, change an existing MX, or alter a static NAT, and I'm confident you can put the device into its role as your gateway mail server. The security services that were enabled in the SSW give us thorough protection against spam, phishing, and viruses, without any further configuration. We'll examine what has been set up by the SSW here.

Security filters are part of the work queue, and the settings and actions are configured in *Incoming Mail Policies* and *Outgoing Mail Policies* items under the Mail Policies menu in the WUI. All settings can also be configured in the CLI using the **policyconfig** command, but I find it much easier to use the WUI for this task.

SenderBase and Reputation Filters

The HAT on each listener on the ESA controls how senders can connect. Think of it as *which hosts get what access*. The table groups senders, and applies policies to each group. You have a variety of methods of determining the policy, but the chief means of determining sender group is the score of the connecting IP, as determined by the Cisco database of email sending IPs called SenderBase. That score is called the SenderBase Reputation Score (SBRS), and it is one of the most well-known features that ESA offers. Deservedly so—properly configured, it will stop some 80–90% of spam messages at the connection level. Figure 2-15 shows the default HAT after you complete the SSW in a single-arm configuration.

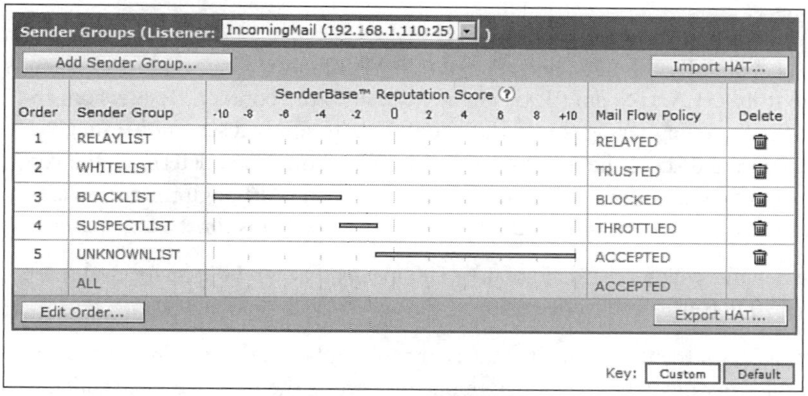

Figure 2-15 *Default HAT*

Cisco gathers the data for reputation score from many places: reports of spam submissions from all over the globe, registrar and ISP data, reports from ESA appliances from Cisco customers, and increasingly, information about IPs from other Cisco products like Firewalls, Intrusion Prevention, and Web Filtering. SenderBase is continually updated, and the queries for reputation score are always done at connection time, subject to some caching.

SBRS for a given IP ranges from -10.0 to +10.0, plus a special score of **None.** As you can see, the default HAT covers that entire range. Connecting IPs with SBRS from -10.0 up to -3.0 are rejected, because they are grouped into the **BLACKLIST** and applied a policy of **BLOCKED.** SBRS slightly above that are **THROTTLED**, which generally means they can't make many connections and are limited in terms of the overall volume of email they can send. All other scores go into the **UNKNOWNLIST**, which gets the basic **ACCEPTED** policy.

No entries are included in the **WHITELIST** by default. Because the **TRUSTED** policy turns off anti-spam filtering, you must be careful even when manually adding senders to the groups. In fact, I strongly recommend against turning off anti-spam for any senders, regardless of trust; even good senders get virus infections and compromised accounts that can turn them into spam sources.

The **RELAYLIST** contains internal IPs. We have this group and policy created because we told the SSW that we would relay email on this interface. The only entries in this table should be those that you specifically list, either in the SSW or by editing the group. The **RELAYED** privilege is wide open and allows the client to send to any Internet destination with few limits. As such, it should be restricted to a small range of IPs.

The basic HAT policy setup from the factory is ideal in most cases. It's not as aggressive as some companies like, but still makes for a good starting point. I do not recommend changing the default values until you're much more comfortable with the settings. Cisco has designed the HAT defaults to match the accepted best practices of customers worldwide.

IronPort Anti-Spam

For messages accepted by the ESA, and treated to a Mail Flow Policy where anti-spam is turned on, the IronPort Anti-Spam (IPAS) engine examines the content. IPAS is conceptually simple: Break down messages into their components, apply a series of tests given by a rules database, and score the result of each test. The scores then determine the verdict category: Not Spam, Suspected Spam, and Positive Spam. Although the scores aren't accessible from the message data, you can configure the thresholds for the categories.

SSW uses the default, which on a scale of 1 to 100 means that 50–90 is suspected to be spam, and over 90 is considered to be spam.

The rules that make up the tests come from Cisco and number in the hundreds of thousands of new rules per day. The rules operate on any part of the message: the sender, the sending IP and its reputation, the headers, or body of a message. Rules are processed in an order so that the least effort/highest catch rate rules are processed first. Early exit from rules is possible so that filtering is efficient.

As with the HAT, the policy defaults are ideal for a starting point. They are focused on keeping false positives to an absolute minimum, and so they may not be as aggressive in stopping spam as some customers like. I recommend leaving the defaults until you're more comfortable with the settings.

What may not be ideal defaults are the actions taken on messages found to be spam or suspect spam. The default actions can either be to deliver the messages with an altered subject or, if you've enabled the ISQ, to quarantine spam and suspect messages. The ISQ default is shown in Figure 2-16.

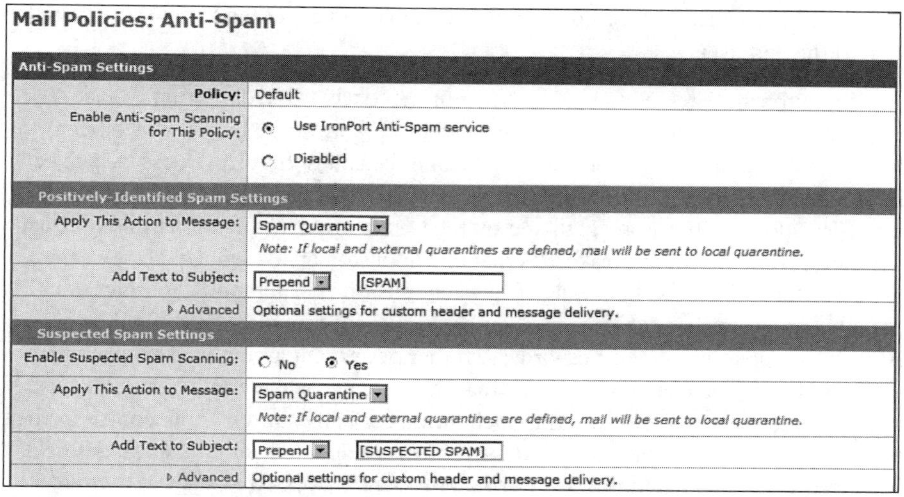

Figure 2-16 *Default IPAS Actions*

What you do with messages determined to be spam is an organizational decision, but delivering the messages to the end users will likely result in complaints and confusion. Quarantining the messages is ideal, especially when sent to a centralized quarantine running on an SMA. The quarantine features include notification and message controls via a summary digest message, allowing end users to manage their own spam messages. If you're quarantining, there's less reason to mark up the message **Subject**, but it's also not harmful to leave it.

These basic settings are a good place to start if you're evaluating the product, or are deploying for the first time and want to review the messages being caught by the Anti-Spam engine. There is much more to cover with spam filtering, including the repercussions of changing the default thresholds, and so we cover IPAS in more depth in Chapter 8.

Antivirus Features

The last engine enabled by the SSW is one, or both, binary antivirus engines provided on the ESA, and the virus outbreak filter feature. The ESA provides this multilayer, multivendor approach to provide the broadest coverage for new virus types and variants of existing viruses. Because the virus writer's techniques are constantly changing, all the engines provide regular update, sometimes dozens per day, and the ESA checks for updates every 5 minutes.

Both Sophos and McAfee apply a number of different techniques for detecting malicious files attached to email messages, including signatures, patterns, heuristics, and emulation. Both engines can open archives and compressed files in order to inspect executables and documents contained within. When the engine finds a match between the rules contained in its signature database, and a file attached to an email message, a virus positive verdict is found and action taken. Both engines can also repair some virus-infected files, such as Word documents with macro viruses, and pass the repaired files on to the end user.

The Cisco Outbreak Filters (OF) takes a different approach, using data from global Internet traffic trends to identify threats. Instead of looking at the binary attachment data, it looks at message and attachment metadata: filenames, file sizes, message subjects, URLs in message bodies, and tries to identify *possible* viral messages based on global patterns. The global patterns are gathered by the Cisco security operations, and unusual patterns are codified into outbreak rules that all OF customers download. For example, when 300 different ESAs, at hundreds of different customers, all report the exact same filename being received, it can trigger an outbreak rule for that file. Unlike Sophos or McAfee, which positively identifies viruses so that permanent action (like drop) can be taken, an outbreak rule match only means that the message is likely to be viral. Because of this, the action taken is to quarantine such messages, and wait. Over the course of the following hours, outbreak rules and virus signatures are updated, and the messages held in quarantine are re-evaluated. If they are viral, they are processed as such. If the rule is repealed, they are released from quarantine. After a certain period of time, all messages not identified as viral will be released.

The SSW provides a basic policy for any antivirus engine that you chose to enable during setup. Each engine provides four possible verdicts:

- **Repaired:** This verdict only occurs if message scanning is set to **Scan and repair** and is reached when either the infected attachments have been dropped or macro viruses in documents have been removed.
- **Encrypted:** Some, or all, of the message was not scanned because of encryption or protected files. This can include password-protected zip files, documents, protected cells in a spreadsheet, PGP, S/MIME, or others. Usually not harmful.
- **Unscannable:** Some, or all, of the messages was not scanned because of a reason other than encryption. Most often, this is due to a corrupted attachment, a timeout, or another error of the engine itself. Usually not harmful, and really should be a rare occurrence. If timeouts are routinely occurring, system load needs to be examined and the AV timeout setting changed.
- **Virus Infected:** The message contains at least one viral attachment. You should not let these messages be delivered to the end users. You can quarantine these infected messages for historical record or other security analysis, or simply drop them.

The default AV policy is shown in Figure 2-17.

Figure 2-17 *Default Antivirus Actions*

Appropriate policy depends on your organization's security practices. The defaults are effective against malicious files without being intrusive. Normally, I recommend **Deliver As Is** as an action for all these verdicts, except Virus Infected, where I recommend drop. I also recommend not modifying Subject lines on delivered messages or sending any kind of notification to the sender or recipient. Notifying end users with a message like WARNING: MESSAGE ENCRYPTED usually just results in confusion and panic. You may decide to quarantine Unscannable messages, but stopping encrypted messages is only going to prevent the transmission of legitimate protected content.

For outgoing mail policies, again, I recommend **Deliver As Is** for all verdicts, except Virus Infected. Again, the default actions match my general recommendations, although you should consider adding a notification to the Virus Infected verdict to let an administrator or security manager know when the ESA detects viral content originating internally.

SSW also provides a basic policy for VOF, which is moderate sensitivity to rules, and an action of quarantine of messages that match the rules. There's really not much else to configure here, and the defaults match my recommendations. There is an option to skip VOF scanning for certain attachment types, but because the false positive rate for VOF is near-zero and its quarantine action is non-destructive, I don't recommend skipping the scanning for any reason.

The quarantine parameters for VOF are not controlled in the mail policy, but rather on the system quarantine space set aside for VOF. The settings for this are available on the *Quarantines* item in the Monitor menu.

Summary

In this chapter, I've covered the basic ESA appliance models and their features. The ESA is available in 1U and 2U rack mount formats and have essentially the same features, but differ in capacity and throughput.

From there, I described the initial setup process of a new appliance, from initial connection to the ESA to running the System Setup Wizard to configure basic appliance information. We covered some external dependencies, like DNS configuration and firewall access rules. Because the wizard establishes many default settings, I described the results of using the wizard to set up an ESA. If you're following these steps on a new installed ESA, you have a basic but secure configuration that you can deploy immediately.

We'll next look at all stages of the product's email pipeline and describe the features available at each stage of the lifecycle of an email message.

Chapter 3

ESA Email Pipeline

In this chapter, you will learn the following:

- The full email-processing pipeline for all accepted messages
- How the system performs connection handling and rate limiting
- Operations performed in the ESA work queue
- How to configure options for acceptance and delivery of messages

Simple Mail Transfer Protocol (SMTP) connections and email messages handled by the Email Security Appliance (ESA) move from connection acceptance to SMTP conversation, to message acceptance, and then to filtering and delivery in a step-by-step process known as the *email security pipeline*. The pipeline is important because the fixed order of certain steps dictates configuration and architecture, and the flexibility of other steps means we have a great deal of leeway in designing and deploying an email environment based on ESA.

ESA Pipeline

The ESA pipeline has some stages that are fixed in order, apply to all messages, and other components that are either optional based on the message or completely optional for all messages. For example, spam filtering may not be performed on mail from certain senders, and virus scanning need not be performed at all on the pipeline. *Direction* of messages also dictates the order and stages that messages travel through. Messages that arrive at the ESA can pass through either an *incoming* pipeline or an *outgoing* pipeline, although we'll see that this distinction is not always clear. Incoming and outgoing are not really separate pipelines or queues; in fact, they don't refer to any distinct features, as all messages arriving at an ESA are treated more or less the same. They really only distinguish between which filtering steps occur and which don't, and how the filtering affects the messages.

We can broadly group the pipeline stages into three: First, the connection and SMTP conversation stages, that control how and whether connections are accepted, and if accepted, whether the messages being transmitted and their sender and recipient addresses should be accepted. Second, after the message data has been accepted, filtering of the message occurs in steps, with each table and engine examining senders, recipients, headers, and body, as appropriate. Finally, if a message continues past all filtering, intact or modified, it proceeds to delivery, where a number of features can affect the final destination and rate at which messages are delivered.

Some messages do not proceed through the entire pipeline. There are a number of places where connections and messages from remote senders can be rejected or messages dropped. Messages generated on the ESA, such as notifications, reporting, alerts, and administrative copies of messages, do not pass through the acceptance and filtering stages and move directly to delivery.

Note When it comes to stopping an email message for any reason, the term *blocked* is often used, such as the troubleshooting question, "Why was this message blocked?" I dislike this imprecise term and try to avoid it. Because of the ESA's email pipeline, and the store-and-forward nature of MTAs, it's more appropriate to say

- A message or connection was *rejected* or *refused* if the delivery of the message was halted during TCP connection or SMTP conversation. I usually use the phrases *message or recipient rejected* and *connection refused.*
- A message was *dropped* if the ESA stopped processing and discarded the entire contents of a message.
- A message was *bounced* if the ESA dropped the original message, and created a new message in the delivery status notification (DSN) format that informs the sender of the delivery failure. If a DSN message is also undeliverable, it's considered a *double bounce.*
- A recipient was *rejected* if, during receipt or delivery, the response to a RCPT TO command was 4yz or 5yz error codes. Because a recipient that was met with a 4yz code is only temporarily rejected, we may refer to that recipient as *attempted.*

It might be fine to refer to a message as being blocked when speaking casually about filtering, such as, "We're blocking the messages caused by that virus outbreak," but in ESA terms, using the precise terminology will aid understanding and troubleshooting.

We'll closely examine each stage and the steps within each stage. First, we need to define and discuss one of the most important concepts on an ESA, that of a listener. The listener is the primary controller for the first stage of the email pipeline, as shown in Figure 3-1.

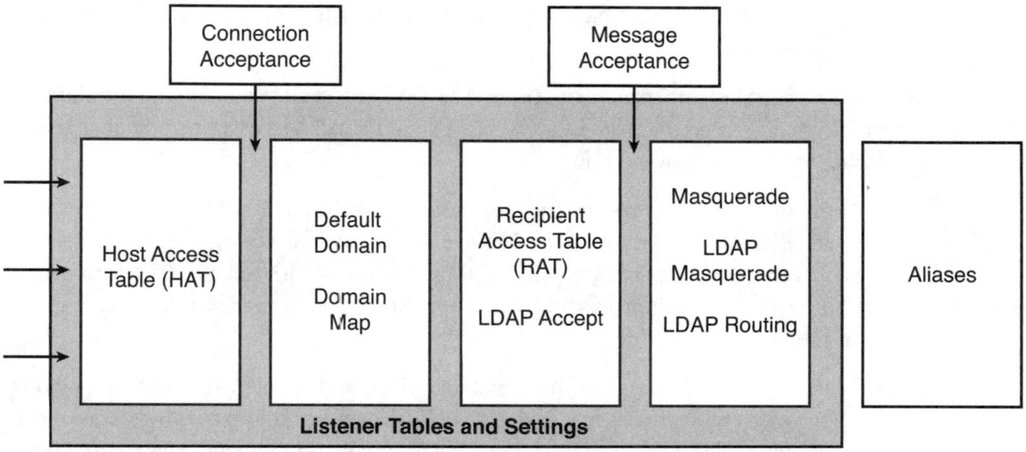

Figure 3-1 *First Portion of the ESA Email Pipeline*

Listeners

The ESA listens for connections on the interface and port specified in one or more SMTP ***listeners***. You can think of a listener as an SMTP server daemon bound to a specific interface and port. A listener controls all of the aspects of the first third of the pipeline, the connection and SMTP conversation. These settings are global for a specific listener, and major features like Host Access Table (HAT) and Recipient Access Table (RAT) are tied to each specific listener. It's certainly valid to have more than one listener on an ESA. In fact, there are good reasons to have multiple listeners on a single appliance, but for this chapter, we work with just a single listener. In addition to deciding whether to accept or reject connections, and at what rates, the listener also provides:

- **Sender and recipient checks:** The envelope sender and all envelope recipients can be validated during SMTP conversation, and this allows the ESA to reject undesirable senders and invalid recipients.
  - The envelope sender's domain can be tested against DNS, and senders from nonexistent domains can be rejected.
  - The envelope sender address can be checked against the exception table to override a reject or accept decision.
  - The envelope recipients are checked against the RAT and can be tested against an LDAP query for validation. Usually, this is just a test to see that the email address exists. The ESA can reject, drop, or bounce messages that fail an LDAP acceptance test.
  - Partial recipient addresses (those that do not contain a fully qualified domain name after the @ sign) can have a *default domain added*. This is typically only used for internal email traffic. For example, some application servers might send messages to webmaster@host1, but the proper delivery address would be

webmaster@host1.example.com. Default domain adds the example.com domain to addresses that don't have it.

- **Sender and recipient transformations:** The envelope sender, some or all envelope recipients, and even message headers that contain email addresses can be changed during the SMTP conversation.
    - **Domain map:** A one-to-one transformation of the domain portion of recipient email addresses. For example, if I have a domain map entry of *@ironport.com* with a target of *@cisco.com*, any RCPT TO address with form *user@ironport.com* is transformed into *user@cisco.com*. No change is made to the user portion of the email address.
    - **Masquerading:** The transformation of envelope and visible email addresses, done either with static entries in a table or via LDAP query. This is most often used on outgoing mail to change *internal* email addresses into *external* email addresses.
- **LDAP queries:** All the LDAP queries that will be used on inbound messages must be assigned on the listener. We'll look at LDAP queries and using them in policies later in this chapter and in Chapter 8, "Security Filtering."
- **Address and message content restrictions:** Each listener has settings to control whether the system accepts 8-bit data, whether certain characters are allowed in recipient addresses, and whether to *fix* issues with illegal CR and LF characters.
- **Miscellaneous other settings:** There are a number of other message actions that are configured on the listener settings. Most of these can be overridden later in the pipeline.
    - A disclaimer, which is text added to the top or bottom of a message, can be chosen for the messages arriving at the listener. These are also referred to as headers or footers, respectively. These can also be assigned using filters.
    - A bounce profile can be chosen for messages. A bounce profile really should be called a *retry and bounce profile*, because it controls how often, and for how long, a delayed message should be retried. If a message exceeds that schedule, the message is *bounced*, and that behavior is controlled here. These can also be assigned using filters, or in the destination controls table during the delivery stage of the pipeline.
    - Connection timeouts. To deal with stuck senders, we can limit the maximum time allowed for an inbound SMTP conversation. There are separate limits for SMTP connections that have actually attempted to send email, versus unproductive connections that haven't.

Host Access Table (HAT) and Reputation Filters

The pipeline for any message begins with the standard TCP connection handshake. Based on the source IP in the TCP packets, the ESA takes a number of actions even before presenting an SMTP welcome (or rejection) banner. These actions include the following:

- A DNS PTR (reverse) lookup is performed to find the fully qualified hostname of the connecting IP. If no PTR is available, or the lookup times out, that fact is recorded. Note that all allocated IP addresses in use on the Internet need to have PTRs defined; we'll examine this requirement later.
- A DNS A (forward) lookup is performed to determine the IP addresses mapped to the hostname returned in the first step, if any. If at least one of the IPs returned in this lookup matches the connecting IP, the DNS derived host and domain information is considered *verified*.
- A SenderBase Reputation Score (SBRS) lookup is performed, using DNS as the transport mechanism. The value returned is a real number in the range of –10.0 to +10.0, or the special value of *None*. Although this is a real number, in practice, the value returned has only one digit after the decimal point. SBRS reflects the likelihood that a given IP is sending spam, viruses, or other unwanted email. The lower the score, the more likely it is to be junk. Scores below –3.0 are almost always junk.
- Other DNS lookups are performed. If you've configured such features as DNS Blacklists (DNSBL) to third-party lookup services, these will be performed.

As you can see, an ESA depends heavily on DNS for its lookups. Once all these lookups are complete, the ESA now has the source IP, hostname (if any), SBRS, and DNSBL results. It also knows if a PTR exists, and if it does, whether there's a forward and reverse DNS match. These attributes are used to classify the connection in a sender group in the HAT. Any single criteria match suffices for a sender group match. A default HAT includes some predefined sender groups, and you can define your own or modify the default groups. The default HAT includes a WHITELIST group, which starts empty, a BLACKLIST group for SBRS ranges of –10.0 to –3.0, a SUSPECTLIST group for SBRS from –3.0 to –1.0, UNKNOWNLIST for –1.0 to +10.0, and a default group ALL. Matches are performed from top to bottom and any connecting IP that doesn't match a specific group fall into the ALL default group.

Essentially, the fate of a connection is determined entirely based on source IP, or information about the IP or host derived from these lookups. It's not based on any information from the message—in fact, we haven't even started the SMTP conversation yet. Once a HAT group is determined, it is fixed, and no later stage of the pipeline will alter that group. Because the first match wins, you should put the groups with more specific criteria first. For example, because WHITELIST lists specific IP addresses and hostnames, it should come before groups that use DNS conditions or SBRS. Because the WHITELIST is first, you can place a particular sender there to avoid false positives, overriding the classification based on SBRS.

The result of a connecting IP being classified in a group is the application of a Mail Flow Policy that controls how, and whether, connections are accepted. Every sender group has a corresponding policy, like the BLOCKED policy for the BLACKLIST sender group. The Mail Flow Policy encapsulates all the connection controls and rate limits at SMTP conversation time and controls many of the security filters that will apply to messages accepted under the policy. Policies are defined separately from groups to keep classification of senders distinct from actions taken. You can even use the same mail flow policy with more than one group, allowing for reporting and filtering based on group membership while still applying consistent policy. Mail flow policies are flexible, and you can create your own in addition to the built-in policies. All mail flow policies boil down to just four fundamental actions:

- **Accept:** The connection will be accepted and the SMTP conversation will start. The sender is limited to recipients in the domains specified in the RAT and may be subject to further checks on the recipient addresses. Messages received over an accepted connection are treated as incoming for policy purposes. This is the default action for most policies.
- **Relay:** The connection will be accepted, and the SMTP conversation will start. The sender is not limited to recipients in the RAT—in fact, the RAT is not checked at all. The sending IP is allowed to issue RCPT TO commands to any email address. The ability to send to any email address is a high level of privilege to grant any sender, so use it carefully by limiting it to very specific sending IPs (typically only your internal mail servers). Limiting access to relay policies to absolutely trustworthy hosts is a cornerstone of HAT security.
- **TCP Refuse:** The TCP connection is closed. The ESA issues a FIN to the sender to indicate that the connection is over before it even starts. Because this is usually confusing to the sender and is not RFC compliant, I strongly recommend against using this setting, as satisfying as it may be to refuse senders. Most senders will treat the ESA as *down* and reattempt connections for hours or days.
- **Reject:** The TCP connection is accepted, but the ESA greets the sender with an SMTP 554 banner to indicate that they are not welcome here. That's immediately followed by a TCP FIN to close the connection. This banner code and text is customizable, so you can give the sender some information about why he has been rejected. This is the default action for the BLOCKED policy.

Any connection that continues into the SMTP conversation proper must have been greeted with either an Accept or Relay behavior. This means that all messages making it into the pipeline must have arrived on one of those two behaviors. For policy purposes, all messages that have been accepted are classified as *incoming* messages, and relayed are considered *outgoing* messages.

Note Understanding the distinction between the labels *incoming* and *outgoing* is critical. You need to understand the distinction to create policies and troubleshoot. The label applied to a message is determined solely by the behavior of the mail flow policy that was applied to the connection: Accept means incoming and Relay means outgoing. The only exception to this is messages generated on the ESA itself, and because these messages don't go through the full pipeline, the distinction is not important.

For accepted and relayed connections, the SMTP conversation starts with the ESA issuing a 250 <hostname> banner (by default). The client proceeds at this point with EHLO. The EHLO hostname string is recorded, and may be used in sender authentication tests, a topic covered in Chapter 15, "Advanced Topics." You can't reject connections in the HAT based on the hostname string or write filters or invoke anti-spam policies against it. There's not much reason to: Although the RFC requires the client to send a resolvable host or domain name, and allows servers to verify the hostname/IP match, it prohibits servers from refusing messages on a mismatch.

Rate Limiting with Mail Flow Policies

If a mail flow policy has a behavior of *accept*, you can further specify exactly how much mail is accepted. This rate-limiting capability is exceptionally important for managing the email injection rates from individual senders so that no system can overwhelm the ESA. It's also effective at slowing down possible spam senders that use a *hit-and-run* technique to deliver new spam content quickly, before anti-spam rules can be updated. This process of rate-limiting suspicious senders is called throttling, and the built-in HAT group SUSPECTLIST and its policy THROTTLED make use of these limits to control possible spam senders.

Figure 3-2 shows the mail flow policy connection and message limits.

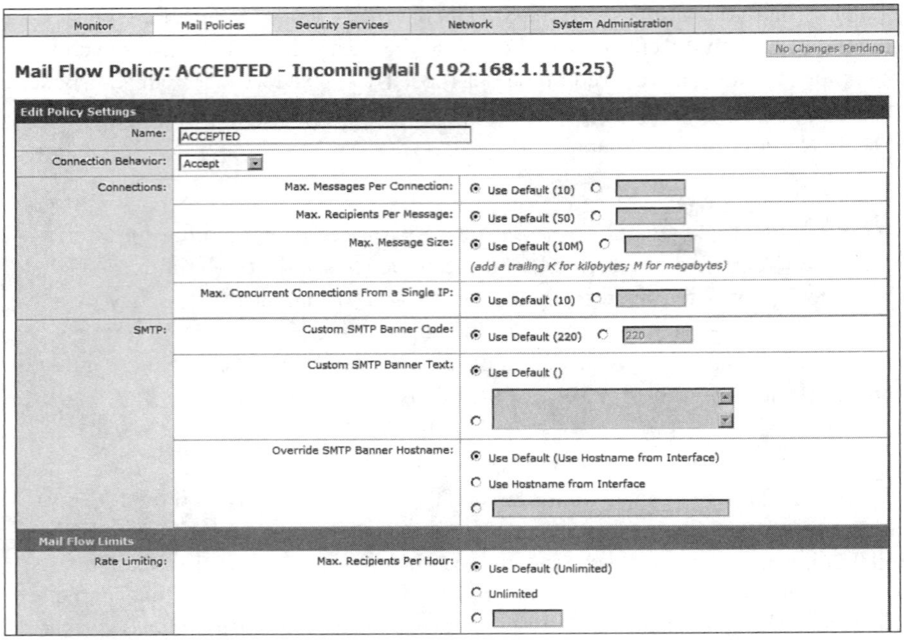

Figure 3-2 *Mail Flow Policy Connection and Message Limits*

Figure 3-3 shows the mail flow policy rate-limiting options.

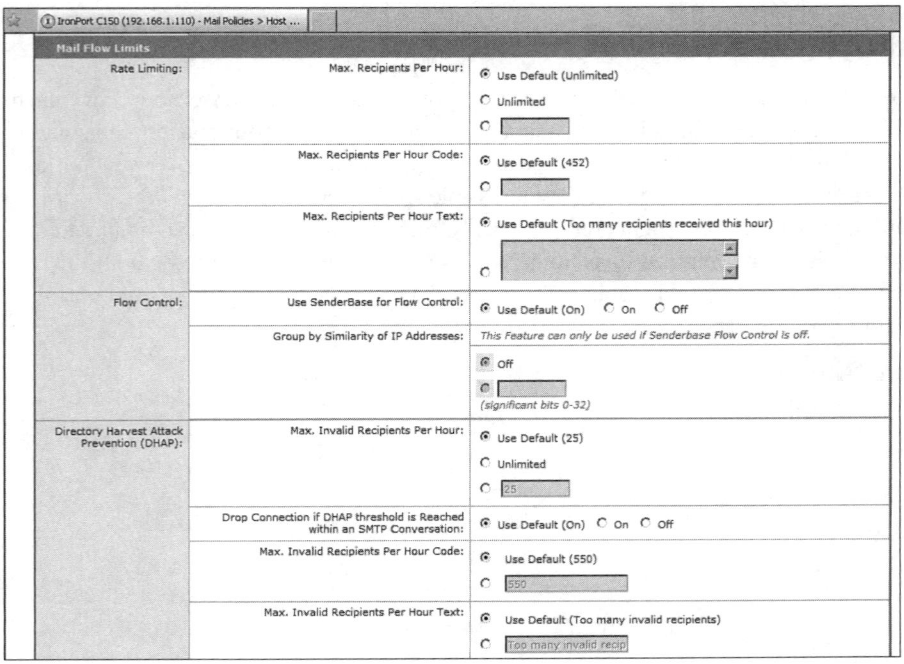

Figure 3-3 *Mail Flow Policy Rate Limiting*

DNS and Envelope Checks

After greetings are exchanged, the sender begins his message with the MAIL FROM command. There are a couple of features we can use to stop the sender right at this point. The mail flow policy has a feature called Envelope Sender DNS verification, which checks the domain of the MAIL FROM address to ensure that it exists in DNS. The closely related Exception Table (more properly, the Sender Verification Exception Table) defines sender addresses that should always be allowed or always rejected. Here's what it looks like to the client to be rejected at this stage, because the domain ironport0.com doesn't exist:

```
EHLO cisco.com
250-esa02.cisco.com
250-8BITMIME
250-SIZE 20971520
250 STARTTLS
MAIL FROM: <chris@ironport0.com>
553 Envelope sender <chris@ironport0.com> rejected
```

Why would you want to do this? Well, a sender whose domain can't be found in DNS can't have replies or bounces sent back to it, for one. Some groupware servers won't accept these irresolvable sender addresses, and it's pointless to accept a message on the ESA that ultimately won't be delivered to the groupware server. Another use is to explicitly reject any sender connecting to your public MXs but attempting to use an internal domain or local address as the sender—akin to rejecting internal networks on the outside interface of a firewall. It all sounds like an ideal way to stop some junk, but there's a false positive problem because some legitimate senders don't have their DNS house in order. As we examine techniques to stop unwanted mail, I highlight the cost-benefit balance of each feature. Sender DNS verification will stop some junk, but be warned that it also occasionally stops some legitimate traffic that may require you to investigate and correct.

Sender Authentication

Sender authentication lookups are performed. If you're configured to check Sender Policy Framework (SPF) records, new in AsyncOS 7.1 is the ability to perform such checks in the SMTP conversation and reject senders that fail the SPF test. DNS lookups for SPF verification are done here. Sender authentication is thoroughly covered in Chapter 15.

Recipient Access Table and LDAP Accept

In response to each RCPT TO command issued by the sender, the ESA checks the Recipient Access Table (RAT) to determine if the recipient, or the domain portion of the recipient, is allowed. If configured, an LDAP lookup for the recipient is also performed here. The goal in both cases is to avoid accepting messages for recipients that don't exist locally and to prevent the abuse of the ESA as a relay for other domains. You must list in the RAT all local domains that you plan to accept messages for, even if you're using LDAP recipient checks. To be accepted, a recipient must pass both checks. The RAT also acts as a backup if LDAP becomes unavailable.

The RAT takes entries in a few different forms, and can include usernames or just the host or domain portion after the @ symbol. Each entry has a basic action—Accept or Reject—and a few options. Table 3-1 describes the types of RAT entries.

Table 3-1 *RAT Table Entries*

Entry Format	Description and Example
Hostname or domain name	Accept all usernames at the particular host or domain name. Adding *cisco.com* means to accept any address of the form *anyuser@cisco.com*. An entry of *newyork.cisco.com* accepts mail for that subdomain. The wildcard notation of *.cisco.com* means to accept addresses of the form *anyuser@anyhost.cisco.com*.To provide a full wildcard for a domain and all of its subdomains, you need two entries: *domain.com* for the root level and *.domain.com* for the subdomains. You can also add a RAT entry like this with a Reject action, for example, to allow subdomains in general, but to explicitly reject some.
IP address literal	Accept all usernames addressed to the specific IP, such as user@[204.15.82.79]. This is not normally something you would use unless you want strict RFC compliance or have a need to accept messages addressed directly to this machine. If the ESA is replacing an existing server that supported local mailboxes, this type of entry may be necessary. Because this is often an exploit attempt, ESA blocks it by default.
Full email address	Allows the specific full email address, in an exact match. *chriport@cisco.com* is an example. It is possible to populate the RAT with every single valid email address for your organization, rather than accept mail for the whole domain. This gets you user-level validation without having to make LDAP queries from ESA. The challenge is keeping such a static list updated. The RAT table provides import and export features, and the CLI commands can be scripted for automatic updates. You can also add full email addresses with a Reject action. This is useful for overriding LDAP or a domain-level Accept action.
Username portion only	An entry like *postmaster@* or *webmaster@* means to accept the messages for this user for all domains. Highly dangerous with an Accept action, because including *postmaster@* forces the ESA to accept for the postmaster address at any and all Internet domains. Effectively creates an open relay for that username. It can be useful with a Reject action to stop external senders from reaching specific users.

Every RAT entry has a few options associated with it:

- **Accept or Reject:** Basic action to be taken. You will mostly use Accept here because the RAT default is Reject, but it is possible to selectively reject individual usernames within a domain that you would normally accept.
- **Bypass LDAP:** For recipients to be accepted, you can decide whether the address should further be checked by LDAP. This is perfect if some domains have addresses stored in a directory but others don't or to make an exception to LDAP validation for a specific recipient. I often see this used to explicitly allow *postmaster@company.com* even though the address may not be stored in a directory.
- **Custom SMTP Response:** Tells the ESA to use a custom response when rejecting or accepting a particular recipient domain or address. There's very little call for this, but some companies put a specific rejection message on specific user addresses. For example, imagine a PR disaster that makes an executive's email address a popular target. You might reject that recipient address, with a polite but firm message that indicates that the recipient isn't available anymore.
- **Bypass Receiving Control:** When turned on, this option overrides the various rate limits that count recipients. The only case where you'd ever want to do this would be for abuse-reporting addresses, like abuse@ or postmaster@, so that these addresses can be used by senders that are trying to resolve problems with abuse reports. Even with this, it's not going to allow a BLACKLIST sender past a connection rejection.

LDAP operations are normally performed later in the email pipeline, but LDAP Accept queries are an exception to that rule. This is so that the ESA can check, validate, and respond to the sender during the RCPT TO command. This recipient validation during conversation is extremely valuable and, if directory information is available, strongly recommended. If you have multiple Internet domains, but not all have LDAP available, deploy it for the ones that do.

Validating the recipient reduces the volume of messages that must be accepted, filtered, and attempted for delivery. In some environments, invalid recipient addresses can be more than 50% of the messages accepted, requiring much more work and potentially more equipment to handle. Further, validating recipients allows the ESAs to keep track of senders that have suspiciously high rates of invalid recipient accounts. These *directory harvesters* are up to no good, and the ESA can dynamically block this behavior. Lastly, validating the recipient address notifies the sender client immediately, avoiding the process of generating a bounce message later.

> **Note** If LDAP is not available for recipient validation and a static list of recipients is too large or too dynamic to continually import, another option is to use SMTP as a recipient validation protocol, using the new SMTP call-ahead feature in AsyncOS 7.5.
>
> The process is simple: The ESA receives an SMTP connection and allows the client to proceed. At the point when the RCPT TO command is issued, the ESA makes a simultaneous SMTP connection to a specified backend host. This backend connection proceeds like a normal SMTP conversation, and the ESA uses the results of this RCPT TO command to provide a response back to the sender on the first connection.

Recipient and Sender Manipulation

At this point, a sender whose message has passed all the HAT rules, and has at least one valid recipient, continues with the DATA command to deliver the message body. At this point, the ESA accepts the message, as no checks will be done on message content during the SMTP conversation. After all the data is sent, as indicated by the client concluding with <CRLF>.<CRLF>, the ESA writes the message contents to disk, and responds to the sender with a 250 code indicating message success. That response means that the ESA is taking responsibility for the message and the sender can consider it delivered.

At this point, message processing continues down the ESA pipeline independent of the SMTP connection that sent it. If the ESA doesn't close the connection because of policy, the sender can either quit the conversation and close the connection or start from the beginning and deliver another message by issuing another MAIL FROM command.

Default Domain, Domain Map, and Aliases

Most MTAs have historically supported the ability to rewrite portions of recipient addresses, and the ESA provides this through several features. Note that the rewrite changes I'm talking about are happening to the envelope recipient address, and not the visible To: header that users see. For example, a message addressed to *cporter@ironport.com* but aliased to *chriport@cisco.com* still shows me *cporter@ironport.com* in the To: field when I receive it at my Cisco mailbox. The envelope recipient is used to route the message to the right place.

The recipient transform features are

- **Default Domain:** A setting on the listener that applies a domain name to recipient addresses that are injected without a fully qualified domain name (FQDN).
- **Domain Map:** A table on the listener that provides a one-to-one mapping of the domain portion of recipient addresses. For example, an entry of *@ironport.com* → *@cisco.com* changes all recipients of the form *user@ironport.com* into *user@cisco.com*. No change is made to the username portion.
- **Aliases:** A global table whose entries are managed through the CLI command aliasconfig. Aliases can change recipient addresses in one-to-one, one-to-many, and

many-to-one mappings. One-to-one mappings are used to rewrite a single email address to another, such as cporter@ironport.com → chriport@cisco.com. One-to-many mappings are like distribution lists, allowing a message to a single address to be delivered to many recipients, such as sales@ironport.com. Many-to-one mappings allow a single recipient to receive all messages for a given domain. You may want to use this mapping on Internet domains that are used only for websites, for example, routing all the mail for the domain to a PR or marketing department employee.

Note Technically, the domain map does support fully qualified email address entries and not just domains. Why? Because domain mapping happens early in the pipeline. In fact, domain map occurs even before the RAT check is done, so that you if you have a domain map entry of left.com → right.com, only right.com needs to be in the RAT; the RAT never even sees the left.com recipient.

This creates a problem. Suppose you've acquired another company, *subsidiary.com*, and moved all the users to your organization's mail environment with addresses at *company.com*. However, you want to maintain the address *sales@subsidiary.com*, and it can't be mapped to *sales@company.com* because that address is already in use.

The natural solution would be to create an alias mapping *sales@subsidiary.com* to a new address, such as *sales-subsidiary@company.com*. But, this won't work on ESA, because the domain map happens before aliases are processed; the domain map would transform *sales@subsidiary.com* into *sales@company.com* and the alias wouldn't match. The solution is to do this mapping in the domain map table and not in the alias table. The domain map's transformations happen earlier in the pipeline than aliases.

Note that aliasing is also available through LDAP by using the LDAP Routing feature described later in this chapter.

Masquerading

The complement to recipient address rewrites is called sender masquerading. If you need to change or hide addresses sent from within your organization, masquerading is the right tool. The masquerade transforms are typically performed on envelope sender addresses, but can also affect the addresses that users will see in the To, From, CC, and Reply-To headers. Masquerading address rewrites are performed only on outgoing email messages.

Each listener has a masquerade table that performs static mappings, and which lists the headers that should be examined for rewrites. Although individual user entries can be made, the most common use of masquerading is to *flatten* email address domain hierarchies or to hide *internal* or acquired domains that shouldn't be used on the Internet.

For example, suppose your organization uses the domain recycling.org on the Internet but has separate departments for plastics, aluminum, and paper. Users in each department might use addresses such as csmith@plastics.recycling.org and al@aluminum.recycling.org. These addresses are useful for maintaining separate email environments, but might not be valid addresses on the Internet. Assuming that there's no clash of usernames, a masquerade entry of

```
@.recycling.org  @recycling.org
```

transforms all addresses of the form *user@subdomain.recycling.org* to the top-level *user@recycling.org*.

Note that masquerading is also available through LDAP, described next.

LDAP Operations

ESA supports LDAP queries for a wide variety of tasks, from validating and routing mail to authenticating users and clients. Thorough coverage of LDAP is provided in Chapter 7, "Directories and Policies," but it's instructive to know which queries are applied in this part of the pipeline.

LDAP Accept

We covered LDAP Accept for recipient validation in a previous section, but it makes another appearance here because LDAP Accept queries have two possible places in the pipeline: during the SMTP conversation immediately after the RAT check or after message acceptance and address transformations. When you add an LDAP Accept query to a listener, you have the choice of where in the pipeline the action should occur.

It's not really much of a choice: The SMTP conversation check is definitely the right place to do it. LDAP Accept in the work queue means that the message must be accepted by the ESA; whether the recipient is valid or not, the sender has delivered the message and disconnected. You only have two options at this point if the recipient is invalid: bounce, which means composing a new message back to the purported sending address, or drop, which silently throws the message away. Because of bounce storms and forged sender addresses, bouncing is not a good substitute for in-conversation rejection.

The only possible justification in using the work queue would be for safety in the event of an LDAP outage: The work queue check allows the ESA to queue the messages while it waits for LDAP to become available. The SMTP conversation check is time-sensitive and cannot wait for LDAP to be available. However, this still isn't a good reason to move to work-queue validation, as you can also set the SMTP conversation policy to *allow mail in* if LDAP is unavailable.

I recommend using SMTP conversation checks for LDAP Accept in all cases.

LDAP Routing and Masquerading

The operations just described under aliases and masquerading based on listener tables are also possible to perform on a per-user basis with LDAP. Masquerading is similar to the masquerade table, but the individual destination addresses are retrieved via an LDAP query rather than from the table.

LDAP routing incorporates the same recipient address rewriting that aliases can do, but adds another feature. The LDAP routing configuration must specify the source address in order to find the recipient, and then specifies either the rewrite address, the target hostname for the user, or both. A recipient can be rewritten and routed based on the new target address, or the recipient can simply be routed to another host. If your LDAP directory includes alias information for users, and hostname for mailbox servers, doing the lookup on the ESA and routing messages appropriately is ideal.

Unlike Accept queries, a failed routing or masquerading lookup doesn't stop the message. No rewrite is performed, and the message continues on unchanged. For this reason, it's safe to perform routing and masquerading even on users that don't have the appropriate attributes in the directory.

Groups

An LDAP group query poses this simple question to the directory: Does this recipient (or sender) address have an attribute called *X* with value *Y*? It's referred to as grouping because the most common form of the query is actually "does this user have a memberOf field with a value Y?" You can use it for any kind of user grouping you like: organizational groups or departments, physical location, spoken language, privilege level… anything that's stored in an LDAP attribute associated with the email address.

The most common use of LDAP group queries is organizing users into different processing policies. This is commonly based on organizational information, like department, location, or job function. For example, you can create separate filtering policies for members of your legal department or create aggressive anti-spam policies for company executives.

The group queries are performed before any of the security policies or content filtering. The results of the group lookups are available to filters and policies in the work queue. A failed lookup is not harmful, so it's safe to perform group queries on users that don't have the appropriate attributes in the directory.

Work Queue and Filtering Engines

The second major stage of the email pipeline is organized into what's called the ESA work queue. This section is shown in Figure 3-4.

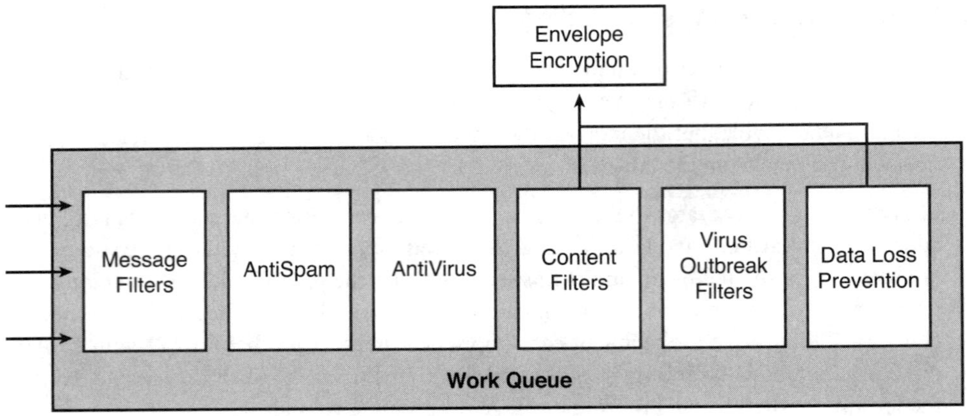

Figure 3-4 *Second Portion of the Email Pipeline: the Work Queue*

The processing steps taken on a given message in the work queue is mostly configured through *Incoming Mail Policies* and *Outgoing Mail Policies* in the Mail Policies menu of the WUI.

Work Queue Overview

The work queue is the place where, not surprisingly, most of the work on the appliance is done. All the custom filtering and security filtering is done here. What's not so apparent is that, at this point, the ESA is also moving to multiprocessing to take advantage of modern multicore CPUs. The individual filtering engines run in their own process, and multiple instances are run to take advantage of the hardware.

The work queue is really a place where messages line up until they can be picked up by an available process for filtering. When message throughput exceeds the throughput of all the filtering engines, the messages wait in the work queue until they can be processed.

Incoming and Outgoing Mail Policies

Every message that is accepted by the ESA is classified as either incoming or outgoing. The determination is made by the *connection behavior* of the mail flow policy that was applied at the HAT. Every message that is *accepted* is considered incoming, and every message that is *relayed* is considered outgoing.

Within incoming and outgoing, messages are further broken down into one or more incoming or outgoing mail policies. These policies are determined by sender or recipient addresses. Each policy lists sender and/or recipient addresses, either individually, by domain or subdomain, or by LDAP grouping. After a policy is defined, you can customize the settings and action of each stage of the work queue.

Effectively, the single ESA pipeline now splits into separate pipelines depending on the policy that applies. Messages continue down separate paths until they exit the work queue and are put into the last section of the pipeline: delivery. When a recipient matches more than one policy, the ordering of policies is important: first match wins.

One important feature of policies is *message splintering*. When the ESA examines a message with multiple recipients, it's possible that the various recipients each match on different policies. For example, you might have users in the IT department that are allowed to receive binary executable files, while the rest of the employees are not. What happens to a message addressed to two users, one in the IT department and one in marketing? The ESA actually separates the two recipients, breaking up the message and simultaneously sending it down both policy pipelines. In this way, the appropriate action is taken for each user.

Message Filters

Message filters are the first module that runs on messages after all the address transformation work is done. Message filters provide a script-like interface for custom rules and can compare any part of a message with regular expression patterns. Because they run before most other processing, they also have some actions that can control work queue processing, such as skipping anti-spam or antivirus scanning.

Message filters are similar to the content filters engine that's a few steps later in the pipeline—in fact, they're really just two interfaces into the same engine. Because content filters are available in the WUI, and message filters only in the CLI, it's far more typical to use content filters for custom rules. We cover the differences in depth in Chapter 11, "Message and Content Filters."

Here are some tasks where you might use message filters:

- Rerouting messages based on sender, recipient, message size, or subject
- Bypassing anti-spam or antivirus filtering based on some message attribute
- Using advanced filter conditions that are only available here, like checking S/MIME signatures
- Conditionally adding or removing headers from messages

For general filtering tasks, like stopping profanity, dropping attachments, or adding disclaimers, it's better to use content filters, because these run after the anti-spam and antivirus engines can drop the junk messages. There's not much reason to filter content that will only be dropped or quarantined later in the pipeline.

Anti-Spam Engine

IronPort Anti-Spam (IPAS) runs in multiple instances, each in a separate AsyncOS process, to spread the scanning load across the available CPU cores. AsyncOS handles this automatically, running an appropriate number of processes for the given hardware and message load. This is why ESA models with 8 CPU cores have peak throughput of about twice that of models that have 4 CPU cores when running IPAS. IPAS only runs with a valid feature key installed on the system.

Under the hood, the engine that powers both IPAS and Virus Outbreak Filters (VOF) is called the Context-Adaptive Scanning Engine (CASE). CASE handles all parts of the message-scanning process: breaking down the message into component parts, decoding attachments, opening archive and compressed formats, and then applying the rules contained in the latest rule definition update. For IPAS, CASE applies the rules for spam messages.

Several actions can be taken with messages found to be spam positive or spam suspect, and some affect further processing in the pipeline:

- **Drop:** The message is immediately thrown away. Message processing does not continue in the work queue. It is possible to archive a copy of the message to disk in case recovery is required.
- **Deliver:** The message continues normal processing and moves on to antivirus scanning. The message can be modified, with changes to subject or header, or sent to an alternate recipient, but the message will go through the other scanning engines.
- **Spam Quarantine:** The message is marked for delivery to the local or external spam quarantine configured in the Security Services menu. The message continues through the work queue to the remaining filtering engines. This is important, because antivirus and any configured content filter rules will be run on these messages before the message is delivered to the quarantine. If a filter drops a message later in the pipeline, it will not appear in the quarantine.
- **Bounce:** The original message is immediately dropped, and a bounce message is generated and sent to the envelope sender of the original. Because of the widespread fraud of sender addresses, this is never a good idea. You should *never* bounce spam or virus messages.

Antivirus Engines

Like IPAS, the available antivirus engines run in a separate process and handle their own message breakdown, archive opening, and rules processing. If a message is found to be viral by one engine, or both, the message is considered viral. When a final verdict is reached, the ESA can take several actions:

- **Drop:** The message is immediately thrown away. This is the default for virus-infected messages. Message processing does NOT continue in the work queue. It is possible to archive a copy of the message to disk in case recovery is required and to optionally send a notification about the event.
- **Deliver:** The message continues normal processing and moves on to content filtering. This is the default action for Repaired, Encrypted, and Unscannable verdicts. It's possible to modify the message with a custom header or a new subject or to deliver the original message as an attachment to a new message. Whatever method is chosen, message processing continues to content filters.

- **Deliver with modification:** For messages that have malicious attachments, it is possible to drop the attachments and deliver the rest of the message intact. The message data that is delivered will continue processing through the work queue.
- **Quarantine:** The message is marked for delivery to the local virus quarantine that's part of the default ESA configuration. The message continues through the work queue to the remaining filtering engines.

Content Filtering

Content filters are the primary policy feature for writing custom rules. It's a Swiss army knife of conditions and actions, allowing you to write rules that test almost any aspect of the message and its parts, the senders, and the recipients. For every incoming and outgoing policy, a selection of content filters is applied to all of the messages passing through that policy. Because of the depth of features, we cover this topic in Chapter 11.

Some common tasks for content filters include the following:

- **Filtering attachments:** Content filters can quarantine or drop messages with certain attachment types or drop the attachments and leave the rest of the message intact.
- **Adding disclaimers:** Additional text can be appended to messages, either above or below the message body.
- **Rerouting messages to other systems:** Filters can identify specific messages by header, sender, recipient, or other data and reroute a message to another host or recipient. You can integrate external encryption, archiving, or DLP systems by using filters to direct messages.
- **Filtering for message content:** Although I don't recommend using content filter rules to stop spam or other junk messages, your organization may prohibit certain message content, like profanity. **You can also use content filters to stop some sensitive information, such as U.S. Social Security numbers, credit-card numbers, or ABA routing numbers.**

Content filters are created globally, but then are selectively applied on a per-policy basis. This allows you to create custom filtering rules for different groups of users. Because content filters run after the anti-spam and antivirus engines, they cannot skip those engines. It is possible to skip outbreak filters, however, and create message tags that can affect processing of DLP. Content filters are run in a well-defined order and offer an action to skip remaining content filters. Unless a content filter uses a final action like drop or bounce, or explicitly skips remaining filters, processing simply moves on to the next filter in the list for that policy.

Virus Outbreak Filters

Virus Outbreak Filters (VOF) actions are applied after content filtering. The purpose is to examine messages that were found to be nonviral by the binary engines, but may be part of a new virus outbreak. The rule examination actually happens with the CASE engine, in one pass, so if IPAS is running the additional work required to run the VOF engine is minimal. Actions are applied at this stage in the pipeline, after content filters, so that VOF doesn't quarantine messages that your custom rules dictate be dropped. For example, if your organization doesn't allow, as a blanket rule, commonly exploited file types, such as .pif and .exe, content filters can drop these attachments and VOF won't act on them.

Every outbreak rule identifies an attachment type or other message attribute, and a severity level from 1–5. The more certain Cisco is about an outbreak, and how widespread it is, the higher the security level will be. Most rules top out at level 3. To date, the false positive rate (where messages were quarantined by rules but turned out to be nonviral) has been vanishingly low—zero for most customers.

Although it's not a "black box," VOF really only has one action that can be taken: quarantine. You can examine the rules associated with a given outbreak and, when a message is quarantined, you'll have visibility into the reason for that action. There are three main configurable options. The first is the global severity level at which to start quarantining, which can be lowered for more aggressive filtering. I generally recommend the default, 3, because most rules are published at 3 and stay there. A rule published with severity 1 or 2 means that there's a lot of uncertainty about the threat, and that any threat is likely contained within a few customers. The second option is the per-policy list of attachment types to be excluded from VOF rules. This list is empty by default, and I recommend keeping it that way—meaning not skipping VOF for any attachment types. One of the greatest features of VOF is the ability for Cisco to publish rules for any file type, and if a common file type, like XLS or PPT, suddenly has a security exploit in the wild, VOF can react. The third option is to enable Adaptive rules, which can be described as local VOF rules, based on message history and attachment types seen locally on this ESA. We examine VOF options in Chapter 9, "Automating Tasks."

DLP and Encryption

Data Loss Prevention (DLP) is provided on the ESA with technology from RSA, a division of EMC Corporation. It requires a valid feature key to enable and use. The DLP engine examines content passed to it by the ESA, which extracts text from any attachments.

The primary purpose of DLP is to take action on messages containing sensitive information that are being sent from local senders to Internet destinations. Because of this purpose, DLP is only available on outgoing messages, and so it only appears as a pipeline stage for outgoing mail messages.

DLP rules are organized into policies, and because the ESA uses the word "policy" for so many different things, we use the term DLP policy to refer specifically to those created in the DLP Policy Manager for use by the RSA engine. The featureset includes a large number of built-in policies and the ability to create custom policies. Chapter 15 covers these policies.

When a message is found to have one or more matches according to a policy, the message is said to contain a DLP violation and has a severity setting from 0–100. Based on the DLP policy, violations are classified as Low, Medium, High, or Critical severities, and each classification can have a different action assigned. The actions that DLP supports are

- **Deliver:** Let the message continue to delivery, potentially with modifications to recipient or destination.
- **Deliver with encryption:** Let the message continue, but use one of the encryption methods available to secure the content. Encryption is supported gateway to gateway using Transport Layer Security (TLS) or through encryption of the actual message data through the Cisco Envelope Encryption technology.
- **Quarantine:** Hold the message in one of the ESA's system quarantines. Each quarantine space specifies how much, and for how long, messages should be held, and what action is to be taken after they expire. The system quarantines are storage areas particular to each appliance.
- **Drop:** The message is discarded. **No further processing is done.**

Other actions like sending a copy of the message to another recipient (BCC) or sending a notification about the violation can be combined with these actions. DLP notifications can be composed with a custom message, including variables that refer to attributes of the message and the violation, such as sender, subject, recipient, and the policy name and the content that matched.

Encryption through Cisco IronPort's Envelope Encryption engine is an optional stage of the email pipeline, usually triggered by content filters or DLP actions. The approach is called envelope encryption because the engine wraps the original message in an encrypted HTML file that adds security and authentication to the message. Authentication of users is handled by the Cisco Registered Email Service (CRES) and, because the technology is based on standard web technologies, is usable by anyone with a web browser or web-enabled mail client.

ESA also supports TLS for delivering email over a secure connection. TLS is covered in Chapter 12, "Advanced Networking."

Delivery of Messages

Any messages that have not been dropped or bounced now proceed into the delivery stage. I often use the term "delivery queue" to refer to this stage, but in reality, the ESA uses more of a tree structure to organize messages. There is no single disk or memory queue where all messages line up to be delivered in order. The ESA creates a node in its tree for every delivery destination and can simultaneously connect and deliver to all active destinations. Figure 3-5 illustrates the steps taken during the delivery stages.

Figure 3-5 *Delivery Stages of the ESA Pipeline*

Most of these tables and settings in this section are optional. The default ESA settings are adequate in the vast majority of environments, with the major exception of the SMTP Routes table. If you used the System Setup Wizard to specify the delivery destination for your local domains, you shouldn't have much reason to change it.

Selecting the Delivery Interface (Virtual Gateways)

When a single ESA has more than one interface, it must choose which interface should be the source of the connection. There are a couple of rules regarding interface selection. On an ESA with no other rules to override it, source interface for SMTP connections follows the source rules for any other kind of connection:

1. If the destination IP is on the same subnet as an ESA interface, use that source interface to send the packet.
2. If the destination IP is not on the same subnet as any ESA interface, send the packet to the default gateway, using the interface that's on the same subnet as the gateway.
3. If the destination IP is on a network listed in a static route, send the packet to the gateway listed in that static route entry.
4. If the ESA has virtual gateways (that is, it has more than one interface on the same subnet as the gateway), then multiple source IPs would be eligible based on these three rules. The ESA chooses the numerically lowest IP based on an alphanumeric sort.

The strict alphanumeric sort can be a bit confusing. For example, if your ESA has these IPs in a DMZ:

```
192.168.1.28
192.168.1.9
192.168.1.100
```

Then a strict numeric sort puts them in this order because 1 is less than 9 when looking only at the first digit in the last octet:

```
192.168.1.100
192.168.1.28
192.168.1.9
```

As a result, 192.168.1.100 will be used as the source interface. This last rule on selecting delivery interfaces can be overridden in a couple of ways: using the *altsrchost* table or using the message or content filter action that selects a delivery interface. (Chapter 12 reviews both of these.)

Destination Controls

The destination controls table provides settings for connection and message rates when ESA is delivering to remote destinations. It also provides settings for attempting or enforcing the use of TLS to these destinations. You can think of it as the corollary to the HAT: instead of rate limiting remote senders, destination controls rate limits the ESA when delivering to remote servers.

Even without hard limits in this table, the ESA follows what is called the *good neighbor algorithm* when delivering mail to a remote destination. Instead of opening numerous connections all at once, it starts with a single connection and only makes another if the message volume warrants it. By slowly increasing connection counts, the ESA can avoid being forcibly rate limited by remote servers that see a large volume of connections as an attack.

In most environments, the connection and message rates in the table by default, combined with the good neighbor approach, are sufficient. Generally, you'll be creating entries in this table to set TLS preferences and not rate limits.

Global Unsubscribe

Global unsubscribe is a rarely used table that comes in handy for certain tasks. It is only available in the CLI through the **unsubscribe** command. It tells the ESA that it should never send messages to certain recipients or domains. For any listed recipient or recipient domain, you have two actions: drop or bounce.

This can be useful if you have machine-generated messaging, like bills, statements, or marketing, and need to prevent it from being sent to sensitive domains or individuals. Normally, automated message subscription lists should be updated to exclude recipients that don't want to receive the mailings, but those updates can often take days to process. Global unsubscribe is an immediate change that ensures that delivery is never made to that recipient or domain.

SMTP Routes

The determination of the host used to deliver a given recipient is primarily done through the global SMTP routes table, available through both the CLI and the WUI. Every SMTP route table specifies a domain and one or more destinations for the domain. Each destination for a domain is given a priority, or cost, that determines the order that destinations are tried in. Lower cost destinations are preferred. Only full domains and subdomains are allowed as entries; per-recipient destinations must be done with aliases, LDAP routing, or filters. For every entry, there are a few types of destinations supported, as listed in Table 3-2.

Table 3-2 *SMTP Routes Destination Types*

Destination Type	Description
Domain name	Full domain names, like cisco.com, can be added as destinations. The ESA first looks up the domain's MX records, and then looks up A records for any hosts returned from the MX lookup. If no MX lookup exists for the domain, an A record for the domain is queried.
Hostname	Treated exactly like a domain, the ESA first queries for an MX record for an entry like email.cisco.com, and only looks up an A record if the MX lookup fails. If you are sending local mail to a server called mailstore.company.com, for example, you may want to skip the MX record lookup by using the square bracket notation.
Host or domain name in square brackets	An entry specified in the form [email.cisco.com] skips the initial MX record lookup and forces the resolution via A record only.
IP address	Destination IP for this domain. No DNS lookup is performed.

Special destination USEDNS	Reverts to using the normal DNS rules (MX record, then A record if no MX exists) for this destination. This type of entry is usually only used for making an exception to a wildcard rule. For example, suppose you had this entry in the SMTPRoutes table:
	`.cisco.com: 10.10.20.30, 10.10.23.30`
	But, you had a subdomain called external.cisco.com that has published MX records in DNS. With this entry, this subdomain will be delivered to the two IPs listed. Adding this entry overrides that behavior:
	`external.cisco.com: usedns`

Special destination /dev/null	Provided for compatibility with some other MTA software. Drops the message immediately at the point of delivery, after all scanning has been completed. If you want to accept, scan, and then drop messages, this is one way to do it, but for performance, it's better to refuse or drop earlier in the pipeline. Not recommended except for test systems, obviously!

The table also has a default route that matches any destination, if no specific route entry exists. The default SMTP route works like other entries and uses the same destination types. The ESA typically has an empty default route, and you would normally only provide an entry for ESAs that handle internal traffic only. If no specific entry for the destination exists in the SMTP Routes, ESA uses the default route. With an empty default route, ESA uses the normal DNS process for determining destination host: Look up an MX record and the A record for any host returned in the MX result. If no MX record is found, ESA then looks up an A record for the domain. If no records are found at all, the message is immediately bounced as an unrecoverable error.

Each SMTP route entry can have more than one destination. Providing multiple destinations allows for load balancing or failover across the available destinations. As of AsyncOS 7.1, each destination can have a priority value, with lower numbers being higher priority as with MX records. Zero is the highest priority. Connections to equal-priority hosts are load-balanced in a round-robin fashion. Connections to lower-priority hosts are only made if all of the higher-priority hosts are unavailable.

Lastly, if delivery to a specific destination requires that the SMTP client (in this case, the ESA), authenticate in order to be able to deliver email, you must configure SMTP Auth profiles and specify them in the appropriate destination entries.

Selecting Bounce Profiles

Bounce profiles aren't really a separate stage of the pipeline, but rather a small policy attached to each message that determines what to do if the message can't be delivered. Bounce profiles decide how many times, and how often, a message should be retried before the ESA gives up and declares it permanently undeliverable. For permanently undeliverable messages, the bounce profile also determines whether a delivery status notification (DSN) or bounce is generated and where it is sent. Bounce messages are also called non-delivery records (NDR) and usually go to the envelope sender of the message.

Bounce profiles can be assigned to a message in several places in the pipeline, and assigning a different profile later in the pipeline overrides earlier settings. The three places where bounce profiles can be assigned are

1. The listener that the message was received on. Every listener assigns a bounce profile as the message is accepted.
2. Message filters can assign a bounce profile using the bounce-profile action.
3. Destination controls can assign a bounce profile to recipients within a specific destination domain.

These assignments occur in this order and the last match wins, so any bounce profile chosen in a filter overrides the listener setting. Choosing a bounce profile in destination controls overrides both the listener and any filter settings, except if the value **Default** is chosen, which can be interpreted more accurately as "use the Default if no other bounce profile has been chosen." If you set a custom bounce profile in a filter, it will not be overridden by a destination control that chooses Default.

Handling Delivery Errors with Bounce Profiles

Not every recipient on every message is always going to be deliverable. Users mistype addresses, employees leave companies, and mail servers don't always accept messages.

Delivery errors boil down to two general classes: temporary and permanent. Permanent errors include DNS errors, like a nonexistent domain, or email address problems, like a nonexistent or permanently disabled account.

Temporary errors include being unable to make a connection to a remote server, not being able to negotiate connection parameters (such as TLS), or any kind of 4yz SMTP error code returned from the remote server. Eventually, all temporary errors can become permanent errors if the message exceeds the retry limits defined in the bounce profile.

Retry limits for messages are controlled in the individual settings for each bounce profile created through Bounce Profiles in the Network menu of the WUI or the CLI command **bounceconfig**. Each profile encapsulates settings like the maximum number of retries to make, the maximum time a message may stay in queue, and what action to take if the message exceeds those limits. For example, you can create a bounce profile with a short lifetime like 4 hours and apply it to outgoing messages, while another profile applies a 72-hour limit to incoming messages. You can even create a *no bounce* profile to prevent some messages from generating a bounce, which can be useful for automated systems that send email.

Retry limits for unreachable hosts are controlled globally, not per-profile. All retry settings for both hosts and messages are expressed in a minimum and maximum time between attempts. The ESA uses a retreating schedule of attempts, starting from the minimum. For example, if the minimum retry is 60s, the first attempt is one minute later, the next two minutes after that, the next four minutes, and so on until the maximum one hour limit is reached.

When a temporary error exceeds the retry limits, the error becomes permanent and ESA can generate a DSN. The default setting is to generate a DSN or bounce message and send it back to the sender, and include information about the error in the message. You can send bounces to another address—for example, when the sender is an automated system. You can also customize the DSN text using a bounce notification template. Customized DSNs can include additional information about the delivery error or about the original message that caused the bounce. If you want the end-user text in a non-English language, you can use customized DSNs to create them.

One last option with bounce profiles is to generate a DSN when a message is undeliverable for some period. The DSN simply states that the message has not been delivered and that the system will continue to attempt to deliver it. Because most users are usually just confused by these status messages, they are off by default, but you can enable them and provide a single or multiple delay warnings at any interval.

Final Disposition

The ESA can never be the final destination for a message because it does not host a mail store. As a result, there are only three possible final states for a message: dropped, bounced, or delivered. There are several non-final states that a message can be in: queued, in process, quarantined, or active, but eventually these will all have a final state. Active messages and recipients are those awaiting delivery and are further broken down into attempted and unattempted.

Messages that are not in a final state have an active MID on the system, and logging for the message continues until it reaches a final state. Because the final state may be determined days after the initial injection, the MID value may span across log files.

There are several places where the final disposition of a message can be determined. Message tracking on the ESA directly, or centralized on an SMA, is probably the most convenient, because it provides a thorough search capability and fast search times. Message disposition is also recorded directly in the IronPort Text Mail logs or in an optional log format called delivery logs. Delivery logs are stored in binary and require additional processing, but the text mail logs are, of course, in plain ASCII text and can be searched directly.

Once a message reaches final disposition, all of its contents are removed from memory and disk and only the record in the logs and tracking is kept on the ESA. It is possible to archive message contents locally on the ESA using a filter action, but it's not possible to directly reinject messages from those archives.

For delivered messages, ESA waits until the message has been acknowledged with a 2yz response code from the SMTP server. Any text accompanying the response code is logged.

Summary

This chapter describes the entirety of the message lifecycle in the ESA pipeline, from initial SMTP connection to final delivery. We covered basic message transport capabilities, LDAP features, and security filtering. You should have a good understanding of the stages of the ESA email pipeline and the order in which they occur.

Now that we have a lot of the theory of operation covered, we're next going to dive into the full management capabilities of the appliance, first in the web user interface in Chapter 4, and then in the command-line interface in Chapter 5.

Chapter 4

ESA Web User Interface

In this chapter, you will learn the following:

- The complete tour of all WUI pages and options
- Details of all menu items and their command-line equivalent
- How to make configuration changes and the commit process

Overview

The Cisco IronPort Email Security Appliance (ESA) offer a rich web-based user interface for almost all management, monitoring, and reporting tasks that you will encounter in your email security environment. When you are working with the ESA, you'll likely be in the web user interface (WUI).

Connecting to the WUI

The WUI is available using HTTP or HTTPS on any IP interface that you've configured to support those protocols and can be run on any port. If you allow both, you also have the option of forcing HTTP connections to be redirected to HTTPS to enforce the use of Secure Socket Layer (SSL) for management tasks.

If you use HTTPS, be aware that the ESA ships from the factory with a self-signed demo certificate that will cause a browser warning when you connect. This default should be replaced before deploying in production, either with a locally generated self-signed certificate, or with a certificate that you've purchased from a reputable Internet root certificate authority.

WUI Tour

The ESA WUI is intended to be straightforward and intuitive. All the menus and menu items should be fairly self-explanatory if you are familiar with email security, MTAs, and general servers. I give you a brief tour and then provide more details for configuration sections that are unique to the Cisco IronPort security appliances.

Monitor Menu

The monitor menu includes all of the pages that provide reports for the ESA. It includes the live, drill-down reporting pages for incoming and outgoing mail, security engines, user statistics, and system monitoring pages. It also includes system quarantines and, if enabled locally, the message tracking page. The monitor menu is shown in Figure 4-1.

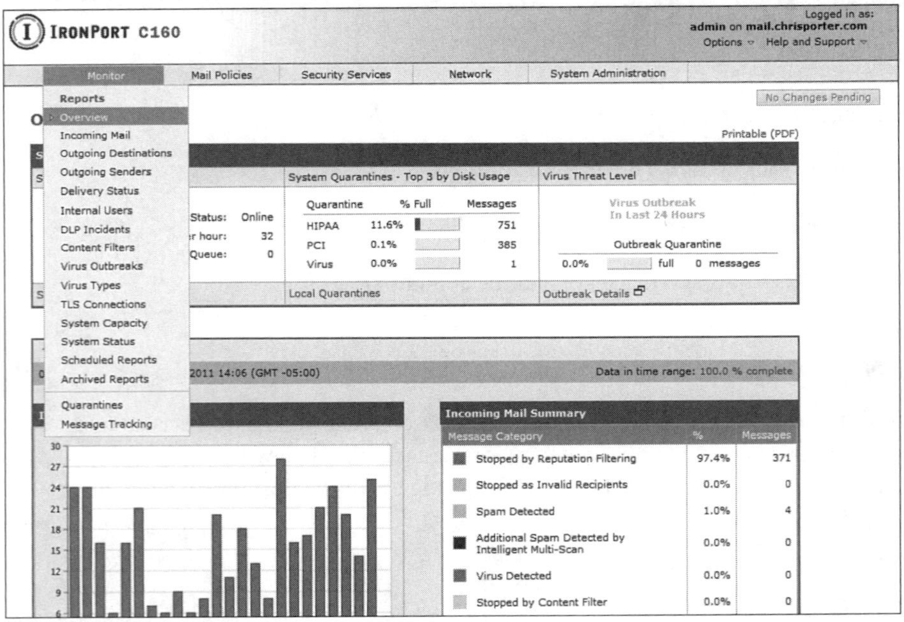

Figure 4-1 *Monitor Menu*

Most of the reporting pages are arranged similarly. Each report has a top-level **Overview** report, with graphs displaying relevant data for the selected time range. The **time range** drop-down box gives you a choice of past hour, day, week, 30 days, 90 days, previous day, previous month, or a custom time range. If you are using an SMA with its centralized reporting feature, the ESA is limited to past hour, day, and week, because the month, quarter, and year views are only on the SMA. When you choose a time range for reports, all the report and status pages will reflect the time range choice until you change it again.

Almost every report page provides two common elements. Near the upper right is a link called **Printable (PDF)** that exports the current report view into a PDF document, including all graphs. In many reports, there's also a link called **Export...** that can give you a comma-separated values (CSV) file containing the data included in the report. There's more on this reporting export in Chapter 9, "Automating Tasks."

Reporting pages do not have a CLI equivalent, with a few noted exceptions.

Overview

As its name suggests, the **Overview** page provides a summary of all email operations on this ESA. At the top, you'll see a brief system status, a snapshot of up to three system quarantines ordered by disk usage, and an outbreak status. Below that is a graph and table for **Incoming Mail** and then below that is **Outgoing Mail**. Incoming and outgoing follow the general ESA rule for determining email direction: incoming are messages that are accepted; outgoing are messages that are relayed.

Incoming Mail

Incoming mail is the launch point for a variety of pages that cover all the mail accepted by the ESA. The first page you're brought to from this menu covers mail received by the ESA, sorted by the domain of the connecting hosts. There are also IP address and network owner views of the data.

This page, like most of the reports in the ESA WUI, offers a considerable amount of detail in drill-down. For example, if you click a domain in the chart or table, you'll see a report on email statistics and global sender information for this specific sending domain. If you click the IP address in a domain report, you'll see the stats for that particular IP. All these reports offer an **Add to Sender Group...** link, which allows you to quickly add the sender to a whitelist, blacklist, or other Host Access Table (HAT) sender group.

One of the hidden gems of the WUI is only available through the default **Incoming Mail** page: At the bottom is a link for the **Sender Groups report**, which shows how the ESA has categorized the connections made to the ESA. If you can't find it, it's also available through the URL on your ESA:

https://<hostname>/monitor/reports/sender_groups

The sender groups report shows you how the ESA is classifying incoming connections into the sender groups, and the relative percentages and absolute connection count for each group. It won't show an entry for groups that have no matches, so it can show you when sender conditions aren't being matched or when your HAT ordering is incorrect. It's also a great way to report on different senders without necessarily taking specific action. For example, you could use DNS mismatches to categorize senders into a group called DNSMISMATCH that uses the standard ACCEPTED policy. This report will show you the number of connections that meet the conditions for that group.

There's no drill-down to individual users or messages. For this level of detail, you can look at the **Internal Users** report or go to **Message Tracking**.

Outgoing Destinations

Outgoing destinations is the opposite of incoming mail, focusing on destinations of delivered messages rather than their source. The graphs and tables show you where your users are sending messages.

You can sort the columns and choose the number of items displayed, but there's no further drill-down in this report. For details on messages delivered to a specific destination, go to the **Message Tracking** page.

Note that this page is historical: It shows messages that have reach a final disposition, either delivered or bounced. For details on messages that are in the process of being delivered or are queued for delivery, see the Delivery Status report.

Outgoing Senders

Outgoing senders provides you with a view of the domains and IP addresses that are responsible for your outgoing mail. This should show you all the groupware and application servers that are using your ESA relay mail flow policies. It can also show you unexpected sources: Hosts in your network that shouldn't be sending messages directly. Because the table provides statistics on virus and spam filtering, this report is useful for tracking down infected hosts or users.

There is no drill-down available here for more detail. For information on messages sent out by users and hosts in your organization, use the **Message Tracking** feature.

Delivery Status

Delivery Status provides an ordered list of active destinations in the ESA. Active refers to a destination domain that the ESA has recently or currently queued messages. If there are active recipients for a particular destination, you can **Retry All Delivery** with a button at the top right.

Drill-down on each destination domain provides a summary of that domain, including the delivery details, time of oldest message, and a historical summary of delivery and bounces. You can force the ESA to make a delivery attempt with the **Retry All Delivery** button. If the remote destination is rejecting connections with an SMTP 5yz error code, the most recent such error will be displayed here.

The same information is available in the CLI with the commands **tophosts** and **hoststatus**. Chapter 6, "Additional Management Services," has a detailed example of delivery troubleshooting with these commands.

Internal Users

The Internal Users report summarizes both incoming and outgoing mail based on the statistics for your local users. Local user addresses are the senders of email on relay HAT connections, and the recipients of email on accepted HAT connections.

The graphs provide a view of top senders and recipients of email in your organization, and the table below total statistics for individual users by email address. Want to see who receives the most spam? Who sends the most virus-laden messages? Sort the columns in the table here for the view that you want.

You can also drill-down on specific users by clicking their email address. The detail report for a user shows security filtering and content filtering results. The content filter results for a user allow drill-down to a content filter report for that filter.

DLP Incidents

If you have a feature key for the RSA DLP engine and are scanning outgoing email for data loss prevention policy violations, any matches will be recorded here.

DLP match results are similar to content filter matches, with the addition of a severity score that roughly correlates with the number of entity matches in the message. You can drill-down on the policy names to get to a detailed DLP report, which lists local email addresses causing policy matches.

Chapter 15, "Advanced Topics," covers DLP.

Content Filters

The Content Filters report summarizes content filter matches for incoming and outgoing mail. This report shows the totals for your content filters by name—a good reason to use descriptive names when you create content filters. A content filter match means that either one or all conditions matched, depending on the logic you used in the filter. Any message that matches the filter conditions is considered a match, even if no permanent action is taken.

This feature makes the content filters report wonderfully flexible, allowing you to gather statistics on a wide variety of message conditions that don't have dedicated reports. If you want to know how many messages are sent out with ZIP file attachments, or those larger than a specific size, or almost any other message condition, simply create a filter with that condition and a low impact action, like **Add Header**. Matches are recorded for every message where the filter is applied and the condition clause matches.

Drill-down on any filter name shows a graph of match results over time, and a list of internal users whose messages have matched the filter. Clicking the user email address brings you to the Internal Users report for that user.

Outbreak Filters

Outbreak Filters (OF) reports details the type of threat messages acted on by the outbreak filters engine. In versions prior to 7.5, this report is known as Virus Outbreak Filters (VOF). The entries in this report describe the classification of threat messages and the count of messages in each category.

The use of OFs to scan for and stop zero-day viruses, phishing, and malware messages are covered in Chapter 8, "Security Filtering."

Virus Types

The Virus Types report is a detail of all email attachment viruses that have been sent or received in the current timeframe. It displays the name provided by the AV vendor, and some virus names will vary across different vendors.

The outgoing virus types graph should ideally be empty. If there are hits for outgoing viruses, use the Internal Users or Outgoing Senders reports, or the **Message Tracking** feature to find the source of these viruses in your organization.

TLS Connections

The TLS Connections report is similar to the Incoming Mail report, but focused on message statistics received over connections that used Transport Layer Security (TLS) to encrypt the SMTP conversation. If you're not using TLS, the report will be empty.

The goal of this report is to give you a snapshot for how much TLS is being used, and with which senders and recipients. It's the first place to look if you're receiving alerts about TLS being required but not available, and a good place to look for senders that you can move from Preferred to Required TLS.

You can drill-down on incoming TLS domains to get a domain-specific TLS report that includes individual sending IP addresses.

System Capacity

System Capacity collects all the operational conditions of the ESA into one place. There are separate pages for the work queue, incoming mail, outgoing mail, and system load, or you can just click the **All** link to see everything in one page.

These reports are an easy way to zero in on capacity issues, queue backups, and corresponding events. Work queue backups can usually be correlated with a spike in connections, message count, or message size.

System Status

The System Status page collects the current running statistics for the ESA and displays them all in one page. The results are collected at the time the page is requested, so the statistics here will change each time you reload the page.

Most of the gauges are self-explanatory, but the rates and counters warrant a bit of explanation. The rates refer to events per hour, but measured over the last 1, 5, or 15 minutes. The ESA measures the rate at which these events occur and extrapolates the per-hour rate from that measurement period. For example, if the page displays 600 in the 1-minute column for messages received, that means the ESA received 10 messages in 1 minute and extrapolated from that a rate of 600 per hour. You can think of this as somewhat like speed in a car: On the highway, you might say that you've been driving at 60 mph for the last minute. Because they measure a longer interval, the 15-minute samples are the most accurate.

The counters are straightforward enough, but have three measures by which they count: reset, uptime, and lifetime. Lifetime is a count from the time when the system was first imaged and shipped, and it can never be reset. Uptime counts events from the last reboot of the system. Reset refers to events since the last time counters were reset, either with the **Reset Counters** button on this page or the **resetcounters** command.

You can obtain the same information in the CLI with the command **status detail** or with the XML status pages. There is more detail on these approaches in Chapter 5, "Command-Line Interface," and Chapter 9, respectively.

Scheduled Reports

Scheduled Reports is where you schedule any of the previously mentioned reports to be generated on a regular cycle. There are even some scheduled report types, like the domain-based executive summary, that aren't available anywhere else.

Note that if you are using an SMA for centralized reporting, you should generate scheduled reports there, as they are disabled on the individual ESAs. Because the SMA can generate reports for individual appliances, it's not necessary to have this on the ESA.

Archived Reports

This page is the historical collection of all the results of the scheduled reports that archive their results. Reports are stored in either PDF or CSV, and the report title link allows you to download it directly to your local computer. You can delete old reports to save space, but the appliance will also do this for you, deleting the oldest reports first when space is limited.

If you aren't already receiving a copy of reports every day, suggest that, as a minimum, you schedule an Executive Summary and System Capacity report generated on a daily basis for the previous calendar day. You might not examine these reports every day, but having them available will give you some insight into long-term trends. If you're using the DLP feature, the DLP Incident Summary report is another good daily report to archive.

Quarantines

Quarantines are storage space on the appliance for messages of interest. There are two basic kinds of quarantines. The IronPort Spam Quarantine (ISQ) provides storage for spam or suspected spam messages and optionally allows for direct end user access and management. The other type are system quarantines, which are intended to hold messages for administrator review; there are no end-user access capabilities for system quarantines. Within system quarantines, there is some space reserved for Outbreak Filters quarantining and two quarantines (called Policy and Virus) that are created by default.

This page in the WUI gives you access to the quarantines for message management or, if you have administrator or operator rights, the ability to manage the quarantine settings for space, retention time, and expiration action.

Administrators and operators have the rights to release or delete messages in any quarantine. Guest and Help Desk users do not, but can be granted privileges on a per-quarantine basis. For example, if you create a quarantine called PCI for the purposes of storing messages that contain credit-card numbers, you can grant access to that quarantine to a guest user in your legal department who is responsible for investigations. This type of task delegation allows that person to perform policy review without having other administrative rights.

Many of the quarantine settings are available in the CLI with **quarantineconfig**, but managing messages in quarantine for release or delete is best done through the WUI.

Message Tracking

Message Tracking is a single, simple interface for searching the ESA history for message events. The search fields allow you to query the history for messages based on sender, recipient, subject, or attachment name, and to restrict the search to specific date and time range. The interface also allows you to search by message event so that you can search for all DLP violations or virus positive messages in the past day, for example.

The results of a search are a summary of all matching messages that can be exported to a CSV file. Every message in the match list has a **Show Details** link that provides a complete summary of that particular message. This cradle-to-grave report of the message shows the source IP, message sender and recipient, and all the processing details, including the verdicts of the security filtering engines.

If you have an SMA in your environment configured for centralized message tracking, this feature will be disabled on the ESA. The SMA will have message tracking history for all ESAs in the environment.

There's nothing quite like message tracking in the CLI; however, you can search the text mail logs with CLI commands, like **grep**, **tail**, and **findevent**.

Mail Policies Menu

The Mail Policies menu is where almost all of the controls related to email filtering happens. All the security and content filtering policies are set here, so it's likely that, as an ESA administrator, the pages on this menu are where you are likely to spend most of your time. The Mail Policies menu is shown in Figure 4-2.

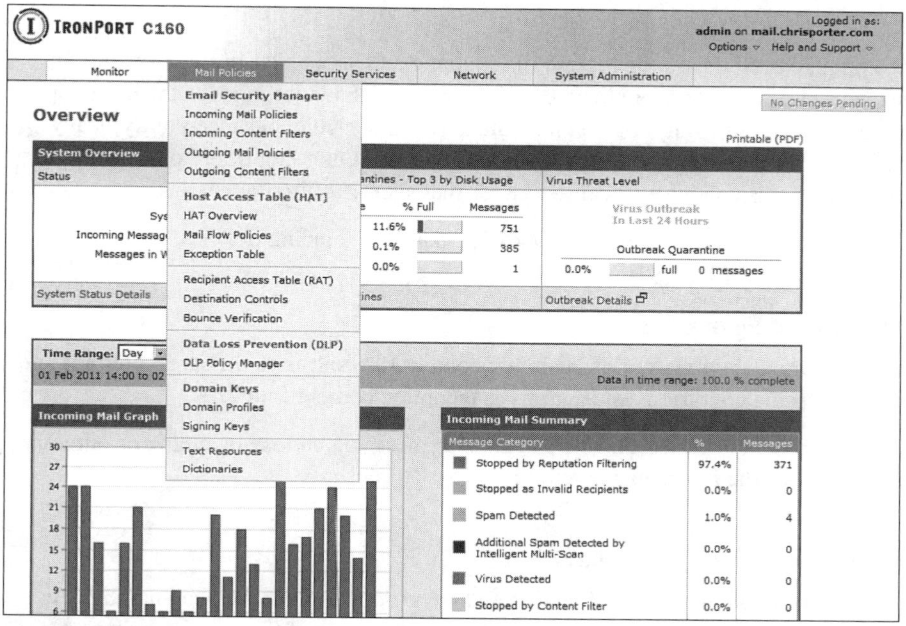

Figure 4-2 *Mail Policies Menu*

Mail Policies also provides WUI pages for creating and managing the resources, such as DLP policies, notifications, and dictionaries that you will use elsewhere in constructing policies.

Incoming Mail Policies

Incoming Mail Policies graphically displays the filtering steps of the email security pipeline starting with anti-spam.

The ESA pipeline, including incoming and outgoing policies, is covered in Chapter 3, "ESA Email Pipeline."

The CLI equivalent is **policyconfig**.

Incoming Content Filters

Content filters are the ESA Swiss army knife with flexible conditions and Boolean logic to identify messages of interest. Content filters must be managed separately for incoming and outgoing traffic.

This WUI page allows you to create and manage a library of filters that you then apply by editing the **Content Filters** column in **Incoming Mail Policies.**

The CLI equivalent is buried under **policyconfig**; after you choose incoming or outgoing policies, you see the **filters** menu item.

Outgoing Mail Policies

Outgoing mail policies are the inverse of incoming and are similar in function and appearance. There are two key differences. First, the default settings for the outgoing policies are different from those on incoming. This is sensible, because you typically won't be spam-scanning your outgoing traffic. Second, Outgoing Mail Policies has a column for DLP if you have a license key for that security filtering engine.

The CLI equivalent is also under **policyconfig**, just like incoming policies.

Outgoing Content Filters

This is the outgoing equivalent of incoming content filters. It uses the same interface and provides the same conditions and actions as incoming content filters.

The CLI equivalent is buried under **policyconfig**; after you choose incoming or outgoing policies, you see the **filters** menu item.

Host Access Table (HAT) Overview

The next three menu items are all related and are grouped under the heading HAT. As discussed in Chapter 3, the HAT controls the parameters the ESA uses in the first part of the SMTP server pipeline: connection management, SMTP conversation, and related tasks, like recipient validation.

The HAT is a table composed of two portions: the sender groups and the mail flow policies. Sender groups do just what it sounds like: lumps email senders into groups based on criteria that you specify. Every sender group has a name and one or more entries that define which senders are members of that group. You can do this manually by entering IPs, CIDR ranges, or hostnames, or you can use dynamic categorization like SenderBase Reputation Scores (SBRS), DNS blocklists, or other DNS parameters. For the vast majority of customers, SBRS is the primary means of sender sorting, and sensible defaults are established by the System Setup Wizard or whenever you create a new public listener.

Once a connecting IP is categorized, the mail flow policy associated with the sender groups is applied. Mail flow policies control basic connection behavior as well as rate limits, SMTP responses, TLS, security, authentication, and verification. The mail flow policy has effects on the pipeline deeper than the immediate SMTP connection behavior it dictates.

The HAT offers a good deal of depth, and because it's such an integral part of the pipeline its features are covered in Chapter 3. The security nature of SBRS and Reputation Filters is covered in Chapter 8.

Each listener on your ESA has its own HAT and, for that reason, the command-line equivalent is in the **hostaccess** item under the **edit** menu in **listenerconfig**.

Mail Flow Policies

Mail flow policies collects all the parameters associated with accepting and handling SMTP connections that are applied to sender groups. It also affects a number of other pipeline components, such as anti-spam and antivirus, by deciding whether such scanning will be performed on messages accepted under this policy.

The HAT and its corresponding mail flow policies are described in Chapter 3.

Exception Table

The exception table is used only for overriding the results of the Sender Verification features in HAT mail flow policies. To use it, you must turn on the **Use Sender Verification Exception Table** option in one or more mail flow policies.

This table is here because DNS Sender Verification can be problematic. Sender Verification attempts to look up the domain of the email sender of messages in DNS. The logic of this lookup is that you may want to reject messages whose senders don't exist in DNS and whose messages you can't reply to. Years ago, before spam and fraud senders got wise, this could be used to discard junk email. Today, these sophisticated senders use legitimate return addresses stolen from other sources, so most junk messages will pass the sender verification step.

The problems with sender verification are that DNS can occasionally return indecisive results, like temporary lookup failures, and queries can timeout. Further, some legitimate senders don't have their DNS house in order and can fail this test, resulting in your ESA rejecting legitimate messages.

It's this last problem that the exception table is designed to solve.

Recipient Access Table (RAT)

The Recipient Access Table (RAT) is simple: It controls whether the ESA will accept email for a given recipient, or recipient domain, or not. The default is to reject all recipients at all domains to avoid the ESA being configured as an open relay. During the system setup wizard, you normally specify your local domains for the ESA to accept on incoming mail connections.

If the RAT specifies that a domain or address is to be accepted, you can also specify that LDAP queries be bypassed. The RAT is discussed in more detail in Chapter 3.

An ESA may have more than one RAT, because each listener has one RAT table. As a result, the CLI command equivalent is in the **listenerconfig** command in the **rcptaccess** option within the **edit** command for each listener.

Destination Controls

You can think of destination controls as the opposite of the HAT. This table is where you specify connection and SMTP parameters at the end of the pipeline for delivery. You can modify settings for delivery on a per-domain basis for attributes such as TLS, concurrent connections, messages per hour, and recipients in a unit of time. You can also decide which bounce profile to assign to messages queued for delivery to each destination.

The equivalent CLI command is **destconfig**. I cover different components of this table in other chapters. Bounce profiles are in Chapter 3, and TLS (encrypted SMTP delivery) is covered in Chapter 12, "Advanced Networking."

Bounce Verification

Bounce verification is an interesting feature, one that most customers likely won't need, but a lifesaver for some environments. The purpose is to stop *bounce storms*, a type of SMTP application layer attack roughly akin to a distributed denial of service (DDOS) attack. Such attacks can be intentional or just a side effect of the spam and fraud messages that traverse the Internet daily.

These attacks take advantage of the fact that SMTP sender address specified in the MAIL FROM command can be forged. If the fraudulent sender uses an address from your organization in their message, you will sometimes get non-delivery records (NDR, or bounces) sent back to your organization. This happens every day, and the occasional bounce message might be confusing to users, but ultimately not terribly harmful. The anti-spam engine on the ESA can often filter these messages.

The harm comes when a fraudulent sender composes tens of millions of these messages, all using the same address in your organization. The result can be millions of bounced messages, sent by many organizations across the globe, all during the same time period. This traffic can swamp even the largest email systems.

Bounce verification can solve this by marking up messages that leave your environment. If these messages bounce, the markup is recognized, and the bounce is accepted by your ESA and delivered. If a bounce arrives at the gateway without the markup, it can be assumed that the original message was not from one of your users and can be rejected. The markup used by bounce verification is actually a modification of the SMTP envelope sender and includes a timestamp and a secret key so that attackers can't forge the return addresses.

There are a number of potential problems to consider with bounce verification, and I cover it in detail in Chapter 14, "Recommended Configurations." The CLI command equivalent is **bvconfig**.

DLP Policy Manager

If you have a license key for the DLP scanning engine, configuration of policies is done here. Like content filters, policies are created in a library and then applied to individual outgoing mail policies.

Prebuilt policies are available for many U.S. Federal and State regulations and some industry-specific ones; others are available for common intellectual property and confidentiality protection needs. In addition, built-in and blank policies are customizable, and you have access to the dictionaries, classifiers, and entities that the RSA DLP engine provides. These entities include content-matching patterns for identifiers from many countries that go beyond regular expressions, such as for payment card numbers, bank routing numbers, social insurance, and drivers' licenses.

DLP is covered in Chapter 15. There's no CLI equivalent.

Domain Profiles

Domain Profiles is for managing Domain Keys Identified Mail (DKIM) policies. DKIM is a form of sender authentication that cryptographically signs email messages to prove their provenance. This page allows you to specify which messages are signed, what DKIM options are used, and what signing key is used.

You can also create profiles that use the older Domain Keys (DK) standard, but unless you have a need to support legacy signatures, you should use DKIM.

Chapter 15 covers DKIM and other sender authentication standards. You can manage DKIM keys and profiles in the CLI with **domainkeysconfig**.

Signing Keys

DKIM signing requires cryptographic public key pairs using the RSA algorithm, and the ESA gives you this page to create and manage your key pairs. Keys can be generated locally or pasted in if you've generated them with another tool.

Chapter 15 covers DKIM and other sender authentication standards.

Text Resources

Text Resources is a single place to manage templates for all kinds of administrative and user-facing text. Notifications, disclaimers (footers and headers), encryption text, and even bounce message text can be managed here.

Text messages are created in a library here and then used in other places, like filters, bounce profiles, and antivirus policies. You can create notifications in any language, provided that your browser supports Unicode or other character sets.

Text resources can also make use of a number of action variables that include information from the ESA or from the message being acted on. These include data like message size, senders, recipients, attachment names, filter name, ESA hostname, timestamp, and so on. An action variable is a string beginning with a dollar sign character, such as $bodysize.

The equivalent CLI command is **textconfig**.

Dictionaries

Dictionaries are lists of words, phrases, and regular expressions that are used for matching content in message or content filters. You can use dictionaries to test simple Boolean logic, such as "does this message match any single entry in this dictionary?" and weighted logic by assigning a score to each dictionary entry and building a filter whose conditions trigger only when the total score match reaches a threshold you specify.

Chapter 11, "Message and Content Filters," discusses dictionaries in the context of message and content filters. The equivalent CLI for managing dictionaries is **dictionaryconfig.**

Security Services Menu

The Security Services menu provides global settings and status for all of the optional filtering engines on the ESA. Some menu items only appear here if the corresponding license key is available and active on the system. For example, you won't see a license for McAfee Antivirus if the key is expired. The Security Services menu is shown in Figure 4-3.

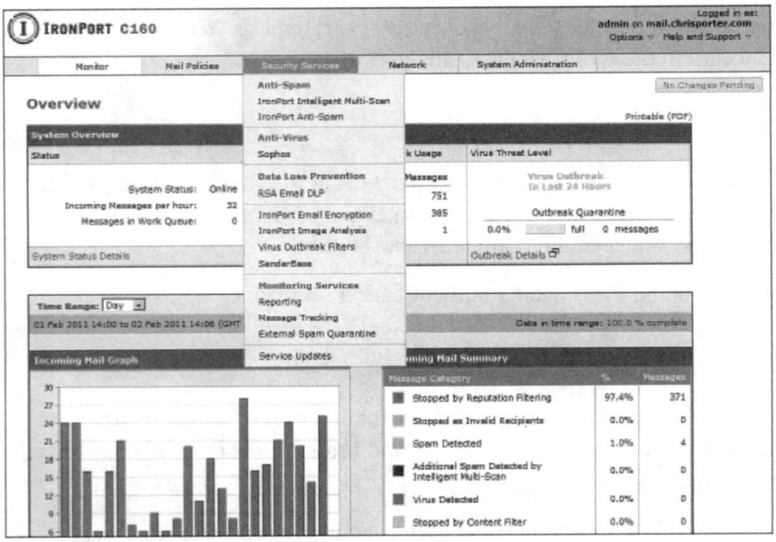

Figure 4-3 *Security Services Menu*

Anti-Spam

The global settings for each engine generally cover size thresholds, timeouts, and other options that apply to the engine as a whole. Specific policy actions are handled in **Incoming and Outgoing Mail Policies** pages in the **Mail Policies** menu and, as a result, most configuration for the security and content engines is handled there, not in the **Security Services** menu.

The Security Services menu does provide a status for each engine, where relevant. This includes the individual engine version, rules database versions, and the timestamp of last update. For anti-spam, the rules are in a number of different databases that are updated independently. You can also manually force an update of rules downloads.

The CLI equivalent is **antispamconfig.**

Antivirus

There are two possible menu items for antivirus: Sophos and McAfee, depending on which engine technology is licensed on the ESA. It is possible to show both if there is an active license key for each.

The global options are similar for the two antivirus engines. The menu item for each engine also shows the status of latest rules downloads, including the version number and timestamp. You can also manually force an update of rules.

The CLI equivalent is **antivirusconfig.** Both engines configuration is available under this single command.

RSA Email DLP

If you have a feature key for the RSA DLP engine, you can enable it here. There is also an option to enable or disable **Matched Content Logging**, which records an excerpt of text that causes a DLP match, and makes it available during message tracking searches.

Matched content logging is extremely useful, but it does expose message content to any user with message tracking privileges.

IronPort Email Encryption

Here, email encryption refers to the message-based envelope encryption that Cisco offers as an optional license key and service. When used as a content filter or DLP action, message contents are encrypted using strong symmetric encryption, and sent to the recipients with that encrypted bundle attached. The recipient can open the message using only a web browser.

The encryption options that are used when a particular message is encrypted are selected by an encryption profile. An encryption profile encapsulates settings such as encryption strength and algorithm, envelope branding logos, notification text, and reply options. You can have multiple encryption profiles on one ESA, for multiple notification types or for multiple brands. If you send encrypted messages from separate divisions within your organization, you may want to have separate brands for each division's encrypted mail.

Once an encryption profile is created and provisioned, the Encrypt action is available in incoming and outgoing content filters.

IronPort Image Analysis

Image analysis is another optional engine that will only appear here if you have a valid license key. The purpose of this engine is singular: to open and examine image attachments to messages and make a determination of whether the image is business inappropriate. In other words, it determines if a still image is pornographic.

You have a number of configurable options for sensitivity. Image attachments are scored from 0 to 100, with 100 being most likely to contain adult content. This range is broken up into three verdicts: clean, suspected, and inappropriate. You can modify the thresholds here.

The other option is for minimum size threshold, and this is important for two reasons: First, small images, such as icons and logos, are not likely to have adult content, and skipping them avoids any false positives. Second, these icons and logos are common attachments, such as those in email signatures, and skipping them saves a huge amount of work. The default threshold is 100 pixels in either width or height, but I recommend increasing this to 150 or 200, if you plan to use this feature.

Once this engine is enabled, the Image Analysis verdict is available in incoming and outgoing content filters. Because such machine image recognition has an inherent false positive rate, quarantining is the preferred action to take on positive verdicts.

Outbreak Filters

One of the primary functions of the ESA is to keep dangerous messages that contain virus attachments or URL links to virus or malware laden websites out of your environment. The anti-spam and antivirus engines provide most of the filtering, but Cisco created Outbreak Filters (OF) to incorporate one more layer of protection. This type of filtering is usually known as "zero-day" protection, because it can effectively stop newly released malware before antivirus signatures are published.

The global options for OFs are configured on this page, and it also provides a snapshot of the current outbreak rules that the ESA has in place. This list of rules is constantly changing, updated by the ESA automatically every 5 minutes.

As with all the security engines, the configuration provided here is fairly minimal. Most of the configuration options are in the **Incoming and Outgoing Mail Policies.**

Chapter 8 covers outbreak filters and its interaction with antivirus features. The CLI equivalent is **outbreakconfig.**

SenderBase

This page provides configuration and status for two separate components lumped together under the name **SenderBase.** The first is SenderBase Network Participation (SBNP), which allows your ESA to share a limited amount of anonymized data with Cisco, to help improve the security services. For the most part, this data consists of security engine verdicts for Internet IPs, and hashed filenames of message attachments. Not only does this help to improve scores globally, it can provide a boost in capture rates for your environment.

The bottom part of the page shows the connectivity for both SBNP and SBRS lookups. Any problem with a status check here should be investigated.

The CLI equivalents are **senderbaseconfig** and **sbstatus.**

Reporting

ESA Reporting (in the **Monitor** menu) is configured here, and it's a simple single option: whether to use local or centralized reporting. Centralized reporting provides a single place to look at reports across all of your ESAs and provides more storage for longer-term reports, but it requires that you have a separate Security Management Appliance (SMA), in the Cisco M-series of IronPort appliances.

Unlike with message tracking, using centralized reporting does not completely disable reporting on your ESA. Reporting is still available for past hour, day, and week durations. Longer durations, for past month and year, are only available on the SMA.

The CLI equivalent is **reportingconfig**.

Message Tracking

As its name implies, message tracking is configured here. The main choice is whether to use local or centralized message tracking. Centralized message tracking provides a single place to look up message history and provides more storage, but it requires that you have a separate SMA. You have the choice of whether to track rejected IP addresses, which allows for more detail, but requires more storage space, which reduces the duration of message history you can track.

The CLI equivalent is **trackingconfig**.

External Spam Quarantine

This page allows you to enable and define an external end-user IronPort Spam Quarantine (ISQ) host on a separate SMA appliance. If you're using the ISQ locally on the EUQ, you won't need this page. You don't have to quarantine spam messages at all, in fact, and so you may not need this page.

There's no CLI equivalent.

Service Updates

All the services that dynamically update their rules and engines honor the settings in the Service Updates page of the Security Services menu. This page is also where you would specify a proxy server if the ESA cannot reach Internet destinations on port 80 and 443 directly. The Service Updates are globally set to a 5-minute update interval, and I recommend that this value not be changed. Updates longer than 5 minutes, especially for anti-spam rules, will cause the ESA to miss spam messages. In the ever-changing world of email threats, having timely updates dramatically improves filtering results.

This is also why I do not recommend using a proxy server for downloading updates, preferring instead to allow the ESA direct access on port 80 and 443 to all Internet destinations. In some environments, this may not be preferable from a security perspective, but using a proxy adds one more layer that can potentially fail, reducing effectiveness of filtering and lowering the level of security that the ESA provides to your environment.

Warning The ESA requires both port 80 (HTTP) and 443 (HTTPS) access to *all* Internet destinations in order to be able to download rule and engine updates. If the ESA is behind a firewall or other security device, that firewall needs to allow all connections with destination ports 80 and 443.

Don't be tempted by the hostnames in the URLs that the ESA displays in the WUI in the Service Updates page. If you, or your firewall administrator, look up the hostnames from this page in DNS, and use the resulting IPs to create destination rules, you will cause updates to fail periodically and make for a frustrating troubleshooting experience. The hosts that Cisco uses for hosting these updates are dynamic, using a third-party content delivery network (CDN). The IP addresses are selected based on proximity to your network, and these can and do change over time.

If you must have static firewall rules that allow the ESA to get to specific IP destinations, you can do so, but you must also make changes to the Service Updates settings on each ESA. Note that this static updates setting compromises the performance benefit of using a CDN.

Network Menu

The **Network** menu provides pages for all of the TCP and SMTP network settings. Most of the options here are settings you would establish at the initial installation of the ESA and then rarely configure again, but if you are changing deployments or taking advantage of additional ESA features, you'll find them useful. Note that there are several networking related areas that are not available in the WUI: physical Ethernet port settings, VLANs, and loopback addresses are in the CLI command **etherconfig**. Figure 4-4 shows the WUI Network menu.

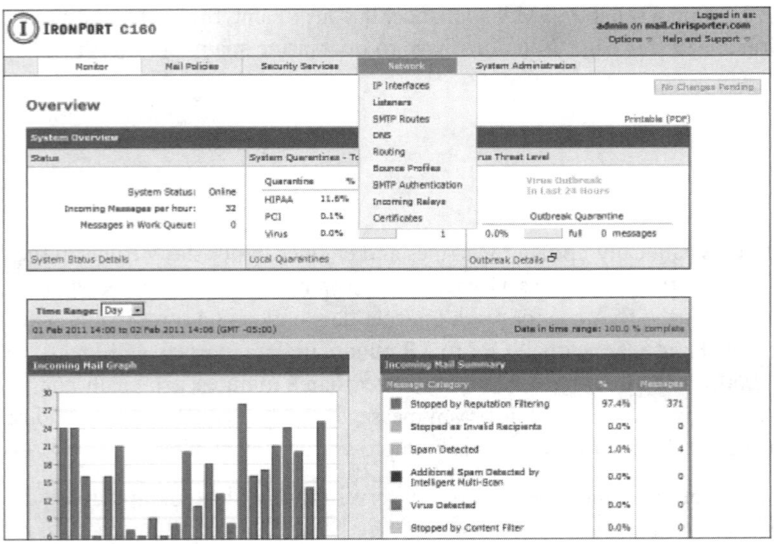

Figure 4-4 *Network Menu*

IP Interfaces

This is where you create and manage the IP addresses and hostnames that your ESA occupies on the network. You can configure multiple IP interfaces on each physical port and even multiple interfaces on a single port.

If you reconfigure or delete an interface that you're currently using to log into the WUI or CLI, you'll get a warning about losing access to the appliance. If you delete an interface that has an associated listener or is being used in delivery as a virtual gateway, you'll get a warning. If you remove all the administrative interfaces on an ESA, you'll have to resort to access through the console on the serial port.

There are a lot of capabilities related to IP interfaces, and the topic is more thoroughly covered in Chapter 12.

The CLI equivalent is **interfaceconfig** or, for those with a preference for UNIX commands, **ifconfig**.

Listeners

Listeners are an SMTP daemon that accepts inbound SMTP connections on an IP interface and port combination. As such, they cover a huge amount of the ESA SMTP server functionality. Each listener has its own HAT and RAT whose settings are covered elsewhere in the WUI, as are LDAP queries that can be tied to a listener.

Because the settings that the listener provides cover a wide range of topics, I address them in different chapters: HAT and RAT in Chapter 3, LDAP in Chapter 7, and multiple interfaces and listeners in Chapter 12.

The CLI equivalent is **listenerconfig**.

SMTP Routes

SMTP routes controls delivery destinations for email domains. It's a simple table specifying one or more destinations for an email domain or subdomain. Destinations can be IP addresses or other domains or hosts, and each destination for a given domain has a weight or cost associated with it. If you use weighted routes, the ESA will attempt delivery in order from highest priority (lowest weight) to lowest, failing over only when connection attempts to a host fail. For equally weighted hosts, the ESA load-balances its connections.

Don't confuse this with IP routing, which is two menu items below. This is only for the purposes of directing messages to their next hop. When delivering email to a destination domain that does not appear explicitly in the SMTP routes table, it drops to the default route, which is usually empty. An empty default route means to use DNS for delivery, and that's the default for an ESA.

SMTP routes are covered in Chapter 3 as part of the last stage of the pipeline.

The equivalent CLI command is **smtproutes**.

DNS

DNS is a critical network service for the operation of any MTA, including ESA. Aside from providing the MX record lookups that email delivery requires, DNS queries are also used by reputation filters, sender groups, DNSBLs, and sender verification and authentication features. In short, good DNS is a requirement, and it's configured here in the WUI. The ESA can act as its own DNS server or you can configure it to make queries to your local DNS servers. For redundancy, you can configure multiple DNS hosts.

More on DNS, especially on more complex split-DNS, is included in Chapter 12. The equivalent CLI command is **dnsconfig.** The **Clear DNS Cache** button on the WUI page has an equivalent in the CLI command **dnsflush.**

Routing

Routing here refers to IP static routing. Because the ESA is not a packet router and does not support dynamic routing protocols, all network destinations that cannot be reached through adjacency will be sent to the default router. To override that behavior, you must provide a static route for any destination network that uses a different gateway.

Because most ESA deployments only have interfaces on one network, it's not common to need a static route other than the default. Static routing is covered in Chapter 12. The equivalent CLI command is **routeconfig.** The default gateway for an ESA is configured using **setgateway.**

SMTP Call-Ahead

SMTP Call-Ahead is an alternative to LDAP for recipient validation, added in AsyncOS 7.5. Instead of querying a directory for valid recipients, it uses an independent SMTP connection to the delivery host or to a specified static host. The ESA makes an SMTP connection and uses the RCPT TO command to test each recipient. A 2yz response code indicates a valid recipient, while a 5yz indicates a non-existent recipient.

If LDAP is not available or complete in your environment, you may be able to use SMTP Call-Ahead instead. You must have a mail server that's capable of replying appropriately to the RCPT TO command, and you must disable any kind of harvesting protection or rate limiting on the call-ahead server.

SMTP Call-Ahead provides the same features to the ESA as LDAP Accept queries: listener assignment, conversational rejection, and directory harvest attack prevention. The CLI equivalent is **callaheadconfig.**

Bounce Profiles

Bounce profiles would be better described as retry profiles, because that's the configuration they cover. At message delivery, the bounce profile assigned to a message determines whether, and how often, a message or host is retried before the ESA gives up. When a message can't be delivered, the profile also controls if and when a user should be notified and whether to generate a bounce.

Bounce profiles are covered in depth in Chapter 3. The equivalent CLI command is **bounceconfig.**

SMTP Authentication

One of the services you can offer with your ESA is the ability to authenticate remote senders using the ESMTP AUTH extension. Control over this service is given here. The ESA acts only as a bridge for credentials and does not authenticate the sender against local accounts. To authorize senders, you must have either an LDAP server or another SMTP server that supports AUTH for the ESA to make connections to using the supplied credentials. Another use of SMTP AUTH is when the ESA is acting as a client and must provide authentication credentials to another MTA. The CLI equivalent is **smtpauthconfig.**

Incoming Relays

ESAs depend heavily on information about connecting IP addresses to arrive at a verdict in the security engines. If the ESA is not receiving connections directly from the public Internet from senders, but is instead behind another MTA, the security engines will be hampered. Incoming relays can help by looking through the messages received from another server for the original source IP.

This feature allows you to specify the MTAs where the ESA will receive its incoming mail and which headers to search for the original IP. Luckily, the SMTP-standard received header is written by most MTAs in a standard format with this information.

This isn't a perfect solution, because it prevents the ESA from using any of the HAT-based connection controls. Therefore, it's not a recommended configuration except in some cases; for example, in evaluation prior to a production deployment or where only a small fraction of incoming messages are coming from another server.

The CLI equivalent is **incomingrelayconfig.**

Certificates

X.509 certificates are used for a number of different features on the ESA related to encryption: HTTPS for WUI access, for secure LDAP connections to servers that require it, and for encrypted SMTP connections using TLS. This page is where you create and manage your certificates. You can also manage the list of root certificates that your ESA trusts when verifying TLS connections.

Most environments require that a certificate be purchased from a well-known root certificate authority (CA). In some cases, the certificate provider has tools to allow you to request certificates. For others, you may need to provide a certificate signing request (CSR), and you can generate that on the ESA.

If you don't need a certificate signed by a public root CA, you can also generate and use a self-signed certificate. I recommend that you take at least this step, because the self-signed certificate that Cisco provides on each ESA is identical across all new ESAs and is not secure.

Chapter 12 provides more information on TLS, including what information you need to provide to acquire an appropriate certificate.

The CLI equivalent is **certconfig**, but there are some important differences. The WUI allows you to import certificates in PKCS format, while **certconfig** requires separate key and certificate files in PEM format.

System Administration Menu

The System Administration menu fits in all the miscellaneous WUI tasks for the appliance as a whole. Figure 4-5 shows this menu.

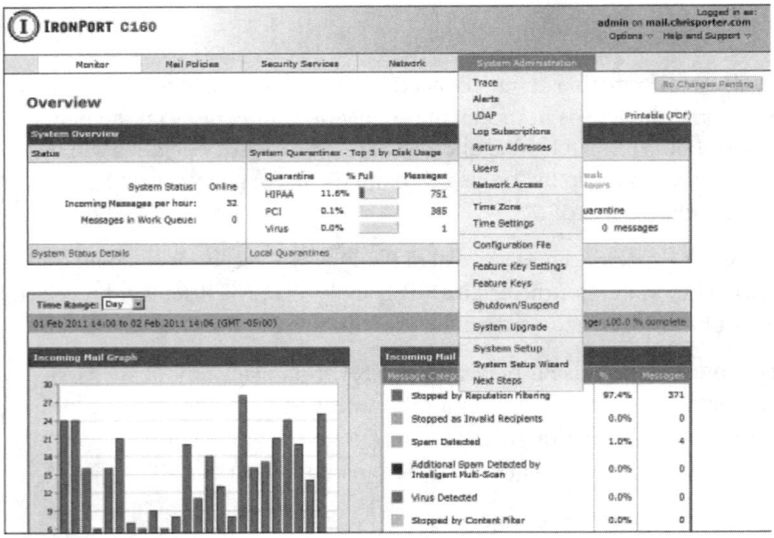

Figure 4-5 *System Administration Menu*

Trace Tool

The trace tool is an extremely useful page for troubleshooting and configuration planning. Trace allows you to simulate an email message injected into the ESA. You can specify the attributes: sending IP and host, sender's SBRS, the listener on the ESA, and all the message attributes, such as sender, recipients, and even the entire message body. Clicking **Start Trace** runs the message through all the appropriate tables and filters, providing a verdict for each stage of processing. The final disposition of the message is provided, allowing you to determine whether the message would be delivered or if it would be bounced, dropped, or quarantined. It does not actually inject a message or make any attempt to deliver it. Trace acts on uncommitted changes, so it's extremely useful for testing new policy before you commit them.

Trace is especially useful for troubleshooting content filters, because it shows in detail which conditions matched on the supplied message. It's easy to uncover logic issues in filters this way.

In the CLI, the equivalent command is **trace**.

Alerts

Alerts are email messages generated by the appliance about events occurring on the system that warrant a notification. Most of these alerts require some action from an administrator.

Alerts are grouped into categories, and then into severities within each category. By default, ESA sends all alerts to the email address specified during the System Setup Wizard, but you can create additional recipients and limit the messages sent to specific categories or severities.

Because some alerts can be repeated many times, the system has the ability to suppress and summarize duplicates instead of sending individual alerts thousands of times. The repeat interval is something you can modify, but the default settings are recommended.

The equivalent CLI command is **alertconfig**.

LDAP

Directory integration via LDAP is one of the most common ESA configuration tasks. ESA is known to work with a wide variety of commercial and open source LDAP servers. LDAP integration is important for security, policy, and remote access features. This page in the WUI allows you to create and test LDAP server profiles and their associated queries.

Because of the number of options for LDAP configuration, and the relationship between LDAP and policy, Chapter 7 is dedicated to the topic.

Related CLI commands include **ldapconfig**, **ldaptest**, and **ldapflush**.

Log Subscriptions

For any network security appliance, logging is critical for troubleshooting and post mortem, and ESA is no different. The appliances provide many different types of logs in various formats and a number of options on storage and rollover. There are logs for each major subsystem of the ESA pipeline, and a global text mail log format that records all message events for all messages and connections.

Logs on the ESA are arranged into subscriptions, where each subscription defines the log type, the size of the log files, the number of files, and what to do when the subscription reaches the limit. The logs can be stored locally and retrieved via FTP or SCP, or the ESA can push these files to a remote server using FTP or SCP or send log lines via syslog. This WUI page also gives you a button to force a log rollover.

You can have multiple log subscriptions of the same type. For example, you may want the text mail logs sent to a central log server via syslog for long-term archiving, but it's always convenient to have logs stored locally on the appliance for troubleshooting using **grep** and **tail**. You can easily do this with a new log subscription of the same type as the on-box subscription.

Most of the log formats support various levels of detail, from Error (reports errors only) to Warning, Information, Debug, and Trace, with more information recorded at each level. There are also log types that are specifically for debugging, such as LDAP debug or injection debug logs. Chapter 7 discusses logging in detail.

The equivalent CLI commands are **logconfig** and **rollovernow**.

Return Addresses

Every email message generated by the ESA has a return address in the From: header, and these can be specified here. By default, the ESA uses "Mail Delivery System" <MAILER-DAEMON@hostname> as the sending address.

The ESA generates messages like alerts and notifications that go to administrative users, but also some messages, like bounces and quarantine notifications, that your end users will see. If you want your users to be able to reply to these, you'll need to set valid addresses for your environment. Each type of notification can be configured separately. Return addresses for administrative alerts are not configured here, but under the Alerts menu.

The equivalent CLI command is **addressconfig**.

Users

The Users page provides settings for local or remotely authenticated user accounts for ESA administration. This is strictly for administrative users with a variety of privilege levels and not for end users. End user authentication for such features as ISQ is strictly performed through LDAP.

The user accounts that you create here can have one of five available fixed roles. Administrator is a super-user account with the ability to make changes in almost every configuration area. In AsyncOS versions prior to 7.5, certain tasks, like system upgrades, were limited to the "admin" account, but with 7.5 and later, the Administrator level includes all configuration options. Operators have access to most configuration areas with some important exceptions, like user-account creation. A read-only operator is just that: An account that can see all settings but not make configuration changes. A Guest has minimal access, only to reporting, and cannot make configuration changes. Helpdesk User has minimal reporting access and message tracking ability, making it ideal for a group that services end users' queries about message delivery. The privileges that each user has can also be individually specified in some cases, such as access to quarantines.

Administrative users do not need to have local accounts. You can also allow for authentication to an external LDAP directory or a RADIUS server. RADIUS server settings are configured on the External Authentication settings page, but LDAP authentication requires that you already have an LDAP server profile and query created.

The equivalent CLI command is **userconfig.**

User Roles

User Roles is a new features in AsyncOS 7.5 that allows an administrator to create named roles to assign to other administrative users. It expands upon the earlier role-based access control by allowing roles to be assigned and limited to specific policies, reports, filters, and quarantines.

Creating roles for specific configuration areas allows you to delegate a portion of the configuration to specific users. For example, you can delegate configuration of DLP policies to a regulatory compliance officer, allow departments to manage their own anti-spam settings, or even have a separate administrator for specific domains.

You can manage user roles in the CLI command **userconfig.**

Network Access

Network access allows you to limit the network address sources that can use the ESA's administrative interfaces. You can think of it as a simple firewall rule that specifies who can connect to the administrative ports on the appliance. By default, the ESA allows any source to connect, but you can change this to only allow certain sources to connect either directly or through a proxy. Another option on this page is the WUI inactivity timeout.

Valid source ranges can be specified as individual IP addresses, IP ranges, or CIDR blocks. The equivalent CLI command is **adminaccessconfig**, although that command also allows you to create a login banner that is displayed to anyone that connects to the ESA via SSH or HTTP before login. This banner is a typical place to display warnings about unauthorized access.

Time Zone and Time Settings

These two related pages in the WUI allow you to set your local time zone and either manually or automatically set your current date and time. Time zones can be set by geography or to a specific GMT offset. Automatic time settings use Network Time Protocol (NTP) and require that the ESA can reach the specified NTP servers on port 123 UDP. Time zone information is updated automatically and you can force a request for updates here.

Accurate time is required for proper functioning of any MTA, including the ESA. Aside from logging and header timestamps, many anti-spam rules depend on time accuracy.

The equivalent CLI commands are **settz**, **settime**, **ntpconfig**, and **tzupdate.**

Configuration File

The configuration file page allows you to import and export the entire ESA configuration file in XML format. You can save the file to your local computer or to the ESA's disk storage, or have it sent via email. You can restore configurations from a local or uploaded XML file. You can also separately manage the database file for the end user safelist/blocklist spam filter feature.

Chapter 10, "Configuration Files," covers managing the XML configuration.

The equivalent CLI commands are **saveconfig**, **mailconfig**, and **loadconfig**.

Feature Keys and Feature Key Settings

Feature keys control the availability and expiration of features on the ESA. There are two types of keys: perpetual (which never expire) and duration (which expires at the end of your contract). When you purchase an ESA, you'll typically receive a perpetual key for incoming mail handling and duration keys for the length of the support contract you purchased. Some features will not appear in the WUI unless you have an active feature key for them. New ESAs ship with a 30-day evaluation key for all individual features.

Feature keys are typically downloaded by each ESA automatically after they become available. Some keys are applied automatically, but others require that you accept the EULA before the key becomes active. The **Feature Key Settings** page allows you to specify how, and whether, new keys are automatically downloaded and applied. The default is to allow both to happen automatically, and I recommend leaving this default setting. Feature key downloads use the interval and method that's specified in the **Service Updates** page on the **Security Services** menu.

The **Feature Keys Settings** page also allows you to paste in a feature key string manually if that becomes necessary.

The equivalent CLI commands are **featurekey** and **featurekeyconfig**.

Shutdown/Suspend

As the name suggests, this page allows you to shut down or reboot the ESA, but also suspend and resume some email services.

Shutdown, reboot, and suspend don't abruptly halt all services and connections, instead using a friendlier method. New connections are refused, but the system waits for existing open connections to finish, waiting as long as the time limit that you specify here. At that point, existing open connections are reset and the restart or shutdown proceeds.

You can independently suspend individual listeners, or email delivery, with the check boxes in the Mail Operations section. Suspending a listener stops it from accepting new connections and is extremely useful for taking an ESA out of production for upgrade, replacement, or major configuration changes. Suspending delivery allows the ESA to continue accepting and filtering messages, but prevents it from delivering them; this can be useful if you are performing maintenance on other servers in your email environment, because the ESA can easily hold several hours worth of mail in most environments without ill effect. This page allows you to resume these operations if they are currently suspended. Suspended delivery or receiving is a state that is preserved when you restart the system, so you must resume operations after a restart to let mail flow again.

The related CLI commands for mail operations are **suspend**, **suspenddel**, **suspendlistener**, **resumedel**, **resumelistener**, and **resume**. The commands for shutting down or restarting are **shutdown** and **reboot**.

System Upgrade

The System Upgrade page is only available to administrators. An upgrade in this context refers to a new version of AsyncOS—a complete replacement of the software running on the ESA. The **Available Upgrades...** button checks the Cisco servers for any available new version, and then lets you select an upgrade from the list and start the process.

There may be multiple upgrade versions available in the list, especially if you haven't upgraded for an extended period. It's safe to upgrade to any version in the list. You do not need to upgrade sequentially across version numbers. If an upgrade version appears in the list, it means that the upgrade path from your current version to that target version has been tested and approved. If an upgrade path has not been tested and approved, the version simply won't appear in the list.

If your ESA is running older software, you may have to upgrade more than once to get to the latest version. Only certain upgrade paths are tested and approved. When you complete an upgrade, it's worthwhile to check again for upgrades, because new versions may be available that weren't on the upgrade path from the version you started with.

The upgrade process requires several confirmations at the start and a confirmation at the end before a mandatory reboot. Until you click Reboot, the ESA continues to operate as normal. WUI upgrades are *resumable*—that is, you can close your browser session or go out to lunch, and the upgrade will continue. You may be required to log back in to the WUI, and the system will send you back to the upgrade in progress.

Although you can perform an upgrade while the ESA is in production, it's recommended to suspend incoming email traffic while you're doing the upgrade. If nothing else, the upgrade proceeds faster if the ESA is not busy processing messages.

The CLI equivalent is **upgrade**, but be aware that the upgrade here is not resumable. If your CLI session is interrupted, the upgrade halts and you have to run the command again.

System Setup Wizard

This page offers to let you run the initial System Setup Wizard again, just as with a factory-new configuration. Be aware, however, that this is destructive: All of your current configuration, including network settings, is restored to factory default. The WUI page warns you of this. It's likely you'll be disconnected from the WUI and not able to reconnect.

Because of its destructiveness, there's little reason to use this on a production ESA. Email messages on the system can be lost and unrecoverable.

The CLI equivalent is **systemsetup**. The command **resetconfig** will restore the system to its factory state, which will prompt you to run the **systemsetup** command.

Next Steps

The Next Steps page is normally only displayed after you complete the System Setup Wizard, and it gives you points to common configuration steps that are useful on a newly setup system. You can reach all the tools listed here through other WUI pages, so there's not much reason to come to this page.

Options Menu

The Options menu collects a couple of important items for your interaction with the ESA WUI. This drop-down menu is in the upper right-most portion of the WUI page. ESAs running AsyncOS versions before 7.5 will have only two options: **Change Password** and **Log Out**. However, if you have a key for WUI localization, this is where you'll see the selection box for the 11 languages that the WUI is available in. With AsyncOS 7.5, a localization key is no longer required. A menu item called Active Sessions has also been added in 7.5. Figure 4-6 shows the Options menu.

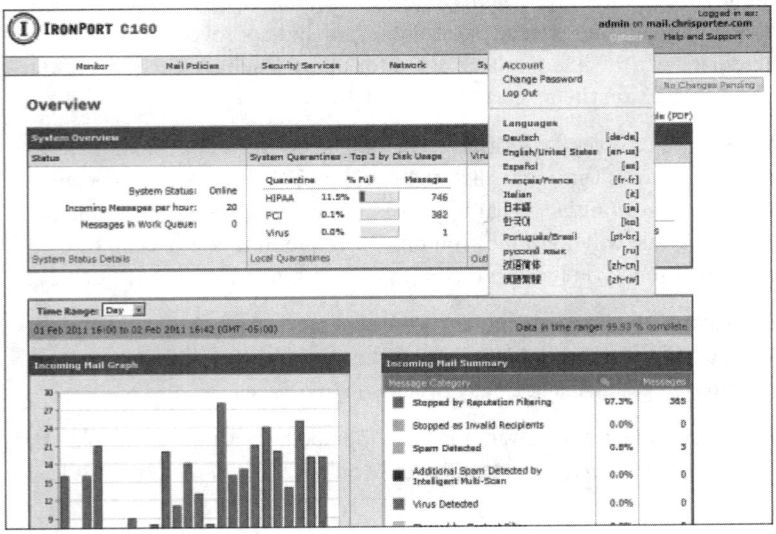

Figure 4-6 *Options Menu*

Active Sessions

Active Sessions shows all currently active sessions by administrative users for both the WUI and the CLI. The output on this page shows the username, role, login time, and duration, and the IP address of the remote host that opened the session. You can't forcibly close another session.

In AsyncOS 7.5, the **who** or **w** command in the CLI has been enhanced to show both CLI and WUI sessions.

Change Password

The Change Password page allows you to change the password on the account currently logged into the WUI. If you are logged in with an administrator account, you can change the password for any user account in the **Users** page of the **System Administration** menu.

The CLI equivalent is **password.**

Log Out

This is self-explanatory. Log Out literally logs you out of your WUI session and returns you to the login page of the ESA. There's no confirmation page, unless you have uncommitted changes pending. In that case, you will get an error and the **Uncommitted Changes** page that requires you to commit or abandon your change.

The CLI equivalents are the **quit** or **exit** command. Like in the WUI, these warn you if you have changes pending.

Help and Support Menu

The Help and Support menu gathers a couple of important tools: documentation, online support, and some troubleshooting tools. Figure 4-7 shows the Help and Support menu in the upper right-most portion of the WUI.

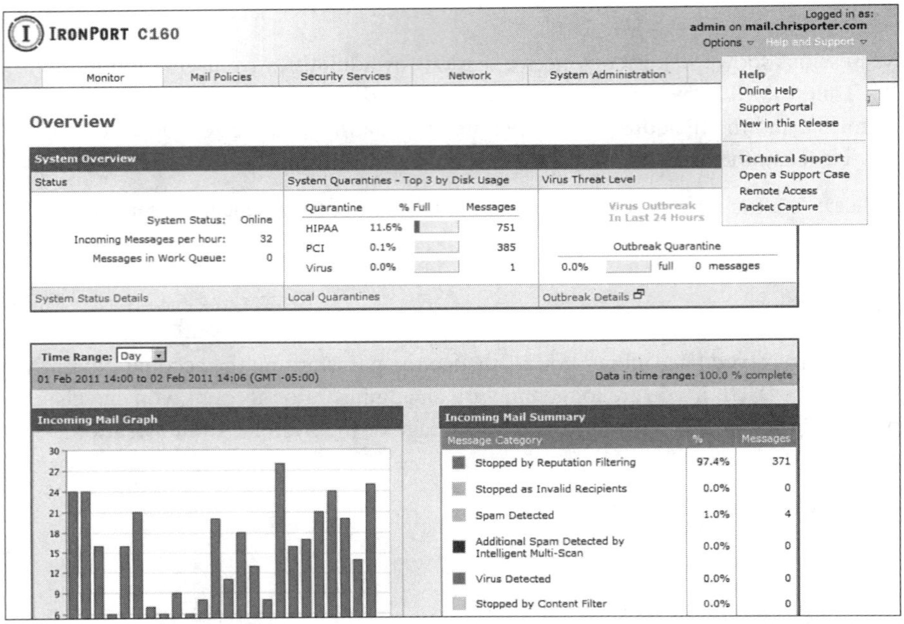

Figure 4-7 *Help and Support Menu*

Online Help

The online help provides you with a searchable HTML version of the entire documentation suite for the ESA. This includes the Configuration Guide, Advanced Configuration Guide, and the Daily Management Guide. The help is context sensitive and will open to the section of the help for the WUI page you're currently on. There's no equivalent documentation in the CLI, but the **help** command can give you syntax and command descriptions.

Support Portal

This entry provides a link to the IronPort customer support portion of the Cisco website. The support portal provides documentation and tools for download, and a page to submit a support request. You need a cisco.com login to access the tools.

New in This Release

This pops up another browser window or tab with an HTML version of the release notes. Release notes cover notable new features, bugs fixed, and outstanding known issues in the current release.

Open a Support Case

Choosing this option brings you to a page that prompts you for information about a question or problem you might have with the ESA. Clicking **Send** creates an email message and sends it to support along with the provided information. This opens a Cisco IronPort support request.

This is a great way to get support, from minor issues to serious problems. It provides the support engineer with a serial number and configuration of the system where the request is generated and includes additional logging and debugging information. This means issues are resolved quickly because the request includes commonly needed information from the appliance configuration.

Because it depends on email, you shouldn't use this method of contacting support if email operations on the ESA are severely impacted.

You can send yourself a copy of the support request if you're interested in knowing what it is composed of. The equivalent CLI command is **supportrequest**, which prompts you for the issue description and contact information.

Remote Access

Remote access is a support tool that you might be asked to use during a support issue. This tool allows remote access to an authorized customer care engineer using an SSH *reverse tunnel*. A reverse tunnel uses SSH to connect from your ESA to the Cisco IronPort support portal, and then allows an engineer to use SSH to connect from Cisco to your ESA. This remote access can help Cisco identify and troubleshoot issues more quickly than any other way or monitor for situations that only occur occasionally.

This access method is extremely valuable and will help you get issues resolved more quickly. However, many ESA owners are naturally wary of opening a *back door* into their environments.

To ease these concerns, the remote access tool has been designed with a few important features:

1. The remote-access tunnel cannot be enabled from anywhere other than the CLI or WUI, is not turned on by default, and not turned on automatically under any circumstances. You or a delegated administrator must enable it.

2. Using the remote-access tunnel requires a session password, which is different from the ESA admin password, that you share with a support engineer. No Cisco engineer can access your appliance without this password.

3. The WUI and CLI indicate when an engineer is remotely logged into your appliance.

4. You control when the tunnel is closed. When you disable the tunnel session, it cannot be re-enabled remotely.

The CLI equivalent is **techsupport**.

Packet Capture

The last tool in the Support menu is a packet-capture tool for recording network traffic on one or more ESA IP interfaces. Like the tcpdump application that it's based on, it provides a variety of filtering expressions to allow you to narrow your packet capture to the traffic you're interested in. It records the selected traffic until a maximum size is reached or you manually stop the capture, and the resulting data is stored on disk in a file that you can download from this page.

Using packet captures and troubleshooting IP and TCP packets is beyond the scope of this guide. If you're familiar with captures and with tools to analyze them, you'll have no trouble with this tool. Even if you're not, it's a simple interface, if a packet capture is necessary for support to troubleshoot an issue.

The CLI equivalent is **packetcapture**.

WUI with Centralized Management

The ESA supports a secure, robust Centralized Management (CM) feature to synchronize changes across multiple appliances without any additional software or hardware. We'll discuss CM further in Chapter 13, "Multiple Device Deployments," but because it affects what you'll see in the WUI, an introduction is in order here. A set of ESAs using CM to manage settings is referred to as a *cluster*. CM organizes the ESA configuration into a hierarchy: There are machine-specific settings like IP addresses and hostnames, and there are cluster-wide settings like anti-spam policy. In between, you can create logical CM *groups* of ESAs and specify settings that are configured per group. For example, you might have groups named East and West and have separate DNS server settings for each group.

When using the ESA CM features, the WUI changes to reflect the fact that the ESA is a member of a cluster. At the top of each page, below the menu bar, there are some additional options, and a drop-down box to select the cluster *mode*. The mode refers to the level in the hierarchy that you're currently configuring: machine, group, or cluster.

Figure 4-8 shows an example of the WUI where the ESA is a member of the cluster.

Whenever you're in a cluster, the WUI attempts to guide you toward the correct mode. For example, if you're on the **Network à IP Interfaces** page, the WUI will tell you that the settings are at machine level. If you're in Cluster or Group mode, the settings are grayed out until you change to Machine mode.

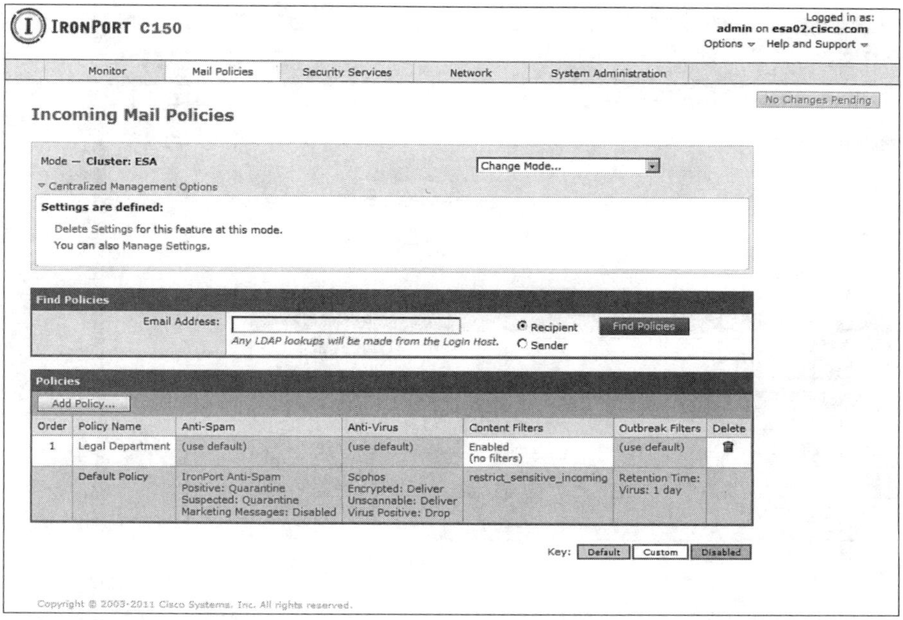

Figure 4-8 *Cluster Mode in the WUI*

Selecting Cluster Mode

When you are configuring an ESA that's part of a cluster, you'll likely find that you need to change the configuration mode often. The WUI makes this easy. Every page offers a mode drop-down box to select cluster, group, or machine mode. You can even select Machine mode for a different ESA, all from the same login, except for Reporting and Monitoring pages, which are only available for the ESA you're currently logged into. Take care with this feature, however, and always be sure you know which ESA you're currently configuring. The ESA that you logged into is displayed in the far upper-right hand portion of the WUI. The ESA machine mode that you're currently in is displayed in the CM options box below the main menu.

To change mode, simply select it from the drop-down, as shown in Figure 4-9.

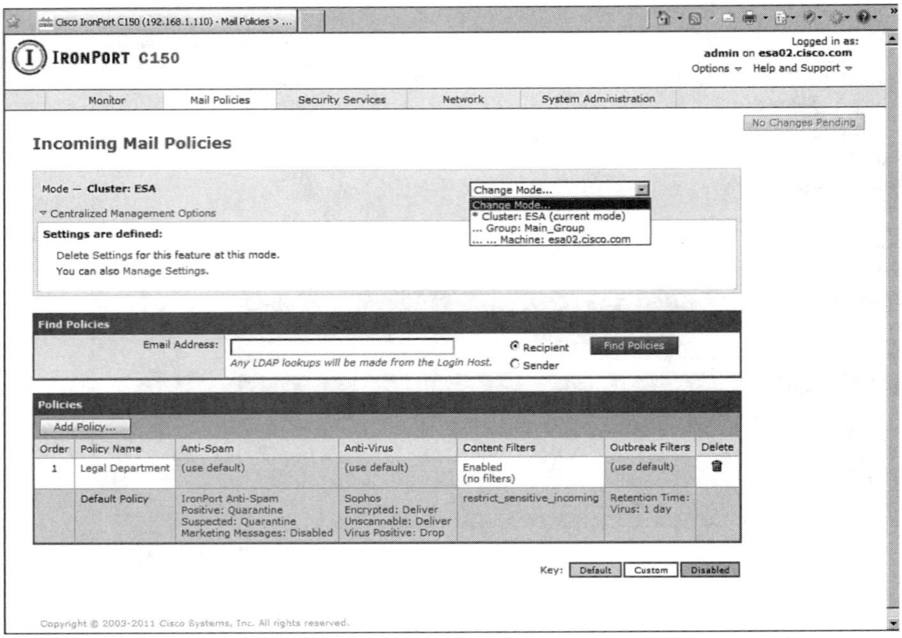

Figure 4-9 *Centralized Management Mode Selection*

If you arrive at a page that is not configured at the mode you're in, you'll see a preview of the settings grayed out, as shown in Figure 4-10.

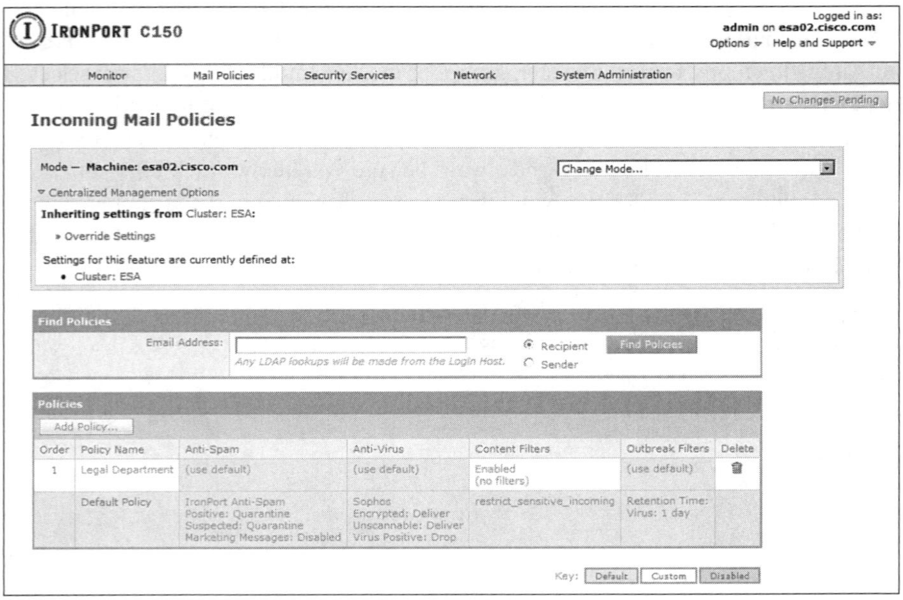

Figure 4-10 *Centralized Management Preview Screen*

If you want to change how a particular table is configured within the cluster, you can do that right from the WUI.

Modify CM Options in the WUI

You can modify where in the cluster hierarchy a particular feature is configured here in the WUI with the CM controls at the top of the page.

Figure 4-11 shows an example. I'm changing the way DNS is configured in the CM hierarchy, by moving the settings from cluster level (which is the default) to group level. This is a common scenario if you have ESAs in more than one physical location, and each location has its own DNS servers. Create a CM group for each location, move the DNS settings to the group level, and make sure the individual machines are members of the appropriate group.

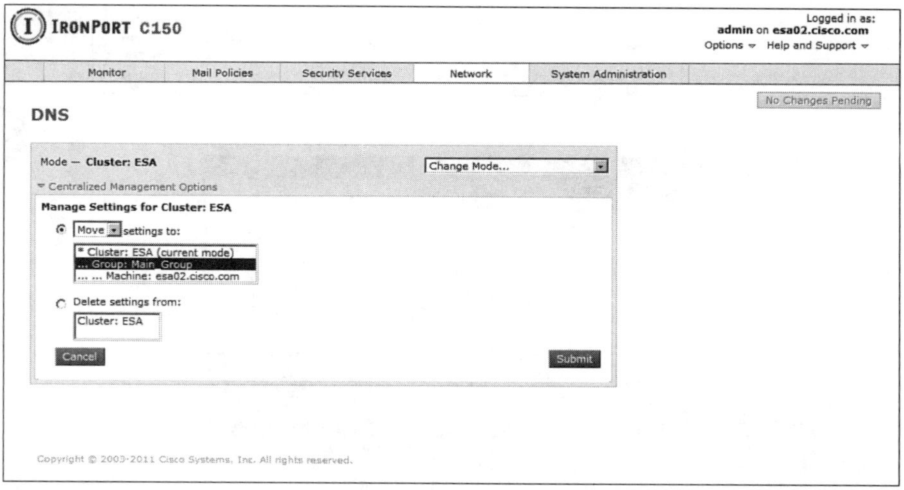

Figure 4-11 *Modifying CM Options for DNS Settings*

You can also copy settings from one level to another, but take care—this can be confusing. When a feature is configured at more than one level, the most specific setting wins. For example, if DNS is configured at the cluster and group level, any ESA members of the group will use the group settings for DNS, and the cluster settings will be ignored.

Modifying Cluster Settings

To modify other cluster settings or to add or remove machines from the cluster, you need to use the CLI **clusterconfig** command. Another useful CLI command, for troubleshooting cluster communications issues, is the **clustercheck** command.

Other WUI Features

The WUI has a couple of other features that aren't obvious if you're just logged in to a single ESA with the admin account. The WUI takes on a different appearance if you're logged in with other credentials or if you log into an ESA that's part of an active CM cluster.

Variable WUI Appearance

Up to this point, all the figures and descriptions have described the UI as it looks to a super user logged in using the admin account. What about other user roles? Administrator, Operator, and Read-Only Operator have a couple of minor differences, but essentially, see the same WUI that I discussed in this chapter.

Guest users see a radical change from the administrative interface. Figure 4-12 shows the view of a guest user login.

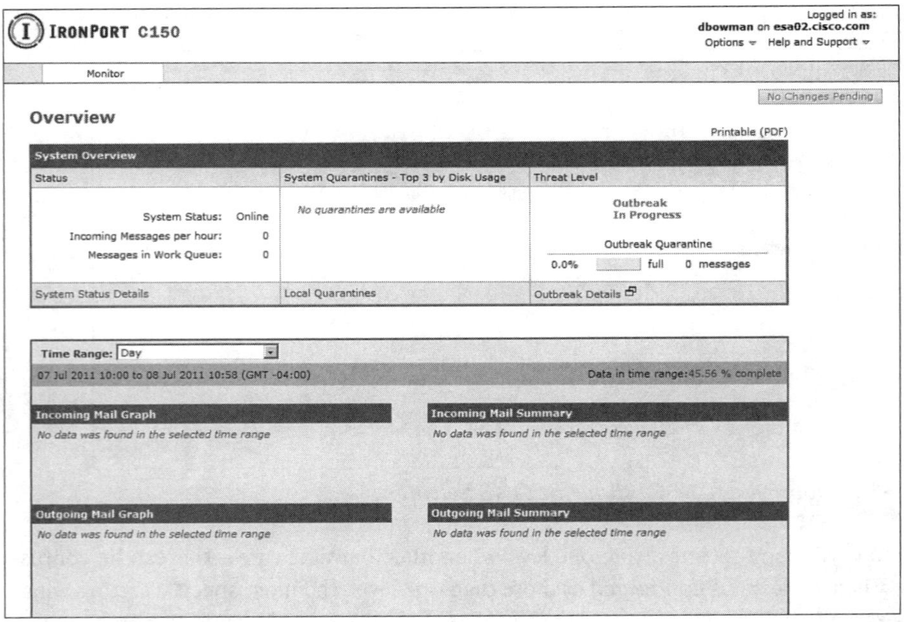

Figure 4-12 *WUI Appearance for a Guest User*

As you can see, the WUI contains only the **Monitor** menu, plus the **Options, Help**, and **Support** menus, and even these menus are limited in the options that they provide. A Helpdesk user will see a similar interface, but the **Message Tracking** menu item will be exposed.

Committing Changes

The ESA uses an explicit configuration change model that requires a commit before changes become effective. In the CLI, you would issue the **commit** command to make your changes to the running configuration. In the WUI, the **No Changes Pending** button in the upper right of every page changes to a yellow **Commit Changes** button whenever there are pending configuration changes. You must click this button to get to the **Uncommitted Changes** confirmation page, and then click **Commit Changes** after adding an optional comment.

Somewhat counter-intuitively, you can clear your current pending configuration changes by clicking the **Commit Changes** button, and then clicking **Abandon Changes** on the **Uncommitted Changes** page.

The comment that you enter here is entirely optional, but I strongly recommend that you get into the habit of commenting your changes. These comments are recorded along with a timestamp and username in the system logs on the ESA:

```
Tue Jul  5 10:31:13 2011 Info: PID 1085: User admin commit changes: deleted @
  cisco.com from the HAT exception table
```

Because the comments space is limited, another practice is strongly recommended: making your changes granular. That is, if you have multiple changes to make, make the changes individually or in related groups, and commit as often as you can. This allows the comments to be relevant to the precise change that you're making. For example, if you have to add a domain to the RAT, set up a new LDAP server profile for redundancy, and modify the text resource for email disclaimers, you should do them individually and commit after each change. For changes that are related, like adding a domain to the RAT and the corresponding entry to SMTPRoutes, it's better to commit the changes all at once. Granular commits also make it easier for you to remember what you've changed in your session, because the ESA provides no easy way to review the changes you've made before you commit them.

With AsyncOS 7.5, a new Configuration History log records your configuration changes and saves a copy of the configuration file when you commit. It is extremely valuable in the event of a mistaken configuration change. This log subscription is not enabled by default and, therefore, must be created by an administrator.

Summary

Administration of the ESA means using the web user interface, and we've covered the layout and workflow of the WUI in this chapter. You should have a thorough familiarity with the WUI and where to find all of the configuration settings you'll need to manage the ESA. Where there is an equivalent in the command-line interface, the command is listed, and any differences between the two are noted. We also examined the two-step configuration change and commit process.

In the next chapter, we'll look at similar tasks through the command-line interface, including how to connect to the ESA, run commands, and make configuration changes.

Chapter 5

Command-Line Interface

In this chapter, you will learn the following:

- How to access the CLI of ESAs via SSH
- How to use CLI commands for setup, monitoring, and configuring ESA
- How to use batch commands to automate complex tasks
- Some of the hidden/undocumented commands and their purpose

Overview of the ESA Command-Line Interface

AsyncOS provides a complete command-line interface (CLI) in addition to the web user interface (WUI). The CLI can be used for configuration, monitoring, and troubleshooting. It is the only means by which certain advanced features, like static aliases, can be configured.

The AsyncOS CLI is primarily intended for interactive use by humans, not for automated or schedule operations. As such, it does not natively provide any means of scheduling or repeating commands, like UNIX's cron or Windows' Scheduled Tasks. This does not mean that we can't automate tasks on the ESA, but it does mean that we need to use an external system to schedule them.

There are other limitations to the CLI. There is no direct access to the appliance filesystem, and no access to UNIX shell commands, compilers, or interpreters. There is no means of installing third-party binary software executables, monitoring tools, or scripts.

Using SSH or Telnet to Access the CLI

You can access the CLI with a Secure Shell (SSH) client on port 22. Telnet is not available on the Email Security Appliance (ESA) unless you specifically enable it. SSH and

Telnet are permitted on any active ESA interface, but you may have to enable these protocols when creating an interface. If an interface was set up during the System Setup Wizard (SSW), SSH is enabled. If not, navigate to the IP Interfaces page on the Network tab of the WUI. Figure 5-1 shows the check boxes for SSH and Telnet in the WUI. You can also use the **interfaceconfig** command to enable these protocols.

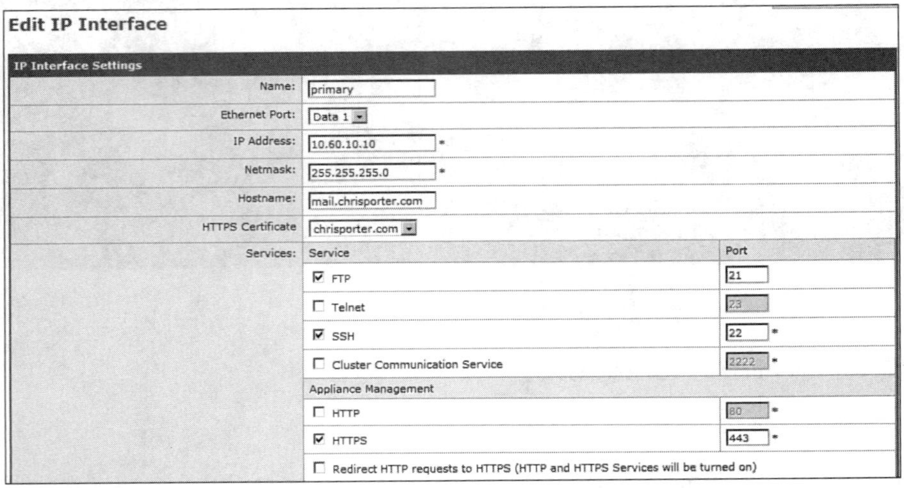

Figure 5-1 *Enabling SSH*

Although using Telnet is convenient, a Telnet session is not secure in any way and login credentials are passed in the clear. For this reason, Telnet is never enabled by default on ESAs, and SSH is preferred in all cases. SSH provides the same look and feel as a Telnet session, but all login credentials and data for the session are encrypted. This chapter focuses on using SSH to get to the CLI on the ESA.

Many free and commercial SSH clients are available. All UNIX-like systems, such as BSD, Linux, and MacOS, either have an SSH client installed or make it easy to do so. It's difficult to imagine a Linux distribution without an SSH client. For Microsoft Windows, a free SSH client called PuTTY is available online. Any SSHv2-capable client can be used.

Note I use Macintosh day-to-day, including an iMac desktop and a Macbook pro laptop, running MacOS 10.6. It includes the OpenSSH client, based on the OpenSSL toolkit. MacOS has at least part of its pedigree based in FreeBSD and has a rich set of UNIX command-line tools.

You can also connect to the CLI via the hardware 9-pin serial port using the null modem cable that's supplied in the ESA shipping carton. The null modem cable can be plugged into a PC serial port or serial console server with connection parameters set to 9600bps, 8 data, no parity, and 1 stop bit (96008N1).

Once you connect, you are prompted to log in, unless you've created and shared an SSH public key for authorization. Any local username, or a valid username found by external authentication (if configured), can be used to log in to the CLI. The commands available once logged in depends on the role of the user account.

From a bash shell in MacOS, the following command will connect to a host named **esa02** using **admin** as the username:

```
ssh admin@esa02
```

The ESA responds with a challenge for the password for the admin user. If the password matches (comparing MD5 hashes), the CLI session begins:

```
Password:
Last login: Tue Jan  3 21:17:51 2012 from 172.16.9.25
Copyright (c) 2001-2011, Cisco Systems, Inc.


AsyncOS 7.5.1 for IronPort C670 build 029

Welcome to the IronPort C670 Messaging Gateway(tm) Appliance
```

The session starts with a record of last login and a copyright banner, followed by the AsyncOS version and build number, and a welcome message. If a SSH banner has been defined, that banner is displayed before the password prompt. (See the **adminaccessconfig** command for details on defining an SSH banner.)

PuTTY on Microsoft Windows

For any version of Microsoft Windows, free graphical SSH client is available: PuTTY. PuTTY is distributed with the MIT license, similar to a BSD license: free for all use, including commercial use, without fee. You can easily find it by searching for "putty"; for many years, it has been hosted at this URL: www.chiark.greenend.org.uk/~sgtatham/putty/.

Note that there's no windows installer for PuTTY, just a win32 executable. When you run it, the basic login page is presented, as shown in Figure 5-2.

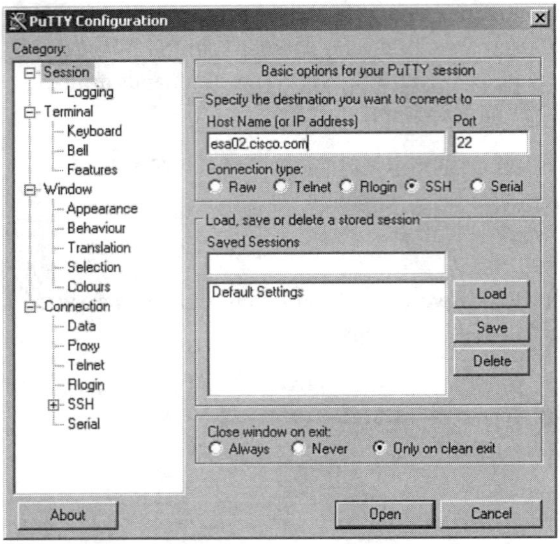

Figure 5-2 *PuTTY Basic Options Page*

To connect to an ESA via SSH, specify the hostname or IP in the Host Name text box. SSH on port 22 is the default. Once connected, the PuTTY window displays the same login text as when you logged in with SSH:

```
login as: admin
Authorized users only. All activity is logged.
Using keyboard-interactive authentication.
Password:
Last login: Fri Aug 13 15:23:46 2010 from 173.37.9.25
Copyright (c) 2001-2010, Cisco Systems, Inc.


AsyncOS 7.1 for IronPort C60 build 020

Welcome to the IronPort C60 Messaging Gateway(tm) Appliance
```

In this case, the ESA has an administrative banner configured, beginning with "Authorized users only." You can configure this optional banner with the **adminaccess-config** command to display a banner to all management login sessions. Once you connect to the ESA with an SSH client, you are placed at the root prompt, indicated by the hostname of the appliance followed by the greater-than character:

```
esa02.cisco.com>
```

This indicates that the system is awaiting entry of a command. Note that the hostname displayed is the global hostname of the appliance, not necessarily the name assigned to any network interfaces. The global hostname is set during the System Setup Wizard or via the **sethostname** command. After you run the wizard, the global hostname cannot be changed in the WUI.

Simple CLI Examples

AsyncOS CLI commands can be divided into two categories. The first is simple commands, which execute immediately and don't change the running configuration. These may or may not have menus with options. The second is configuration commands, which move the CLI prompt into a menu specific to each command. Configuration commands alter the configuration in a temporary memory space; configuration changes aren't effective until the **commit** command runs.

> **Note** For those familiar with Cisco IOS: Some of the ESA terminology and configuration process is similar to IOS, but the configuration change and commit process definitely differs from IOS. When making configuration changes in the ESA CLI or WUI, the various pages and commands always show the latest values that have been set during the management session. However, these changes are not actually effective until the **commit** command runs. You could say that a **commit** writes the changes to both running-config and startup-config, and it gets those changes from a "change buffer" that you are working in during a CLI or WUI session.
>
> For example, if you change the IP address on an interface using the WUI, the **IP Interfaces** page reflects this after you submit the change. However, the new IP won't actually be in use and the ESA won't answer on that interface. Furthermore, another user with a separate WUI or CLI session won't reflect the new IP. After the **commit**, the new IP address will be available for use.
>
> Speaking of separate WUI or CLI sessions: Because each administrative session maintains its own buffer of changes, avoid making configuration changes in multiple simultaneous sessions. The most recent change overwrites the other sessions upon commit, losing configuration changes you've made.

Commands in the CLI, and options in all submenus, are *tab-completable*, like most Windows and UNIX shells. This means that you can type the first few characters of a command, press the Tab key on your keyboard, and the CLI will complete the rest of the command name if it can uniquely determine the command. If there is more than one possible match, the CLI displays a list of possible matches. You have to type additional characters to determine the unique command. The CLI provides tab completion on all documented commands; you must type the full name of hidden (undocumented) commands.

For example:

```
esa02.cisco.com> lda<tab>
ldapconfig, ldapflush, ldaptest
esa02.cisco.com> ldaptest
```

The CLI is not case sensitive for either commands or arguments. Some input to commands is case sensitive, such as the names of listeners and interfaces, but mostly, the ESA is a case-insensitive system.

One of the simplest commands in the ESA is the **version** command. It displays the hardware and software details of the ESA model you're logged in to:

```
esa02.cisco.com> version

Current Version
===============
Model: C60
Version: 7.1.2-020
Build Date: 2010-07-29
Install Date: 2010-08-13 14:15:05
Serial #: 00C09F3AEB36-1Y5CR41
BIOS: A00I
RAID: 02
RAID Status: READY
RAID Type: 1
BMC: NA
```

A simple configuration command is **userconfig**, which allows an administrator to create, edit, or delete additional (local) user accounts on the ESA:

```
esa02.cisco.com> userconfig

Users:
1. admin - "Administrator" (admin)

External authentication: Disabled

Choose the operation you want to perform: - NEW - Create a new account.
- EDIT - Modify an account.
- DELETE - Remove an account.
- POLICY - Change password and account policy settings.
- PASSWORD - Change the password for a user.
- ROLE - Create/modify user roles.
- STATUS - Change the account status.
- EXTERNAL - Configure external authentication.
- DLPTRACKING - Configure DLP tracking privileges.
[]>
```

Like most configuration commands, **userconfig** changes the root prompt of the CLI to a menu prompt for the command. The prompt changes from the hostname to the characters []>. A list of available options in this command is presented. Some of the options result in a new submenu view where additional choices are available. Other options simply ask for input from the administrator.

You can exit any command by pressing **Enter** at the []> prompt of the top menu. You can also use **Ctrl-C** to break out of any configuration command, but be aware that this clears any changes that you made while in this menu. For example, if you add a user account, but hit **Ctrl-C** before you finish, all the data that you entered is discarded. The CLI indicates this with this line:

```
-- Changes not recorded.
```

Example 5-1 shows how to create a new Operator user account on the ESA. Just follow the prompts, pressing **Enter** after each entry.

Example 5-1 *Creating an Operator Account with* **userconfig**

```
esa02.cisco.com> userconfig

Users:
1. admin - "Administrator" (admin)

External authentication: Disabled

Choose the operation you want to perform:
- NEW - Create a new account.
- EDIT - Modify an account.
- DELETE - Remove an account.
- POLICY - Change password and account policy settings.
- PASSWORD - Change the password for a user.
- ROLE - Create/modify user roles.
- STATUS - Change the account status.
- EXTERNAL - Configure external authentication.
- DLPTRACKING - Configure DLP tracking privileges.
[]> new

Enter the new username.
[]> cporter

Enter the full name for cporter.
[]> Chris Porter

Assign a role to "cporter":
1. Administrators - Administrators have full access to all settings of the system.
2. Operators - Operators are restricted from creating new user accounts.
3. Read-Only Operators - Read-Only operators may only view settings and status
information.
```

```
4. Guests - Guest users may only view status information.
5. Help Desk Users - Help Desk users have access only to ISQ and Message Tracking.
[1]> 2

Enter the password for cporter.
>
Please enter the new password again.
>

Users:
1. admin - "Administrator" (admin)
2. cporter - "Chris Porter" (operators)

External authentication: Disabled

Choose the operation you want to perform:
- NEW - Create a new account.
- EDIT - Modify an account.
- DELETE - Remove an account.
- POLICY - Change password and account policy settings.
- PASSWORD - Change the password for a user.
- ROLE - Create/modify user roles.
- STATUS - Change the account status.
- EXTERNAL - Configure external authentication.
- DLPTRACKING - Configure DLP tracking privileges.
[]>
```

The menus and submenus create a logical hierarchy of commands, sometimes several layers deep. Whenever you are done with a menu or submenu and want to return to the next higher-level menu, press **Enter**. Repeat to move up additional levels, finally reaching back to the root prompt where the system hostname is displayed. We refer to this often, either as "press **Enter** to get back to the previous menu" or "return until you reach the root prompt."

To refer to a specific submenu or subcommand, we will use the hierarchy to specify the location. For example, to create a new user account in the CLI as we just did, go to **userconfig → new**. This means that you should type **userconfig** at the root prompt, **Enter**, and then **new** at the userconfig menu.

Getting Help

AsyncOS provides help for all commands, except undocumented ones. The list of all available simple and configuration commands is found by running the command help.

Help on any individual command is available by running **help** command. Help for an individual command typically consists of a list of options that the command supports (if any) and a short description of the command:

```
esa02.cisco.com> help ldaptest

ldaptest [<smtpauth_query_name> [<user_identity>]]
ldaptest [<group_query_name> [<address> [<group_name>]]]
ldaptest [<other_query_name> [<address>]]

 Perform a single LDAP query test based on the parameters given.
 Any information which is omitted will be prompted for interactively.

 Different parameters are required based on the type of the query
 you are testing, as indicated in the respective synopses.

 Note that ldaptest will only attempt to connect to the first
 server on the failover list.
```

Committing Configuration Changes

No change to the actual running configuration of the ESA takes effect until the change is committed, much as in the WUI. The **commit** command must be run to make all changes effective. As in the WUI, you have an option to record comments about the changes being made, and it is highly recommended to do so:

```
Please enter some comments describing your changes:
[]> Added user cporter to Operators

Changes committed: Fri Aug 13 16:21:01 2010 GMT
```

The comments you enter here are recorded in the system logs. Comments for all commit actions made within the current CLI session can be viewed with the command **commit-detail.**

Care is needed in a CLI session when you're making configuration changes. There's no visible change to the CLI prompt, or any other indicator, when there are uncommitted changes. If there are no changes currently pending, running commit indicates that

```
esa02.cisco.com> commit

There is no data to commit.
```

If you attempt to exit a CLI session by using **quit** or **exit**, when there are uncommitted changes, you are warned about them and given the option to remain in the CLI.

You can clear any changes that you've made in a session by running the **clear** command and answering Y if you're sure that you want to abandon all pending changes. AsyncOS does not provide a thorough means of reviewing uncommitted changes while they're still pending. The comments you add to the commit are one of the few records of who made a configuration change and what changes were made. There is a keylog record of all CLI sessions recorded in the CLI audit logs if they're enabled (see Chapter 6, "Additional Management Services," for details on logging).

Note What I've said about reviewing uncommitted changes isn't entirely true. There is a hidden command called **showchanges** that can give you a look at the uncommitted data, but it's the raw AsyncOS configuration data structure and it's difficult to read. (See the section, "Hidden/Undocumented Commands," later in this chapter.)

Because of these features and limitations, here are some good practices to follow when working in the CLI:

- Always save a copy of the configuration file to disk, or your local computer, before embarking on a configuration change session. There's no automated configuration "rollback."
- Always add comments to your commits when prompted. The ESA has no automated means of auditing configuration changes, but commit comments are recorded in the system logs.
- Keep your changes granular. Because there's no way to view pending changes, it's easy to forget what you've changed so far. You can always view the pending value of a particular configuration area, but you'd have to remember all the commands you visited to be sure of what's changed. If you plan to make several changes in one session, make your changes one at a time, and then issue **commit** after each change. For example, if you need to add a user, change an SMTP destination, enable FTP on an interface, and make the changes after each one rather than collecting them all for the end. Some changes require that you set values in two places without a commit in between, such as changing IP addresses and default gateway at the same time. (If you do one of these without the other, you lose connectivity to the ESA.) I recommend keeping changes as simple as possible rather than committing all at once.
- Don't exit the SSH or Telnet session using your software's controls. You won't be prompted about uncommitted changes if the session is terminated at the client end. Always use the **quit** or **exit** commands to end your sessions.

Keeping the ESA CLI Secure

Access to the AsyncOS CLI should be restricted, for obvious reasons. If possible, firewall rules, access control lists (ACL), or other network access controls should be in place to prevent unauthorized users from connecting to the ESA CLI. The same rules should apply to any of the management interfaces to the appliance, including HTTP and HTTPS for the WUI and FTP for filesystem access. As with any network resource, the principle of least necessary restriction should apply. If you can restrict access to the appliance to a specific source IP range, you should do so. An example of restrictive network rules is shown in Figure 5-3.

Warning The management login interfaces, including SSH, do not by default support controls for maximum login attempts or maximum failed login attempts, and can theoretically be vulnerable to dictionary attacks. Preventing connection to the SSH, HTTP, and HTTPS ports is critical.

As of AsyncOS 7.5, new account and password settings are available on the **Users** page of the **System Administration** menu. These include requirements for password length and complexity, forcing password changes, and account locking based on number of failed login attempts. You can also manually lock an account in this release. In previous versions, you had to change the password or delete an account to rescind access.

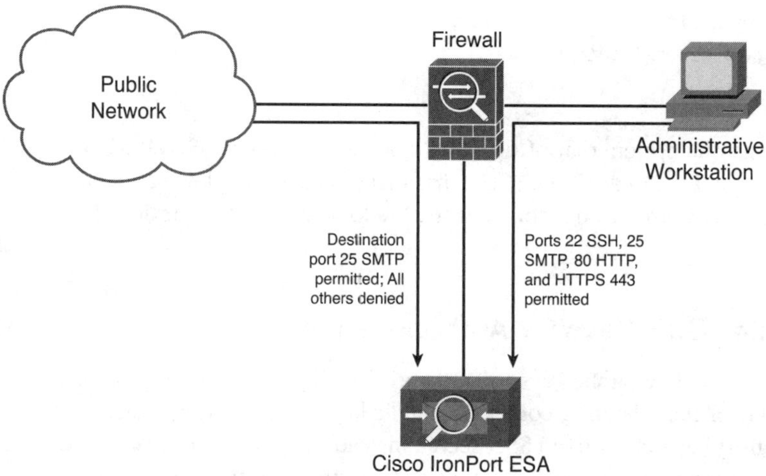

Figure 5-3 *Network Restrictions on Access to the Management Interfaces*

SSH Options on the ESA

SSH and Telnet are only available on interfaces where it's specifically turned on. Ideally, any public-facing interface on the ESA will have only a single port open, 25, for receiving inbound SMTP connections. For single IP deployments, where all services are running on a single IP address, it's important to have network controls in place to prevent unauthorized access.

SSH on the ESA is server only. There is no SSH client available from the CLI. SSH is used as a protocol for some outbound connections, such as centralized management, but this is not exposed and is not available for administrators to use.

Of course, SSH is secure, and by using a combination of configuration settings and strong user passwords tied to an external authentication system, it is reasonable to allow SSH connections without network layer restrictions, even allowing connections from public Internet sources. The **sshconfig** command provides us with some of the important configuration settings:

```
mail.chrisporter.com> sshconfig

Currently installed keys for admin:
1. ssh-rsa AAAAB3NzaC1yc2EAA...AJ1AJKPQ== (cporter@Chris-Porter.local)
2. ssh-dss AAAAB3NzaC1kc3MAA...wrYASjmP4= (cporter@new-host-2)


Choose the operation you want to perform:
- NEW - Add a new key.
- DELETE - Remove a key.
- PRINT - Display a key.
- USER - Switch to a different user to edit.
- SETUP - Configure general settings.
[]>
```

setup only contains one option: that of deciding whether to support SSHv1. It's not enabled by default, and it shouldn't be. SSHv1 has many security exploits associated with it. SSHv2 is widely supported among clients. We look at the other options in the next section.

Creating and Using SSH Keys for Authentication

AsyncOS supports installing public keys for authentication by copying and pasting them into the options under the **sshconfig** command. Public key authentication is an alternative means of identifying a client to an SSH server, instead of typing a password at the prompt. It takes some work to set up, but once up and running, it makes login easier, and it's absolutely essential to running commands noninteractively, as from a script running on an external server. Public key authentication is just as secure as (or more secure than) typing a password and much more convenient once configured.

Warning AsyncOS does not currently offer a means to disable interactive (password) logins, even after SSH public keys are installed. Password logins are always available for any account, limited only by IP ranges specified in the **adminaccessconfig** command.

The reasons for setting up SSH keys are for flexibility and convenience, not really for security. It's possible that the product will be changed in the future to disable interactive logins.

To use public key authentication, your SSH client must support it, and you must generate a key pair in either RSA or DSS algorithms. The key pair consists of a public key, which anyone can know and which will be copied into the ESA configuration, and a private key that is kept secret on your local workstation and is used by the SSH client. The SSH client generates a signature using the private key and presents the signature to the SSH server (the ESA, in this case), and the ESA uses the public key it has in its configuration to verify the signature as genuine. A new signature is generated for each session.

On most UNIX systems, ssh-keygen is the provided tool that can generate key pairs in a variety of lengths. The command **ssh-keygen –t rsa** generates a 2048-bit private key and corresponding public key. It prompts you for an output filename and directory. The defaults are id_rsa for private and id_rsa.pub for public, both created in the hidden directory called **.ssh** in your home directory. These defaults are ideal for UNIX SSH clients.

Note **ssh-keygen** prompts you for a passphrase. This passphrase is used by the SSH client to access the client's public key. Obviously, this makes the private key file secure, but it means that you now have a password to remember and you are required to type this in for any CLI session. You can leave the passphrase blank, which is necessary for any automation of SSH commands by external servers. I recommend leaving the passphrase blank, but be sure that the file and directory permissions are appropriately set.

Generating key pairs for the PuTTY tool is done with the PuTTYgen tool, which is available from the same sources as the PuTTY. When you start the tool, simply select a key length and click the **Generate** button, as shown in Figure 5-4.

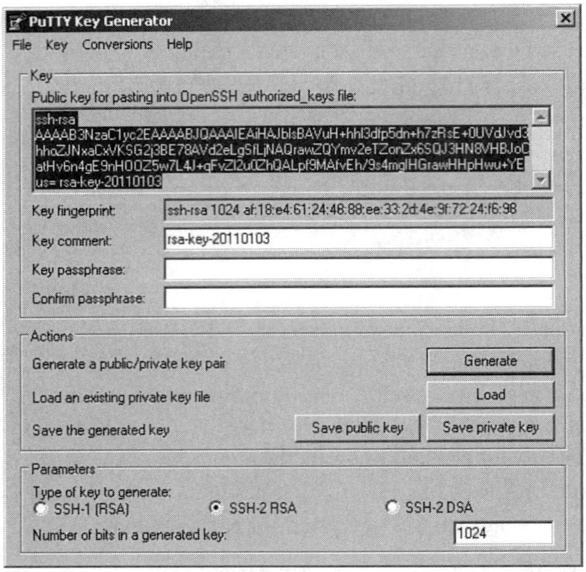

Figure 5-4 *PuTTYgen Used to Create SSH Key Pair*

Once you have your public and private key pair, copy the entire contents of the public key file and paste it into the **sshconfig → new** command. Keys are created and managed by user accounts on the ESA. This means that you or another administrator must install SSH keys from each client that logs in with SSH keys, on the **sshconfig** user settings for their target account. To keep things straight in your environment, it's best to create usernames that match individual's known user credentials. In this example, we create a public key for the admin user, but the **user** menu item can switch to another username before adding the key, as shown in Example 5-2.

Example 5-2 *Installing Public SSH Key Using* **sshconfig**

```
esa02.cisco.com> sshconfig

Currently installed keys for admin:

Choose the operation you want to perform:
- NEW - Add a new key.
- USER - Switch to a different user to edit.
- SETUP - Configure general settings.
[]> new

Please enter the public SSH key for authorization.
Press enter on a blank line to finish.
ssh-rsa AAAAB3NzaC1yc2EAAAABJQAAAQEAt0+Amb6yUn83yIxiQqAn4OresxMjBuYNjY+QQSC0QAy8m
JpEi7zqkESTNFf7nsgLyecVZ/5RtQafgMOPI6iBxiq+v2we01SxYGiR7Mc+Iplbhxe4TDzChMRyCz4feO
IqWWhMqXAEwmm2gw5sey5K1ugI1ykqGdsGutm+wllTSjeJ0ygJRRuy3jmK8hxR4p/bmbCOI3URwBL+y
```

```
TXAsukWGZoBWbqT3pzx/XuduAoNQqEtdjSArgsQTMXq0Aest8x3HmkgIfwBR9hTFa5S6b1pkftpjX-
tHxoeHq1f6feKqjOdnQm5ZeudL305srqxruS4j5iS8oSKtCiEuhx7tDrQMiw== rsa-key-20100813

Currently installed keys for admin:
1. ssh-rsa AAAAB3NzaC1yc2EAA...7tDrQMiw== (rsa-key-20100813)

Choose the operation you want to perform:
- NEW - Add a new key.
- DELETE - Remove a key.
- PRINT - Display a key.
- USER - Switch to a different user to edit.
- SETUP - Configure general settings.
[]>
```

From here, remember to press **Enter** to get to the root prompt, and then run the **commit** command. To test, exit your CLI session and reconnect; you should not be prompted for a password, just greeted with the CLI welcome banner. If you are prompted for a password, something went wrong.

sshconfig also gives you the ability to display the public keys for a user and delete a key. If something isn't working with a particular installed key, delete it and reinstall it. Whitespace and line breaks won't cause format troubles with the key, but missing or garbling any single character results in failed import or failed logins.

After you install the key, press **Enter** to get back to the root prompt and run **commit**. Just like any other configuration change, adding SSH keys requires a **commit** before it's actually in use.

There's not much troubleshooting or logging information on the ESA side for connections. The log cli_logs shows user logins and logouts, along with a keystroke log of all activity, but it doesn't show the port or protocol used to login. If you create a log subscription of type Authentication Logs, you see the record of username logins, but again no record of port or protocol. For troubleshooting SSH connections, it's best to look at the debug output that the SSH client can offer:

```
ssh -v admin@esa1.example.com
```

Troubleshooting OpenSSH and PuTTY connections is beyond the scope here, but errors in the process should stand out. In particular, it's important that the SSH client is finding your local private key file, which is indicated by a line like this in the debug output:

```
debug1: identify file /home/username/.ssh/id_rsa type 1
```

Login Banners

Login banners are akin to a "message of the day" warning that greets anyone that connects to the management interfaces, whether HTTP, HTTPS, Telnet, or SSH. The **adminaccessconfig** command allows you to set the banner text.

The text can be multiline and appears before the copyright message during a CLI login. It appears next to the login boxes on the WUI.

Restricting Access to SSH

adminaccessconfig can be used to restrict the source IP range that is permitted to connect on the management interfaces, including SSH. By default, all IP ranges are allowed to connect to the listening port. Using the **restrict** command and entering at least one IP or IP range will then reject all connections to the management interfaces, unless connecting from one of the listed ranges. An example of restricting administrative login is shown in Example 5-3. Be careful about NAT-ting and other network features that can hide your true source IP. The command warns you about restricting logins when your current login session would be excluded.

Example 5-3 *Restricting Administrative Login*

```
esa02.cisco.com> adminaccessconfig

Choose the operation you want to perform:
- BANNER - Configure login message(banner) for appliance administrator login.
- IPACCESS - Configure IP-based access for appliance administrative interface.
[]> ipaccess

Current mode: Allow All.
Please select the mode:
- ALL - All IP addresses will be allowed to access the administrative interface.
- RESTRICT - Specify IP addresses/Subnets/Ranges to be allowed access.
[]> restrict


List of allowed IP addresses/Subnets/Ranges:


Choose the operation you want to perform:
- NEW - Add a new IP address/subnet/range.
[]> new

Please enter IP address, subnet or range.
[]> 10/8
```

```
List of allowed IP addresses/Subnets/Ranges:
1.  10.0.0.0/8

Choose the operation you want to perform:
- NEW - Add a new IP address/subnet/range.
- EDIT - Modify an existing entry.
- DELETE - Remove an existing entry.
- CLEAR - Remove all the entries.
[]> new

Please enter IP address, subnet or range.
[]> 172.16/16

List of allowed IP addresses/Subnets/Ranges:

1.  10.0.0.0/8
2.  172.16.0.0/16

Choose the operation you want to perform:
- NEW - Add a new IP address/subnet/range.
- EDIT - Modify an existing entry.
- DELETE - Remove an existing entry.
- CLEAR - Remove all the entries.
[]>

Warning: The host you are currently using [192.168.1.107] is not included in the
User Access list.  Excluding it will prevent your host from connecting to the
administrative interface. Are you sure you want to continue? [N]>
```

adminaccessconfig supports CIDR ranges with a format of network/mask. The **who** command (or just **w**) displays a list of everyone logged into the CLI and their source IP. This is convenient for figuring out from where you're logged in.

ESA Setup Using the CLI

We've seen how to set up an ESA using the WUI and, most of the time, that's sufficient for basic setup. But, what if the SSW isn't available because you're on a console or SSH session? What if you just wanted a basic setup without all the additional features that the SSW configures? You might want a basic network-only configuration if you plan to load an existing configuration file or join the ESA to an existing centralized management cluster.

Of course, you can just run the command **systemsetup** from the root prompt, which takes you through all the required setup features. But, that wouldn't be much fun, would it?

Basics of Setup

The list of commands required to set up an ESA is short, if you don't mind the defaults. The following commands are enough to get an ESA responding on the network and get rid of the **run the setup wizard** prompt:

- **interfaceconfig** allows you to create an IP interface and turn on the management services.
- **setgateway** sets the system's default gateway IP.
- **sethostname** changes the global hostname. This is what actually triggers the **run the setup wizard** prompt.

You should run **dnsconfig** to give the ESA an IP of a DNS server, unless it can connect to the public Internet on port 53 UDP and port 53 TCP. The ESAs are not very happy without access to DNS.

commit your changes and use **ping** and **telnet** to verify network connectivity. If you don't get good results, check **etherconfig → media** to see if the physical interfaces are up, and then check your cabling. If all is well, you can proceed with tasks like loading a configuration file or joining a cluster, which are tasks that addressed in another chapter. You can also continue a manual setup by running a few more commands.

Next Setup Steps

At this point, if you've used the just discussed commands and have network connectivity verified, you have a running ESA, but it's not accepting SMTP connections. You can fix that by running **listenerconfig**, and then using **new** to create a new listener. Because listeners control most of the parameters involved in accepting email, it's a big step. For these next steps, I assume that you have a single IP interface on the physical data 1 NIC.

As discussed in Chapter 2, "ESA Product Basics," the listener includes a Host Access Table (HAT) with parameters for accepting connections, limiting sender rates, and controlling sender permissions. Every listener has a HAT predefined, and the contents of that table are dictated by whether you choose a public or a private listener. Other than setting some default values (that can be changed later), the choice of public or private is not important, although the general practice is that public listeners accept incoming mail from the Internet, and private listeners accept only outgoing mail from a limited list of internal senders. I choose to create a public listener, but I call it AllMail, because I plan to use it for both incoming and outgoing mail. Example 5-4 illustrates this process.

Example 5-4 *Using* **listenerconfig** *to Create a Listener*

```
esa02.cisco.com> listenerconfig

Currently configured listeners:

Choose the operation you want to perform:
- NEW - Create a new listener.
[]> new

Please select the type of listener you want to create.
1. Private
2. Public
3. Blackhole
[2]> 2

Please create a name for this listener (Ex: "InboundMail"):
[]> AllMail

Please choose an IP interface for this Listener.
1. mgmt (192.168.42.42/24: esa02mgmt.cisco.com)
2. primary (10.60.10.10/24: esa02.cisco.com)
[1]> 2

Enter the domain names or specific email addresses you want to accept mail for.
[]> cisco.com

Do you want to enable filtering based on SenderBase Reputation Service (SBRS)
Scores for this listener? (Your selection will be used to filter all incoming mail
based on its SBRS Score.) [Y]>

Do you want to enable rate limiting for this listener? (Rate limiting defines the
maximum number of recipients per hour you are willing to receive from a remote
domain.) [Y]>

Enter the maximum number of recipients per hour to accept from a remote domain.
[]> 25

Default Policy Parameters
==========================
Maximum Message Size: 10M
Maximum Number Of Concurrent Connections From A Single IP: 10
Maximum Number Of Messages Per Connection: 10
Maximum Number Of Recipients Per Message: 50
Directory Harvest Attack Prevention: Enabled
Maximum Number Of Invalid Recipients Per Hour: 25
```

```
Maximum Number Of Recipients Per Hour: 25
Maximum Recipients Per Hour SMTP Response:
    452 Too many recipients received this hour
Use SenderBase for Flow Control:  Yes
Spam Detection Enabled:  Yes
Virus Detection Enabled:  Yes
Allow TLS Connections: No
Allow SMTP Authentication: No
Require TLS To Offer SMTP authentication: No
DKIM/DomainKeys Signing Enabled: No
DKIM Verification Enabled: No
SPF/SIDF Verification Enabled: No
Envelope Sender DNS Verification Enabled: No
Domain Exception Table Enabled: No
Accept untagged bounces:  No
Would you like to change the default host access policy? [N]>

Please choose a bounce profile to apply.
1. Default
2. standard
3. test
[1]>

Listener AllMail created.
Defaults have been set for a Public listener.
Use the listenerconfig->EDIT command to customize the listener.

Currently configured listeners:
1. AllMail (on primary, 10.60.10.10) SMTP TCP Port 25 Public

Choose the operation you want to perform:
- NEW - Create a new listener.
- EDIT - Modify a listener.
- DELETE - Remove a listener.
- SETUP - Change global settings.
[]>
```

Pretty simple, really. **listenerconfig** prompts us for some basic options when setting up the HAT, and we accepted the defaults. It also prompts for a recipient domain to accept mail for, which is used to create the Recipient Address Table (RAT). Once you press **Enter**, and **commit** at the root prompt, the ESA starts listening for mail on port 25 on the selected interface.

Note In addition to public and private listeners, ESA also supports something called a blackhole listener. You can only create a blackhole listener in the CLI—the option isn't even displayed in the GUI. A blackhole does exactly what you'd guess: It accepts and then just dumps messages. There aren't many real-world scenarios that call for a blackhole listener, but they can be useful for testing as a sink for other systems or for the ESA to deliver back to itself. Just be careful; as with a real blackhole, anything that goes in is lost forever.

At this point, you have a running ESA, and because of the defaults in the HAT and incoming mail policies, you have a fairly secure setup that can actually be used right away, provided that you gave accurate information to **listenerconfig** prompts. There are a few other things that you normally want to configure before you do that, however. These tasks are normally taken care of by the SSW, but you need to do them manually:

1. Make sure DNS servers are specified using **dnsconfig**. ESAs need one or more DNS servers to resolve names and IPs, or need access on port 53/UDP and port 53/TCP to the Internet so that they can act as their own caching DNS resolver. The ESA will be extremely unhappy if DNS is not working: Connections will be slow to accept as DNS queries time out; SenderBase queries will fail, causing the system to accept potential junk connections; and email accepted by the system will likely not be deliverable. **nslookup** (and the hidden command **dig**) are available to test name resolution.

2. Set the time zone, date, and time, or set up NTP servers. Having accurate time and date is critical for email. **settz** allows you to pick a time zone or use a GMT offset. **settime** allows you to manually set both the date and time, but a better option is to use Network Time Protocol (NTP) synchronized to a local or public time server that you specify in **ntpconfig**. If you don't have one, you can use time.ironport.com.

3. Specify delivery destinations using **smtproutes**. Without a destination specified for a given domain, the ESA defaults to using DNS MX lookups to resolve delivery hosts. For your local domains, this is almost certainly wrong, and you need to add entries to use **smtproutes** to override this.

4. Set up alerts. Alerts are email messages generated by the ESA for error, warning, or informational events. **alertconfig** is where you establish email addresses that should receive these alerts, and each entry allows you to specify which categories and severities (or all) should be sent to whom. It's recommended to have at least one email address that will receive all categories and all severities. From there, if you have different roles for individuals on your team or across groups, you can set up categories appropriately.

Remember to **commit** all of your changes. Forgetting to **commit** changes is the most common cause of head scratching during troubleshooting. Running **commit** isn't harmful if there are no changes to commit, so just get into the habit of committing often.

Commands in Depth

We looked at a few CLI commands in this chapter, and there will be references to CLI commands throughout the rest of this book. Suffice to say, you need to know how to use them. Now, we examine the CLI commands in depth, organized by their functional area and demonstrated through some real-world examples.

The focus here is on information and configuration that can't be done in the WUI or on commands that have expanded capabilities compared with the WUI.

Troubleshooting Example

To better illustrate the use of CLI commands, we'll follow a typical mail delivery troubleshooting procedure. In this case, imagine that we have an unknown problem whose symptom is that outbound mail isn't being delivered to an external company. Users have complained to the IT helpdesk, and the helpdesk investigation found that the users' email clients and the company's groupware servers show that the message has been delivered. Because the groupware servers deliver all outgoing mail to the ESAs, they've escalated the problem to the messaging technicians, and that's you. There's no more information available. We're going to exclusively use the CLI to find the root cause of the delivery problem.

Status and Performance Commands

The WUI provides a quick-glance overview of the status of an ESA, but for critical, real-time information on status and performance, the CLI commands are ideal. The best place to start is the **status** command, but using the *status detail* option gives us all the same information, with additional performance and queue statistics. Example 5-5 shows the output of the **status detail** command.

Example 5-5 *Output of the* **status detail** *Command*

```
esa02.cisco.com> status detail

Status as of:                  Wed Aug 18 16:10:12 2010 EDT
Up since:                      Sat Aug 07 12:24:19 2010 EDT (11d 3h 45m 53s)
Last counter reset:            Never
System status:                 Online
Oldest Message:                15 mins 43 secs
Feature - Bounce Verification: Perpetual
Feature - Virus Outbreak Filters: 723 days
Feature - IronPort Email Encryption: 723 days
Feature - IronPort Anti-Spam:  723 days
Feature - Incoming Mail Handling: Perpetual
Feature - IronPort Intelligent Multi-Scan: 79 days
Feature - RSA Email Data Loss Prevention: 79 days
Feature - Sophos Anti-Virus:   723 days
```

```
Counters:                               Reset          Uptime        Lifetime
  Receiving
    Messages Received                 143,126           3,932         143,126
    Recipients Received               154,609           3,939         154,609
    Gen. Bounce Recipients                267              19             267
  Rejection
    Rejected Recipients               506,679          14,359         506,679
    Dropped Messages                       40               0              40
  Queue
    Soft Bounced Events                     3               0               3
  Completion
    Completed Recipients              153,425           3,917         153,425
      Hard Bounced Recipients             524              38             524
        DNS Hard Bounces                  254              19             254
        5XX Hard Bounces                  259              19             259
        Expired Hard Bounces                4               0               4
        Filter Hard Bounces                 7               0               7
        Other Hard Bounces                  0               0               0
      Delivered Recipients            109,741           2,630         109,741
      Deleted Recipients               43,160           1,249          43,160
        Global Unsub. Hits                  0               0               0
    DomainKeys Signed Msgs             60,719           2,529          60,719
  Current IDs
    Message ID (MID)                                                   154987
    Injection Conn. ID (ICID)                                          697826
    Delivery Conn. ID (DCID)                                            74870

Rates (Events Per Hour):             1-Minute       5-Minutes      15-Minutes
  Receiving
    Messages Received                     416             536             528
    Recipients Received                   416             536             528
  Queue
    Soft Bounced Events                     0               0               0
  Completion
    Completed Recipients                    0              72              32
      Hard Bounced Recipients               0               0               0
      Delivered Recipients                  0              36              16

Gauges:                               Current
  System
    RAM Utilization                        4%
    CPU Utilization
      Total                                2%
```

```
    MGA                              2%
    Anti-Spam                        5%
    Anti-Virus                       0%
    Reporting                        0%
    Quarantine                       0%
  Disk I/O Utilization               0%
  Resource Conservation              0
  Logging Disk Usage                14%
  Logging Disk Available            42G
Connections
  Current Inbound Conn.              2
  Current Outbound Conn.             5
Queue
  Active Recipients                435
    Unattempted Recipients         432
    Attempted Recipients             3
  Messages In Work Queue             0
  Messages In Quarantine         1,143
  Destinations In Memory             8
  Kilobytes Used                29,877
    Kilobytes In Quarantine     29,877
  Kilobytes Free             8,358,731
```

From this output, we can begin troubleshooting. You can see at the top that the system status is online, which means that the ESA is actively accepting connections and delivering mail. The next line shows the oldest message age of more than 15 minutes, which is not necessarily cause for concern, but it's worth looking into.

The next lines of output start with the word Feature and refers to the active feature keys on the system. All of these show either perpetual or a non-zero duration, and so expired keys are not the source of the delivery problem. If any keys are expired or near expiration, the ESA generates email alerts to notify administrators, and you or someone in your group pays diligent attention to those kinds of alerts.

The next section of output shows combined statistics for messages and recipients accepted and completed. Data on messages is shown, because it's more straightforward for users and administrators to think in terms of messages. More pertinent information is shown based on recipients, because multirecipient messages require that each recipient be filtered, processed, and delivered separately. It's possible that a message with two recipients ends up delivered to one of the recipients and not to the other or delivered at a much later time. You must be familiar with thinking in terms of recipients, because most of the ESA troubleshooting tools work on a recipient basis, and most of the filtering and delivery rules do, too. The counters here show three columns: Reset, which is since the last counter reset (using the **resetcounters** command); Uptime, which is since the last reboot or shutdown; and Lifetime, which is, of course, since the ESA came from the factory.

The Gauges section is of most interest to us in our delivery troubleshooting. The first gauges are for system performance: CPU load, broken out by component, Disk I/O, and use of physical disk space on the system. Because all the gauges in this report show very low usage, this is not the source of our delivery problem, and we'll move on.

Below the Gauges, we see Connections, organized into inbound and outbound connections. These are live values at the time when the command is run. In this context, inbound refers to the direction of the SMTP connection, not the direction of email. Inbound means initiated by any external IP in to the ESA, whereas outbound means initiated by the ESA to any external IP. We can have inbound connections from our internal groupware server, over which outgoing email is transmitted. An outbound connection could be from the ESA to local groupware, delivering incoming messages from an Internet sender to a local recipient. Only successful SMTP connections are shown here. Connections that are still being initiated, or which are rejected either by ESA or the remote server, are not added to the count.

In this troubleshooting example, we have both inbound and outbound SMTP connections, so we can conclude that the system is actively receiving and delivering email. The number of connections is important, but needs to be taken into context with how busy the system is. ESA automatically opens as many connections as it needs to deliver mail efficiently, subject to limits set on the system and subject to its *Good Neighbor* algorithm, which avoids flooding destination servers with massive numbers of connections.

The Queue section starts with Active Recipients, which is a count of all recipients on all messages that have completed filtering and are waiting to be delivered. You can think of it as the total count of all recipients in a delivery queue, although ESA does not actually use a disk or memory queue to store them. Recipients are actually organized in a tree structure, grouped by recipient domain. Barring a problem with a remote server, the ESA should either be actively attempting to deliver them or waiting to make another delivery attempt based on the retry schedule configured in the appropriate bounce profile. If there is a problem with any remote server, recipients are counted here until they are delivered or the message exceeds its maximum time in queue and is bounced.

Active Recipients is broken out into Attempted Recipients and Unattempted Recipients and, in this example, output most are unattempted. Unattempted Recipients are those whose destination hosts have never been reached, so the SMTP RCPT TO command has never been attempted. This can mean that the host is down and not responding or is refusing or rejecting connections. It can also mean that the ESA has the maximum number of connections open, due to system settings, and is waiting to open more. ESA continues delivery attempts by periodically trying to open SMTP connections to these hosts, but recipients are not marked as attempted until SMTP is successful. Attempted Recipients refer to recipients that have been presented to the receiving host using the SMTP RCPT TO command, but received a temporary (4yz) error code in response to that recipient. This response could be caused by a busy server, an unavailable mailbox, or rate limiting by the remote host. Recipients in the Attempted category are reattempted until either the maximum number of retries or maximum time in queue has been exceeded. Getting to the SMTP RCPT TO command presumes that ESA was able to make a successful SMTP connection at some point.

Back to this example, we have five outbound SMTP connections, but 432 recipients in queue have never been attempted because the ESA can't make connections to the various remote servers. Although this isn't necessarily a severe problem all the time, it could certainly be the root of the delivery problem. The combination of a low number of outbound connections combined with a high number of active recipients may mean that we're experiencing delivery delays, so it is worth investigating.

Before we move on to the next step, we must examine the last lines of output. The next, Messages in Work Queue, is a count of those messages that are awaiting processing by the security engines. All the processing for AntiSpam, AntiVirus, Content Filtering, Outbreak Filters, Encryption, and DLP is performed in the work queue. Messages that will be scanned by one or more of these engines go into the work queue where they are handed off to an available security engine running in a separate process. Because the security engines are the performance bottleneck in most ESA configurations, having a non-zero value in the **Messages In Work Queue** field can be the first indication that an ESA has reached its maximum throughput, at least for the current instant. Because this value is zero here, this is not the source of our delivery delays.

If you have a value in this field, you can drill further into work queue statistics. For status on the work queue and specific engines, or for a view of performance, see the commands in Table 5-1.

Table 5-1 *Work Queue and Filtering Engine Commands*

Command	Description
workqueue status	Displays the status of the work queue (operational or paused) and the number of messages in the work queue.
workqueue rate	Shows a continual running count of messages entering and leaving the work queue, updated by the interval it prompts you for.
antispamstatus	Status of any enabled anti-spam engines, including date and time of last engine and rule update.
antivirusstatus	Status of any enabled antivirus engines, including date and time of last engine and rule update.
vofstatus	Virus Outbreak Filters, shows last rule update and all current active outbreak rules.
encryptionstatus	Shows date and time of last encryption engine update.
sbstatus	Shows the status of the SenderBase lookups, including the queries used to find reputation scores, but also for the queries submitted as part of SenderBase Network Participation (SBNP).

This same information about the status of the security engines is also available in the WUI in the Security Services menu, but the **workqueue rate** command is not.

After the work queue stats, the output from **status detail** shows the count of Messages In Quarantine for policy reasons. For the troubleshooting example, it's possible that messaging delays could be caused by a security engine or filter-quarantining messages, so we need to investigate.

Destinations In Memory refers to a count of destination domains that have had recent activity. For efficiency, information about any destination that has had activity in the last three hours is kept in memory. After three hours of activity, the stats are cleared and the destination is no longer displayed as an active host. New activity for the destination would trigger the start of new statistics, and by activity, it means that at least one recipient has been queued for delivery to that destination. Because of the three-hour window, it means that some domains will only occasionally have any stats whatsoever, and other destinations, like local internal servers, will almost never be cleared; stats will be cumulative for the uptime of the ESA.

Kilobytes Used refers to disk usage of the queue partition on disk. ESAs dedicate an entire disk partition for queued messages, using a journaling filesystem called *AsyncFS*. All messages accepted by ESA are written to disk, while processing continues on the message in memory. The messages are not removed from disk until a final disposition (delivered or bounced) is reached. The ESA has much more disk than memory, so disk-queuing capacity is rarely a concern.

At this point in our troubleshooting, we have some idea of where the problem may lie. We know that the messages are on the ESA but not delivered to the destination host, so the messages we're interested in are among the 435 in queue for delivery. They're not stuck in processing on a security engine, because the work queue is empty. We need to see what's in those queues. The next set of commands we'll use focus on messages in the delivery queues. Each destination domains in memory has a separate record for the history of connections and delivery to that host.

Caution Many of the ESA commands refer to *hosts*, but don't actually refer to individual machines. When referring to hosts in the context of mail delivery, the ESA really means *destination domain*, as derived from the portion of recipient email addresses after the @ sign. The distinction is subtle, but important. If you know that mail bound for your local domain is sent to hosts named exch1.company.com and exch2.company.com, the mail that is being delivered to those hosts won't be listed by those hostnames, but rather for the company.com destination domain.

If you do see what looks like a full-qualified hostname in a list of destinations, or even an IP address, that's because, at some point, one of the messages on the ESA had at least one recipient email address of user@fqdn.company.com or even user@192.168.1.1. These are valid SMTP recipient addresses, even though they may not be valid in your environment.

The **tophosts** command is the best place to go next. Despite the name, it actually doesn't show hosts, but destination domains. It lists the top 20 destination domains, ordered by the parameter you select (see Example 5-6).

Example 5-6 *Output of* **tophosts**, *Sorted by Active Recipients*

```
esa02.cisco.com> tophosts

Sort results by:

1. Active Recipients
2. Connections Out
3. Delivered Recipients
4. Hard Bounced Recipients
5. Soft Bounced Events
[1]> 1

Status as of:                   Fri Aug 20 12:59:36 2010 EDT
Hosts marked with '*' were down as of the last delivery attempt.

                                 Active  Conn.    Deliv.      Soft      Hard
#   Recipient Host               Recip.    Out    Recip.   Bounced   Bounced

1   external.com                    115      0     2,966         0         0
2   isp.com                           1      1         2         0         0
3   othercompany.com                  0      0         0         0         0
4   ironport.com                      0      0         4         0         0
5   the.euq.release.queue             0      0         0         0         0

6   the.encryption.queue              0      0         0         0         0
7   the.euq.queue                     0      0         4         0         0
8   the.euq.release.queue             0      0         0         0         0
```

This command gives us a critical piece of information: The top destination domain is external.com, where we have 115 active recipients waiting to be delivered, but with no outbound connections. We need to drill deeper into this. You can look at the details for a specific destination host, like external.com, by using the command **hoststatus**. The **hoststatus** command can be run interactively, where it prompts you for the name of the destination domain. You can also use the batch mode, as shown in Example 5-7.

Example 5-7 hoststatus *Run in Batch Mode*

```
esa02.cisco.com> hoststatus external.com

Host mail status for: 'external.com'
Status as of:         Mon Aug 23 15:37:33 2010 EDT
Host up/down:         down

Counters:
  Queue
    Soft Bounced Events                          0
  Completion
    Completed Recipients                     3,670
      Hard Bounced Recipients                    0
        DNS Hard Bounces                         0
        5XX Hard Bounces                         0
        Filter Hard Bounces                      0
        Expired Hard Bounces                     0
        Other Hard Bounces                       0
      Delivered Recipients                   3,670
      Deleted Recipients                         0

Gauges:
  Queue
    Active Recipients                          115
      Unattempted Recipients                   115
      Attempted Recipients                       0
    Connections
      Current Outbound Connections               0
      Pending Outbound Connections               0

Oldest Message        23 mins 36 secs
Last Activity         Mon Aug 23 15:30:06 2010 EDT
Ordered IP addresses: (expiring at Tue Aug 24 14:45:09 2010 EDT)
    Preference   IPs
    10           128.107.243.13
                 128.107.243.14
                 128.107.234.207

    20           64.103.36.153

    25           64.104.252.248

MX Records:
    Preference   TTL        Hostname
```

```
10          23h7m35s    inbound.external.com
20          23h7m35s    backup1.external.com
25          23h7m35s    backup2.external.com
```

From this output, we can see many interesting things about delivery history to this domain. The first interesting item is a couple of lines down from the top. The host's status is being displayed as down. Clearly, this is not a good situation if we are trying to deliver mail to this domain. A host is listed as down when the ESA cannot successfully establish an SMTP session to any IP address returned for all MX records for the destination domain.

We drilled down to the point where it looks like the problem lies outside the ESA. We used the **status detail** command, which confirmed that there aren't any system-wide problems, like performance or connection limits. We used the **tophosts** command and discovered that most mail is being delivered, but email to our host of interest is not. The output of **hoststatus** tells us that we can't reach the destination domain to deliver mail, and the ESA is queuing email to that domain while it tries to make a connection. The MX records listed in the **hoststatus** output tells us that DNS resolution is working and the domain has primary and secondary hosts listed.

We can't stop there, however. Responding back to the users with "it's not on our side" isn't usually an acceptable answer. The problem may lie outside the ESA, but with a little more digging, we can find where the problem may lie. Because we see that the ESA can't make a successful connection to the remote ESA, there are two possibilities: The TCP connection attempt is failing or the TCP connection is succeeding, but the SMTP connection is being rejected. Let's examine each possibility from the ESA perspective.

To test network connectivity, start with **telnet**. We can use **ping** and **traceroute** to determine connectivity and network path if that fails.

A successful **telnet** to a destination host looks like this:

```
esa02.cisco.com> telnet 128.107.243.14

Trying 128.107.243.14...
Connected to sj-inbound-e.cisco.com.
Escape character is '^]'.
220 sj-inbound-e.cisco.com ESMTP
```

Remember that, on the ESA, **telnet** defaults to port 25, so we don't have to specify that port here. In this case, we've successfully connected to the remote host on port 25, and the SMTP conversation has started because the remote host greeted us with a welcome banner.

A connectivity failure can take two forms. One is a timeout, either because the packets are being dropped or lost somewhere, or the response packets aren't being routed back to the ESA. The second is a refusal or reset, where the destination, or an intervening network security device, is terminating the connection. A timeout looks like this, providing the result only after 30 seconds:

```
mail.chrisporter.com> telnet 128.107.243.14

Trying 128.107.243.14...
telnet: connect to address 128.107.243.14: Operation timed out
telnet: Unable to connect to remote host
```

By comparison, a refusal or rejection is immediately returned:

```
mail.chrisporter.com> telnet 128.107.243.14

Trying 128.107.243.14...
telnet: connect to address 128.107.243.14: Connection refused
telnet: Unable to connect to remote host
```

Back to the example, let's assume that TCP network connectivity is confirmed, but instead of a 220 banner, we get one that looks like this:

```
mail.chrisporter.com> telnet 128.107.243.14

Trying 128.107.243.14...
Connected to 128.107.243.14.
Escape character is '^]'.
550 sj-inbound-e.cisco.com
Connection closed by foreign host.
```

The 550 code indicates a permanent failure, and your ESA treats this banner response as a host that's down. This could very well be the cause of the delivery delays: The recipient domain has blacklisted your sending IPs, or the receiving servers really are down and unavailable. However, for mail servers that are running but whose services are unavailable, the more likely response code is a banner 4yz code instead of 5yz:

```
mail.chrisporter.com> telnet 128.107.243.14

Trying 128.107.243.14...
Connected to 128.107.243.14.
Escape character is '^]'.
421 #4.4.5 Too many connections from your host.
Connection closed by foreign host.
```

Command Listing by Functional Area

Now that we've seen some concrete examples of using the CLI, we'll review all of the available CLI commands, organized by functional area. The word *command* here refers to CLI actions that display information or alter message processing but don't permanently change the ESA configuration, with a few exceptions.

All of these commands, with the exception of the hidden and undocumented ones, has online help available in the CLI by typing *help <command>*.

Mail Delivery Troubleshooting

Hopefully, troubleshooting mail delivery won't be a major day-to-day task with ESA. It's designed to operate with extremely low administration time, delivering mail reliably without having to manually manipulate queues or remove undeliverable messages. However, as we saw in the earlier example, there are quite a few tools for investigating and handling delivery issues. The ESA's delivery troubleshooting commands are listed in Table 5-2.

Table 5-2 *Mail Delivery Commands*

Command	Description
tophosts	As in the example, displays a list of the top destination domains, ordered by one of the columns it displays: active recipients, active connections, delivered recipients, and soft or hard bounce recipients.
hoststatus	Displays status about any destination domain with recent activity (last three hours). Includes a breakdown of delivery or bounces and count of message waiting to be delivered. Also includes destination details, like all MX records and IP addresses for those hosts.
topin	Displays the top connectors (such as the client hosts connecting to a listener with the most simultaneous connections).
delivernow	Forces the ESA to reattempt delivery of all messages or messages for a specific destination, regardless of the current retry schedule. Useful after you make a configuration change, such as changing the smtproutes destination of a domain.

Network Troubleshooting

Traditional UNIX or Windows Shell utilities are only available on ESA in the CLI, and there are a few other similar ESA-specific commands that are also CLI-only. The available network troubleshooting tools are listed in Table 5-3.

Table 5-3 *Network Troubleshooting Commands*

Command	Description
ping	Standard ping utility, used to confirm connectivity to a remote host using ICMP echo.
telnet	Establishes a TCP connection to a remote host. On the ESA, telnet defaults to using port 25 if the port isn't specified. Extremely useful for checking TCP connectivity on all ports, not just for manually testing SMTP.
traceroute	Displays the route path across networks to destination. Output is exactly like that of the common tool of the same name.
netstat	Shows information about active sockets and interfaces, routing table contents, packet statistics, and listen queues. Like the common netstat utility, but wrapped in a menu-driven command.
packetcapture	A wrapper for the tcpdump utility that stores TCP connection data in a format that can be displayed in a packet analyzer, like wireshark or ethereal. The packetcapture menu allows you to specify source and destination, interface, and ports, or a custom filter based on tcpdump syntax. The capture file is available for download from the ESA either via FTP, SCP, or the WUI.
tcpdump	Now deprecated as of 7.1 in favor of packetcapture, this was just a wrapper around the built-in tcpdump command. Harder to use than packetcapture, because you had to know the flags and filter formats.
nslookup	Like the familiar OS command, queries DNS for information about a host, domain, or IP. The interactive form allows you to specify the type of lookup.

Controlling Services

For maintenance work or troubleshooting, the ESAs have a series of commands for stopping and restarting various services. The status of the system when one or more services are stopped is displayed in the GUI or in the output of the **status** command.

When pausing delivery or listening, these commands ask you how long to wait before abruptly closing connections. The default is 30 seconds. This delay allows the system to gracefully shut off the service: Active connections are allowed to continue transmitting, but no new connections are accepted or made. Once the time limit is reached, any remaining active connections are forcibly terminated. Table 5-4 lists the service control commands.

Table 5-4 *Commands for Controlling Services*

Command	Description
suspenddel	Suspend delivery. Stops the ESA from delivering mail, but allows it to continue to accept new mail connections. Forces the ESA to queue messages. This stops all delivery of email, incoming and outgoing.
resumedel	Restarts the mail-delivery process and lets the ESA make outbound SMTP connections again.
suspendlistener	Stops one or more listeners from accepting connections. Connections to a suspended listener will be refused. Delivery will still continue, so this is useful for "draining" an ESA of all mail (for example, when moving or replacing machines or even upgrading).
resumelistener	Restarts one or more listeners to allow inbound connections.
suspend	Stops everything—inbound and outbound.
resume	Restarts all delivery and listeners, if stopped. Useful if you've been starting and stopping services and not keeping track; resume starts all delivery and all listeners.
shutdown/reboot	Self-explanatory. shutdown powers off the system as its last step, requiring a physical button push on the ESA to start up again.
workqueue/workqueue pause/workqueue resume	Shows the status and allows for the pausing or resuming of the work queue. ESA continues to accept messages, but prevents any of the messages from going into the work queue to be processed by the filtering engines. The net effect is to halt all filtering—both incoming and outgoing.

Performance and Statistics

Almost every action taken on an ESA is logged and counted. The counts of actions and rates are available through numerous commands. Performance and statistics commands are listed in Table 5-5. Many of the attributes and values displayed by these commands are available for monitoring through other methods, a topic discussed in Chapter 6.

Table 5-5 *Performance and Statistics Commands*

Command	Description
status/status detail	Broad overview of all statistics on the ESA, as mentioned earlier in this chapter. It's the only command that shows statistics on message and recipient rates, expressed in terms of events per hour.

Command	Description
rate	A live view of message rates, updated every *n* seconds as prompted for when you start the command. Each line shows, for an *n*-second interval, how many connections and recipients were received, and how many were completed. The delta indicates the change from the last interval. When run as *rate 1*, the update interval is 1 second, allowing you to see connection and recipient changes per second.
hostrate	Like **rate**, shows a continually updating live view of message rates, but limited to a specific destination domain. It offers more detail, breaking down the number of completed recipients into active, delivered, bounced, or soft bounced.
workqueue rate	Another live view command, with just three important stats: the number of messages in, out, and pending for the work queue during every interval update. This command gives you a quick view into message backups and delays due to processing by the engines in the work queue.

Logging and Log Searches

By default, the ESA has 23 log subscriptions running by default, and you can create additional logs, and even have multiple subscriptions of the same type—for example, for storing one copy on the ESA and pushing off another copy to a remote server. We examine logging thoroughly in Chapter 6. The logging and log search commands are listed in Table 5-6.

Table 5-6 *Logging and Log Searches*

Command	Description
logconfig	Main configuration command for creating, editing, and deleting log subscriptions. I prefer to work in the WUI for managing log subscriptions. The CLI allows you to manage SSH keys for subscriptions transferred via SCP.
tail	Like the UNIX tail command, prints the selected log-file output to screen, live as the log lines are written. Use Ctrl-C to break out.
grep	Similar to the UNIX grep command, this version allows you to search any log file for a given regular expression. The interactive mode gives you a list of log subscriptions to choose from and several search options. Batch mode is run by specifying the search pattern and log subscription name. The ESA grep has an option to "tail the logs," and using this option is like the command sequence *tail –f file | grep pattern* on a UNIX system.

Command	Description
findevent	A more sophisticated search tool that allows you to find log entries for a specified sender, recipient, subject, or message ID with one command. Automatically finds matching messages and presents them as a list. Choosing from the list gives all log entries for that message. Searches only logs of type IronPort text mail logs.
rollovernow	Causes a log subscription to roll itself over, starting a new log file and archiving the previous. There may be other actions associated with a rollover, depending on the subscription, such as an FTP or SCP push.

Queue Management and Viewing

Day-to-day management of the mail queues on an ESA is not really necessary, because the system handles all of it for you. There are times, however, when you want to dig deeper into what exactly is sitting in queue or remove messages that are stuck in queue. I use this group of commands when I'm repurposing or removing an ESA from commission and want to look at any remaining messages.

We've already seen that the output of **hoststatus** includes aggregate counts and status of a single delivery host. It doesn't show any individual message data, however. For that, we need the additional commands listed in Table 5-7.

Table 5-7 *Queue Management and Viewing Commands*

Command	Description
showrecipients	Shows a summary table of all the messages and recipients on the ESA, all those from a given sender or all for a given destination domain.
deleterecipients	Deletes multiple messages in queue, specified by sender, destination domain, or all messages. Dangerous, because the action is unrecoverable. I only use this in emergencies, such as deleting email from out-of-control applications or compromised user accounts.
bouncerecipients	Like deleterecipients, this acts on multiple messages, but bounces the messages. Bouncing means dropping the original message while composing a delivery status notification message to the sender, informing them that the message is undeliverable. Again, this is dangerous in production.
redirectrecipients	Delivers all active queued messages to another destination. This command prompts you for the delivery IP or hostname. Useful when replacing an appliance, because it allows you to send any remaining undelivered messages to another ESA before shutting down.
oldmessage	Provides details about the oldest message in the queue.

Command	Description
archivemessage	Writes a copy of a given message to disk. You must have the MID for the message.
removemessage	Removes a message currently in queue. You must have the MID for the message. Obviously, this is dangerous, because the message is discarded and not delivered.
showmessage	Dumps the actual message content to screen in its native ASCII, including any encoded binary data. All message data is shown.

Configuration File Management

The configuration of an ESA can be exported in XML to disk or by email to any address. In addition, configuration information can be shared across systems using Centralized Management, which requires a feature key from Cisco. Managing configuration files can be done from the CLI, and these commands are exceptionally useful in automating configuration changes or configuration backups. Table 5-8 describes these commands.

Table 5-8 *Commands for Configuration Management*

Command	Description
mailconfig	Emails a copy of the configuration XML export to a given email address. It will ask you if you want to include passwords, which you should answer Yes to if you want to be able to load this configuration file later. This question is actually misleading: Answering Yes still means that user account passwords are hashed, but others are in the clear; answering No means that passwords are replaced by five asterisks (*****) in the output, and private keys get the same treatment.
saveconfig	Like **mailconfig**, but it writes the data to a file on the ESA filesystem. You can retrieve it using FTP or SCP. The file is written to the /configuration directory.
loadconfig	Allows you to restore an XML configuration file from disk or by directly pasting it into the CLI. Stick with the disk option. SSH clients can't usually handle such a huge influx of pasted text. Be aware that the XML format changes from release to release and older XML may not import. This is addressed in Chapter 10, "Configuration Files."
showconfig	Displays the configuration information directly to the screen. It's almost always better to examine the configuration by using the appropriate commands or going into the WUI, but if you want to have a look at the config, this will do it. Pages across the console; use Ctrl-C to break out.

Command	Description
resetconfig	Resets the configuration back to the default factory config. Extremely destructive. Resets *everything*, including network interfaces, so you're likely to be disconnected as soon as this runs. Be careful with this command. It should really only be used if an ESA is being returned or permanently decommissioned. If you're just changing a machine to a new config, there's no need to reset the existing configuration before loading a new one.

AsyncOS Version Management

Table 5-9 shows the commands for changing the version of the AsyncOS firmware on the ESA. Upgrades start by checking with the Cisco upgrade servers for available images. If available, and a version is selected, the ESA downloads the appropriate image file through a worldwide content delivery network and installs it on a separate partition. All ESAs must upgrade independently, each downloading their own image. The upgrade and revert commands are described in Table 5-9.

Table 5-9 *AsyncOS Version Management*

Command	Description
upgrade	Checks for new versions of AsyncOS that are available to download and install. If selected, performs the upgrade by installing the image to a new disk partition that will be used at reboot. If that new partition fails, the system rolls back to the earlier boot partition. **upgrade** prompts you for a reboot at the end. The ESA continues to function during the installation process, and gracefully stops connections at the point of reboot. You can upgrade a system while it's in production and processing mail, although suspending the listeners first will make the upgrade faster. Note that, if there are multiple versions available in the upgrade list, you can safely install any listed upgrade. If a version is not listed, that upgrade path isn't available or hasn't been tested; versions that are listed have been tested for upgrade process. If you haven't upgraded in a while, you may have to go through several upgrades to get to the latest release.
revert	Rolls back the AsyncOS version to one of the previously installed versions. Because the ESA installs new versions of AsyncOS on separate partitions, it is possible to return to a previous version. All configuration information is lost, except for the network configuration, so it's a good idea to store a configuration file for every version you upgrade to, in case you need to return to it. This command is extremely destructive—all messages in queue or stored in quarantine are deleted—so run this only on empty ESAs.

Configuration Testing Commands

When you spend time configuring an ESA, either via CLI or WUI, it's handy to be able to test the configuration without actually having to inject messages. These commands give you just that, although it's always wise to send test messages through a system before deploying into production. Consider the commands in Table 5-10 to be your first-stage unit test, after which you should proceed to integration testing.

Table 5-10 *Configuration Testing Commands*

Command	Description
ldaptest	Tests LDAP queries, even before they are committed or assigned to a listener. **ldaptest** prompts you for the arguments, depending on the query type, and then connects to and performs the query against the LDAP server. The output tells you the server that it contacted, query result, and any errors it encountered. Extremely useful for testing connectivity and credentials in addition to the queries themselves.
trace	A testing simulator for email messages that tests the entire policy pipeline, from connection to filtering and policies and to delivery. Allows you to specify all the attributes of a message: source IP, sender and recipient addresses, and the entire message body. Output includes all stages of the email pipeline that apply to this message and gives a final disposition. No message data is actually sent, so you can test without impacting production email.
dnslisttest	If you're using external blacklists that are queried via DNS, it's recommended that you test those queries using this command. It actually querys the DNSBLs for values and provides the results. Test with an IP address that you know is in the list, and another that is not, for certainty of the responses. A nonworking query can continually timeout or, worse, provide a false-positive match that results in legitimate connections being rejected.
tlsverify	Tests a remote host and recipient domain for Transport Layer Security (TLS) connectivity and certificate validity. This is extremely useful and mandatory to use if you're considering using the Verify option for outgoing TLS connections. It checks that TLS is available and validates the server's certificate against the hostname and recipient domain. We discuss TLS in Chapter 12, "Advanced Networking."

Support Related Commands

The ESA is a highly reliable product, but it's not perfect, and Cisco backs up the product line with industry-leading 24/7 support by phone, email (naturally), and through the system itself, with a variety of commands that let you do some troubleshooting locally and, when needed, to provide information to Cisco TAC. The commands shown in Table 5-11 are all related to the support process.

Table 5-11 *Support Commands*

Command	Description
supportrequest	Creates and sends a support request to Cisco, which opens a ticket automatically. This is a better approach to starting the support process than emailing or calling Cisco, because it automatically bundles up configuration and diagnostic information. If you do phone or email, you'll often be asked to issue a supportrequest on the affected system. Of course, it does so using SMTP, and if your ESA is down or unable to send email, you should call instead. You can run this command and choose not to send the information to Cisco, but to another email address, so you can send yourself a copy if you're curious about what information is sent.
techsupport	A clever support tool that allows you to establish remote access for a Cisco TAC engineer during the support process. It does so by one of two means: either by SSH directly on an outside interface (which I never use) or by the TUNNEL method, which uses an SSH connection to Cisco and an SSH reverse tunnel that allows for the TAC engineer to connect directly to the CLI of the ESA. Because the tunnel is an SSH connection from your ESA to Cisco, on port 25 by default, it's much easier and more secure than trying to arrange for remote SSH access to an ESA. Speaking of security, this command may sound like a back door to the ESA, but security has been a consideration from the start. First, the tunnel uses a session password that you specify, and provide to the engineer working the case. Second, the CLI prompt changes when a support engineer is logged in, adding the text SERVICE to the prompt. Finally, you have the ability to close the session at any time.

There's another command that can be grouped with the support commands: **diagnostic**. The **diagnostic** command in the CLI has a number of useful utilities, but it exposes some fairly dangerous options that can reset configurations and delete important data or email messages. You are advised to use caution and respect the warnings that the CLI provides you about certain commands. When you instruct the system to delete the reporting database, all the old data is gone for good. Table 5-12 describes the options available in the **diagnostic** command.

Table 5-12 diagnostic *Command*

Subcommand	Description
RAID	Performs a full diagnostic using the RAID card firmware or OS software. This is not something you would casually run, but only do so if Cisco TAC requested the information. You can find out the current status of the RAID subsystem by using the version command. If there is something wrong with a RAID component, you will see email alerts and SNMP traps from the ESA and should contact Cisco support.

Subcommand	Description
DISK_USAGE	Displays disk quota and usage for the spam quarantine, reporting, and tracking components. Quotas for these components are assigned in commands specific to each one.
NETWORK	Provides a number of network utilities, some of which are exposed elsewhere. FLUSH is the equivalent of running **dnsflush** and **ldapflush**, but it also flushes the ESA ARP cache. ARPSHOW displays the contents of that cache, which is a mapping of IP to MAC addresses. SMTPPING is an application layer connectivity test for SMTP connections to a remote host, verifying that a TCP connection can be made, SMTP commands to be issued, and even to send a test message. Useful for determining basic message delivery. TCPDUMP is another name for the **packetcapture** command.
REPORTING	Two options here: The first is to completely disable reporting for the entire ESA so that neither local nor centralized reporting will gather data. The second deletes all the data in the reporting database. The DELETEDB command is permanent and unrecoverable.
TRACKING	Provides a low-level debug command for when Cisco needs troubleshooting information to resolve tracking problems. Also provides a DELETEDB command, which as you can guess is permanent and unrecoverable.
RELOAD	An extremely destructive wipe of the entire ESA, including all configuration and data. Everything is set back to the manufacturing default. Obviously, if you absolutely have to run this, you should only use this when a machine is being decommissioned or returned. Even feature keys are cleared, requiring new keys to restore functionality.

General Administration Commands

While you're logged into the CLI, there are a few commands you can use to get information about your own session and other login sessions. There's also a command for determining the license status of the ESA. These administration commands are described in Table 5-13.

Table 5-13 *General Administration Commands*

Command	Description
passwd	Changes the password of the currently logged-in user. You must know the old password.
w, who	Who is logged into the ESA CLI and from where. CLI only.

Command	Description
whoami	Tells you the username you're logged in as. Not as useless as it sounds, if you're accustomed to logging in with multiple accounts and lost track. Also provides information on the ESA user roles that affect the privileges of your current login. CLI only, although WUI displays this in the upper-right corner.
last	Displays the last few dozen login attempts, including the username, remote IP, date and time of login, and session time. On systems that have multiple administrative or operator users, this is the first thing I look at when I need to answer the question, "Who made this configuration change?"
featurekey	Displays the current state of the keys used to control the basic and optional features of the appliance. To run a filtering engine, or the ESA platform itself, you must have either a temporary evaluation key or a full-duration key that is issued when the feature is purchased. Feature keys are automatically checked for and downloaded, although you may have to accept an EULA for a new feature the first time the keys are found.

Miscellaneous Commands

The last few commands that we haven't described are simple and mostly self-explanatory. The commands of the form **<engine>status** give a simple output of the state of that engine or daemon, and usually the date and time of the last update. The corresponding **<engine>update** forces the ESA to check for and download any new updates, if available. When there is more than one engine controlled by a command, as could happen with **antivirusstatus** and **antivirusupdate**, the command will further prompt for the engine name. The status and update commands are **antispamstatus**, **antispamupdate**, **antivirusstatus**, **antivirusupdate**, **dnsstatus**, **encryptionstatus**, **encryptionupdate**, **sbstatus**, **vofstatus**, and **vofupdate**. Another related command is **vofflush**, which clears the cache of rules for the outbreak engine.

In AsyncOS 7.5, the VOF engine has been renamed to **Outbreak Filters**, and the relevant commands are now named **outbreakstatus**, **outbreakflush**, and **outbreakupdate**, although the original VOF commands are still supported.

Although the status commands are occasionally useful, you should never have to spend time day to day running the update commands. Once network connectivity is available, the ESA automatically checks for and downloads updates without intervention and issues alerts if it's unable to do so. These commands only kick off the appropriate update, so you have to check the corresponding **<engine>status** command, or the logs, to be sure the update succeeded.

Configuration Listing by Functional Area

Configuration in the CLI refers to actions that actually change ESA configuration. The ESA provides either a configuration menu, or asks further configuration questions, when you run any of these commands. They're organized here by functional area.

It bears repeating that you must use the *commit* command to make any configuration changes effective. The single most common administrative mistake is to make changes but forget to commit them, resulting in very frustrating troubleshooting.

Network Setup

As a TCP/IP host, the ESA provides access host-level network configuration. It's tempting to think of the ESA as a network device, but more accurate to think of it as a host. It supports no routing protocols, no packet filtering, and no packet forwarding across interfaces. TCP connections terminate at the ESA if they are destined for one of its interfaces. As a host on an IP network, commands are provided to configure the relevant interface and routing rules. The network configuration commands are described in Table 5-14.

Table 5-14 *Network Configuration Commands*

Command	Description
interfaceconfig	Creates, edits, and deletes active interfaces and interface groups. You can add many IPv4 addresses to each physical NIC, up to 32 per ESA. Why would you want to do this? We discuss virtual gateways in Chapter 12.
setgateway	Sets the default gateway for the system. Packets destined for any network that's not on the same subnet as the ESA, and not defined in a static route, will be sent to the default gateway.
sethostname	Sets the ESA global hostname. This can be different from the hostnames on the individual interfaces. It's mainly used to identify the ESA to you and to other ESAs or SMAs that interact with it. This setting is CLI-only.
routeconfig	Manages the ESA static route table for defining alternate gateways for specific destination networks. There's only one static routing table per ESA.
etherconfig	Controls the low-level settings for the Ethernet NICs on the ESA. This is not available in the WUI. Allows you to set port speeds and duplex on each port, adjust MTU, and to assign VLANs that each NIC supports. Loopback addressing can be enabled here, for the purposes of supporting a load-balancing scheme called Direct Server Return. On ESA models that support it, NIC pairing can be enabled from the MEDIA submenu. NIC pairing, designed to provide redundant network paths in case of cable, port, or switch failure, is only available on the 2U ESA models.

Command	Description
dnsconfig	Configuration of the DNS client on the ESA. There are two basic modes: ESA as a pure client to a specified DNS server or servers or ESA acting as its own recursive server, contacting the Internet root servers to build its lookup tree. There's also a hybrid mode that allows both; Chapter 12 examines this split DNS.
snmpconfig	Enables and configures the SNMP daemon, including community string and password, trap targets, and acceptable network ranges for Network Monitoring Software. Also allows customization of certain traps, like CPU and RAM utilization traps.
ntpconfig	Enables the Network Time Protocol (NTP) client that gets date and time information from a local or Internet server. Highly recommended, as email highly depends on accurate time and setting it manually is so 20th Century.
certconfig	Creation and management of TLS certificates on the system. Chapter 12 looks at TLS and certificates.
sslconfig	Controls which versions of SSL and TLS protocols are available on the ESA, and which SSL ciphers are available during protocol negotiation (see Chapter 12 for details).

Listeners

The **listenerconfig** command has a deep command tree and, because it controls almost every aspect of the first part of the email pipeline, from connection acceptance to recipient manipulation, it deserves a thorough examination in this section. Like most CLI commands, listener settings can be controlled in the WUI and for certain features, like the Host Access Table (HAT), the WUI is much more straightforward to work in. However, knowing the complete **listenerconfig** tree is extremely valuable, because there are listener settings that are only available in the CLI. If you ever find that you need to automate the settings or periodically import tables, the CLI is the way to go, because **listenerconfig** has thorough batch command support.

The complete **listenerconfig** menu is shown here. The submenus and subcommands are detailed in Table 5-15 through Table 5-20. For many of the listener settings, values are stored in tables, and most of the tables have a simple common set of manipulation options. Options like **New**, **Edit**, **Delete**, **Print**, **Import**, **Export**, and **Clear** are self-explanatory and identical for each table. For **Import** and **Export**, you should know that the source or destination file is stored on the appliance filesystem in the **configuration** directory; they can't be saved to your local workstation. Under the listener, the RAT, domain map, and masquerade use those common table commands:

listenerconfig

- NEW
- EDIT
  - (Listener Name or Number)
    - NAME
    - INTERFACE
    - CERTIFICATE
    - LIMITS
    - SETUP
      - DEFAULTDOMAIN
      - RECEIVED
      - CLEANSMTP
      - SENDERBASE
      - FOOTER
      - HEADING
      - ADDRESS
    - HOSTACCESS
      - NEW
      - EDIT
      - DELETE
      - MOVE
      - DEFAULT
      - PRINT
      - IMPORT
      - EXPORT
      - CLEAR
    - RCPTACCESS
      - NEW
      - EDIT
      - DELETE
      - PRINT
      - IMPORT
      - EXPORT
      - CLEAR
    - BOUNCECONFIG
    - MASQUERADE
      - NEW

DELETE
PRINT
IMPORT
EXPORT
CONFIG
CLEAR
DOMAINMAP
NEW
EDIT
DELETE
PRINT
IMPORT
EXPORT
CLEAR
LDAPACCEPT
LDAPGROUP
SETUP

Table 5-15 describes the top-level menu of listenerconfig. If you have no listeners on your ESA, you'll only see NEW and SETUP.

Table 5-15 listenerconfig *Top-Level Menu Items*

Menu	Description
NEW	Creates a new listener on a given interface and port. You can have more than one listener on an interface but each must have a separate port. We reviewed creating listeners in the CLI earlier in this chapter.
EDIT	Changes settings for an existing listener. An extensive menu whose submenu tree is described in Table 5-16.
DELETE	Removes a listener and all settings. When you commit this change, any active connections to a deleted listener are terminated, so use this with caution.
SETUP	Global miscellaneous options for all listeners on the ESA, including connection limits, SenderBase caching, counters, timeouts, and adding headers. The defaults should be maintained for most of these settings, but I usually set the connection timeouts down to their minimum: 1 minute for unproductive SMTP connections and 5 minutes for all SMTP connections. This frees the ESA from managing connections that aren't going to result in messages.

The EDIT submenu has a long list of commands, described in Table 5-16, for modifying settings or tables on the listener. To get to this menu, select a listener by name or number.

Table 5-16 listenerconfig → *EDIT Submenu*

Submenu	Description
NAME	The name that the listener is referred to. Important to keep this name consistent for corresponding listeners on multiple systems, especially for clustered (centrally managed) ESAs.
INTERFACE	The IP interface and port that this listener is bound to. Again, for centralized management, this should be consistent across ESAs.
CERTIFICATE	Chooses a certificate to use for TLS from a list of certs that have been installed. This certificate is presented when the ESA is accepting inbound SMTP connections and STARTTLS is issued.
LIMITS	Controls overall concurrent connection limits to this listener (the number of active SMTP connections that can be open at one time), and how large the kernel listen queue can be. It's tempting to set the connection limit high to avoid becoming connection bound, but this can be self-defeating. We discuss concurrency settings when we discuss performance and deployment. It's not recommended to increase the kernel listen queue.
SETUP	Miscellaneous settings for each individual listener. Table 5-18 describes the setup options.
HOSTACCESS	Manipulates the HAT for this listener. This submenu has a long list of commands to manage the HAT, as detailed in Table 5-17.
RCPTACCESS	Manipulates the RAT for this listener. This submenu has commands that are common to all the "table" settings in the listener. This is also in the WUI, where it's easier to manage.
BOUNCECONFIG	Chooses a bounce profile to be assigned to all messages received on this listener. Bounce profiles are created in bounceconfig, described later in this chapter.and the assigned bounce profile can be changed later in the pipeline by filter action or destination controls.
MASQUERADE	Table for mapping of transformation of email addresses or email domains. Masquerading can be considered the complement of aliasing: Instead of rewriting a recipient address from an "outside" address to an "inside," this table rewrites "inside" addresses in the From, To, CC, and envelope to an acceptable "outside" form. Can be done on an address-by-address basis or on whole domains or subdomains. A common case is to "flatten" internal addresses, like user@east.company.com to user@company.com. Aside from this table, masquerading can also be done with LDAP, and if you have a query created, it gives you that option here. The table portion of this command is available in the CLI only; LDAP is also in the WUI.

Submenu	Description
DOMAINMAP	Transforms recipient addresses like aliases, but at the domain level only. Designed to transform an entire domain from source to destination, leaving the user portion untouched. You cannot configure this in the WUI; it's CLI-only.
LDAPACCEPT	Chooses an existing LDAP accept query to be applied to this listener. Be absolutely certain that your query is tested and working before assigning it here, as lookup failures result in delays or rejection of legitimate mail. Chapter 7, "Directories and Policies," covers LDAP.
LDAPROUTING	Chooses an existing LDAP routing query to be applied to this listener. Recommended to have this query working before you assign it, but it's not destructive, like LDAPACCEPT.
LDAPGROUP	Chooses an existing LDAP group query to be applied to this listener. Recommended to have this query working before you assign it, but it's not destructive, like LDAPACCEPT.

Table 5-17 describes the HOSTACCESS submenu options for modifying HAT settings on the listener.

Table 5-17 listenerconfig → *EDIT* → *HOSTACCESS Submenu*

Submenu	Description
NEW	Creates a new sender group or mail flow policy. As discussed in Chapter 3, a sender group is IP addresses, listed explicitly or conditionally by some lookup. Each group then applies a mail flow policy, which controls all aspects of message acceptance and limits. I would normally add new groups and policies in the WUI, but regardless of where you do this, it's not something you would do every day.
EDIT	Changes settings for an existing sender group or policy. You can add new hosts to sender groups, change the policy applied, or rename the group. For policies, you can edit any of the connection, message, or filtering settings, but honestly, this is easier to visualize and manipulate in the WUI.
DELETE	Deletes a group or policy. Once you commit this change, it's gone for good, so be sure to back up your configuration files.
MOVE	The order of sender groups is important, because the first match wins. It's good practice, therefore, to keep groups that have elevated privileges, like whitelists and relaylists, at the top. This allows you to reorder.

Submenu	Description
DEFAULT	Alters the default mail flow policies on a listener. From the factory, most mail flow policies use the default settings for most of their parameters, only altering from the default for specific needs.
PRINT	Displays the HAT and all mail flow policies to the screen. You need a terminal with scrollback to see all the lines; a typical HAT is hundreds of lines long.
IMPORT / EXPORT	Like other tables, the HAT can be written to files on the ESA filesystem accessible through FTP or SCP. You can also import the table from those files. If you want to import a huge blacklist or whitelist (something I don't recommend), editing the HAT in an external editor is the way to do it.
CLEAR	Doesn't really empty the table, but sets all the groups and policies back to factory defaults for the listener type.

The menu item SETUP appears both at the top layer of listenerconfig, and on each individual listener. The top level SETUP, described previously in Table 5-15, covers global settings that apply to all listeners. Table 5-18 describes the per-listener SETUP menu, whose settings apply to a particular listener.

Table 5-18 *Individual Listener SETUP Menu*

Submenu	Description
DEFAULTDOMAIN	Can be used to add a fully qualified domain to sender email addresses that lack one. For example, if the default domain is cisco.com, addresses like chris@stbu will have the default domain added to become chris@stbu.cisco.com. Sender addresses that are not fully qualified shouldn't be sent to Internet destinations, because they cannot be bounced or replied to, and many sites will simply reject them.
RECEIVED	Chooses whether or not a Received: header is added to messages. Because the RFCs require that every email hop add this header, you shouldn't disable this, but in some environments, it's desirable to "hide" the internal architecture by omitting this on outgoing mail. It's critical for troubleshooting incoming mail, however, so I recommend leaving it on there. There are other tables and filters where we can manipulate headers, including the Received header.

Submenu	Description
CLEANSMTP	"Cleaning" SMTP data means dealing with messages that have Carriage Return (CR or hex 0x0D) or Linefeed (LF or hex 0x0A) characters by themselves. These two characters combined constitute a line break sequence, but are prohibited from appearing individually in SMTP. Despite the RFC prohibition, some systems still inject these characters. You can be nice and accept these messages, converting the bare characters into a legal CRLF sequence, or accept and just leave them as-is. You can also reject these messages, but you are likely to reject many legitimate messages. The default is to clean the messages of bare CRs and LFs.
SENDERBASE	Enables the use of **SenderBase** queries on this listener and specifies the timeouts for lookups. The default is enabled, of course, with 5-second timeouts.
FOOTER	You can add a disclaimer at the bottom of every message body received by this listener, selected from those created in textconfig. This is a common requirement, but I dislike doing this on the ESA because of character-set incompatibility issues. You can also specify footers in filters.
HEADING	Like **Footer**, adds a disclaimer, but at the top of the message body.
ADDRESS	Covers a variety of email address restrictions for SMTP envelope addresses. The TYPE option sets either a loose parser (default) or strict parser, which requires that email addresses follow the formats required in RFCs. Being strict is a nice idea, but it causes problems. There are two options for 8-bit addresses for accepting data in characters beyond the standard 7-bit US ASCII character set. The other options are for handling source routing (see warning), or accepting literal addresses to non-IPv4 address literals. For an IPv4 or host address literal, like user@[1.2.3.4] or user@[host.cisco.com], the RAT controls acceptance.

Warning Source routing addresses are those that contain the characters @, !, or % in the user portion of the recipient email address (for example, *chriport@cisco.com@ironport.com* or *chriport%cisco.com@senderbase.org*). The purpose of these formats was to instruct the recipient domain, after the last @ sign, that it should accept the message, strip out the last *@domain* portion, and forward it on to the email address that results. Addresses that include one or more ! characters, chained together in what's known as a bang path, were used in UUCP mail to specify the route emails should travel to get to their destination. Because of the once common use of these addresses, especially in transition from UUCP mail systems, the SMTP RFCs explicitly provided support for these address forms.

Do you see the problem with automatic forwarding? That's right—a nice feature got abused and as a result, it began to be disabled, and now virtually no system on the Internet honors them. If a system accepts and actually forwards messages in these formats, it becomes a forwarding relay that anyone can use, including spammers. Even when tightly controlled, source routing is extremely problematic.

These routing formats are also unnecessary with Internet DNS MX records providing routing information for email without having to provide explicit paths.

At this point, the only use of source routing is for exploit purposes. RFC 5321 explicitly deprecates this practice and states that clients should NOT generate such addresses. On the ESA, I highly recommend leaving the defaults, which is to reject source routing and, in fact, reject any message with a username portion with these special characters.

Mail Routing and Delivery

Obviously, because the primary mission of the ESA is reliable email delivery, there are a large number of configuration commands for mail routing and delivery, as shown in Table 5-19.

Table 5-19 *Mail Routing and Delivery Commands*

Command	Description
deliveryconfig	This seems like it should be a useful configuration command with a lot of settings for mail delivery. It's not. It covers four items and all are best left at the defaults. It allows you to choose the default delivery interface, but Auto is the default and is the only valid choice here. If you have a multinetwork configuration and find you need to run deliveryconfig to force a particular interface, something isn't right. Instead, you should be using altsrchost or filter actions to choose delivery interfaces. Likewise, you should never disable the Possible Delivery feature—it allows the ESA to deal with non-RFC compliant mail servers that don't acknowledge delivered messages. Finally, although you might conceivably need to raise the global TLS concurrency limit on high-end ESAs, the global max connections limit shouldn't be altered.

Command	Description
smtproutes	Defines the destination hosts for domains given in the table. Any entries here override DNS for the specified domain. When a domain is not listed, the ESA uses standard DNS MX records to route messages. It is possible for other tables or filter actions to override an entry here.
destconfig	Destination controls, which allows you to set delivery parameters and control delivery rates to specific destinations. Extremely handy for keeping rates low to domains that react badly to floods of messages. It's also the place to specify that you want to attempt, or require, the use of TLS when delivering mail to a domain.
altsrchost	Defines alternate source interfaces for outgoing messages. If you have multiple outside IP interfaces, you can originate SMTP connections from any or all of them, and this table controls how that mapping is done. It's also possible to do this through a filter action. This table is CLI-only.
bounceconfig	Creates and manages bounce profiles, which can also be thought of as "retry profiles." Each profile specifies how long messages can stay in queue, and how often they should be retried, and if either limit is exceeded, whether bounce messages should be sent and to whom. Also controls the global host retry schedules, which I can't think of any good reason to modify.

Policy and Filtering

You can manage incoming and outgoing mail policies from the CLI, including actions for anti-spam, antivirus, VOFs, and even content filters, using the commands shown in Table 5-20. To be honest, unless I'm under duress, I do not work with these features in the CLI. Creating and managing policies is much easier in the WUI. On the other hand, message filters are only available in the CLI.

Table 5-20 *Policy and Filtering Commands*

Command	Description
policyconfig	Manages incoming and outgoing mail policies, including all the security engines and filters. This is a deep command tree with many options. Best left for the WUI, but handy in a pinch.
textconfig	Allows you to manage text resources used by the system, such as notifications, disclaimers, bounce templates, and the introduction message included with encrypted messages.
dictionaryconfig	Manages lists of words and phrases organized into dictionaries. Dictionaries can be used in content filtering or DLP rules. Again, the CLI is not as convenient as the WUI for manual administration, but the CLI is perfect for automating changes to dictionaries.
filters	Message filter creation and management. Filters are covered in Chapter 11, "Message and Content Filters."

Managing Users and Alerts

As an administrator, you have the ability to manage the entirety of an ESA configuration but also the roles and responsibilities of other users on the system. The configuration commands for users and other administrative topics are described in Table 5-21.

Table 5-21 *User, Role, and Alert Commands*

Command	Description
userconfig	As shown earlier, this creates and manages administrative accounts on the ESA.
alertconfig	Manages alert "subscriptions," which sends email to defined addresses based on class and severity. Typically alerts cover hardware and software faults. At least one person in your organization should get all alerts, with the possible exception of the directory harvest attack prevention (DHAP) alerts, which are needlessly noisy.
addressconfig	Specifies the source address of email messages generated on the ESA, such as security notifications, reports, and delivery status notifications (DSN, or bounces). These default to MAILER-DAEMON@esahostname, which is probably not a valid address in your environment. If you want your users to be able to reply to notifications, make this a valid return address.

Configuring Global Engine and Services Options

Most of the components on the ESA have a configuration command that controls global options on the engine, including basic enabled/disabled state and, for filtering engines, maximum scanning size and time. Other engines, like tracking and reporting, have simpler settings. Each engine may have additional global options, like regional scanning for anti-spam or depth of scanning for attachment filtering.

The commands in Table 5-22 offer a short list of options, because the actions taken on messages and rules for notifications are controlled on the relevant policy. Normally, these configuration commands are rarely used—you will almost always be configuring the relevant policy actions rather than the global settings.

Table 5-22 *Global Engine and Services Configuration*

Command	Description
antispamconfig	Configures only global settings for one or more anti-spam engine, including IPAS. The global settings are maximum message size and scanning timeout and whether to enable the regional scanning features. Actions and thresholds used by IPAS are configured in the relevant policy.

Command	Description
antivirusconfig	Like **antispamconfig**, only controls the global settings for any configured antivirus engines.
scanconfig	Controls the behavior of the various text-scanning capabilities of the ESA. It sets the limits for depth of recursion (zips within zips, for example) and maximum size to scan, and configures the list of attachment types to be skipped. Because it doesn't make sense to scan image or multimedia types for text content, these are skipped by default.
vofconfig/outbreak-config	VOF settings, including threshold value and the use of adaptive rules. (These are described in Chapter 8.) One interesting option is the ability to receive Outbreak Filter alerts, which is a nice idea until you get hundreds a day. In AsyncOS 7.5, this command name changed to outbreakconfig, but the older commands are still supported.
encryptionconfig	Global options for the encryption engine, and the ability to create and provision encryption profiles. Because encryption is intimately connected with content filtering and DLP, I stick to the WUI for this command.
senderbaseconfig	Configures the SBNP feature, which gathers aggregate and anonymous data from messages and reports back to Cisco to improve the security services. Because this gathers no personally identifiable information and can improve spam capture rates, I recommend enabling this.
bvconfig	Configures the bounce verification feature, which "marks up" outgoing messages
trackingconfig	Sets options for the message-tracking feature, which is basically limited to on/off and whether it's running locally or centralized through the SMA.
reportingconfig	Like **trackingconfig**, sets options for off, on, and local versus centralized.
quarantineconfig	Manages the policy quarantines on the ESA, which are used by filters and DLP actions to hold messages for administrative reasons, such as banned attachment types or DLP violations. This is distinct from the end-user IronPort Spam Quarantine (ISQ), which is used to hold suspected spam messages and allows end users to self-manage. Policy quarantines can be created and managed here, but it's so much easier to configure in the WUI that I almost never use this CLI command. One nice feature is the bulk release of messages from quarantine, using the quarantineconfig releasemsg <MID Range> command, which doesn't come up often, but is handy if it does.

CLI-Only Tables

A few configuration tables are only available through the CLI, and these are described in Table 5-23. For most tables, it's easier to add, edit, or remove entries using the WUI, but for these, we don't have that choice. Most organizations won't need these tables, however.

Table 5-23 *CLI-Only Configuration Tables*

Command	Description
aliasconfig	An alias is a transformation of envelope recipient addresses, either one-to-one, as in a mapping of cporter@ironport.com to chriport@cisco.com, or one-to-many, as in distribution lists.
unsubscribe	Allows the ESA to store a list of addresses that it should never deliver mail to, under any circumstances. Matching recipients can be bounced or dropped. It can be used as a last-second check (for example, to stop the delivery of machine-generated mail to addresses that don't want the content, hence the name unsubscribe). It's much better for the application generating such mail to keep track of unsubscribed users rather than filtering here.
stripheaders	Strips all instances of headers listed by name in this table. Useful for removing locally significant headers on messages outgoing to Internet destinations. All matching headers are removed. You can also take this action with filters, which offer more precision because they can be applied based on other conditions.

Configuration for External Communication

In all likelihood, your ESAs make up only one component of your email system, and communication to the other components is critical. For protocols other than SMTP, there are specific commands, which are listed in Table 5-24.

At the very least, an ESA needs connectivity to the Internet to reach the Cisco update services, either directly or through a proxy.

Table 5-24 *External Communication Configuration*

Command	Description
updateconfig	Controls how the various engines connect to the Cisco update services. Specifies the URLs for retrieving updates, and the use of HTTP and HTTPS proxies for retrieving these updates. Ideally, the ESAs will have unrestricted access out on ports 80 and 443 for these updates; if this is not possible, the dynamic URLs can be changed to static URLs provided by Cisco.

Command	Description
featurekeyconfig	Toggles just two settings for feature keys: whether keys are automatically downloaded from Cisco when available, and if available, whether they are automatically applied. I can't imagine why you would disable these.
ldapconfig	Configures LDAP servers and queries and provides testing tools. I prefer to use the WUI, but the CLI command gives you the same abilities. We cover LDAP in Chapter 7.
logconfig	Although logs are mostly concerned with files on-ESA, I included it here because logs can be pushed to remote systems and are often critical for external monitoring. Logging is covered in Chapter 6.
dnslistconfig	Controls the lookup and timeout parameters for any external DNSBLs you've used in HAT sender groups. Keep the timeout short to avoid inbound connection delays while lookups occur. CLI-only.
smtpauthconfig	Controls how and where SMTP AUTH is used by the ESA. There are three kinds of SMTP AUTH profiles. The first mode, LDAP, ESA acts as SMTP AUTH server, allowing connected clients to provide credentials and checking those credentials by binding to a configured LDAP server. In the other two modes, the ESA uses SMTP AUTH to another MTA. In FORWARD, the ESA passes on credentials it got from a client, acting as a middleman for authentication. In OUTGOING, the ESA is the SMTP client and uses the configured username and password to authenticate itself so that it can deliver outgoing mail to another MTA.

Miscellaneous

The remaining configuration commands don't neatly fit into a single category, so I compiled them into Table 5-25. One configuration, **clusterconfig**, is not available in the CLI unless you have an active license for it. Licenses are controlled through feature keys that must be downloaded or pasted into the WUI or CLI.

Table 5-25 *Miscellaneous Configuration*

Command	Description
localeconfig	Configures the behavior of the ESA when modifying message headers and bodies, such as with add-header filter actions or footer stamping. The behavior in question is encoding and character sets, and how the ESA should handle mismatches between the message to be modified and the content being added. In general, the ESA tries to make the inserted content use the same encoding or character set as the message. This is almost always the right thing to do, but there are cases where you need to change that behavior. This character set mismatch is one of the reasons I don't recommend doing disclaimers on the ESA.

Command	Description
incomingrelayconfig	Configures the incoming relays feature, which allows an ESA to be the "second hop" in your environment, but gather some information from incoming messages so that it can reconstruct source IP information, such as reputation score. It allows the reporting engine to use the original source IP so that the senders can be displayed. Despite the capabilities, this is still a compromise as all connection control and rate limiting is unavailable. Can be useful in an evaluation, but putting the ESA behind another system is neutering its capabilities.
domainkeysconfig	Allows you to create signing keys and profiles for Domain Keys Identified Mail (DKIM) signing. DKIM is a joint standard defined in RFC 6376 and originally proposed by Yahoo! and Cisco. DKIM is a domain-level sender authentication standard that uses public-private key pairs to prove identity. We discuss sender authentication in Chapter 15, "Advanced Topics."
exceptionconfig	Configures domain exceptions, which are sender email addresses that should be excluded from the normal DNS lookups. This feature should be part of the HAT, because its use is dictated by HAT mail flow policies. You would put an address in the exception table, if you knew that the sender ordinarily wouldn't pass the envelope sender DNS verification policy that you have in place. By doing so, you tell the system to always accept mail from that sender as defined by SMTP envelope from. You can also list a sender and apply a Reject behavior. Because it operates at SMTP connection time, it is an efficient way of rejecting messages based on the sender address or the domain of the sender address.
clusterconfig	This command is only available in the CLI if a valid feature key for centralized management (CM) is installed on the system. It covers the global options for creating CM clusters and adding ESAs to clusters. It also provides status and troubleshooting tools to allow you to check for connection problems and configuration inconsistencies. Once a cluster is created, several major changes to the CLI will be apparent. We cover this in Chapter 13.

Batch Commands

We looked at a large number of commands and, for the most part, have used these commands *interactively*, meaning that we've typed the name of the command followed by **Enter**. The CLI responds either with a menu in the case of configuration or asks us for parameters in the case of commands.

Many of the CLI commands also work in *batch mode*, which is where all the arguments are supplied in a single line with the command name. A good example of this is **hoststatus <domain>** used earlier. Another good example is **ping**, the standard network tool. AsyncOS just wraps the basic UNIX command:

```
esa02.cisco.com> ping 10.60.10.1

Press Ctrl-C to stop.
PING 10.60.10.1 (10.60.10.1): 56 data bytes
64 bytes from 10.60.10.1: icmp_seq=0 ttl=255 time=0.589 ms
64 bytes from 10.60.10.1: icmp_seq=1 ttl=255 time=0.517 ms
64 bytes from 10.60.10.1: icmp_seq=2 ttl=255 time=4.514 ms
64 bytes from 10.60.10.1: icmp_seq=3 ttl=255 time=3.039 ms
```

In fact, you're probably used to seeing **ping** only in its batch mode, but **ping** also offers an interactive mode, where there's an option to pick a source interface:

```
mail.chrisporter.com> ping

Which interface do you want to send the pings from?
1. Auto
2. mgmt (192.168.42.42/24: mail.chrisporter.com)
3. primary (10.60.10.10/24: mail.chrisporter.com)
[1]> 3

Please enter the host you wish to ping.
[]> 10.60.10.1

Press Ctrl-C to stop.
PING 10.60.10.1 (10.60.10.1) from 10.60.10.10: 56 data bytes
64 bytes from 10.60.10.1: icmp_seq=0 ttl=255 time=0.578 ms
64 bytes from 10.60.10.1: icmp_seq=1 ttl=255 time=0.514 ms
```

Many of the configuration commands also offer batch modes. You can often string together command name, menu option, and all arguments rather than being prompted for each one. To see the appropriate syntax for a command, run **help <command>**:

```
esa02.cisco.com> help tophosts

tophosts [sort_key]

    Display the top hosts by queue size.

    sort_key - Optional value, one of "active_rcpts", "concurrency",
               "rcpts_sent", "soft_bounces", "hard_bounces".
               Default is active_rcpts.
```

If you see a response from a command like this:

```
esa02.cisco.com> snmpconfig setup
The command "snmpconfig" does not take any arguments!
```

The batch commands aren't implemented or aren't applicable for that feature, and they must be used interactively.

Why would you want to use batch commands? For some commands, it's natural, and you're probably used to using them in batch mode, like **traceroute** and **telnet**. In fact, you're likely to forget that these commands also have interactive modes. For other commands, the shortcut offered by batch commands makes for easier work when you have multiple entries to make. For example, if you have email aliases to add to **aliasconfig**, this will do it in a single line:

```
esa02.cisco.com> aliasconfig new global chris@cisco.com chriport@cisco.com
```

That naturally points to the most powerful reason to use batch commands: automating configuration or monitoring tasks on the ESA through scripts running on another server. We explore that topic in Chapter 9, "Automating Tasks."

Hidden/Undocumented Commands

Over the course of its development, AsyncOS has occasionally implemented new features in the CLI-only, and left out of the documentation. This is not to say that they don't work, or that they are not being QA'd by Cisco, but they are seldom used by customers. They don't appear in the help, aren't listed in the documentation, and cannot be *Tab-complete* the way other commands can be. There are a few reasons that commands are implemented in this way:

- **Emergency or last-minute inclusion:** Some features were needed specifically by certain customers or market segments or were added to a release near the end of the development cycle. Because of time constraint, documentation was not produced, and WUI pages could not be designed or developed in time for the release. This situation only lasts for a release or two and then transitions to fully documented and WUI-enabled features.
- **Oversight:** Oops! Cisco forgot to get this command included in the Tab-completion list or documentation wasn't ready for the release. Usually corrected within the next point release, so you won't see many of these.
- **They offer advanced functionality:** These expert commands aren't documented because they cover advanced functionality. These are wrappers around underlying UNIX commands. They are there for the convenience of expert users, but documenting them is beyond the scope of the ESA documentation. Most of these over the years, like **tcpdump** and **netstat**, have transitioned to documented AsyncOS commands or even entire new features, like **packetcapture**, which replaces **tcpdump**.

- **They don't have wide appeal:** Some of the hidden CLI commands have use only within a specific kind of environment, or only with specific back-end groupware, mailstore, or LDAP server.
- **They duplicate existing functionality:** In some cases, a CLI table or command has been effectively replaced by other features. The legacy command is still supported for backwards compatibility.
- **They are simply an alias for another command:** These hidden commands are just another name for a documented command. **w** (for **who**) and **ifconfig** (for **interfaceconfig**) are good examples.
- **They're dangerous:** Some commands are intentionally hidden because their use is destructive. These are commands that reset configurations, for example.

Because of these reasons, it's important that you are aware of the risks associated with hidden or undocumented commands. They do go through a QA process, but because they're hidden, get very little use in production by customers. They're not supported by Cisco TAC, which means that if you run into an issue with them, you may not be able to get help.

That being said, some of these are extremely useful, and I use them regularly. Because the list of hidden commands continually shrinks as Cisco provides full documentation and support, I expect that these commands will not be hidden in future releases. Table 5-26 describes the hidden commands.

Table 5-26 *AsyncOS Hidden Commands*

Command	Description
dig	A wrapper around the domain information groper, a tool for querying DNS. On most Linux distributions, dig has become the de-facto replacement for nslookup, because the syntax is friendlier. Provides more information than nslookup.
sievechar	A sieve character, named after the Sieve mail-filtering language, is a delimiter that can appear in email addresses, typically a + character, and is typically used to separate the actual username from some other string identifier, such as folder name. The string after the sieve character is processed by the mail store or other system and is not significant to the ESA. An example is chriport+alerts@cisco.com. Assuming my groupware account had a folder called alerts, and supported sieve-sorting, it would put all messages addressed that way into that folder. Common in academic organizations, but almost no corporate mail systems support such features. The ESA needs to know what character is in use for the delimiter in order to be able to validate the recipient address. Because chriport+alerts@cisco.com won't appear in a directory, the ESA uses the sieve character to split the address and validate only chriport@cisco.com.

Command	Description
injectorconfig	An alias for **listenerconfig**, left over from the days when listeners were called injectors.
secondaryconfig	Allows an ESA to export its reporting and tracking data to a second SMA. Normally, only a single SMA is supported in ESA environments: Each ESA can only export data to one SMA. For redundancy, this command forces the ESA to record data in a second directory so that a secondary SMA can also retrieve the data. As of the release of AsyncOS 7.2 for SMA in November 2010, however, a proper backup/restore capability has been added to the SMA. I recommend using the backup features rather than secondaryconfig.
redirectrecipients	As you might guess, forces the ESA to send messages to another host. It affects all messages on the ESA, so you would only use this if you were decommissioning an ESA and needed to empty all the queues. The same thing can be accomplished using smtproutes to change destination, followed by delivernow.
ipcheck	Displays hardware, firmware, and software details of the ESA.
showchanges	Shows configuration changes that have been made but not committed; essentially a "pending changes" display. However, the list of changes is not displayed in the XML configuration format, but a nested tree format that may be difficult to understand.
snmptrap	Forces the ESA to generate an SNMP trap to the configured trap targets. You can generate any of the 13 different trap types, and the relevant trap object and value. Useful for testing SNMP and the target Network Management System.
setrcptsperdelivery	Sets the maximum number of recipients the ESA will attempt in a single SMTP connection. Global setting that applies to all connections. This command is completely replaced by enhancements to the Destination Controls table found in destconfig.
tarpit	Controls behavior of the ESA when the system reaches overload state and allows you to specify work queue threshold. When the ESA starts running out of resources, like RAM and disk, because it can't deliver all of its mail, it protects itself by slowing, and eventually stopping, incoming connections. The thresholds for this are controlled here, although you should really never change these values. The other option is to pause and resume connection acceptance when the work queue reaches user-defined thresholds. Use this with caution, because it is natural for an ESA to use the work queue to temporarily buffer incoming messages. If you set this low, you end up with a "flapping" state of connections on the ESA.

Summary

The ESA's CLI is a powerful tool for administration that provides more than just an alternative to the WUI for configuration. CLI commands also allow you to examine the operational status of the ESA, view performance and delivery statistics, search logs, test connections, and make DNS lookups. Knowing how to use the CLI is a requirement for effective administration. You'll find it convenient to access the CLI via an SSH client that supports public key authentication, and we discussed how to set that up.

In this chapter, we've covered all of the ESA commands, documented or otherwise, and provided some recommendations on their use. In the next chapter, we'll discuss a few other means of accessing reporting data and operational statistics.

Chapter 6

Additional Management Services

In this chapter, you will learn the following:

- Reporting and monitoring of ESAs with SNMP
- Managing files on the ESA with FTP and SCP
- Understanding ESA logging

The Need for Additional Protocol Support

We've seen that the primary administrative interfaces to the Email Security Appliance (ESA) are the web user interface (WUI) and the command-line interface (CLI). These are perfect for human administrators, because they provide an easy to use and complete interface to all aspects of management and reporting. For automated systems, they're not always ideal, and integration with third-party products requires other options. Other peripheral protocols are available on the ESA for monitoring the systems, reporting on data, and manipulating configuration and data files.

This chapter starts with using Simple Network Management Protocol (SNMP) to integrate the ESA into external network management tools and what you should monitor on production ESAs. For configuring and managing the system, using File Transfer Protocol (FTP) or secure copy (SCP) to transfer files to and from the ESA is critical, so we look at the ESA filesystem.

Logging is critical to all aspects of product operation and troubleshooting, and an email administrator must be able to read and understand the logs that the ESA can record. The IronPort Text Mail logs are especially critical in this regard, so this chapter covers that format in depth.

Simple Network Management Protocol (SNMP)

SNMP is a widespread industry-standard protocol for monitoring and managing network devices. The protocol specifies how a managed network device exposes data in variables and defines the way that these variables are organized and queried. The variables exposed by a device are defined, along with metadata, in a hierarchy called a Management Information Base (MIB). Network Management Software (NMS) on a separate server is used to query a managed device, like an ESA. SNMP also supports notifications called *traps* from managed device to an NMS.

An SNMP MIB is a tree structure, and the custom MIB for the ESA has its root nodes in the RFC defined SNMPv2-SMI MIB. This tree structure somewhat resembles Domain Name System (DNS) and, like DNS, the root-level portions are Internet standards, but with leaf nodes controlled by the organization. Also like DNS, the data is entirely numerical, but with a name-to-number mapping mechanism.

Cisco publishes MIBs for all ESA platforms in two parts. The filenames as supplied by Cisco are **IRONPORT-SMI.txt** and **ASYNCOS-MAIL-MIB.txt**. The **IRONPORT-SMI.txt** file defines the top-level enterprise specific identifiers. **ASYNCOS-MAIL-MIB.txt** defines the specific variables and traps for the ESA.

Note SNMP MIBs have different revision numbers, and the ESA MIB has changed over time as SNMP capabilities expanded. You can always download the latest SNMP MIBs from the Cisco IronPort support website or from the ESA appliance filesystem in the /configuration directory.

The ESA's SNMP attributes are read-only; there is no support for changing configuration values via SNMP.

Enabling SNMP

SNMP is disabled on the ESA by default and must be enabled and set up in the CLI using the **snmpconfig** command. If SNMP hasn't been configured, the only option available will be SETUP.

The setup on the ESA side is straightforward. You must choose a local IP interface to service requests, a v3 passphrase, a trap target and community string, and then decide which traps should be enabled. You must also decide whether to support SNMP v1/v2c requests, and the answer to that depends on compatibility with your NMS and some important topics in SNMP security.

You should also accurately enter the system location and contact information. You may know what this system is and where it's installed, but entering this correctly allows others in your organization to contact the right folks when their NMS starts generating alerts because of your ESA.

SNMP Security

SNMP as a protocol is somewhat notorious for its security problems. Older versions don't encrypt credentials and, in fact, often don't require credentials at all. For that reason, I recommend using SNMPv3 only, which support cryptographic security and authentication.

Because so many NMS support SNMPv2c, support is provided in the ESA for that version. In an attempt to improve security, you must define the subnets that will be allowed to access the ESA SNMP daemon and which ESA IP the daemon will listen on. You should make this as restrictive as possible.

SNMPv3 requires that you enter a passphrase that any SNMP management system must use to read the ESA variables.

Enterprise MIBs

For your NMS to recognize the variables and traps that the ESA supports through SNMP, you must define them by importing the Cisco IronPort ESA MIB definition files. The MIB defines the variables and values, and provides human-readable descriptions for them; the NMS uses this hierarchy to monitor and display the values. These files are supplied as plain text and are available on the ESA filesystem or by download from Cisco IronPort support. There are two files. The first, IRONPORT-SMI.txt, defines the top-level enterprise and appliance object identifiers (OID). The second, ASYNCOS-MAIL-MIB.txt, defines all the variables for the ESA. As of this writing, the ESA still uses the IronPort enterprise identifier and not the Cisco identifier, and the MIBs are not published as part of any Cisco MIB package.

The MIB definition files are intended for human readability, too, and can be viewed in any text editor. The MIB provides a name-to-number mapping so that your NMS can display the relevant variable and trap names. The ESA MIB uses the enterprise identifier of 15497 under the global SNMPv2-SMI.enterprises root. Beneath that root, all the available objects and traps fall into the hierarchy. For example, the OID

```
1.3.6.1.4.1.15497.1.1.1.5.0
```

represents the object from the ASYNCOS-MAIL-MIB for queueAvailabilityStatus, an indicator of whether the ESA's mail queues are full. It has possible values of queueSpaceAvailable(1), queueSpaceShortage(2), or queueFull(3). This OID can be broken down into its components, as shown in Figure 6-1.

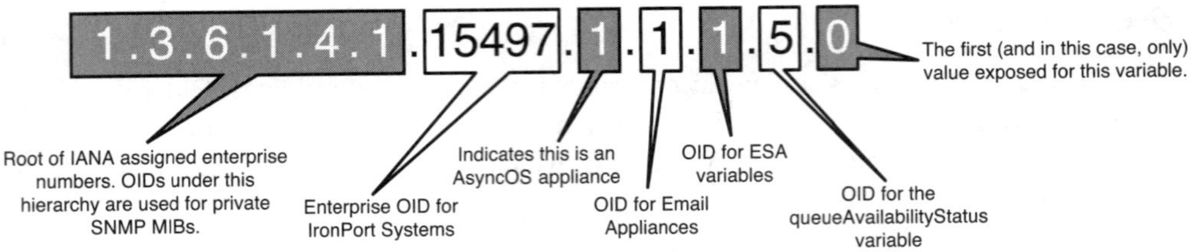

Figure 6-1 *Breakdown of Enterprise OID for Queue Availability Status*

Other objects, like powerSupplyTable, have a deeper hierarchy, which enumerates the table that defines all the power supplies and each of their possible states. The good news is that modern NMS hide this complexity, exposing easily readable variables like percentMemoryUtilization with a description of **Percent Memory Utilization** and a value range of 0 to 100.

Other MIBs

In addition to the enterprise-specific MIB for the ESA, the ESA supports many other MIBs, defined in other RFCs, such as 1213, 1907, and 4293. Although the ESA supports these standard MIBs, Cisco does not supply a MIB definition file for it. Your NMS should already have the definitions for these MIBs, but you can also download the MIBs from many Internet sources. These other MIBs define only variables and no traps.

If you use your NMS to poll the SNMP daemon on the ESA, you should see a series of variables rooted at the OID of:

```
1.3.6.1.2.1
```

If your NMS recognizes the name mappings for these OIDs, you may see variables such as:

```
SNMPv2-MIB::sysDescr.0
RFC1213-MIB::ipRouteDest.0.0.0.0
IF-MIB::ifNumber.0
```

The collected set of variables here cover system information, physical interfaces, and attributes and counters for IP, UDP, TCP, and SNMP. Table 6-1 provides a brief description of the top-level variable groups.

Table 6-1 *SNMP MIB-II Variable Groups Supported by ESA*

SNMP MIB Name	Description
SNMPv2-MIB	Collects system-level variables, like description, location, and uptime. Also lists the MIBs that this device exposes.
IF-MIB	Enumeration of physical network interfaces.
IP-MIB	IP networking variables and statistics. Enumerates the ESA's IP addresses, netmasks, and broadcast addresses. Stats include packets sent and received, discards, and fragmentation.

SNMP MIB Name	Description
TCP-MIB	Information on active and recent TCP connections and ports. Includes an enumeration of all TCP ports the ESA is listening on, all open TCP connections and their local and remote IP addresses, and connection counters and errors. Similar to information you can obtain from the netstat CLI command.
UDP-MIB	Like the TCP MIB, but enumerates UDP ports and connections.
RFC1213-MIB	Miscellaneous network variables. On ESA, this covers network routes, protocols, and metrics. Because the ESA supports only static routing, the data enumerated here should match the ESA's configured routes table.

Monitoring Recommendations

Monitoring the health of the ESAs in your environment is a critical part of maintaining reliable email delivery. Some of the traps should be acted on immediately in all cases; others need to be investigated if they occur repeatedly in a short time or periodically over a longer time. Most of the variables require that you establish a *baseline* value range and act when the value of that variable exceeds the baseline dramatically.

The most important items to monitor are the traps. SNMP traps include information that is available in the email alerts, but in a situation where email alerts are undeliverable, the SNMP traps provide an alternate path of notification. The available traps should be acted on:

- **keyExpiration:** Key expiration notices for any active feature should be investigated. A key expiration means that a security scanning engine, or even email receiving, will be halted.
- **RAIDStatusChange, fanFailure, highTemperature, powerSupplyStatusChange:** These four traps indicate a hardware problem and should be investigated immediately. The RAID and power supply traps may not indicate an immediate problem, but should be examined to determine what the current hardware state is. In the event of hardware failure, you need to contact Cisco TAC for replacement.
- **resourceConservationMode:** Resource Conservation is a state the ESA enters when it is running low on main memory. The most common cause of high memory usage is large amounts of undelivered mail queued on the system. Resource conservation is serious—by default, this state is only reached at 75% of memory utilization, when an ESA typically has millions of undelivered messages. It warrants an immediate investigation as to why messages aren't being delivered. The variables resourceConservationReason and memoryAvailabilityStatus are related.
- **connectivityFailure and updateFailure:** connectivityFailure indicates that a test that the ESA uses to connect to an Internet URL (downloads.ironport.com as of this

writing) has failed. This could mean that the ESA will be unable to download new security rule updates and that causes the ESA to issue the updateFailure trap.

Aside from the traps, these variables should be an important part of your monitoring strategy:

- **queueAvailabilityStatus:** A value in this variable other than queueSpaceAvailable could potentially be a problem. The ESA mail queues are very large, and a status that indicates a space shortage or a queue full state means your ESA likely has millions of messages stored on it, undelivered.
- **PerCentQueueUtilization:** Related to queue availability, this variable tells you exactly what percentage of queue disk space is used. In normal conditions, this should be a small percentage (under 10% in most cases).
- **powerSupplyRedundancy:** There are several SNMP variables related to the electrical power supplies in the appliance chassis and their status, but this one is most critical. It indicates simply whether the appliance has power redundancy or not. On the 2U ESA models, each of the two power supplies can power the entire appliance, but when one is out, you have a single point of failure.
- **WorkQueueMessages:** The number of messages in the queue waiting to be processed by the security or content filtering engines. Although it's normal during daily operation to have some messages in the work queue, having a consistent non-zero value indicates that the ESA is overburdened. You shouldn't worry much about this unless it's over a few hundred messages, and even then, it should only cause concern if it stays high.
- **raidTable:** The RAID table is a list of RAID entries that describe the physical disks in the ESA and their status. These variables provide you with the condition of the redundant storage, either hardware RAID (in the 2U enterprise appliances) or software RAID (in the 1U appliances). Any status other than driveHealthy (1) should be investigated. You'll receive email alerts and a trap from the ESA should any drive's condition change, but it's also wise to monitor the current status.

For an NMS that maintains long-term records of variable values, it makes sense to include all the ESA variables, for long-term trending purposes. For example, mailTransferThreads records the number of active SMTP threads on the system. There's no particular value that would necessarily indicate a problem, but both short-term and long-term trends can help you understand the load on the appliances. Likewise, an individual reading from pendingDNSRequests will not be terribly revealing, but the long-term ups and downs can be.

PerCentCPUUtilization, perCentMemoryUtilization, and perCentDiskIOUtilization also fall into this recommendation: Monitor these to establish baselines, and then alert on sustained values 50% higher than baseline average. However, because these are percentages expressed as integers from 0–100, any consistent reading above 90 should be of concern. Memory utilization is straightforward in this concern: High usage indicates high load and undeliverable messages.

CPU and Disk I/O readings are not as straightforward. First, the CPU value is calculated as a composite of the various processes across all available CPU cores to estimate a total CPU usage percentage. This works reasonably well on a fully burdened ESA running many different security services that use all the available CPU cores. On systems with less running, the extra cores won't ever be used but will be reported as idle.

Disk I/O is calculated as ratio of current IOPS (operations per second) to the maximum IOPS, but the maximum is determined by a "high water mark" experienced by the ESA rather than a fixed maximum. For instance, if the ESA has seen 400 IOPS at peak traffic, and current load is 300 IOPS, this gauge will show 75% even though the appliance might in the future see 1000 IOPS. Over time, the maximum high water mark will attain something like the real hardware maximum, so this gauge becomes more useful over time.

For the Internet standard MIBs that the ESA supports, like IP-MIB and TCP-MIB, there's not a compelling reason to monitor the exposed variables. These are provided for consistency with other TCP/IP network devices and for base compatibility with NMS. If your organization typically monitors server and appliance TCP/IP networking stats via NMS, the ESA will fit right in.

Working with the ESA Filesystem

The ESA naturally has hard drives and a disk filesystem for storing data like email queues. In the appliance form factor, however, access to that filesystem is limited to a specific directory and its subdirectories. That access is provided for transferring configuration and diagnostic files to and from the system and for storing log files. What is available of the ESA filesystem can be accessed through FTP or SCP, although you can only browse the directory structure with FTP.

A typical ESA top-level folder list looks something like Example 6-1.

Example 6-1 *ESA Top-Level FTP Listing*

```
drwxrwx---   5 root     config    3584 Oct 26 08:22 configuration
drwxrwx---   2 root     log        512 Oct 20 10:19 authentication
drwxrwx---   2 root     log        512 Oct 26 08:22 system_logs
drwxrwx---   2 root     log        512 Oct 31 03:39 cli_logs
drwxrwx---   2 root     log        512 Oct 26 08:22 ftpd_logs
drwxrwx---   2 root     log        512 Oct 26 08:22 sntpd_logs
drwxrwx---   2 root     log        512 Oct 26 08:22 trackerd_logs
drwxrwx---   2 root     log    1688576 Nov  1 11:57 slbl_db
drwxrwx---   2 root     log        512 Oct 26 08:22 updater_logs
drwxrwx---   2 root     log        512 Nov  1 00:33 reportd_logs
drwxrwx---   2 root     log        512 Oct 26 08:22 gui_logs
drwxrwx---   2 root     log        512 Oct 26 08:23 reportqueryd_logs
```

```
drwxrwx---   2 root     log        512 Oct 26 08:22 euq_logs
drwxrwx---   2 root     log        512 Oct 26 08:22 euqgui_logs
drwxrwx---   2 root     log       1024 Oct 30 13:22 mail_logs
drwxrwx---   2 root     log        512 Oct 26 08:23 status
drwxrwx---   2 root     log        512 Aug 14  2009 asarchive
drwxrwx---   2 root     log        512 Oct 26 08:23 bounces
drwxrwx---   2 root     log        512 Oct 26 08:23 error_logs
drwxrwx---   2 root     log       1024 Oct 26 08:23 avarchive
drwxrwx---   2 root     log       1024 Oct 26 08:23 scanning
drwxrwx---   2 root     log        512 Oct 26 08:23 antispam
drwxrwx---   2 root     log        512 Oct 29 10:56 antivirus
drwxrwx---   2 root     log        512 Nov  1 03:57 encryption
drwxr-xr-x   6 root     log        512 Aug 14  2009 periodic_reports
drwxrwx---   2 root     log        512 Nov  1 09:44 mbox drwxrwx---   3 root
log        512 Aug 14  2009 export
drwxrwx---   2 root     log        512 Oct 26 08:22 snmp_logs
drwxrwx---   2 root     log        512 Oct 26 08:23 ldap
drwxr-xr-x   3 root     log        512 Aug 14  2009 reporting
drwxrwx---   2 root     log        512 Oct  2  2009 diagnostic
drwxrwx---   2 root     log        512 May  3  2010 slbld_logs
drwxrwx---   2 root     log        512 May  3  2010 slbl_isq_db
drwxrwx---   2 root     log        512 Oct 26 08:22 authlogs
drwxrwx---   2 root     log        512 Nov  1 08:17 ConfigHistory
drwxrwx---   2 root     log        512 Oct 13 15:03 injection
```

Almost every folder in this list is for logging, which is discussed in the next section. A folder is created for every log subscription, and each log subscription has one or more files for the actual log. A typical FTP listing of a log directory looks like this:

```
-rw-rw----   2 root     log      4956202 Nov  1 12:11 mail.current
-rw-rw----   2 root     log      4956202 Nov  1 12:11 mail.@20111030T132219.c
-rw-rw----   1 root     log     10481862 Oct 18 02:55 mail.@20111013T002910.s
-rw-rw----   1 root     log      8853447 Oct 26 08:16 mail.@20111022T144551.s
-rw-rw----   1 root     log     10480348 Oct 30 13:22 mail.@20111026T082340.s
```

The **.s** file extension indicates a stored log file, **.c** indicates the current open log file, and **.current** is an alias for the current open log file. You can download and even delete the **.s** extension files at any time, but be aware that the **.c** and **.current** files are open and their contents will change over time. If you delete the currently open log, you won't be able to use tail or grep in the CLI until the log is recreated with an automatic or manual rollover. In other words, don't delete the **.c** or **.current** files.

The other folders are used to store data that needs to be transferred to and from the system:

- **configuration:** Contains all configuration file and table exports, and it's the location where you need to place files for import. When the ESA, WUI, or CLI refers to a filename to import or export, it is expected to be in this directory.
- **captures:** Packet capture files from the WUI or tcpdump utility available in the CLI **diagnostic** command are stored here. There will be one capture file, with extension **.cap**, for each capture session you record.
- **reporting:** Data for the reporting system that is being transferred from the ESA to an SMA for centralized reporting. Only used if you have an SMA that is configured to pull data from this ESA.
- **export:** Data for message tracking that is being transferred from ESA to SMA for centralized tracking. Only used if you have an SMA that is configured to pull data from this ESA.
- **slbl_db:** Storage for the spam quarantine's Safelist/Blocklist feature. Typically used only on the SMA. If you're using this feature on ESA, it's better to do backup and restore through the WUI Configuration File page on the System Administration menu.
- **diagnostic:** Storage for some types of diagnostic data that is gathered by tools from the **diagnostic** CLI command. These tools can affect mail operations, so you normally won't run them without direction from Cisco support.

Transferring files from the ESA works like it does with any other file server. To transfer data from the ESA to a local workstation using FTP, use the commands **GET** or **MGET** in a command-line FTP client, or drag and drop files in a GUI FTP client. For SCP, you need to know the path of the folder where you're transferring data to or from. The exposed ESA filesystem starts at root, indicated by /, so a transfer from the configuration folder can be done with this **scp** command:

```
scp admin@esa02.cisco.com:/configuration/hat.txt /usr/data/hat.txt
```

Transferring log files is similar—you must know the folder name, which matches the log subscription name:

```
scp admin@esa02.cisco.com:/mail_logs/*.s .
```

Note Many GUI SCP clients, like winscp, won't work with the ESA filesystem, because they depend on an SSH shell being available on the remote filesystem, and ESA does not expose the filesystem via the SSH CLI. Some GUI clients that claim to support scp in reality only support SFTP, which the ESA does not provide.

ESA Logging

The ESA has extensive logging capabilities. Logs are organized into log subscriptions, which encapsulate both the type of information logged (the log type), the level of detail, and the storage and rollover settings. It's possible to have multiple log subscriptions of the same type, recording different levels of detail, or having one subscription store logs locally and another transfer to a remote system.

The ESA ships by default with 20 to 23 active log subscriptions, depending on which features are enabled by the System Setup Wizard.

ESA Subsystem Logs

All the various subsystems of the ESA have their own log, akin to a UNIX-style daemon log. These are chiefly for troubleshooting and debugging. You would normally have no reason to transfer or permanently store these logs, or even to look at them day to day. If a component is failing, though, these logs provide valuable troubleshooting information.

Table 6-2 lists the subsystem logs.

Table 6-2 *ESA Subsystem Logs*

Log Format Name	Description
NTP logs	Network time daemon. See the ntpconfig command or the time page under the System Administration menu.
FTP server logs	FTP daemon. Records activity of both connections in and out of the ESA via FTP.
SNMP logs	SNMP daemon. Records connections in and out of the SNMP daemon; only used if you have SNMP enabled.
Reporting logs	Activities of the reporting system, typically the writing and purging of data intervals.
Reporting query logs	Any reporting queries are listed here; activity in this log is generated when you use any of the reporting pages in the Monitor menu of the WUI.
Tracking logs	Events related to the message tracking data being imported. In most organizations, the message tracking features should be run on the SMA, not on the ESA.
Updater logs	Records activities of all the security engine updates: anti-spam rules, outbreak rules, and antivirus signatures.
Encryption logs	Message encryption activity (using the envelope encryption features) is recorded here chiefly for debugging by Cisco personnel should errors occur. Although it's easy to interpret some of the messages, many will refer to internal engine details and won't be useful for your troubleshooting.

The updater logs warrant further attention as they record all the rule updates for the security engines and the engines themselves. Context-Adaptive Scanning Engine (CASE) is the name for the underlying scanning software for IPAS and Outbreak Filters, so you'll see a lot of messages referring to CASE actions. If you're using VOF or OF, you'll also see a long list of current outbreak rules and their plain-text descriptions. If any updates fail, you'll see exactly which engine and component caused the failure.

Administrative and Auditing Logs

Components of the appliance software that deal with administrative interfaces like CLI and WUI have their own logs. These logs typically record who's logged in and what actions they've taken in the CLI or WUI.

The important available administrative logs are listed in Table 6-3.

Table 6-3 *Administrative Log Types*

Log Format Name	Description
CLI audit logs	A keystroke logger of all CLI sessions that includes a record of username, date, time, and all commands issued.
HTTP logs	A log for the HTTP WUI web server. Not really an audit log, but it records the page requests from the browser of a logged in user, so it can be revealing of who was logged in and when.
Spam quarantine GUI logs	User and daemon activity for the spam quarantine user interface. Will only have data recorded if you've enabled and are using the spam quarantine on ESA. For most environments, the spam quarantine is better suited to running on the SMA.
Configuration history logs	This log records committed changes that are made to the ESA configuration.
Authentication logs	Records all login activity, both by administrative users and system users like the SMA (M-series daemon).

From this list, it's worth discussing the configuration history logs, which are new in AsyncOS 7.5, but not enabled by default. When enabled, this log subscription records a copy of the XML configuration file for the appliance whenever you commit a configuration change. The ESA also attempts to describe the changes that were made during this commit. Of course, it can't read your mind, but it can indicate which sections of the configuration were changed. It also records the commit comment (which you always enter accurately, every time, correct?), the current time, and the user doing the commit. Subsequent commits record new configuration XML concatenated until the log file reaches its rollover point.

Unlike most other log types, you cannot search or display the configuration history log. You must transfer it to a local workstation to read the configuration data. By opening the log and copying a complete XML configuration section, you can restore the ESA to an earlier configuration state.

Email Activity Logs

The IronPort Text Mail logs format is the primary log for all email activity. Every event that occurs in the processing of SMTP connections and messages is recorded here. In addition to the main email logs, many other log types record email activity (see Table 6-4).

Not all these logs are stored in plain text, but the ones that are can be searched or displayed in the CLI using **grep**, **findevent**, or **tail** commands.

Table 6-4 *Email Activity Logs*

Log Format Name	Description
IronPort text mail logs	The primary mail activity log where all inbound and outbound connections, and all accepted messages, are recorded. Even rejected connections and rate limited recipients are recorded. When you need to troubleshoot message activity beyond the information in the WUI or CLI, this is the first place you should turn. Reading the text mail logs is critical for effective administration of ESAs.
Anti-spam logs	Records the scanning verdicts for the anti-spam engine on messages, and other activities like rules downloads and restarts.
Antivirus logs	Records the scanning verdicts for the antivirus engines, and other engine activity, like signature downloads.
Delivery logs	The delivery logs record each email message in a single line summary. It sounds extremely useful, but it's not recorded in plain text, so it can't be searched natively. These logs must be downloaded from the ESA and converted from their compressed binary format to CSV or XML text formats, using tools you can download from Cisco.com.
Bounce logs	Records only bounce activity—both soft bounces (as a result of 4yz SMTP responses) and hard bounces (a result of 5yz SMTP responses).
Qmail format logs	Only used if you have a listener that accepts connections in the QMQP protocol. This is not a widely adopted protocol, so it's unlikely you would ever use it.

Because the text mail logs are such an important troubleshooting tool, we examine them in a later section.

Debugging Logs

Numerous logs are dedicated to troubleshooting configuration or message traffic. These aren't solely intended for Cisco; these are intended as customer tools to investigate and resolve mail traffic, delivery, or directory-lookup problems. The list is shown in Table 6-5.

Table 6-5 *Debugging Log Types*

Log Format Name	Description
Domain debug	Record all parts of the SMTP conversation to a specific destination. Everything is recorded, including every byte of the message data.
Injection debug	Injection debugs are the reverse of the domain debug log—they record the verbatim SMTP conversation for all mail from a specific source. Again, like domain debug, every byte of the message is recorded.
LDAP debug	Details of all LDAP queries composed and sent to the LDAP servers and a record of the replies. Extremely useful when first setting up LDAP or whenever trouble arises. This is covered in detail in Chapter 8, "Security Filtering."
SMTP conversation logs	This log provides a verbatim recording of the SMTP conversation for all email up to the DATA command. Useful for troubleshooting, and because running this log is not a performance problem, you can even leave it running continually.
Status logs	Writes a large number of counters and gauges every minute, corresponding to the values seen in the CLI status command.

The ones that warrant real attention in the list are the injection debug and delivery debug logs. Both provide the same information: verbatim record of the entirety of an SMTP conversation. Injection debug records messages on inbound connections, where ESA is the server. You must specify the remote sending IP addresses that you want to record. Domain debug records the details of outbound connections, where ESA is the client. You must specify the destination domains to record.

Both record a limited number of sessions, for good reason. This detail recording can cause performance problems by keeping the CPU and disk very busy, so the ESA only records for a limited number of connections, based on source or destination, and only records a small number of sessions.

Even with a small number of sessions, the injection debug and domain debug logs are extremely revealing for certain email troubleshooting tasks. Whenever I'm dealing with a problem with delivery to a specific destination or accepting messages from a specific source, and the mail logs don't reveal enough information, these logs are the first tool I turn to. They're also extremely useful for investigating issues with message or MIME attachment corruption. If you suspect the ESA is corrupting a message, these debug logs are the right place to turn, because they allow you to compare what's being accepted with what's being delivered.

Another situation that warrants these debug logs—both types—is when you want to see the results of message modification on the ESA itself. For example, when you're using the ESA disclaimer feature to add a header or a footer to a message, and something doesn't look right, you can investigate the before and after with a combination of these two logs.

Here's the steps to take to set up a before-and-after debug session:

1. Create an injection debug log to record the incoming message. Specify the source IP where you'll be injecting the message and set the log to record a few sessions. I used 10.60.10.0/24, which includes a lab server capable of telnet to the ESA.
2. Create a domain debug log for the destination domain. In this case, I used cisco.com as the destination domain.
3. Commit the changes: These logs don't record data until you commit.

After both logs are running, send a test message that matches your criteria, and then look at the logs. You can transfer the logs files from the ESA and open them in a text editor, but I just used the CLI **tail** command to view them directly.

Here is the relevant injection debug output, as the message is received:

```
Tue Sep 27 17:05:20 2011 Info: 1026671 Rcvd from '10.60.10.134': 'Message-ID:
<4E823A8F.1010405@chrisporter.com>\r\nDate: Tue, 27 Sep 2011 17:05:19 -0400\r\
nFrom: Chris Porter <cporter@chrisporter.com>\r\nUser-Agent: Mozilla/5.0
(Macintosh; Intel Mac OS X 10.6; rv:6.0.2) Gecko/20110902 Thunderbird/6.0.2\r\
nMIME-Version: 1.0\r\nTo: Chris Porter <chriport@cisco.com>\r\nSubject:
testing\r\nContent-Type: text/plain; charset=ISO-8859-1; format=flowed\r\nCon-
tent-Transfer-Encoding: 7bit\r\n\r\nSending a test message...\r\n\r\nchris\r\n\
r\n'
```

Here is the relevant domain debug output, as the message is delivered:

```
Tue Sep 27 17:05:21 2011 Info: 172412 Sent: 'from mailhost.chrisporter.com(HELO
[10.60.10.134]) ([10.60.10.134])\r\n  by mail.chrisporter.com with ESMTP/TLS/DHE-
RSA-CAMELLIA256-SHA; 27 Sep 2011 17:05:20 -0400\r\nMessage-ID: <4E823A8F.1010405@
chrisporter.com>\r\nDate: Tue, 27 Sep 2011 17:05:19 -0400\r\nFrom: Chris Porter
<cporter@chrisporter.com>\r\nUser-Agent: Mozilla/5.0 (Macintosh; Intel Mac OS
X 10.6; rv:6.0.2) Gecko/20110902 Thunderbird/6.0.2\r\nMIME-Version: 1.0\r\nTo:
Chris Porter <chriport@cisco.com>\r\nSubject: testing\r\nContent-Type: text/
plain; charset="iso-8859-1"; format="flowed"\r\nContent-Transfer-Encoding:
quoted-printable\r\n\r\Sending a test message...\r\n\r\nchris\r\n\r\n--\r\nThis
message was sent via Cisco IronPort ESA\r\n\r\n'
```

In this case, the relevant difference is the addition of the text at the bottom of the message. You can see that the message body content delivered by the ESA is identical to that received, plus the addition of the footer.

You'll have a challenge with this approach in a groupware environment, such as Exchange or Notes; there are too many messages coming from a single server to get lucky to catch your test message before the log exceeds the session count. In those cases, I resort to manual telnet or a mail user agent (MUA), like Mozilla Thunderbird, that can send directly to an SMTP server.

Archive Logs

Archive logs really aren't logs at all, in the sense that they don't record system or mail activity. These log types record entire messages, including all headers and attachments. It's a verbatim byte copy of the messages on the ESA. However, these archive files share their storage, transfer, and rollover characteristics with logs, so we discuss them here.

The ESA archive logs are recorded in plain text in a format customarily called mbox or mailbox format, after the typical personal mailbox format on many UNIX operating systems. This format can be parsed by many different text console and GUI MUAs, or even a plain-text editor. Mozilla Thunderbird is a free MUA that can handle these files. The archive is essentially just a plain-text concatenation of the RFC 2822 Internet Message format, with a delimiter at the beginning of each message consisting of the word **From** followed by a space.

An archive log subscription is created for the anti-spam and antivirus engines by default on a new ESA. The description and use of these archives is detailed in Table 6-6.

Table 6-6 *Standard ESA Archive Types*

Log Format Name	Description
Anti-Spam archive	Stores the full content of messages when you choose to archive messages in the Advanced section of the anti-spam verdict settings.
Antivirus archive	Stores the full content of messages when you choose the Archive Original Message under each antivirus verdict setting.

In addition, whenever you use the message filter action *archive*, a new log subscription is created to store messages, using the name passed into the archive action. For example, the content filter

```
archive_to_cisco:
if (rcpt-to == "@cisco\\.com$") {
   archive ("cisco");
}
```

creates a log subscription called "cisco" written to a directory on the ESA of /cisco, and which uses a base filename of **cisco.mbox**. The ESA will create the log directory and files as soon as you commit the new filter. You can transfer, **grep** search, or **tail** this log data as you would any other log type.

Note Archive log subscriptions created by the archive filter action can be viewed and transferred as other log types are, but you can't manage them the same way. If you look, you'll find that these log subscriptions are not available in the WUI log subscriptions page or via the **logconfig** CLI command.

In fact, they're managed through the filters CLI command in the subcommand **logconfig**. You have all the same options that you would have for other log subscriptions, except that syslog is not available for any archive log type.

Archives are most useful for troubleshooting message receipt or delivery issues or to see the raw message data. You can use these archive files to restore or redeliver messages, but there's no automatic way to do so. To restore an archived message, you need to download the relevant archive log file and use a text editor or MUA to extract the message of interest, and a MUA to redeliver the message. For this reason, and because of the limited storage available on the ESA, this feature is not a general-purpose message-archiving solution. It is a fantastic troubleshooting tool, however, and if you encounter a reproducible message issue, create a filter and record an archive copy.

Creating a Log Subscription

Creating a log subscription is simple. You can create a subscription in the WUI in the Log Subscriptions page of the System Administration menu.

You can delete a log subscription from the same WUI page. Deleting a subscription stops the log from being recorded, effective as soon as the change is committed, but it does not delete pre-existing log files.

To create a log subscription, at a minimum, you need only specify two things: the type of log (chosen from the drop-down box) and a subscription name that must be unique for that host. The subscription name is used to name the folder where logs are stored. The rest of the options are set by default and are suitable for most cases where the logs are to remain on the ESA; I discuss automatic log transfers later in this chapter.

Like any other configuration change, you must commit that change for it to be effective. Log folders and files will be created after the change is committed.

Logging Recommendations

Logging is another case where the default settings are ideal for most organizations. There are logs created for the various subsystems to aid in troubleshooting, and the default detail level is suitable for day to day operations.

Even if you plan to transfer logs from the ESA to another server for archiving, it's always a good idea to have copies of logs stored locally on the ESA. For that reason, when you need to set up a log transfer, I recommend creating a new log subscription with the remote transfer settings rather than modifying the existing one. For example, if you want to use syslog to transfer the text mail logs, create a new log subscription named **mail_syslog** with type **IronPort Text Mail Logs** and the appropriate syslog settings. I discuss transferring logs in the next section.

Note In any environment with more than one ESA, you may run into a naming problem if you plan to transfer logs to a centralized server. By default, the ESA log filenames for a given log type are the same—so that two separate ESAs will both use the filename prefix **mail.text.** for log files. At worst, this can result in a filename collision if the log rollovers on two ESAs happen in the same second, but that's fairly unlikely. Even so, the similarity in filenames makes things confusing when dealing with large numbers of files.

The solution is simple: Choose a subscription name and a filename that reflects the ESA hostname. For example, if I create mail log subscriptions named **esa01mail** and **esa02mail** with filenames to match, the resulting logs have the format *esa01mail.text.<timestamp>.s*, which allows you to easily distinguish the hosts.

Performance of logging may be a concern in some conditions. In general, logging only creates performance problems when using the specific debug logs, or setting one of the standard log types to Debug or Trace log level. The LDAP debug, injection debug, and domain debug logs all cause additional CPU and disk I/O to record. For this reason, injection and domain debug logs only run for a limited number of sessions. LDAP debug logs run continuously, and so should only be used during troubleshooting or on lightly loaded ESAs. Likewise, setting the IronPort text mail logs to debug or trace level causes much more data to be written, so they should only be enabled during troubleshooting.

Don't set your log subscription file sizes too small. Ten MB is the default and should be considered a minimum file size. If you set this value too small and traffic is high, many of the log types will roll over so often that it becomes a resource burden to the ESA. In a busy environment, 1 MB of mail-log data can be written in a few seconds. Setting this value higher, even as high as 100 MB, results in fewer rollovers, but obviously, requires transferring larger files.

Transferring Logs for Permanent Storage

The ESA ultimately has finite storage space for logs. If your organization requires retention of log data for an extended period of time, or permanent retention, you must transfer the files away from the ESA before the rollover process.

Rollover is the process of closing the current log file and starting a new one. Rollover also deletes or transfers older files. A log file is closed because it reaches its maximum file size or its maximum time period since the last rollover. Older log files are deleted when the maximum file count is reached. Both parameters are set in the log subscription that records the logs. Each subscription has a maximum log size per file and a maximum number of log files to keep. Most subscriptions, by default, use a maximum of 10 files and 100 MB per file, resulting in 1 GB of total storage at maximum. Each ESA model differs in how much log storage it offers, but it's in the range of 30–200 GB. You can safely raise the default limits, but take care that the total size won't encroach on the maximum size of the log partition. You can see what the current log partition availability is by using the **status detail** command, and you'll receive alerts from the system if the log partition is filling up.

To transfer files from the ESA to another storage location, you can do it manually with FTP or SCP. If you want to automate the process, you can script an external system to do so, but it's far easier to use the built-in transfer tools that the ESA provides.

HTTP to the ESA

If you're using the ESA WUI, you can access log files directly from the **Log Subscriptions** page. Each log subscription has a link in the **Log Files** column. All log files currently stored on the ESA can be accessed here, and there is a check box next to each for deleting individual files. You don't have to manually manage these files, though—the ESA will delete older files when the rollover and storage maximums are met.

FTP to the ESA

You can also list and retrieve log files from the ESA with FTP, provided that FTP is enabled on one of the ESA's IP interfaces. Log in using any valid ESA user account. Note that FTP is an unencrypted protocol and all credentials and file transfers are transmitted in the clear, so I recommend only enabling FTP on internal-facing interfaces and using a firewall to control access to the port.

Any FTP client can be used. FTP and HTTP are the only access methods that allow log files to be manually deleted. Log files are normally deleted only at rollover, when the subscription file limits have been reached, or when the files are automatically transferred. SCP cannot be used to delete log files.

FTP to a Remote Server

File Transfer Protocol (FTP) is the natural choice for transferring files from the ESA to another server automatically. FTP is widely supported on a variety of operating systems (OS).

After you create the log subscription and commit the changes, the ESA begins recording the log until it reaches the maximum file size or duration and only attempts to transfer the files when the rollover conditions are met. To test log transfers, use the Rollover Now button on the Log Subscriptions page or the CLI command **rollovernow**. The options for FTP push are shown in Figure 6-2.

Figure 6-2 *FTP Push Options for Log Subscriptions*

Once created, the ESA attempts to transfer log files at each rollover event, and so the *maximum files retained* will only have an effect if logs cannot be transferred to the remote server. On any error in transferring files via FTP, you will receive an email alert from the ESA.

SCP to a Remote Server

You can also use secure copy (scp) to transfer log files to a remote server. Unlike FTP, this connection is encrypted using SSH between the ESA and the target remote server. For further security, you cannot use an interactive login, and the settings for SCP push do not ask for a password, as shown in Figure 6-3.

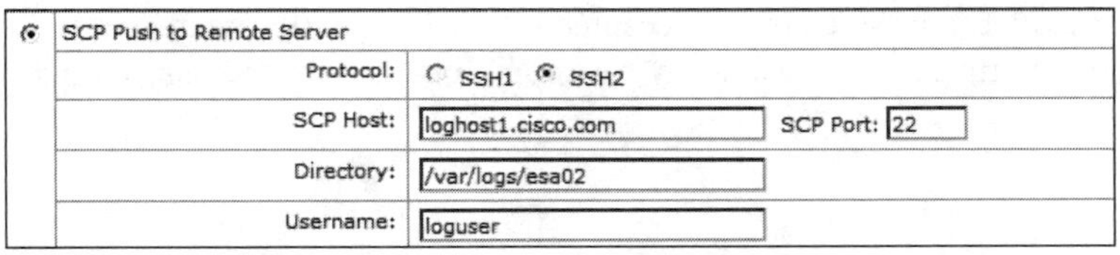

Figure 6-3 *SCP Push Options: No Provision for a Password Exists*

Instead, you must install the ESA's user public key on the remote server. You can get this key (or keys; the ESA has both an RSA and a DSS key) from the CLI command **logconfig → hostkeyconfig → user**. You place this key in the remote server's SSH configuration, which will depend on the particular installation. On most Linux and BSD servers, this will be in the remote user's **.ssh/authorized_keys** file. In the previous SCP log push settings example, I would put the ESA keys in the file **/home/loguser/.ssh/authorized_keys.**

SCP push events are triggered by the rollover conditions, which is either based on size of the log file or, for some log subscriptions, a scheduled rollover.

Syslog Transfer

Syslog is a logging protocol that includes support for remote transfer of logging messages over UDP. It was specifically created for logging of the sendmail MTA package, but has now evolved into an RFC standard that documents the protocol. ESA supports syslog push over traditional UDP transport, or optionally over TCP that some syslog servers support.

Unlike FTP or SCP, syslog transfer log subscriptions don't rollover. Instead, they transmit logging information line by line as the events occur. Because of this, and because the data isn't compressed in transit, syslog can create a lot of network traffic in busy environments, so you should ideally have your syslog servers close to the ESAs, topology-wise, or even separated onto a separate network segment.

Syslog log subscriptions require that you select the *facility* to log to. The facility is simply a code that represents the type of service being logged, with *mail* being the obvious facility choice for ESA logging. In practice, you can use any facility that you like since it's an arbitrary identifier. Most syslog servers write the accepted log data to separate files for each facility, so if mail is already in use, you can use any of the others.

Understanding IronPort Text Mail Logs

The ESA text mail logs are the primary mail log format for all message activity. They are critical to troubleshooting, and you need to be comfortable reading these logs and extracting useful information about message history from them.

Mail logs record events as they occur, arranged chronologically, not arranged on a per-message basis. Each event is written as one line, which includes its timestamp. This means that all the activity for a given message is spread over many lines, each potentially separated in time, and thus spread across the log file or potentially even spread across multiple files. For example, a message that is accepted by the ESA at 10:05 a.m., but not successfully delivered until 1:22 p.m., will likely have its events scattered across multiple log files.

Message Events

Because of the huge variety of events that can occur on a connection or message, there needs to be some unifying identifier so we can trace the history of a single message. You need to be familiar with four major identifiers:

1. **ICID** (inbound connection ID): Refers to SMTP connections made by a remote client to the ESA. ICIDs are created for all SMTP connections made where the ESA is the destination. This could be either Internet mail senders or your own internal hosts.

2. **MID** (message ID): The internal 32-bit number used to track events for a given message. Every accepted message is assigned a MID and all logging events relevant to that message and any recipient display the MID. MIDs do not change, although certain events like address rewrites or message modifications like footer stamping can result in a new MID being created from an old one.

3. **RID** (recipient ID): Every message has one or more envelope recipients, indicated by a numeric recipient ID. These IDs start from zero for the first recipient and are only locally significant to their message.

4. **DCID** (delivery connection ID): Refers to an SMTP connection made by the ESA to a remote SMTP server. DCIDs are created for all SMTP connections where ESA is the source. The destination can be any other server, whether locally or Internet.

The MID is distinct from the SMTP message-ID header, which is also recorded in the logs. Message-ID headers are an alphanumeric identifier for a message typically created by the sending mail client and not by the ESA. The MID is a purely numeric ID assigned by the ESA based on incrementing a 32-bit counter. Each new message gets assigned the next available number from that counter.

The relationships are typically one-to-many: One ICID can (potentially) be the source of many messages. One MID can have many RIDs. One DCID can (potentially) deliver many messages.

Every event line starts with the timestamp in local date and time, in 24-hour format, and a log level for the event: Error, Warning, Info, Debug, or Trace. Each log subscription determines which log levels are recorded, and they're cumulative. Error level logs include only Error level log entries, while Info level (the default) includes Info, Warning, and Error log entries. For the most part, examining the mail logs means examining Info log entries that all start like this:

```
Fri Jun 26 03:00:41 2009 Info:
```

Following that prefix, the real event data starts, whether it's a message attribute, policy decision, a scanning verdict, or a routing action. If you have ESAs across multiple time zones, each will record actions in their own local time, and you may want to pick a single time zone or use UTC to keep them consistent.

Lifecycle of a Message in the Log

All email messages on the ESA either start with an inbound connection or are created on the ESA itself. I expect that, most of the time, you'll be interested in messages that were accepted from a remote client by the ESA, and then delivered by the ESA to a remote server. That starts with a new ICID line:

```
Fri Jun 26 03:00:41 2009 Info: New SMTP ICID 143 interface INBOUND (10.1.1.17)
  address 68.244.174.120 reverse dns host mail1.example.com verified no
```

That inbound connection is either accepted or rejected. If it's rejected, the ICID is immediately closed. That process is logged across two lines:

```
Fri Jun 26 03:00:41 2009 Info: ICID 142 REJECT SG BLACKLIST match sbrs[-10.0:-
  2.5] SBRS -7.1
Fri Jun 26 03:00:41 2009 Info: ICID 142 close
```

The string **REJECT SG BLACKLIST** means that the connecting IP was classified in that sender group and that the connection was rejected. The connecting IP had SBRS of –7.1, which fell into the range defined for that sender group, which is listed here as –10.0:-2.5.

If the inbound connection is accepted, you'll see the creation of a new MID as a message delivery is started. This line is a critical one: It's the first place where the ICID and the MID are linked:

```
Fri Jun 26 03:00:41 2009 Info: Start MID 325651 ICID 143
```

The ESA then logs the sender address and all recipients. In this case, these are the envelope sender and envelope recipient addresses, not the header From and To addresses that users will see. These addresses come from the MAIL FROM and RCPT TO commands, respectively. These lines also log both the MID and ICID:

```
Fri Jun 26 03:00:41 2009 Info: MID 325651 ICID 918198 From: <sender@example.net>

Fri Jun 26 03:00:41 2009 Info: MID 325651 ICID 918198 RID 0 To: user@example.com
```

Assuming that at least one recipient is valid, and no other policy prevents message acceptance, you'll see a series of log entries for that MID, including the message size and subject. After that come the various entries for address transformations like aliasing or masquerading, which policy is applied, and the verdicts and actions of the security and content filters. At the end of the pipeline, as the message goes to delivery queues, you see this line:

```
Fri Jun 26 03:00:41 2009 Info: MID 325651 queued for delivery
```

Queued for delivery doesn't mean the message has been delivered, only that it's ready for delivery if a connection to the proper destination domain can be opened. Message logging for a given MID typically ends with the delivery of the message to another host via an available delivery connection (DCID). That situation is indicated by these lines:

```
Thu Nov  3 12:05:03 2011 Info: Delivery start DCID 179770 MID 348707 to RID [0]
Thu Nov  3 12:05:04 2011 Info: Message done DCID 179770 MID 348707 to RID [0]
Thu Nov  3 12:05:04 2011 Info: MID 348707 RID [0] Response 'ok:  Message 11441796
  accepted'
Thu Nov  3 12:05:04 2011 Info: Message finished MID 348707 done
```

Note that between the MID event **queued for delivery** and the DCID/MID event **Delivery start**, there can be a long delay in time. You won't see any events related to a MID that's queued for delivery until a successful SMTP connection to the destination is made. You will see the logging events for connection attempts indicated by this line:

```
Fri Oct  7 11:26:13 2011 Info: New SMTP DCID 174615 interface 10.60.10.10 address
  66.94.237.139 port 25
```

As you can see, there's no mention of a MID in this line, only the DCID. The DCID and MID do not come together until the DCID is successfully established and the message recipients are actually attempted. If the ESA cannot make a successful connection, ultimately the MID will timeout, and the last you'll see of that MID is a line like this:

```
Thu Jun 30 16:51:33 2011 Info: Bounced: DCID 6914 MID 2629 to RID 0 - Bounced
  by destination server with response: 5.4.7 - Delivery expired (message too old)
  ('000', ['timeout'])
```

Another possible end to a message is being dropped, which can happen for a variety of reasons, usually policy-based like anti-spam (CASE) or by a filter. A filter drop displays the name of the filter:

```
Fri Jun 26 03:23:28 2009 Info: Message aborted MID 72902 Dropped by filter
  'banned_attachments'
```

An anti-spam drop action shows CASE as the reason:

```
Fri Jun 26 03:23:29 2009 Info: Message aborted MID 72904 Dropped by CASE
```

Another possible outcome is a quarantine, which actually isn't a final state, because the message will either be deleted or released and delivered later. Quarantine events display the reason for it:

```
Thu Jun 18 19:31:03 2009 Info: MID 334420 quarantined to "Policy" (content
  filter:quarantine_all)
```

Log events for a given connection or message always occur in the same order. For example, **Start MID** occurs before **Subject** and **CASE spam negative** events, and of course, those will all be recorded before **queued for delivery**.

Tracing Message History

If you want to become an expert ESA admin, familiarity with logs is critical, and one of the most common log-based tasks is tracing the history of a message. Of course, you could just use the message-tracking features that make this easy, but I assume you want to do this manually, because the skill comes in handy in many situations.

Let's start with an example: I need to find out who sent the message with the subject *Happy Birthday Chris*, and I need to know who it came from, what host injected it, who it went to, and whether it was delivered. Because all we know about the message is the subject, we have to start there.

I'll demonstrate searching just using the ESA CLI grep tool, but you can use any text editor or search tool—the process is the same. I start by searching for that subject:

```
grep "Happy Birthday Chris" mail_logs
```

In this case, I get back one result:

```
Fri Oct 28 11:05:01 2011 Info: MID 346564 Subject 'Happy Birthday Chris'
```

Now that I have the MID, I can search for that to get the other data:

```
grep "MID 346564" mail_logs
```

I'm searching for both the word MID and the numeric MID itself to avoid any search results that match other numeric values in the log. The result is everything in the log that corresponds to that MID:

```
Fri Oct 28 11:05:01 2011 Info: Start MID 346564 ICID 1042862
Fri Oct 28 11:05:01 2011 Info: MID 346564 ICID 1042862 From: <dave@example.com>
Fri Oct 28 11:05:01 2011 Info: MID 346564 ICID 1042862 RID 0 To: <chriport@cisco.
  com>
Fri Oct 28 11:05:01 2011 Info: MID 346564 Message-ID '<112067.438985349-em02@
  granite>'
Fri Oct 28 11:05:01 2011 Info: MID 346564 Subject 'Happy Birthday Chris'
Fri Oct 28 11:05:02 2011 Info: MID 346564 ready 864 bytes from <dave@example.com>
```

```
Fri Oct 28 11:05:02 2011 Info: MID 346564 matched all recipients for per-
  recipient policy local domains in the outbound table
Fri Oct 28 11:05:03 2011 Info: MID 346564 interim AV verdict using Sophos CLEAN
Fri Oct 28 11:05:03 2011 Info: MID 346564 antivirus negative
Fri Oct 28 11:05:03 2011 Info: MID 346564 DLP no violation
Fri Oct 28 11:05:03 2011 Info: MID 346564 queued for delivery
Fri Oct 28 11:05:03 2011 Info: Delivery start DCID 178987 MID 346564 to RID [0]
Fri Oct 28 11:05:04 2011 Info: Message done DCID 178987 MID 346564 to RID [0]
Fri Oct 28 11:05:04 2011 Info: MID 346564 RID [0] Response 'ok:  Message 10569973
  accepted'
Fri Oct 28 11:05:04 2011 Info: Message finished MID 346564 done
```

This covers most of the information I need. It's an outgoing message based on the policy selection. I can see the sender, recipient, size, security verdicts, and the final result. The response from the remote server is recorded. However, it doesn't tell me what the injecting host was, because that's part of the ICID, and not the MID. So, I need to perform one more search, this time for the ICID that was revealed in the last search:

```
grep "ICID 1042862" mail_logs
```

The result from that search includes the host that connected to the ESA to deliver this message:

```
Fri Oct 28 11:05:01 2011 Info: New SMTP ICID 1042862 interface primary
  (10.60.10.10) address 10.22.18.105 reverse dns host unknown verified no
```

So, finally, we know that this message was injected from 10.22.18.105, a host without DNS information, and relayed outbound. It was delivered, and we even have the response from the remote MTA that accepted the message.

A shortcut version of this example uses the CLI command **findevent** to search for the relevant messages. **findevent** consolidates the search steps into a single command, asks you which log to search, and correlates MIDs and ICIDs for you. If multiple messages match, it provides a list of matching MIDs from which to select. Here's an example of the same search using **findevent** interactively:

```
esa02.cisco.com> findevent
Please choose which type of search you want to perform:
1. Search by envelope FROM
2. Search by Message ID
3. Search by Subject
4. Search by envelope TO
[1]> 3
Enter the regular expression to search for.
[]> Happy Birthday Chris
```

```
Currently configured logs:
    Log Name             Log Type                       Retrieval           Interval
 ---------------------------------------------------------------------------------
 1. mail_logs            IronPort Text Mail Logs        Manual Download     None
Enter the number of the log you wish to use for message tracking.
[1]> 1

Please choose which set of logs to search:
1. All available log files
2. Select log files by date list
3. Current log file
[3]> 3

The following matching message IDs were found. Please choose one to show
  additional log information:
1. MID 373351 (Thu Jan 12 15:29:01 2012) Happy Birthday Chris
2. MID 373359 (Thu Jan 12 15:44:02 2012) Happy Birthday Chris
[1]> 1
Thu Jan 12 15:29:01 2012 Info: New SMTP ICID 1077703 interface primary
  (10.60.10.10) address 10.60.10.20 reverse dns host unknown verified no
Thu Jan 12 15:29:01 2012 Info: ICID 1077703 RELAY SG RELAYLIST match
  10.60.10.0/24 SBRS rfc1918
Thu Jan 12 15:29:01 2012 Info: Start MID 373351 ICID 1077703
Thu Jan 12 15:29:01 2012 Info: MID 373351 ICID 1077703 From: <dave@example.com>
Thu Jan 12 15:29:01 2012 Info: MID 373351 ICID 1077703 RID 0 To: <chriport@cisco.com>
Thu Jan 12 15:29:01 2012 Info: MID 373351 Message-ID '<648851.85900809-em02@granite>'
Thu Jan 12 15:29:01 2012 Info: MID 373351 Subject 'Happy Birthday Chris'
```

Parsing Message Events

If you plan to extract any data from the logs, there are two steps: Decide what data you're looking for and which event(s) contains that information, and then search for it and extract it. If the information you're looking for is contained in a single line of the log, the task is straightforward, and regular expressions are an ideal way to do this.

For example, the log event that records the MID and its sender is easily matched with this regex:

```
Info: MID \d+ ICID \d+ From: .+
```

The log event for the creation of a new MID and its association with ICID can be matched with this regex:

```
Info: Start MID \d+ ICID \d+
```

Another important log event is the message size, which can be matched with this regex. In this case, I include a Perl-style regex capture so that I can use the message size and sender values later:

```
Info: MID (\d+) ready (\d+) bytes from <.+>
```

When you're looking for more than one piece of data, spread across multiple log lines, you need to do some more advanced parsing to keep track of multiple lines tied together through their MID. We look at that in the next section.

A Practical Example of Log Parsing

If you want to dive into parsing logs directly, it helps to have a practical example. I'm going to turn to my tool of choice for text processing, Perl 5, to demonstrate a program that parses logs for a practical use. Suppose you have a business policy that allows email messages up to 25 MB in size, and that during some busy periods, some users are sending out a few messages that approach the maximum size. These larger messages, at peak periods, cause brief workqueue backups as the ESAs process them. Who's sending these messages, and where are they going?

The built-in tools are of limited help. Message tracking doesn't allow for a search by size. The system capacity reports provide information on average message size and total bytes transferred, in aggregate for all traffic on the appliance. You can certainly grep the logs for the line that indicates the message size:

```
Mon Aug 29 11:56:01 2011 Info: MID 320877 ready 53036 bytes from <user@example.com>
```

That log entry includes the sender address, but not the recipients, and if you extract all the message sizes events from the log, you still need to sort them and then look up the MIDs on the largest to get other message information. We can do better with a script that only examines messages above a given minimum size.

It would seem that such a script would have straightforward logic: Look for the **bytes from** lines and extract the MID. Add the MIDs that meet the minimum size threshold to a list, and then finally look for the lines for recipients (RID) and record them. Lastly, print out the list at the end. Unfortunately, if you're parsing log lines in order, this won't work because the message-size line is *after* the lines that record the sender address and the recipient addresses. They always occur in this order for a given message:

```
Fri Oct 28 11:05:01 2011 Info: MID 346564 ICID 1042862 From: <dave@example.com>
Fri Oct 28 11:05:01 2011 Info: MID 346564 ICID 1042862 RID 0 To: <chriport@cisco.com>
Fri Oct 28 11:05:02 2011 Info: MID 346564 ready 864 bytes from <dave@example.com>
```

To avoid double- or triple-parsing the log files, we need to record *every* MID in the log when we see the **From:** event, and then add the recipient information when we see the **To:** event. Finally, when we see the **bytes** event, we can finally decide if the MID meets our minimum size and either discard or save it. This *running collection* of MIDs is an approach that works for almost any program extracting data from the logs.

The script provides the list of MIDs that meet the minimum size and the sender and recipients. (The source code is shown in Example 6-2.) Like the other source code examples in this guide, I'm not assiduously checking input or properly handling errors, because to do so would make for a very long example.

Example 6-2 *Source Code for bigsender.pl, a Log Parsing Script*

```
#!/usr/bin/perl

#####################################################
#
# Perl script to examine ESA mail log MIDs and display information
#     about messages larger than a specified size.
# Intended to give ESA admins information about the largest messages and
#     their senders and recipients

use strict;

# global variables
my %mids = ();
my $filename;
my @filenames;
my $mid;
my $size;
my $minSize;

sub usage () {
      print <<USAGE;
bigsender.pl <minimum size> <log files to parse>

example:
bigsender.pl 32K /logs/*.s

All arguments are mandatory. Size is interpreted as bytes, kilobtyes (if size is
  followed by K), or megabytes (if size is followed by M)
USAGE
}

# main
if (scalar @ARGV < 2) {
        usage ();
        exit (1);
}
```

```
# get the arguments
$minSize = shift @ARGV;
if ($minSize =~ /[mM]$/) {
        $minSize = $minSize * 1024 * 1024;
}
elsif ($minSize =~ /[kK]$/) {
      $minSize = $minSize * 1024;
}

@filenames = map { glob($_) } @ARGV;

# print a header
print "MID      size       sender       recipients\n";

while ($filename = shift @filenames) {

      open INPUT, $filename;

      while (<INPUT>) {
             if (/Info: MID (\d+) ICID \d+ From: (.*)$/) {
                    push ( @{$mids{$1}}, $2 );
             }
             elsif (/Info: MID (\d+) ICID \d+ RID \d+ To: (.*)$/) {
                    push ( @{$mids{$1}}, $2 );
             }
             elsif (/Info: MID (\d+) ready (\d+) bytes from/) {
                    $mid = $1;
                    $size = $2;

                    if ($size < $minSize) {
                          # this message is below minimum size
                          delete $mids{$mid};
                    }
                    else {
                          # this message is above the threshold
                          print "$mid $size @{$mids{$mid}}\n" if $mids{$mid};
                          delete $mids{$mid};
                    }
             }
      }

      close INPUT;

}
```

When you run it like this:

```
Bigsender.pl 5M mail.@20100615T084118.s
```

The output might look like this:

```
MID      size      sender      recipients
72901275 6088112 <dave@example.com> <chriport@cisco.com>
72901393 2817478 <joe@example.com> <chris@chrisporter.com>
72901553 26672132 <bill@example.com> <chriport@cisco.com> <cporter@chrisporter.
  com> <dave@example.com>
72901586 1912897 <Julie@example.com> <chris.porter@cisco.com>
```

This script can be repurposed as a framework for a number of different tasks.

Using Custom Log Entries

If you plan to regularly search the logs for specific information on messages, you can use the Content Filter action **Add Log Entry** or the log-entry message filter action to record arbitrary data in the logs. Custom log entries can be free-form text or include filter action variables for message attributes. You can use this to record information that's not normally in the logs, like attachment filenames, or to consolidate information that is normally recorded across multiple lines. Custom log entries can also be written based on specific conditions so that you can record interesting events for searching later. Of course, recording a custom log entry adds to log sizes, so if you're taking that action on every message, or you're using multiple log entries, expect that expansion in file sizes.

Let's look again at the previous section's log parsing example. If you expected to have to routinely look through the logs for large file senders, you can actually take a shortcut. You could add a custom log entry that records the sender, recipient, and message size all in one line, as shown in Figure 6-4. You don't need to add the MID; every custom log entry starts with it.

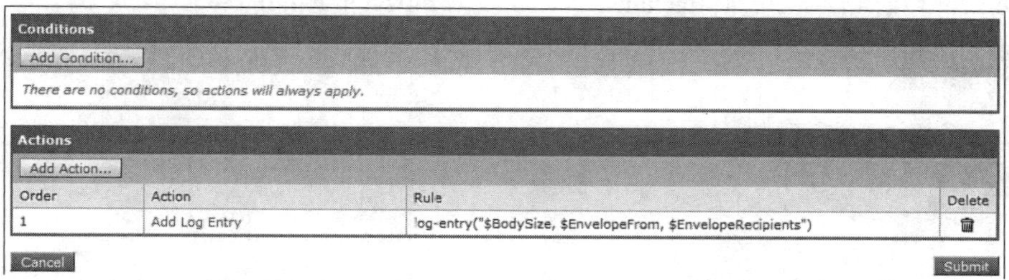

Figure 6-4 *Custom Log Entry with Sender, Recipient, and Size*

The output in the logs for a message looks like this:

```
Fri Nov  4 10:33:04 2011 Info: MID 349047 Custom Log Entry: 54495, chriport@
  cisco.com, chris@chrisporter.com
```

To avoid adding this entry for every single message, restrict it to messages above a specific threshold with a condition, as shown in Figure 6-5.

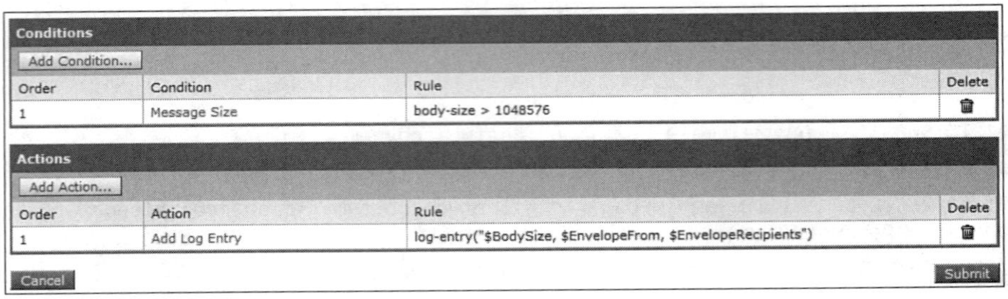

Figure 6-5 *Custom Log Entry Restricted to Large Messages*

Now, to reproduce the report for large senders, you only need to search for the Custom Log Entry string. The custom log entry includes the MID, which will allow you to use message tracking, **grep**, or **findevent** to display the rest of the message details.

Another example covers attachment filenames, which are not logged in the mail logs by default. You can add this by using the action variable $filenames, but there's a catch you should be aware of. Normally on ESA, messages with attachments are not decoded from their MIME parts unless a message or content filter examines the data. This is for performance: The ESA does not incur the overhead of message body decoding unless you ask for data in the message body. As a result, attachment filenames are not available to message tracking, or the $filenames variable, unless you're already doing message decoding. Any content filter condition that examines message body—attachment or body text rules, file type, or filename rules, and such—causes the decoding process to happen and, hence, make the filenames available. If you're already doing this, you're all set and there is no additional performance consideration. If you're not already doing body searches, be aware that you won't see the filenames unless you start doing it, and those filter conditions could impact performance.

A content filter that records attachment filenames is shown in Figure 6-6.

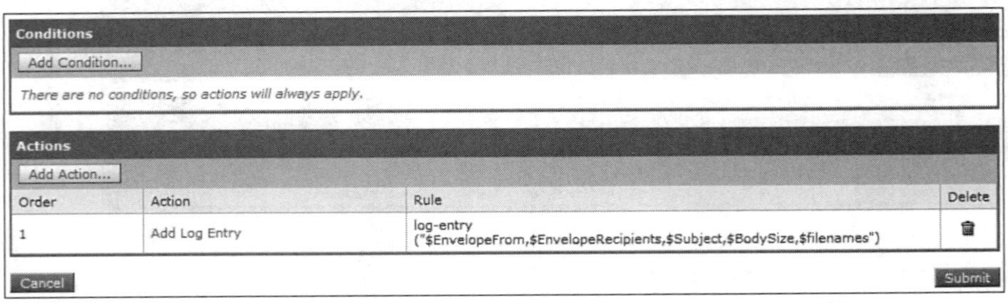

Figure 6-6 *Custom Log Entry to Record Attachment Filenames*

The result in the logs of this action is:

```
Fri Nov  4 10:33:04 2011 Info: MID 349047 Custom Log Entry: chriport@cisco.
  com,chris@chrisporter.com,Capacity Docs,54495,CapacityPlan.xls
```

Summary

In this chapter, we've looked at several ways of peering under the hood of the ESA for detailed monitoring and troubleshooting, and how to access the ESA filesystem for transferring logs and configurations.

One of the most critical skills for troubleshooting delivery, performance, and system errors on the ESA is reading and understanding the logs. The IronPort mail logs format provides a complete history of every connection and message that your ESA handles, and the system and engine logs provide details on errors that can affect delivery or security. For monitoring the health of your ESAs, the WUI and CLI provide convenient reporting and status tools, but the best way to continually monitor appliance health is with SNMP, and we discussed setting up and monitoring your ESAs with **snmpconfig**.

To this point, we have focused on accessing, administering, troubleshooting, and monitoring, but in the next chapter we'll dig deeply into mail policy, and interaction with LDAP.

Chapter 7

Directories and Policies

In this chapter, you will learn the following:

- How to integrate ESA with LDAP directories, including Microsoft Active Directory
- How to create and use LDAP server profiles and basic and advanced LDAP queries
- How to create incoming and outgoing mail policies and tie those policies to directory information

Directory Integration

Email systems have a close relationship with other services in the network. Most prominent among these is Domain Name System (DNS), because of the dependency of Simple Mail Transfer Protocol (SMTP) on DNS. In most organizations today, however, directory services provided through Lightweight Directory Access Protocol (LDAP) are critical to email environments. In addition to providing information like address books for mail user agents (MUA), information in a directory can be used for routing email messages and applying policy to individual senders or recipients. Directories are also typically used to authenticate users for network services and applications, and email is no exception.

The Email Security Appliance (ESA) supports LDAP and LDAP over SSL/TLS, referred to as LDAPS. ESA does not provide any directory services—it's only an LDAP client—but does cache results returned from queries.

The single-most common LDAP server in use is Microsoft's Active Directory (AD). It's so common that most of the ESA documentation refers to AD integration, instead of LDAP, and most configuration examples are targeted toward AD environments. In fact, the ESA has a Wizard mode that eases setup for AD, and most of the setup defaults use AD defaults. Because of its ubiquity, we refer to AD most often, including examples based on AD attributes and queries. Note, however, that the ESA speaks LDAP only, and AD is just another LDAP server as far as it is concerned.

The Need for Directory Integration

Directory integration with your ESA provides many important advantages for your email environment:

- **Lower message volumes:** Using LDAP recipient validation through LDAP accept queries reduces the number of messages your ESA has to accept. It's a lot of unnecessary work to accept and filter messages that cannot be delivered because there's no valid user with that address.
- **Lower administration:** Policy changes can be done at the directory instead of on the ESA. For example, grouping users by their language or location can make adding disclaimers or sending notifications in the correct language easy.
- **Improved security:** Using SMTP-conversation recipient validation with the *dictionary attack prevention* feature helps the ESA identify bad SMTP clients and keeps your valid email address list from being discovered and sold.

For some policy tasks, there's simply no feasible alternative to using a directory. In large environments, the capacity of the ESA tables may become an issue, and administration of large static tables is a headache. The maintenance and security risk from other approaches far outweighs any drawbacks to ESA LDAP integration.

Security Concerns

The idea of exposing internal directory access to a gateway security device installed in the demilitarized zone (DMZ) is sometimes unpopular from a security perspective. The legitimate concern is that an attacker could gain access to an ESA and use it as a bastion to attack other systems; information installed in the directory could be stolen or modified. The first step is to prevent unauthorized access to an ESA in the first place. Cisco takes significant precautions against the exploitation of the ESA appliance software, and in fact, the appliance software doesn't include the basic tools that could be used for such attacks. Appropriate network layer security can control access to the administrative interfaces on the ESA. Taking a few precautions minimizes any risk.

There are a few general recommendations for minimizing the perceived risks that LDAP queries from the ESA to an organization's directory servers could create:

- The ESA should authenticate to LDAP with a username and password created specifically for the purpose.
- The username associated with ESA LDAP queries should have the minimum required privileges and be read-only if possible. Don't use any kind of administrative account.
- Use LDAP over SSL/TLS (LDAPS) to encrypt the communications between the ESAs and the LDAP directory.

- Have an LDAP server available directly in the DMZ, eliminating the need to make LDAP connections inside; many LDAP servers support read-only instances to support this model, with synchronization performed by pushing updates from inside to the DMZ. If you plan to dedicate LDAP servers for messaging, it may be possible to expose only a portion of the directory to the ESA.
- If you're crossing network boundaries, the firewalls or other network security devices should have rules that include the specific source (ESA) and destination IP and ports of the LDAP servers.

If direct access to LDAP servers is absolutely forbidden, you have other options for certain policy tasks. SMTP recipient validation can be performed with the Recipient Access Table (RAT). Recipient or sender policy grouping can be done with static entries in the appropriate policy. Both create a maintenance headache, and I'm left wondering this: Is having a list of email addresses in a static table on the ESA preferable to giving the ESA minimal directory access?

Another alternative introduced in AsyncOS 7.5 is SMTP call-ahead, which allows the ESA to use SMTP as a recipient validation protocol. It is only for recipient validation, so it can only replace LDAP accept queries. Call-ahead requires that there is an available SMTP server that can provide a clear acceptance and rejection response for the RCPT TO command.

Brief LDAP Overview

The LDAP was developed as a low-overhead alternative to the standard client protocols for X.500 directories. Although it is, technically, only a directory access protocol, it also necessarily defines the structure of the data being accessed. Under the hood, the directory can store its data in a variety of ways—LDAP does not constrain the architecture of the server software itself. Some servers use relational databases to store the directory attributes and values, while others use flat files, but the backend storage method does not impact ESA.

The current specification for the protocol is provided in RFC 4510, along with a number of others. The protocol defines a number of operations that can occur between a client and a server, but in the case of ESA and a directory server, only a few are relevant:

- **StartTLS:** Begins the negotiation for a TLS connection so that credentials and query data are sent over an encrypted channel. ESA supports secure connections for LDAP.
- **Bind:** In LDAP terminology, *bind* is the term for authentication of a client to an LDAP server. ESA uses a bind operation to connect to the server for making queries, but also as an authentication mechanism for administrators and end users.
- **Search:** Query the LDAP server for attributes of a specific value. Returns the count of matches and the matching values.

- **Compare:** Query the LDAP server to test if a named attribute has a specific value. LDAP is always case-insensitive when matching attribute names or values.

The ESA does not support any operations that modify the directory, like adding or removing entries or editing any attributes. It's a read-only client.

LDAP envisions a directory as a tree starting at a root node. Every node is itself a directory tree, with subnodes that contain entries and other nodes. Entries in the directory are *name: value* pairs, called attributes, and can have one or more values.

Figure 7-1 shows a conceptual diagram of an LDAP directory tree.

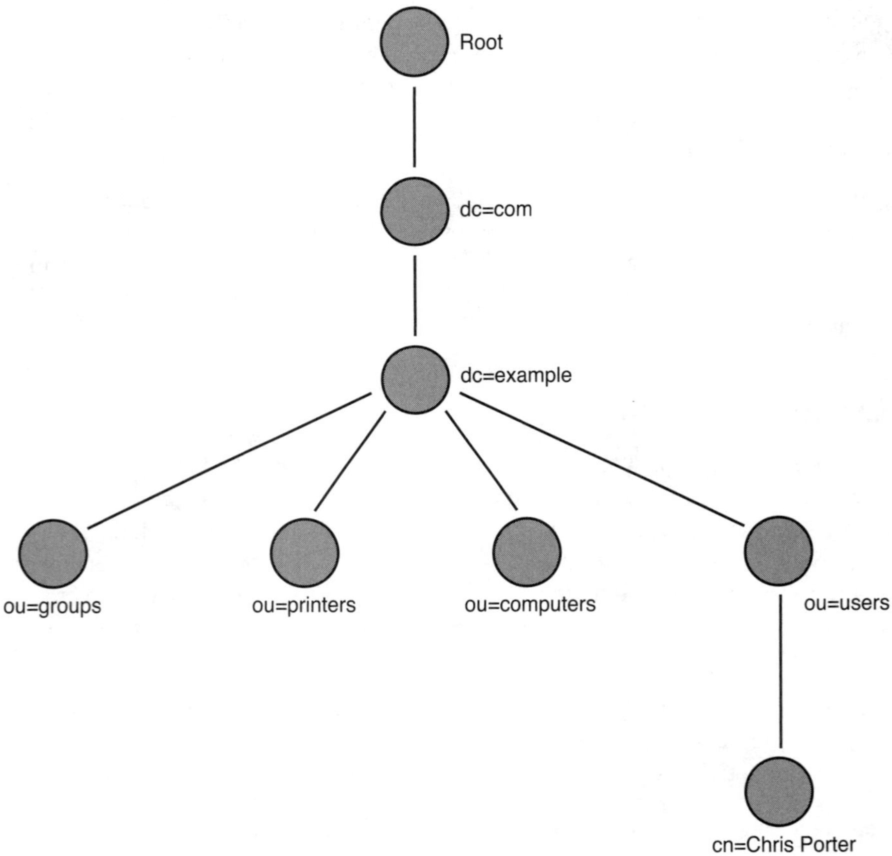

Figure 7-1 *Simplified Conceptual LDAP Tree*

The unique path from root to the actual node where attributes are recorded is called the distinguished name (DN) and is often, but not always, recorded as an attribute on the entry itself. For example, the DN of the user account in Figure 7-1 is just a comma-separated list of all the node names:

```
dn:cn=Chris Porter,ou=users,dc=example,dc=com
```

Although LDAP is a binary protocol, it's convenient to represent attributes in text format for our discussions, and the LDAP Interchange Format (LDIF) provides just that. An LDIF representation of the user account from Figure 7-1 might be displayed as

```
dn: cn=Chris Porter,ou=users,dc=example,dc=com
objectClass: person
cn: Chris Porter
c: US
mail: chriport@cisco.com
proxyAddresses: SMTP:chriport@cisco.com
proxyAddresses: smtp:cporter@ironport.com
memberOf: ou=ESA Admins,ou=groups,dc=example,dc=com
memberOf: ou=IT Security,ou=groups,dc=example,dc=com
```

At the top is the attribute dn, or Distinguished Name, which uniquely identifies this particular node in the LDAP tree by its complete path back to the root. Aside from this object's DN, there are other attributes that have values that are LDAP DNs, which is perfectly valid, and a fact that I use later when we see LDAP group queries. I use this type of LDIF text layout in examples in this chapter. Because the ESA is focused on email, the LDAP objects you'll deal with most are users—real people—so, the examples revolve around those kinds of entries.

There's one note about LDAP directory servers being used with the ESA. The ESA has a fairly short LDAP query timeout, necessitated by the need to react at SMTP conversation time, and so expects the LDAP server to respond quickly. Most LDAP servers perform a process called *indexing* to speed up search times for commonly used attributes. Any attribute you intend to query with the ESA needs to be indexed. Configuring indexing varies with the LDAP server software, and most servers index the email-related attributes in their default configuration. If you're querying other attributes, however, it makes sense to double-check that they are indexed, and be aware that unindexed attributes can be a cause of LDAP timeouts on the ESA. The ESA response to timeouts on LDAP recipient validation queries depends on your configuration. You can set it to accept messages if LDAP is unreachable, relying only on the RAT for recipient checks, or set it to temporarily reject messages until LDAP is restored. For other LDAP queries, the ESA queues messages until LDAP is available. Timeouts and other connection errors result in alerts being sent from the ESA.

LDAP Setup on ESA

To start using LDAP, you need one or more LDAP server profiles. You can set these up manually or, if you're using AD, you can use the AD Wizard. The wizard makes LDAP setup faster because it preconfigures attributes common to most AD deployments. Either way, you can always modify an LDAP server profile later.

To create an LDAP server profile, you need all the following information, at a minimum:

- **A name for the LDAP profile:** This is just a friendly identifier to distinguish profiles from each other and to name the queries attached to the profile.
- **Hostnames or IP addresses of one or more LDAP servers:** This is the directory server or servers to contact for all the queries under this profile. The servers should be identical, meaning that they should support the same queries and contain the same data. Support for multiple servers is provided here for failover and load balancing. If you have multiple directories with disparate data, see the "Advanced LDAP Queries" section later in this chapter.
- **Base DN:** In the LDAP directory tree, this is the root node that all searches should start from. When you specify a base DN, all searches are relative to that base and the search is limited to nodes and subnodes of that base. You may be tempted to set an empty base, starting at the root of the LDAP directory. This is allowed, but narrowing the base DN to make it as specific as possible improves performance. In the example, we could choose dc=example,dc=com as the base, because all relevant entries are below that node, or you might go further and specify ou=users,dc=example,dc=com if you're only querying users.
- **Credentials for access to the directory:** You need a username and password for an account that has at least read-only privileges; the ESA does not make changes to any directory. You can also use anonymous access if the directory permits.
- **Port to contact the LDAP server on:** LDAP customarily uses 389 for LDAP and 636 for TLS LDAP. AD uses these ports also, but you're better off using the Global Catalog (GC) ports of 3268 and 3269.
- **At least one query:** Although you're technically not required to create an LDAP profile, the queries are the fundamental part of any profile. We cover basic and advanced queries later in this chapter.

After the profile is created, you can use the associated queries in relevant parts of the configuration. Note that creating a profile and queries does not put the queries into use; you must configure other features to use LDAP before they actually apply to accepted or relayed messages. For example, creating and testing an LDAP accept query does not enable recipient validations until you assign that query to a listener. Group queries don't sort users until you assign the query to a listener and either create a filter condition or define policy membership.

Figure 7-2 shows the basic setup of an LDAP server profile.

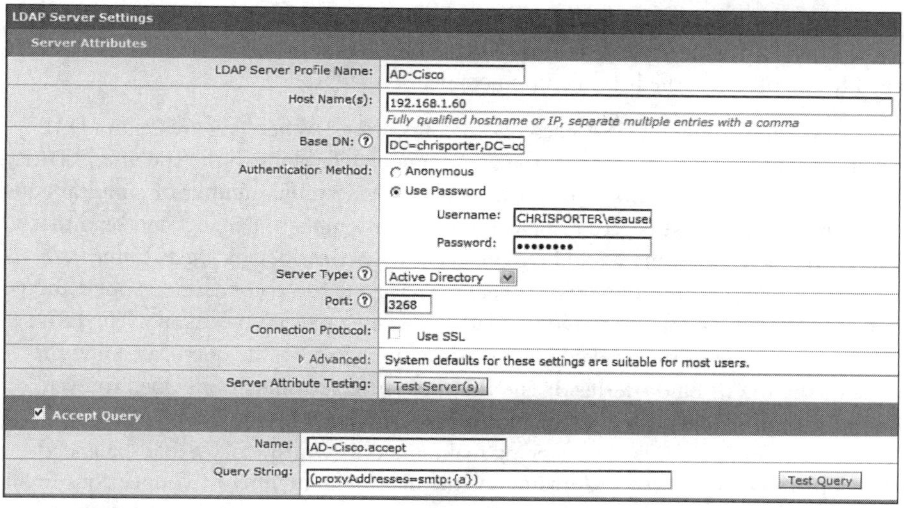

Figure 7-2 *LDAP Server Profile Setup*

This profile contains all the elements in the previous list, with a single recipient validation query configured.

Note Credentials entered into an LDAP server profile are stored in the clear in the XML configuration files unless you choose the option to exclude passwords when generating the configuration. Any administrator or operator user on the ESA can export the configuration and obtain the LDAP passwords in plaintext. I recommend that you use an LDAP account specifically created for use by the ESAs. That account should have minimal read-only privileges.

Advanced Profile Settings

The **Advanced** drop-down on any LDAP profile provides configuration for a few connection related settings. Normally, the defaults are sensible, but it's worth taking a look to understand how changing these settings can improve performance.

The first is caching for LDAP lookups. Caching makes lookups more efficient by storing both the positive and negative results of recent queries. The Time to Live (TTL) sets how long the results are good for, and the maximum cache entries is of course how many entries will be used. I recommend using longer TTLs, if you can. If the attributes that the ESA is querying don't change that often, setting this to 4 hours (14,400 seconds) or even a whole day (86,400 s) will have benefits for performance. Increasing the cache size uses more memory on the ESA, but the default of 10,000 is fairly anemic; I recommend 4 hour TTLs and 100,000 entries in cache. In most environments, that's enough to cache all the active email recipients.

The other advanced settings are for connections, controlling the number of connections the ESA can make and how to handle multiple hosts in a single profile. Multiple hosts can either be load-balanced so that queries are made round-robin to all the hosts in the list, or failover so that queries are normally made to the first LDAP server in the list and proceed to the others in the list only upon connection failure.

It's worth explaining how the ESA uses LDAP connections. When you create an LDAP server profile and commit the change, the ESA immediately binds to the specified LDAP server and keeps the connection open. If the value in **Maximum number of simultaneous connections for each host** is greater than 1, the ESA attempts to connect and bind that number of times. This setting could be more accurately described as *always maintain this number of active simultaneous connections.* Having these connections open, even when no LDAP queries are active, reduces latency when a query is necessary. The ESA's LDAP client uses one of the available open connections to send the query, avoiding the expense of the LDAP Bind overhead. The ESA keeps these connections open forever, if allowed to, and reopens any connection that is terminated by the LDAP server so that the maximum number is always being maintained. If you specify a load-balanced relationship among hosts, the ESA maintains the maximum number of connections to all the hosts in the list.

You can see the connection behavior of the LDAP client in the LDAP debug logs, which are discussed later in this chapter. These logs show the ESA opening new connections immediately as the LDAP server terminates them.

Basic Query Types

The basic ESA LDAP queries are

- **Recipient validation:** A simple check to determine whether a recipient exists in the directory. Essentially just a true/false query; any non-zero result from the directory is assumed to mean that the recipient exists.
- **Group queries:** Used for checking some attribute of a recipient or sender address to associate that address with some organizational group. A flexible query that can be used for various purposes.
- **Routing query:** I also refer to this as *LDAP aliasing* because these queries are designed to rewrite or redirect recipient addresses or both. Rewriting actually changes an individual address to one or more other addresses, so it can be used for either altering a single address or expanding a single address to multiple addresses, as with a distribution list. It can also redirect the recipient to a specific delivery host, either separate from or in conjunction with recipient rewrites. This capability is commonly used in Internet server provider (ISP) and university environments, less so in AD environments.
- **Masquerading:** You can think of masquerading as the opposite of aliasing. Instead of rewriting recipient addresses, it rewrites sender addresses. The purpose is to change any *internal only* addressing into externally resolvable full email addresses.

- **SMTP authentication:** Configures queries for the ESMTP extension SMTP-AUTH, which provides for authentication to mail servers. The ESA can act as either an SMTP AUTH client or server, but for LDAP purposes, we're concerned with how remote clients authenticate to the ESA. SMTP-AUTH is specified in RFC 4954.
- **External authentication:** Provides for LDAP authentication to a directory for the purpose of logging into the ESA. If you want to allow administrative users that have accounts in AD or other LDAP directory to use those credentials for ESA administration, you must configure an LDAP query and define access levels.
- **Spam quarantine authentication:** Like external authentication, this is intended to allow login via credentials stored in an LDAP directory. In this case, however, the users are your user population accessing their stored spam messages in the spam quarantine. This is not the only means of allowing end user access to the quarantine, but if you want them to use the credentials they already have and are familiar with, you must configure the LDAP query first.
- **Spam quarantine alias consolidation:** If you are allowing end users to access the spam quarantine, you might also consider consolidating multiple email addresses per user into a single view. The quarantine can only do this if it can query LDAP to determine all the email addresses for a given user.

The most commonly used queries are the LDAP recipient validation and group queries, so I dedicate large sections on those subjects. Routing (aliasing) and masquerading are critical in certain environments, if the right directory information is available. If it's at all possible, I strongly recommend using LDAP recipient validation, because it improves performance and security, so I discuss this next.

Recipient Validation with LDAP

The single most common use for LDAP on a Message Transfer Agent (MTA) is to validate recipients. This means querying an LDAP server with a simple "does this user exist?" question. A positive response means that the recipient (and message) is accepted; a negative response means that the recipient is rejected or bounced. Even with LDAP recipient validation, you still must list the valid recipient domains in the RAT, which the ESA checks before making an LDAP query.

Recipient validation has a few differences from the other LDAP query types:

- Can act at SMTP connection time. Lookups are performed while the client is still connected, at each instance of the SMTP RCPT TO command. The response is given back to the sender immediately. Most of the other query types are performed after the message is accepted.
- Negative results are *harmful* to messages. For most queries, a negative result means *does not apply* and message processing continues. Not so with LDAP accept: A negative response means that recipients are rejected or dropped. Note that error responses aren't considered negative; a negative response is one where the connection and query succeeded, but the result was 0 matches.

- Only applied on HAT policies with accept behavior. LDAP accept is effectively bypassed on Relay (outgoing) behavior HAT mail flow policies, to avoid performing recipient validation on messages sent from your organization out to Internet recipients. Other LDAP query types are performed on all messages received at a particular listener.

For most corporate LDAP servers, the attribute named *mail* stores the valid email address for a user. It doesn't matter if there are multiple instances of the same attribute because our query is essentially "does *any* mail attribute in the search path have value *user@example.com?*" The ESA doesn't care what the values are, or how many matches there are, only whether there is a match or not. The query for the mail attribute is:

```
(mail={a})
```

Microsoft Exchange and AD use two attributes: *mail* and *proxyAddresses*. There's an instance of the proxyAddresses attribute for every address for the user, and the value starts with smtp: or SMTP: for those types of addresses. The *primary* email address for the user is stored with a capital SMTP prefix and is copied into the mail attribute. Unfortunately, LDAP queries aren't case sensitive, so ESA can't see the difference between the primary and other proxyAddresses values. It's no matter, however, because all we care about is whether there's a matching value in the directory regardless of case, and this query accomplishes that. You'll find that in the ESA web user interface (WUI), this query is the default for accept queries on AD profiles:

```
(proxyAddresses=smtp:{a})
```

When the recipient address isn't found in the directory, you can choose to reject the recipient at SMTP conversation time or to bounce the message at the work queue. Of these two options, there's not really much debate: You should use SMTP rejection. This is preferable because the sending client knows immediately that the recipient isn't valid, and you avoid the trouble of accepting and bouncing the message later.

LDAP accept queries don't have to be so simple. You can query multiple attributes and query using only a part of the recipient address with the {u} user or {d} domain variables. For example, to test only if the domain is valid, you can use a query like this:

```
(localdomain={d})
```

To test both the username and the full address, you can use a query like this:

```
(¦(mail={a})(uid={u}))
```

The vertical bar or *pipe* character is a logical *or* condition, making the search result true if either an instance of the mail attribute matches the full recipient address or the uid attribute matches the username portion to the left of the @ sign. You don't have to worry about the domain portion being local as long as the RAT is correctly configured. Logical *and* is the ampersand character, as in this test:

```
(&(mail={a})(externalMail=true))
```

That query tests whether the recipient address exists, but also that the attribute externalMail has the string value, true. You use this sort of query to limit inbound messages to addresses that are specifically enabled to receive mail from outside the organization.

Recipient Routing with LDAP

LDAP routing on the ESA is designed to support the delivery of individual recipients to the appropriate host after the ESA finished message processing. The phrase *routing* actually refers to two specific capabilities: rewriting envelope recipient addresses (aliasing) and setting delivery destination host (routing). Routing LDAP queries are less frequently used than other LDAP features simply because most corporate LDAP directories don't have appropriate attributes for it, and because most groupware servers, like Exchange and Notes, have the ability to route messages themselves for their local users.

As mentioned, routing queries have two parts: aliasing and destination host. You can use one or the other or both on incoming mail. For example, aliasing is the process of looking up an original recipient address, like

```
chris.porter@cisco.com
```

Rewriting the entire address to something else, like

```
chriport@cisco.com
```

The source and target address don't need to be in the same domain. One common use case is to rewrite external-facing addresses to internal addresses that are only relevant inside your network. For example, an Internet email address like

```
alice.smith@example.com
```

might internally need to be transformed into

```
asmith@boston.example.com
```

The ESA can perform this rewrite based on an LDAP lookup on each recipient, and will then route the message according to the new address, hence the term *LDAP routing*. In this example, the ESA delivers the message via SMTPRoutes or DNS lookup for boston.example.com. Only the envelope recipient addresses are rewritten; the visible headers, like To: and CC:, are not modified by this process.

The other feature of LDAP routing is to change the delivery destination for the recipient without rewriting. This requires that the directory have an attribute that stores the fully qualified domain name (FQDN) of the delivery destination for the user.

To use LDAP routing, you need to have this information stored in LDAP for this to work. Routing setup requires two things: a query to *locate* the user in the directory and the name of the attribute(s) to use when rewriting or rerouting. Locating the user works just like it does with LDAP accept, but the query is doing more than a simple yes/no test. The ESA is actually asking the LDAP server, "What is the value of attribute X for user with email address user@example.com?", and then using that address to rewrite or reroute. The second part of the equation is the actual attribute to use for rewriting or rerouting. Here's an LDIF excerpt that includes suitable attributes for use with both LDAP routing features:

```
dn: cn=alice smith,ou=users,dc=example,dc=com
cn: Alice Smith
mailRoutingAddress: asmith@internal.example.com
mail: asmith@example.com
mail: asmith@internal.example.com
mail: asmith@otherdomain.com
mailhost: webmail.example.com
```

In this case, the LDAP locator query will be:

```
(mail={a})
```

The attribute to use for rewrite is *mailRoutingAddress* and for destination host is *mailhost*. Again, you can use either one of those or both.

If you only have information for a subset of users, you can still use LDAP routing, because if the locator query fails to find the user, the rewrite step is simply bypassed and the recipient is routed as normal. No harm is done if the address can't be found.

Warning LDAP routing requires that the target attributes for rewrite and host route be unique for that user. LDAP allows for multiple copies of the same attribute with different values, but you must use a single instance attribute for routing. If more than one exists, it's not well defined as to which one would actually be used and the result will be inconsistent behavior.

To avoid this, use an LDAP browser client that allows you to see an entire user record, and test your queries extensively before putting into a production configuration.

Sender Masquerading

If you're using LDAP aliasing to hide internal SMTP architecture by rewriting external addresses to internal addresses for incoming mail, you'll probably want to reverse that process for outgoing mail. That is, when a user sends a message from an internal address, the local address needs to be rewritten to an externally facing one.

In the most common case, masquerading is used simply to flatten internal subdomains into a single external domain, without changing the user portion, as in this transformation:

```
jdoe@chicago.example.com: jdoe@example.com
```

You don't have to use LDAP for this; the static masquerade table on the listener accomplishes this directly. It's available in the CLI command **listenerconfig** under the settings for individual listeners. The static table also supports individual user address rewrites. As is the case with most of the static tables, however, maintaining the user-by-user rewrites may be easier if the appropriate information is available in LDAP. Similar to LDAP routing, you must have both the source (internal) address and the destination (external) address in an attribute for each user, and the destination attribute must be single-instance.

When you are using masquerading, LDAP or otherwise, the important configuration option is deciding which headers to rewrite. For outbound messages, it's possible that local (internal) addresses are used in **To**, **CC**, and **Reply-To**, in addition to the **From** header. The selection is made in the listener configuration when you're assigning the query to the listener. Make sure that you enable these header rewrites appropriately; I recommend turning them all on, with the possible exception of the envelope sender address. The envelope sender should only be used in the event of a bounce or other system message, and the internal address is likely what you need to be used. For messages that are delivered, the **From** address determines replies and the like, and should be masqueraded.

Group Queries

When using LDAP to invoke policy on the ESA, I am generally referring to using LDAP group queries. Group queries might sound complex, but they are really quite simple: They query the directory using the supplied query string, and if there's at least one match, the sender or recipient is considered a member of the group. Recipient addresses are tested (individually) for incoming mail, and sender addresses are tested for outgoing mail.

The complexity for these queries can come in the query string. These strings are essentially arbitrary—you can query anything. In general, you need at least two attributes to test: an attribute that identifies the user, whether by a username or full email address. I call this part of the query the *locator*. You also need at least one other attribute to test for group membership.

Here's an example that uses the full email address as the locator and an attribute called departmentName as the group test:

```
(&(mail={a})(departmentName={g}))
```

When this is applied to incoming mail, a substitution occurs for the {a} and {g} variables. The variable {a} (for address) refers to either the sender or recipient, depending on context. (More on the context later in this chapter.) The {g} variable refers to the group name, which is supplied as either the argument to the policy membership, or by the argument to a content filter. In this example, we assume that this is incoming mail, and we have a policy called *Legal*, which uses the string Legal as the group query string. The result of the substitution is

```
(&(mail=chriport@cisco.com)(departmentName=Legal))
```

which is passed to the LDAP directory. Assuming the query is a success, the address is considered a part of the group if there is a non-zero result set. Zero results means that the user is not considered a member of the group. You can use any query that works—if you can compose the LDAP filter logic to return what you want, you can use it here. For example, if I want to narrow the previous example to the Legal department in one country, I use this:

```
(&(mail={a})(departmentName={g})(countryCode=US))
```

In this example, I'm hard-coding the string US for the countryCode. Because you only get one group variable, {g}, you have to use it wisely. You can use it in more than one place, if you carefully consider what that means. For example, suppose you have this query:

```
(&(mail={a})(|(departmentName={g})(countryCode={g})))
```

You're using this query with two policies that use the strings Legal and US as the group policy membership criteria. During message processing, the two policies cause these LDAP queries to be sent:

```
(&(mail={a})(|(departmentName=Legal)(countryCode=Legal)))
```

```
(&(mail={a})(|(departmentName=US)(countryCode=US)))
```

If only one query returns a positive match, obviously, the message falls into the corresponding policy. If both queries return a positive match, order determines the policy, based on top-down evaluation of policy order. If you have users that match both policies (because they are in the Legal department in the U.S.), you must decide which policy takes precedence and order it higher in the list.

This only begins to hint at some of the flexibility of group queries. You can use such a query for any attribute that distinguishes users, provided that they're indexed for fast searches. You can use any of the LDAP logical operators, like and &, or |, and not !, and you're not limited to one or two attributes. You don't even necessarily have to use the {g} variable, as we see later in this chapter. Table 7-1 gives some examples with a description.

Table 7-1 *Compound Group Query Examples*

Query	Description
(&(mail={a})(objectclass=group))	Recipient or sender address is a group of users.
(&(mail={a})(!(objectclass=group)))	Recipient or sender address is *not* a group.
(&(proxyAddress=smtp:{a})(|(&(objectCategory=user)(homeMDB=*))(objectCategory=contact)))	Address is a real human user and has a mailbox on any server or is a contact record. Using the wildcard * value means *search for any value* and is true if the attribute exists.
(&(proxyAddresses=smtp:{a})(objectCategory={g}))	Group based on object category; for example, contractors, users, groups, public folders.
(&(proxyAddresses=smtp:{a})(displayName=Chris*))	Users whose display name starts with "Chris."

Warning Although objectclass is a perfectly valid attribute to query, it's often not indexed and in AD, it may not be feasible to index it.

In AD environments, use the objectCategory attribute to distinguish between the types of available objects stored in the directory. However, because the ESA LDAP queries are focused on valid email addresses, it's not often that you'll need to limit your query to specific object types.

Authentication Queries

LDAP is used for a number of authentication tasks on the ESA. You can use LDAP to authenticate administrative users, replacing the local username and password logins. If you're using the spam quarantine features, you can, optionally, force end users to authenticate. You can also authenticate connecting SMTP clients using SMTP-AUTH. All function in essentially the same way: Credentials are received from the client, and those credentials are used to bind to the relevant LDAP server. A successful bind means that the user is authenticated. SMTP AUTH queries also allow retrieval of a password attribute, to be compared with the supplied password, but that approach is uncommon.

External authentication for administrative users also provides the ability to group users based on organizational information in the directory. Based on this query, you can map group names in the directory to roles on the ESA.

AD Specifics

In commercial enterprise environments, AD is the most common directory server, and as a result, the ESA has default settings and specific features for supporting AD. It's important to note, however, that the ESA still treats an AD server as an LDAP server.

There are a couple of important things worth knowing about AD in regards to the ESA LDAP client:

- AD can answer LDAP queries on port 389, the LDAP standard, and port 3268, which queries the AD global catalog. In multidomain environments, the AD GC contains information for all domains, while the LDAP port is limited to a specific domain. For this reason, LDAP queries to AD default to 3268, and unless you have good reason, you should always search the GC. The secure (LDAPS) port equivalents are 636 and 3269, respectively.
- The mail attribute only lists the primary SMTP address for a user or group. AD uses the proxyAddresses field to store all addresses for a user, and the primary proxyAddresses attribute is also copied to the mail attribute. The default ESA queries for AD use proxyAddresses, so you shouldn't change that unless you have good reason.
- Some attributes aren't indexed by default. Whatever attributes in AD you plan to query, either standard or custom, make sure that they're indexed.

- AD doesn't expose an FQDN hostname for the server storing the user's messages. This means it's not possible to use the ESA LDAP routing features directly, but it's rarely necessary because Exchange servers can route messages between themselves. I discuss a workaround for this using group queries later in this chapter.

Testing LDAP Queries

The ESA provides tools to test your queries before putting them into production. You can test queries from the WUI, right as you create the LDAP server profile.

There are two tests available in the WUI:

- **Server profile tests the server attributes only:** Hostname or IP, port and bind credentials. The base DN is tested, too, because the base is part of the parameters to the LDAP bind operation.
- **The query tests individually test the configured queries:** To test the queries, you should have already tested the server profile, because there is no sense in testing the query format and attribute availability if you haven't tested server connectivity.

Both sets of tests run against the values you currently have in the WUI boxes on the page. There's no need to commit or even submit the page to make changes and test.

In addition, the CLI has the command **ldaptest**, which can be run interactively or in batch mode:

```
ldaptest active_directory.accept cporter@ironport.com
```

When you are testing LDAP queries, after you have a working query that is returning a successful result, be sure to test thoroughly. If you have entries in more than one directory, make sure to include those in a test. Test both negative and positive results—it is easy to create a query that always matches at least one record, defeating the purpose of accept and group queries.

Take particular care with LDAP accept queries, because a negative result here means the ESA will reject some recipients, causing lost, or at least delayed, messages.

Advanced LDAP Queries

After you have one or more basic LDAP queries created and tested, you have the option of using a couple types of advanced queries:

- **Per-domain queries:** Performs LDAP searches based on the domain portion of the recipient or sender email address. If may have information about different domains stored in different directories, this allows the ESA to select the relevant query for each domain. This allows ESA configurations that would otherwise normally require separate listeners or appliances.

- **Daisy chained queries:** Chained queries allow the LDAP subsystem to make multiple queries, one after the other, to find a match. This allows you to make queries to completely different directories, or even to the same directory, but with different search base and query filter. ESA follows the chain in order, stopping as soon as it gets a match.

Both advanced query types are created by combining two or more basic query types. You must first create the basic LDAP server profiles and their relevant queries before you have the option of creating advanced queries.

The per-domain queries are, of course, used where you have separate LDAP servers or queries for different domains or where you have LDAP for some domains, but not others. As an example, consider the situation when a company acquires a smaller one. We'll use the example of Cisco acquiring IronPort. Within a week of the acquisition, all the users with email addresses @ironport.com need to also have @cisco.com addresses, but for continuity purposes, we need to continue to accept and route both domains on the same ESA infrastructure. Figure 7-3 conceptually shows this consolidated ESA environment.

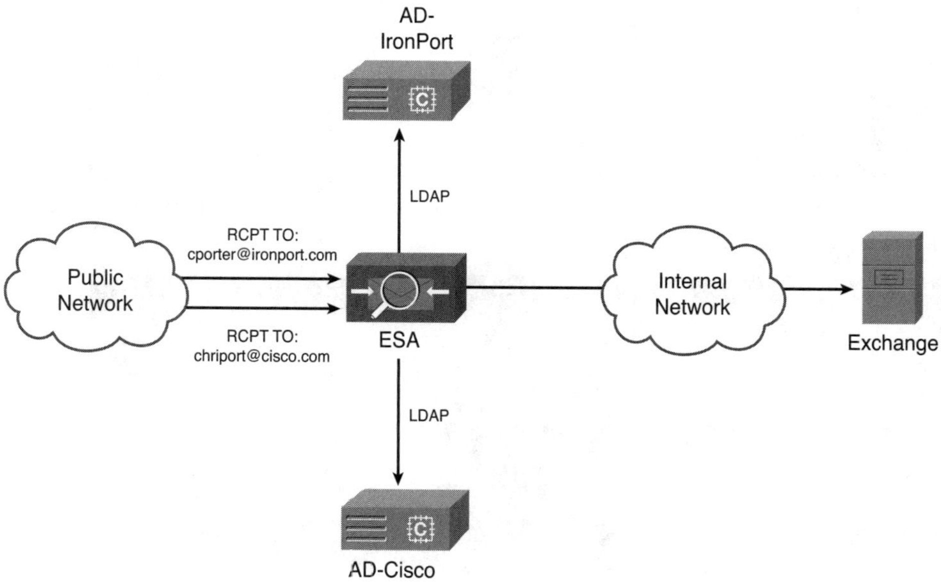

Figure 7-3 *Consolidated LDAP Environment Supported by Per-Domain LDAP Queries*

To support this configuration on the ESA, follow these steps:

1. Create the LDAP server profile and query for the first environment. In my example, I'm using AD-Cisco for the cisco.com addresses. The accept query is called AD-Cisco.accept. Test the query and submit the change.

2. Create the LDAP server profile and query for the second environment. Here, I'm using AD-IronPort for the ironport.com addresses. The accept query is called

AD-IronPort.accept. Test and submit. If you have more than two LDAP environments, repeat this for each one.

3. On the LDAP page of the System Administration menu, click **Advanced** and **Add Domain Assignments**. Give it a name, and choose the Accept query type in the drop-down. Add each individual recipient domain and select the appropriate query. You can select the same query for multiple domains, but in my case, I have one domain for each profile. Test and submit.

Figure 7-4 shows the resulting advanced query setup.

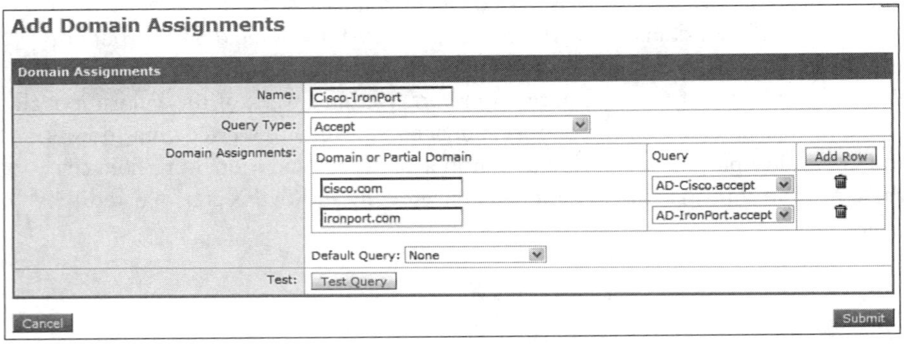

Figure 7-4 *Per-Domain LDAP Query*

Figure 7-5 shows the LDAP server profile and advanced query created in the WUI. The new per-domain accept query has its own unique name and can be used anywhere an LDAP accept query can be used.

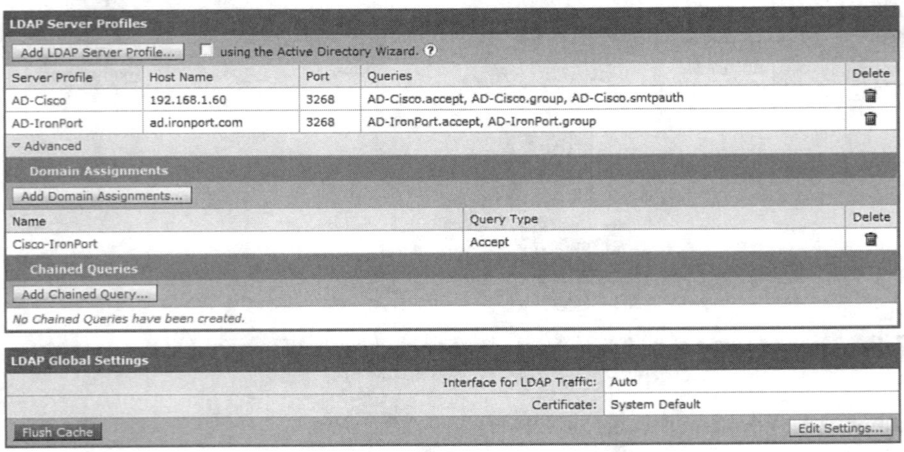

Figure 7-5 *LDAP Server Profiles and Per-Domain Query*

Daisy-chained queries are useful when all the information for a given domain may reside in more than one LDAP server. For example, suppose that, in addition to the regular corporate user directory, your organization also has a client database application that stores customer email addresses and makes them available via LDAP queries. Your business requires that whenever one of your user emails a client, a copy of the message is sent to an email archiving address using BCC. The concept is illustrated in Figure 7-6.

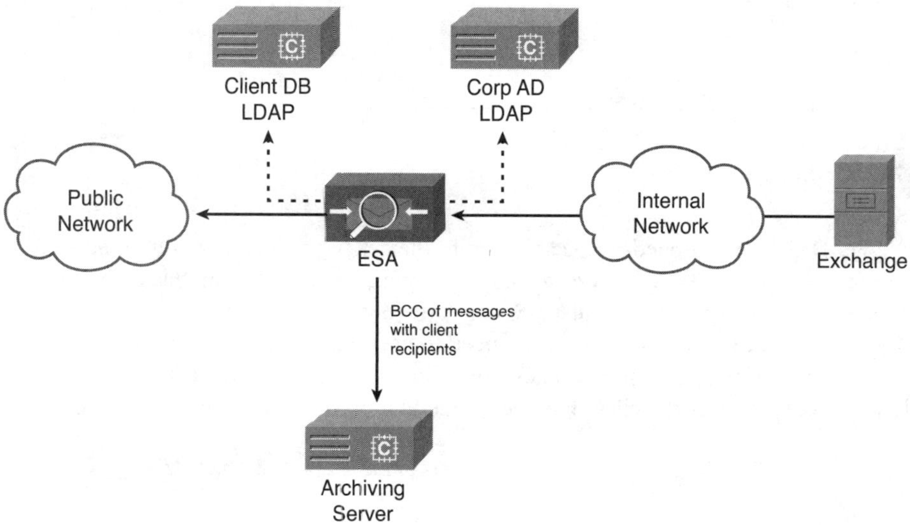

Figure 7-6 *LDAP Server Profiles and Per-Domain Query*

The challenge here is this: How do you identify which are client addresses? You could maintain a static list of recipients in an outgoing mail policy, but you would have quite a bit of maintenance to keep that up to date. The better approach is, of course, to use LDAP and to compose a group query to the client database server. Because you're already using your main organizational LDAP server for group queries, I'll show you how to use a chained query to do both. A chained query can contact multiple LDAP servers until it gets a successful answer; a query fails only when all LDAP servers respond negatively. The queries in the chain don't have to query the same attributes or use the same variables. In this case, we can ask the client database about the recipient address and the corporate LDAP server about the sender addresses. The client database query looks like this, keying on the objectclass attribute:

```
(&(contactEmail={a})(objectclass={g}))
```

While the regular corporate directory query looks like this:

```
(&(memberOf={g})(proxyAddresses=smtp:{a}))
```

First, create and test the two LDAP server profiles with their corresponding group queries, as you did with the per-domain advanced query. Here, however, you select **Group** from the drop-down, and there's no need to assign domains for the queries. Figure 7-7 shows the resulting chained query in the ESA WUI.

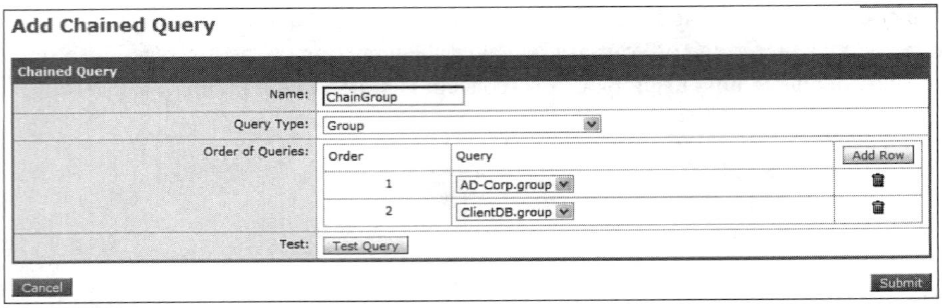

Figure 7-7 *Chained LDAP Query*

Like any LDAP query, it needs to be assigned to the listener that handles outgoing mail. Once assigned, you still need to create an incoming mail policy that supplies the group membership values for {g} in the query. Because the business use case is concerned with outgoing mail sent to client recipients, we need to create an outgoing mail policy that uses LDAP group values. Be sure to click the radio button for **Recipient**. The resulting policy configuration for the client member in the ESA WUI is shown in Figure 7-8.

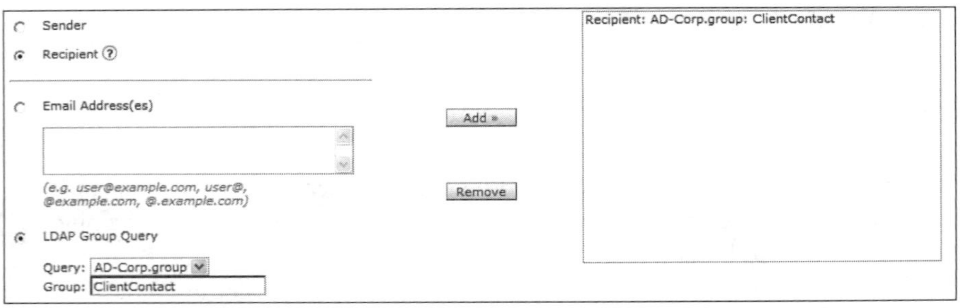

Figure 7-8 *Recipient-Based Membership for Client Policy*

For our local corporate users that are *not* sending to clients, the normal group rules apply, perhaps for policies corresponding to archiving, DLP, or encryption. Suppose you have an encryption policy for users in the Legal department. In this case, you want to create policies that apply to the sender, not the recipient, as shown in Figure 7-9.

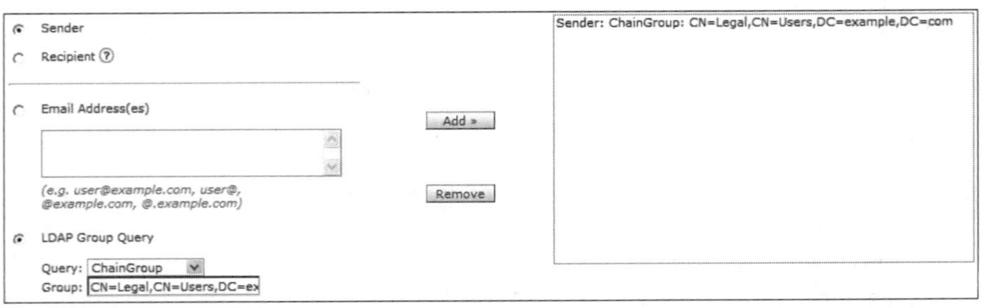

Figure 7-9 *Sender-Based Membership for Corporate Policy*

You would follow the same pattern for creating your other corporate policies. Order matters here: not the order of LDAP queries, but on the order of the policies. In the case of our client archiving example, it's possible that a message matches more than one policy, because the sender is in the legal department and the recipient is in the client database. The policy that's applied is the first one in the list from top to bottom. If the client policy is first, the client archiving content filter will be applied, but not any of the Legal department filters. You can resolve this with a content filter.

Let's suppose that the business rule requires the client archiving to take precedent over all the others, so it's the first policy in the list. However, the Legal department still needs its encryption policy. If the client policy includes no filters to account for this, messages from the Legal department to a client may not be encrypted as mandated. The solution is to test for the Legal department senders and the encryption conditions in a filter, and apply that filter to the client policy. Figure 7-10 shows the content filter that accomplishes this.

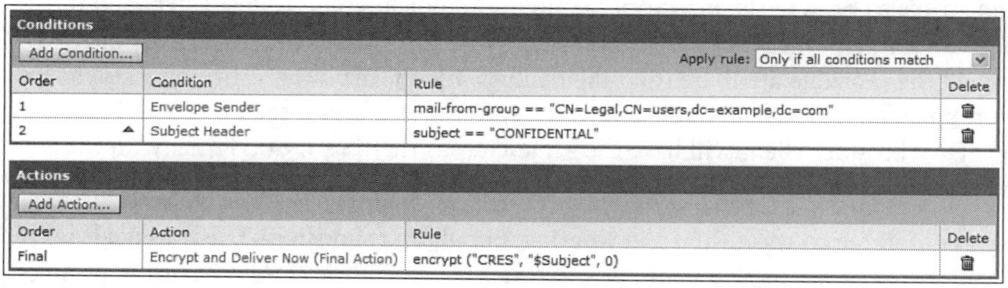

Figure 7-10 *Content Filter Testing for Senders in the Legal Department*

As you can see, I'm just using the same string that we used for defining the Legal department policy in the envelope sender condition, in the Matches LDAP group field. In this way, we have effectively enforced an action based on both sender and recipient via a filter condition and a policy, respectively.

These examples focused on LDAP accept and group queries, but per-domain and daisy-chained advanced queries can be used for any type of query.

Troubleshooting LDAP

Using LDAP integration on the ESA is essentially creating a dependency between two systems, and as a result, it can be difficult to troubleshoot. First, I assume that you tested your LDAP profiles and queries thoroughly and now have put the queries into production.

First, how would you know that something is going wrong? Obviously, with so many different uses for LDAP queries, the symptoms differ, but most LDAP issues start with an alert from the ESA. These alerts are classified as critical and list the affected LDAP query. The alert text looks something like this:

```
LDAP: query AD.group result LDAP Query Syntax Error: Invalid character 'o' at
  position 29 of query "(&(mail=chriport@cisco.com)(!objectclass=group))"
```

In many cases, the alert text will be enough to troubleshoot the issue. I should have tested this query before I committed it; it's missing a pair of parentheses.

If the source of the problem is not immediately obvious, enable an LDAP debug log subscription. You'll see the full text of the error and all the connection activity (or lack thereof) to each server.

The most challenging LDAP problems to solve are the intermittent ones—the problems affecting certain users or policies, but not all of them. If you know the user address or group that's experiencing an issue, single it out and run ldaptest or use the WUI testing features to see the results of the queries. Try clearing the LDAP cache and test again. If the issue doesn't appear obvious, you may have to resort to packet capture of the LDAP session.

Because the ldaptest tool is fairly limited unless you know precisely what you're looking for, you may want to look at the LDAP directory in a different way. Most LDAP servers include tools to browse the directory hierarchy, graphically, and to test filters and queries. There are also third-party LDAP browsers that give you extraordinary visibility by listing all the available attributes and their values. It's an easy way to troubleshoot access and privilege limitations, attribute and value spelling errors, and search scope (base DN). Your LDAP browser client will have the same view as the ESA if you log in with the same credentials and base DN.

If your configuration was tested and working, but all of a sudden isn't, ask yourself what changed. Some of the most common issues I've seen with ESA LDAP hiccups in production environments have been

- **Account expiration or password lockout:** The user account being used by the ESA has had its password expired or been locked out because of incorrect password guesses. This can happen for many reasons, both automatic and manual. The account that the ESA uses for LDAP queries should be set to never expire and never be required to change the password. Any account restriction that could suddenly result in suspension should not be applied to the ESA account.

- **Query timeouts:** These are fairly obvious if you have an LDAP debug log running, and are usually caused by querying unindexed attributes. You should only query indexed attributes, and these kinds of timeouts should be uncovered in testing. Query timeouts can also occur on overburdened LDAP servers.

- **Firewall rule changes:** All it takes is one short-sighted change in rules to shut off LDAP access, resulting in an email outage. The ESA is somewhat resilient to this and can let mail in if accept queries can't be resolved, and by queuing messages for the other query types. Luckily, this is fairly easy to troubleshoot because the alert messages are clear and a simple ldaptest can confirm connectivity.

- **Routing updates:** The ESA only supports static routing, so if network topology in the DMZ changes in a way that affects the ESA's ability to reach DNS or LDAP, you will have an outage unless you manually update the routes on the ESA.

Incoming and Outgoing Mail Policies

Aside from using LDAP to verify local email addresses, the most common use of directory integration is to group senders and recipients for the purpose of applying policies. We discussed incoming and outgoing mail policies in Chapter 4, "ESA Web User Interface," when describing the ESA pipeline, and earlier in this chapter. We look again at the effect of policies in Chapter 8, "Security Filtering," regarding security scanning. I hope you get the sense that mail policies are a crucial topic in ESA administration!

Group-Based Policies

In this chapter, we're interested in the application of policies based on LDAP information. This is done through group queries. Group queries are wonderfully flexible, allowing you to test the values of any attributes or even multiple attributes. A query that returns a match means that the recipient or sender address is part of the group, and hence a member of the policy. Figure 7-11 shows an outgoing mail policy showing membership by using a value to be tested in a group query.

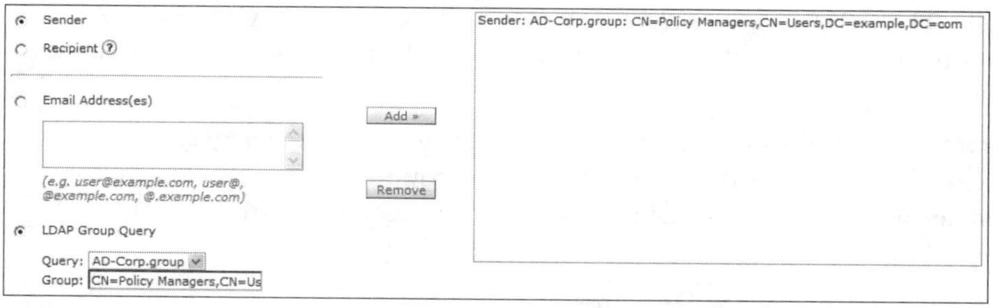

Figure 7-11 *Group Query Used as a Membership Test for a Policy*

You can certainly add multiple group query conditions, providing different values for the membership test. If you're using a chained or per-domain query, you can use a completely separate query as membership test. Lastly, you can also combine static email address, domains, or partial domains with LDAP membership, and freely mix conditions applying to senders and recipients.

Group Matches in Filters

You can also use the content filter conditions *Envelope Sender* or *Envelope Recipient Matches LDAP Group* to enact conditional rules on particular groups of senders and recipients.

When should you use policy membership versus one of the content filter conditions? In general, you should always use policy membership for recipient rules whenever possible, because of the problem with multirecipient messages, which was described in Chapter 3, "ESA Email Pipeline." Using policy membership allows multirecipient messages to be processed correctly, with each recipient falling into the appropriate policy via the splintering process. The content filter conditions are evaluated after this point in the pipeline.

For sender rules, applying policy is easier, because there's only one sender to any given message, and splintering doesn't occur. It's still a good idea to prefer policy-based sender sorting, however, simply because it's easier to understand and maintain.

There may be cases where you need to use *both* policy and content-filter based user grouping. This comes up with any business rule that requires a specific policy on messages sent by specific groups of users to specific groups of recipients, like my earlier example of Legal department senders and external client recipients. Because mail policies can only group users by either recipient address or sender address, but not both, we have to use both policies and filters to accomplish the task.

Because of the multirecipient problem, you should prefer using recipient policy membership and content filter sender tests.

Other LDAP Techniques

You're most likely to have a need for LDAP for recipient validation, and that's where I recommend you start with directory integration. Recipient validation provides several tangible benefits in an email environment. Beyond that, you're likely to need LDAP group queries for applying policy to inbound and outbound messages to meet business requirements.

In some cases, some requirements aren't quite met by the built-in query types, at least not directly. Necessity is the mother of invention, however, and the flexibility of the LDAP features on ESA mean that we can put group queries to creative use.

Using Group Queries for Routing

Sometimes, you'll have a need to make email delivery decisions based on non-hostname information in an LDAP directory. For example, suppose you have a set of recipient email addresses that are used by applications, not people, and these messages should all be delivered to the same host. The relevant attributes in the LDAP object for these applications look like this:

```
dn: cn=Customer Database,cn=users,dc=example,dc=com
memberOf: cn=applications,cn=users,dc=example,dc=com
cn:Customer Database
mail: crm@example.com
proxyAddresses: SMTP:crm@example.com
proxyAddresses: smtp:customercontact@example.com
```

Because there's nothing in this node that looks like a hostname, and the mail attribute doesn't look like it can route messages, we can't use LDAP routing. We can, however, use ESA group queries and filters to do the routing. I use the familiar group query recipe, which includes these ingredients:

1. Construct a group query that includes the user address {a} to locate the user and the group variable {g} that positively identifies the group. Test and then assign the group query to the listener.

2. Create an incoming mail policy whose membership is based on the LDAP group value you want to match. This value becomes the {g} variable in your query. Use the recipient condition for the test.

3. Create a content filter that performs the action you require—in this case, *Send to Alternate Destination Host*—and apply it to the policy you created in Step 2.

For the routing example, the group query needs to distinguish applications from users. It looks like we can use the memberOf field to do that, so our query is:

```
(&(proxyAddresses=smtp:{a})(memberOf={g})
```

The group variable that I'll use in the policy membership test is in this case the value of memberOf in the LDAP node. This must be the actual value stored in the attribute, which, in this case, is itself an LDAP DN:

```
cn=applications,cn=users,dc=example,dc=com
```

Don't let this confuse you! Even though we're passing in an LDAP DN, it has no further meaning here; to the ESA, it's just a string of bytes that needs to be compared to the values in the directory. The ESA isn't going to parse that string DN value or use it for a separate query. The resulting queries, at runtime, will be passed to the LDAP server, like this:

```
(&(proxyAddresses=smtp:crm@example.com)(memberOf= cn=applications,cn=users,
  dc=example,dc=com))
```

If that query is successful and has at least one match, the group query is true and the address is considered part of the group. The incoming mail policy, with the example LDAP group query value, is shown in Figure 7-12.

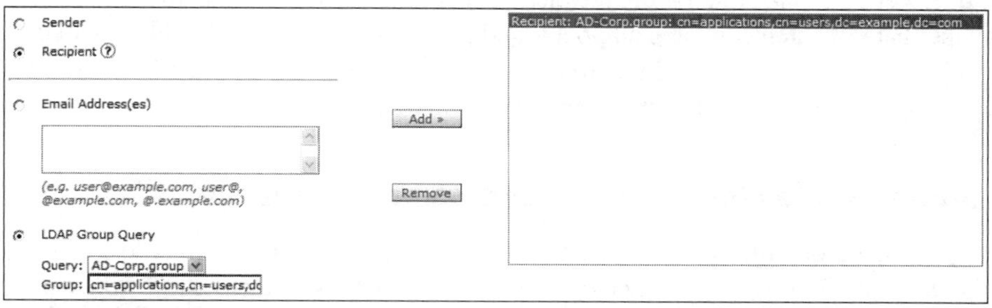

Figure 7-12 *Incoming Mail Policy for Applications*

The content filter is simple in this case, with no conditions and a single action, *Send to Alternate Destination Host*. Just take care to apply this filter only to the relevant application mail policy, because it has no condition and hence applies to all messages that it runs on. Make sure that it only runs on application mail by restricting it to that policy. The content filter is shown in Figure 7-13.

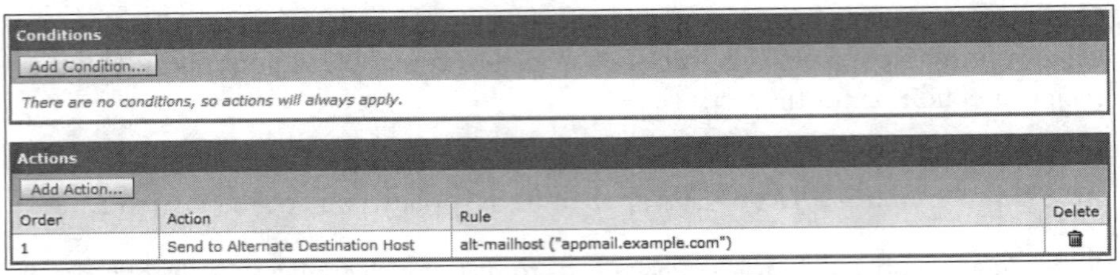

Figure 7-13 *Routing Content Filter to Be Applied to Application Mail Policy*

Per-Recipient Routing with AD and Exchange

AD and Exchange warrant a special mention because it does not directly expose the fully qualified hostname that stores the user mailbox account, and so the ESA cannot use AD to route messages on a per-recipient basis. Instead, the DN of the user's mailbox server is stored in the homeMDB attributes, like this:

```
homeMDB: CN=Mailbox Store (E2K7),CN=First Storage Group,CN=Information
  Store,CN=E2K7,CN=Servers,CN=first administrative group,CN=Administrative
  Groups,CN=EXAMPLE,CN=Microsoft Exchange,CN=Services,CN=Configuration,DC=example,
  DC=com
```

Using the previous technique, we can actually route using a group query that looks like this:

```
(&(proxyAddresses=smtp:{a})(homeMDB: CN=Mailbox Store ({g}),CN=First
  Storage Group,CN=InformationStore,CN={g},CN=Servers,CN=first administrative
  group,CN=Administrative Groups,CN=EXAMPLE,CN=Microsoft Exchange,CN=Services,
  CN=Configuration,DC=example,DC=com))
```

That query evaluates to true for any recipient whose mailbox is stored on that server. Combine that with an incoming mail policy, and an incoming content filter like the one shown in Figure 7-13, and you can deliver messages directly to the right Exchange server from the ESA. Repeat this for each server in your environment.

Using Group Queries for Recipient and Sender Validation

As explained, a group query is nothing more than a simple comparison, akin to asking the directory, "Do you have any entries with an attribute with this value?" You can exploit this simple query to do recipient validation, too. The idea is simply to group recipient addresses into two groups: those that are in the directory and those that aren't. By using a group query, we can ascertain that the email address is in the directory and use that test to apply an incoming mail policy. The addresses that aren't fall into the default policy.

Why would you want to do this, considering that LDAP accept is purpose-built for this very task? The answer is that LDAP accept is limited to a one of two actions on a negative result: either reject or drop. Either way, if the recipient address isn't in the directory, it's removed from the message and if that's the only recipient, the whole message is dropped or rejected. In order to use it, you have to be certain that your directory is authoritative. If you want to take another action, like quarantine, you can't use LDAP accept, but you can use LDAP group queries.

Like the other group query examples, we start with the query itself. This is pretty simple, because we're just going to use an LDAP accept query:

```
(proxyAddresses=smtp:{a})
```

We don't need the {g} variable because we're not actually querying for it. This also makes the incoming mail policy simple, because the LDAP group membership value can be any string. The resulting incoming mail policies are shown in Figure 7-14.

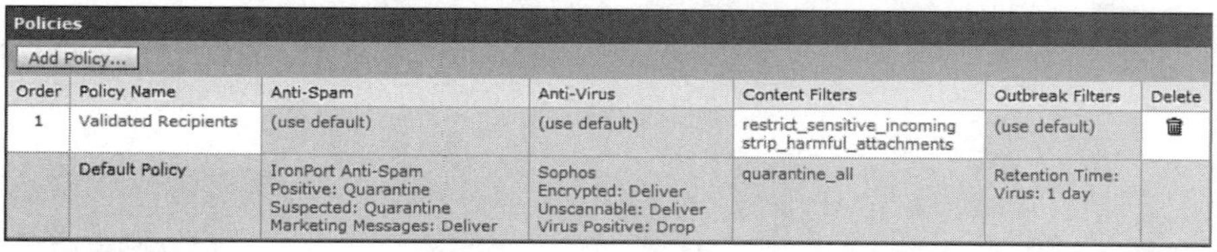

Figure 7-14 *Incoming Mail Policies to Support Recipient Validation via Group Query*

The accepted mail policy will be followed for any recipient that appears in the directory, and the default mail policy will be followed for any recipient not in the directory. To quarantine or redirect the recipients that don't resolve, create a content filter and apply it to the default. If you quarantine, the messages will be recoverable.

If you're using this approach as a crutch to start doing recipient validation, without taking hard action, be aware that performance is better when you actually reject the recipients, because you're not actually accepting the messages.

Summary

Almost every organization that uses the ESA can benefit from its LDAP integration features for security, routing, and policy. We covered how organizations can benefit, what the directory requirements are, and how to configure, test, and deploy LDAP queries. We explored the relationship between LDAP and incoming and outgoing mail policies, with examples of group queries for applying appropriate policies to individuals and groups of users.

We'll use incoming and outgoing mail policies in the next chapter where configuration of the security engines are covered: anti-spam, anti-virus, and outbreak filters.

Chapter 8

Security Filtering

In this chapter, you will learn the following:

- Security filtering engines that are available on the Email Security Appliance
- Technology underlying each filtering engine
- Enabling and configuration actions taken on identified messages

Overview

Security filtering is clearly the *sine qua non* of a product called the Email Security Appliance (ESA). This chapter explores the security filtering features—like anti-spam and antivirus—in depth. It also covers the zero-day virus capabilities of the Cisco Outbreak Filters feature and the use of other features, like content filters for security purposes.

The goal is to eliminate all kinds of unwanted messages from the environment entirely. At the very least, these junk messages are time-wasting, aggravating, and intrusive. At worst, they can be extremely dangerous—malicious software attached to, or linked from, email messages can be used for security breaches, allowing an attacker inside access to networks and servers in your organization.

Email spam has been a part of the Internet since the early days of Simple Mail Transfer Protocol (SMTP). Because the protocol doesn't require authentication of sending addresses or any other part of message content, it can be forged, hiding the identity of the sender or allowing them to continually shift their sending identity. Spam, and the battle against it, has taken the form of an arms race, with each side developing new measures and countermeasures to combat the other's techniques.

The Criminal Ecosystem

In general, security for email means dealing with unsolicited commercial email (UCE, or spam) and computer viruses or other malicious software (generally lumped together as *malware*). The two threats are typically related: Some spam messages propagate viruses, which infect systems and put them under the control of a botnet. There are thousands of botnets running on the Internet at any time, and there is competition among them for resources. Botnet systems are used to send out more spam and viruses.

In most jurisdictions, sending unsolicited commercial email is illegal. Unfortunately, the cross-jurisdictional nature of the Internet and the stolen resources by which the messages are propagated makes it extremely difficult to enforce these laws. Effective steps have been taken in some cases to stop the payment process that ultimately provide the profit for spam, but the senders have found means to continue their operations through front organizations, and operating in jurisdictions that have no laws or lax enforcement.

Spam typically makes money for the senders in one of a few ways. Advertisements promoting product sales are common, typically for pharmaceuticals or diet drugs, which can be legitimate but still illegally sold, or the drugs themselves can be imitation, placebo, or a dangerous substitute. Some spam is straight-up fraud, engaging in an email conversation with the recipient to extract funds. Other fraudulent messages seek to have users provide access credentials to email accounts, banking sites, or other websites by purporting to be an account or fraud alert, or by offering free products, gift cards, coupons, or rebates. These fraud messages are called *phishing*, but all the variants are fraud, and ESA doesn't try to distinguish between one form of junk and another.

Computer viruses aren't new, but the growth of Internet email made their spread much easier. Combining a malicious attachment with a message using various social engineering techniques has been an effective means of transmitting malicious software. Simply asking individuals to download and install software has been such an effective technique, in fact, that it's difficult to describe this kind of software as a virus, as they are not self-propagating. Cisco describes any unwanted software, whether attached to email, hiding inside a useful software package, or downloaded from the web, as malware.

Reputation Filters and SenderBase Reputation Scores

Reputation filters refers to the process where the ESA makes a decision about accepting connections from remote SMTP clients based on a lookup criteria that occurs as the connection starts. Essentially, the ESA categorizes each incoming SMTP connection into groups and applies a policy to all the connections in that group. The primary criterion for this grouping is the Cisco SenderBase database, using a rating system called the SenderBase Reputation Score (SBRS).

SenderBase tracks the history of email-sending IP addresses on the public Internet. Not every IP address has a score, but virtually all IPs that have made connections on port 25 in the last 30 days are listed.

The process of categorizing IPs and applying the relevant connection policy happens in the Host Access Table (HAT). From Chapter 3, "ESA Email Pipeline," you know that the HAT is the first part of the ESA pipeline, affecting the TCP connection and SMTP conversation. The policy that you apply also continues to affect message processing later in the pipeline, for messages that have been accepted by the ESA.

Enabling Reputation Filters

If you set up an ESA using the System Setup Wizard (SSW) and chose the option to accept incoming mail, you already have a basic HAT with groups and policies that use SBRSs. Figure 8-1 shows the default HAT that results from the SSW.

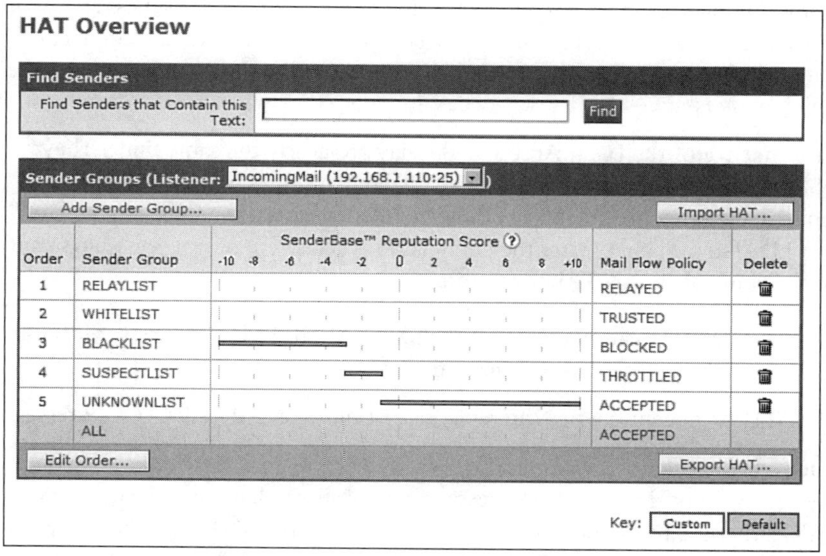

Figure 8-1 *Default HAT, Including Reputation Score Ranges*

The HAT is easily customizable. You can adjust the score ranges that each group represents, or even create your own groups with different score ranges. It's always a good idea to overlap your reputation score ranges (for example, a BLACKLIST with the range –10.0 to –3.0 and a SUSPECTLIST of –3.0 to –1.0). In such a scenario, an IP with exactly –3.0 SBRS falls into the first matching policy, which is the BLACKLIST in the default table.

Reputation Scores

Reputation scores range from –10.0 to +10.0, with –10.0 being the worst. An IP address that scores –10.0 is a certain, confirmed source of junk mail. The scores are calculated as real numbers, rounded to the nearest tenth of a point. So, although an IP can have a reputation score of -3.4867, you only see scores like –3.5 in the WUI reports, message tracking, and mail logs.

Connection Actions

Once a connection is grouped, the corresponding policy is applied. The grouping decision and policy application is final; connections are not reevaluated later in the pipeline, although certain features can change the outcome of the SMTP conversation. Mail flow policies, as part of the HAT, are created by default when you run the SSW, but can be modified any time after that. All mail flow policies boil down to four possible actions, as detailed in Chapter 3: TCP Refuse, Reject, Accept, and Relay. I recommend against using TCP Refuse; it's not part of any default policy, so you're really left with Reject, Accept, or Relay.

A Reject, or refuse, action is immutable. Even when using the optional **Delayed HAT Reject** option, a connection that has a Reject action applied never allows messages in. In fact, the ESA doesn't even allocate a full SMTP server thread to handle the connection: Although it looks like an SMTP server, the ESA is just servicing the connection with the absolute minimum resources.

From the perspective of the HAT, Accept and Relay are nearly the same thing: They allow the SMTP conversation to continue. The difference comes with the Recipient Access Table (RAT), where recipients are either validated against the table or not, and then against LDAP if available. After the connection is accepted, only a few things can change the outcome of the SMTP conversation:

- Envelope sender verification can reject the SMTP MAIL FROM address if it fails DNS checks. This feature must be enabled.
- RAT and LDAP Accept queries can reject one or more SMTP RCPT TO addresses.
- Messages that exceed the maximum size allowed by the mail flow policy can be rejected. This is not the only place message size limits can have an effect, and in fact, it's fairly rare. In most cases, ESMTP clients parse the SIZE extension that the ESA provides in response to EHLO and not deliver messages that exceed the ESA's maximum advertised size. Some senders ignore this or only support standard SMTP HELO and attempt to deliver large messages.

Of course, the HAT mail flow policies can all have different settings, so the behavior that a given SMTP client sees varies with the policy applied. You can find out which sender group and policy is applied to a given sender from the Incoming Mail reports, message tracking, or the mail logs.

HAT Policy Recommendations

The default HAT created by the SSW, or when you create a new public listener, has sensible groups and policies. These defaults are designed to provide good security with low false positives and a minimum of rate limiting. More restrictive filtering is possible and recommended if you understand the implications of tightening some of the controls. Here are some things to keep in mind while modifying HAT settings:

- **Don't WHITELIST.** If you can, avoid the temptation to bypass anti-spam scanning for any senders whatsoever. Even with a good reputation, a known sender can suddenly become a spam or virus source because of compromised hosts in their network. Reputation and anti-spam can handle these outbreaks, but not if you manually bypass these security features explicitly for certain senders. As an alternative, consider modifying the TRUSTED policy so that it performs anti-spam scanning while maintaining the higher connection limits that are part of the default.
- **Don't set your connection limits too high.** The default for most policies is to allow ten simultaneous connections from a given SMTP source. This is actually very high, and I recommend setting this lower—to just 1 or 2 per sender. Even a single connection is enough for a sender to deliver many, many messages in a short period. Save the high bandwidth settings for the TRUSTED policy.
- **Overlap your SBRS ranges.** Notice that the defaults include ranges like –10.0 to –3.0 for BLACKLIST and –3.0 to –1.0 for SUSPECTLIST. This is intentional. A score of –3.0 falls into the BLACKLIST, but don't be tempted to set the SUSPECTLIST lower bound to –2.9. SBRS scores are only granular to one-tenth of a point today, but they are actually calculated to three digits or more. If Cisco decided that there was a need to publish more granular scores, you could find senders that would go unclassified.
- **Decide on the organization's email message size limit and consistently apply it.** It's frustrating to troubleshoot message-size delivery problems if one policy is set to allow 10 MB messages while the others allow 20 MB.

Once established, a HAT policy should not require constant tending. If you find yourself manually adding senders to the BLACKLIST to manage spam and virus sources, consider making your policies more aggressive based on SBRS. If you are manually WHITELISTing senders, consider opening the default restrictions to avoid inflicting rate limits on legitimate senders.

IronPort Anti-Spam (IPAS)

Anti-spam filtering means simply to stop any message with unwanted content from entering your environment. It sounds simple, but what's obvious to a human being reading a message is not something a machine system understands. What machines are good at is processing a lot of simple comparisons, very quickly. A good anti-spam engine processes many, many rules very quickly and updates those rules very often.

Most spam filter engines work in roughly the same way: They open and examine messages, decoding attachments if necessary, and apply a series of tests. The series of tests, in total, produce a spam score, and the engine arrives at a verdict based on the score. The difference, then, is in the quality of the rules and the throughput of the engine.

When examining a spam filter, it's typical to talk about how effective it is—how well it identifies spam. The *catch rate* or *false negative* (FN) rate refers to the number of spam messages that the rules fail to identify as such. Filters with low catch rate let a lot of spam through, so this is an important measure, and a good filter should let less than 1% of spam messages through. On the other side, the dirty secret of anti-spam filtering is how often a given engine reaches a spam verdict on a legitimate message. This *false positive* (FP) rate is the other key number by which to measure the effectiveness of a spam filter. Many spam-filtering technologies have low FN rates, but unfortunately also have high FP rates. In other words, they catch a lot of spam, but at the expense of catching legitimate messages, too. An accurate spam filter should have an FP rate lower than 1-in-1000.

The IPAS design goal is to exceed a 99% catch rate, while maintaining a 1-in-1 million (0.0001%) false positive rate.

Enabling IPAS

If you have a new ESA that you've run the SSW, IPAS will be enabled automatically unless you uncheck the box during setup.

If IPAS is currently disabled, or the feature key expired, you may need to enable the engine from the Security Services menu under the IronPort Anti-Spam page. If you previously configured IPAS, and the key expired or the feature was manually disabled, your earlier settings will be preserved. If this is the first time you enabled it, you are given a default policy for IPAS.

The global options page for IPAS is shown in Figure 8-2.

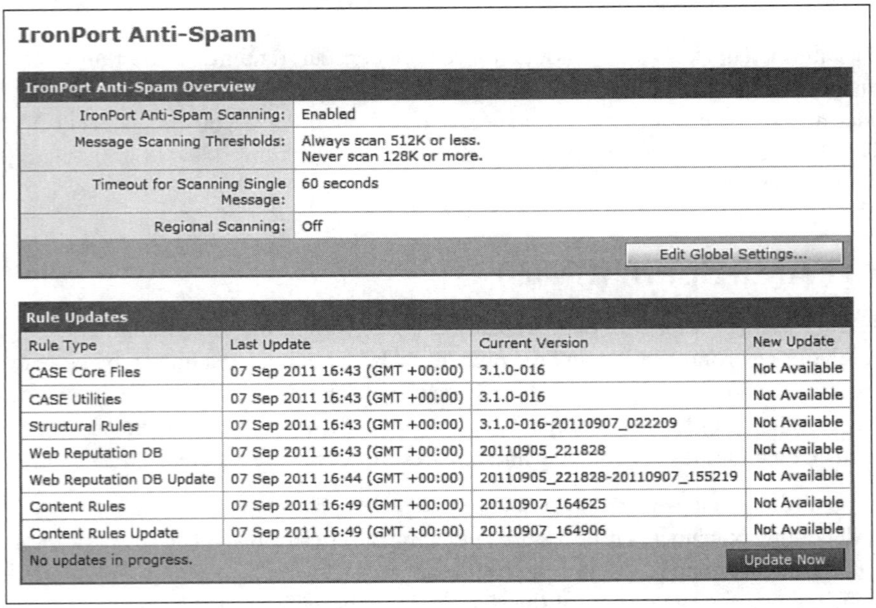

Figure 8-2 *IPAS Global Options*

All the security engines have only their global options enabled under the Security Services menu.

The configuration for anti-spam settings, like thresholds, verdicts, and actions, is on individual mail policy pages. If you're starting from a new ESA setup, you'll have only a default incoming and outgoing mail policy. The incoming default will have a basic IPAS configuration; outgoing will have anti-spam disabled. Because all the thresholds and actions are configured on a per-policy basis, you can have different spam settings for different groups of users.

The default IPAS policy page is shown in Figure 8-3.

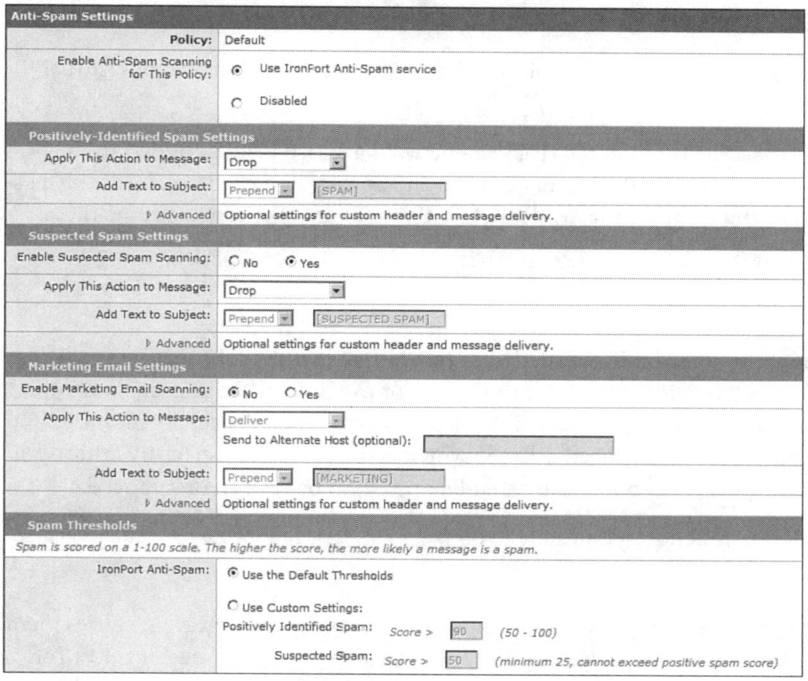

Figure 8-3 *Anti-Spam Policy Settings*

IPAS Verdicts

The IPAS engine computes a numerical score (hidden) for each message. The numerical scores are then compared with the verdict thresholds. There are three possible spam verdicts: not spam (clean), suspected spam, and spam.

There's another verdict that's possible, if the message is considered not spam: marketing. IPAS distinguishes between the illegal, and fraudulent, spam messages, and the legal marketing and advertising that is often sent in bulk. Because it is legal, it's not considered spam, but you may not want these messages delivered to your users. The marketing verdict is the way to treat these messages separately from clean messages.

IPAS does not render a separate verdict for phishing, fraud, 419 scam, or adult content. In general, if it can be described as bulk and unsolicited, or outright illegal, it will be classed as spam. If you have a need to filter legal adult content, for acceptable use policies, you need to consider using content filters and content dictionaries.

As IPAS evaluates its current rule set against each message, a total score is computed and a verdict rendered. Messages then pass into the actions specified for that verdict category. For performance, the IPAS engine always seeks an early exit, evaluating the lowest cost, but highest capture rules first, and exiting after a definitive match is made.

IPAS Actions

By default, clean messages continue in the next stage of the pipeline with no further action taken.

All messages that pass through the IPAS engine will have two headers added to them. These record the fact that IPAS scanned them, and an encoded header records the message verdict. If you examine the headers of an IPAS scanned message, you see these:

X-IronPort-Anti-Spam-Filtered:

X-IronPort-Anti-Spam-Result:

The anti-spam result header is encoded with rule hits so that the information can be used for improving results if it is submitted to Cisco. For example, if the message was found to be clean, but is submitted as spam, The Cisco Security Intelligence Operations (SIO) team can examine the results header to see why it scored low. It's especially critical for examining false positives, so that the offending rules can be revised or removed.

There are four basic actions you can take on messages that fall into a particular verdict category:

- **Drop:** Immediately stops all processing and discards the message. Log entries record the verdict and the drop. Unless you choose to archive the message, it is lost forever. Because these messages do not continue in the pipeline, they are not checked by antivirus and cannot be acted on by content filters. Because messages continue no further, this option is good for performance.
- **Deliver:** Allows the message to continue, potentially with modification, and proceed through the pipeline to antivirus, content filters, and outbreak filters. If you choose not to modify the message, the only indication of the verdict will be in the encoded X-IronPort-Anti-Spam header, which cannot be decoded other than by Cisco.
- **Spam Quarantine:** Schedules the message to be delivered to the on-box or centralized end-user quarantine. Under the hood, this action only modifies the delivery destination, so the message continues through the pipeline to the other security engines.
- **Bounce:** Sends an NDR back to the envelope sender address, and drops the original message. Although this may seem useful, providing notification to the sender in the case of false positives, it is an extremely bad idea. Simply put: You should

never use this option, because it creates *backscatter*—you become a spam relay system back to the envelope addresses. Because spam senders forge these addresses, you'll be sending notifications to innocent third parties, and will likely end up with your external IPs on a DNS blacklist. Frankly, this setting is so problematic that it shouldn't even be available in the product.

Note that IPAS actions apply to all messages that pass through the relevant mail policy; per-user and per-group actions are possible by using multiple incoming or outgoing mail policies. More complex actions can be achieved by using content filters.

Content Filters and IPAS

Content filters can be used to act on messages that have passed through the IPAS engine, because content filters are evaluated near the end of the work queue pipeline, after anti-spam and antivirus. To distinguish between the verdicts, however, you have to use the IPAS options to modify the message by adding a header and looking for that header with a content filter. There is no native condition to check the IPAS verdict on a message, and no way to access the numerical score of the message. So, you must combine a message markup with a filter condition that checks for that markup.

This interaction between filters and IPAS comes up when using dictionaries in a content filter for scanning messages for words and phrases. Suppose your organization has a policy against using profanity in email messages, and your naughty words are organized into a dictionary. Further, you want to redirect, or just drop, these profanity-laden messages. At the same time, your IPAS policy is to send spam to the spam quarantine. It seems simple: Set your IPAS policy to quarantine and create a simple content filter like the one shown in Figure 8-4. This one redirects the profanity to an administrator.

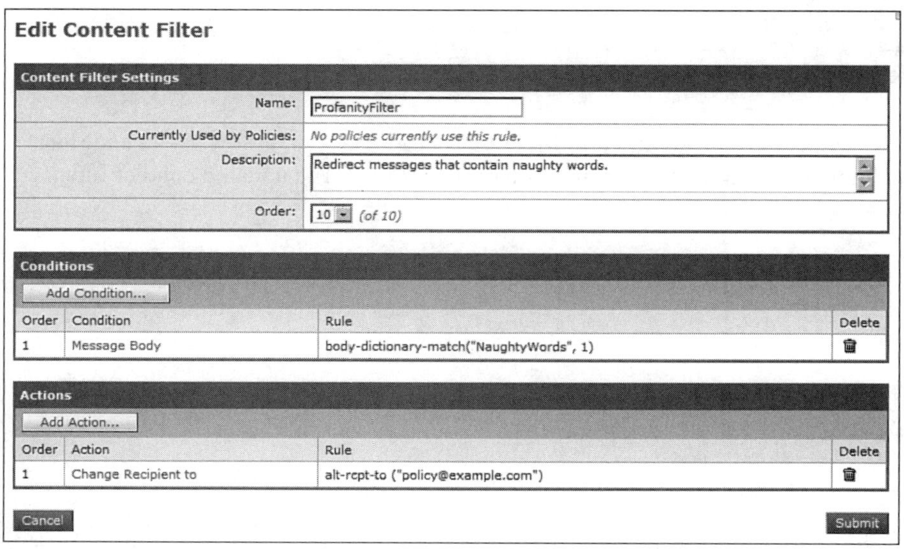

Figure 8-4 *Simple Profanity Filter*

If you were to use this filter, however, you would find that some spam messages are being redirected, because a lot of spam contains profanity. This example doesn't have to be profanity; it could be any kind of content you're looking for in messages. Attachment filters are affected, too. If you're using the spam quarantine action, you are allowing the spam to continue through the pipeline for further filtering, and that may not be what you want.

The solution is to keep the quarantine action, but use the Advanced actions in each verdict configuration to add a header to the message. This is shown in Figure 8-5, where I use a header called X-AS with a value of True for both positive and suspect verdicts.

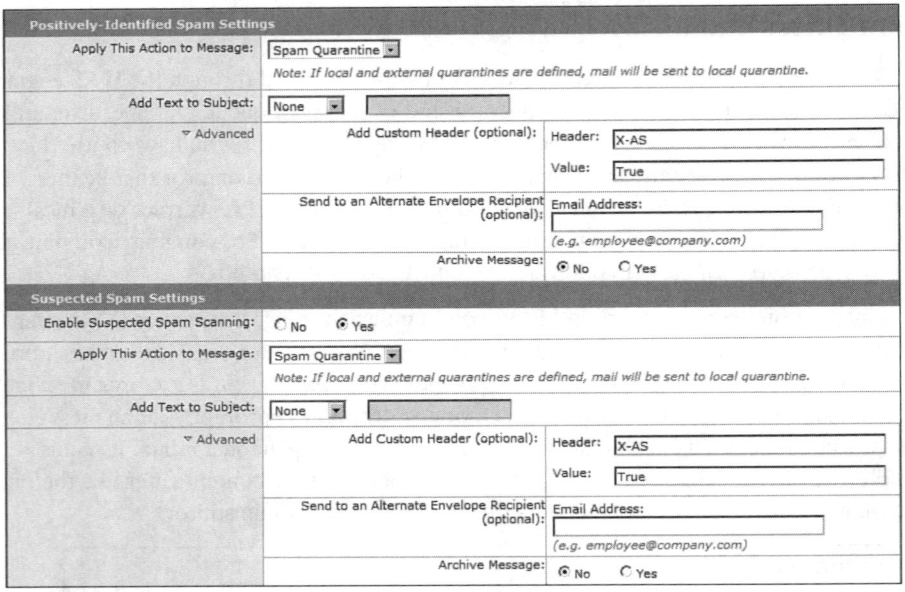

Figure 8-5 *Advanced Settings for Spam-Handling Actions*

The filter needs to be modified to handle this header as well. It now has an additional condition, checking that the spam header wasn't added. The updated content filter is shown in Figure 8-6.

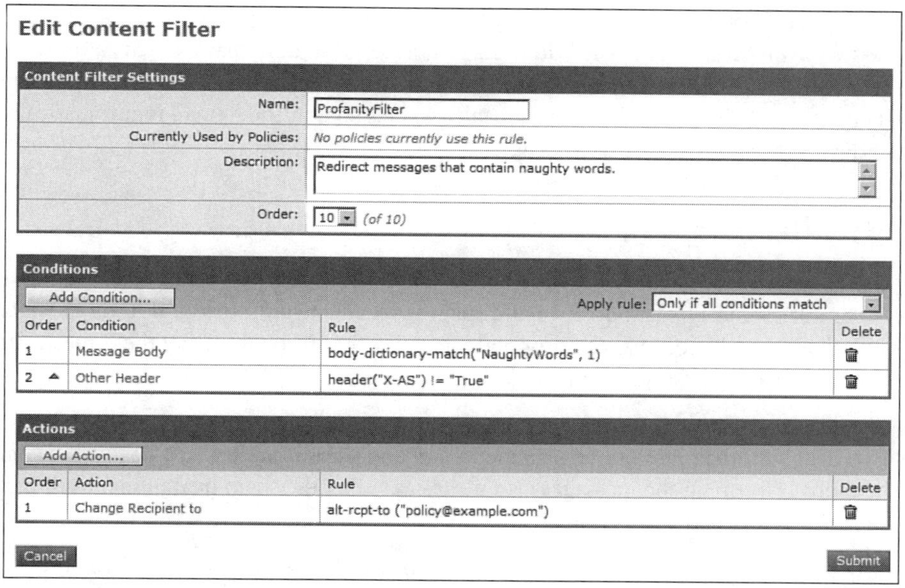

Figure 8-6 *Updated Content Filter*

Recommended Anti-Spam Settings

If you've run the ESA SSW and turned IPAS on, the default settings closely match the recommendations I would make for you in a new Cisco email security deployment. The spam capture rate is high, with a focus on keeping false positive rates low.

If you are transitioning to the Cisco Email Security technology from another product, you may want to create a policy that closely matches your current environment. IPAS has settings and options that are analogous to those in other products and services. Because of the very high accuracy of IPAS, you may be able to get more aggressive with spam filtering than you are with other products.

Spam Thresholds

The default spam thresholds classify scores of 90–100 as positive spam and 50–90 as suspected spam. These are good settings, if a bit conservative. They focus on providing good capture rates but maintaining a low false positive rate.

If you want to be more aggressive, you should lower the thresholds. I recommend doing so incrementally, by no more than 5 points per shift. From the default, that would make the first step to move the spam positive lower bound to 85, and the spam suspect to 45.

When you do have need for more aggressive settings, another option is to create an aggressive spam filter policy, and add users to it as requested. In many organizations, the preference for ultra-aggressive spam filtering is limited to a few vocal users. You can even create an LDAP group for these squeaky wheels so that their email is automatically treated with the more aggressive settings.

Actions for the Bold

If your focus is on removing as much spam as possible, an aggressive anti-spam policy is pretty simple: Set your spam positive and spam suspect actions to drop. IPAS is accurate enough that you will not miss the dropped messages, and throwing away these messages has advantages for performance.

Removing the messages from the environment means that you, as an administrator, don't have to deal with them in your environment, and end users don't have to deal with them in the inbox. Dropping the messages also means avoiding the spam quarantine, both for administrators and end users.

Slightly less aggressive would be to drop spam positive but quarantine or deliver suspected spam.

In the world of anti-spam, the ideal technology would always catch every spam message, never catch a legitimate message, and never require that users review and release messages. IPAS with a drop action is as close to this technology nirvana as you can get, and it's very close.

Actions for the Middle-of-the-Road

If you've come to trust the IPAS verdicts, as I have, but want to have a recovery option, or if you want to be more aggressive and test lower spam thresholds, you should quarantine the messages. You can quarantine locally on the ESA or on an SMA, if you have one in your environment.

When using the spam quarantine, you can choose whether you allow end users to manage their own messages, or leave it strictly administrator access only. The middle-of-the-road approach is to leave the quarantine admin-only, sparing end users the burden of having to sort messages, but giving your administrators a means of retrieving messages should a legitimate message be caught as spam.

The drawback of an admin-only quarantine is additional work in the IT department to search for and release these messages, and for end users, the additional time it takes to have a message released.

Actions for the Conservative

If your organization must simply never encounter an unrecoverable false positive, you should configure the ESA to use the deliver or spam quarantine actions. Delivering the messages allows end users to deal with messages as they prefer. In most environments, the strategy is to deliver the message with a specific Subject or other header modification, allowing end users or administrators to create client mail user agent (MUA) rules to folder or delete messages. Some MUAs support flexible filtering rules that are applied at the time of final delivery; these rules can act on header presence or values or specific strings in the Subject.

The end-user quarantine always provides administrative oversight and optionally, end user access and periodic summary digest notifications. Messages are stored in the spam quarantine until either they expire or the quarantine storage space is exceeded.

Outgoing Anti-Spam Scanning

In environments where the end users are not under organizational control, spam leaving your organization from infected machines or compromised account credentials can be a serious problem. For example, service providers for residential or mobile broadband servers and higher education are often in a role of providing outgoing mail services, but don't control the devices and software used to send email.

IPAS can be used on outgoing policies, but should not be the only security policy for controlling infected clients. Filtering effectiveness for outgoing mail originating in RFC 1918 address spaces is lower than for incoming mail. It's more effective and much lower overhead to use HAT mail flow policies to rate limit individual clients. We cover this and other architectural solutions to compromised internal clients in Chapter 14, "Recommended Configuration."

Sophos and McAfee Antivirus (AV)

Antivirus (AV) is the examination of email attachments for malicious content. Modern AV engines use a wide range of techniques to detect malicious content, and rely on regular updates to the rules packages that they operate on. You can think of AV as a test platform, with the message as subject and the downloaded rules as the test. The rules are generally dubbed *signatures* and are routinely updated. In fact, what distinguished AV today between the different vendors is how quickly a signature is created when a new virus type is identified.

The ESA provides two signature-based AV engines on the platform, each from a different vendor: Sophos and McAfee. Both products use both industry-standard and their own proprietary techniques for analyzing messages. Dynamic updates allow both the rules engine, and the rules themselves, to be updated at any time. As an ESA administrator, you can choose to run one, or the other, or both, provided you have a license key.

The motivation behind virus writing has changed. Gone are the days of *graffiti* and other electronic vandalism that served to enhance the author's reputation. Virus writing has moved out of the world of motivated amateurs and into professional criminal operations. With the rapid growth of Internet usage and e-commerce, a lot of money is at stake and so has come the rapid growth of criminal activity. Computer systems running malware can be remotely controlled, with such computers being called *bots* organized into *botnets*. These bots then send out more infected messages or host landing pages for fraudulent activity or for spreading more viruses.

Because of the ubiquity of email, the credulousness of users, and the amount of money at stake, it makes a compelling infection vector for the criminals behind such activity.

As of this writing, another change in the nature of email viruses is under way. There's a shift away from malware email attachments and a move to messages that contain a URL. This URL serves as a *call to action* in the message, enticing users to click on the link using social-engineering techniques. The link—usually to a website hosted on a botnet—actually delivers the malware, infecting the user through known browser exploits, or more simply, encouraging them to download and install the software, hiding the malware behind a purportedly useful package. The Cisco focus on web security and URL reputation provides the information that allows the anti-spam engine to recognize malicious URLs in email messages.

Enabling AV

As with all the security engines, the global options are available on the Security Services menu, but the individual mail policies control the actions taken by the engine for a given message. Just like with anti-spam, you can specify AV policies on a per-group or per-user basis, but there's hardly ever a call to do so. Most organizations have a single, global AV policy.

The only configurable option on the Security Services menu is the global AV scanning timeout, in seconds. The AV engine gives up scanning a message after this amount of time, to protect the engine and the ESA from corrupted or deliberately malformed attachments, like *zip bombs*, that would otherwise continue scanning forever.

On a new configuration from the SSW, some sensible defaults for AV are created, and AV is enabled for both incoming and outgoing mail policies. If AV is not enabled during the SSW, you can do so by clicking the Enable button on the individual engine pages under the Security Services menu or by using the CLI **antivirusconfig** command. You must have a valid feature key to enable AV.

The mail policy options for Anti-Virus are shown in Figure 8-7 and Figure 8-8. You have a choice of engines, depending on which engines are keyed and enabled. You can choose Sophos, McAfee, or both. From there, you have two choices for scanning: scan for viruses only or scan and repair. Although it seems like repairing messages is a good idea, it just creates noise and confusion for end users, so I recommend the **Scan for viruses only** option. I go into details about this recommendation later in this chapter.

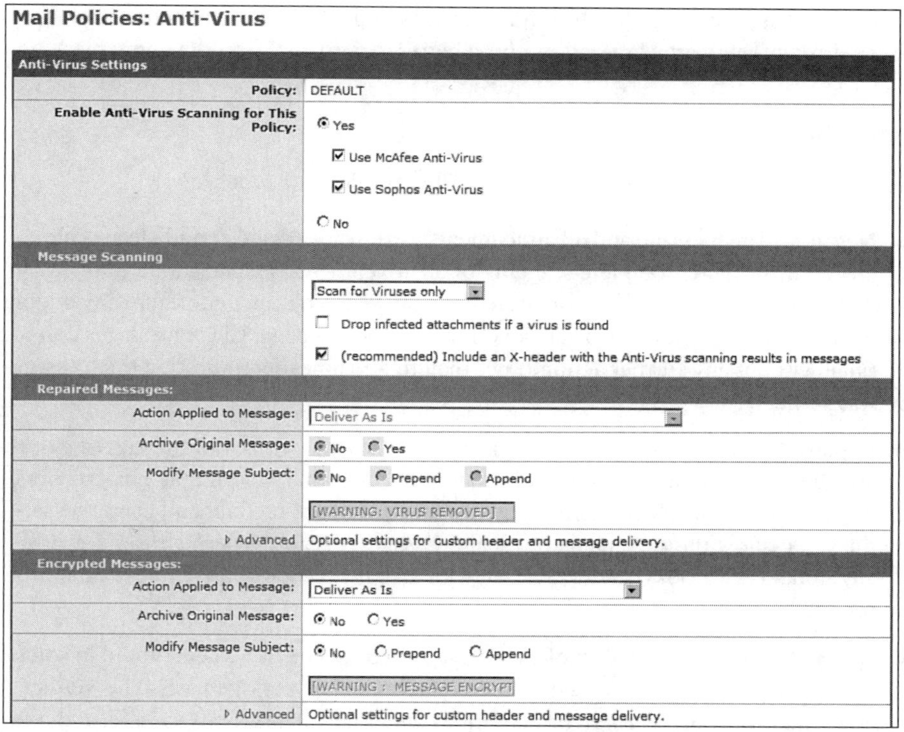

Figure 8-7 *AV Scanning Options and Repaired and Encrypted Actions*

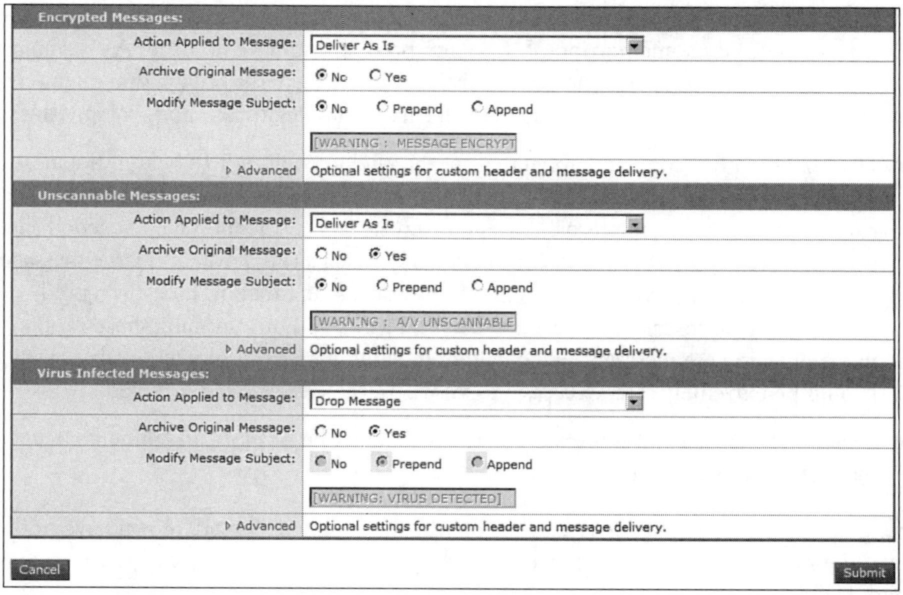

Figure 8-8 *AV Scanning Options: Encrypted, Unscannable, and Virus Detected*

I recommend against using the **Drop infected attachments** option. It sounds like a good idea to drop infected attachments, but it's a better idea to just drop the entire message.

AV Verdicts

The AV engines can arrive at one of five possible verdicts for a message:

- **Not viral:** The message and all attachments were scanned and found clean. The engine was able to complete scanning of all attachments, reaching a definitive verdict. No timeout or other errors were encountered. You can't configure any actions for this verdict, as it is not available on the AV policy page. Clean messages continue without any further action other than to add a header indicating the message was scanned.
- **Repaired:** The message contained an attachment with a virus, but the message or the attachment was modified to remove that virus. This could mean that a macro virus was removed from a document or spreadsheet. I do not recommend using the settings that allow the AV engine to repair messages, because macro viruses are virtually nonexistent today, and a message with a viral executable attachment cannot be repaired.
- **Encrypted:** At least one part of the message or attachment was encrypted in some way, preventing the AV engine from fully scanning all message parts. This verdict is reached for a large variety of conditions and attachments. For example, archives with passwords, *protected* documents, and even spreadsheets with protected cells will return an encrypted verdict. It does not mean that the message contains a virus or that it's even likely; it just means that the engine could not scan every byte of the message because some portion of it is encrypted. If you have no other AV scanning in the environment or have an absolutely zero-tolerance virus policy, you might consider quarantining these, but doing so will catch many legitimate nonviral messages.
- **Unscannable:** For some unknown reason, the engine could not fully scan the message. This could be because some portion of the message or attachment was corrupted or truncated, an internal AV engine error, or that the message exceeded the maximum scanning timeout. If you continually receive this verdict on large messages during busy periods, you can increase the AV scanning timeout. Like encrypted messages, most unscannable verdicts are NOT viral, and quarantining these results in many legitimate messages being halted. In daily operation, an unscannable verdict should be extremely rare, except in cases where the ESA is overburdened.
- **Virus Infected:** The message was found to contain one or more attachments that matched a virus signature.

The same verdicts are available regardless of which AV engine is used. If you have both enabled, only one engine has to arrive at a viral verdict for the entire message to be considered viral.

AV Actions

Just like anti-spam, you have a choice of actions for each verdict that the AV engine can reach. Those actions are

- **Deliver As Is:** Delivers the message exactly as it was received. You have the option of modifying the message subject, adding a header, delivering to an alternate recipient or host, and generating a notification about the message.
- **Deliver As Attachment to New Message:** Delivers the original message as either a text/plain or rfc822 MIME attachment to a new message.
- **Quarantine:** Delivers the message to the virus system quarantine. The message is delivered to the local system quarantine where it can be reviewed, released, or deleted by an administrative user. The system quarantines are not accessible to end users.
- **Drop:** All message processing halts and the message is discarded. You can choose to archive a copy. Because the message does not continue in the pipeline, you cannot act on these messages in content filters.

The actions available differ slightly depending on the verdict. For example, Drop is not available as an action for repaired messages.

When you use the Drop action, you have the additional option of archiving a copy of the message on disk in a log archive format. This can be a peace-of-mind last resort for dropped messages.

AV Notifications

Sending automated notifications is a common need for virus verdicts, and the ESA makes special provisions to support notifications for this task. Like all notifications, the text of an AV notification is controlled through a template that you create and manage in the Text Resources page of the Mail Policies menu or in the CLI *textconfig* command. The system-generated notifications are in U.S. English, but you can use a custom notification to craft messages in any language.

There are two types of text resources associate with anti-virus: container templates and notification templates. Container templates are only used when you choose a **Deliver As Attachment to New Message** action. Notification templates are the messages sent in place of the original message.

Like any other text notification, you can use action variables that are substituted with system and message values when the notification is generated. Action variables start with a $. For AV, some additional action variables are supported, which are above and beyond the normal notifications. Table 8-1 lists these antivirus action variables. The most informative variables are the various TABLEs that can be added, and I recommend that you use these for human-readable notifications.

Table 8-1 *AV Notification Action Variables*

Variable	Description
$AV_VIRUS_TABLE	An HTML table that includes each virus-infected part and the name of the virus. It just shows the virus name, and does not indicate what action was taken.
$AV_DROPPED_TABLE	Similar to the AV_VIRUS_TABLE, but only shows attachments that were dropped.
$AV_REPAIRED_TABLE	Similar to the other tables, but only shows attachments that were repaired. This table is usually empty, because it's extremely rare to encounter repairable virus-infected files.
$AV_REPAIRED_PARTS	Like the repaired table, but it just uses a comma-separated list of the files or MIME parts that were repaired.
$AV_UNSCANNABLE_PARTS	List of unscannable parts. This is an extremely useful variable if you're trying to track down a consistent problem with unscannable attachments. If you can capture a file that consistently yields an unscannable verdict, send it to Cisco for analysis.
$AV_VIRUSES	A list of all the viruses found anywhere in the message. Not useful, because it does not list the filenames or parts; instead, use AV_VIRUS_TABLE.
$AV_VERDICT	The overall AV verdict for the message. If any one part of the message is found to be encrypted, unscannable, or viral, that will be the verdict for the entire message.
$AV_REPAIRED_VIRUSES	List of the viruses found and repaired. Because repairable viruses are so rare today, this will likely always be empty.
$AV_DROPPED_PARTS	List of the message parts that were dropped. This will only have a value if you're using the "dropped infected attachments" option. The AV_DROPPED_TABLE contains more information.
$AV_ENCRYPTED_PARTS	List of the MIME parts that were at least partially encrypted.
$AV_INFECTED_PARTS	All the infected MIME parts. The AV_VIRUS_TABLE is more informative than this simple list.

Notifications should be used on outgoing virus positive messages, alerting IT security that a user or host is sending infected messages through your email environment. The notification should include enough information from the original message to allow you and your team to identify the source and type of the virus.

Content Filters and AV

You can act on messages that have been scanned by the AV engines in content filters in much the same way that you can act on spam filtered messages. By default, the AV verdict on a message is not recorded anywhere in the headers, but you can use the AV message modification options to easily add such a header.

One example of AV and content filter interaction is to augment the ability of the ESA to detect encrypted content. If your organization restricts the use of encrypted content, you can use the ability of the AV engine alongside the ESA's native encryption detection.

Figure 8-9 shows an example of such a content filter. This example shows a quarantine action being taken on these messages, but any of the content filter actions are available. You could drop, redirect, BCC the messages, add disclaimers, send notifications, or add a custom log entry. You could also bounce the messages, but that results in your ESA sending potentially viral messages back to some third party whose address has been forged, which is obviously not recommended.

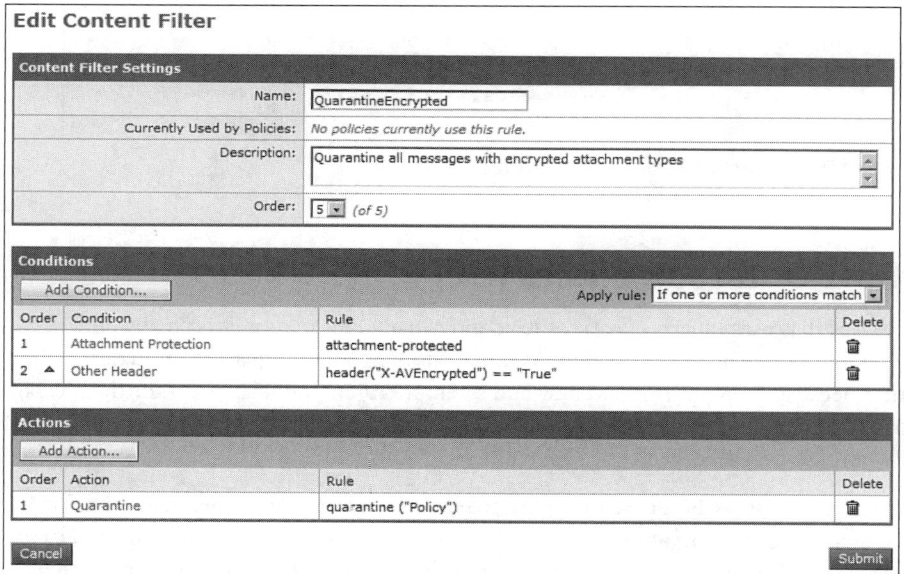

Figure 8-9 *Content Filter for Acting on Messages That Are Encrypted*

This content filter requires that you add an X- header to the message using the action in the Encrypted Messages verdict in the AV policy. To do this, click the AV settings in the appropriate policy to get to the Antivirus Settings page. Scroll down to the section for Encrypted Messages. Click **Advanced** to reveal the message modification options and click **Yes** to **Add Custom Header to Message.** Be sure to use the same header name and value in the AV settings and in the content filter.

Figure 8-10 shows the Advanced header option in the Encrypted verdict of the AV settings.

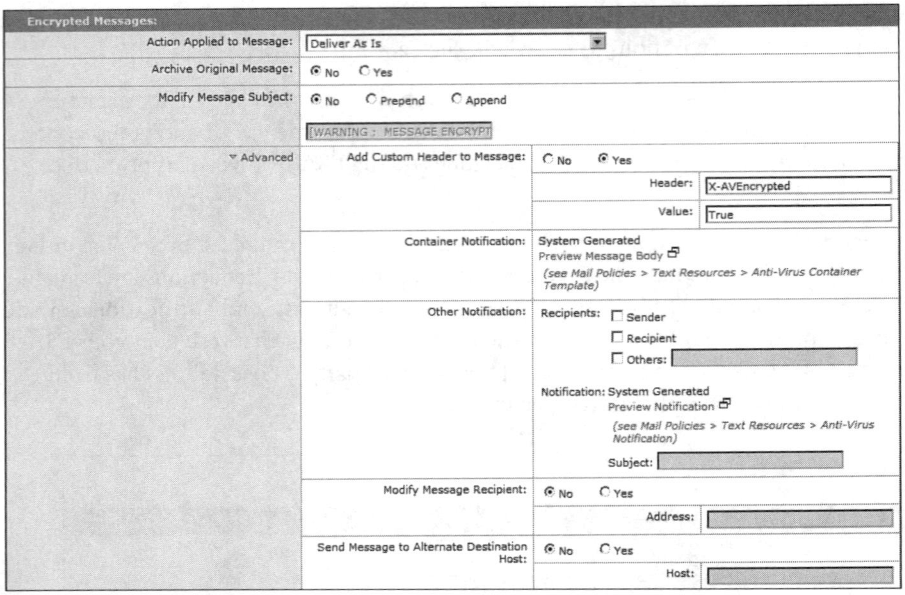

Figure 8-10 *Adding a Header to Encrypted Messages*

IronPort Outbreak Filters (OF)

Antivirus that uses binary signatures to identify malicious messages is an absolute necessity in modern email environments. At times, though, binary signatures aren't enough, either because the virus is brand new and signatures aren't published yet, or the message doesn't actually contain any viral attachments, instead using a URL that brings the user to viral content on the web.

The Cisco Outbreak Filters (OF) engine covers these *corner cases* and makes intelligent judgment about potentially viral content or URLs. It is not a signature engine and cannot replace the McAfee or Sophos engines on the ESA; in fact, it's a complement to these technologies, offering an advanced zero-day protection while relying on the verdicts from the AV engines for final action.

Because it's not a signature engine, and it is possible that OF rules will catch legitimate content, the filtering approach is wait-and-see: Quarantine matching messages until the AV engines have a chance to update, or until the outbreak passes and the content can be confirmed non-threatening and released. In this way, additional threat messages can be stopped without much of a penalty for false positives. Messages are rescanned when AV signatures are updated, allowing the system to release or drop as soon as the threat is identified. When messages are released from quarantine, they are scanned again, giving the anti-spam and antivirus engines a second chance to render a verdict.

Enabling OF

It's the same story with OF as it was for the other engines: Enable it on the Security Services menu, but configure the verdicts and actions on the individual mail policies.

The global outbreak filters options page shows you the global settings, along with a status report of the latest rule and engine updates. The page also shows the actual rule identifiers and descriptions so you can understand what outbreaks are underway. Note that this page lists all active outbreak rules, whether those threats are being encountered in your environment or not. If you want to see only the threats affecting your environment, look at the Outbreak Filters report on the Monitor tab.

Figure 8-11 shows the global OF options for editing. You can enable or disable the engine, set a maximum message size to scan, and opt in to email alerts. The email alerts are a nice feature, but in most environments, they will be very noisy—several to dozens per day.

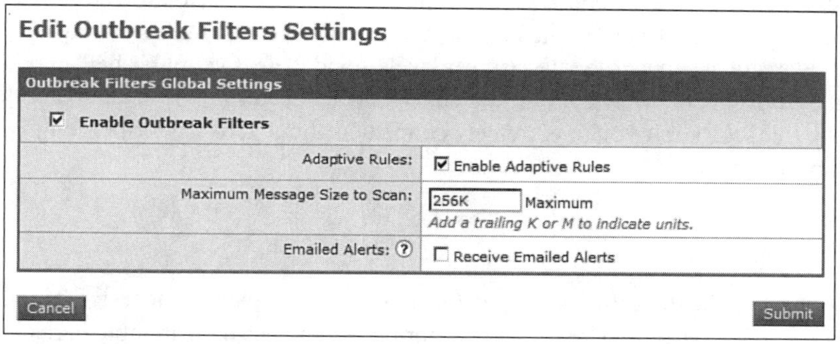

Figure 8-11 *Global OF Options*

The other option is whether to enable adaptive rules. Adaptive OF rules can be described as "local" outbreak rules that are always active. Instead of using the global information, they examine volume trends on attachments locally, focusing on typically dangerous attachments like executables, or archives that contain executables. These rules can help protect against an outbreak that effects your environment, like a compromised host or account that begins sending virus attachments to emails. When a large volume of executables is sent in an atypical pattern by one host or user, the adaptive rules can key in on that threat and quarantine the messages.

OF Verdicts

There are, effectively, only two possible verdicts for messages when it reaches OF: clean or suspicious. Clean messages move on to the rest of the pipeline. Suspicious messages are quarantined, in a special system quarantine called Outbreak, where they are held for re-evaluation. Messages can also, optionally, be modified to alter malicious URLs, or mark up the message to make end users aware of the potential threat.

The thresholds that you configure in OF are related to the threat level published by Cisco for a given outbreak rule. Throughout the day, new outbreak rules are published that include

- An outbreak ID that uniquely identifies the rule set.
- An outbreak threat level that indicates the severity of the outbreak. Most will use threat level 3; higher is more dangerous.
- An attachment filename, file extension, or other attributes. For example, a rule might specify that it is for bat, pif, scr, or an archive type, like zip(exe). You can see these attachment details in the WUI.
- Suspicious threat URLs. If the outbreak is for messages that use a URL to malicious files instead of an attachment, the rule will include those URL patterns. The actual URLs are not available in the WUI.

You must decide for your environment at what threat level the ESA should take action on these messages. Threat level 3 is the default, and there isn't much reason to change this. Very few *slightly suspicious* rules (threat levels 1 and 2) are ever published, and by the time an outbreak reaches level 4 or 5, you likely have missed some viruses. I recommend leaving this set to 3; if you're extremely concerned about zero-day or phishing messages, lower it to 2.

OF Actions

The OF actions are, like the verdicts, simple: Quarantine the suspicious messages, potentially modifying them when they're released. Your policy choices then are not so much what to do with messages (you can only quarantine), but rather to determine how long to quarantine for. The default is to quarantine suspected viral content for 1 day, and all other threats for 4 hours. Note that these are only the defaults; messages may actually spend more or less time in quarantine, depending on several possible events:

- When entering quarantine, the rule that determined the suspicious nature may recommend a quarantine period that is shorter than the default.
- Updates to outbreak rules may cause a reevaluation of the quarantined content. This occurs most often when an outbreak is confirmed viral and an AV signature is available, allowing the message to be released and rescanned. It's also possible that an outbreak continues, without a determinate solution, and the message continues to be held.
- Administrative release. Any administrative user with appropriate privileges can release messages manually.

After the release, messages pass through IPAS and AV engines again, giving those engines a chance to render another verdict. Messages with suspicious URLs, like click-to-download Trojans, phishing, or 419 scam fraud are caught by IPAS. The AV engines catch viral attachments.

The Outbreak Filters mail policies page is shown in Figure 8-12.

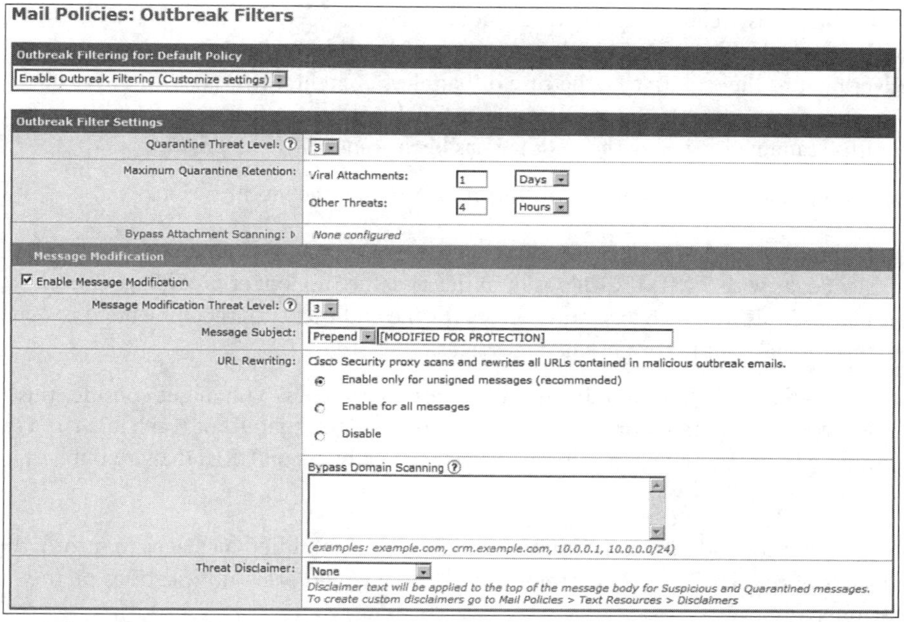

Figure 8-12 *Outbreak Filters Settings*

You also have the option of bypassing outbreak filter scanning for particular file extensions. Outbreak rules for a given extension will not be evaluated when configured. You would generally use this capability if you have a strong concern about false positives and want to be certain that attachments, like spreadsheets, are never held for quarantine. Because OF has an extremely low false positive rate to begin with, and bypassing defeats the central idea behind OF, creating a security hole, I recommend against it.

Message Modification

Message modification is a new OF action, and it's specifically designed to eliminate the threat from messages containing URLs to malicious content. If such a message is released from quarantine and is not caught by the IPAS engine after that release, it can go to the user with its URLs modified.

The modification rewrites the URLs so that the original link, when requested through a click from the user, is first passed through the Cisco-hosted security service before being delivered to the end user.

Message modification of URLs is only possible in HTML format messages or multipart messages with an HTML section. An original URL that looks like

http://fraud.example.com/mal.js

is rewritten so that the original URL is part of a new Cisco URL:

http://outbreak.cisco.com/url=fraud.example.com/mal.js

Note that this URL is just for example. It's not actually a valid URL for this service. The valid URL depends on your software version, the Cisco infrastructure, and other conditions. When a user clicks the new URL, though, the end user's browser contacts Cisco, not the original web server. This allows Cisco to filter the content, if necessary, before delivering it to the end user. In the case of harmless content, the end user notices no difference, but if the content is malicious, they'll be given an error page. Think of it as antivirus scanning long after the message has been scanned by the ESA.

There are just a couple of configurable options for message modification:

- **Skipping signed messages.** Modifying messages that have been cryptographically signed, as with S/MIME, will result in the signature no longer providing a match. Because this will probably cause errors for the end users, it's recommended to leave this to enable only for unsigned messages.
- **You can disable URL modification for certain domains.** You might consider this for your own intranet or corporate pages, or any URL that is not reachable from the public Internet. The Cisco filtering service can only act on URLs that are publicly available.

The ESA uses a standard text notification at the top of modified messages to inform the end users of the risk. You can customize this as you would other notifications on the system.

Content Filters and OF

Because outbreak filters occur in the pipeline near the end after content filters, you can't act on OF verdicts in filters. However, you can use content filters to affect their OF processing.

When OF is enabled, you'll be able to use the Bypass Outbreak Filter Scanning action in content filters, or the **skip-outbreakcheck** action in message filters. Skipping OF is the only control that you have, and there's not much call for it: Skipping the engine creates a slight but real security hole. If you want to skip OF for certain attachment types only, do that with the OF policy settings. If you want to skip OF for certain senders or recipients, do that with an appropriate incoming or outgoing mail policy for those users.

Recommended AV Settings

AV seems like a simple policy decision: Get rid of the bad stuff. Depending on your organization's security stance, though, there may be more to it than that. If the ESA is the only place for virus-scanning email messages, you may want to take action on unscannable or encrypted messages on the off chance these contain some viral content. If you have anti-virus scanning at other layers, like groupware and desktop client, you may choose to deliver everything except virus positive verdicts.

The first question for AV policy is: to repair or not? Repairing messages seems like a good idea, as it could allow an infected, but otherwise valid, document sent from a legitimate sender to be received. In practice, though, this kind of repairable message has disappeared from email altogether. You're not likely to ever see a message that can be repaired.

Dropping infected attachments is also problematic. When you remove the infected attachment, the remaining clean portion of the message is delivered to the original recipient. When the rest of the message is a spam-like, plain-text message enticing the user to open the attachment, confusion results. This husk of the message is useless and confusing to the end user. Better to throw the whole thing away and forget about it.

In short, my recommendation closely matches the default:

- **Don't repair messages.** You're not likely to see repairable messages.
- **Don't drop infected attachments.** This just leaves the empty message remnants to confuse the end user.
- **Drop virus-infected messages.** Don't send notifications to sender because that causes backscatter, and don't send notifications to recipients because that causes confusion.
- **Deliver encrypted messages.** These are rarely, if ever, viral and dropping encrypted messages will result in many legitimate messages being lost.
- **Deliver unscannable messages.** You should consider sending a notification about this verdict to an administrator. Unscannable can indicate a bug, malformed message, or a timeout.

Incoming AV Recommendations

Incoming email viruses are, unfortunately, a fairly common occurrence. The messages are typically short, plain text or HTML with some form of Windows executable attached. Because they have absolutely no value at all, with or without their attachment, I recommend that you simply drop all messages that reach a viral verdict, without notification either to the sender or the recipient. Notifications to the sender will not actually go to the source; the sender addresses on these messages have been forged, and your notification will go to an innocent third party. Notifications to the recipient often result in the user calling for help or support, or replying to the message over the confusion. Some users will see a familiar sender or attachment name and demand that the original message be restored to them, even though it contains a virus.

If your organization requires a conservative stance, or if you have a morbid curiosity, quarantine the virus-infected messages. Be aware, however, that the message is still dangerous if it's released. Some desktop AV clients will even alert or interrupt your browser if you're viewing the quarantined message. The ESA WUI doesn't actually execute any of the binary content or pass it to your workstation for execution, but the match of byte patterns is often enough to trigger the AV client. It's safe to examine viral content through the browser to the WUI.

You should use OFs on inbound mail policies, for all policies, with the default threat level of 3. Don't skip any attachment types. You might be interested in the outbreak email alerts, but the volume of these alerts means that you'll quickly turn it off. The beauty of OF is that it runs, quietly, and quarantines the suspicious threats. It's rarely wrong, so the typical OF suspect is released from quarantine and dealt with by anti-spam or antivirus on the second pass.

Outgoing AV Recommendations

An infected message in your outgoing mail stream is more of a concern: It could be the result of a virus-infected or otherwise compromised host, or could be sent by an automated mail source that itself has been compromised. Either way, it's important to investigate any outgoing email viruses.

For this reason, I recommend quarantining virus-positive outgoing messages and sending a notification to an administrator or administrative alias. The notification should include enough information that you can track down the source and should include the MID, sending host, and email address, the date and time, and the type of viral content. Example 8-1 shows the text listing of such a notification.

Example 8-1 *Administrative AV Notification*

```
A virus was detected in outgoing MID $MID:

Sender: $EnvelopeFrom
Source: $remotehost
Timestamp: $Date $Time
Subject: $Subject
Filenames: $filenames
Verdict:  $AV_VERDICT
Viruses: $AV_VIRUSES

Virus detail:
$AV_VIRUS_TABLE

Infected parts:
$AV_INFECTED_PARTS

Encrypted detail:
$AV_ENCRYPTED_PARTS

Unscannable detail:
$AV_UNSCANNABLE_PARTS
```

Because of the possibility of local infected hosts, it's also a good idea to enable OF on outgoing mail policies, if available.

Using Content Filters for Security

In many environments, custom-written rules form an important part of email security. I'm not going to strongly recommend against doing so, but I put a warning here that using content filters to do the jobs that anti-spam and antivirus do is administratively intense and can affect the performance of the ESA.

That being said, there are a couple of filters you should consider if you want to be preemptive about security. The first to start with are attachment filters. Virtually every organization restricts attachments to email in some way, because the reality is that many attachment types have no legitimate use in email, and their presence almost always indicates a threat.

Attachment Conditions and Actions

There are a few ways that the ESA can identify attachments, and you'll likely want to use more than one approach combined:

- **Filename:** ESA compares the filenames reported in the MIME part for each attachment against the regular expression that you supply. Because this matches against the filename supplied in the message itself, it will not recognize files correctly if the sender modified the filename. For example, if a win32 executable has been renamed "photo.jpg," a regular expression \.exe will not detect it.
- **File type:** The ESA decodes the attachments and compares the file to a database of known *magic numbers* that identify many common file types. Because this identification compares the bytes of the attachment, it will detect attachments that have been renamed.
- **File MIME type:** This is the file type as reported in the email MIME headers. It consists of a general type and a specific type indicator, like **audio/mp3** or **text/html**. Many binary attachments will use a generic type of **application/octet-stream** limiting the use of filters to stop attachments by MIME type. You can specify rules with wildcards, like **video/***, which will match any general MIME type that starts with video.

Once identified, you have a few good choices for the action you can take:

- **Drop:** You can simply throw away the message.
- **Quarantine:** This parks the message in a system quarantine that requires an administrator to review and release it. If it's possible that your end users may come looking for these messages, and your organization permits them to request its release, quarantine with a notification is a good choice.

- **Strip the attachments:** This modifies the message body, removing the attachments that match the filename, file type, or MIME type specified, replacing it with a custom message. Because these actions do both the comparison and the strip, you don't need to have the attachment conditions in the same filter.
- **Bounce:** I strongly recommend against this. Bouncing messages, for any reason, is almost never a good idea.

My recommendation is to use both the filename and file type detection methods, and then either drop or quarantine the message. For incoming messages, if you worry that your users will miss these messages, send them a notification with the message details. For most of the potentially harmful attachment types, the message will have no value whatsoever, and the end user will be confused if he receives a modified message.

If your organization restricts the use of attachments that have some legitimate use, like ZIP archives, but prevent the use of executables, you may want to compose separate filters for the *likely harmful* and *possibly harmful but useful* attachment types.

Figure 8-13 shows a content filter that identifies *likely harmful* types and drops the message silently.

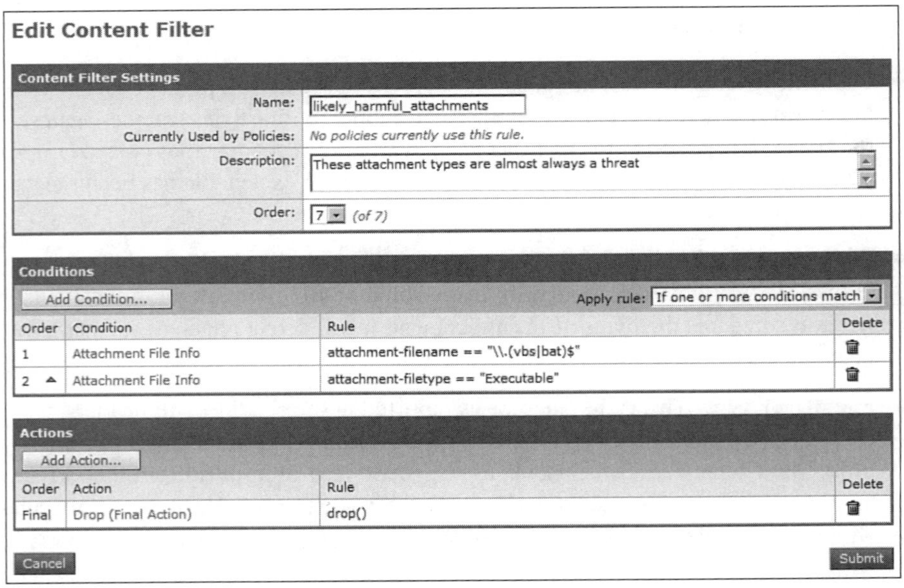

Figure 8-13 *Likely Harmful Attachment Types Filter*

Figure 8-14 shows a content filter that identifies *possibly harmful* types and quarantines the message while sending the recipient a notification.

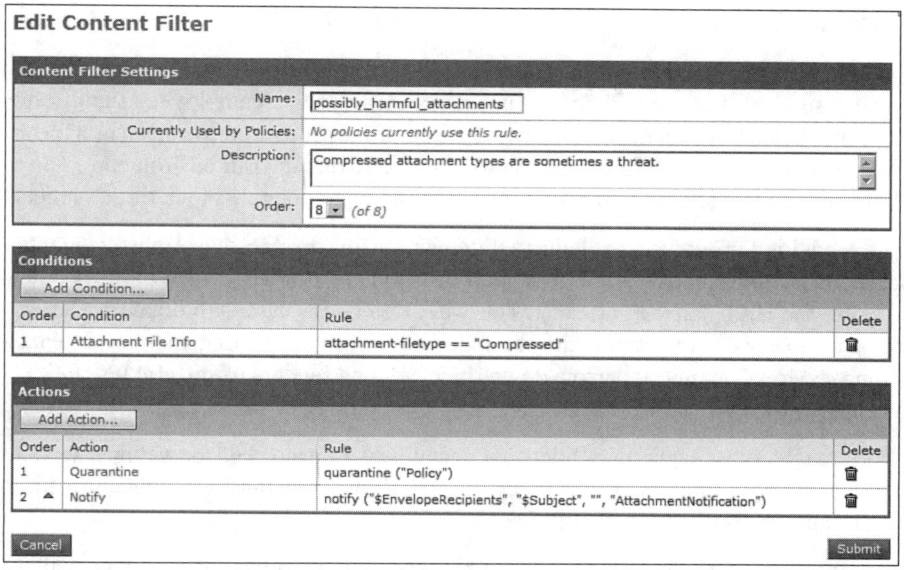

Figure 8-14 *Possibly Harmful Attachment Types, with Quarantine and Notify*

Figure 8-15 shows a content filter that strips various file types from the message. The notification to the end user is in the form of a text string that replaces the original attachment.

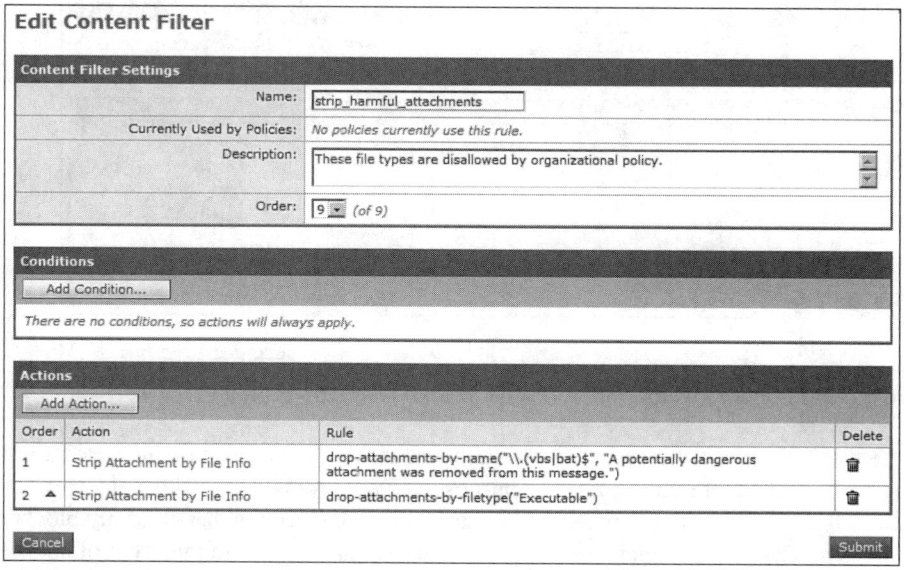

Figure 8-15 *Attachment Stripping*

Filtering Bad Senders

In every environment, some email senders are not welcome, above and beyond the spam and virus senders. These could be disgruntled ex-employees, an employee's significant other, or a hostile outsider. Any motivated group or individual can use email as a means of harassing employees in your organization. It's likely that in your environment, you will, from time to time, have to respond to requests to completely block these senders.

If the sender is a group using a dedicated domain or specific Message Transfer Agents (MTA), the simple solution is to simply add that domain, or the IP range of the sending MTAs, to the HAT's built-in blacklist. This will often be the case with organized letter-writing campaigns and websites with the specific purpose of offering anonymous email-sending services. If you can narrow down the offending senders to specific IPs, and those IPs aren't used for other legitimate mail, this is the right solution.

Unfortunately, most harassing senders use accounts with major ISPs or webmail service providers that you cannot add to a blacklist. In that case, you must use policies or filters that examine the sending email addresses.

My recommended approach is to create a **Blocked Senders** policy on incoming mail, with the senders in question as members of the policy. When adding users, make sure to click the **Sender** radio button. Figure 8-16 shows an Incoming Mail Policies table with such a policy at the top.

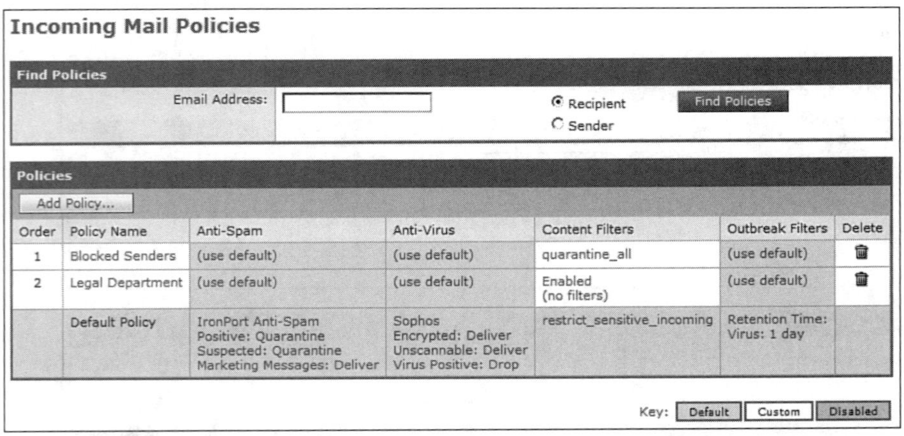

Figure 8-16 *Incoming Mail Policies with a Blocked Senders Policy at the Top*

Note that I disabled the standard content filters for this policy, and instead added a single filter called **quarantine_all**. The purpose of that filter is, as you'd expect, to quarantine all messages that are processed by that policy. The result is that all of my blocked sender's messages will funnel into this policy and be quarantined. In the event of another problematic email sender, simply add the address to the policy; there's no need to modify the content filter.

There are other approaches to filtering bad-sender addresses, namely with content filter conditions that match the envelope sender against a regular expression or a dictionary, but managing those is more hassle than simply modifying a policy.

I want to caution you against using this sender-filtering approach for spam filtering: Addresses are easily forged and constantly changing, so blocking an individual spam sender is completely ineffective.

Filtering Subject or Body

If you have a security situation that requires that messages be filtered by some content in the message—in a header, or in a subject, or in the body or attachments of messages—you should think carefully before doing so. Using content filters as a security mechanism suffers from many problems:

- **Performance.** Examining the body of every message, and its attachments, is an expensive operation. The more terms that have to be searched, the lower the performance. There are some techniques for optimizing body scanning, but it is almost always a performance drain. If your filtering needs can be met by blocking source IPs, sender or recipient addresses, or headers, you should take that approach first.
- **Maintenance.** Filters require maintenance. When a filter is no longer matching any messages, it should be removed so that it's not a drain on resources. It's easy to forget why a filter was added, and so the filters and conditions pile up, leading to performance problems.
- **Regular expression mistakes.** It is easy for even experienced filter writers to make mistakes, especially with regular expressions. A mistake that simply fails to catch messages is not a big problem, but an overly broad expression can result in hundreds, or thousands, of matches, potentially dropping or quarantining a lot of legitimate messages. Take care.

These aren't limitations or problems of ESA content filtering per se, it's just the nature of trying to filter junk messages with words, phrases, and regular expressions. If, despite all these drawbacks, you still find that a content (or message) filter is required, I recommend following a few guidelines:

- **Use dictionaries and dictionary match rules, even if you only intend to filter on a few keywords or phrases.** Performance is better because only a single regular expression call is made by a content filter condition that matches against a dictionary. Maintenance is easier, because the content filter does not need modification—only the dictionary changes. It's easy to add or remove terms from a dictionary.
- **Apply these filters sparingly.** If they can be limited to a specific mail policy (and therefore to a subset of users), they'll be less of a performance drain and have less impact in the case of false positives.
- **Maintenance.** Take care not to let filters or dictionaries get too long or contain too many terms. Once the particular filtering need passes, the terms should be removed. Consider a policy for a 30-day filter window; every 30 days, clear the filter or dictionary of all terms and start over.

- **Be careful with regular expressions.** Avoid using expensive wildcards and make use of anchors and search minimum/maximum regex controls to avoid searching the entirety of every message body.

Summary

We covered the configuration of the ESA security engines and explored some techniques for security using content filters. For the most part, the actual spam and virus identification is handled by rules that are automatically updated, so the configuration work is focused on deciding on the actions to take for various message verdicts. It's important to know the differences between the verdicts and the repercussions of using the various verdicts.

Some of the configuration settings, like spam thresholds, affect security, and you have to decide which of the risks we covered warrant more or less open policies. We also covered creating custom security rules, and the best way to craft policies and filters to address common organization security needs.

The next chapter explores some options for controlling the ESA and retrieving its data using external tools that access the CLI and WUI.

Chapter 9

Automating Tasks

In this chapter, you will learn the following:

- Creating and running scripts that can access the CLI and WUI
- Using CLI batch commands for simple automation
- Managing configuration files with external scripts

Administering ESA from Outside Servers

Chapter 5, "Command-Line Interface," and Chapter 6, "Additional Management Services," covered the AsyncOS web user interface (WUI) and command-line interface (CLI) in depth with the intent of giving an administrator the knowledge and skills he needs to manage Email Security Appliance (ESA). This chapter uses the CLI and WUI as interfaces for machine interaction, using commands and scripts on external servers to poll information from the ESAs and even to send data and change configuration.

The ESA does not make provision for any third-party scripting or software to be installed and run locally. However, it does provide a CLI that can be used in batch mode and several WUI interaction features that can be used for automation.

Using CLI batch commands is simple, and it's ideal for accomplishing tasks for which the ESA has no built-in feature. Those generally fall into a few categories:

- **Monitoring:** You may have a need for retrieving data from an ESA on a regular basis for monitoring the system for availability, response time, and performance. Although SNMP is designed specifically for monitoring by external services, a number of interesting operational attributes are simply not included in SNMP. You might have a need to monitor specific performance attributes or check email delivery status to specific destinations. For example, if you want to monitor the number of active inbound or outbound connections, the amount of disk space for logging, or the last date and time of an anti-virus (AV) rules update, you must use an external script.

- **Configuration backup:** An administrator can always manually export configuration files from the WUI or CLI, but if you want regular backups on a particular schedule, you can automate the export.
- **Automatic configuration changes:** If you regularly need to change the data in a table or feature of the ESA, based on input from an external source, scripting the change is the best approach. Many of the WUI and CLI tables can be scripted, although some are easier than others. For example, if your valid recipient addresses are stored in a SQL database and not available through LDAP, you can export a static list of recipients and import the result into the ESA RAT. Another common configuration change is to add or replace items in a dictionary of words and phrases, like confidential terms used by a filter for intellectual property protection.
- **External reporting systems:** You may want to export data for summarization and long-term storage, or compare data from the ESA with other inputs. Although much of the reporting and tracking can be manually exported in the WUI, you might have a need for regular exports at specified intervals.

Warning This chapter contains many shell command and scripting-language automation examples. All these examples are intentionally short and simple to illustrate a given approach to automation.

None of the examples have thorough error checking and perform no argument checking, blindly assuming that the input is correctly formatted. Some of the scripts, if used in production, would require that they store passwords in the clear. All of this is dangerous from a security perspective: Anyone that can run the scripts would be able to change ESA configuration and possibly compromise security.

It is strongly recommended that any automation scripts you use take this into account and perform proper error and argument checking rather than blindly trusting user input. I also suggest using accounts other than the superuser "admin" account, running scripts with the minimum privilege level necessary to execute the task.

CLI Automation Examples

To run CLI commands in batch mode (as opposed to interactively), you need to have tools that can automate connecting to a remote host and executing commands. If you're using Telnet to access the CLI on your ESA, you'll have a lot of options available, as it is not difficult to simply read and write from a Telnet connection. As previously stated, Telnet is not a good choice because it lacks security, and SSH is altogether better even for CLI connections entirely within your own network. For these reasons, I focus on CLI interactions that exclusively use SSH. Of course, if you prefer to use Telnet, this chapter is still directly applicable.

SSH Clients

SSH is the natural protocol for automating CLI tasks from a remote server. Virtually all UNIX-like systems, including Linux, BSD, and MacOS X, include an SSH client. For Windows, we previously described PuTTY in Chapter 5. Another utility provided by the PuTTY project is *plink.exe*, a command-prompt version of PuTTY that functions much like any other SSH client. Plink can be used to automate CLI tasks on the ESA.

To support truly noninteractive scripting, you must set up SSH keys on the SSH server (in this case, on the ESA using sshconfig) and on the SSH client. This process is described for Windows and UNIX systems in Chapter 5. Before experimenting with scripting, test to confirm that you can connect an SSH client to the ESA without being prompted for a password.

For example, here's a simple SSH command that runs the ESA command **mailconfig** in batch mode:

```
ssh admin@10.1.1.70 "mailconfig chriport@cisco.com y"
```

Here's the equivalent under Windows command shell using Plink:

```
plink.exe admin@10.1.1.70 "mailconfig chriport@cisco.com y"
```

Note that it is possible to provide the plink program with a password via the –pw argument, but I recommend against this; instead, I highly recommend using SSH key authentication. Storing passwords in remote scripts in plain text is a massive security hole. Using SSH keys in place of passwords also means that your scripts won't be affected by password changes on the ESA. You don't have to use the admin account; any account with a role that allows the appropriate CLI command to be run will work.

Expect

Expect is a standard UNIX-scripting tool for automating command-line–based protocols, like Telnet. It can also be used for SSH and is ideal for manipulating the ESA CLI. In addition to the expect tool itself, many programming languages have built-in support for expect or expect-like scripting features. Expect scripts are written in plain ASCII text, in a syntax derived from Tcl. (It's freely available from http://expect.nist.gov/.)

Expect gets its name from one of the two major commands in any script: **send** and **expect**. These are fairly self-explanatory. **send** takes a string argument, which is passed directly to the program being controlled. **expect** parses the output of the program being controlled, waiting for a match on the string argument that you provide.

For ESA automation, send/expect work in pairs to issue commands and wait for the ESA to respond with another prompt. For example, this pair:

```
send "hoststatus\n"
expect "[]> "
```

Issues the **hoststatus** command to the CLI and waits for the ESA to display a prompt. A script that automates **hoststatus** would then issue the domain with another **send** command.

Example 9-1 shows a simple expect script that adds a domain entry to the destination controls table, setting TLS to required. This script uses SSH to log in, but for simplicity, it does not deal with password logins. You must have SSH keys installed on your ESA for this script to work, or modify the script to support password logins to SSH. The domain to be added to the destination controls table for TLS required is passed as an argument to the script.

Example 9-1 *Expect Script Example for Automating Destination Controls*

```
#!/usr/bin/expect -f

set domain [lindex $argv 0]

spawn ssh admin@192.168.1.110

expect "> "
send "destconfig\n"
expect "[]> "
send "new\n"
expect "[]> "
send "$domain\n"
expect "]> "
send "N\n"
expect "]> "
send "N\n"
expect "]> "
send "N\n"
expect "]> "
send "Y\n"
expect "]> "
send "3\n"
expect "]> "
send "N\n"
expect "]> "
send "N\n"
expect "]> "
send "\n"
expect "> "
send "commit\n"
expect "[]> "

send "added $domain to destconfig for TLS required\n"
expect "> "
send "exit\n"
```

You can run this script from any system with expect, either by invoking it directly:

```
expect destconfig.exp cisco.com
```

Or, on UNIX systems where expect is installed, you can execute this script:

```
./destconfig.exp cisco.com
```

Just remember that your script file needs to have execute permissions set in the shell.

Perl

Of numerous languages that can be used for automating command-line tasks, Perl is my favorite. Normally, I won't resort to a Perl script for simple tasks, like exporting a configuration file, where you are not really concerned about the output; I save scripting for tasks that require formatting input, parsing output or stringing together multiple commands.

> **Note** All the Perl scripts listed in this section are targeted and tested on UNIX-based Perl distributions version 5.8 and later. They further assume that SSH keys have been installed on the ESA, as described in Chapter 5. You must have SSH keys installed and tested before these scripts work noninteractively.
>
> A number of SSH modules are available for Perl, notably the Net::SSH used here, which is a wrapper around an SSH client. There's also Net::SSH::Perl for a Perl-native SSH implementation, and Net::SSH2, which is a Perl interface to the libssh2 library. (For more information, see the Perl archive at hwww.cpan.org.)
>
> Perl has distributions available for Windows, but because of the lack of a native SSH client or library, the Net::SSH module simply won't work. We'll address some of the issues with Perl on Windows later.

As an example, suppose I wanted to check a group of ESAs on a regular basis and monitor its RAID status. Like many monitoring tasks, you can do this via SNMP, but for this example, let's assume we need another way to do it. A Perl script is ideal for this, allowing us to loop through a list of ESAs, outputting the serial number and RAID status of each. Because the output of the **version** command lists a series of attributes and values separated by a colon character, I'm using the Perl split function to extract the values. The complete listing is shown in Example 9-2.

Example 9-2 *Source Code for RAIDstatus.pl, an ESA Monitoring Script*

```
#!/usr/bin/perl

use strict;
use Net::SSH qw (sshopen2);

my @hostList = ("esa01.cisco.com", "esa02.cisco.com");
my $esaHost;
```

```
foreach $esaHost (@hostList) {
      my ($reader, $writer);
      my ($name, $value) = "";
      my $serial = "";
      my $raidstatus = "";

      # open the connection to the current host
      if (sshopen2("admin\@$esaHost", *reader, *writer, "version")) {
             while (<reader>) {
                    chomp;    # remove newline character if present
                     ($name, $value) = split /:/; # break the line into attribute /
  value pairs
                    if ($name =~ /Serial #/) {
                           $serial = $value;
                    }
                    elsif ($name =~ /RAID Status/) {
                           $raidstatus = $value;
                    }
             }

             print "$esaHost, serial $serial, RAID $raidstatus\n";

             close reader;
             close writer;
      }
}
```

In these examples, we're using the Net::SSH module for Perl, which is commonly available under most UNIX Perl distributions. If you don't have this module, or would rather not use it, but have a regular UNIX SSH client, instead of using the module, you can use the *system* function call to invoke the SSH client directly. Gathering output from the command is handled simply with the Perl **open** function. Example 9-3 shows a snippet of code that accomplishes this.

Example 9-3 *Source Code Snippet for RAIDstatus.pl That Invokes an SSH Client*

```
#!/usr/bin/perl

use strict;

my @hostList = ("esa01.cisco.com", "esa02.cisco.com");
my $esaHost;
```

```
foreach $esaHost (@hostList) {

    my ($name, $value) = "";
    my $serial = "";
    my $raidstatus = "";

    if (open (SSH, "ssh admin\@$esaHost version¦")) {
        while (<SSH>) {
            chomp;
             ($name, $value) = split /:/;
            if ($name =~ /Serial #/) {
                $serial = $value;
            }
            elsif ($name =~ /RAID Status/) {
                $raidstatus = $value;
            }
        }

        print "$esaHost, serial $serial, RAID $raidstatus\n";


    }
}
```

CLI Automation from Microsoft Windows Servers

Most of the CLI automation examples to this point focused on tools found only on UNIX or UNIX-like systems, or that have limitations when run on Windows operating systems (OS). SSH is a particular sore point, because the protocol is not natively available in the OS as a client or programmatically in libraries.

You have a few options to automate ESA tasks from Windows servers:

- Use the free plink.exe program from the PuTTY project in place of SSH commands and pscp.exe in place of SCP. Plink provides support for SSH v2 and commands can be sent just as with any UNIX SSH client. In conjunction with a Perl interpreter for Windows, you can run Perl scripts that issue commands over SSH with plink.
- Use a commercially available component library for SSH that is compatible with the programming environment you're using. With the establishment of the .NET component standard, many vendors provide components for Internet protocols like SSH that are not traditionally used under Windows.

- Use Telnet in place of, or in addition to, SSH on the ESAs. Telnet is widely supported, and the ESA CLI can be automated with any script that can open a TCP connection. The drawback is that the Telnet protocol is not encrypted, and login credentials are sent in the clear, so take other security precautions to prevent interception or sniffing.
- Use the Cygwin project to support Linux tools and utilities under Windows. The Perl and Python interpreters are supported under Cygwin, as are SSH clients and libraries. There's even a version of Expect under Cygwin.
- Use a commercially available automation software package or library. There are commercially available versions of Expect for Windows.

Another option that we'll address later in this chapter is to skip the CLI and use the WUI for automation tasks. Because it's just HTTP (or HTTPS), there is a lot of native client support in Windows.

Let's look at a Perl example of the RAIDstatus tool, written in Perl that will run under a Perl interpreter for Windows. The source code is shown in Example 9-4. It's similar to Example 9-2, but instead of using SSH, it uses plink.exe. For simplicity, this script assumes that plink and the putty private key are in the current working directory or in an accessible path. Plink offers the ability to provide both a username and password as arguments, which is convenient and avoids the need for installing SSH keys on the ESA. If you choose to include a password in your script, take care to protect the script contents. This example assumes that your SSH public key has been installed in the ESA. Refer to Chapter 5 for details on using SSH keys with PuTTY.

Example 9-4 *Source Code for RAIDstatus.pl, Suitable for Running in Windows*

```
#!/usr/bin/perl

use strict;

my @hostList = ("esa01.cisco.com", "esa02.cisco.com");
my $esaHost;

foreach $esaHost (@hostList) {

      my ($name, $value) = "";
      my $serial = "";
      my $raidstatus = "";

      if (open (PLINK, "plink.exe -i id_rsa.ppk admin\@$esaHost version|")) {
             while (<PLINK>) {
                    chomp;
                     ($name, $value) = split /:/;
                    if ($name =~ /Serial #/) {
```

```
                        $serial = $value;
                }
                elsif ($name =~ /RAID Status/) {
                        $raidstatus = $value;
                }
        }

        print "$esaHost, serial $serial, RAID $raidstatus\n";


    }
}
```

WUI Automation Examples

Compared to the process of automating tasks via the CLI, scripting the WUI is more complex. Although the primary intent of both the CLI and WUI is interaction with a live, human administrator, the practice of scripting a shell login is long established, and the various SSH clients in the industry have extensive support for noninteractive logins. Also, when using documented and supported CLI commands, the format and availability of the commands is unlikely to change across releases of AsyncOS. No such consistency is promised for the WUI; while the forms, pages, and asset locations have remained stable over many ESA software releases, it's not guaranteed to remain the same in the future.

Despite the warnings, there are many good reasons to automate using the WUI. In some cases, like for reporting or XML data, there is simply no other way to access the information.

Polling Data from the ESA

Most of the data from the WUI and CLI is intended for a human audience using those interfaces directly. However, there are a number of ways to do automatic monitoring. The primary means of machine monitoring is via SNMP, which is covered in Chapter 6. SNMP MIBs do not cover all possible metrics on the ESA, so if you're looking to monitor counters, like performance or connection counts, or look at the delivery status of a particular destination, you have to find other means.

Retrieving XML Data Pages

The CLI examples provided in the first part of this chapter can be used to pull monitoring data from a running ESA. For example, a SSH command like

```
ssh admin@10.1.1.70 "antispamstatus"
```

gives you information about the latest anti-spam rule updates. Similarly, running the command **version**, like we did for our RAID status tool

```
ssh admin@10.1.1.70 "version"
```

results in output that's easy to parse. The output of **version** is a simple list of name: value pairs separated by colon; any script can easily parse and examine the content.

What if you need other data from the CLI, such as that given by the command **status detail**? You can also run this command remotely and parse the data. You'll have to learn the format and parse the values that this command provides. If you'd prefer not to use SSH or want something more structured, the ESA offers an XML format export for some of its monitoring commands, including **status detail**.

You reach the XML pages like you would any URL, but these are not linked anywhere in the WUI; you have to manually enter them:

```
https://esa02.cisco.com/xml/status
```

You are prompted by the browser to log in, using any active credentials on the ESA. This is an HTTP login prompt, so the actual behavior depends on your browser. This authentication is different from the normal form-based authentication that the WUI uses, and your script must handle it. Another way of providing authentication is to embed it in the URL, like this:

```
https://report:ironport@esa02.cisco.com/xml/status
```

But, this requires that you store those credentials in your script or in a bookmark. At the very least, you should create a guest user account for this purpose.

Depending on what your browser does with unformatted XML, you may be prompted to save the file, or it may display in the browser window. Here's typical output from the XML status URL:


```
  <?xml version="1.0" encoding="ISO-8859-1" standalone="yes" ?>
- <status build="phoebe 7.5.0-472" hostname="esa02.cisco.com" time
  stamp="20110630141053">
  <birth_time timestamp="20110630083158 (5h 38m 55s)" />
  <last_counter_reset timestamp="" />
  <system status="online" />
  <oldest_message secs="0" mid="0" />
- <features>
  <feature name="Sophos" time_remaining="-2502703" />
  <feature name="Bounce Verification" time_remaining="Dormant/Perpetual" />
  <feature name="Central Mgmt" time_remaining="-1031362" />
  <feature name="IronPort Anti-Spam" time_remaining="-2502703" />
  <feature name="IronPort Email Encryption" time_remaining="-2502703" />
  <feature name="RSA Email Data Loss Prevention" time_remaining="-2502703" />
  <feature name="Receiving" time_remaining="Dormant/Perpetual" />
  <feature name="Outbreak Filters" time_remaining="-2502703" />
```

```
</features>
- <counters>
<counter name="inj_msgs" reset="10" uptime="0" lifetime="10" />
<counter name="inj_recips" reset="10" uptime="0" lifetime="10" />
<counter name="gen_bounce_recips" reset="5" uptime="0" lifetime="5" />
<counter name="rejected_recips" reset="0" uptime="0" lifetime="0" />
<counter name="dropped_msgs" reset="0" uptime="0" lifetime="0" />
<counter name="soft_bounced_evts" reset="0" uptime="0" lifetime="0" />
<counter name="completed_recips" reset="10" uptime="0" lifetime="10" />
<counter name="hard_bounced_recips" reset="10" uptime="0" lifetime="10" />
<counter name="dns_hard_bounced_recips" reset="5" uptime="0" lifetime="5" />
<counter name="5xx_hard_bounced_recips" reset="0" uptime="0" lifetime="0" />
<counter name="filter_hard_bounced_recips" reset="0" uptime="0" lifetime="0" />
<counter name="expired_hard_bounced_recips" reset="5" uptime="0" lifetime="5" />
<counter name="other_hard_bounced_recips" reset="0" uptime="0" lifetime="0" />
<counter name="delivered_recips" reset="0" uptime="0" lifetime="0" />
<counter name="deleted_recips" reset="0" uptime="0" lifetime="0" />
<counter name="global_unsub_hits" reset="0" uptime="0" lifetime="0" />
  </counters>
<current_ids message_id="10" injection_conn_id="7" delivery_conn_id="36" />
<rates>
<rate name="inj_msgs" last_1_min="0" last_5_min="0" last_15_min="0" />
<rate name="inj_recips" last_1_min="0" last_5_min="0" last_15_min="0" />
<rate name="soft_bounced_evts" last_1_min="0" last_5_min="0" last_15_min="0" />
<rate name="completed_recips" last_1_min="0" last_5_min="0" last_15_min="0" />
<rate name="hard_bounced_recips" last_1_min="0" last_5_min="0" last_15_min="0" />
<rate name="delivered_recips" last_1_min="0" last_5_min="0" last_15_min="0" />
</rates>
<gauges>
<gauge name="ram_utilization" current="1" />
<gauge name="total_utilization" current="0" />
<gauge name="cpu_utilization" current="0" />
<gauge name="av_utilization" current="0" />
<gauge name="case_utilization" current="0" />
<gauge name="bm_utilization" current="0" />
<gauge name="disk_utilization" current="0" />
<gauge name="resource_conservation" current="0" />
<gauge name="log_used" current="5" />
<gauge name="log_available" current="46G" />
<gauge name="conn_in" current="0" />
<gauge name="conn_out" current="0" />
<gauge name="active_recips" current="0" />
<gauge name="unattempted_recips" current="0" />
<gauge name="attempted_recips" current="0" />
<gauge name="msgs_in_work_queue" current="0" />
```

```
<gauge name="dests_in_memory" current="3" />
<gauge name="kbytes_used" current="0" />
<gauge name="kbytes_free" current="8388608" />
<gauge name="msgs_in_quarantine" current="0" />
<gauge name="kbytes_in_quarantine" current="0" />
<gauge name="reporting_utilization" current="0" />
<gauge name="quarantine_utilization" current="0" />
</gauges>
</status>
```

As you can see, this includes all the data in the **status detail** command, but it's organized into a hierarchical XML format.

There are other XML pages. Table 9-1 lists all the available XML URLs.

Table 9-1 *XML Data URLs*

ESA URL	Description
/xml/status	Gauges, counters, and rates from the status page. Contains the same information that the System Status page and the CLI command **status detail** have.
/xml/hoststatus?hostname=example.com	Equivalent to the output of the CLI command **hoststatus** for the supplied destination. Includes information about queued, delivered, and bounce messages, delivery MX and IP, and the last 5yz error code.
/xml/dnsstatus	Statistics of DNS queries, equivalent to the CLI command **dnsstatus**.
/xml/topin	Equivalent to the CLI command **topin**, shows the hostname and IP of remote SMTP clients that have active connections to this ESA.
/xml/tophosts	Equivalent to the CLI command **tophosts**, or the WUI Delivery Status page. Shows the top destination domains with active recipients.

Using XML Export for Monitoring

Let's look at a script example that uses the hoststatus XML data to monitor a given destination. The ESA does not generate alerts when delivery queues have undelivered messages, unless the queues reach such a depth that the appliance is running out of resources. Resource conservation of that type usually means that there are millions of undelivered messages, when the problem has been ongoing for many hours. Queued messages are normal, and storing them until they can be delivered is one of the primary tasks of a Message Transfer Agent (MTA), but you may be interested to know if the ESA is queuing messages that should be delivered immediately. It could indicate that reliable delivery hosts, like your internal groupware servers, are down or not accepting connections.

SNMP can provide monitoring for the work queue and overall queue disk usage, but what if you're interested in queue depth to a specific destination, such as your local domains? You might want to be alerted if there are more than 100 messages currently queued for delivery to your groupware servers, because that might indicate a network or server issue, and it certainly means that messages are being delayed in delivery.

Example 9-5 shows the complete Perl script that pulls the **hoststatus** information, parses the output, and prints a message if the queue depth for the specified domain exceeds the supplied threshold.

Example 9-5 *Simple Perl Script for Polling XML Data*

```
#!/usr/bin/perl
use strict;

# load the modules for web (HTTP) and SSL requests
use LWP::UserAgent;
use HTTP::Request::Common;
use Crypt::SSLeay;

# ESA host and credentials. You could easily make these specified as arguments to
  the script
my $user = "admin";
my $pass = "ironport";
my $host = "esa02.cisco.com';
my $domain = "cisco.com";
my $threshold = 100;

# make the web request and pass credentials
my $request = new HTTP::Request (GET=>"https://$host/xml/
  hoststatus?hostname=$domain") or die $!;
$request->authorization_basic ($user, $pass);
my $response;

my $agent = new LWP::UserAgent;

# check the status of the request; if it's empty, quit the script
if ($request) {
        $response = $agent->request ($request);
}
else {
        die $!;
}


my $xmlHostData;
```

```
# check the result, and if it's not an error, extract the body content
if ($response->is_error) {
        print $response->error_as_HTML();
        exit;
}
else {
        $xmlHostData = $response->content;
}

# search through the XML data for the active recipients line, and extract the cur
  rent count
if ($xmlHostData =~ /active_recips" current="(\d+)"/) {
        if ($1 > $threshold) {
                print "Alert threshold exceeded: found $1 active recipients for
$domain\n";
        }
}
```

This script can be used as the basis for a full alert system, either writing data to a remote logging host or sending an email to an administrator or administrative alias. If you are going to use email, it's not a good idea to send alert messages through an ESA with a queue backup, especially for your local domains.

Normally, this is something you would want to run on a regular schedule, either using a job scheduler like **cron** on a UNIX-like system or Windows Scheduled Tasks under Windows. Running it every 5 minutes is adequate for catching serious queue backup problems.

Pushing Data to the ESA and Making Configuration Changes

If you have configuration changes that need to be made on a regular basis, you'll be interested in automating those changes, especially if those changes depend on data from an external source.

Some common automatic configuration needs include

- **Email aliases:** If you have a table of aliases for recipient routing or address list expansion, and this data is not available for lookup in LDAP, you can import the data using the **aliasconfig** command. This can easily be automated with SCP and SSH commands.

- **Recipient Access Table:** You can import domains or individual email addresses to the RAT. If you don't have your recipient information in LDAP, or the domains you accept mail for changes often, you can import this data automatically.
- **Dictionaries:** If you're filtering based on keywords and phrases, and these change on a regular basis, you can use the **dictionaryconfig** command to add entries to a dictionary or even to replace the entire dictionary.

For any command that you need for automation, the first step to take is to determine if the configuration change is available using a CLI batch command. You can use **help <command>** in the CLI to get a complete list of supported batch options and examples of their use. For example, the tasks in the previous list can be automated respectively with

```
aliasconfig import alias.txt
listenerconfig edit IncomingMail rcptaccess new cisco.com
dictionaryconfig edit Confidential new Secret
```

After each, you also need to commit the change. I dig deeper into these topics in the following sections.

Changing Configuration Settings Using the CLI

Scripting can also be used to string together multiple steps required to automate some task. For example, suppose your ESA environment makes use of aliases to rewrite recipient addresses. An outside username, like cporter@ironport.com, needs to be rewritten to chriport@cisco.com. Further, suppose the list of aliases is hundreds or thousands of entries long, and changes daily. Ideally, this kind of aliasing should be done via LDAP routing queries on the ESA, but what if the information isn't available via LDAP and instead is in a database or in a text file? A shell, batch, or Perl script can handle this. The two steps required here are to transfer the file to the ESA using FTP or SCP, and then issue the **aliasconfig** batch command to import the file. Finally, as with any configuration change, we must commit the change.

Suppose your aliases are stored in a plain ASCII text file, in a format like this:

```
cporter@ironport.com:   chriport@cisco.com
```

Here, the text file contains one alias entry per line. Example 9-6 shows the complete listing for a UNIX shell script that does this. Note that we are not parsing or modifying the input; the script assumes that the alias file is in the correct format for ESA import.

To commit the change, we simply append the **commit** command to **aliasconfig import** so that it's all done in a single session. Issuing two separate SSH commands does not work, because the first SSH command exits its login session and closes the connection after it issues **aliasconfig**. These must be done in one SSH session, separating the commands with a semicolon.

Example 9-6 *Source Code for aliasimport.sh, a Shell Script for Importing Aliases from a Text File*

```
#!/bin/bash

scp alias.txt admin@esa02.cisco.com:/configuration

ssh admin@esa02.cisco.com "aliasconfig import alias.txt; commit alias"
```

The Windows equivalent, using plink.exe for SSH commands and pscp.exe for SCP, is a batch file shown in Example 9-7. This hardly requires anything as complex as a batch file, but it's useful for grouping together the commands. If the alias file was being extracted from a database, for example, you could pull and format the data before copying the file over and importing it into the ESA.

Example 9-7 *Windows Batch File for Alias Import Tasks*

```
pscp.exe -pw ironport alias.txt admin@esa02.cisco.com:/configuration

plink.exe -pw ironport admin@esa02 "aliasconfig import alias.txt; commit alias"
```

Another situation where a script comes in handy is in automating provisioning. Most organizations own just a few email domains and a small list of delivery destinations for those domains, and maintenance is very low. But, in environments that deal with hundreds or thousands of domains, such as service providers, web-hosting firms, or email archiving services, maintaining the list of local requires more effort. This is especially true if the list changes regularly.

Example 9-8 is a listing for domainProvision.pl, which adds a given email domain to the ESA RAT and SMTPRoutes table.

Example 9-8 *Source Code for domainProvision.pl*

```
#!/usr/bin/perl
use strict;
use Net::SSH qw(sshopen2);

sub usage () {
        print "usage:\n $0 <domain to add> <smtproute destination>\n";
        exit (0);
}

if (@ARGV < 2) {
```

```
        usage ();
}

my $domain = $ARGV[0];
my $destination = $ARGV[1];

my $rcptAccessCommand = "listenerconfig edit IncomingMail rcptaccess new
  $domain\n";
my $smtpRoutesCommand = "smtproutes new $domain $destination\n";
my $commitCommand = "commit \"added RAT and SMTPRoutes entry for $domain\"\n";

my $tmp;

if (sshopen2("admin\@192.168.1.110", *READER, *WRITER)) {
        print WRITER $rcptAccessCommand;
        $tmp = <READER>;
        print WRITER $smtpRoutesCommand;
        $tmp = <READER>;
        print WRITER $commitCommand;
        $tmp = <READER>;
        print WRITER "exit\n";
        $tmp = <READER>;
}
```

You can run this script with just two arguments—the domain and the delivery destination:

```
domainProvision.pl cisco.com 10.1.17.122
```

The script could easily be expanded to support two or more destinations for a given domain.

Committing Changes Using the CLI

To make configuration changes to the ESA with the CLI, you must issue the **commit** command and supply a comment (or just press Enter). The same is required of automated configuration changes.

If you're using a batch command, like we saw earlier, you need to string the **commit** command together with the configuration batch command. In other words, you must do this:

```
aliasconfig import alias.txt; commit alias
```

And not this:

```
aliasconfig import alias.txt
commit alias
```

Running commands through an SSH client in multiple calls creates multiple sessions, losing any configuration changes. You must issue all of your commands in a single session, and the ESA provides the semicolon notation for this.

Changing Configuration Settings Using the WUI

Changing the configuration settings using the WUI is less straightforward than using the CLI, chiefly because the WUI is intended for human interaction using a browser. It has the further difficulty that, unlike when retrieving XML status pages, the WUI doesn't allow for web server login directly, but rather requires that the script actually login using the ESA's login forms.

Most configuration changes in the WUI are performed using HTML forms that use either GET or POST methods. Manipulating data with GET URLs is fairly easy, once you identify the appropriate argument names and values. Most of the POST forms can actually be converted into a GET method.

Despite these challenges, once the basics of logging in, using cookies, and manipulating form URLs is done, you'll have a framework that you can build additional configuration scripts with.

Every script that manipulates configuration through the WUI must perform three basic tasks (at a minimum):

1. Log in to the ESA using the https://hostname/login GET URL. Save the sid cookie for use in the next steps; sid represents the session id of the currently logged in user.
2. Make configuration changes using GET URLs. Each HTTP request must include the sid cookie from the first step.
3. Commit the changes using the https://hostname/commit GET URL. Again, this request must include the sid cookie from the first step.

We deal with committing the changes in the next section. We first look at logging in and making a configuration change. Example 9-9 provides a VBScript listing of a script that logs into an ESA.

Example 9-9 *VBScript Example of ESA WUI Login*

```
''''''''''''''''''''''''''''''''
' esalogin.vbs
'
' VBScript example for logging into WUI
```

```
'  on Cisco IronPort ESA, and SMA appliances
' Created by: Chris Porter
'  chriport@cisco.com
' Apr 2011
'
'


dim user
user = "admin"
dim pass
pass = "password"

dim loginURL
loginURL = "https://esa02.cisco.com/login?username=" & user & "&password=" & pass &
  "&action:Login=Login"

dim sidCookie

Set webClient = WScript.CreateObject ("MSXML2. serverXMLHttp")

webClient.open "GET", loginURL, False    ' use the login GET URL
webClient.setOption 2, 13056             ' ignore HTTPS cert issues
webClient.send ""

If err.Number = 0 Then
      sidCookie = webClient.getResponseHeader ("Set-Cookie")    '
retrieve the SID cookie if we logged in properly
Else
      WScript.Echo "Error: ' & err.Number & ": " & err.Description
End If
```

All this script does at this point is log in and save the cookies that the login script sends via the Set-Cookie header. For the script to be able to make configuration changes, or to commit them, you need to save the sid cookie. Whenever you make a subsequent request, the sid cookie will need to be submitted with that request.

Example 9-10 shows the next step, which is actually making a configuration change. In this case, we add a domain to the destination controls table, setting TLS connections to Required.

Example 9-10 *ESA Configuration Change*

```
dim configURL
configURL = configURL = "https://esa02.cisco.com/mail_policies/destination_control?
  action=Add&pg=1&screen=mail_policies.destination_control&no_goodtable_action=
  0&new_name=example.com&host_concurrency=0&messages_per_connection=0&recipient=
  0&table_tls=2"

webClient.open "GET", configURL, False
webClient.setRequestHeader "Cookie", sidCookie    ' return the SID
webClient.send
```

The URLs for configuration changes aren't documented, but the HTML source of the ESA WUI pages can easily be examined for the scripts and their arguments. Most of the ESA configuration changes are done through POST or GET form submissions, and the POST submissions can be converted to GET by supplying the correct arguments. Most browsers offer web-development tools or plugins that can make it easier to dissect the forms and URLs in the ESA WUI.

Committing Changes Using the WUI

After the required configuration changes are submitted, a script must commit the changes. This can be done with yet another GET URL, as shown in Example 9-11.

Example 9-11 *ESA Commit Changes*

```
dim commitURL
commitURL = "https://esa02.cisco.com/commit?action=Commit&screen=commit&logout=
  &comment=TLS%20required%20for%20new%20domain"

webClient.open "GET", commitURL, False
webClient.setRequestHeader "Cookie", sidCookie    ' return the SID
webClient.send
```

At this point, we have a framework for a script that logs in, issues a configuration change, and commits the change. The configuration change can be anything that suits your purpose; just change the configURL parameter in the appropriate place in the script.

Retrieving Reporting Data from the WUI

The data that makes up the reports in the WUI is available for export. If you're browsing a report, each of the tables and charts has an Export... link at its lower right that produces a comma-separated values (CSV) text file containing the relevant data.

The data that is exported reflects the current selected time range in the WUI. Each export link is just a URL, though, with CGI arguments reflecting the time range and report type. Because each report is an HTTP GET URL, you can easily write a script that retrieves reporting data.

Data Export URLs

There are a large number of report pages in the WUI, and each report has multiple export links. The export URLs can all be accessed with the same base URL to the report engine:

```
https://<esa hostname>/monitor/reports/report
```

The parameters to this URL determine the report type, time range, and export format. You must use the parameter names and values that the ESA expects or you'll get 404 not found or other error responses from the ESA. If you specify a set of parameters that yields a report that has no data, you won't get an error. Instead, you get an empty file.

The report type is dictated by two parameters, which specify which particular chunk of data you want to export. The first parameter is *report_def_id*, and it signifies the high-level report you're retrieving. The possible values for this parameter, listed in Table 9-2, correspond to the reports in the Monitor menu in the WUI.

Table 9-2 *ESA Export Report Types: Parameter Report_def_id*

Report_def_id Value	Corresponding WUI Report
mga_incoming_mail	Incoming Mail
mga_destination_domains	Outgoing Destinations
mga_internal_senders	Outgoing Senders
mga_outgoing_delivery_status	Delivery Status
mga_internal_users	Internal Users
mga_dlp_incident_summary	DLP Incidents
mga_content_filters	Content Filters
mga_virus_outbreaks	Outbreak Filters
mga_virus_types	Virus Types
mga_tls_connections	TLS Connections
mga_system_capacity	System Capacity

The other pages in the WUI Monitor menu don't have exportable data in this format. System Status can be exported several other ways, as we have seen.

After you specify the global report type, you need to specify the actual data to be exported in the parameter named report_query_id. The values for this parameter are listed in Table 9-3. Not all pairs of report_def_id and report_query_id are valid; only combinations of query ID that correspond with their global report types will generate data. Luckily, it's easy to determine the relationship just from the name, because the report_query_id values all start with their corresponding report_def_id values.

Table 9-3 *ESA Export Report Types: Parameter report_query_id*

Report_query_id Value	Corresponding WUI Element
mga_incoming_mail_top_domain_threat_messages	Top Senders by Threat Messages bar chart, ordered by domain. You can get the IP or Network Owner view by using the profile_type parameter.
mga_incoming_mail_top_domain_clean_messages	Top Senders by Clean Messages bar chart.
mga_incoming_mail_domain_search	Incoming Mail Details table.
mga_destination_domains_top_threat	Destinations by Threat Messages bar chart.
mga_destination_domains_top_clean	Destinations by Clean Messages bar chart.
mga_destination_domains_virus_types_detail	Outgoing Destinations details table.
mga_internal_senders_top_threat	Top senders by Threat Messages bar chart.
mga_internal_senders_top_clean	Top senders by Clean Messages bar chart.
mga_internal_senders_sender_detail	Sender Details table.
mga_outgoing_delivery_status_status_table	Exports the only table on this page: delivery status. You can get this data from other places, like the CLI command **tophosts** or from the XML status pages.
mga_internal_users_top_incoming_messages	Top Users by Clean Incoming bar chart.
mga_internal_users_top_outgoing_messages	Top Users by Clean Outgoing bar chart.
mga_internal_users_user_monitoring	User Mail Flow Details table.
mga_dlp_incident_summary_top_incidents_by_severity	Top Incidents by Severity line graph.
mga_dlp_incident_summary_incident_summary	Incident Summary table.
mga_dlp_incident_summary_top_dlp_policy_matches	Top DLP Policy Matches bar graph.
mga_dlp_incident_summary_dlp_incident_details	DLP Incident Details table.
mga_content_filters_top_incoming_cf_matches	Top Incoming Content Filter matches bar chart.
mga_content_filters_top_outgoing_cf_matches	Top Outgoing Content Filter matches bar chart.

mga_content_filters_incoming_cf_matches	Incoming Content Filter Matches counts table.
mga_content_filters_outgoing_cf_matches	Outgoing Content Filter Matches counts table.
mga_virus_outbreaks_threats_by_type	Threats by Type bar chart.
mga_virus_outbreaks_threat_detail	Threat Details table.
mga_virus_outbreaks_outbreak_detail	Past Year Outbreaks history table.
mga_virus_types_top_incoming_virus_types	Top Incoming Virus Types bar chart.
mga_virus_types_top_outgoing_virus_types	Top Outgoing Virus Types bar chart.
mga_virus_types_virus_types_detail	Virus Types Detail table.
mga_tls_connections_received_tls_graph	Incoming TLS Connections graph.
mga_tls_connections_received_tls_table	Incoming TLS Connections Summary table.
mga_tls_connections_received_tls_msg_table	Incoming TLS Messages Summary table.
mga_tls_connections_received_tls_detail	Incoming TLS Connections Details table.
mga_tls_connections_sent_tls_graph	Outgoing TLS Connections graph.
mga_tls_connections_sent_tls_table	Outgoing TLS Connections Summary table.
mga_tls_connections_sent_tls_msg_table	Outgoing TLS Messages Summary table.
mga_tls_connections_sent_tls_detail	Outgoing TLS Connections Details table.
mga_system_capacity_average_time_workqueue	Average Time Spent in Work Queue graph.
mga_system_capacity_average_messages_workqueue	Average Messages in Work Queue graph.
mga_system_capacity_max_messages_workqueue	Max Messages in Work Queue graph.
mga_system_capacity_total_incoming_connections	Total Incoming Connections graph.
mga_system_capacity_total_incoming_messages	Total Incoming Messages graph.
mga_system_capacity_average_incoming_message_size	Average Incoming Size (Bytes) graph.
mga_system_capacity_total_incoming_message_size	Total Incoming Size (Bytes) graph.
mga_system_capacity_total_outgoing_connections	Total Outgoing Connections graph.

mga_system_capacity_total_outgoing_messages	Total Outgoing Messages graph.
mga_system_capacity_average_outgoing_message_size	Average Outgoing Size (Bytes) graph.
mga_system_capacity_total_outgoing_message_size	Total Outgoing Size (Bytes) graph.
mga_system_capacity_overall_cpu_usage	Overall CPU Usage graph.
mga_system_capacity_cpu_by_function	CPU by Function graph.
mga_system_capacity_swap_page_out	Memory Page Swapping graph.

For example, to export the data from the **Top Users by Clean Incoming Messages** graph on the upper left of the WUI Internal Users report, you would add these arguments to the URL:

```
https://<esa hostname>/monitor/reports/report?report_def_id=mga_internal_
  users&report_query_id=mga_internal_top_incoming_messages
```

Next, you need to specify the time range for the exported data. The start and end date and times of the exported data are controlled through the date_range parameter, which can be current_hour, current_day, current_week, or current_month. Continuing with the example, looking at the data for the last day gives us a URL like this:

```
https://<esa hostname>/monitor/reports/report?report_def_id=mga_internal_
  users&report_query_id=mga_internal_top_incoming_messages&date_range=current_day
```

Finally, to get a complete URL, we need to specify the export format. The export format is simple; the parameter name is format and the only possible value is CSV because that's the only format the ESA supports for export:

```
https://<esa hostname>/monitor/reports/report?report_def_id=mga_inter
  nal_users&report_query_id=mga_internal_users_top_incoming_messages&date_
  range=current_day&format=csv
```

To get some reports in a different view, or the data in a different sort order, you need to pass a couple of other parameters in the URL. For the incoming mail reports, you add the profile_type parameter to get data by IP or network owner. If you exclude the parameter entirely, you get the Domain view:

```
https://<esa hostname>/monitor/reports/report?report_def_id=mga_incom
  ing_mail&report_query_id=mga_incoming_mail_top_domain_threat_messages&date_
  range=current_day&format=csv&profile_type=ipaddr
```

Other Data Export Topics

If you build some export URLs and request them with a browser or scripting tool, you'll get a feel for what kind of data is in each report export. In most cases, there's more data in the Export than you see on the screen in the WUI, and it's arranged differently. The first thing you're likely to notice is that most of the reports include timestamp information, in both UNIX epoch and human-readable formats.

This is because the data that you'll see in the exported CSV is not quite the same as what you see in the WUI—it's actually the raw data that goes into making up the charts and tables that you see on each report page. Each CSV breaks up the requested time period into intervals, so that, for example, an export of a table with a Time Range of Day actually exports data by the hour.

Let's look at a concrete example. Figure 9-1 is the Past Day view of Incoming Mail on an ESA. It shows the top-ten domains attempting to send unwanted messages to this ESA.

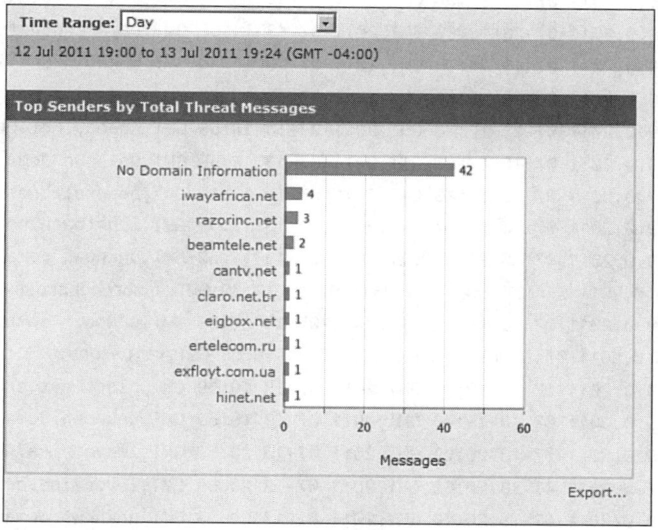

Figure 9-1 *Past Day Chart for Top Threat Message Senders*

The export of the chart, however, gives us that same data broken into hourly segments, and it includes more data. In fact, it includes *all* domains that have at least one threat message attempt in the last day. The CSV listing of this export is shown in Example 9-12.

Example 9-12 *CSV Export of Daily Data Showing Hourly Segments*

```
Begin Timestamp,End Timestamp,Begin Date,End Date,Domain,Messages
1310511600.0,1310515199.0,2011-07-12 23:00 GMT,2011-07-12 23:59 GMT,unknown domain,1
1310518800.0,1310522399.0,2011-07-13 01:00 GMT,2011-07-13 01:59 GMT,irtel.ru,1
1310518800.0,1310522399.0,2011-07-13 01:00 GMT,2011-07-13 01:59 GMT,prima.net.ar,1
1310518800.0,1310522399.0,2011-07-13 01:00 GMT,2011-07-13 01:59 GMT,speedy.com.ar,1
1310518800.0,1310522399.0,2011-07-13 01:00 GMT,2011-07-13 01:59 GMT,unknown domain,1
1310518800.0,1310522399.0,2011-07-13 01:00 GMT,2011-07-13 01:59 GMT,virtua.com.br,1
1310522400.0,1310525999.0,2011-07-13 02:00 GMT,2011-07-13 02:59 GMT,unknown domain,2
1310551200.0,1310554799.0,2011-07-13 10:00 GMT,2011-07-13 10:59 GMT,ertelecom.ru,1
1310551200.0,1310554799.0,2011-07-13 10:00 GMT,2011-07-13 10:59 GMT,hinet.net,1
1310551200.0,1310554799.0,2011-07-13 10:00 GMT,2011-07-13 10:59 GMT,hol.gr,1
1310551200.0,1310554799.0,2011-07-13 10:00 GMT,2011-07-13 10:59 GMT,romtelecom.net,1
```

```
1310551200.0,1310554799.0,2011-07-13 10:00 GMT,2011-07-13 10:59 GMT,triolan.net,1
1310551200.0,1310554799.0,2011-07-13 10:00 GMT,2011-07-13 10:59 GMT,unknown domain,1
1310551200.0,1310554799.0,2011-07-13 10:00 GMT,2011-07-13 10:59 GMT,wateen.net,1
1310554800.0,1310558399.0,2011-07-13 11:00 GMT,2011-07-13 11:59 GMT,eigbox.net,1
1310558400.0,1310561999.0,2011-07-13 12:00 GMT,2011-07-13 12:59 GMT,seed.net.tw,1
1310558400.0,1310561999.0,2011-07-13 12:00 GMT,2011-07-13 12:59 GMT,unknown domain,4
1310562000.0,1310565599.0,2011-07-13 13:00 GMT,2011-07-13 13:59 GMT,unknown domain,1
1310565600.0,1310569199.0,2011-07-13 14:00 GMT,2011-07-13 14:59 GMT,razorinc.net,1
1310565600.0,1310569199.0,2011-07-13 14:00 GMT,2011-07-13 14:59 GMT,unknown domain,7
1310569200.0,1310572799.0,2011-07-13 15:00 GMT,2011-07-13 15:59 GMT,razorinc.net,1
1310572800.0,1310576399.0,2011-07-13 16:00 GMT,2011-07-13 16:59 GMT,speedy.net.pe,1
1310572800.0,1310576399.0,2011-07-13 16:00 GMT,2011-07-13 16:59 GMT,unknown domain,7
1310576400.0,1310579999.0,2011-07-13 17:00 GMT,2011-07-13 17:59 GMT,beamtele.net,2
1310576400.0,1310579999.0,2011-07-13 17:00 GMT,2011-07-13 17:59 GMT,lightpath.net,1
1310576400.0,1310579999.0,2011-07-13 17:00 GMT,2011-07-13 17:59 GMT,unknown domain,6
1310576400.0,1310579999.0,2011-07-13 17:00 GMT,2011-07-13 17:59 GMT,upcbroadband.cz,1
1310580000.0,1310583599.0,2011-07-13 18:00 GMT,2011-07-13 18:59 GMT,unknown domain,2
1310580000.0,1310583599.0,2011-07-13 18:00 GMT,2011-07-13 18:59 GMT,veloxzone.com.br,1
1310583600.0,1310587199.0,2011-07-13 19:00 GMT,2011-07-13 19:59 GMT,claro.net.br,1
1310583600.0,1310587199.0,2011-07-13 19:00 GMT,2011-07-13 19:59 GMT,unknown domain,2
1310587200.0,1310590799.0,2011-07-13 20:00 GMT,2011-07-13 20:59 GMT,iwayafrica.net,4
1310587200.0,1310590799.0,2011-07-13 20:00 GMT,2011-07-13 20:59 GMT,levonline.com,1
1310587200.0,1310590799.0,2011-07-13 20:00 GMT,2011-07-13 20:59 GMT,unknown domain,6
1310590800.0,1310594399.0,2011-07-13 21:00 GMT,2011-07-13 21:59 GMT,cantv.net,1
1310590800.0,1310594399.0,2011-07-13 21:00 GMT,2011-07-13 21:59 GMT,exfloyt.com.ua,1
1310590800.0,1310594399.0,2011-07-13 21:00 GMT,2011-07-13 21:59 GMT,razorinc.net,1
1310590800.0,1310594399.0,2011-07-13 21:00 GMT,2011-07-13 21:59 GMT,telkom.net.id,1
1310590800.0,1310594399.0,2011-07-13 21:00 GMT,2011-07-13 21:59 GMT,unknown domain,1
1310594400.0,1310597999.0,2011-07-13 22:00 GMT,2011-07-13 22:59 GMT,unknown domain,1
1310598000.0,1310601599.0,2011-07-13 23:00 GMT,2011-07-13 23:59 GMT,rr.com,1
```

This difference in export can be frustrating if you just want what you see in the WUI, but it delivers more data (in this case, more domains) and adds time interval information about each sender. If you really want to summarize the data for a particular day, you have two choices: Export the weekly report and find the particular day you're interested in, or export the daily report and summarize the totals across all hourly periods.

In the example in the next section, I take the second approach, summing the data across all hours to create a report for a single day.

Example Script

Now that we are able to retrieve the data, what should we do with it? Because the resulting format is in CSV and is ideal for use in spreadsheets and charts, let's add it to a spreadsheet and graph the data.

Example 9-13 is a listing for a VBScript program that uses Microsoft Excel objects to graph data about incoming threat messages. Essentially, I recreated the graph from the Incoming Mail page for the past day, but with all the data available for that 24-hour period rather than just the top senders. With the flexibility of scripting, and the data ending up in Excel, you'll be able to do whatever you like with it.

Example 9-13 *Data Export and Manipulation from WUI*

```
''''''''''''''''''''''''''
' threatReport.vbs
'
' VBScript example for retrieving data from report Export
'  on Cisco IronPort ESA appliances
' Created by: Chris Porter
'  chriport@cisco.com
' Jun 2011
'
'


dim user
user = "report"
dim pass
pass = "ironport"

dim loginURL
loginURL = "https://esa02.cisco.com/login?username=" & user & "&password=" & pass &
  "&action:Login=Login"

dim reportURL
reportURL = "https://esa02.cisco.com/monitor/reports/report?date_range=current_
  day&report_def_id=mga_incoming_mail&profile_type=domain&report_query_id=mga_
  incoming_mail_top_domain_threat_messages&format=csv"
dim sidCookie

Set webClient = WScript.CreateObject ("MSXML2.serverXMLHttp")

' log in to the ESA, ignoring HTTPS cert errors
webClient.open "GET", loginURL, False
webClient.setOption 2, 13056
webClient.send ""
' store the SID cookie if we logged in properly
```

```
If err.Number = 0 Then
      sidCookie = webClient.getResponseHeader ("Set-Cookie")
Else
      WScript.Echo "Error: " & err.Number & ": " & err.Description
End If

' retrieve the report data
webClient.open "GET", reportURL, False
' return the SID cookie we got when we logged in
webClient.setRequestHeader "Cookie", sidCookie
webClient.send
If err.Number > 0 Then
      WScript.Echo "Error: " & err.Number & ": " & err.Description
End If

' examine the returned data
dim responseLines
responseLines = Split (webClient.responseText, vbCrLf)     ' split the response by
  line
responseLineCount = ubound(responseLines)
redim preserve responseLines (responseLineCount-1)         ' get rid of last,blank
  line

' use a dictionary to keep track of unique domains
Set resultsDictionary = WScript.CreateObject ("Scripting.Dictionary")

for each csvLine in responseLines
      csvArr = Split (csvLine, ",")
      domain = csvArr(4)
      msgcount = csvArr(5)
      If (resultsDictionary.Exists (domain)) Then
             resultsDictionary.Item (domain) = CInt(resultsDictionary.Item(domain))
  + msgcount
      Else
             resultsDictionary.Add domain, msgcount
      End If
next

' put the results into an array
dim connectionArray ()
redim connectionArray (resultsDictionary.Count, 2)

i=0
for each domain in resultsDictionary
      connectionArray (i,0) = domain
      connectionArray (i,1) = resultsDictionary.Item(domain)
      i = i+1
```

```
next

' create an Excel worksheet and chart
dim appExcel
set appExcel = createobject("Excel.Application")
appExcel.Visible = true

dim wb
set wb = appExcel.workbooks.add

dim reportRange
set reportRange = wb.ActiveSheet.Range("A1").Resize(resultsDictionary.Count, 2)
reportRange.value = connectionArray

wb.Charts.Add
wb.ActiveChart.SetSourceData appExcel.Sheets ("Sheet1").Range("A:B")
wb.ActiveChart.ChartType = 54 ' xl3DColumnClustered

appExcel.UserControl = true

WScript.Quit
```

Figure 9-2 shows the resulting graph, as displayed in Microsoft Excel 2007.

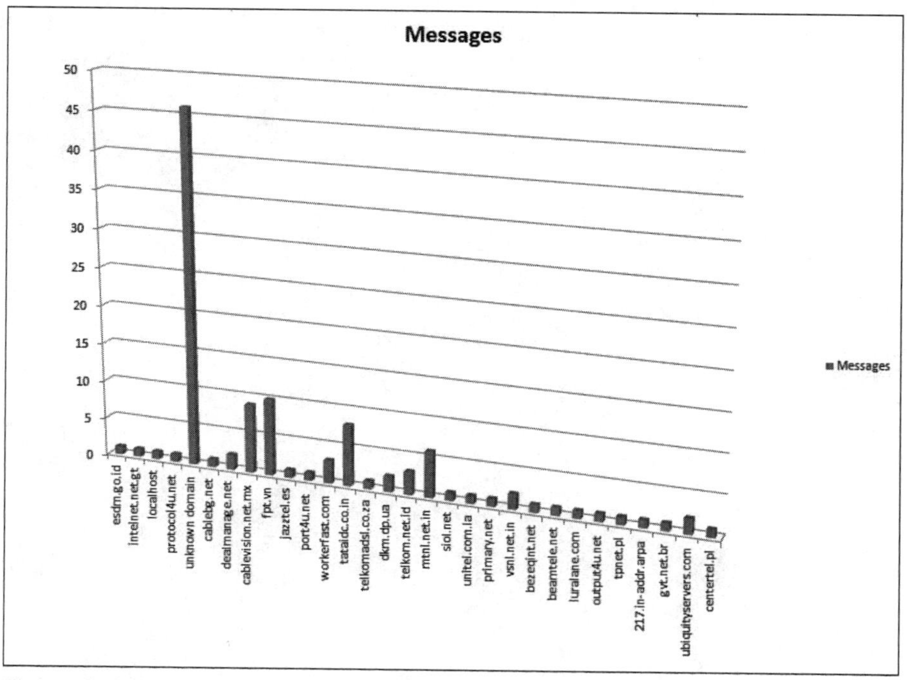

Figure 9-2 *Results of the ThreatReport Script*

Summary

Much of the ESA monitoring, reporting, and configuration is intended for interactive use by humans, but we've shed some light on using CLI batch commands and WUI reporting URLs with scripts running on external systems. Hopefully, the examples give you a place to start for your own automation needs.

Cisco provides batch commands for all CLI operations that we have put to good use in making simple configuration commands. Some examples of scripts that can compile and transfer text data for import into an ESA table were also shown.

The next chapter examines another critical administrative topic: configuration files in XML format.

Chapter 10

Configuration Files

In this chapter, you will learn the following:

- Structure of XML configuration files
- Process of exporting and importing XML configuration files
- Editing complete or partial XML configuration files

ESA and the XML Configuration Format

Every Email Security Appliance (ESA) maintains an internal configuration repository that's minimally exposed to administrators. The only interface to this configuration is through the supported XML configuration format provided in files by export from a running ESA. This XML document is defined by the Document Type Definition (DTD) file config.dtd on the ESA filesystem in the configuration directory.

The XML configuration file contains all the configuration settings for that particular appliance. It does not contain any of the data on the system, namely messages in queue or in any quarantine, or any files on the ESA filesystem. It records the log subscriptions and options, but not any logging data. In other words, if you're replacing an ESA, you need to take separate steps to get the messages delivered and log files transferred away from the ESA. It stores the settings for the end user Safelist and Blocklist (SLBL), but not the actual entries, so if you're using that feature, you need to export that table.

The configuration file from an appliance is suitable for use as a complete backup for restoring to the same appliance, or to another appliance, including different models of ESA. Because of that, you can use it when replacing appliances or upgrading to new hardware models, and if you're willing to tinker with the files, you can even propagate a single appliance configuration across multiple appliances.

Configuration File Structure

The XML format that the ESA uses is well-formed XML that should be parsable by any browser or editor capable of handling the format, but it's often easier to treat it as plain text and open it in a text editor. The ESA uses UNIX-style line endings, so some Windows editors (like Notepad) won't display it legibly. Most web browsers can display XML data, too, but may require that the DTD document be available. Because they don't allow editing of XML, web browsers are of limited use for config files.

Being XML, the configuration file structure is hierarchical. If you plan on editing the configuration files, you need to maintain this hierarchy. Like all XML format files, the configuration begins with the XML header:

```
<?xml version="1.0" encoding="ISO-8859-1"?>
<!DOCTYPE config SYSTEM "config.dtd">
```

The next section is information about the specific appliance that the file was exported from, contained in a multiline XML comment. The ESA ignores these comments when importing a configuration, so this section is just for your reference. When editing XML, you don't need to preserve the comments. Example 10-1 shows a sample configuration comments section.

Example 10-1 *XML Configuration Comments*

```
<!--
  Product: IronPort C670 Messaging Gateway(tm) Appliance
  Model Number: C670
  Version: 7.1.3-010
  Serial Number: 11C09F3AEB36-1005CR41
  Number of CPUs: 8
  Memory (GB): 4
  Current Time: Thu Nov 17 14:05:16 2011
  Feature "IronPort Anti-Spam": Quantity = 1, Time Remaining = "30 days"
  Feature "Sophos": Quantity = 1, Time Remaining = "30 days"
  Feature "Virus Outbreak Filters": Quantity = 1, Time Remaining = "30 days"
  Feature "Bounce Verification": Quantity = 1, Time Remaining = "Perpetual"
-->
```

The actual ESA configuration data starts and ends with the config element that is the root of the document tree. Every configuration import must have this top-level config element, even if you're only importing a partial configuration, which is a subject discussed later in this chapter. From there, the subelements of the configuration are grouped logically. The first portion of the config is demarcated by the XML comment header that reads **Network Configuration**. This section is chiefly concerned with local-machine settings: hostnames, interfaces, Domain Name System (DNS), gateways, routing, and other network settings. If you were comparing configuration files from different ESAs that are similarly configured, this is where you would see all the differences. By contrast, the remainder of the configuration is less machine-specific: policy, logging, delivery, and so on. The organization is similar to the way *machine* versus *group* or *cluster* settings are managed in a centralized management cluster, and that's not just coincidence. The goal of the XML structure was to clearly separate per-machine configuration from global policy settings, a fact that we put to use later in this chapter when we modify and import configuration files.

Here are the major sections of the configuration (in order):

1. **Network Configuration:** Basic IP networking and host-specific settings. In this section, you'll find all the configured IP interfaces, your DNS settings, the default gateway and any static routes, and the configuration of the physical Ethernet ports.

2. **System Configuration:** Miscellaneous appliance configurations, other than policy. NTP server settings, all TLS certificates, local user accounts, and service update rules are stored in this section. Most of these are considered cluster-level settings because they would be identical across multiple appliances, but TLS certificates are more often configured per ESA. You would only use the same TLS certificates across multiple ESAs if they were load balanced with a shared VIP.

3. **Mail Configuration:** The bulk of the policy, filtering, and email routing configuration is stored in this section. All listener configuration and subcomponents, like HAT and RAT, are here. Also includes LDAP, bounce profiles, system quarantines, destination controls, SMTP routes, dictionaries, message filters, DKIM signing profiles and keys, and SPF policies.

4. **Log File and Alert Configuration:** As its name suggests, this section starts with log subscriptions and system alerts, but also includes masquerading, global security services settings, SNMP, and text resources (like notifications and bounce templates). It also contains all the incoming and outgoing mail policies and their associated content filters.

5. **End User Quarantine Configuration:** A short section with just the **<euq>** element. Contains the configuration settings for the end-user quarantine, whether enabled or not. If you're using the centralized quarantine on an SMA, this section contains only the ESA portion of that configuration. The SMA side of the configuration is stored in the SMA's configuration file.

6. **Bounce Verification:** As you'd expect, this section contains the configuration for the bounce verification feature, but also includes global reporting settings and a record for all the periodic scheduled reports configuration on this appliance.

7. **Security Management:** Includes the configuration settings for centralized reporting and tracking when those SMA features are in use. Also includes SSL cipher settings and envelope encryption profiles.

8. **RSA Email Data Loss Prevention:** Settings for the local RSA DLP engine. Includes all the enabled policies, custom classifiers, custom dictionaries, and DLP actions.

9. **System Packet Capture:** A single element, **<system_packet_trace>**, includes the settings for recording packets passing through the ESA.

The XML element names are usually self-explanatory, and you'll be able to tell which configuration sections correspond to which CLI command or WUI pages. The <listeners> element corresponds to the **listenerconfig** CLI command or the Listeners page under the Network menu in the WUI. <log_subscriptions> correspond to **logconfig** or the Log Subscriptions page. Not all are quite so easily correlated. Table 10-1 lists these elements and their corresponding CLI command or WUI page.

Table 10-1 *Obscure XML Configuration Elements*

Configuration Element	Description
<thirdparty>	Global options for the security engines: anti-spam and antivirus. Corresponds to the pages in the Security Services menu in the WUI or the **antispamconfig** and **antivirusconfig** in the CLI.
<body_scanner>	Scanning options for message bodies and attachments: maximum scan size, depth, and MIME types. Settings are controlled by the CLI command **scanconfig.**
<unsubscribe>, <unsubscribe_enabled>, <unsubscribe_do_bounce>	Global unsubscribe table, accessible via **unsubscribe** in the CLI.
<delivery_interface>, <delivery_max_concurrency>, <delivery_max_tls_concurrency>, <possible_delivery>	Global delivery behavior and limits, as set in the **deliveryconfig** command.
<hostkeys>	SSH host keys for remote systems, for authentication to remote SSH servers in SCP log transfers. Since this is for log subscriptions, these settings are in that WUI page in the System Administration menu, or in **logconfig.**
<slbl>	The Safelist and Blocklist (SLBL) feature for the end-user spam quarantine. Enabled through the Spam Quarantines settings in the Quarantines page. Note that this contains only the settings, not the actual entries! The SLBL entries must be backed up separately.
<percpt_policies>	Incoming and outgoing mail policies and content filters are organized under this element.
<smad>	Settings for this ESA's communication with a security management appliance (SMA). Most of these settings will actually be on the SMA, with the exception of those under the **secondaryconfig** CLI command.

<iccm>	Placeholder for centralized management features. Not used on the ESA as of this writing.
<encryption>	Despite the general-sounding name, this corresponds only to the envelope encryption profiles. TLS, SSH, certificates, and other encryption topics are stored separately.
<system_packet_trace>	Settings for the packet capture features available on the Help and Support menu or via the CLI **diagnostic** command.

Importing and Exporting Configuration Files

The chief purpose of the XML configuration format is for backup and restoration of configuration settings, either on the same appliance or when copying configurations to another appliance. You can export the configuration to the ESA filesystem or to your local workstation from the tools in the WUI, and the ESA can, naturally, send you a copy via email. In the WUI, configuration file management is all available in the Configuration File page of the System Administration menu. In the CLI, the commands are **saveconfig**, **mailconfig**, and **loadconfig**.

When you perform an AsyncOS upgrade, the ESA automatically preserves all configuration settings, so there's no need to import and export manually as part of the upgrade process. Existing settings will be preserved, and any new features introduced in the new AsyncOS version will have a default configuration applied. In some cases, when a feature is overhauled, your older settings will be maintained as close to the original interpretation as possible. If such a translation between versions will affect operation of the appliance, the change will be noted in the release notes for the new version.

If you don't need to export the configuration for upgrade, what reasons would you have for exporting and importing the XML configuration files? There are a few reasons:

- In the event of hardware failure, you can easily replace one ESA hardware chassis with a new one by importing the configuration into the new device. Having recent configuration files for all of your ESAs makes the individual appliances easier to replace.
- Backing out configuration changes. If a configuration change has undesirable affects, it's easy to revert to an earlier configuration, if you've saved one. The ESA does not have an automatic configuration revert process.
- Modifying portions of the configuration. If you want to make bulk changes to a configuration, or import just a portion of a configuration, you can directly edit the XML file.

In general, I recommend exporting the configuration file on a regular basis (see the section "Automating Configuration File Backup" later in this chapter), or at least on each of these events:

- **Before any upgrade:** Having a configuration export at your current AsyncOS version allows you to restore the configuration if you had to roll back the upgrade with the **revert** command. The revert process clears the ESA configuration.
- **After any upgrade:** You should save a copy of the new configuration immediately after an upgrade just to have an original at the new version. It's usually difficult to restore a configuration from a different version of AsyncOS.
- **Before and after any major configuration changes:** If you're changing IP addresses and hostnames, altering security settings, or other high-impact changes, having a pre-change configuration file allows for easy back-out should something go wrong. This should be a part of every change control process.

Exporting

Exporting the configuration file from the ESA is trivial from either the WUI Configuration File page in the System Administration menu, or the CLI commands **mailconfig** or **saveconfig.** From the WUI, you can choose to save the exported configuration directly to your computer. Other options are to have the ESA email you the configuration (of course) or save it to the ESA's filesystem. If you're saving a configuration for archive or backup purposes, you can use the email or local appliance save, but if you're planning to manipulate the configuration file, save it to your local workstation to save the extra steps.

There's really only one thing to decide during export: whether to mask passwords or not. This description is misleading, because choosing to exclude passwords actually does the following:

- Replaces the password strings for all local accounts with a line of asterisks. Local user accounts are MD5 hashed in unmasked configuration files anyway, but masking passwords removes the hashes.
- Replaces the private key portion of any installed certificates with asterisks.
- Replaces any DKIM private (signing) keys with asterisks.
- Replaces the password strings for credentials to external systems, like LDAP and FTP, with asterisks. These are stored in the clear in unmasked configuration files.

The purpose of masking passwords is to exclude the sensitive information in this list when sharing configuration files with others. Whenever you export a configuration for a human audience, or when you plan to send the file outside of your department or organization, it's a good idea to use the Mask Passwords option.

> **Warning** If you expect to import the configuration file at some later date, you must choose to include passwords by unchecking the box marked **Mask passwords in the configuration files.** Without the passwords and other secret information, the import process will fail.
>
> It is possible to hand-edit and restore a masked-password configuration file so that it can be imported, but you really don't want that hassle.

In recent AsyncOS versions, the upgrade wizard prompts you to save a copy of the configuration before upgrade. I recommend that you do this, but you should also save a copy of the configuration immediately *after* upgrade. The ESA doesn't prompt you for this post-upgrade export, but it's extremely valuable to have. In all likelihood, you won't be able to easily import an older configuration file on a new AsyncOS version.

Importing

If you're completely replacing one ESA with another, you can simply import the entire thing without editing. If the two ESAs are running the same version, the configuration will import without errors. For ESAs running the same major/minor version on different builds, it will probably import cleanly, but it varies depending on releases. For ESAs with different major/minor versions, it's unlikely to import cleanly.

If the import process encounters an error parsing the loaded configuration file, the entire import fails and an error message is displayed. No portion of the configuration file is loaded unless the entire configuration is valid. Once imported, the changes are not committed automatically and you must commit for the configuration to take effect. Before committing changes, you can view the imported configuration settings in all WUI pages, which is a good idea for validating the new configuration before commit.

If the file does not import cleanly, the import page will display an error and indicate the line number of the configuration file where the error occurred, as shown in Figure 10-1.

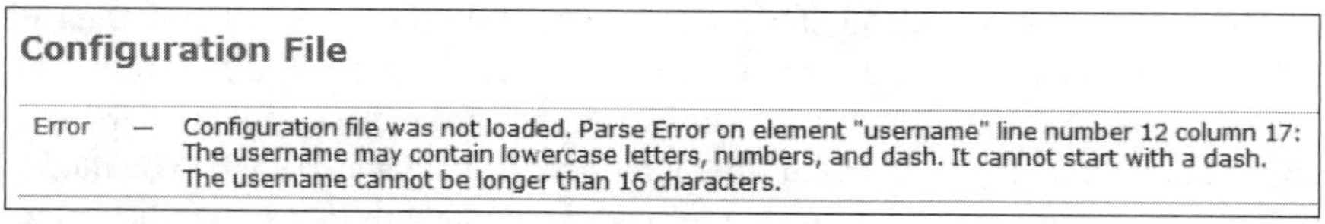

Figure 10-1 *Configuration File Import Error*

The WUI will only show the first error, as the import process bails out after the first parse problem. There's no way to know ahead of time about each error, so you have to continually fix, upload, and import to correct all the errors.

Note these things that are not imported by this process:

- **Interface MAC addresses:** The ESA won't change the hardware addresses of the physical interfaces. The MACs are fixed on each appliance.
- **Hardware serial number:** The ESA won't change its serial number.
- **License keys:** Keys are tied to a specific hardware serial number and must be issued independently for each appliance. You can import configuration settings for an engine, like anti-spam, into an appliance that does not have a feature key for it, but that will not import a valid key for it.
- **Spam quarantine SLBL entries:** If you're using this quarantine feature that allows end users to manage their own list of senders, the database is stored separately from the configuration and has its own backup.

If present in the imported configuration file, these elements will just be ignored. All other settings will be replaced by the values in the configuration file.

> **Warning** If you're importing a configuration file that has enabled security services into a new appliance that has those security engines disabled, the import will not enable the engines. The configuration will be imported, but the engine will still be disabled. You'll have to manually enable the engine, including accepting the license agreement, but at that point, the configuration you imported will be intact.
>
> In other words, if your new appliance hasn't been set up yet, or has its feature keys expired, or for some other reason, has engines like anti-spam or antivirus disabled, importing a configuration won't fix that. For this reason, I recommend that brand-new appliances be set up using the System Setup Wizard before you import an existing configuration.

If you're importing a configuration on a different appliance model than the one that produced the file, you have to deal with the potential differences in the hardware. For models in the same class (such as C660 and C670), the configuration should import cleanly. The 1U units like the C160 only have two physical Ethernet interfaces, Data 1 and Data 2, and importing a C670 configuration with a management interface results in an error. Simply delete the section of the configuration for the management interface. The same holds true of appliances with fiber interfaces (Data 3 and Data 4). You might have to move the IP address and hostname settings from one interface to another, or even rethink your network installation.

Editing Configuration Files

Up to this point, we discussed exporting and importing complete configuration files, and that's adequate for basic ESA backup and restore. If you simply want to revert to an older configuration or replace one appliance with another in a one-for-one swap, you shouldn't have to dig any deeper.

For other tasks, such as duplicating configuration from one appliance to many or copying settings for a specific feature from one appliance to another, you need to delve into the configuration file and edit the values stored in the XML elements.

Duplicating a Configuration

When you have a stable *master* configuration on one ESA, but need an identical configuration on other *target* appliances, you can manually create a configuration file for the new ESA by editing this master configuration. Conveniently, the XML elements in the configuration that need editing in such a situation are grouped near the top. To start, export a configuration from your master ESA and open the file for editing. After the XML header and system comments, you'll come across the Network Configuration section, where you'll need to edit these elements, at a minimum:

- **<hostname>:** The global hostname for the appliance, which is displayed in the WUI and CLI and used as an identifier in reporting, tracking, and centralized management.
- **<interfaces>:** You need to change the <ip>, <interface_hostname>, and <netmask> subelements to change this ESA's network information. Don't change the <phys_interface> value, because this needs to be consistent with the <port_name> element that defines the name of the physical Ethernet jacks on the ESA.
- **<ethernet_settings>:** Best practice is to leave all the interfaces set to autoselect, but if you have specific settings, you may need to modify this between appliances. Don't worry about the <macaddr> element, because the target ESA will not import this.
- **<dns>:** If your master and target ESA will have different DNS server settings, you can modify them here. You can also modify this after the import.
- **<default_gateway>:** The default route for all packets destined for nonlocal networks. It's critical that this be correct for the target machine.
- **<routes>:** The static routing table, critical in multiinterface network deployments.

You need to modify these basic elements to give your target ESA a network identity that differs from the master. Take care—if you import a configuration with an invalid network setting, you could lose connectivity to the new ESA. If the network settings conflict with another, like a duplicate IP address, you'll cause both appliances to be unavailable. You can certainly edit other elements in the XML, but I prefer to modify *only* the critical network elements, and then import the configuration. Before I commit, I review the imported network settings and make any other required changes.

If your target ESA is a brand-new appliance, start by running the System Setup Wizard (SSW), even if you plan on completely overwriting the configuration. For one reason, the full WUI of the ESA won't even be available until you complete the wizard and install the basic configuration. For another, the SSW also takes care of basic setup tasks that a configuration import will not do, like enabling security engines.

Remember that importing a configuration imports every setting that's present in the file. Existing settings are overwritten completely. Because this process falls into the category of *major configuration change*, I recommend saving the existing ESA configuration before importing another.

Partial Configuration Files

If you want to duplicate the settings for a single feature of the ESA, most of the time, the right approach is to export the relevant table, copy the exported file, and import into the target ESA using the WUI Configuration File page or the CLI command **loadconfig**. This works perfectly for tables like HAT, RAT, SMPTRoutes, and Destination Controls, but it's simply unavailable for other features that don't support an individual import/export.

One good example is the table of administrative users. In the WUI, controls are provided for creating, editing, and deleting user accounts, but you can't import/export en masse. Further, without knowing what each user's account password is, you can't even manually recreate the accounts on another ESA, because the password strings are not stored directly, but as MD5 hashes. User accounts will certainly be duplicated if you export the entire XML configuration file, but let's suppose that you only want to duplicate the user account information and not the entire appliance configuration. You can accomplish this with a partial configuration file.

As the name suggests, a partial configuration doesn't have every single XML element present. To be imported, it must be valid XML, include the declarations at the top, and must include the top level <config> element. In fact, that's technically all that's required for a minimal partial configuration, as shown in Example 10-2.

Example 10-2 *Absolutely Minimal Partial Configuration*

```
<?xml version="1.0" encoding="ISO-8859-1"?>
<!DOCTYPE config SYSTEM "config.dtd">
<config>

</config>
```

Of course, that partial configuration contains no actual configuration settings, and so it isn't much use to us as is. The ESA runs the import process and notes that there are no settings changed. However, we can use it as a framework to build more useful files for import.

To accomplish the goal of importing only user account information, you can create a partial configuration from scratch or by taking an exported configuration and deleting the unnecessary elements. In the case of the user accounts, I simply copied that section of a configuration file into my framework. You must include the entire second-level <users> element and all of its subelements, even if those elements have no value. Example 10-3 shows the resulting partial config file.

Example 10-3 *Partial XML Config File for Users*

```
<?xml version="1.0" encoding="ISO-8859-1"?>
<!DOCTYPE config SYSTEM "config.dtd">
<config>
  <users>
    <user>
      <username>admin</username>
      <fullname>Administrator</fullname>
      <group>admin</group>
      <enc_password>$1$VvOyFxKd$OF2Cs/W0ZTWuGTtMvT5zc/</enc_password>
    </user>
    <user>
      <username>chriport</username>
      <fullname>Chris Porter</fullname>
      <group>operators</group>
      <enc_password>$1$fv.kJkLL$0SFOluOghTpr2u1ibXjqU/</enc_password>
    </user>
    <user>
      <username>reports</username>
      <fullname>Report Scripts</fullname>
      <group>guest</group>
      <enc_password>$1$M614l0Ia$d2bxYzjRFJGT84mYB.hmr0</enc_password>
    </user>
  </users>
</config>
```

Importing this configuration file completely replaces the table of users. Any config section not represented in the imported XML configuration is simply ignored; the target appliance retains its configuration for those settings. As with any other configuration import, you can view the updated configuration before you commit the changes.

This approach works for a variety of configuration settings, but you must include the element hierarchy all the way back to the root <config> element, and you must include all the subelements of every element. This set of requirements makes it impractical to partial-import certain settings.

For example, I might want to copy just the incoming content filters from one ESA to another. However, incoming content filters are grouped in the element <content_filters>, whose parent element is <inbound_policies>. That element's immediate parent is <per-rcpt_policies>, which is a direct subelement of <config>. To have a valid configuration, you need to include that entire hierarchy, including all incoming and outgoing mail policy settings and all incoming and outgoing content filters.

Automating Configuration File Backup

Good ESA management practices include keeping recent backups of all of your appliance configurations to enable appliance replacement or roll back configuration changes. In many environments, asking the administrators to follow backup best practices simply isn't enough, and you must have an automated backup facility.

You must have an external system capable of running CLI commands or connecting to the WUI to back up the configuration on a regular schedule, as the ESA has no capabilities for running commands at arbitrary times.

Automatic configuration history is recorded when changes are committed if you enabled a Configuration History log subscription, but as discussed in Chapter 6, "Additional Management Services," restoring a configuration from an exported file is much easier than from the log subscription.

The simplest means of regularly exporting the configuration is to use an external SSH or Telnet client to connect to the ESA and issue the **mailconfig** CLI command to have the ESA send the configuration file as an attachment to a specified email address:

```
mailconfig email_team@example.com y
```

The `y` argument at the end tells the ESA to include passwords and private keys in the exported configuration.

Configuration Backup via CLI

Using **mailconfig** to email the configuration on regular intervals is adequate in most cases, but if you prefer a method that does not rely on SMTP (in the event of outages), there is another approach: Export the configuration to the ESA filesystem and the retrieve the file via FTP or SCP.

The CLI **saveconfig** command can be batch scripted, but unfortunately, the ESA chooses the export filename based on the ESA serial number and the current timestamp. You have to parse the output of this command to get the filename. Here's what the **saveconfig** command output looks like when run in batch mode:

```
ssh admin@esa02.cisco.com "saveconfig n"
File written on machine "esa02.cisco.com" to the location
"/configuration/C160-00221D61A91-4ZPTNK1-20111126T212236.xml".
Configuration saved.
```

The output includes the full path and filename, which makes it convenient to script. A simple regex parse on the script output gives the full path to use with scp. Like other scripts that use SSH, you need to install SSH keys on the ESA for this script to run without being prompted for passwords, as described in Chapter 5, "Command-Line Interface."

Example 10-4 shows the complete Perl script.

Example 10-4 *Perl Script to Save and Retrieve XML Configuration Files*

```
#!/usr/bin/perl
use strict;

my $hostname = "esa.example.com";
my $username = "admin";
my $port = 22;
my $fname;

open SSH, "ssh -p $port $username\@$hostname \"saveconfig y\"|";

while (<SSH>) {
        if (/"(\/configuration\/.*\.xml)\"/) {
                $fname = $1;

                print "found config file $fname\n";

                system "scp -P $port $username\@$hostname:$fname .";
        }
}

close SSH;
```

It would be easy to extend this script to copy the configuration file to network storage, a database, or to use a version-control system to check in the configuration file. For multiple ESAs, you can run the script multiple times or modify it to loop through a list of ESAs.

Configuration Backup via WUI

Chapter 9, "Automating Tasks," presented some scripts that used the HTTP WUI to make configuration changes to an ESA, automating the same steps a human user would with a browser. You can use the same technique to export configuration files via HTTP or HTTPS.

Using the HTTP WUI for this export might be preferable if you don't have SSH access, or if exchanging SSH keys isn't possible. This method is essentially the same as logging in with a browser—as long as you can reach the WUI, you can run this script. Like the examples in Chapter 9, the script has to log in so it can get an authentication session cookie; then, it can use the cookie for the subsequent request.

The complete listing is shown in Example 10-5.

Example 10-5 *Configuration Backup via WUI*

```
''''''''''''''''''''''''''''
' esaConfigRetrieve.vbs
'
' VBScript example for retrieving configuration file from ESA / SMA
'  on Cisco IronPort ESA, WSA, and SMA appliances
' Created by: Chris Porter
'  chriport@cisco.com
' Nov 2011
'
'


dim user
user = "admin"
dim pass
pass = "ironport"

dim loginURL
loginURL = "https://esa.example.com/login?username=" & user & "&password=" & pass &
  "&action:Login=Login"
dim configURL
configURL = "https://esa.example.com/system_administration/configuration_file?
  action=Save&operation=download&mask_passwords=0&load_from=from_appliance"
dim sidCookie

Set wget = WScript.CreateObject ("MSXML2.serverXMLHttp")

wget.open "GET", loginURL, False                 ' first, log in to the appliance
wget.setOption 2, 13056                                'ignore HTTPS cert issues
wget.send ""
If err.Number = 0 Then
                  sidCookie = wget.getResponseHeader ("Set-Cookie")    ' retrieve
  the sid cookie if we logged in properly
Else
                  WScript.Echo "Error: " & err.Number & ": " & err.Description
End If


wget.open "GET", configURL, False
```

```
wget.setRequestHeader "Cookie", sidCookie          ' return the sid value we got
  when logging in
wget.send
If err.Number = 0 Then
                  WScript.Echo wget.responseText               ' dump the config
  to stdout
Else
                  WScript.Echo "Error: " & err.Number & ": " & err.Description
End If

WScript.Quit
```

Configuration Files in Centralized Management Clusters

The ESA peer-to-peer centralized management features mostly obviate the need for saving configuration files. ESA CM was designed to have that level of configuration redundancy: Every appliance in the cluster has the entire configuration for all cluster, group, and machine settings. Replacing an individual appliance is a fairly simple process: Install the ESA on the network, upgrade it to the same AsyncOS version, and join the cluster. The collected cluster settings effectively back up all the policy and system settings. As long as you have at least one ESA in the cluster, all of your settings are preserved. In fact, it's often easier to temporarily add machines to a cluster to duplicate configurations than it is to edit configuration files.

Still, you might want to have a valid configuration file, for all the reasons mentioned earlier in this chapter. When you use the **saveconfig** command, however, this message is displayed after the configuration file is saved:

```
WARNING: Clustered machines do not support loadconfig.  Your configuration file
has complete data for the entire cluster, but cannot be used to restore a con-
figuration.
```

Likewise, the WUI has a similar message on the **Configuration File** page under the **Load Configuration** section. Exporting the configuration works, but the resulting file differs from a normal ESA XML file in that it adds a number of elements specifically for supporting clusters. You'll see, right from the top, some of the differences:

```
<?xml version="1.0" encoding="ISO-8859-1"?>
<!DOCTYPE cluster_config SYSTEM "cluster_config.dtd">
<cluster_config>
<cluster>
```

The XML for CM uses a different DTD altogether. This configuration file actually has multiple <config> elements: one for the cluster, one for each group, and one for each machine. The child elements of <config> are the normal configuration settings, arranged under machine, group, and cluster level as appropriate. Because settings can exist at multiple levels, you may see the same child elements in different sections. For example, if DNS servers are configured at the cluster level, you'll see the <dns> element near the top of the file, in the <cluster_config>.

This presents a big problem for restoring configurations: Restoring with loadconfig isn't supported, and the cluster config file you have can't be used for that purpose anyway. To export and import a single-system ESA configuration file, you must remove the machine from the cluster, which forces the ESA to flatten the configuration to a single-system version. Temporarily disconnecting from the cluster won't do this—you must remove the machine. In fact, if your intent is to restore an earlier configuration, you have to take all the machines out and destroy the cluster, because an ESA that joins the cluster takes its settings from the other machines in the cluster, so it will lose the configuration you just imported.

The ultimate lesson is not to rely on configuration export for backup of clustered machines. You should, under normal circumstances, never need a backup—even replacing entire machines can be done without the manual configuration file process.

However, if you find yourself in a situation with nothing but a clustered ESA configuration file and a need to restore that file to an individual ESA, it is possible to construct a single-system configuration. Here are the steps to follow:

1. Start by creating a template for the single-system configuration, including the XML header, DTD, and the top-level <config> element.
2. From the <machine> element, copy the network configuration elements (like <hostname> and <interfaces>) into your template.
3. From the <clustergroup> and <cluster> elements, copy the relevant settings (like <listeners> and <perrcpt_policies>) into your template. Don't copy any elements with names that start with "cluster." Remember that, if an element isn't included, the current ESA settings are retained, so you don't necessarily have to copy it all.
4. Import the configuration file, read the ESA's error message (if any), and correct the error. You'll likely have XML parse errors and missing required elements the first few times. Repeat this step until the configuration imports successfully. Examine the configuration in the WUI before committing.

This should only be a last resort. The work involved varies depending on the AsyncOS version. You'll have much more difficulty if the source and target ESAs are on different versions, so do yourself a favor and make sure that they're the same before you start. In a CM environment, once this ESA configuration is imported and everything is to your liking, use this master ESA to create a new cluster.

Summary

This chapter examined the XML configuration file format thoroughly, including using the basic WUI and CLI features and some advanced techniques, like partial-configuration files. Because it's strongly recommended that you back up your configuration files on a regular basis, we covered a variety of ways to automate this. Finally, we covered the limitations of configuration files in centralized management clusters.

In the next chapter, we dive into message and content filters, a versatile tool for security, acceptable use filtering, and message modification. Because there are two similar engines, we examine both and cover their similarities and differences.

Chapter 11

Message and Content Filters

In this chapter, you will learn the following:

- What the message filters and content filters features are used for and the differences between the two engines
- When to use message filters over content filters
- Low-level information on filter conditions and actions and performance considerations

Filtering Email Messages with Custom Rules

The Email Security Appliance (ESA) platform and its AsyncOS software has a huge number of features for almost any email task that would be encountered in production, from connection controls, through message routing and address rewriting, to control over final delivery. Tables like HAT, RAT, SMTPRoutes, and Destination Controls offer extensive control. Security filtering is handled automatically by IPAS and the antivirus engines.

Inevitably, however, a certain problem will need a custom solution that can't be solved using a table or setting. You'll need to compose and use our own custom filter rules that can act on individual messages and recipients, and the ESA provides two points in the pipeline where you can use them, as shown in Figure 11-1.

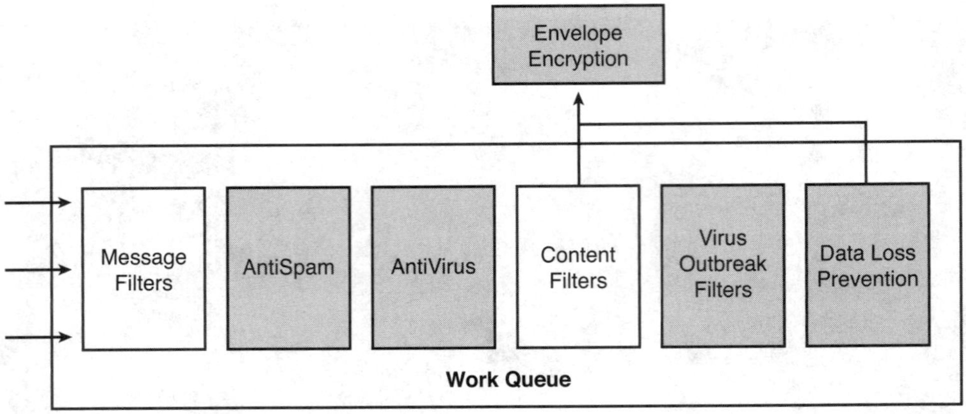

Figure 11-1 *Location of the Message Filter and Content Filter Steps in the ESA Pipeline*

Message filters are only configured in the command-line interface (CLI) using the **filters** command. Message filters were the first such feature on the ESA, implemented early in the product development for tasks like removing, modifying, or adding message headers, and for selecting delivery source IPs. Content filters are available in both the CLI and the web user interface (WUI), but are fairly cumbersome to use in the CLI, so we'll stick to the WUI.

Both message and content filters test one or more *conditions*, and based on the logical truth or falsehood of the condition statement, apply one or more *actions*. Both types of filters have conditions to test almost every message attribute: source, sender, recipients, size, headers, body, and attachments. Both types of filters offer flexible actions that can be combined together, including dropping, bouncing, redirecting, quarantining, or modifying messages. In most cases, we can do the same tasks in a message or a content filter, so why choose one over the other? Should we stick to message filters, because they're "more powerful?" Is it simply easier to always use content filters because they're in the WUI? The answer is that you need both, and at times when the task at hand can be done in either engine, there will be a critical difference between the two that will make the decision for you. Other times, it's purely your preference.

Message Filters Versus Content Filters

The most obvious difference between the two engines (or, more correctly, the two interfaces into the same engine) is the CLI versus WUI. Message filters get typed into or copy-and-pasted into the CLI, and content filters are built step by step in the WUI.

Example 11-1 is a simple message filter.

Example 11-1 *Simple Message Filter*

```
simple_sender_check_and_drop:
if mail-from == "sender@somewhere\\.com" {
      drop();
}
```

Example 11-2 shows a CLI session to add that filter to the configuration.

Example 11-2 *Adding a Message Filter*

```
esa02.cisco.com> filters

Choose the operation you want to perform:
- NEW - Create a new filter.
- DELETE - Remove a filter.
- IMPORT - Import a filter script from a file.
- EXPORT - Export filters to a file
- MOVE - Move a filter to a different position.
- SET - Set a filter attribute.
- LIST - List the filters.
- DETAIL - Get detailed information on the filters.
- LOGCONFIG - Configure log subscriptions used by filters.
- ROLLOVERNOW - Roll over a filter log file.
[]> new

Enter filter script.  Enter '.' on its own line to end.
simple_sender_check_and_drop:
if mail-from == "sender@example\\.com" {
    drop();
}
.
1 filters added.
```

First, we see the CLI **filters** command, which is where we create and examine message filters on the system. You can also enable or disable individual filters and deal with filter logging. One filter action, *archive*, writes data to log files and that logging is managed here. *List*, of course, provides all the filter names in a list, and *detail* shows you the body of one or more filters. Note that there is no **edit** command—there is no way to modify a filter that's already in the list. To change a filter, you must delete it and reenter it. For this reason, and for the fact that the space provided to enter your filter doesn't even come close to being considered an editor, I recommend that you create and edit your filters elsewhere, and then just paste only the final result into the *filters → new* option. If you have the option, use an editor that's designed for editing source code or has a "programmers" or source-code mode. I prefer vi, but anything that can give you a line count and some ability to match pairs of parenthesis or brackets makes for easier filter-mangling.

> **Note** This simple example includes a regular expression as the condition being tested against. The double-backslash is an escape sequence. In English, the three-letter regular expression \\. tells the ESA to match a single period (or "dot") character—and nothing else. We examine regular expressions in filters later in this chapter.

This brings us to a good question: Is filter writing programming? If you're familiar with Perl, C, PHP, or Java programming, the syntax here might look familiar. Filters support constructs that look like branching, subroutines, and combinatorial logic. But, there are some important differences, most of which are limitations on filters:

- **Filters have no state:** Every filter is evaluated in the context only of the current message being evaluated. No storage of values or results across messages is possible. No counters can be incremented or compared against. We can cheat a bit and use SMTP message headers as signals or temporary storage.
- **Filters operate independently of each other:** It's not possible to call one filter from another, or pass values between filters. They're not subroutines, and they have no return values.
- **Filters have limited access:** With a couple of minor exceptions, filters have no access to files, memory, or any other local or remote services. You can only evaluate conditions about the message and its sender, and the results of lookups already performed.
- **Filters get only one shot at a message:** A message passes through each filter at most once, unless we intentionally loop messages back into the ESA. This technique, called reinjection, can be useful but has some undesirable side effects. We discuss this later in this chapter.

Despite the limitations, there is still a great deal of flexibility, power, and creative ways to get around some of the limitations. We dig deeply into all of that.

All message filters must have a few things. First, it must have a unique name. Any name works, provided that it doesn't have whitespace or other nonalphanumeric characters, but descriptive is better. A colon follows the name. The filter body is one *if* statement, although this can have nested *ifs* below it. An *else* statement is optional, but supported. The filter must have at least one *condition* to test and at least one *action* to perform. We go into more depth on writing message filters after we examine the same exact logic in a content filter in the GUI. Figure 11-2 shows the content filter.

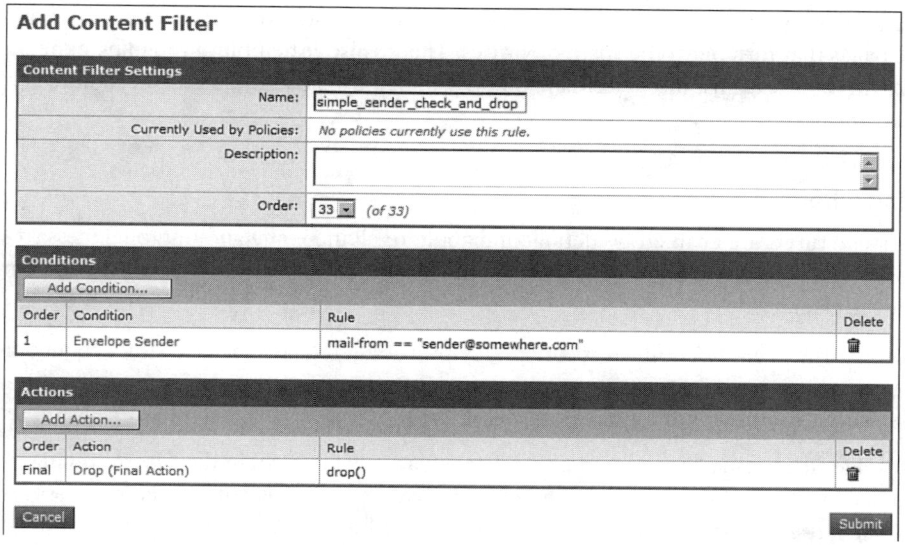

Figure 11-2 *Content Filter Example*

To create this filter, I started by clicking **Add Filter...** in the **WUI** page **Incoming Content Filters** under the **Mail Policies** tab. The example would be the same if I were working on Outgoing. On the new filter page, we must provide a unique name with no whitespace. A description is optional, but recommended, especially for complex or dangerous filters. Below that, you can see that I've added one condition, **Envelope Sender** (numbered 1, oddly enough), and one action, **Drop** (listed as *Final*). To add the conditions and actions, you naturally just click the corresponding button and, to edit a rule, click the name of the condition or action. This editability makes it immediately evident why content filters are easier to work with than message filters. Also notice that the value in the **Rule** column looks much like the filter condition shown in Example 11-1. This is not a coincidence, because both types of filters are going into the same rule-parsing engine.

Processing Order

Another fundamental difference between the two filter interfaces is their placement in the pipeline. As we saw in Chapter 3, "ESA Email Pipeline," message filters are the first stage in the work queue portion of the pipeline. They are processed after message acceptance and after any sender or recipient address manipulation, like aliases or masquerading. Most importantly, message filters are evaluated before any of the security engines, including anti-spam, antivirus, Virus Outbreak Filters (VOF), and DLP. They're also before the content filters, and messages that are acted on here are evaluated again in content filters. That leads to some interesting interactions that we'll look at.

The early position of message filters means that we can take certain actions, like skipping anti-spam or antivirus engines, that aren't possible to do in content filters. It also means that message filters are usually the wrong place to take other actions, like encryption, message body scanning, or disclaimers, because we don't want to take these actions on messages that turn out to be spam or viruses. There's also little point in running expensive filter tests against messages that will be dropped by those engines and can hurt performance.

Enabling Filters

Message filters are enabled by default and apply to all incoming and outgoing messages. To apply a message filter to your message traffic, you simply have to submit it and commit the change.

Content filters are not applied to any policy by default and are specific either to incoming or outgoing messages. To apply a content filter to traffic, you must submit it and then add it to one or more policies.

Message filters can also be set *inactive* through a toggle control in the **filters** command. An inactive filter is still present in the ESA configuration, but is not applied to messages until it is toggled back to the active state. Content filters don't have an inactive status, but a content filter that is created but not applied to any policy is effectively inactive.

Some filter conditions and actions refer to other named entities on the system, like dictionaries, notifications, interfaces, or listeners. Content filters require that these entries exist or they won't be available in the form for that condition or action. For example, you cannot specify a notification template that doesn't already exist on the ESA; the notify action requires you to select an existing notification from a drop-down list. Message filters are different, however, because they allow for arbitrary names to be provided as arguments. If you specify an entity that does not exist, the message filter will be accepted but marked as *invalid*. An invalid message filter is not applied to messages. You can correct this by editing the filter or creating the named entity.

Combinatorial Logic

Both message and content filters can combine multiple test conditions using AND and OR Boolean logic. In message filters, combinations of AND and OR clauses can be used to test complex conditions. Message filters can also nest conditions, such as in this example:

```
complex_logic:
if (rcpt-to == "chriport@cisco\\.com" OR header("Received") ==
"chrisporter\\.com$") {
    if (body-size > 1024k) {
          bcc ("chris@chrisporter.com");
    }
}
```

The filter in this header sends a BCC copy of the message if it's larger than 1MB in size and has either a recipient of chriport@cisco.com or a Received header that contains the string chrisporter.com. Note that, in both the recipient and header conditions, I'm using a regular expression.

By comparison, content filters have more limited logic. When multiple conditions are added to a filter, you have a choice of matching when all conditions or true (i.e., all conditions are ANDed together) or matching when any condition is true (i.e., all conditions are ORed together). You cannot create content filter condition logic that includes both AND and OR. It's possible, in some cases, to get around this limitation by using multiple content filters, one after another, to affect more complex decision making.

Message filters can also create nested rules that content filters don't support, with the if/else conditional, as in this example:

```
message_size_src_host:
if (body-size > 128k) {
    if (body-size > 256k) {
          alt-src-host ("LargeMessage");
    }
    else {
          alt-src-host ("MediumMessage");
    }
}
else {
    alt-src-host ("Default");
}
```

This filter sorts messages by size and selects the appropriate delivery interface. First, messages larger than 128 KB are selected in the first condition. The second, nested, condition picks the LargeMessage interface for messages over 256 KB, and the else clause applies to messages between 128 KB and 256 KB and uses the MediumMessage interface. All other messages, those smaller than 128 KB, use the Default interface for delivery.

Scope of Message Filters

Message filters apply to all messages, incoming and outgoing, for all policies and senders. If you want to limit the scope of a filter, you must explicitly do so using the available conditions. Content filters must be created as either incoming or outgoing, and are assigned to mail policies and can thus be restricted to certain policies that affect only some senders or recipients.

To limit the scope of message filters, you must use qualifying conditions, such as *recv-listener*, *sendergroup*, *rcpt-to*, or *mail-from*, in addition to the other conditions you want to test.

Handling Multirecipient Messages

To write effective filters, there's an important filter logic issue that you should understand. It occurs when a filter that has recipient conditions evaluates a message containing more than one recipient. Take this message filter as an example:

```
if (rcpt-to == "chriport@cisco\\.com") {
   drop();
}
```

You might be tempted to describe this filter as "drops messages where the recipient is chriport@cisco.com," but that's slightly inaccurate. More accurate would be "drops messages where *any* recipient is chriport@cisco.com." With a multirecipient message, if *any* of the recipients match the condition, the message is dropped for *all* recipients.

Filters actions affect entire messages, but recipient conditions can match any recipients. When writing a filter that uses recipient conditions like rcpt-to or rcpt-to-group, you need to keep this fact in mind.

With most filter actions, this is not a problem and, in fact, is the desirable effect. Take this example, which sends a copy of mail, silently, to another address:

```
if (rcpt-to == "chriport@cisco.com") {
    bcc ("supervisor@it.cisco.com");
}
```

You might write such a filter to monitor a particular user's mail traffic. You would certainly want this to apply to messages where chriport@cisco.com is the only recipient or is one of many recipients.

If you do need actions to apply only to a single recipient, the better approach is to use incoming or outgoing mail policies to splinter messages and use content filters to take action. We describe that later in this chapter.

Availability of Conditions and Actions

The last major difference between content and message filters is that some conditions and actions are simply not available in content filters in the WUI. Some, like *skip-spam-check*, are missing because they're not relevant to content filters; spam checking occurs before content filters in the ESA pipeline. But, others just aren't included in the list of conditions and actions available to content filters. For the most part, these advanced features aren't used often, but if you find that you need them, obviously the choice is made for you—you must write a message filter.

Filter Conditions

Filter conditions refer to the tests performed against a message by the filters engine. Conditions vary about what is being tested. Some take no arguments and are essentially simple true/false tests, such as encrypted and valid. Each message filter or content filter can incorporate multiple conditions, combined with AND and OR into a Boolean logic. When the entire condition expression evaluates as true, the actions listed in the filter are taken.

Content filters do not necessarily need conditions; a filter with no condition is considered always true, and the actions will always be taken. In message filters, the true condition can be used to the same effect:

```
always_add_originator:
if (true) {
   strip-header ("X-OriginatingIP");
   insert-header ("X-OriginatingIP", "$RemoteIP");
}
```

Filter conditions often have multiple forms: a unary test, which is a simple true or false result, and a binary, or comparison, form that tests against a supplied value. For example, the condition header ("CC") by itself tests whether the CC: header is present in a message. The condition header("CC") == "cisco" tests whether the CC header exists and contains the string "cisco" anywhere in it.

Conditions That Test Message Data

The most commonly used filter conditions are those that test something about the message itself: sender, recipients, headers, and body. Attachment conditions are discussed later in this chapter. Table 11-1 lists these filter conditions and gives examples of their use.

Table 11-1 *Conditions for Testing Message Data*

Message Filter Condition	Content Filter Condition	Description
mail-from and mail-from-dictionary-match	Envelope sender	Tests the sender email address transmitted in the SMTP MAIL FROM command.
mail-from-group	Envelope sender	Tests the envelope sender address against an LDAP group value. An LDAP group query must be configured and active on the listener this message was received on.
rcpt-to and rcpt-to-dictionary-match	Envelope recipient	Does *any* recipient on the message match the given pattern? Applies to all the addresses supplied during SMTP RCPT TO command.
rcpt-to-group	Envelope recipient	Does *any* recipient on the message belong to the given LDAP group value?

subject and subject-dictionary-match	Subject header	Does the subject of the message match the supplied regular expression?
header and header-dictionary-match	Other header	Does a particular header exist and match some pattern? Works for both RFC-defined headers and custom X-headers. If multiple headers of the same name are present, this condition is true if *any* of the instances match.
body-contains, dictionary-match	Body or attachment	Searches all the SMTP message body, which includes what users think of as the message body and all attachments.
only-body-contains, body-dictionary-match	N/A	Searches the MIME parts that users normally consider the "message body," and does not search attachments of other types.

Operating on Message Metadata

Many filter conditions are provided for testing message metadata—that is, data about the message rather than the actual message content. This category includes the conditions that show the results of message processing earlier in the pipeline. Table 11-2 describes metadata conditions.

Table 11-2 *Conditions for Testing Metadata and Scanning Results*

Message Filter Condition	Content Filter Condition	Description
body-size	Message size	How does the number of bytes in the body of the message compare with the supplied value? This measures the actual byte count transmitted for the entire message including attachments.
attachment-size	N/A	Does any individual attachment meet the size comparison?
remote-ip	Remote IP	Was the sending SMTP host's IP an exact or range match? Supports IPs, IP ranges, and CIDR notation IPs with netmasks.
recv-listener	Receiving listener	Was this message received on the named listener? Useful for filter-based routing or policy bypass configurations.
recv-int	N/A	Was this message received on the named interface? Useful for filter-based routing, like recv-listener, or for private submission.

Reputation, no-reputation	Reputation score	How does the reputation score of the sender compare to some value? Does the sender have a reputation? Normally, acting on SBRS is done in the HAT, but the filter condition can be useful in two-layer environments.
sendergroup	N/A	What sendergroup applied to the connection that delivered the message? Must be an exact match to a HAT sendergroup name.
valid	N/A	Attempts to determine if the message has any unparseable MIME parts. A valid message means that all MIME boundaries are correct and the message has no unparseable parts.
rcpt-count	N/A	How does the count of all recipients compare to some value? Includes all envelope recipients.
addr-count	N/A	How does the count of "visible" recipients compare to some value? Includes recipients in the To and CC: headers, but doesn't include BCC'd recipients.
Signed, signed-certificate	N/A	Is the message S/MIME signed? Does the signature X.509 certificate match the regex pattern?
encrypted	Attachment protection is similar	Encrypted detects PGP and S/MIME encrypted data. More thorough detection of encrypted and password protected files is provided in the content filter condition.
spf-status and spf-passed	SPF verification	What is the status of SPF lookups for the sender of this message? Can be compared to a list of verdicts, including pass, fail, softfail, and temperror.
dkim-authentication	DKIM authentication	What is the status of DKIM signature verification for the sender of this message? Can be compared to a list of verdicts, including pass, fail, softfail, and temperror.

Attachment Conditions

The ESA has thorough capabilities to open and examine text content within binary attachments, and supports more than 400 different kinds of attachment types. When this conversion is done, it makes the text content of attached documents available for filters to test. It supports archive formats, like TAR and ZIP, providing scanning results against the files contained in a compressed archive. The ESA also treats some document types, like Microsoft Office documents, as containers and can unpack and examine content embedded within. For example, the ESA can find content in a spreadsheet object embedded in a Word document.

When using a content or message filter condition that examines the body of the message, attachments are automatically unpacked, if needed, and converted to plain text.

The filter comparisons are then performed against this plain text. Because this process can be resource intensive, the ESA only does the decoding and conversion when the message in question will actually hit a filter condition that requires it. Any filter condition that examines message body content, like body-contains, or attachment data or metadata, like attachment-type, will cause the message to be converted. The process is performed only once, regardless of the number of separate filters that examine the data.

Table 11-3 describes the attachment filtering conditions.

Table 11-3 *Attachment Conditions*

Message Filter Condition	Content Filter Condition	Description
Attachment-filetype	Attachment file info	Compares the actual file type with the supplied value. The file type is determined by fingerprinting the contents of the attachment, not by examining file extensions or MIME types.
Attachment-filename	Attachment file info	Compares the filename of the attachment with the supplied regular expression. The filename is taken from the MIME header for the attachment part; the file extension may not accurately identify the file type. If the attachment is an archive, the filenames from within the archive will be tested.
Attachment-mimetype	Attachment file info	Compares the MIME type of the attachment with the supplied value, which can either be a complete MIME type or a MIME wildcard. The type is taken from the MIME header.
Attachment-type	N/A	Similar to attachment-mimetype, but this determines the MIME type by signature and not by reading the MIME header.
Attachment-binary-contains	N/A	Searches through attachment data, but performs the search on the raw binary data of the file, not the converted text. Can be useful in some cases to write custom signatures or look for nonvisible text.
Attachment-protected and attachment-unprotected	Attachment protected	Is any attachment to the message encrypted or password protected in some way? Or is any attachment unprotected?
Attachment-size	N/A	How does the size of individual attachments compare to the stated value? Values can be expressed in bytes, kilobytes, or megabytes. True if any attachment matches the condition.

Attachment-contains, attachment-dictionary-match	Attachment content	Does at least one attachment to the message match this pattern?
Every-attachment-contains	N/A	Does every attachment to the message match this pattern?

Attachment filtering on the ESA has a subtle problem in some cases when combining multiple attachment rules. Like the issue with multiple recipients to messages described previously, this problem arises when messages have multiple attachments.

Suppose, for example, that you want to quarantine all messages that had a PDF attachment with the phrases "sensitive and confidential" in it. You might write this message filter or the equivalent in content filters:

```
detect_sensitive_pdf:
if (attachment-type == "pdf" and attachment-contains "sensitive and confiden
  tial") {
   quarantine ("Policy");
}
```

This seems to cover the requirement, and it will indeed stop messages that contain a PDF with such a phrase in it. But, what happens when you have more than one attachment? If a message arrived at the filter that had a PDF attachment without the phrase, that would meet the first condition; if the message also has a Word document with the phrase "sensitive and confidential," that would meet the second condition. This two-attachment message would trigger the quarantine action, even though the phrase doesn't appear in the PDF.

A better description of the **detect_sensitive_pdf** filter in the previous example would be "if any attachment to the message is a PDF, and any attachment contains this phrase, then quarantine." That's a slightly different case than the original business requirement. Unfortunately, there's no way to guarantee that two separate attachment conditions are matching on the same attachment.

System State Conditions

A few convenience conditions are available that test various system states or external data. All are available only in message filters and have no content filter equivalent. These are listed in Table 11-4.

Table 11-4 *System State Conditions*

Message Filter Condition	Description
date	Tests the current date and time against the supplied value.

dnslist	Does the sender's IP address return a positive result when looked up on the configured DNSBL? Can be used in a unary form to test membership or, in comparison, form to test for a particular value.
workqueue-count	Tests the supplied value against the current number of messages in the work queue. Can be useful for detecting overloaded systems and redirecting messages.
destqueue-count	Does the number of messages in queue for a given destination compare to some value? Note that this is an undocumented filter condition at time of writing.

Miscellaneous Filter Conditions

The remaining filter conditions don't easily fit into a single category, so they are grouped in Table 11-5 for completeness.

Table 11-5 *Other Filter Conditions*

Message Filter Condition	Content Filter Condition	Description
true	N/A; a content filter with no conditions is equivalent	This condition is always true; useful for filters where the action needs to be applied to all messages. You can use not true for a test that is always false, but that's rarely useful.
random	N/A	Tests the supplied value against a randomly generated value in the range specified. Can be useful for some pseudo load balancing or for BCCing a sample of messages matching another condition.
image-verdict	Attachment file info	Are there any image attachments to the message that fall into the particular category? Requires a feature license key for image analysis, which examines image attachments for inappropriate adult content.

Filter Actions

Actions are the operations that are performed when the conditional expression of a filter evaluates to true. You can have more than one action on a filter, and they will typically run in the order specified. Final actions, such as drop, bounce, or skip-filters, really are final and no further processing is taken on a message that hits them. In content filters, the filter-building WUI will always put final actions as the last action in your filter.

Changing Message Data

Table 11-6 lists the available actions that change basic message data or metadata. Certain attributes, like sender, message size, reputation, remote IP, and others, are not modifiable.

Table 11-6 *Message Metadata Actions*

Message Filter Action	Content Filter Action	Description
alt-rcpt-to	Change recipient to	Changes all recipients on the message to the string that you specify. If you need per-recipient rewriting, look at aliases or LDAP routing instead.
alt-mailhost	Send to alternate destination host	Overrides the normal delivery destination and sends the message to the specified host and port. Extremely useful for integrating external systems; see the examples later in this chapter.
alt-src-host	Deliver from IP interface	Tells the ESA to choose the named interface when delivering this message at the end of the pipeline. Useful only in configurations where the ESA has multiple IP interfaces. Commonly used with virtual gateways. Note that the CLI command **altsrchost** provides a table that does the same thing, but filters can be more flexible in identifying messages.
insert-header	Add header	Adds an SMTP header to the message. You can add any header that you like, but you should adhere to the custom of using X- as the prefix name for any custom headers. If the header already exists in the message, another instance of the header is added.
strip-header	Strip header	Removes all instances of the named header.
edit-header-text	N/A	A search and replace is performed on the specified header.

Altering Message Body

ESA provides filter actions to modify the actual message data. You can add disclaimers to messages either at the top (header) or bottom (footer) of a message. You can drop attachments based on the same conditions used to identify attachments. In one case, you can actually modify the body of plain text messages, but it is not possible to modify binary attachments.

Table 11-7 lists the actions that modify messages in some way.

Table 11-7 *Message Modification Actions*

Message Filter Action	Content Filter Action	Description
Edit-body-text	N/A	Performs a search and replace of text in HTML and plain text in the message body parts. Does not apply to attachments. This can be useful for content redaction, but it's not for the faint of heart, because modifying message bodies can have unintended side effects.
Html-convert	N/A	Drops HTML parts of multipart/alternative messages, and strips HTML body parts of their HTML tags, leaving plain text in unformatted lines. This is a sledgehammer solution if your organization deems HTML email a security threat. This conversion process will negatively affect many legitimate emails.
Drop-attachments-by-name, drop-attachments-by-type, drop-attachments-by-mimetype, drop-attachments-by-filetype, drop-attachments-by-size	Strip attachment by file info	Like the attachment conditions, identifies attachment by metadata, but then removes the attachment from the message by deleting the MIME part. You have the option of including text to replace the missing attachments.
Drop-attachment-where-contains and drop-attachment-where-dictionary-match	Strip attachment by content	Removes attachments from messages based on their content.
Drop-attachments-where-image-verdict	Strip attachment by file info	Removes image attachments from messages based on the verdict of the image analyzer engine; requires a license key.
Add-footer and add-heading	Add disclaimer text	Adds a chunk of plain text to message bodies, either at the top or at the bottom. The disclaimer text must be created as a text resource. Note that this message body modification affects performance and can cause trouble in cases where character sets differ between body and disclaimer. Use with care.
Encrypt and encrypt-deferred	Encrypt and deliver now, and encrypt on delivery	Encrypts the message with the on-box PXE engine, either exiting the pipeline and encrypting immediately or waiting until the message moves into the delivery queues. Messages that are encrypted immediately are not available for scanning by remaining content filters or DLP; to make sure that later scanning is performed, use the encrypt on delivery action.

Affecting Message Delivery

Table 11-8 lists the actions that modify message delivery in some way, by altering delivery destination or adding or changing recipients.

Table 11-8 *Filter Actions That Affect Message Delivery*

Message Filter Action	Content Filter Action	Description
drop	Drop (final action)	Immediately halts all processing on the message and discards it from memory. No further filters are evaluated. No recipient receives any of the message data. Obviously, this is dangerous.
bounce	Bounce (final action)	Generates a bounce back to the sender address in the DSN format. This action takes place immediately; no further filters are evaluated. The composition of the DSN is determined by the bounce profile of the original message.
deliver	Skip remaining content filters (final action)	The deliver and skip-filters actions are exactly the same: These final actions cause the message to bypass any remaining filters, moving the message to the next stage of the pipeline.
Quarantine and duplicate-quarantine	Quarantine	Tags the message for delivery to a system quarantine. Note that message processing does not halt immediately; all remaining filters and scanning is performed. When the message exits the work queue, it is delivered to the quarantine. duplicate-quarantine has the ability to quarantine a copy, letting the original be delivered normally.
Notify and notify-copy	Notify	Creates a new message, sent to specified recipients, that typically includes data about the original message. Very flexible. Arguments to this action include specifying the recipient, sender, and subject of the notification message, and whether to include a copy of the original message. Notifications can also be customized with a notification template that must be created in the Text Resources page or via **textconfig**. Using a custom notification template allows you to compose the exact text in that notification.

Bcc and bcc-scan	Send a copy (BCC)	Creates a new message with the specified email address as the sole envelope recipient. With BCC, the new message bypasses all remaining filters and scanning engines. bcc-scan pushes the new message through filters and scanning. This action takes several arguments in addition to the recipient: the subject of the new message, the return path which is the sender address, and an alternate mail host if the message copy should be sent to a different delivery host. If unspecified, all these arguments use the values from the original message.
Bounce-profile	N/A	Applies a particular bounce profile to the message. Bounce profiles include settings for message retry and maximum delivery attempts.

Altering Message Processing

Table 11-9 lists the filter actions that alter the processing steps that a message goes through, skipping the upcoming pipeline stages. These actions take no arguments.

Table 11-9 *Message-Processing Actions*

Message Filter Action	Content Filter Action	Description
Skip-filters	Skip remaining content filters	Skips remaining filters in the list. For message filters, this means that it skips all remaining message filters, but will not skip content filters. For content filters, this action skips all remaining filters that would have been executed. No security scanning is skipped.
Skip-dksign	N/A	Skips the DKIM signing process.
Skip-spamcheck	N/A	Skips spam scanning by all engines. The message will not have any of the AS scan headers added.
Skip-viruscheck	N/A	Skips virus scanning by all engines. The message will not have any of the AV scan verdict headers added.
Skip-vofcheck	Bypass Outbreak Filter scanning	Skips the VOF scanning.

Miscellaneous Filter Actions

The remaining filter actions are listed in Table 11-10.

Table 11-10 *Miscellaneous Filter Actions*

Message Filter Action	Content Filter Action	Description
log-entry	Add log entry	Adds an arbitrary log entry to the text mail logs during processing. Can be any text, including action variables. For example, if you wanted to log all the attachment filenames, you can use the action variable $filenames.
tag-message	Add message tag	Adds a hidden markup to the message so that the data loss prevention (DLP) engine can identify messages. This allows you to do some preprocessing of messages, flagging relevant content as it goes into DLP processing.
archive	N/A	Writes a copy to disk in plain-text mbox format, in a destination file that's managed like a log subscription. Messages are written one after the other, until the log subscription hits rollover limits. To recover messages from the archive, you have to retrieve these files and separate the messages for reinjection.

Action Variables

In most filters that perform notifications, whether to sender, recipient, or another party, the notification should include data about the message triggering the filter. This is especially true of notifications about dropped or modified messages, or messages that match sensitive data rules. You could create notifications with custom text for each possible matching condition, but it's far better to include data from the message in question. Users who know exactly why a message was modified or undeliverable will open fewer support tickets and have a clear idea of the rules being enforced. The filters engine on the ESA provides action variables that allow you to include this data.

Action variables start with a $ and are limited to a specific list of supplied variables. You've already seen several examples of action variables in this chapter. I used $RemoteIP to add the sender's IP address to the headers of a message.

Other useful action variables include $EnvelopeFrom, $EnvelopeRecipients, $Subject, and $Filenames. Variable names are not case sensitive. The action variables available to you in notifications and other filter actions are described in Table 11-11. There are additional action variables available for anti-virus notifications and those are described in Chapter 8, "Security Filtering," in the section "AV Notifications."

Table 11-11 *ESA Action Variables*

Variable	Description
$EnvelopeFrom	Envelope sender address as injected with the SMTP MAIL FROM command.
$From	Contents of the From header, which users normally see.
$EnvelopeRecipients	All of the envelope recipients as injected with the SMTP RCPT TO command. If there is more than one recipient, they are comma separated. Be careful because this can reveal BCC recipients.
$To	Contents of the To header, which users normally see. Will not display recipients that are CC or BCC.
$Subject	Subject of the message. Reflects changes made by an earlier filters.
$AllHeaders	Names and values of all SMTP headers in the message, including those added by earlier filters or engine actions.
$Header["*Name*"]	Value of any header quoted in brackets. If there is more than one copy of the header, only the last value is returned.
$BodySize	The size of the entire message, in bytes, including all headers and attachments. Reflects the encoded size of MIME attachments as received by the ESA.
$Hostname	Name of the ESA that generated the notification. Exceptionally useful when using the quarantine action, as this will reveal which ESA host quarantined the message.
$Filtername	The name of the filter that generated the notification.
$MatchedContent	Contains the value that caused a match in a filter condition like body-contains or dictionary-match. Not populated for matches with filename or filetype rules.
$Filenames	Comma separated list of file attachment names. Like other attachment rules, the first MIME part of type text/plain, text./html, or multipart/alternative is considered body, not attachment.
$Filetypes	Comma-separated list of attachment MIME types.
$Filesizes	Comma-separated list of attachment file sizes.
$Dropped_Filetypes, $Dropped_Filetype	The plural version of this variable is a comma-separated list of MIME types of any attachments that have been dropped using a strip-attachments filter action. The singular version lists only the most recent dropped attachment type. If no files were dropped, this will have the value **None**.
$Dropped_Filenames, $Dropped_Filename	Comma-separated list of dropped filenames. The singular version lists only the most recently dropped attachment filename. If no files were dropped, this will have the value **None**.
$RemoteIP	Client IP address that sent this message.

$RemoteHost	Client hostname that sent this message, if available.
$Reputation	The SenderBase Reputation Score of the connecting IP.
$OrgID	SenderBase Network Owner ID, a unique number assigned by SenderBase to individual network and domain owners.
$RecvInt	The name of the IP interface on the ESA that received the message.
$RecvListener	The name of the listener on the ESA that received the message.
$Group	The HAT sender group name that classified the connecting IP.
$Policy	The HAT mail flow policy that was applied to the connecting IP. The policy names will have a leading $ (dollar sign), a legacy of the HAT table format.
$MID	The internal message ID assigned to the message. Highly recommended for inclusion in notifications as the MID can be used to track the original message.
$Timestamp	Current ESA local date, time, and timezone. For example, "10 Feb 2012 10:08:06 -0500".
$Time	Current local time.
$GMTimestamp	Current GMT date, time, and timezone. For example, "10 Feb 2012 15:08:06 -0000".
$Date	Current ESA local date in MM/DD/YYYY.
$BouncedRecipient	Only usable within Bounce and Encryption Failure Notification types. Contains the undeliverable recipient address.
$BounceReason	Only usable within Bounce and Encryption Failure Notification types. Contains the response code from the remote server that rejected the message.
$DLPPolicy	Only usable within Disclaimer or Data Loss Prevention (DLP) notifications. Names the policy that generated the notification.
$DLPSeverity	Name of the severity category for DLP violation, either Low, Medium, High, or Critical.
$DLPRiskFactor	Numeric DLP violation score, in the range 0–100.

Regular Expressions in Filters

Almost every filter condition that looks for matching content in a message is expecting a regular expression (regex) as the argument. Regular expressions are a mathematical language for expressing character, word, and string matches. The characters between the quotes of a message filter condition, or entered in the text box in the WUI, are always treated as a regular expression. The ESA generally follows the Python regular expression syntax, and most regex metacharacter, character set, and compilation flags are supported. The filter conditions only support regex matching expressions and do not support modifications like substrings, splitting, or replacement.

There are many great online and text references to regular expressions, so I do not make an attempt to be an authoritative guide. However, some regular expression metacharacters and character classes repeatedly come up in ESA filters.

An important topic in filters is the use of the escape special character, \, the backslash. In regular expressions, the backslash serves two purposes: to indicate a character class, such as \s or \d, which refers to whitespace characters and digits, respectively. The other is to undo the special nature of characters like +, *, and ^. If you want to match an actual asterisk, you must use the sequence *, and if you want to match an actual backslash character, you must use \\.

Table 11-12 lists some of the important regex entities commonly used in ESA filters.

Table 11-12 *Important ESA Regular Expression Entities*

Entity	Description	Example
\	Escape character; doesn't match anything itself, but tells the regex engine that the next character should be interpreted literally or that the next character indicates a character class.	\.com matches a dot com, as in cisco.com and ironport.com.
\s	Whitespace character class; matches characters like space, tab, and newline.	`up\sstairs` matches **up stairs** and **up<tab>stairs** but not **upstairs.**
\d	Digit character class; matches a single digit in the range [0–9].	`ID:\d\d` matches **ID:32** and **ID:001** but not **ID:1A** or **ID:T2.**
\w	Word characters; matches a single alphanumeric character or the underscore character.	`\w\w:\d\d` matches **ID:32** and **SS:14.**
.	Single-character wildcard. Matches any single character, including a period. If you want to match only a period character, use \.	`flight 239.` matches **flight 239A** and **flight 239** and **flight 2391.**
?	Not a character matcher itself, but a modifier for the previous character or class. Makes the previous match optional.	`sports?` matches both **sport** and **sports.**
+	Modifier for the previous character or class, which matches when one, or more, of the previous character is repeated. When used after a period, takes the place of the dos-style * wildcard, because **.+** matches any string of characters.	`Patent \d+` matches **Patent 12913** and **Patent 9.**

*	Modifier for the previous character or class, which matches when zero, or more, of the previous character is repeated. Note that although the asterisk is a sort of wildcard character, its behavior is considerably different than the file glob asterisk or DOS wildcard.	`Cisco.*IronPort` matches **Cisco IronPort** and **Cisco Acquired IronPort in 2007**, but also **CiscoIronPort.**
[ ]	Brackets enclosing a list of characters tells the regex engine to match any one of the characters in the brackets. Character ranges are supported, too; as noted previously, the regex `[0-9]` is equivalent to \d. Note that this applies to single characters only; `[0-255]` does not match digits in the range of 0 to 255, but rather a single digit 0, 1, 2 or 5.	`[a-z]` matches any single lowercase character. `dr[aiu]nk` matches **drink**, **drank**, and **drunk**.
^	Matches the beginning of a line. This character *anchors* the regex to the start of a line or to the start of the header being examined.	`^chris` matches **chris@chris-porter.com** and **chris@cisco.com**, but not **porter.chris@cisco.com.**
$	Matches the end of the line. Anchors the regex to the end of the line.	`cisco\.com$` matches any **user@cisco.com** and **sanfran-cisco.com.**
(|)	The combination of parenthesis for grouping and the pipe character for *or* allows regex matches to *choose* one of the patterns.	`\.(exe|com|bat)$` matches filenames like notepad.exe, rundll32.com, and upload.bat.

There are some other items to note about regular expressions in the ESA:

- All regular expressions have an implicit .* sequence at the beginning and end. Effectively, this means that unless you anchor your regex, you are asking for a substring match. For example, when a regex such as `bit` is written, the pattern matches the word **bit**, but also **arbitrary** and **gambit**. This is why the pattern `ID:\d\d` matches **ID:001** and **SID:23A.**
- Some filter conditions, like *remote-ip*, support ranges of matching values but not proper regular expressions. *remote-ip* allows for matches against inclusive IP ranges, such as **192.168.1.34-37**, or with CIDR notation, such as **10.1.0.0/16** or **10/8.**
- Regular expressions are always case-sensitive by default. On the ESA, you can make regular expressions case-insensitive by using the (?i) directive at the start of your regex.
- The use of the backslash \ character as an escape differs across content filters and message filters. Because the backslash is first parsed by the ESA filters engine, and then passed to the Python regex engine, all backslash characters must be doubled. In

message filters, you must include the two backslashes in your filter code. In content filters, the ESA automatically adds a backslash to every one that you enter, so you must always use one backslash in your regular expressions.

As an example of this, take this message filter from earlier in this chapter:

```
simple_sender_check_and_drop:
if mail-from == "sender@somewhere\\.com" {
   drop();
}
```

The equivalent content filter condition, as entered by the ESA administrator, is shown in Figure 11-3.

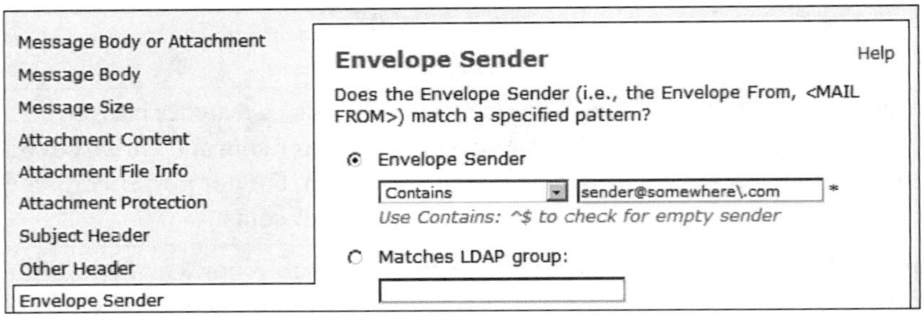

Figure 11-3 *Content Filter Condition, as Entered by the Admin; Note the Single Backslash*

The resulting content filter, with the single backslash converted into two, is shown in Figure 11-4.

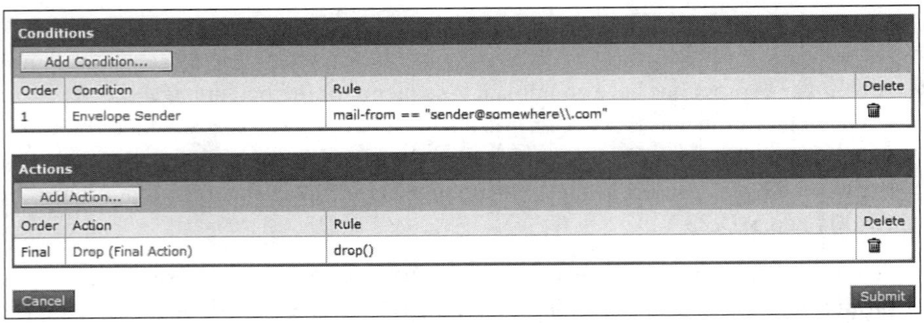

Figure 11-4 *Content Filter Results*

Dictionaries

Many of the filter conditions I describe refer to *dictionaries* on the ESA. Dictionaries refer to collections of words, phrases, and regexes, and can be used to test messages for matches. In general, the conditions that refer to a dictionary will evaluate to true if the message matches at least one term in the dictionary that you specify.

Dictionaries also support *weighting* of terms, where each word, phrase, or pattern is assigned a numeric value. Each match adds the corresponding score to a running total for that message. Every message scanned by the filter has a total score calculated and compared to the threshold you provide.

For example, assume that a dictionary contains these terms and scores:

```
Confidential, 1
Copyright, 1
Secret, 5
Do Not Distribute, 10
```

A message with the sentences, "This material is confidential. Do not distribute under any circumstances," compared against this dictionary would score 11 points. You can create filter conditions that trigger after a particular score threshold is reached, as in this example:

```
sensitive_information:
if (dictionary-match ("Sensitive", 10)) {
    quarantine ("Sensitive");
}
```

In our examples, a single instance of the phrase **Do Not Disturb** is enough to trigger the quarantine action, but would require multiple matches of the other terms. Any repeated matching terms are each added to the score, so three instances of the word Confidential would score 3 points for that message.

Dictionaries are managed on the ESA through the **dictionaryconfig** command or in the WUI on the Mail Policies → Dictionaries page.

Notification Templates

Another topic closely related to filters is that of notification templates, which are a type of text resource on the ESA. Text resources are customizable versions of the various email text that can go to end users, like bounce messages. Although the ESA provides defaults, you can customize them in the WUI by going to Mail Policies → Text Resources or in the CLI to *textconfig*.

Notification templates are used by the filter action notify. You have the option of specifying a notification template that you've created or use the default system notification. Because the notification action in content filters only allows you to choose templates already created, you should create your notification templates before creating the filter. Message filter notify actions that don't refer to a valid template name will be marked invalid and will not be run against messages.

The distinct advantage of using a custom notification template is that it will contain exactly the information you want, including data from the message that triggered the filter. Notifications support a wide range of action variables that are written with real data from the message at the time the notification is generated in the filter.

Here's an example notification as created in the ESA interface, complete with action variables:

```
I'm sorry, your message to $enveloperecipients sent at $timestamp with Subject
'$Subject' was not delivered because the message violated the company's sensitive
information disclosure rules.
Specifically, this content:
$MatchedContent
Was sent in plain text over an unencrypted channel. To send this material, please
encrypt the message contents before resending.
```

Here's what the resulting text would be, if triggered by a message or content filter:

```
I'm sorry, your message to chriport@cisco.com sent at 25 Apr 2011 14:23:36 -0500
with Subject 'Legal documents' was not delivered because the message violated the
company's sensitive information disclosure rules.
Specifically, this content:
Copyright 2011 Sensitive and Confidential.

Was sent in plain text over an unencrypted channel. To send this material, please
encrypt the message contents before resending.
```

Smart Identifiers

In addition to the rich regular expression syntax, the ESA filters support the comparison of message data with *smart identifiers*. Smart identifiers are like a predefined regex pattern, in that they match sequences of characters, but have additional smarts to recognize particular data entities.

The four smart identifiers provided in the ESA are

- **ABA routing numbers:** This identifies 9-digit numerical sequences that uniquely identify a financial organization in the United States, also known as a routing transit number (RTN). This code appears on checks and other payment forms and consists of a federal reserve routing portion, an ABA institution identifier, and a check digit.
- **Credit card number:** Identifies 14-, 15-, or 16-digit payment card numbers issued by U.S. banks or credit unions. This smart identifier calculates the check digit by using the Luhn algorithm to verify that the sequence is actually a valid credit card number.
- **CUSIP:** A 9-digit alphanumeric code that uniquely identifies U.S. securities, like stocks or mutual funds, maintained and published by S&P. Like the first two smart identifiers, it has a check digit algorithm.
- **U.S. Social Security Numbers (SSN):** The 9-digit number issued to U.S. citizens and permanent residents working in the U.S. by the Social Security Administration. Although SSNs do not have a checksum, there are requirements for the area and group numbers that are part of every SSN. This smart identifier applies those rules to sequences that are potentially SSNs.

Smart identifiers can be used in message or content filter conditions that examine the body of messages. Furthermore, a smart identifier can be used as an element in a dictionary. Compared with writing regexes for possible combinations and formats of this data, smart identifiers save a lot of time and trouble.

Using smart identifiers in place of a regular expression helps to improve matching accuracy by reducing the number of false positives. For example, if you want a filter to match 16-digit credit card numbers, with groups of 4 separated by dashes, you could use this regex:

```
\d{4}-\d{4}-\d{4}-\d{4}
```

Applied to these sequences, both would be a match for this regex:

```
5105-1051-0510-4902
5105-1051-0510-5100
```

However, only the second is actually a valid credit card number that passes the Luhn checksum algorithm. The smart identifier would correctly match on the second, but not the first.

Using Smart Identifiers

Using smart identifiers in content filters is easy. When adding a content filter condition that tests a message body, like **Message Body or Attachment**, **Message Body**, or **Attachment Content**, one of the selectable options is **Contains smart identifier.** A drop-down box allows you to select the type, as shown in Figure 11-5.

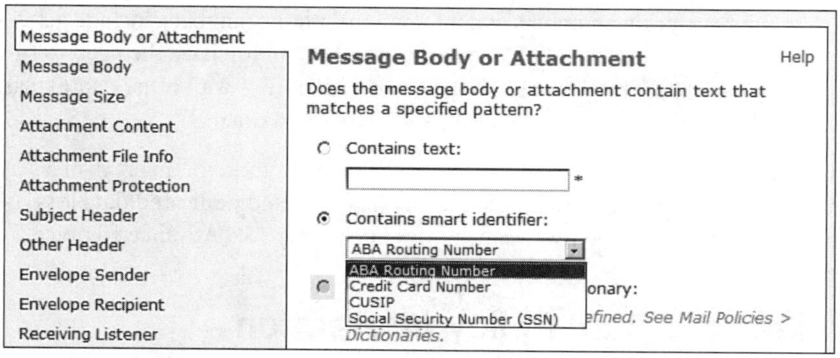

Figure 11-5 *Using Smart Identifier in Content Filters*

Using smart identifiers in message filters requires using a specialized keyword that starts with an asterisk. This keyword must be used alone and cannot be combined with another smart identifier or a regular expression. For example:

```
check_ssn:
if (body-contains ("*ssn")) {
    quarantine ("SSN");
}
```

If you're using smart identifiers as an entry in a dictionary, just apply the dictionary match to the filter condition as you would any other dictionary.

Smart Identifier Best Practices

Smart identifiers can be used anywhere there's a requirement to examine email messages and attachments for the entities that they match. It is common for organizations to have a policy in place to prevent the transmission of personally identifiable information (PII) or sensitive financial information via email. This may be driven by corporate data-protection practices, regulatory compliance, or industry requirements.

However, it's rarely a good idea to use regular expressions or even smart identifiers to take action on messages. This is because smart identifiers lack any context within the message and are looking only for alphanumeric or numeric sequences that follow a particular format. Not every 16-digit number, even those that pass the Luhn checksum, are actually an example of payment card data. Using smart identifiers alone will likely result in many false positive hits, and actions being taken on messages that do not actually represent data loss.

Best practice for using smart identifiers for the purpose of identifying data loss is to provide context along with the smart identifier match. You should, at a minimum, combine your smart identifier rules with other corroborating data—for example, credit card issuer names, expiration date regexes, and the phrases "credit card," "debit," and so on. When initially deploying such policies, I recommend a nonintrusive action, like quarantine-copy, so that you can review the matches and modify the filters based on what is being caught.

U.S. SSNs represent a particular challenge. Many 9-digit numbers fall into valid SSN ranges, and the numbers do not have a checksum or other verification. Many common numeric sequences, like shipper tracking numbers and international phone numbers, include a 3-2-4 pattern of digits that fully meet the SSN format requirements. If you have the need to filter U.S. SSNs, it's imperative that you combine the smart identifiers with other contextual information, like the phrase "Social Security," "SSN," "SS#," and others.

Crafting data loss-prevention policies using smart identifiers is more of an art than a science. To make this process easier, the ESA recently incorporated dedicated data loss prevention features. We examine these capabilities in Chapter 15, "Advanced Topics."

Content Filter and Mail Policy Interaction

Earlier, this chapter mentioned a subtle detail with message or content filters that have conditions that test recipients. In message filters, this is the rcpt-to condition, and in content filters, it's the envelope recipient condition. The issue occurs when messages have multiple recipients; the condition tests if *any* recipient matches the condition, whether a regular expression, LDAP lookup, or dictionary test.

In the first example, we had a single rcpt-to condition and a simple action, drop. Let's look at a more real-world example, involving intellectual property and encryption. Suppose that your organization is involved in a confidential project, such as an acquisition of another organization that also happens to be a partner and supplier. During a normal day, hundreds of messages pass to and from this organization. Naturally, email will also be used as part of the communication between your organization and the target about the acquisition, but also with a third party, an outside law firm handling the acquisition negotiations.

Suppose that protecting confidentiality in this communication includes the following requirements:

- Outgoing messages to users @targetacq.com and @lawfirm.com, and sent by a group of users in the legal department in your organization, must be encrypted before delivery.
- Outgoing messages to users @targetacq.com and @lawfirm.com, sent by anyone else in your organization, must be dropped and a notification sent back to the sender informing them of the policy.
- Incoming messages sent from users @targetacq.com into your organization are delivered if they are addressed to the Legal department.

Assume that the users in the Legal department have an LDAP attribute identifying them and that there is a working LDAP query on the ESA. What's the best way to approach this problem? We could write filters that check for the recipient domain and encrypt messages, as shown in Example 11-3.

Example 11-3 *Filters for Sensitive Messages*

```
encrypt_sensitive_outgoing:
if ((rcpt-to == "@targetacq\\.com" OR
    rcpt-to == "@lawfirm\\.com")AND
    mail-from-group == "Legal") {
        encrypt();
        skip-filters();
    }

block_sensitive_outgoing:
if (rcpt-to == "@targetacq\\.com" OR
rcpt-to == "@lawfirm\\.com") {
      drop();
      notify ("$EnvelopeFrom", "Your message was dropped", "postmaster@yourco.com",
   "SensitiveTemplate");
}

restrict_sensitive_incoming:
if mail-from == "@targetacq\\.com" {
      if rcpt-to-group == "Legal" {
             skip-filters();
      }
```

```
        else {
                drop();
        }
}
```

There are some subtle issues here. For outgoing mail, this solution has the side effect of encrypting all messages where any recipient in the message matches the rule. For example, if an attorney at your company sends a message to both someuser@cisco.com and otheruser@targetacq.com, the message to Cisco would be encrypted along with the message to the target company. This may not be a terrible problem; the other recipients can simply open the encrypted message.

A similar problem occurs with the second filter. Messages going to more than one recipient will be dropped if at least one of the recipients is in the target or law firm domain.

The far more serious logic issue is in the third filter. For all messages coming from targetacq.com, the rcpt-to-group condition will be true whenever *any* recipient on the message is in the legal department. A message from targetacq.com to local recipients will get through your filter as long as at least one of the recipients is in Legal. Someone can effectively bypass your restriction with a BCC.

The answer to this dilemma is to combine content filters with outgoing mail policies. As you saw earlier in this chapter and in Chapter 3, content filters are processed later in the pipeline and are created and run on a per-policy basis. When a single message has multiple recipients, and those recipients match different policies, the ESA splinters the message into multiple copies, and passes the message down the pipeline independently. Because content filters are processed after the splintering, we need to switch our approach to using content filters.

The solution to the problem presented in the `restrict_sensitive_incoming` filter is to make sure that our test only applies to the right recipients. First, navigate to **Mail Policies → Incoming Mail Policies** and click **Add Policy** to add a new policy. Name it **Legal Department** and leave the order at number 1. Use the drop-down at the bottom for LDAP group and type the department name **Legal**, and then click **Add>>**. The result should look like Figure 11-6. Click **Submit** to add the policy.

This policy only applies to recipients in the Legal department. Now, we can recreate the `restrict_sensitive_incoming` filter. Create a new incoming content filter from **Mail Policies → Incoming Content Filters.** Your new filter should look like Figure 11-7. We do not use filter logic to allow messages to Legal; you'll see what I mean in the next step.

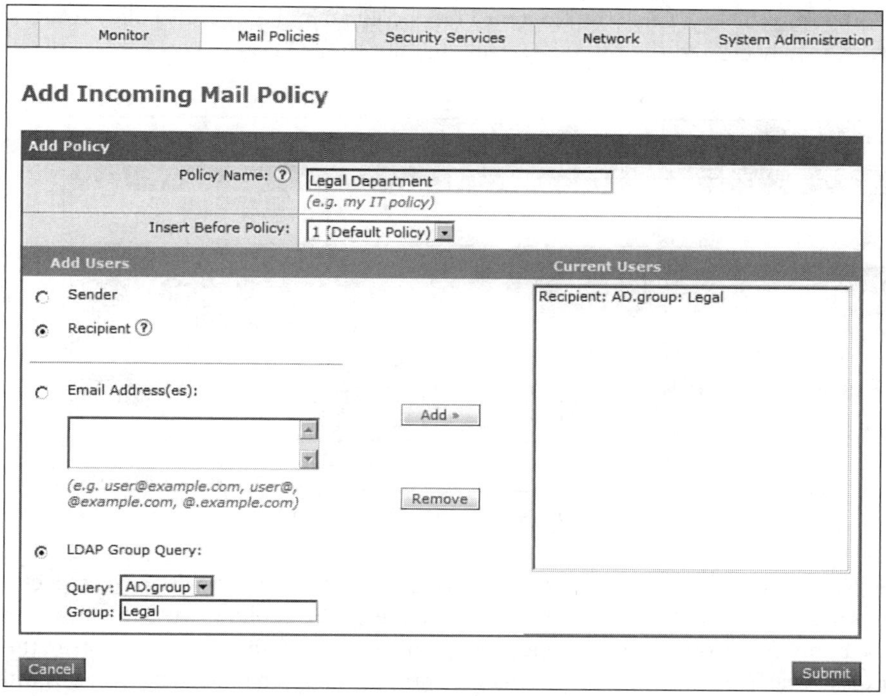

Figure 11-6 *Incoming Mail Policy for Legal Department*

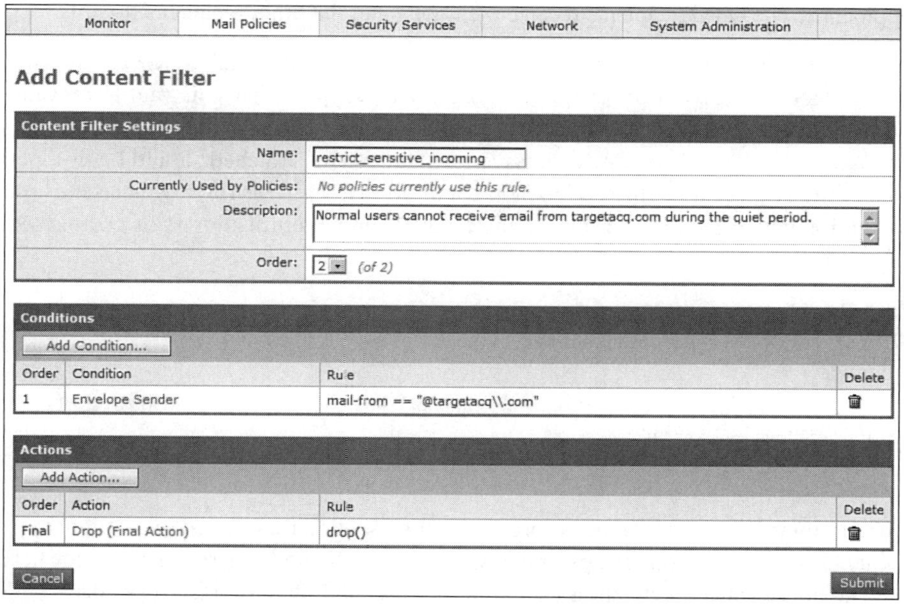

Figure 11-7 *Content Filter to Restrict Incoming Messages*

The last step is the key. Click the **Content Filters** column in the **Default Policy** row to apply the newly created filter to the Default, but not to the Legal Department, as shown in Figure 11-8.

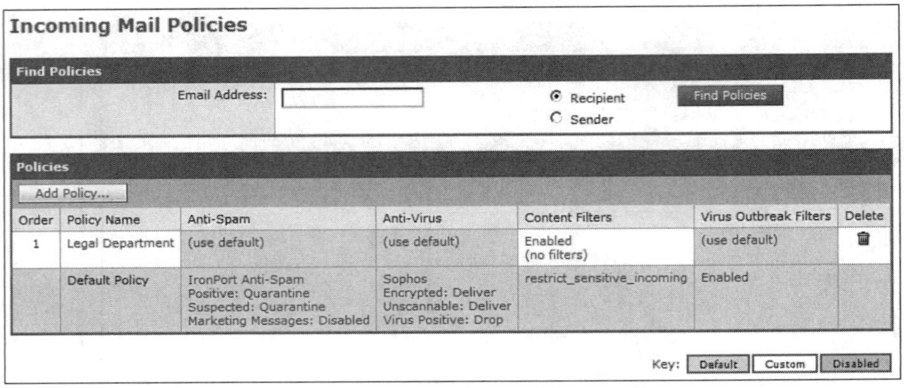

Figure 11-8 *Result of Applying Content Filter to Default Policy*

What happens to incoming messages from targetacq.com now? For single-recipient messages going to a user not in the Legal department, the message follows the default policy and is dropped. For single-recipient messages going to a user in the Legal department, the check isn't even performed, so no messages are dropped. For multirecipient messages with users in both policies, ESA splinters the message into two messages: one with the Legal recipients and one with the other recipients. Each message individually progresses through the pipeline. The Legal recipients receive their copy and the other recipients do not.

Here's another example where you would certainly want to use mail policies to apply per-recipient policies. For protecting corporate data, suppose that you want to prevent your users from sending documents to common webmail domains, like yahoo.com, hotmail.com, and gmail.com. Any message with documents attached should be dropped and a notification sent to the sender. You could do that with this filter, which sends the notification with a customized subject and template and a return address of postmaster@example.com:

```
drop_webmail_doc_messages:
if (rcpt-to == "(yahoo|gmail|hotmail)\\.com$") {
    drop();
    notify ("$EnvelopeFrom", "Your Message Was Not Sent", "postmaster@example.
  com", "WebMailNotify");
}
```

You're again in the same boat as before if someone sends a message to two or more recipients, with at least one recipient at a webmail domain and one recipient somewhere else. The non-webmail recipient is caught in the filter and the message dropped.

One nonfilter solution to this issue is to simply map the webmail domains to the destination /dev/null in SMTPRoutes; that would force messages to those domains to be dropped. However, you would not get the sender notification that you need. The right solution is to create an outgoing mail policy that matches these domains, and apply a content filter that drops and notifies the sender.

Using mail policies to separate recipients or senders is so effective, and so convenient, that whenever a filter seems to call for a rcpt-to or mail-from condition, I opt for mail policies instead. It generally does the right thing with multirecipient messages, it's high performance, and frankly, it's much easier to administer. The approach has my highest recommendation.

Filter Performance Considerations

Filter conditions and actions, when applied to a large number of messages, can add significant scanning effort to any ESA. The good news is that in most ESA configurations, the IPAS scanning process is typically the most resource intensive, because it runs a lot of anti-spam rules against a lot of messages. Typically, filtering is performed on the smaller set of clean incoming and outgoing mail only. This doesn't mean that filters can't cause performance problems, though; at some point, the added work of filters will have a meaningful impact on maximum throughput.

The first performance consideration is the process of decoding, unpacking, and converting MIME attachments. When an ESA receives a message, the system makes no attempt to parse the MIME headers or parts, and simply stores the transmitted message bodies as received. This blob of data remains unparsed until a filter condition or action is executed that requires decoding.

The decoding process starts with parsing the MIME headers to discover the MIME boundaries that separate the message parts. Binary attachments encoded with binary-to-ASCII schemes, like Base64 or uuencode, are decoded to the original binary form. The file-typing process runs on the binary to determine the actual file type. If the resulting binary is an archive format, such as ZIP, TAR, or GZIP, the archive is unpacked and decompressed. At this point, the ESA now has the original binary data, the true file type, and the reported filename and MIME type of each attachment to the message. The files are then passed to the file conversion engine for rendering the file contents into plain text for known file types, like PDF, MS Word, and Excel.

As you might guess, this decoding process can be expensive for large or complex messages. The performance hit on large messages is clear, and the larger the message, the more time it takes to go through the process. Message complexity is more difficult to quantify. Messages with many attachments are more complex. Archive files require decompression and are thus more complex.

Filter conditions and actions that operate on message attributes other than the body, such as sender and recipient rules, header rules, metadata rules, like body-size or remote-ip, are all very fast; the data is stored with the message in memory and the filter test is simply a value comparison. Because these individual message attributes are fairly small, even regular expression matching is not resource intensive.

Filter conditions that modify the message body in some way are the most expensive. The ESA uses a *copy on write* optimization scheme; this means that, to change the message body, a new copy is created in memory and a new MID assigned to the message.

Table 11-13 categorizes the various filter conditions and actions into performance buckets.

Table 11-13 *Performance Categories of Filter Conditions and Actions*

Condition or Action	Intensity Compared with Unburdened
Message metadata, like remote-ip, reputation, sender, and recipient checks.	Very low, less than 10% effect on peak throughput
Header comparisons, including Subject.	Low, less than 25% effect
File information comparisons, like filename or type.	Medium, less than 50% effect
Body scanning, such as body-contains or attachment-contains. Performance depends on size and complexity of messages.	High, 50–75% effect
Message modification: strip-attachment, add-footer, HTML conversion.	Very high, 75% or more

The performance impact here is not stating that body scanning suddenly causes all messages to take twice as long, or even that the capacity of the system will decrease by 50%. These numbers indicate that the peak throughput of an ESA, compared with one running no filters whatsoever, decreases by approximately that value. In general, if you are running anti-spam and antivirus, the performance of those engines dictate the peak throughput of the appliance. Adding a body-scanning filter to a fully burdened system likely results in no loss of peak throughput or increased latency.

Improving Filter Performance

Improving filter performance requires, minimizing the use of expensive filter conditions and keeping regular expressions as specific as possible. Ordering of filters can help in some cases, but because of the optimizations that the ESA performs under the hood, using logical conditions to exempt messages from expensive scans usually won't create a noticeable difference in performance. To avoid calling the regular expression engine multiple times, the ESA checks all filter expressions against each message with a single call and records the results of each pattern, whether that pattern will be used or not.

For example, consider these two filters:

```
one:
if (body-contains ("simple") {
    alt-mailhost ("10.17.23.2");
    skip-filters();
}
```

```
two:
if (body-contains ("Copyright \d\d\d\d") {
    alt-mailhost ("10.17.23.4");
}
```

You might expect that these filters, run in this order, would result in messages containing the string **simple** to not have their content examined for the **Copyright \d\d\d\d** regex. However, the ESA evaluates both of these expressions, because a single scan of the message bytes during a single call to the regex engine is more efficient than doing them separately. It's faster to run all the regular expression tests at once, even if the results won't necessarily be used.

The ESA has other built-in optimizations for filtering messages. The message decoding, decompression, and parsing process happens only once for messages that must be body scanned, to avoid duplicating that expensive process. The best optimization we can do is avoid the decoding step altogether.

Here are some general tips for improving filter performance:

- If you plan to drop messages, such as those with dangerous attachments, like exe, pif, bat, or com, you should do so as early as possible to avoid any unnecessary scanning. Content filters that drop messages should be the first ones in the list. If you can do this work in message filters, even better.
- The fewer the messages that pass through filters, the better the performance will be. Use LDAP recipient validation to ensure the ESAs aren't accepting messages for nonexistent recipients. Set message size limits appropriately in the HAT to avoid accepting large messages that will bounce. If spam messages are to be delivered to the end user or to the ISQ, be aware that these will pass through the content filters engine; we'll address this in a recipe later in this chapter.
- Try to avoid modifying messages, because this is an expensive operation. The most common forms of message modification are disclaimers (footers and headers) and stripping attachments. Disclaimers are best handled by individual user's mail user agent (MUA) because of performance but also because of trouble with character set mismatches. However, many companies mandate the use of a legal disclaimer at the bottom of messages, and this may override concerns about ESA performance. Instead of stripping attachments, drop the messages, or quarantine, and send notifications to the recipient.
- Reduce the number of calls to the regular expression engine. If you're looking for one of many possible patterns, use a single pattern with | (the pipe character) to define *or* terms within the regex. This is an extremely good approach to attachment filtering, for example. Suppose you want to filter attachments by filename and stop all files with file extensions like exe, com, bat, vbs, and pif. Instead of using attachment-filename ("\.exe$") AND attachment-filename ("\.com$"), use a single condition like attachment-filename ("\.(exe|com|bat|vbs|pif)$").

- Avoid regular expression wildcards, like .*, especially in body scans. If you need to search for two separate conditions in the same file, try to use a limited wildcard. For example, if you're searching for the terms "sensitive" and "confidential" when they appear in the same file, you'd be tempted to use a regex of **sensitive.*confidential.** What happens, though, when a file contains the word "sensitive" near the beginning, and "confidential" near the end, or not in the file at all? The regex pattern matching continues all the way until the end of the file, examining all bytes of the message. If you use a couple of these kinds of regexes in your filters, you end up asking the scanning engine to search the content multiple times. Because the words "sensitive" and "confidential" will likely appear near each other in the file, use a regex like **sensitive.{1,100}confidential**, which matches on the words sensitive and confidential when they are separated by no more than 100 characters. Limiting the scope of the regex match in this way considerably improves performance.

Another tactic for improving performance is to move some of the load off system, especially for large messages. The ESA can alter delivery for large messages to avoid processing them on box, using the body-size condition and alt-mailhost action. We discuss two-tier architectures for handling large messages in Chapter 13, "Multiple Device Deployments." Unfortunately, no such simple test exists for message complexity: The complexity of a message isn't known until the decoding is complete.

Filter Recipes

We spent much of this chapter on the details of filter conditions and actions with a few examples to illustrate some of the art of crafting effective filters. Here, we devote time to specific filter *recipes* that solve particular problems. For most of these scenarios, there's more than one way to compose such filters.

Dropping Messages

It may be obvious, but a word of warning about the drop action in either message or content filters. Dropping a message is dangerous: The system immediately discards the content and provides no means of recovery.

Even the best filter writers in the world make mistakes or write overly broad regular expression matches. Take this message filter, for example:

```
drop_virus_messages:
if (subject == "[VIRUS]") {
    drop();
}
```

Seems like a great idea, no? Drop messages that either the ESA or another system have detected as a virus? Do you see the problem? This is a bad regular expression because the [ ] brackets indicate a choice of characters. That means that this filter will drop any messages that contain a single V, I, R, U, or S character anywhere in the subject. This results in a lot of legitimate messages becoming permanently unrecoverable.

For these reasons, if you intend to drop messages to prevent them from reaching the end recipient, I recommend using the quarantine action to hold the messages, giving you a safety net should anything untoward occur. At the very least, use the archive action in a message filter to store a copy-of-last-resort. Once a filter has been running for some time with a nondestructive action, you can consider changing it to a drop action. Even then, I would limit the use of drop to situations where discarding the messages is a matter of life and death, such as traffic storms or other situations that risk the entire email infrastructure.

Basic Message Attribute Filters

This section covers some scenarios that can be addressed with filters that examine basic message data. We've already seen filters that examine sender and recipient to look for specific email addresses, but filters have access to almost all parts of the message body and to metadata like the source IP of the connecting client.

For example, filters can examine message headers, acting if a particular header exists or not, or if it contains some value. Suppose employees in your environment are instructed to mark messages as company confidential when sending sensitive information. The ESA can act on the sensitivity header, like this:

```
encrypt_confidential:
if (header ("Sensitivity") == "Company-Confidential") {
    encrypt();
}
```

Filters can also be used to add information to messages that can make troubleshooting easier:

```
markup_originating_IP:
if (true) {
    strip-header ("X-Originating-IP");
    insert-header ("X-Originating-IP", "$remoteip");
}
```

Attachment filtering is a common solution, and it can be done either through message filters or content filters; the regular expressions are what matters.

First, a basic filter that identifies messages with executable attachments. This identifies executables by file type, not relying on the filename reported in the MIME headers for identification. This will find win32 executables even if they've been renamed, and it will even find them within zip or tar archives:

```
stop_exe_attachment:
if (attachment-filetype == "exe") {
quarantine ("Policy");
}
```

If your security policy requires dropping other kinds of executable software, like installers, dynamic link libraries, screensavers, and Java-based applications, you can do that with an entire category of file type identifications:

```
stop_exe_attachment:
if (attachment-filetype == "Executable") {
    quarantine ("Policy");
}
```

Some types of scripting content, like VBScript or DOS batch files, cannot be identified by type and are not categorized in the executable file type. We must resort to attachment filenames to filter these messages. It's tempting to write individual conditions for these in a filter, like this:

```
stop_script_and_batch:
if (attachment-filename == "\\.bat$" or attachment-filename == "\\.vbs$") {
    quarantine ("Policy");
}
```

Although that filter certainly gets the job done, it's not as efficient as it could be—and if you're stopping a few dozen different file extensions, the overhead of invoking the regex engine many times can be high. A better approach is to invoke the regex engine just once:

```
stop_script_and_batch:
if (attachment-filename == "(?i)\\.(bat|vbs)$") {
    quarantine ("Policy");
}
```

For long lists of file extensions, the regex grouping can be easily extended:

```
attachment-filename == "(?i)\\.(bat|vbs|cmd|wmf)$"
```

Note that I'm using the regex preprocessor flag (?i) that tells the engine that the pattern following it is case-insensitive. This allows the regex to match on filenames regardless of the case the names were created in.

Body and Attachment Scanning

Almost every organization will have a need, at some point, to use filters to scan the bodies of messages, whether for acceptable use, security filtering, intellectual property protection, or regulatory compliance. Here are some examples of how to solve common tasks that involve content in the body of messages, including any attachments.

For matching single terms or regular expressions in filters, we've already seen filter examples that use the **body-contains** condition. Most content filtering needs require matching more than one term, and the best way to search for lists of content is to use a dictionary. For example, if your organization prohibits the use of profanity in email messages, you can use a filter like this:

```
stop_profanity:
if (dictionary-match ("Profanity")) {
    quarantine ("Policy");
}
```

The advantage of using a dictionary is that modifying the list of search terms is as simple as modifying the dictionary. You don't need to change the message filter to add or remove terms. Composing a dictionary of profanity terms is left as an exercise for you.

The next example is a common combination of tasks: Stop local users from sending any kind of executable attachment, knowingly or otherwise. Aside from being good policy, this kind of filter can catch local user with infected PCs that are sending malware-laden messages. In this case, we focus on executables, quarantine the message for administrative review, and notify the sender about the action:

```
quarantine_and_notify_exe:
if (sendergroup == "RELAYLIST" AND attachment-filetype == "Executable") {
    quarantine ("Policy");
    notify ("$EnvelopeFrom", "Your message contains a restricted attachment",
"postmaster@example.com", 'AttachmentNotifyTemplate");
}
```

I'm using the sendergroup condition to apply this to outgoing mail only, because I don't want to send notifications to Internet senders of incoming mail. The AttachmentNotifyTemplate uses action variables to describe the message and the policy violation to the sender:

```
Your message contained a dangerous attachment type and was not delivered:

Subject: $Subject:
Recipients: $EnvelopeRecipients:
Filenames: $Filenames

Corporate policy prohibits sending potentially dangerous attachment types. If you
believe this message is in error, please contact the helpdesk.
```

Another common use of filters is to attach a footer disclaimer to the bottom of each outgoing message. However, in the case of a reply, you likely only want to do that if the message doesn't already contain the disclaimer. If you blindly add the disclaimer, a back-and-forth reply conversation will end up having the disclaimer added with each outgoing reply, resulting in messages that grow larger. A simple way to prevent this is to look for the disclaimer text in the message already, as in this filter:

```
add_disclaimer:
if (sendergroup == "RELAYLIST") AND (NOT (body-contains ("This message contains
```

```
sensitive information for the intended recipient only"))) {
    add-footer ("LegalDisclaimer");
}
```

As in the attachment notification filter, I'm using the sendergroup condition to apply this to outgoing mail only.

Complex Combinatorial Logic with Content Filters

Near the beginning of this chapter, we saw this message filter that includes both AND and OR statements:

```
complex_logic:
if (rcpt-to == "chriport@cisco\\.com" OR header("Received") == "chrisporter\\.
com$") {
   if (body-size > 1024k) {
          bcc ("chris@chrisporter.com");
   }
}
```

This filter's logic is "if the recipient is Chris Porter, or the Received header indicates it passed through a host called chrisporter.com, and the message is larger than 1MB, send a copy to chris@chrisporter.com." More formally, the logic of this is if (A OR B) AND C.

I stated that this kind of complex logic isn't possible with content filters, because they are limited to all the conditions being ANDed or ORed together. It's not possible, directly, but you can implement this logic with two filters, using a header to pass values between. Here's how to do that.

The first content filter, shown in Figure 11-9, tests condition (A or B). Instead of directly acting on the message, it adds a header to the message, indicating that the first compound statement is true.

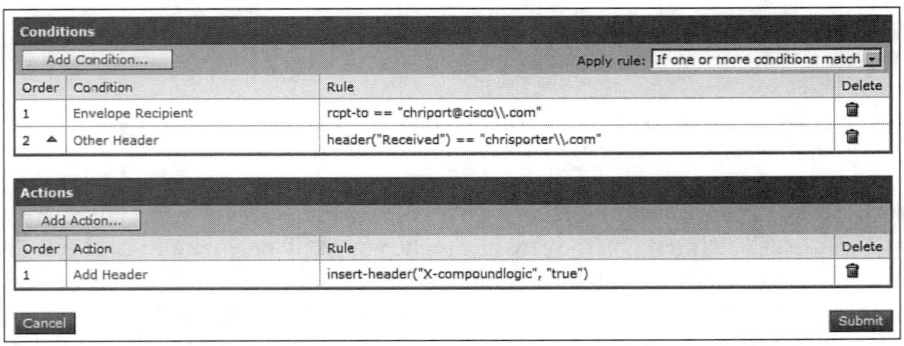

Figure 11-9 *First of a Two-Filter Combination for Some Complex Logic*

The second content filter immediately follows in the processing order. If the header from the first filter is present, and the body is larger than 1MB, it takes action. This filter is shown in Figure 11-10.

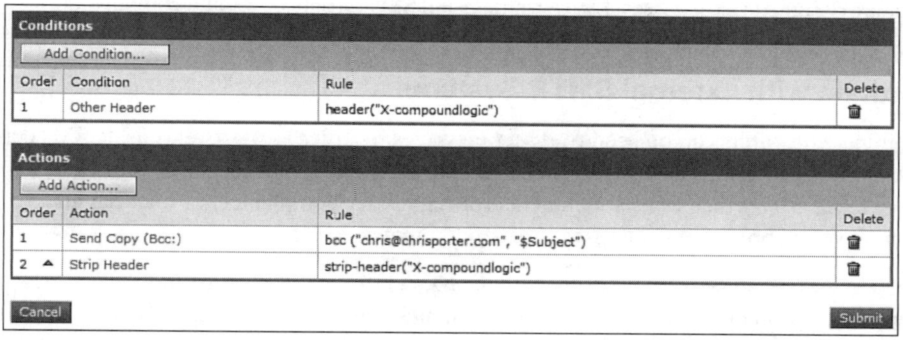

Figure 11-10 *Second Filter in the Two-Filter Combination*

The second filter also removes the header added in Figure 11-9, so this little trick doesn't add unnecessary information to the message.

Routing Messages Using Filters

The filter action alt-mailhost, or "Send to Alternate Destination Host" in content filters, can be used to alter the normal delivery path of a given message. Because of the granularity of filters and mail policies, you can implement some complex routing using filters. If you combine this with information in an LDAP directory, such as Active Directory (AD), you can even route based on user attributes in that directory.

As an example, suppose that your environment has an external server specifically for encrypting email messages, and you want to send messages there when they are confidential or if the sender puts a tag in the Subject. You can use a filter to redirect messages, like this:

```
redirect_confidential:
if (subject == "CONFIDENTIAL" or header("Sensitivity") == "Company-Confidential")
{
   alt-mailhost ("encrypt.company.com");
}
```

Be aware that routing messages does just that—reroutes the entire message, including all recipients. So, a filter that tests for a specific recipient, and reroutes the message, like this, does so for all recipients:

```
redirect_faculty_staff:
if (rcpt-to == "@facstaff\\.university\\.edu") {
alt-mailhost ("factstaff-mail.university.edu");
}
```

This approach risks sending all recipients on a mult-recipient message to the same server. This is an artificial example—the right thing to do in this case is to use SMTPRoutes. If you're going to do some sort of per-recipient routing, it's best to stick with the features on the ESA that are designed for it: aliases, LDAP routing, and SMTPRoutes, or some combination.

Integration with External SMTP Systems

Routing with filters can be used to direct messages to other local systems using SMTP as transport. For example, you might need to deliver certain messages, or all messages, to an external server that scans attachments for regulatory compliance, or one that encrypts or archives a copy of email messages before they're sent out.

For some external systems, like email archiving, all that's needed is a copy of the message. If you don't need to reroute the original message, but just save a copy of the original's content, use the Send Copy (BCC) action or the Notify action with the option to include a copy of the original message.

Warning The BCC action creates a new message (and new MID) with the original content and the BCC recipient as the sole recipient. For archiving purposes, this may not be suitable, because the list of original recipients will not be retained. Although the original To, From, and CC headers are preserved, any recipients that were BCC on the original are lost.

To retain the original recipient list, you might choose to add a header that lists all the recipients, like this:

```
if (true) {
    add-header ("X-rcpt-to", "$EnvelopeRecipients");
    bcc ("archive@server.yourco.com");
}
```

But, that adds another problem: Anyone who receives the message can see all of the recipient addresses, defeating the "blind" of the BCC. There's a simple solution: Delete the header:

```
if (true) {
    add-header ("X-rcpt-to", "$EnvelopeRecipients");
    bcc ("archive@server.yourco.com");
    strip-header ("X-rcpt-to");
}
```

On the face of it, this seems like it shouldn't work. But, it does, because of a subtle pipeline processing fact: The BCC action creates a new message that is not subject to any further processing. So, in this filter, the header is added to the message, and BCC creates a copy of that message, including the new header. The original continues through the actions, and the header is stripped. The BCC copy does not encounter the strip-header action; in fact, it skips all filters and scanning and heads straight to delivery.

In cases where this behavior is not desirable, there is the bcc-scan action.

For other systems, like encryption or large-message storage servers, the original message needs to be rerouted in its entirety. The external system will potentially modify the message and either deliver it directly or return it to the ESA for final delivery.

Cul-de-Sac Architecture

There are several approaches to the problem, depending on the specifics of your environment. The first approach is what I call a *cul-de-sac* model, because messages will be delivered from the ESA to the external system where they're being processed, and the results delivered back to the ESA. This model is conceptually pictured in Figure 11-11.

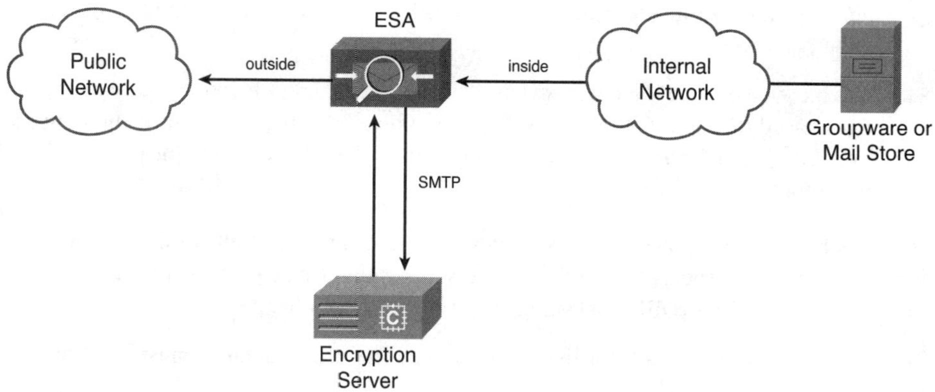

Figure 11-11 *Integration with an External SMTP Server, Such as Encryption or Archiving*

The advantages of this approach are

- The ESA can do some prefiltering and selectively send messages to the external system, instead of all messages having to be sent. This decreases the volume of mail making a double-trip, increasing performance. This is especially important if the rerouting is based on sender or recipient and is limited to small groups.
- The ESA is built for performance and reliability, and won't be impacted if messages cannot be delivered to the external system. Messages destined for the external system will queue until that system is available again, while other messages will be delivered straight through as normal. This limits the impact of any failure of the external system.
- When messages are routed out, and back through the ESA, the ESA continues to act as the final delivery host in your network. This fits in with the recommended *last hop out* placement of ESAs in the email architecture, allowing for consolidated delivery reports, consistent TLS usage, and the use of email authentication features, like DKIM signing.

- The ESA can deliver to multiple external systems for redundancy. This can even be done with filters, if you follow my suggestion on delivering to stand-in hostnames detailed later in the section, "Delivering to Multiple External Hosts."

The problems with this cul-de-sac approach are

- If messages are delivered through the ESA a second time, there will be an additional set of log entries, reporting hits, and tracking entries, because the ESA treats it as a brand-new message.
- When messages are returned, they are for all intents and purposes new messages. The external system may modify the message slightly, or modify it completely, or possibly not even return it at all. Unless the external system has an absolutely predictable behavior, you cannot write filters that depend on message data like attachments, headers or header values, and so on. It's best not to count on message data being preserved.
- You must create the logic to prevent mail loops. A single filter that redirects messages based on an attribute, like Subject, or a header value, risks a hit if the message is returned to the ESA with that attribute intact. The ESA discards messages that loop more than 100 times.

In the **redirect_confidential** filter example, using that filter by itself results in a mail loop if the external encryption server delivers its results back to the ESA, and the message retains the CONFIDENTIAL subject or the Sensitivity header.

To avoid a mail loop, use a filter that short-circuits the process, and it must be above the redirect in the filtering order:

```
short_circuit_encryption:
if (remote-ip == "10.1.17.23-29") {
    skip-filters();
}
```

That creates a maintenance headache; you need to list the IPs for the encryption servers and maintain the filter if it changes. A better approach is to use the HAT to create a sender group for your encryption servers. If you name the sender group ENCRYPTION, you can use this filter to perform the short circuit:

```
short_circuit_encryption:
if (sendergroup == "ENCRYPTION") {
    skip-filters();
}
```

With this filter, maintenance is a bit easier: Simply list the IP addresses of the encryption servers in the HAT sendergroup, and don't touch the filter. The HAT is easier to see and maintain than message or content filters. Furthermore, having a separate HAT group and policy allows you to customize connection control, rate limits, and other SMTP parameters for email originating from your external servers.

The same issue exists with content filters, but the sendergroup condition is not available. You must use the remote IP rule.

Inline Architecture

Alternately, you can use an *inline* model, as shown in Figure 11-12. This model is simpler, because all mail passes through both layers. The ESA configuration is simpler. Messages traverse each layer only once, so message tracking and reporting don't count duplicate data.

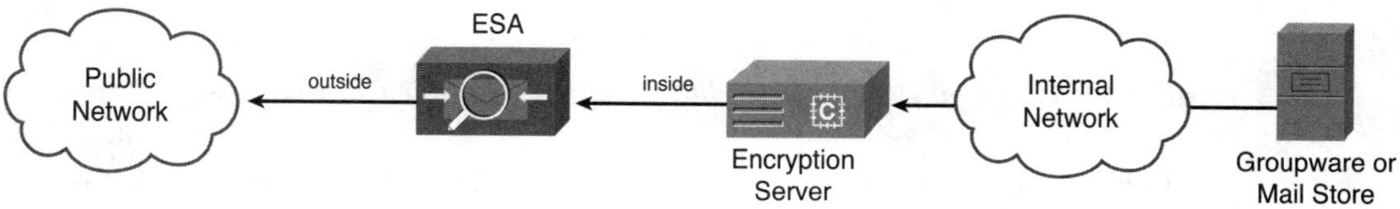

Figure 11-12 *Inline Architecture for ESA with an External SMTP Server*

The problems with the inline approach are

- Failure of either layer stops all mail, reducing effective mean time between failures (MTBF).
- Many email systems, such as DLP, archiving, and encryption, are not intended to handle the kinds of volume and throughput that ESA is designed. The performance of the entire environment is limited by the slowest component in the architecture, so performance will almost certainly be lower with an inline model.
- When the ESA receives all outgoing mail from the external system, you lose the visibility of internal hosts and the ability to create per-host HAT policies.

In general, inline models with ESA should place the ESA as the first hop of incoming mail, delivering messages to the external server after processing. This keeps the ESA security filters in their ideal configuration. For outgoing mail, the external servers should finish their processing and deliver all mail to the ESAs as the last hop of outgoing mail.

Delivering to Multiple External Hosts

When using filters to route messages, be aware of a limitation in the alt-mailhost action: You get only one. If you have multiple alt-mailhost actions, the last one in the filter takes precedence. If multiple filters are hit, each with an alt-mailhost action, only the last one takes effect and the other redirects are lost.

A cul-de-sac model with two external SMTP hosts—one for DLP scanning and another for encryption—looks like Figure 11-13.

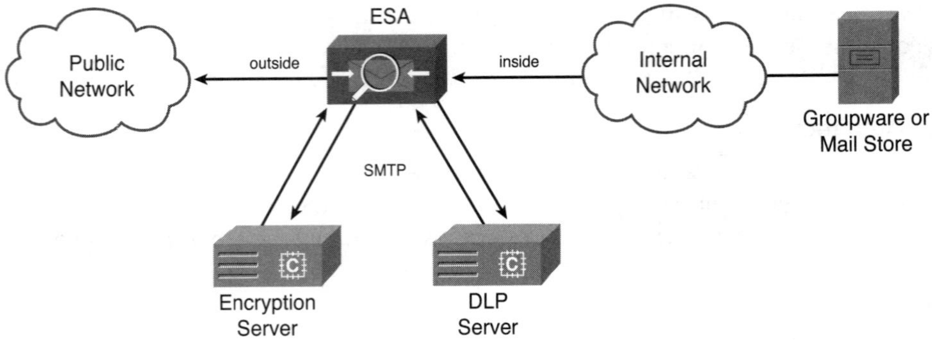

Figure 11-13 *Email Cul-de-Sac Architecture with Multiple External Hosts*

To handle this, we just need to plan our logic carefully and avoid mail loops. Let's assume that messages will traverse this architecture from right to left with ESA acting as the "traffic cop" directing the flow: groupware, ESA, DLP, ESA, encryption, and finally, ESA for delivery.

First, you need short circuits for the external servers. Let's start with the last hop in the architecture, assuming that if the encryption server is sending it, it's ready for delivery:

```
short_circuit_encr:
if (remote-ip == "10.1.17.23-29") {
    skip-filters();
}
```

Second, you need a filter to handle mail that's coming from the DLP servers. You need to short-circuit that process, too, but the message can't go straight to Internet delivery because it must next go to the encryption server. This filter does both:

```
short_circuit_dlp:
if (remote-ip == "10.1.109.63-70") {
    alt-mailhost ("encryption.yourco.com");
    skip-filters();
}
```

The third and final step is to redirect everything else that's outgoing. We don't want to redirect our incoming mail, so we add an additional condition to test the sendergroup and only redirect outgoing relayed mail. We are not skipping any filters, assuming that the first pass through the ESA is the place you want to run any other filters:

```
outgoing_to_dlp:
if (sendergroup == "RELAYLIST") {
    alt-mailhost ("dlp.yourco.com");
}
```

Warning I don't recommend that you use the SMTPRoutes default entry of ALL for this style of integration: The default route affects all mail, incoming and outgoing, and can't be overridden by filter actions. See the discussion in the next section.

Another common reason for multiple external hosts is for redundancy or load balancing. If you have multiple instances of encryption software servers, you must either use a load balancer or account for multiple hosts in the ESA configuration. The problem here is that the alt-mailhost action can only have one destination. The solution to this problem is to combine alt-mailhost with the SMTPRoutes tables. First, we direct the message to a nonexistent hostname; you can use anything you like, as long as it looks like an FQDN:

```
redirect_confidential:
if (subject == "CONFIDENTIAL" or header("Sensitivity") == "Company-Confidential")
{
    alt-mailhost ("encryption.server");
}
```

Then, in the SMTPRoutes table, create a mapping of that host to the destination servers:

```
encryption.server: 10.1.17.23, 10.1.17.24, 10.1.17.25
```

In AsyncOS 7.1 and later, you can even apply a weight to individual destinations in SMTPRoutes, allowing ESA to failover or load-balance multiple hosts. SMTPRoutes are easier to maintain than a filter. Mapping alt-mailhost to an SMTPRoutes entry also avoids a problem where a default SMTPRoute (for the ALL route) can override the alt-mailhost action. For these reasons, I recommend that you *always* set your alt-mailhost action to dummy hostnames and use SMTPRoutes to map to the proper destination.

Interacting with Security Filters

Because content filters run after the anti-spam and antivirus engines, you can create rules that interact with the results of the engines. For the most part, the security engines give you the actions that you need: drop, deliver, and notify.

Messages dropped as spam or viruses will not be processed by the content filters engine; drop is an immediate action that discards the message. If you're not dropping the messages, but instead are delivering to quarantine or to the end user, the messages continue through the pipeline, including filter processing. This may not be desirable: Body-scanning known spam messages adds unnecessary overhead and, if you're scanning for terms that might appear in spam messages, you'll end up with false positives.

For example, take a simple content filter that uses the condition "Body or Attachment Contains" and the pattern "Confidential" to send a notification about matching messages. You might apply this filter to inbound mail going to certain groups within your organization. Whatever the reason, applying this filter to known spam messages is counterproductive. Spammers will at least occasionally use the term Confidential in their messages.

Unfortunately, there's no "is-spam" verdict test to bypass content filters automatically for spam messages. The same logic can be accomplished using the anti-spam engine's advanced markup capabilities to add a header to the message and allowing us to short circuit it. The anti-spam actions for a policy include an advanced section that allows you to add a header to messages found to be spam or suspected to be spam. An example of this setting is shown in Figure 11-14.

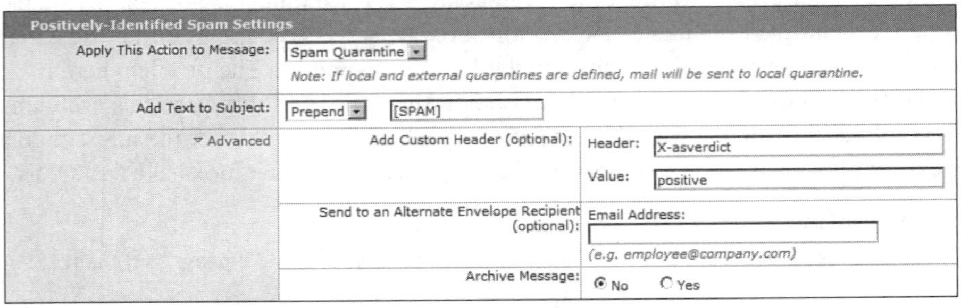

Figure 11-14 *Anti-Spam: Configuring a Header for Spam Positive Verdict*

The header is then used in a simple content filter to short circuit all other processing. An example of this filter is shown in Figure 11-15. I've taken the step of removing the header from the message so that my trick goes unnoticed. Note that the name of the header and its value are arbitrary; you don't even necessarily need to test the value, because the header presence alone will indicate the verdict.

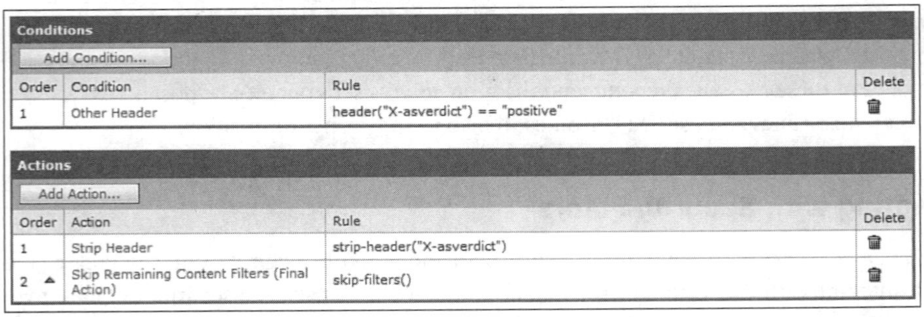

Figure 11-15 *Content Filter to Act on Spam Positive Messages*

Note The IronPort AntiSpam engine and other security filters add some headers to messages by default to indicate that the message was processed and to record the results in an encoded string. Because the string is encoded, you cannot use this header or its value to determine the verdict.

The antivirus engines also write their results into headers. You could possibly act on these headers if they indicate a viral message, but the question then is this: Why do you need to do further processing on viral messages? It's best to drop them and forget it.

Reinjection of Messages

Reinjection refers to changing the delivery destination of the ESA to itself, so that as the message is delivered, the ESA is acting as both SMTP client and server.

Why would you want to reinject messages? There are a few cases where some group of tasks cannot be performed in a single pass and the messages need to be processed a second time. This is because the fixed ordering of the pipeline in the ESA means that most processing cannot be done in order on the same pass. These are usually complex situations; I don't consider reinjection to be a general-purpose approach to any problem, but a solid and reliable solution when nothing else will suit.

In reinjection, the filters that you're writing aren't solving the issue directly, but are routing the messages so that other features can get to the solution.

Suppose that your organization runs two separate email domains, but you're in the process of retiring the old domain and reassigning users to addresses in the new domain. It would be nice if usera@olddomain.com could just be domain-mapped to usera@newdomain.com, but username overlaps prevent this. The ideal solution is to use LDAP routing to look up each user's old and new address, and rewrite the addresses on the fly. This ideal solution allows the migration to proceed as needed.

Problem solved, right? Well, further suppose that at the end of the migration, there are several dozen email addresses at the old domain that haven't been migrated. They don't appear in the directory at all. Either the users have been lost in the shuffle, or these are addresses without real people behind them, and don't have directory information. At some point, perhaps the directory will be updated to include them, but you're under pressure to finalize the migration, and it's decided to simply use aliases or domain-map to rewrite these addresses to addresses in the new domain. In effect, you're adding a little bit of manual rewriting to the automated LDAP rewrites, but if the directory is ever updated with proper addresses, you want that to work the way it should.

The problem with this configuration on the ESA is twofold: First, aliases and domain-map are early stages in the pipeline, before LDAP or filters. Second, there is no means in filters of testing whether LDAP routing queries succeeded or not. You do not know which addresses are failing to lookup or not, other than the fact that they are still of the recipient form @olddomain.com.

This is a case where reinjection can help. (I did say that it only comes up in complex situations.)

The solution that we implement here is simple to describe: Any recipients still being sent to @olddomain.com, because they were not found in LDAP, are reinjected into the ESA so that the domain-map can transform the addresses on a second pass. To ensure that domain-map does not affect any other messages, we create another listener on another port to handle this. This new listener, named Reinject, has a simple configuration with no LDAP and only the domain-map entries we need.

The filters we need are just for doing the reinjection and for short-circuiting the process. First, the short-circuit filter, assumes that anything that comes through the new listener is now on its second pass and should go directly to delivery:

```
short_circuit_reinject:
if (recv-listener == "Reinject") {
   skip-filters();
}
```

The other filter actually performs the reinjection:

```
reinject_old_domain:
if (rcpt-to == "@olddomain\\.com") {
   alt-mailhost ("esa02.cisco.com:2525");
}
```

Astute observers will realize that the multirecipient problem is going to rear its head here, but it's not much to worry about. The other recipients will be reinjected even if they don't need the second pass, but that's not going to cause any harm. The domain-map will not match on them, and the LDAP query won't even be performed. Other than a tiny bit more overhead, there's no harm in reinjecting the other recipients.

The real danger of a reinjection configuration is message loops, where reinjection results in messages being delivered back to the ESA ad infinitum. To avoid loops, the ESA will drop messages that have more than 100 hops, as indicated by the count of Received headers in the message. This drop is permanent and final, and you need filter logic to avoid it. The **short_circuit_reinject** filter, which must be earlier in the process than the reinjection, accomplishes this.

Summary

Message and content filters are the most versatile feature of the ESA, able to act on almost any part of messages. This chapter covered all the available conditions and actions and demonstrated some of those with real examples. Filters bear a resemblance to programming scripts in that they use branch logic for decision making, but there are important differences between filters and a scripting language.

Understanding the difference between message and content filters is critical for administering an ESA environment. Although many organizations will only have a need for content filtering through the WUI, knowledge of the CLI message filters is important, because it can solve numerous issues that can't be addressed anywhere else in the product.

In the next chapter, we revisit some of the networking topics we only briefly touched on in early chapters, and then dive into more advanced network configurations.

Chapter 12

Advanced Networking

In this chapter, you will learn the following:

- Reasons for multinetwork and multi-interface configurations
- Configuring and using virtual gateways on ESA
- Other advanced network topics, including TLS for secure email transmission

The previous chapters deal with simple Email Security Appliance (ESA) network configurations. In most of the examples, the ESA uses a single IP address and hostname for all communications: inbound mail from the Internet, outbound mail from internal mailstores, and for management and monitoring protocols.

There are cases where this configuration is not adequate or simply not desirable. The ESA provides support for many different network topologies to suit your environment.

ESA with Multiple IP Interfaces

During the setup of the ESA described in Chapter 2, "ESA Product Basics," I recommended using a single interface for the entire ESA. This single interface can be used for all Simple Mail Transfer Protocol (SMTP) traffic, both inbound and outbound, as well as for management and monitoring of the ESA. This is a simple, robust, and recommended configuration for most environments. No functionality is lost, it's easier to configure, and there aren't any concerns with network performance issues with a single interface deployment.

However, there are good reasons to use multiple network interfaces on an ESA. If your network design calls for splitting public and private traffic, or you must have a separate out-of-band management network. Multihomed configurations fall into two main categories: multihomed installation for separating functions across different networks and *virtual gateways*, which refer to multiple IP interfaces on the same network. It's also possible to have both: an ESA with multiple IP interfaces, some on the same network and some on different networks.

Multihomed Deployments

Multihomed deployments refer to ESAs with assigned IP addresses on multiple networks. Typically, this means assigning one or more IPs on the same network to each physical Ethernet port. For the 1U units like the C170, there are two separate physical can have IP addresses interfaces on two networks, one per physical Ethernet port. The 2U units like the C370, C670, and X1070 have three physical interfaces and thus can have interfaces on one, two, or three different networks. These aren't strict limits, because you can assign IPs on different networks to the same interface, but your switch and router must be able to support that configuration. You can also raise these limits by using VLANs to extend the count of interfaces, and we discuss VLAN support on the ESA later this chapter. You can even assign IPs.

There's really only one strict rule when planning multihomed deployments: IP addresses on the same subnet cannot span separate physical ports. The ESA has simple network routing capabilities and would be unable to select from two Ethernet interfaces that both have a route to a given destination.

You can get around this (two IPs on the same subnet, but on different physical interfaces) only by separating the two interfaces into different subnets. For example, if you want 192.168.1.4/24 on Data 1, and 192.168.1.27/24 on Data 2, you need to change the subnet mask to /28 or smaller. You can even make the mask on one of the interfaces /32, which puts the interface by itself on its own subnet.

Table 12-1 summarizes the possible network combinations for multihomed ESAs. The port here refers to the physical Ethernet ports or configured VLANs.

Table 12-1 *ESA Multihomed Configurations*

Configuration	Description
IPs on the same subnet, on the same port	Allowed. Common use for virtual gateways. For example, you can assign 10.17.23.20/24, 10.17.23.21/24, and 10.17.23.22/24 to Data 1, subject only to the platform limits on number of virtual gateways.
IPs on the same subnet, each on a different port	Not allowed. The ESA responds with the message: **IPs on the same subnet cannot be on different interfaces. Please try again.**
IPs on different subnets, on the same port	Allowed, but uncommon. Can be useful for creating isolated subnets. Only one of the subnets is likely able to reach the gateway.
IPs on different subnets, on different ports	Allowed. This is the most common configuration for multihomed networks. For example, you can assign 10.17.23.20/24 to Data 1 and 192.168.1.137/24 to Data 2.

Figure 12-1 shows a common multihomed network configuration on an ESA.

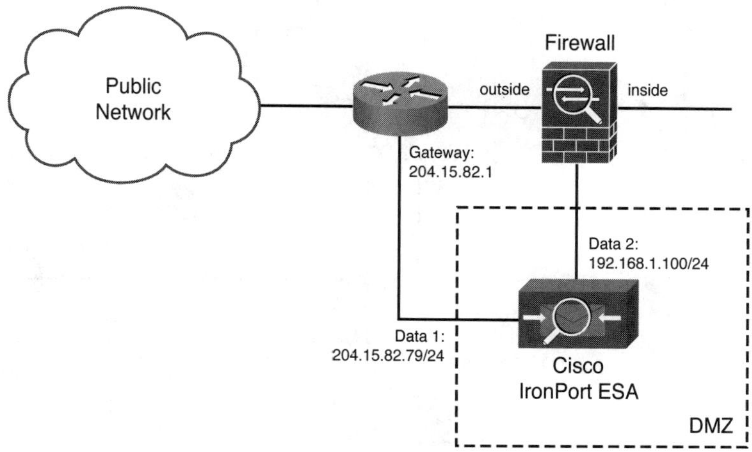

Figure 12-1 *Multihomed ESA Configuration*

Some of the reasons for considering a multihomed deployment include

- The network design dictates that ESA must span networks. This is called for if you have a public or DMZ interface, but the ESA also needs internal access to mail servers, DNS, or LDAP. It's an alternative to making firewall exceptions that would allow the ESA to reach internal servers.
- You want to separate public and private traffic. If your ESAs act as MTA for internal-to-internal email message traffic in addition to being an Internet email gateway, you can isolate the local traffic to an inside interface.
- You need to isolate management interfaces from SMTP-related interfaces. If you have a separate network for common management tasks, like WUI and CLI administration, logging, and SNMP monitoring, you can add an ESA interface on that network, and restrict the management protocols to it.

You want to create a private network for email-related servers. For example, if you want to deploy encryption or DLP servers alongside your ESAs, allowing SMTP delivery to and from, you can segment all that traffic on a private subnet, as shown in Figure 12-2.

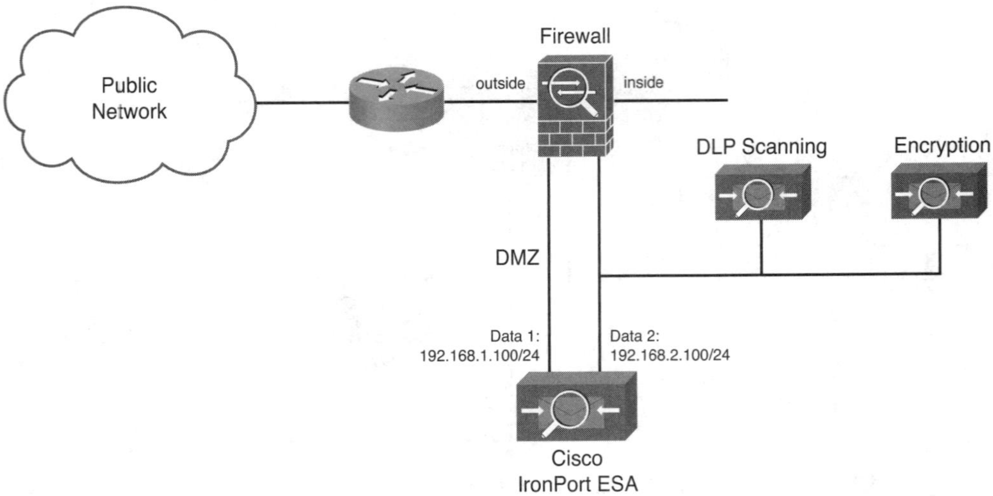

Figure 12-2 *ESA with Private Subnet for Encryption or DLP Servers*

Generally, if your network design calls for servers to have both DMZ and internal interfaces, the ESA can be configured to match. The goal for the ESA is flexibility to match any customer's preferred deployment method.

Virtual Gateways

Virtual gateways refer to the ability of the ESA to have more than one IP address and hostname combination per appliance—virtual gateways bear no relationship to virtual machines or virtualization technology; the term is simply another way of indicating multiple interfaces on the same port, which can be used as additional delivery interfaces. In addition to multihoming, which is having IP addresses on multiple networks, the ESA can also have multiple IPs on the same network, giving the appearance of multiple separate machines. These interfaces work the same as any other and can be used for accepting messages (with a listener configured on them) or for delivering messages.

Support for virtual gateways is limited by platform. Table 12-2 lists the number of supported IP interfaces per appliance.

Table 12-2 *Supported IP Interfaces per Appliance*

Platform	Maximum Number of IP Interfaces
C160, C170	4
C360, C370, C660, C670, X1060, X1070	32
C360D, C370D	254

Why would you use virtual gateways in production? The reasons generally boil down to segmentation of email traffic, whether incoming, outgoing, or both. Some examples of virtual gateway use include delivery, for sending out different kinds of traffic over different IP interfaces, or for receiving SMTP traffic on different IPs. We examine these uses later in this chapter, after I demonstrate how to add IP interfaces and named interface groups.

Adding New Interfaces and Groups

You can add new IP interfaces and hostnames to the ESA through the WUI page at Network à Interfaces or in the CLI using **interfaceconfig.** Every interface has a friendly name that's used to identify it. This can be anything—a description of its usage, like "private" or "management," the switch port number it's connected to, almost anything. You can even make the name the same as the IP address and hostname. The friendly name of an interface is used in a few areas: In Listener setup, it's used to associate the listener and port with an IP. You also see this name in the logs when connections go to and from the interface.

Groups of interfaces are just that—a friendly name for a set of IP interfaces. Groups of interfaces are only used for selecting delivery source for outbound SMTP connections. Instead of selecting a particular delivery interface to use as source IP for new connections, you select a group by name. The ESA then initiates new outbound SMTP connections from the IPs in the group using round-robin rotation.

You can only create groups in the CLI, and you can only use them in the CLI **altsrchost** table once created. Example 12-1 shows how to add interface groups using **interfaceconfig.**

Example 12-1 *Creating Interface Groups*

```
esa02.cisco.com> interfaceconfig



Currently configured interfaces:
1. DMZ (192.168.1.110/24 on Data 1: esa02.cisco.com)
2. DMZ2 (192.168.1.111/24 on Data 1: esa03.cisco.com)
3. DMZ3 (192.168.1.112/24 on Data 1: esa04.cisco.com)

Choose the operation you want to perform:
- NEW - Create a new interface.
- EDIT - Modify an interface.
- GROUPS - Define interface groups.
- DELETE - Remove an interface.
[]> groups



Currently configured IP groups:
No groups defined.
```

```
Choose the operation you want to perform:
- NEW - Create a new group.
[]> new

Enter the name for this group.
[]> Delivery

Enter the name or number of the interfaces to be included in this group.
Separate your choices with commas or specify a range with a dash.
1. DMZ (192.168.1.110/24: esa02.cisco.com)
2. DMZ2 (192.168.1.111/24: esa03.cisco.com)
3. DMZ3 (192.168.1.112/24: esa04.cisco.com)
[1]> 2-3

Group Delivery created.

Currently configured IP groups:
1. Delivery (DMZ3, DMZ2)

Choose the operation you want to perform:
- NEW - Create a new group.
- EDIT - Modify a group.
- DELETE - Remove a group.
[]>
```

As a result, the interface group I created here, Delivery, is now available to use for creating listeners or selecting delivery interfaces.

Using Virtual Gateways for Email Delivery

The primary use of virtual gateways is to segment the delivery of SMTP traffic, which means that you deliver different types of email messages using different VGs. Before I describe how to do this, I answer the "why" of traffic segmentation. Why bother using multiple IP addresses and hostnames to deliver email messages to the Internet?

The answer to this lies in the way that other organizations perceive you and your email traffic. Some sites may treat your email traffic as junk. Given the security and authentication problems with SMTP, and the overwhelming volumes of unwanted email traffic, it's no wonder that many sites take a policy of "shoot first, ask questions later." This means that traffic that might be fraudulent or illegal advertising will be rejected. Your traffic, as legitimate as it might be, can be lumped into the "junk" classification. The reaction that each organization will have varies, making it frustrating to troubleshoot each individual situation. Normally, the concern is that your delivery IPs will be listed with a public DNSBL or reputation service as being a spam source or that your SMTP connections will be rejected by major ISPs. Such an event can disrupt business.

Should everyone consider segmenting traffic across multiple IPs? Not necessarily. Your environment is a good candidate for segmenting if you have one or more of the following situations:

- Your organization sends out automated messaging of some type: statements, confirmations, or alerts, for example. You should segment this traffic from your person-to-person email.
- Your organization has some kind of opt-in advertising messaging. Bulk, automated messages, even when legitimately requested by subscribers, are often not well received. Service providers typically act on customer complaints by rejecting your connections.
- You have different classes of users within your organization. For example, in education, you have students, faculty, and staff. You might have contractors or temporary employees whose messaging should be handled separately.
- Your organization emails on behalf of other organizations, whether internal or external.

The point of segmenting traffic is to ensure that if advertising or other automated emails trigger anti-spam rules or public blacklisting, and the sending IP gets a poor reputation, your other mail delivery interfaces will not be affected by that poor score. If you separate your corporate user traffic from marketing messages using virtual gateways, delivery problems with marketing messages won't affect delivery of your user email.

We discuss segmenting further in Chapter 14, "Recommended Configuration."

Aside from these reasons, you might be interested in creating virtual gateways just in case of an emergency. I'm not suggesting you should actively seek to avoid other organization's junk filtering without addressing the root cause, which won't work anyway. I suggest that in cases where business-critical email is not being delivered because of a blacklisting, having another IP ready for failover can give you the breathing room to address the root cause.

Using virtual gateways is simple. Once an interface or interface group is added to an ESA and the change committed, you simply have to decide when to use them. The ESA must have a rule to determine which messages are delivered from which interface. Messages that do not match any rule are delivered from the default delivery interface. There are three places such a policy can be invoked: using the content filter action "Deliver from IP Interface," the message filter action alt-src-host, or the CLI table available through the **altsrchost** command. The **altsrchost** table is simple, as there are only two criteria for selecting messages: the envelope sender address or the source IP injecting the message into the ESA. In other words, you can use the IP address that sent the message originally to decide which ESA interface will deliver it. Example 12-2 shows a session from the

CLI, where I'm choosing the delivery interface for all the messages originating from a single source IP. I choose to use an interface group called Delivery, which includes two IP interfaces: DMZ2 and DMZ3.

Example 12-2 *Using* altsrchost *to Select Delivery Interfaces*

```
esa02.cisco.com> altsrchost


Choose the operation you want to perform:
- NEW - Create a new mapping.
- IMPORT - Load new mappings from a file.
[]> new

Enter the Envelope From address or client IP address for which you want to set up a
  Virtual Gateway(tm) mapping. Partial addresses such as
"@example.com", "@.com", "user@", or "user@.com" are allowed.
[]> 10.1.17.22

Which interface do you want to send messages for 10.1.17.22 from?
1. DMZ (192.168.1.110/24: esa02.cisco.com)
2. DMZ2 (192.168.1.111/24: esa03.cisco.com)
3. DMZ3 (192.168.1.112/24: esa04.cisco.com)
IP Groups:
4. Delivery (DMZ3, DMZ2)
[1]> 4

Mapping for 10.1.17.22 on interface Delivery created.

Choose the operation you want to perform:
- NEW - Create a new mapping.
- EDIT - Modify a mapping.
- DELETE - Remove a mapping.
- IMPORT - Load new mappings from a file.
- EXPORT - Export all mappings to a file.
- PRINT - Display all mappings.
- CLEAR - Remove all mappings.
[]>
```

If you need to segment traffic by other means, you must use a filter. Figure 12-3 shows an example of an outgoing content filter that delivers using the interface DMZ2 when messages are larger than 1 MB.

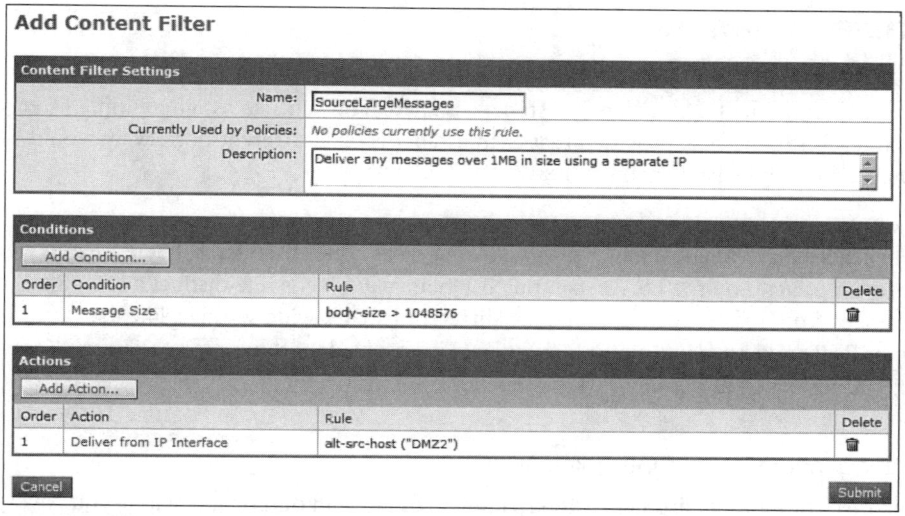

Figure 12-3 *Outgoing Content Filter Showing Source Interface Selection*

Other common selection criteria include recipient email address domain, LDAP group of the sender, or values in headers that indicate the source or use of messages.

Virtual Gateways and Listeners

The name "virtual gateways" implies that a whole new ESA pipeline is created, from listening to delivery. This is not the case. Virtual gateways are additional IPs intended for SMTP delivery, and listeners don't have anything to do with delivery. By default, new interfaces do not automatically have listeners created and assigned to them. Email that is accepted only on a single listener can be separated and delivered across an arbitrary number of delivery interfaces.

This does not mean that you cannot create listeners on newly created interfaces. You can, and there are some good reasons to do so. However, adding additional interfaces, especially on public facing networks, adds complexity: As you make changes to connection controls using the HAT, you must do so for each listener. There's little reason to segment incoming Internet email across multiple listeners. For outgoing email, or internal to internal, however, multiple listeners on a single ESA can segment traffic and policy effectively. We discuss the use cases for multiple listeners later in this chapter.

Note that multiple listeners provide for separate SMTP server capabilities at the start of the pipeline, including HAT, RAT, and LDAP checks. Once the messages are accepted, however, the ESA has only a single work queue and all messages pass through the same security and filtering pipeline.

Multiple Listeners

Virtual gateways can be used for more than just multiple outbound delivery hosts. Every IP interface on the ESA can have a listener assigned. You can also assign multiple listeners to each IP interface, provided that each listener is on a different port. Why would you need multiple listeners on an ESA?

The answer always comes down to the general architecture goal of segmentation. Whenever you have email messages originating from multiple sources, being treated with different policies on the ESA, separating listeners may offer some distinct advantages. If messages from different sources require different listener-wide settings, like masquerading or RAT, you must use multiple listeners. Listener-wide settings are applied to all messages accepted on any listener where they are configured.

Separating Incoming and Outgoing Mail

One case for multiple listeners is to separate incoming and outgoing email. If you have an ESA with a two-network installation, with one network interface "outside" and one "inside," having two listeners may be a requirement.

Having a separate listener for outgoing mail allows you to construct a HAT that is simple and restrictive. An outgoing listener only needs one group and policy, with relay behavior. The default sender group should use the built-in BLOCKED policy. This HAT configuration is preconfigured for you when you create a new listener and choose the Private type.

Your outgoing mail listener is not restricted to a single HAT sender group. You might want to segment your internal sources into different HAT policies. For example, you could create a group and policy for Exchange servers that allow multiple simultaneous connections with no rate limiting, while grouping application servers into a policy that limits mail volume.

Multiple Outgoing Mail Listeners

Most organizations have email from different sources. Commonly, we think of email as "person to person," where a real human being is sending messages to other human beings, whether remote or local. Another common type is machine-generated messages intended for human recipients, and this is a broad category that includes order confirmations, account statements, receipts, alerts, web server notifications, advertisements, flyers, invitations, and more. Rare is a website that doesn't use email for some tasks, like enrollment confirmations, password change requests, or notifications.

These other email sources can be separated for delivery by the ESA using the virtual gateways techniques discussed earlier. You might also have a need to separate the acceptance of these messages into different listeners. There are a few good reasons to consider doing so:

- Do the different types of outgoing mail require different masquerading or domain map settings? These tables are applied to all messages on a given listener, so if you need separate settings for these, you must have different listeners.

- Are any of the outbound applications high volume, high concurrency, or aggressive in other ways? It makes sense to separate listeners to prevent any given application from crowding out other message sources. It's not just public Internet senders that can exhibit bad SMTP behavior. Many internal applications don't respond well to SMTP rate limits, rejected connections, or delays in acceptance, and a separate listener can isolate these problem servers.
- Does your network architecture mean that some application servers can't reach your existing network interfaces?
- Do application servers use a nonstandard port? An individual ESA listener is tied to a single port. If you need to accept or relay mail on other ports, you must create a separate listener.

Separate Public MX from Submission

In some environments, mainly service providers and higher education, users are provided with an SMTP outgoing server IP or host where messages can be sent directly. The user's mail clients send all messages to this IP, usually called a submission host, directly. In many cases, this submission host must be publicly available to support roaming users, and so is often provided right on the same mail servers that are the MX records for the domain, on the same port 25. SMTP AUTH is usually used, sometimes in conjunction with SSL/TLS. ESA supports this model, and can even require that hosts use TLS before being allowed to authenticate. You *must* provide some sort of authentication, either on ESA or another system, to prevent abuse of a submission service. ESA can be configured to not require authentication, so caution must be exercised.

Running submission on the same IP and port as your MX can be a security problem for a number of reasons. First, because the public MX and SMTP AUTH are combined, the HAT cannot control access and message limits separately. Second, such configurations mean that, in order to offer SMTP AUTH to anyone, you must offer it to everyone, because you won't know the source IP of roaming users. Any client connecting to the ESA will see the AUTH extension in the ESMTP extensions list. Third, the general problem with SMTP AUTH, wherever it's running, is that it only requires a username and password, and these can be brute-forced, cracked, stolen, or simply asked for. Spam senders spend a lot of time crafting messages to users seeking their credentials, and too many users happily comply with requests to "reset your account or we will be forced to suspend your email!"

By comparison, a separate submission listener can be run on the same ESA on a separate interface and port, and it has these advantages:

- **Separate HAT:** The separate HAT means completely different settings for the hosts that connect to the submission host. Your public MX listeners will have typical settings for general Internet email senders, while the submission listener will put severe limits on client volume.

- On the submission host, you have access control on a per-IP, CIDR range, or reputation basis. You can exclude entire countries or individual hosts that appear to be a source of exploit attempts.
- You can separately enforce the use of TLS, and specific ciphers, for all clients.
- You can aggressively rate limit all connecting hosts. For example, the submission policy can limit senders to a single simultaneous connection, one message per connection, and a limited number of recipients per hour. A limit of 100 or 250 recipients per hour, per connecting IP, shouldn't bother legitimate users but will foil any attempts to use the service for high-volume spam.

- **Control AUTH:** SMTP authentication, which grants authorized users relay privilege, can be more selectively offered. Connecting clients will not see the AUTH extension on the public MX ESAs.
- **Use a non-standard port:** Although security by obscurity is not something you can rely on to deter attacks, offering a separate submission port can be part of the security strategy. Port 587 is the customary port for email submission, but any port can be used as long as the mail clients are configurable.

If you currently have a combined MX and submission host, and have run into problems with exploited accounts, you can move to a separated architecture. At the very least, separating submission from MX listeners allows you to isolate any problems with exploited clients.

ESA and Virtual LANs

Virtual local-area networks (VLAN) can be used to connect an ESA to more networks than the physical interfaces and routing limits normally allow. When you create a VLAN interface using the **etherconfig** command, you can also have a real IP address on the physical port so that it can handle both VLAN and non-VLAN traffic.

For a server role, like ESA, the chief value of VLAN support is segmentation and security. It's also provided for compatibility with networks that use VLANs.

VLANs are easy to create and must be done in the CLI using the **etherconfig** command. Example 12-3 shows the process of creating the VLAN.

Example 12-3 *Adding a VLAN Using* **etherconfig**

```
esa02.cisco.com> etherconfig



Choose th operation you want to perform:
- MEDIA - View and edit ethernet media settings.
- VLAN - View and configure VLANs.
- LOOPBACK - View and configure Loopback.
```

```
- MTU - View and configure MTU.
[]> vlan

VLAN interfaces:

Choose the operation you want to perform:
- NEW - Create a new VLAN.
[]> new

VLAN tag ID for the interface (Ex: "34"):
[]> 2

Enter the name or number of the ethernet interface you wish bind to:
1. Data 1
2. Data 2
[1]> 1

VLAN interfaces:
1. VLAN    2 (Data 1)

Choose the operation you want to perform:
- NEW - Create a new VLAN.
- EDIT - Edit a VLAN.
- DELETE - Delete a VLAN.
[]>
```

Once the VLAN is created, you can assign IP interfaces to it as you would with any physical interface, as shown in Example 12-4.

Example 12-4 *Assigning an IP Interface to a VLAN*

```
esa02.cisco.com> interfaceconfig

Currently configured interfaces:
1. DMZ (192.168.1.110/24 on Data 1: esa02.cisco.com)

Choose the operation you want to perform:
- NEW - Create a new interface.
- EDIT - Modify an interface.
- GROUPS - Define interface groups.
- DELETE - Remove an interface.
[]> new
```

```
Please enter a name for this IP interface (Ex: "InternalNet"):
[]> ManagementVLAN

IP Address (Ex: 192.168.1.2):
[]> 192.168.3.110

Ethernet interface:
1. Data 1
2. Data 2
3. VLAN    2
[1]> 3

Netmask (Ex: "255.255.255.0" or "0xffffff00"):
[255.255.255.0]>

Hostname:
[]> mgmt02.cisco.com
```

Using VLANs on ESA is not especially common. It's not a feature that I can point to for solving any particular problem. It falls into the category of "there if you need it," and that you will likely know if your environment requires it.

Other Advanced Configurations

ESA offers a lot of features for network compatibility, but at the root, it is a UNIX-like network server. It is not a router, gateway, or firewall, and does not have any packet-routing capabilities or support for dynamic routing protocols. The network features that are available are intended for compatibility with your environment: The product feature focus is on Layer 7, not Layers 2–6.

Static Routing

Because the ESA is not a packet router, you have to explicitly state the routing path for networks that are not immediately Layer 3-adjacent to an interface on the ESA.

If you want to use the ESA to span multiple networks by assigning IP interfaces to the different physical (or VLAN) ports, you'll find that you probably have to use static routing to define the path for packets to take to reach remote networks. The basic example is the default route: This is the destination that all packets will be sent to, if the destination of the packet is not network-adjacent to the ESA. All other routes you define must specify the destination network (using CIDR summaries) and the gateway where these packets should be sent.

Let's look at another example, with a dual-homed ESA that occupies addresses in both the demilitarized zone (DMZ) and internally. Figure 12-4 shows this configuration.

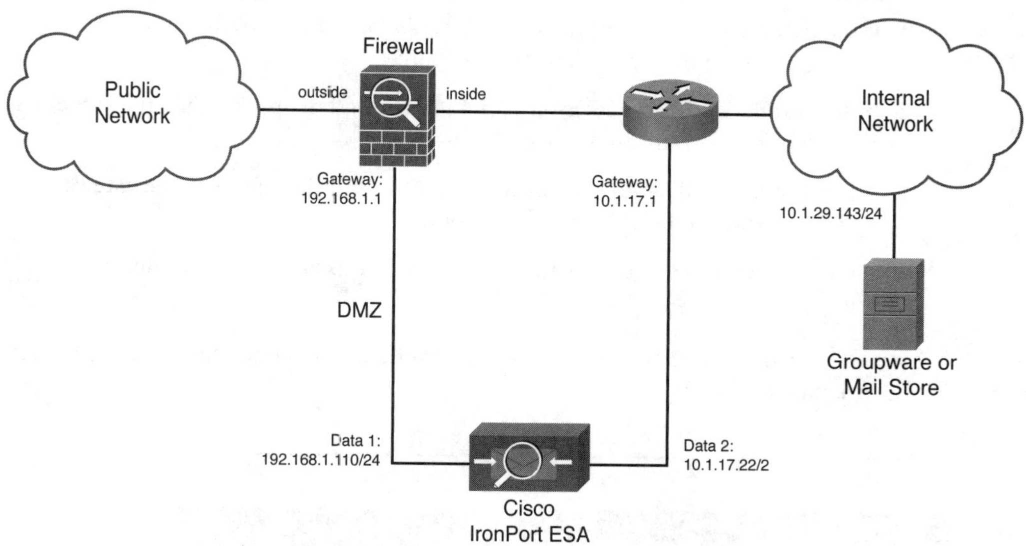

Figure 12-4 *Dual-Homed Configuration*

The default gateway for the system is the DMZ network's router address, which is, in this case, the firewall. This is the proper configuration for a dual-homed ESA: The default gateway must lead "out" to the Internet, because static routes other than the default require destination addresses, and it's not easily possible to summarize all Internet destinations.

If you simply install an ESA on two separate networks, and use a single default gateway, the ESA will not be able to communicate with some hosts in your network. Remember that the ESA has only two basic packet-routing rules (by default):

1. If the destination IP address is on the same subnet as one of the interfaces on the ESA, send the packet directly using that adjacent interface.

2. For all other destination IP addresses, send the packet to the default gateway using the interface adjacent to the default gateway.

In Figure 12-4, the ESA cannot reach or be reached by the network 10.1.29.0/24 because it does not have a route to it. Even if a server on that network sends a packet to the Data 2 interface on the ESA, the ESA sends the reply packet to the default gateway using the Data 1 IP address as the source. Even if this packet were actually routed back to the internal server, it would be discarded.

Luckily, this is easy to fix, by defining a gateway that can be used to reach the internal gateway. Any gateway listed in a static route must be directly adjacent to the ESA or reachable through another static route in the table. To reach this internal network, simply add a static route named Internal with a destination of 10.1.29.0/24 and a gateway of 10.1.17.1. Now, the routing rules for this ESA follow these steps:

1. If the destination IP address is on 192.168.1.0/24, send the packet directly to the destination using the Data 1 interface as source.
2. If the destination IP address is on 10.1.17.0/24, send the packet directly to the destination using the Data 2 interface as source.
3. If the destination IP address is on 10.1.29.0/24, send the packet to the gateway 10.1.17.1 using the Data 2 interface as source.
4. Send all other packets to the gateway 192.168.1.1 using the Data 1 interface as source.

Figure 12-5 shows the static routes for such a configuration in the Routing table in the Network menu of the WUI.

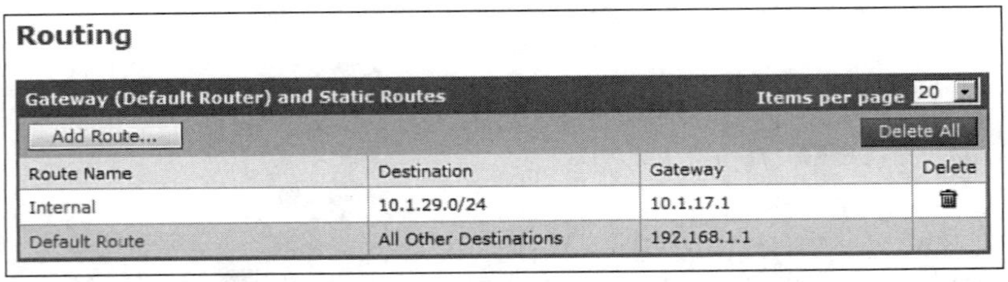

Figure 12-5 *Static Routes for a Dual-Homed ESA That Must Reach an Internal Network*

You can also define static routes in the CLI using the command **routeconfig**, but you can only modify the default gateway using the command **setgateway**.

If there is more than one internal network range, you either have to define the networks and their gateways individually, or by summarizing the internal networks. Many organizations use the RFC 1918 address space for internal networks, and provide a single internal gateway. If that's the case in your network, you can use a static route for destinations, such as 10.0.0.0/8.

Transport Layer Security

SMTP is originally by definition a clear-text transport. From originating mail user agent (MUA) to destination MUA, with all Message Transfer Agent (MTA) hops in between, all SMTP commands and all message data is transmitted in the clear. More recently, RFC 3207 defines support in ESMTP for encrypting the SMTP conversation and all data between client and server using the ESMTP STARTTLS extension command. Transport Layer Security (TLS) is the protocol used for encryption. TLS is more commonly known as Secure Sockets Layer (SSL) and, in fact, TLS 1.0 and SSL 3.1 are identical except for the name. Going forward, new versions of the protocol will use the acronym TLS.

For SMTP, TLS is a point-to-point protocol that establishes an encryption session between two servers, regardless of the number of Layer 3 hops in between. The STARTTLS command begins the process of negotiation, where the client and server must agree on cipher, key length, and padding.

To use TLS, the client and server must both support ESMTP and the client must begin the conversation with EHLO. Then, the server must list STARTTLS in the ESMTP extension list:

```
220 mail.chrisporter.com ESMTP
ehlo cisco.com
250-mail.chrisporter.com
250-8BITMIME
250-SIZE 20971520
250 STARTTLS
```

If advertised, the client machine can request the negotiation by issuing the STARTTLS command. A client may issue STARTTLS even if it's not advertised, and the response from the server will indicate acceptance or not. Typically, STARTTLS is issued as the first command, before MAIL FROM, but this is not strictly required. The ESA accepts TLS negotiation at any point in the conversation.

TLS uses certificates for storing and transmitting information about the server, including identification information and the server's public key. The public key in the certificate is used to encrypt a session key, and that session key is used in a negotiated symmetric cipher for actually encrypting data. The certificate also contains identification information, which you can use for identity verification. We discuss TLS verification next.

If you've used secure websites, indicated by a URL starting with https://, you've used TLS. The web browser requests a certificate from the server, validates the data in the certificate, and uses the certificate public key to encrypt a session key. If the data in the certificate doesn't match the website, or is not issued by a trusted authority, the browser can prompt the user. The process for two SMTP servers is similar, although there's no ability to prompt the user because TLS is strictly machine-to-machine.

Using and Enforcing TLS When Delivering Email

When the ESA is the SMTP client, the Destination Controls table is used to decide if TLS should be attempted. Destination controls provides a default setting, and individual entries in the table can define the TLS policy for an individual destination domain.

Figure 12-6 shows the destination controls table with several entries. This table is used for defining destination-specific policies other than TLS, but we restrict this discussion at this point to encrypting communications.

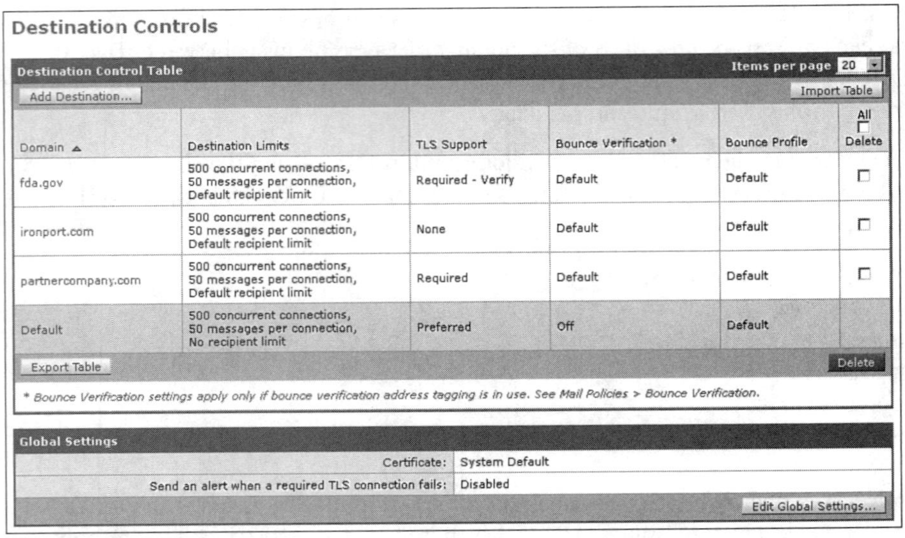

Figure 12-6 *TLS Settings in the Destination Controls Table*

There are five possible settings for TLS in each Destination Controls entry:

- **None:** TLS is not attempted even if the server advertises it. All SMTP data is transferred in the clear.
- **Preferred:** TLS will be attempted if the server advertises it. If TLS negotiation fails, or if the server does not advertise or rejects the STARTTLS command, ESA falls back to plain-text delivery of the message.
- **Required:** TLS will be attempted if the server advertises it. If TLS negotiation fails, or if the server does not advertise or rejects the STARTTLS command, the ESA does not fall back to plain-text delivery. Instead, messages to destinations marked Required will queue, retried periodically until either TLS is available or the message exceeds its maximum time in queue. You can optionally configure the ESA to alert an administrator or even the original sender if TLS cannot be negotiated to a Required domain.
- **Preferred** — Verify: Just as with Preferred, TLS will be attempted if the server advertises it, but the additional step of verifying the server's certificate will be taken. TLS will only proceed if the certificate meets the validity tests, which are described later. If the certificate fails the check, TLS is not used, and the ESA falls back to plain-text delivery of the message.
- **Required** — Verify: TLS must be used, and further, the remote server's certificate must pass the validity checks. ESA does not fall back to plain-text delivery under any circumstance.

Because TLS required does not allow for the delivery of mail in the absence of TLS support, and because many organizations and providers do not support TLS, you should almost never set the Destination Controls default to TLS Required. The only exceptions would be for ESAs that are being used purely internally with no delivery to Internet destinations.

To test TLS connectivity before setting a policy like Required or Verify, use the CLI command **tlsverify**. This command tests a TLS connection to a remote SMTP server and returns the results of a certificate validation test. You need two pieces of information: an envelope recipient domain and a remote server to test. Example 12-5 shows an example of the verification output.

Example 12-5 *Using* **tlsverify** *to Test Secure Connections*

```
esa02.cisco.com> tlsverify

Enter the TLS domain to verify against:
[]> cisco.com

Enter the destination host to connect to. Append the port (example.com:26) if you
  are not connecting on port 25:
[cisco.com]> sj-inbound-e.cisco.com

Connecting to 128.107.243.14 on port 25.
Connected to 128.107.243.14 from interface 10.60.10.10.
Checking TLS connection.
TLS connection established: protocol TLSv1, cipher RC4-SHA.
Verifying peer certificate.
Verifying certificate common name sj-inbound-e.cisco.com.
TLS certificate match sj-inbound-e.cisco.com
TLS certificate verified.
TLS connection to 128.107.243.14 succeeded.

TLS successfully connected to sj-inbound-e.cisco.com.
TLS verification completed.
Would you like to verify another domain? [Y]>
```

Further, because many SMTP servers that support TLS do not have a certificate that will pass verification, I recommend against using Preferred — Verify as a default. Enforcing certificate validity results in ESA not using TLS with most destinations.

Warning Take care with the TLS Required setting and either of the Verify options. TLS Required causes email delivery delays, at a minimum, if a server does not support TLS. You should verify TLS capabilities with the CLI command **tlsverify** before using this setting.

Many SMTP servers on the Internet support TLS, but do not have a certificate that will pass verification. If you choose the verify option, the ESA will not be able to use TLS. Again, verify TLS capabilities and certificate verification status using the **tlsverify** command before using this setting.

Using and Enforcing TLS When Receiving Email

When the ESA is the SMTP server, TLS settings are controlled in the HAT mail flow policy that is applied to the sendergroup that the connecting IP falls into. Because the mail flow policy controls almost all aspects of the ESA's responses to SMTP commands, it makes sense for TLS to be specified here.

From initial setup, most of the HAT mail flow policies inherit their TLS setting from the default mail flow policy. If you just want to support TLS for all senders, and not just specific senders, I recommend changing the default mail flow policy to Preferred.

There are three settings for TLS in each mail flow policy:

- **None:** TLS is not advertised by the ESA in the list of ESMTP extensions, and the ESA responds with *500 #5.5.1 command not recognized* to the STARTTLS command.
- **Preferred:** TLS is advertised by the ESA in the list of ESMTP extensions, but it is left to the client to decide whether to issue the STARTTLS command. Email will be accepted even if TLS is not negotiated.
- **Required:** TLS is advertised by the ESA, and enforces the use by disallowing any command other than STARTTLS. Any other command (except quit) will receive the response **530 #5.7.0 Must issue a STARTTLS command first.**

As you can see, TLS Required is somewhat dangerous: It will prevent a client from delivering email unless TLS is available. If the client is rejected because TLS is not available, the client may decide to queue and retry the message, or may treat it as a permanent failure and bounce the message. Just as with delivery, I recommend *against* setting a default TLS policy of Required, unless the ESA is being used as an internal server and not receiving email from Internet clients.

In most organizations, the policies for TLS on an Internet-facing ESA should be Preferred in the default policy settings, with Required only for a policy like TRUSTED, or better yet in a specific TLSREQUIRED sendergroup and policy. Care should be taken when adding senders to a TLSREQUIRED sendergroup, and you should be certain that the sender is already successfully using TLS in a Preferred policy before adding her to a Required policy.

Notice that the Verify options are not available in Mail Flow Policy TLS settings. This is because the TLS protocol operates chiefly with the server's certificate, and not the client. When acting as the server, it's the certificates installed on the ESA that are potentially being verified by the connecting client. Although TLS does support client certificates, they are rarely used in ESMTP STARTTLS over the public Internet. It is not possible to force ESA to verify a client certificate and it does not require a client certificate during negotiation.

Certificate Validation

When delivering messages to an SMTP server using TLS, the ESA can also optionally verify the server certificate that the ESA, as client, is being presented with by the remote server. TLS certificate verification varies among vendors, but the ESA goes through these steps, all of which must pass for the certificate to be considered verified:

- The certificate must not be expired. X509 certificates have a Validity field with start and end dates; the current date and time must fall into this range. This means that date and time for your ESA must be set accurately.
- The certificate must be signed by either (1) a certificate from a known certificate authority (CA) that the ESA has in its configuration, or (2) signed by an intermediate certificate that in turn is signed by a known root certificate. The process of verifying the signature from the certificate, to the intermediate (and potentially then to other intermediates), to the root certificate is called *chaining*. In other words, the remote certificate must either be signed by a root or be chained back to a root via intermediates.
- The identity of the remote server must match the identity stored in the certificate. There can be several different meanings of identity. At least one of these must match for the identity to be verified:
  - The hostname listed in the certificate's common name (CN) field must match the DNS hostname to which the ESA is connecting.
  - The hostname listed in the certificate's CN field must match the domain portion of the envelope recipient address on the message. For example, it's considered a match if delivering to chriport@cisco.com and the certificate CN is cisco.com.

The ESA ships with a fairly standard list of root certificates from well-known certificate authorities. Most CAs have more than one root certificate, so the list is fairly long and should cover almost every certificate you're likely to encounter on an Internet-facing MTA. The ESA allows you to manage the list of trusted root certificates, so that you can add a trusted root CA certificate, or even to remove some from the standard list. Many government organizations maintain their own root certificate authority that is not signed by any other well-known root. If you want these to pass the verification test, you need to add the root CA to your ESAs. This is easily done in the WUI Network → Certificates page.

Certificate verification also occurs when the ESA is the SMTP server, but in this case, it's the remote client that is doing the verification. Even if remote clients aren't usually performing certificate verification, some always will. If the goal is to use TLS wherever possible, I recommend using a certificate on your ESAs that will pass the verification tests.

Managing Certificates

If you expect to do a lot of TLS communication, and most organizations do, plan to purchase and install a TLS certificate from a well-known Internet root CA. The certificate identifies your ESA and provides a public key for the client to use when exchanging encryption keys for the data to be sent. After the client issues the STARTTLS ESMTP command, the certificate is the first information the client requests.

The process of obtaining a certificate varies with the CA you choose. Most root CAs have a website that allows you to manage and request your certificates. Some CAs require a Certificate Signing Request (CSR) that you can generate directly on the ESA with a new feature that's part of AsyncOS 7.1.

The certificate you buy should pass all the verification steps listed in the previous section. Having a valid, unexpired cert from a well-known root authority is the easy part. It can be a little more confusing to decide what, exactly, should go into the certificate's CN field. In general, you should have the external hostname of your ESAs in the CN field. This is the hostname that external SMTP clients see in your MX records. For example, if your MX records are

```
yourdomain.org.          IN       MX       10 smtp1.yourdomain.org.
yourdomain.org.          IN       MX       20 smtp2.yourdomain.org.
```

You should buy certificates with CNs of smtp1.yourdomain.org and smtp2.yourdomain.org and apply them to the respective ESAs. Simple, right?

It's not always so straightforward. There are a few other possible scenarios, depending on your deployment. For load-balanced ESAs behind a single MX, you might have this in DNS:

```
yourdomain.org.          IN       MX       10 smtp.yourdomain.org.
```

But, that hostname resolves to a VIP on a load balancer, and you have more than one ESA behind that VIP. Again, the CN in the cert should have the external hostname, which in this case, is smtp.yourdomain.org. All the ESAs behind this VIP should have the same hostname, or even the same certificate, regardless of their actual internal hostnames.

Because certificates have such reliance on hostnames, it's worth going over some of the requirements. In addition to the verification steps just described, some SMTP clients go even further in their verification, requiring that the SMTP greeting supplied by the server include a hostname that matches the certificate CN. In other words, SMTP clients want to see this when they connect:

```
220 smtp.yourdomain.org ESMTP
```

The ESA displays in this banner the hostname assigned to the IP interface that is accepting the connection. This hostname should match the external hostname that Internet clients will see. For load-balanced ESAs, this means that the external-facing IP interface should all have the exact same hostname. To keep all the ESAs separate internally, set a different global hostname for each ESA using **sethostname**. You can also override the hostname banner with a custom value using the HAT.

If your ESAs have internal (RFC 1918) addresses and are being NATted to Internet-routable addresses, you may have different internal hostnames for your ESAs. Remember that verification is being done on the hostnames that the external Internet SMTP clients see, and your IP interfaces should match that external hostname.

Another certificate option is *wildcard certificates* that some CAs offer. These are issued and function like any other certificate, but they are valid for more than one hostname. They are generally valid for an unlimited number of hosts or subdomains of your parent domain. For example, the wildcard certificate ***.yourdomain.org** can be used for hosts named smtp1.yourdomain.org, smtp2.yourdomain.org, and smtp3.yourdomain.org. Wildcard certificates tend to be more expensive than single-host certificates and can only wildcard a single level of subdomain. For example, the wildcard certificate ***.mx.yourdomain.org** will not match smtp1.yourdomain.org.

Adding Certificates to the ESA

When you receive certificates that you purchased from a CA, or you generate a self-signed certificate, there are two ways to add it to the ESA configuration. The easiest is through the WUI, in the Certificates page in the Network tab. This is straightforward and requires that you have the certificates available in a local file, in Public Key Cryptography Standard 12 (PKCS12) format, which is the most common format used for distributing certificates. The PKCS12 file has both an X.509 certificate, including the public key, and the corresponding private key, all protected with a password. That single file contains everything you need for importing a certificate on the ESA.

Adding certificates via the CLI is less straightforward and requires a different format. The CLI command **certconfig** is used to create new certificates and manage existing ones. The CLI commands expect the private key, certificate, and any intermediate certificates, each pasted separately in Privacy Enhanced Mail (PEM) format. PEM format represents its data encoded with Base64 to US-ASCII format, much like MIME Base64 encoding.

PEM format certificates are easily recognized because the encoded data is bracketed with these header and footer lines:

```
-----BEGIN CERTIFICATE-----
-----END CERTIFICATE-----
```

PEM format private keys are similar, but bracket the data with these header and footer lines:

```
-----BEGIN RSA PRIVATE KEY-----
-----END RSA PRIVATE KEY-----
```

If you have the certificate and private key in PEM format files, open them in a text editor so that you can copy and paste the data, including the header and footer. Example 12-6 shows the import process that pastes the certificates into the CLI session. I excised some of the actual certificate data for brevity.

Example 12-6 *Using* certconfig *to Import a New TLS Certificate and Private Key*

```
esa02.cisco.com> certconfig



Choose the operation you want to perform:
- CERTIFICATE - Import, Create a request, Edit or Remove Certificate Profiles
- CERTAUTHORITY - Manage System and Customized Authorities
[]> certificate

List of Certificates
Name       Common Name          Issued By            Status        Remaining
---------  -------------------  -------------------  ------------  ---------
Demo       Cisco Appliance Demo Cisco Appliance Demo Active        2797 days

Choose the operation you want to perform:
- IMPORT - Import a certificate from a local PKCS#12 file
- PASTE - Paste a certificate into the CLI
- NEW - Create a self-signed certificate and CSR
- EDIT - Update certificate or view the signing request
- EXPORT - Export a certificate
- DELETE - Remove a certificate
- PRINT - View certificates assigned to services
[]> paste

Enter a name for this certificate profile:
> example

Paste public certificate in PEM format (end with '.'):
-----BEGIN CERTIFICATE-----
MIIDpjCCAo4CCQDdRnDQojP+4DANBgkqhkiG9w0BAQUFADCBlDELMAkGA1UEBhMC
…
sDkZLS756XTpMTPSjB6TZBpLV/NcDERKuXc=
-----END CERTIFICATE-----
```

```
.
C=US,ST=New York,L=New York,O=example.com,CN=mail.example.com,emailAddress=chris@
  example.com

Paste private key in PEM format (end with '.'):
-----BEGIN RSA PRIVATE KEY-----
MIIEpAIBAAKCAQEAqkzgVHRXDknOAePMZICDIQnlQQtd/GHHdTi3lGZQboF/jwOL
…
dqQgnxXod7+X9frXk9RE94pvKen2cfl3QWN5V6Sks03Bis7n02x/Ag==
-----END RSA PRIVATE KEY-----
.

Do you want to add an intermediate certificate? [N]>


List of Certificates
Name       Common Name           Issued By             Status        Remaining
---------  -------------------   -------------------   ------------  ---------
example    mail.chrisporter.com  mail.chrisporter.com  Valid         3270 days
Demo       Cisco Appliance Demo  Cisco Appliance Demo  Active        2797 days
```

If you have certificates in a format other than PKCS12 or PEM, you cannot natively import them into the ESA. The good news is that certificate files are fairly easy to convert from one format to another using the openssl utility for UNIX or Windows, which is available from www.openssl.org if you don't have it already. Most UNIX and similar systems, like MacOS, include the openssl library and utilities. The openssl utility is not available on the ESA, so the following examples must be run on another system.

For example, if you have certificates and keys in the Distinguished Encoding Rules (DER) binary format, you can convert them to PEM with this command:

```
openssl x509 -outform pem -inform der -in cert.der -out cert.perm
```

You can also convert PEM and DER formats to a single PKCS12 package, assuming you have both the certificate and the private key in separate files:

```
openssl pkcs12 -export -out cert.p12 -inkey private.key –in cert.pem
```

The openssl utility has many other certificate features like creating self-signed certificates, viewing certificate details, and converting other formats. These capabilities are beyond the scope of this book, but are useful to know for anyone working with TLS.

TLS Cipher and Security Options

The TLS negotiation process involves selecting a symmetric cipher and key length that will be used to actually encrypt the data being transmitted. Typically, the server lists the available supported ciphers, and the client picks the first in the list that it supports. If the client and server do not share a supported cipher in common, the TLS negotiation fails, and message delivery may be delayed, or may drop to plain-text SMTP delivery.

Because shorter cipher key lengths are higher performance, the ESA defaults to listing ciphers in strength order, starting with the shorter (weakest) ciphers first. This provides good security at fair performance, but you may be interested in higher security

Modifying the TLS and SSL parameters, including ciphers, is only done in the CLI using the **sslconfig** command. The initial menu for **sslconfig**, shown in Example 12-7, shows you the current settings and provides options to modify those settings for each area where TLS is used.

Example 12-7 *Cipher Settings Listed in* **sslconfig**

```
esa02.cisco.com> sslconfig

sslconfig settings:
  GUI HTTPS method:  sslv3tlsv1
  GUI HTTPS ciphers: RC4-SHA:RC4-MD5:ALL
  Inbound SMTP method:  sslv3tlsv1
  Inbound SMTP ciphers: RC4-SHA:RC4-MD5:ALL
  Outbound SMTP method:  sslv3tlsv1
  Outbound SMTP ciphers: RC4-SHA:RC4-MD5:ALL

Choose the operation you want to perform:
- GUI - Edit GUI HTTPS ssl settings.
- INBOUND - Edit Inbound SMTP ssl settings.
- OUTBOUND - Edit Outbound SMTP ssl settings.
- VERIFY - Verify and show ssl cipher list.
[]>
```

The VERIFY submenu shows you all the available SSL ciphers currently available on the ESA. All the other configuration menu items are the same. Example 12-8 shows a modification to the INBOUND settings and ciphers.

Example 12-8 *Modifying Ciphers with* sslconfig

```
esa02.cisco.com> sslconfig

sslconfig settings:
  GUI HTTPS method:  sslv3tlsv1
  GUI HTTPS ciphers: RC4-SHA:RC4-MD5:ALL
  Inbound SMTP method:  sslv3tlsv1
  Inbound SMTP ciphers: RC4-SHA:RC4-MD5:ALL
  Outbound SMTP method:  sslv3tlsv1
  Outbound SMTP ciphers: RC4-SHA:RC4-MD5:ALL

Choose the operation you want to perform:
- GUI - Edit GUI HTTPS ssl settings.
- INBOUND - Edit Inbound SMTP ssl settings.
- OUTBOUND - Edit Outbound SMTP ssl settings.
- VERIFY - Verify and show ssl cipher list.
[]> inbound

Enter the inbound SMTP ssl method you want to use.
1. SSL v2.
2. SSL v3
3. TLS v1
4. SSL v2 and v3
5. SSL v3 and TLS v1
6. SSL v2, v3 and TLS v1
[5]> 3

Enter the inbound SMTP ssl cipher you want to use.
[RC4-SHA:RC4-MD5:ALL]> MEDIUM:HIGH:-aNULL:@STRENGTH
i
sslconfig settings:
  GUI HTTPS method:  sslv3tlsv1
  GUI HTTPS ciphers: RC4-SHA:RC4-MD5:ALL
  Inbound SMTP method:  tlsv1
  Inbound SMTP ciphers: MEDIUM:HIGH:-aNULL:@STRENGTH
  Outbound SMTP method:  sslv3tlsv1
  Outbound SMTP ciphers: RC4-SHA:RC4-MD5:ALL

Choose the operation you want to perform:
- GUI - Edit GUI HTTPS ssl settings.
- INBOUND - Edit Inbound SMTP ssl settings.
- OUTBOUND - Edit Outbound SMTP ssl settings.
- VERIFY - Verify and show ssl cipher list.
[]>
```

The first question that it asks is which protocol versions to allow. Despite the name change, SSL and TLS are similar; you can think of TLS v1.0 as SSL v3.1. Because of known weaknesses, the software no longer supports SSLv1, and it's strongly recommended that you do not use SSLv2. It's still available in the ESA as of this writing, but it's strictly for compatibility reasons. The default is to support SSLv3 and TLSv1 only.

The next question asks you which SMTP SSL ciphers you want to support, and which order to present or select them in. The answer to the SMTP SSL cipher question is a bit odd—it doesn't give you a friendly menu to choose from, but requires that you use an OpenSSL style cipher list. The format is a comma-separated list of cipher names or special keywords. Table 12-3 describes the meaning of these names.

Table 12-3 SSLconfig *Cipher List Entries*

Entry Format	Meaning
DEFAULT	The default cipher list in the suite. This varies across AsyncOS releases as the SSL and TLS standards change.
ALL	All ciphers available in the suite.
RC4-SHA or other cipher name	Refers to a specific cipher in the suite.
RC4, AES, RSA, or other partial cipher name	Refers to all ciphers in the suite that use the specific algorithm. For example, AES refers to any cipher of any length that uses the AES algorithm.
- (dash) preceding an entry	Exclude this cipher or suite; the dash preceding an entry removes that cipher or group from the list.
LOW	A list of all the low-strength ciphers, usually 56- and 64-bit encryption algorithms.
MEDIUM	A list of medium-strength ciphers, typically 128-bit key lengths.
HIGH	A list of the highest-strength ciphers, typically with key lengths higher than 128 bit.
SSLv2	All the ciphers that are part of the SSLv2 specification.
SSLv3	All the ciphers that are part of the SSLv3 specification.
aNULL	A list of ciphers that offer no authentication, sometimes referred to as anonymous ciphers. Because these are vulnerable to attack, they are typically disabled. This can be done by including the entry aNULL in your cipher list.
@STRENGTH	Sorts the list of ciphers, from longest to shortest cipher key length. In general, longer key lengths are more secure, but require more overhead.

In the previous example, I configured the TLS settings to include both the medium- and high-strength ciphers. I disabled the use of NULL ciphers. Finally, the @STRENGTH keyword sorts the list by key length, starting with the strongest ciphers. In essence, this setting can be described as "Exclude the low-strength and anonymous ciphers, and prefer the ciphers with the longest key lengths."

Table 12-4 shows some other common options.

Table 12-4 *Common Cipher Lists for* **sslconfig**

Cipher List	Meaning
MEDIUM:HIGH:-aNULL	Only allow the medium- and high-strength ciphers, and disable null ciphers.
ALL:@STRENGTH	Allow all ciphers, but order them by key length.
MEDIUM:HIGH:-SSLv2:-aNULL	Allow the medium- and high-strength ciphers, but disable the null ciphers and any ciphers that are defined in the SSLv2 specification.

Split DNS

Like any SMTP MTA, the ESAs heavily depend on functioning DNS to perform lookups prior to delivering messages. DNS is also the transport for SenderBase Reputation Scores (SBRS), DNSBL entries, forward (A) and reverse (PTR) lookups, and any domain or host-level matching in HAT sender groups. As a result, an ESA can make as many as seven DNS queries for every inbound connection. More DNS queries are made for delivery, log transfers, and administrative logins. In short, the ESA makes a lot of DNS requests, and its performance and many of its security capabilities depend on DNS servers that can properly handle the volume.

The most common DNS configuration is for ESA to use one or more local caching DNS servers that can answer A, MX, PTR, and TXT queries. These DNS servers can be part of your organization's environment, or provided by your Internet service provider (ISP), but they should be on a "nearby" network via a low-latency path. In large environments, there would ideally be dedicated DNS servers that can handle thousands of queries per second.

If you don't have such dedicated DNS servers, or you'd prefer not to handle it internally, there's another option. The ESAs have a DNS setting for "Internet Root Servers," configurable through the CLI with the **dnsconfig** command or in the WUI under Network → DNS. Here's what the configuration looks like in the CLI:

```
esa02.cisco.com> dnsconfig
Currently using the Internet root DNS servers.
No alternate authoritative servers configured.
Choose the operation you want to perform:
- NEW - Add a new server.
- SETUP - Configure general settings.
[]>
```

The WUI DNS page is shown in Figure 12-7.

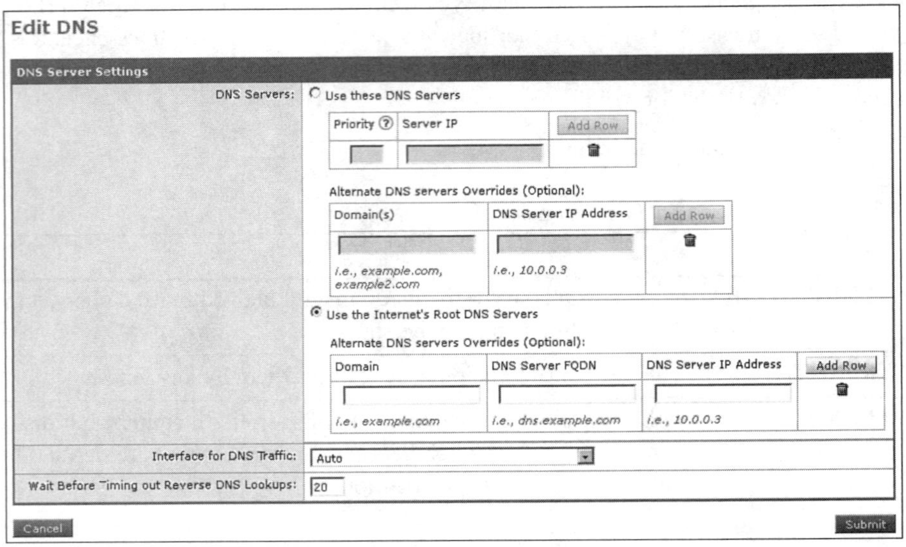

Figure 12-7 *ESA DNS Settings Using the Internet's Root DNS Servers*

In this mode, the ESA acts as its own DNS server. It uses the list of well-known root servers (named a.root-servers.net through m.root-servers.net) to look up name servers for top-level domains, like .com and .net, and then recursively to name servers for each individual domain and subdomain. The ESA can resolve any host or domain that has public name servers available. It caches the results according to the TTLs on the DNS query responses.

The advantage of this configuration is that you no longer have the load of DNS queries falling on your local servers; instead, the queries are performed internally on the ESA, and the DNS resolver contacts the appropriate name servers across the Internet directly, using port 53 UDP and TCP connections.

Some of the disadvantages of this approach are

- Each ESA must act as its own resolver and do not share query results. The ESA cannot act as a DNS server for any other clients. This means that each ESA will make thousands of queries to Internet destinations for name resolution, depending on your connection volume.
- You must open port 53 from the ESAs to all Internet destinations on both UDP and TCP. Name servers to be queried can be found on any Internet address range, and the DNS protocol requires both UDP and TCP connections.

- The Internet DNS name servers have no knowledge of your internal DNS servers, and hence no knowledge of internal hostnames or IP ranges. In particular, RFC 1918 ranges, like 192.168.0.0/16 and 10.0.0.0/8, are not resolvable through public Internet name servers.

We can resolve the last of these by using a split DNS configuration on the ESA. Split DNS tells the ESAs to use the Internet root servers for general DNS lookups, but to use an alternate DNS server for your local domain or domains. Such a configuration is shown in Figure 12-8.

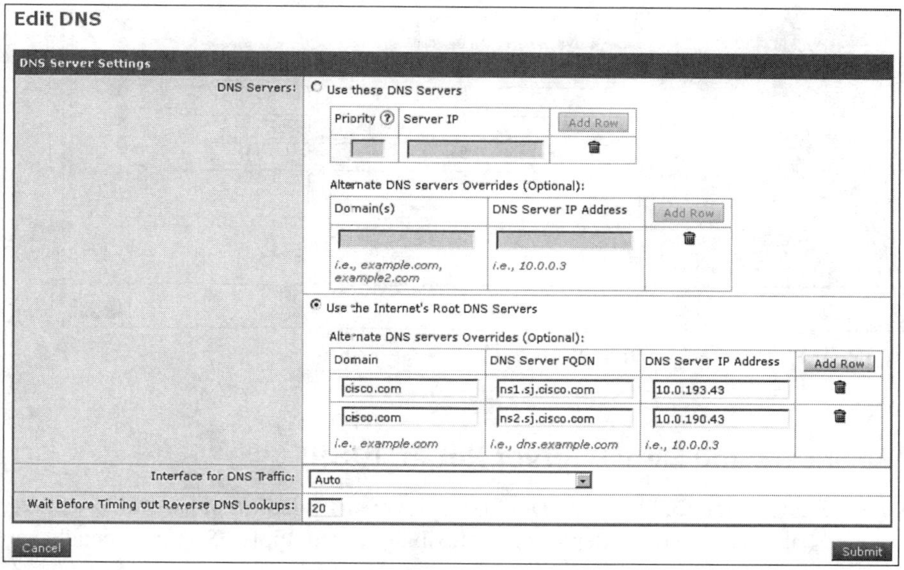

Figure 12-8 *Split DNS Configuration*

In that environment, lookups for hosts like mail.ironport.com, smtp1.fda.gov, and gmail-smtp-in.l.google.com will all be recursively resolved by the ESA itself using the Internet's root DNS servers, but lookups for exchange.cisco.com and encryption.cisco.com would go to one of the two name servers listed for that domain.

What about private address space and PTR lookups? If you try to use the Internet's DNS hierarchy to lookup hostnames for addresses in 10.0.0.0/8 or 192.168.0.0/16, you'll get a "nonexistent hostname" response. To get the ESA to use your local DNS server for these private IP ranges, you need to be creative about your settings in DNS.

Recall that a PTR lookup performed like this:

```
nslookup 10.11.22.33
```

Is actually doing a DNS lookup on a host named 33.22.11.10.in-addr.arpa. The octets of the IP address are reversed, and the domain in-addr.arpa is added. We can exploit this by specifying an alternate DNS server for the domain 10.in-addr.arp for the 10.0.0.0/8 address space, and 168.192.in-addr.arpa for the 192.168.0.0/16 address space. Such a configuration is shown in Figure 12-9.

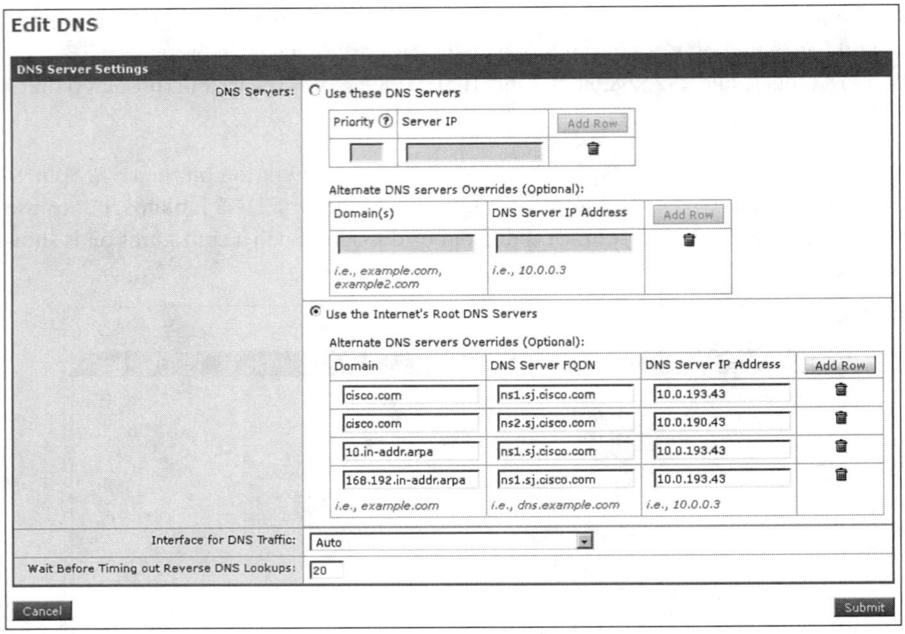

Figure 12-9 *Split DNS Configuration with Reverse Zones*

Load Balancers and Direct Server Return (DSR)

As we see in Chapter 13, "Multiple Device Deployments," dedicated hardware or software load balancers can offer deployment flexibility for multiple ESAs in an email environment.

Normally, using a load balancer requires no change to your ESA configuration, other than planning your architecture and assigning IP addresses appropriately. For load-balancer configurations that use Direct Server Return (DSR), however, the ESA requires a change to create a loopback interface.

Most load balancers support some type of DSR, where the server behind the load balancer responds directly to the client, instead of back to the load balancer. The initial TCP handshake is between the load balancer and the client, but after that traffic from the server to the client is done directly, instead of going back through the load balancer. The response traffic doesn't have to traverse the load balancer, reducing the resource pressure on the load balancer. For protocols that have heavy traffic on the server to client path, like HTTP web servers, this can be a significant advantage. With SMTP, which is conversational in model, and not request-response, it is of less advantage. If you are embarking on a new load-balanced email environment, DSR is not worth the effort for SMTP.

If you already have a DSR environment, you need to configure the ESAs with a loopback address for the direct return to work. This is only available in the CLI with the command **etherconfig**, as shown in Example 12-9.

Example 12-9 *Creating a Loopback Interface with* **etherconfig**

```
esa02.cisco.com> etherconfig


Choose the operation you want to perform:
- MEDIA - View and edit ethernet media settings.
- VLAN - View and configure VLANs.
- LOOPBACK - View and configure Loopback.
- MTU - View and configure MTU.
[]> loopback

Currently configured loopback interface:

Choose the operation you want to perform:
- ENABLE - Enable Loopback Interface.
[]> enable

Currently configured loopback interface:
1. Loopback

Choose the operation you want to perform:
- DISABLE - Disable Loopback Interface.
[]>
```

Once created, you can add IP interfaces to the loopback interface just as you can with the physical Ethernet ports, as shown in Example 12-10.

Example 12-10 *Assigning an IP Address to a Loopback Interface*

```
esa02.cisco.com> interfaceconfig


Currently configured interfaces:
1. DMZ (192.168.1.110/24 on Data 1: esa02.cisco.com)
2. Internal (10.1.17.22/24 on Data 2: mgmt02.cisco.com)

Choose the operation you want to perform:
- NEW - Create a new interface.
- EDIT - Modify an interface.
- GROUPS - Define interface groups.
- DELETE - Remove an interface.
[]> new
```

```
Please enter a name for this IP interface (Ex: "InternalNet"):
[]> Lo0

IP Address (Ex: 192.168.1.2):
[]> 192.168.7.110

Ethernet interface:
1. Data 1
2. Data 2
3. Loopback
[1]> 3
```

DSR works by using MAC address translation. When a new SMTP connection is made to the load balancer's public virtual IP (VIP), the load balancer modifies the destination MAC address of packets from the client to match the MAC of the ESA. It does not modify the original source IP, which is the client's, or the destination IP address, which is the load balancer VIP. Table 12-5 lists the steps in a sample DSR process.

Table 12-5 *Steps in Load Balancer Direct Server Return*

Step	Packet Flow	Source IP	Destination IP	Destination MAC
1	Client to load balancer VIP	204.15.82.70	72.163.7.166	00:0c:29:ab:4f:62 (VIP)
2	Load balancer to ESA	204.15.82.70	72.163.7.166	00:22:18:d6:0a:91 (ESA)
3	ESA to client	72.163.7.166	204.15.82.70	(MAC of default gateway)

When the packet arrives at the ESA because the MAC has been rewritten, the ESA ignores it unless the destination IP matches a local interface. In other words, the ESA is not a promiscuous listener. To get around this, you must assign the load balancer's VIP to the ESA, but having two servers with the same IP would result in Address Resolution Protocol (ARP) errors as two machines with different MACs respond to the same IP. The loopback interface doesn't actually operate on any of the physical Ethernet ports, and doesn't respond to ARP requests, allowing the ESA to accept the packets without conflicting with the load balancer.

Summary

This chapter looked at some of the more complex ways to configure the ESA networking for compatibility with a wide variety of environments. Because the MTA and security capabilities are almost identical regardless of network topology, you should choose a deployment mode that suits your network. In whatever deployment model you use, virtual gateways are extremely useful for segmenting delivery.

We also covered other network features like TLS and their associated certificates, and some less commonly used but important features like VLANs and loopback interfaces.

Up to this point in the book, we focused on configuring an individual ESA, but nearly every single ESA deployment will involve more than one appliance, and so we tackle deploying and managing multiple devices in the next chapter.

Chapter 13

Multiple Device Deployments

In this chapter, you will learn the following:

- Reasons for deploying multiple systems, including performance, capacity growth, redundancy, and disaster recovery
- Decide how to deploy multiple systems to get the most use out of them
- Discussion of common deployment architectures

General Deployment Guidelines

This chapter covers a wide range of deployment scenarios when you want to run more than one Email Security Appliance (ESA). Because this covers virtually all ESA deployments, multiple system deployments are the norm rather than the exception.

Architecture and deployment topics cover the entire email environment from perimeter to end user. This book focuses on the ESA, of course, but issues concerning other components will be addressed. I cover the use of ESAs in various roles and the use of third-party products for tasks like email encryption and archiving. Throughout, I also use the term *groupware* or *mailstore* to refer to servers that accept email messages, store them, and provide a means of retrieval by mail user agents (MUA). Products that fall into the definition of groupware include Microsoft Exchange, Lotus Notes, and many commercial and open source products on UNIX systems that use local mail clients, IMAP, POP, or HTTP webmail interfaces.

I recommend a few general guidelines on deployments to all organizations that use the ESA:

- The ESA should be the first SMTP "hop" in to your network for incoming mail, and the last hop for outgoing mail. Being the first incoming hop allows all the ESA connection-based security filters to effectively do their job. Being the last outgoing hop frees all of your internal email enabled hosts of the hassle of dealing with

Internet email delivery. Making the ESAs your only mail gateway provides a number of advantages:

- Single point of enforcement for all email policies. Whether enforcing rules on attachments, disclaimers, confidential information disclosure, regulatory compliance, or encryption, one set of rules across a cluster of ESAs makes rule enforcement easier.
- Consistent application of authentication standards. The emergence of Sender Policy Framework (SPF) and Domain Keys Identified Mail (DKIM) as standards for host- and message-based sender authentication means that it is more important than ever to control the use of email addresses within your domains, and the IP addresses, which are used to send messages with those domains. Sender authentication is discussed in Chapter 15, "Advanced Topics."
- A single set of ESAs makes enforcement of Transport Layer Security (TLS) encryption policies and any specialized routing for SMTP easier.

- No SMTP connections should be allowed to egress the organization firewalls other than the designated SMTP clients. If you followed recommendation 1, only the ESAs will send and receive email on port 25. Preventing all other systems from directly sending email and instead requiring them to deliver to the ESA allows for policy enforcement. More importantly, any host compromise within your network will be prevented from using SMTP to deliver spam, phishing, or viruses. This "compromise and spam" approach is a favored technique among botnet operators, and while blocking or restricting port 25 is not a solution to the initial infection problem, it avoids one of the nastiest symptoms of such infections.
- Once you restrict the privilege of using SMTP to the Internet, the systems in your network that are authorized to send Internet email through ESAs should be individually enumerated and restricted in policy terms. Groupware systems, such as Lotus Notes and Microsoft Exchange, should be granted relaying privileges through the ESA, possibly with some light restriction on connection counts. Web servers, application servers, and other automated systems should be granted relay privileges, but with severe connection and message volume limits to protect against runaway applications.
- Traffic should be segmented for delivery. When an ESA is handling multiple types of email traffic for your organization, like person-to-person mail, bulk or marketing mail, application generated, or transaction email, all these types should be delivered from separate ESAs or separate virtual gateways (VG) on a group of ESAs. Segmenting traffic is the best way to prevent all traffic from being affected if one of your sending IP addresses is listed on a public DNS blacklist (DNSBL) or is blocked by an ISP. For example, an advertisement email sent by an application server can result in the recipients complaining to their Internet service provider (ISP), who lists the sending IP address in a blocklist. If you use separate IPs for person-to-person mail, those messages continue to be delivered.

Email Availability with Multiple ESAs

If a single ESA meets an organization's capacity needs, continues to run fault-free, has uninterrupted power and network connectivity, that single appliance will provide reliable service and deliver clean email traffic. What happens if all these conditions aren't met?

When discussing an environment of multiple ESAs for the purpose of additional capacity, or reliability in the event of failure, we're really discussing architecture. Multiple ESAs can be configured to fit into a load-balanced or redundant SMTP architecture. Note that this is different than saying that the ESAs support load balancing or failover natively—they don't. Each ESA is its own distinct appliance that does have hardware and network features for redundancy, but does not provide a true means of sharing load or automatically failing over to another appliance. However, if we design an ESA deployment correctly, we can get these capabilities without too much effort or additional cost.

Load-Balancing Strategies

Virtually every email environment in the world will require multiple ESAs for capacity, reliability, or both. If message volumes received by an organization exceeds the throughput rate for a single system, multiple ESAs can be deployed to horizontally scale to the traffic needs. For example, if in your chosen configuration a C370 appliance is expected to handle 70,000 messages per hour, two appliances deployed load balanced will handle 140,000.

Load balancing means spreading the incoming and outgoing connection volume across multiple ESAs. It also implies some fault handling, because connections won't be sent to unavailable servers. The strategy you employ for load balancing ESAs will depend on the method you use and on your organization's requirements.

SMTP MX Records

The good news is that we simply don't need to have built-in load balancing and failover capabilities in the ESA; SMTP provides it natively. As we saw in Chapter 1, "Introduction to Email Security," DNS MX records have a *cost* field that indicates the priority of a given host for the recipient domain. For each recipient domain, list multiple hosts in your MX record, each with an appropriate cost, gives you either load-balanced or tiered failover.

In general, I recommend equal priorities for all ESAs in a given environment. Using equal priorities provides for both load balancing and failover. Sending hosts can connect to any of the available IPs for any of the listed hosts, although the RFCs require honoring the MX priorities and further require random selection among equal-priority hosts. By making all the ESAs equal-priority MXs, load will be evenly spread, and you'll get better use out of all the system that you have.

If an individual host has more than one IP address, RFC 5321 also requires that the sending host connect to them in the order presented by the Domain Name System (DNS) server that returned the results.

Here's an example of four equal-priority MXs for a single domain:

```
cisco.com.          86400   IN    MX    10 smtp1.cisco.com.
cisco.com.          86400   IN    MX    10 smtp2.cisco.com.
cisco.com.          86400   IN    MX    10 smtp3.cisco.com.
cisco.com.          86400   IN    MX    10 smtp4.cisco.com.
```

In this case, we would expect that all four systems listed here would see approximately equal traffic over time. This won't be strictly true, as the method of host selection varies among SMTP clients, but over a long period of time, connection and message rates will be within a few percentage points.

In the event that a host is unavailable, because the connection was refused, or timed out, or because the SMTP server responded with a "service unavailable" error code, the client then attempts a connection to another randomly selected host of equal priority. When all equal-priority hosts have been attempted unsuccessfully, the client moves on to the next priority level of listed hosts. Because of these rules, and because SMTP provides for retrying connections that have been interrupted, you can temporarily or permanently suspend a host without having to remove it from the MX record.

One exception to the SMTP priority rules comes from nonlegitimate senders, such as spam sources. Often, these clients reverse the MX priority rules and attempt higher-cost (lower-priority) MX hosts first. The strategy appears to be to try to exploit less busy or (they hope) less well-protected servers to deliver junk. As a result, whenever you run multiple hosts with unequal MX priorities, the lower-priority systems will still get a small amount of traffic, even if the primary servers are functioning normally.

Domains Without MX Records

Technically, you don't have to publish MX records for a domain. The SMTP RFCs specify that clients should use the A record for the destination domain if an MX lookup fails. For example, if cisco.com does not have any MX records, this A record would be used as the SMTP host:

```
cisco.com.          3600   IN    A     198.133.219.25
```

In practice, you can't account for the behavior of all the possible SMTP clients on the Internet, and there are certainly some that do not properly follow RFCs, and will be unable to deliver email to your domain unless it has at least one MX record. You should always publish MX records for domains you expect to receive email for. That's not to say you shouldn't also publish A records for your domain, because these records are useful for a number of other reasons.

If you own a domain that should not receive email, publish an MX record to a host that will reject that domain's recipients, with the exception of postmaster@ and possibly other important system addresses. Rejecting the domain recipients will give the sender an unambiguous status of the addresses.

Incoming and Outgoing Mail with MX Records

When discussing SMTP MX records we're usually referring to public DNS records advertised to clients on the Internet, and therefore referring to incoming email for your organization. There's no reason MX records can't be used for outgoing mail, with private DNS records that are available to internal hosts. The ESA can query these for delivery to next-hop groupware systems for incoming mail, too.

It can be somewhat difficult to set up a DNS server for this purpose. For internal hosts that need to deliver mail to the Internet, the DNS server must provide MX records for every possible destination, a "wildcard" MX, listing the hostnames of the ESAs that will perform final delivery to the Internet.

For this reason, delivery and load balancing is typically provided through the SMTP client software on the internal hosts, by explicitly listing the ESAs as the destination for all nonlocal domains. This is typically referred to as the *smarthost*. Most SMTP clients can load balance or fail over across multiple smarthost entries, eliminating the need for MX records for outgoing mail. The ESA has this capability, too, by setting the default entry in the SMTPRoutes table.

Single Location with Equal MX Priorities

If you have only a single physical location for email servers, you should run all of your available ESAs as equal-priority MX records for the domains you accept mail for. I generally recommend this equal-priority approach, with all ESAs configured identically.

Equal priority means that all the ESAs see approximately equal load and failover is handled gracefully without manual intervention. If you need to take an ESA out of service, you can do so without changing MX records; just bring down the SMTP service gracefully with the **suspend** command or using the Listeners page in the Network menu of the WUI. Because of the RFC requirements for trying other MX hosts, an unavailable server does not impact client behavior—they just try the next host.

I recommend the equal-priority approach because in primary-secondary architectures, the primary server typically sees all the mail traffic and the secondary, nearly zero. The primary ESA will happily accept overwhelming amounts of messages, possibly causing queue backups and delays, while the secondary ESA handles near-zero volume. In essence, you can have a perceived outage, with users not seeing quick response to email communication, even though, in total, the environment has available capacity. Although it's possible to configure an ESA to more quickly force traffic to other servers, you will still see your primary servers more heavily used.

Multiple Locations with Equal MX Priorities

If your organization runs mail services at more than one physical location, you have a choice to make. If the data centers (DC) are each active DCs, with groupware servers in all locations, I would continue to recommend equal priority for all inbound ESAs.

For example, suppose your organization's users are chiefly in the U.S. and serviced through data center locations in Boston, Atlanta, and Salt Lake City. Each location hosts perimeter ESAs, mailbox servers, and LDAP directories, along with the WAN links and VPN headends that connect the DCs to each other and to various branch offices. Users send and retrieve mail over the internal network through VPN or branch office connections to mailbox servers at one of the three locations depending on their typical work location. A diagram of such architecture is shown in Figure 13-1.

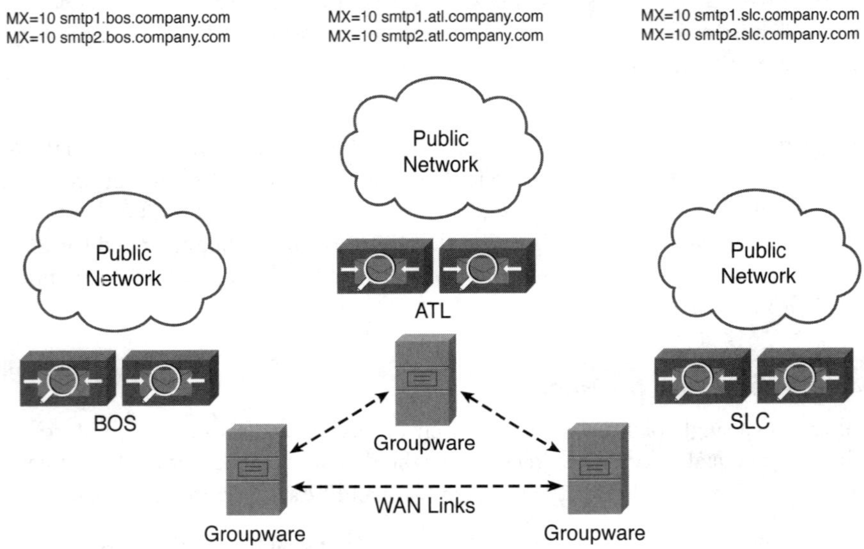

Figure 13-1 *Organization with Multiple Locations and Equal-Priority MXs*

In this case, it really doesn't matter where the messages are received; after the recipients are validated and security filtering is done, each ESA delivers to its local hub transport server, which routes the message within the Groupware environment to the right mailbox server.

Unequal MX Priorities

There are several cases where primary-secondary or primary-secondary-tertiary MX priorities make a good deal of sense. For any organization that has more than one physical data center location, with one location acting as primary and others as subordinate, it makes sense to use MX records to direct the flow to the primary location, but make the subordinate locations secondary MXs.

Another architecture that calls for unequal MX priorities is for organizations that span countries and continents. For example, suppose your organization does business in the U.S. with substantial locations in Europe and Asia. The primary email domain for all users in all counties is *domain.com*, but you also have *domain.de*, *domain.fr*, and *domain.cn*, and DC locations in the U.S., Germany, and China.

Normally, all email to domain.com goes, via primary MX records, to servers in the U.S. and into the MS Exchange environment there. All messages destined to users outside the U.S. travels either to Europe or Asia, depending on where the user's mailbox is. Email to the various country TLDs, like *domain.de*, goes directly to the Europe or Asia locations, as appropriate.

What happens if the MTAs in the U.S. location are down? By making the secondary MX records for domain.com point to Europe and Asia, messages could be accepted, and assuming WAN connectivity to the U.S. is intact, messages could still be delivered to the U.S. exchange servers. For the international domains, the secondary MXs can be set to the hosts in the U.S. In effect, the DCs in each location are a backup to each of the other locations:

```
domain.com.          86400   IN      MX      10 usa.domain.com.
domain.com.          86400   IN      MX      20 eu.domain.com.
domain.com.          86400   IN      MX      30 asia.domain.com.

domain.de.           86400   IN      MX      10 eu.domain.com.
domain.de.           86400   IN      MX      20 us.domain.com.

domain.fr.           86400   IN      MX      10 eu.domain.com.
domain.fr.           86400   IN      MX      20 usa.domain.com.

domain.cn.           86400   IN      MX      10 asia.domain.com.
domain.cn.           86400   IN      MX      20 us.domain.com.
```

The drawback of using multiple MX priorities is that none of the systems other than the primary will receive more than a trickle of mail, unless the primaries are completely unavailable. ESA settings are by default designed to handle large fluctuations in traffic, to allow for natural spikes in connection volumes. In practice, this means that the primary MX systems can be extremely busy, with queue backups, but still available for new connections, while the secondary hosts see little to no traffic. This can be a risk for your email environment: Even in cases where the primary hosts are so busy that deep backups and long delays are occurring, Internet senders will generally not use the secondary.

Disaster Recovery (DR) Sites

Organizations that operate out of one or more primary data centers, but with one or more disaster recovery (DR) sites, should consider using MX records to reflect that. If the DR sites are truly that—to be used only in case of failures at primary locations—assigning secondary MX priorities to the inbound ESAs in those locations makes sense.

Third-Party DR Services

Several companies offer services that act as a "last line of defense" for email outages, accepting and holding Internet email if all MX hosts at your organization are unavailable.

These services queue your email messages, and some even offer your users a means of accessing email while your environment is being restored. Upon restoration, the service provider will deliver the messages that were held during the outage.

Deployment of these third-party services is typically done through MX records. For example, take this list of hosts:

```
cisco.com.          86400    IN      MX      10 smtp1.cisco.com.
cisco.com.          86400    IN      MX      20 smtp2.cisco.com.
cisco.com.          86400    IN      MX      30 cisco.drservice.com.
```

In the event of a failure of both of the first two hosts at cisco.com, the tertiary MX record would see all the connections.

Be aware of a few issues that can occur when using such a third-party service, and the configuration options you have to resolve them:

- Spammers tend to target MX record hosts other than the primary, so even when your hosts are up and running, the DR service is accepting messages, probably spam, for your domain. If they don't perform any spam or virus filtering, or if their filtering is ineffective, they will redeliver spam and virus content to your hosts. Because you need to receive messages from the DR service, you must apply an appropriate HAT policy that ensures that connections are always accepted, but also runs spam and virus filtering on the messages. A further problem is that because the spam messages are delivered through a legitimate server, information about the original sender's IP is lost, reducing the effectiveness of the ESA's spam and reputation filters. The Incoming Relays feature can partially mitigate this, but it is difficult to configure in these situation because you need to know all the DR services' IPs.
- If you are also using the DR service to deliver outgoing email to Internet destinations during an outage, you must account for this in SPF records and DKIM signing. You must add the DR service's IPs to your SPF records. If they don't support DKIM, but you want to sign messages, you must do so before delivery to the DR service.
- DR services may not offer TLS connection encryption and may not follow your established TLS policies with Internet senders and recipients. TLS only encrypts connections between MTAs, so although you can enforce TLS between your servers and the DR service, that encryption won't extend to the next hop.
- DR services cannot typically offer LDAP integration for policy purposes. They may not offer DLP filtering or any other kind of content scanning, creating regulatory compliance risk during an outage.

In general, the needs for redundancy and disaster recovery often outweigh the disadvantages, but you should be aware of the risks.

Limitations of MX Records

Using MX records for failover and redundancy has its drawbacks. There are many reasons why MX records may not be adequate for your architecture:

- MX records cannot provide for fractional load splitting. Client behavior is to choose from equal-priority MX hosts at random, so if you have two at MX cost of 10, each will see half of the traffic; if you have three, each will see a third, and so on. If you want one server to get 50% of traffic and two others to get 25%, or other unequal split, MX cannot help you.
- MX records are more difficult to use for load balancing outbound mail to smart-hosts.
- MX records require individual hosts. This means that each host must have its own public IP address, DNS A and PTR records, and possibly its own TLS certificate. Adding new hosts to the MX list might require allocation of new IPs, changes to DNS, and purchasing a certificate from a root certificate authority (CA).
- Load balancing among multiple hosts with equal priority isn't perfect. Because various SMTP clients differ in how they pick among equals, load will be slightly higher on one of your hosts. Typically, the difference is not high enough to worry about, on the order of 5% more connections to one server than the others.
- MX records are not very dynamic. Like all DNS resource records, MX and A records for mail servers for a domain have a Time to Live (TTL) that varies, but is typically no shorter than 1 hour and often much longer, as much as 1 day or more. It is possible to make MX TTLs shorter, but even if you do so, many SMTP clients don't actually honor the shorter times. This TTL problem means trouble if you need to quickly add or remove systems from your environment.
- Take care not to have too many hosts in your MX records, because of a problem with DNS resolution at many sites with large MX records. DNS is a protocol that requires both UDP and TCP, but UDP is used for the vast majority of responses. When the response is larger than the maximum UDP DNS payload limit of 512 bytes, it switches to TCP. That's where the problem arises: In many environments, the use of TCP by DNS is not understood, and firewalls don't allow the port 53 TCP connection. The result is that your MX record appears to not exist, and email can't be delivered. It's not really your problem, because the issue lies with the client's DNS environment, but of course, when email can't be delivered to your servers, it's your problem.

Most email domains on the Internet today load balance through the use of MX records. With the transition to IPv6, MX records will continue to be the leading approach to load balancing and failover among email servers. If the limitations of MX records are showstoppers for your environment, consider hardware or software load balancers.

Dedicated Load Balancers

Dedicated software or hardware load balancers offer an attractive alternative to using multiple MX records. Load balancers can spread the load based on connection count, connection history, ESA system load, or other attributes rather than counting on the behavior of senders. Load balancers can also direct traffic unevenly—for example, diving the load across four ESAs in a 30/30/20/20 spread rather than the 25/25/25/25 that would result from fours hosts in an MX record. This is ideal if you have different models of ESA, or different data centers with different throughput capabilities.

Making changes to a load balanced environment is typically faster than dealing with MX records, as there is no DNS caching issues when you remove an ESA from the load balance pool.

With a load balancer, deploying ESAs is similar to a standard deployment, but the real IPs of the ESAs are not used in the MX records or smarthost settings. Instead, publish an MX record with a hostname that resolves to a virtual IP (VIP) on the load balancer:

```
cisco.com.        86400    IN      MX      10  inbound.cisco.com
```

The VIP then distributes connections to the internal real IPs of the ESAs.

Load Balancers for Inbound Mail

Load balancers for inbound mail don't give you any fundamentally new capabilities over MX record hosts, but they do give you more flexibility.

Configuring load balancing for ESA is much like configuring load balancing for any other server application, and should either round-robin SMTP connections, or use a least-load connection algorithm. Simple load balancers use only connection count to determine where to send the next connection, but if you have more advanced capabilities, like health checks or SNMP polling, you can use ESA attributes, like CPU usage and work queue count, to determine least-load ESA. In all cases, never use any kind of source Network Address Translation (NAT); the ESAs need to have the originating IP of the client preserved in the TCP connection in order to do accurate SenderBase reputation lookups. Per-host rate limiting and other sender controls also depend heavily on the true source IP being preserved on inbound connections.

For inbound connections from Internet SMTP clients, I recommend using load-balancer stickiness features, if available, to send repeated connections from the same source IP to the same destination ESA; this allows the ESA rate limiting to properly count individual clients and rate limit appropriately. Pure round-robin will result in each ESA enforcing its own limits and bad senders enjoying higher connection rates than they would otherwise.

If you're using simple port 25 SMTP health check probes on the load balancer, make sure the connecting IP is granted a generous HAT policy on the ESAs, or you run the risk of rejecting or rate limiting these connections, forcing the load balancer to drop that ESA out of the pool.

The ESA configuration is not much different from any other deployment. It's important to keep all the ESA configurations in a load-balancer pool synchronized, if for no other reason than troubleshooting: It can be maddening to track down a configuration problem when it's only affecting some of your email messages or connections. You'll even want to keep hostnames the same across the appliances to maintain the illusion of a single large host. Each ESA can maintain its own global hostname so that they can be distinguished, but the hostname assigned to the load-balanced real IP on each ESA should be identical, and it should match the external hostname of the VIP.

For example, suppose Cisco is using this MX record:

```
cisco.com.       86400    IN      MX      10  inbound.cisco.com
```

It resolves to this IP:

```
inbound.cisco.com.   86400    IN      A       128.107.234.204
```

This is a VIP in front of four individual ESAs: smtp1.cisco.com, smtp2.cisco.com, smtp3.cisco.com, and smtp4.cisco.com. All four of these ESAs should have a configuration that looks like this output from **interfaceconfig**:

```
Currently configured interfaces:
1. data (10.1.42.42/24 on Data 1: inbound.cisco.com)

Choose the operation you want to perform:
- NEW - Create a new interface.
- EDIT - Modify an interface.
- GROUPS - Define interface groups.
- DELETE - Remove an interface.
[]>
```

Keeping all four of the interface hostnames identical means that each ESA will use the same banner hostname during SMTP. This comes into play for TLS certificates and certificate verification, and for SPF verification of HELO domains.

Load Balancers for Outgoing Mail

The use of load balancers is especially appropriate for outgoing email, at the point in the architecture where your groupware or mailstore servers are delivering messages to the ESAs for delivery to Internet destinations. Most groupware servers have the ability to send messages to a "smarthost" that accepts email to all nonlocal recipients. This smarthost setting is often limited to a single hostname or IP address or to a list of hosts that have simple round-robin load balancing. For some systems, there is no load-balancing support for smarthosts whatsoever.

It is possible to use MX records for load balancing and failover of smarthosts. However, this requires that you publish a wildcard DNS entry for all nonlocal domains, with host records resolving to your ESA IP addresses. Any internal system needing to send email to an Internet destination does its own MX record lookup for the destination domain; your DNS server always returns the same values, regardless of the domain:

```
gmail.com.       86400    IN      MX      10  esa1.company.com
gmail.com.       86400    IN      MX      20  esa2.company.com
```

```
yahoo.com.      86400   IN      MX      10  esa1.company.com
yahoo.com.      86400   IN      MX      20  esa2.company.com
```

This approach is not usually easy, and depending on the DNS server, may not be possible at all. A hardware or software load balancer is the ideal solution for many of the same reasons previously listed for incoming mail.

Configuration of a load balancer itself is beyond the scope of this book, but many of the guidelines applied to incoming SMTP load balancing also apply to outgoing:

- Load balance based on least-load or round-robin of connections. If the load balancer offers health checks or other load determination features based on SNMP, use them. At the minimum, you should use port 25 health checks. On the ESA, you must whitelist the load balancer health check IPs to avoid rejecting or rate limiting these health check connections.
- Don't use source NAT on connections from internal hosts. The ESA needs to see the connections from individual hosts in order to apply connection and rate limits on a per-host basis. NAT prevents the ESA from being able to distinguish individual internal hosts.
- Load balancers do their work by rewriting destination IPs, making it appear as if the client and server are directly communicating. To avoid asynchronous TCP connections, where the client sends connections through the load balancer, but the server responds directly to the client and to maintain original source IPs, the internal groupware and smarthost ESAs should be on different subnets. Ideally, the ESAs will be separated into their own subnet.

The last problem warrants an example. Suppose an Exchange server has IP 10.10.17.23/24, and you have three ESAs at 10.10.17.130–132/24. The load balancer VIP is 10.10.17.129. If the Exchange server initiates an SMTP connection to the load balancer VIP, the load balancer rewrites the destination IP to that of one of the ESAs. The ESA at 10.10.17.130 recognizes that the Exchange server is on the same subnet and replies directly, creating an asynchronous path. The Exchange server will drop the return packets. Moving the VIP to a different subnet won't help because the ESA still thinks it should reply directly to Exchange.

The solution is to separate ESA from Exchange by changing the network settings or splitting that /24 network into at least two subnets. The other solution is to source NAT the Exchange server, but that will prevent the ESA from being able to distinguish from multiple internal hosts.

Multitier Architectures

I presented some of the many options for running multiple ESAs in parallel, where all devices are doing approximately the same job. All ESAs are handling inbound and outbound mail, all are security filtering, and all are delivering messages to their final destination whether internal or Internet. In general, this is my recommended architecture for deploying ESA—configuration is simple, and the architecture is flexible.

There are cases where separating ESAs into different roles can be of advantage. If your organization routes email between departments or organizations internally, for example, it doesn't always make sense to send that mail through perimeter devices. For network security reasons, you may want to limit the access that perimeter ESAs have to internal networks or directories, requiring multiple layers of ESA.

Any cloud-based email security-as-a-service architecture will necessarily entail a multi-tier architecture: one tier at the service provider, which you may or may not have much involvement with; and a second tier at your premises, even if that tier only includes groupware servers.

There are drawbacks. As you might expect, multitier architectures are inherently more complex to build and administer. When carefully planned, performance should not be adversely impacted and in fact, some multitier architectures have higher average throughput than single tier. Message latency is increased with multiple hops, but not to a degree noticeable to human recipients.

Two-Tiered Architectures

Two-tiered architectures separate ESAs into two groups. The most common two-tier architecture has one group of ESAs facing the Internet directly and a second internal layer. The first layer, at the perimeter, handles incoming email from Internet senders and delivers outgoing messages to Internet destinations. Incoming email destined for local recipients is delivered to the internal ESAs for final delivery. Outgoing mail destined for Internet recipients is first delivered to the internal layer and then to the perimeter layer. Such architecture is shown in Figure 13-2.

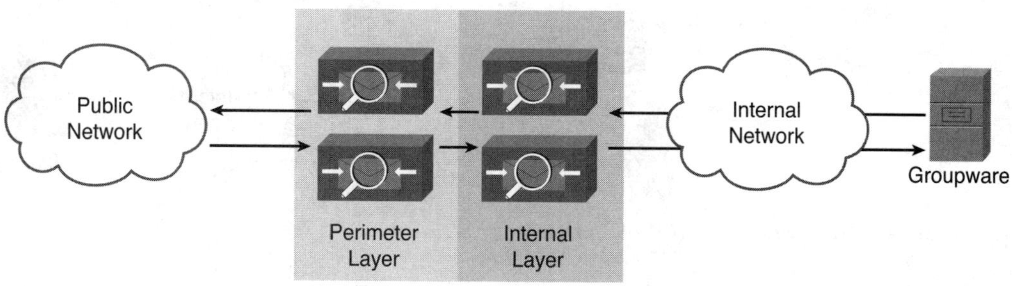

Figure 13-2 *Two-Tiered ESA Email Architecture*

There are a few reasons why you should consider using a two-tiered architecture:

- **Internal messages stay internal:** There's no need to route messages to the perimeter if the source and destination are both internal. If you have multiple internal sources of email traffic, like application and web servers, in addition to person-to-person groupware traffic, ESA can perform the internal routing between these sources, forwarding all Internet messages to the perimeter.

- **Load distribution:** Handling some tasks on an internal layer of ESAs allows you to run fewer perimeter ESAs, making MX record management easier and conserving public IP space. For example, if you want to run two separate antivirus engines, running both on the perimeter systems requires more resources. Or you have a need to scan content for regulatory compliance. Moving one of the AV filtering tasks, or DLP, to an internal layer improves throughput on the perimeter layer, allowing fewer systems to handle the load.
- **Limiting the scope of network access:** General security practices dictate that perimeter devices should not have much, if any, direct access to internal systems. If you have need for extensive directory integration, or are transporting messages to and from other SMTP servers like encryption and DLP, you can perform these tasks on an internal ESA layer, keeping the perimeter layer limited in its access to SMTP with the internal ESAs.

I discuss some other two-tier architectures later in this chapter.

Three-Tiered Architectures

Email architectures can, of course, grow to an arbitrary number of layers, but for practical purposes, it's recommended to keep it as simple as possible. In practice, the most complex email architectures within an organization are three-tiered environments.

A three-tiered architecture is only called for when business requirements dictate a hard separation of tasks for email filtering. An example of a three-tiered architecture is shown in Figure 13-3.

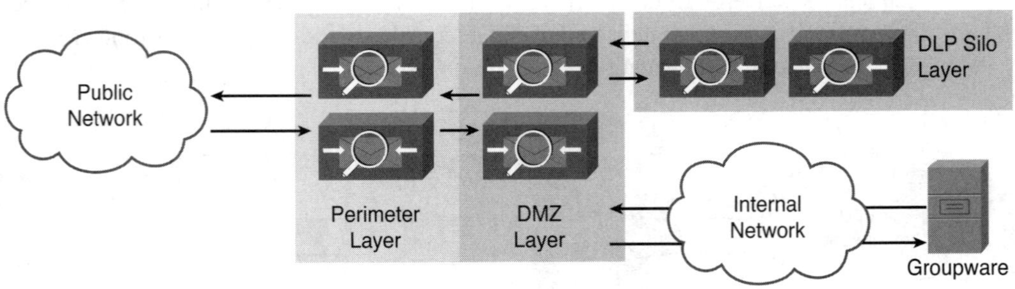

Figure 13-3 *Three-Tiered ESA Email Architecture*

A limited number of scenarios really call for a three-tiered architecture:

- **Security requirements:** Security policies in some organizations dictate that certain tasks, such as DLP or encryption reside on servers separate from security filtering, to allow specific policy officers to create rules and manage rule violations.
- **Network requirements:** Internal email tasks often require access to LDAP servers, DNS, or other resources that are only available internally. If your organization maintains separate resources internally, in the demilitarized zone (DMZ), and externally,

and the ESA needs to access these, it must be placed on a network where the access will be granted. ESAs will happily span two or even three networks, but many environments don't allow for servers to span across firewall borders.

- **Multitiered DMZs:** Strict access control between perimeter, DMZ, and internal can necessitate splitting the email environment into tiers to match.

I have helped companies design and deploy a few three-tiered architectures in my career, and although they solve some serious problems, their complexity means that they shouldn't be used as a general-purpose approach.

Functional Grouping

Some environments call for separating ESAs into groups to accomplish different tasks or to separate administrative duties. These separate ESA roles allow configuration, access, storage, and delivery rules to be customized for each task.

A common example is separating Data Loss Prevention (DLP) and encryption requirements from the rest of the email flow, allowing policy administration and quarantined messages to be separately managed by a regulatory compliance team. These ESAs running DLP could be implemented inline or separately in a cul-de-sac model, which is described in Chapter 11, "Message and Content Filters."

Another common architecture that groups ESAs by their role is separating incoming from outgoing email. Such architecture is shown in Figure 13-4.

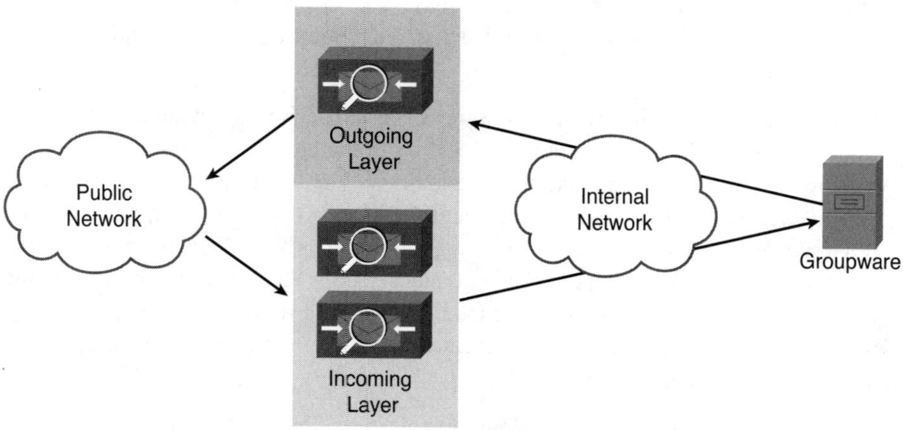

Figure 13-4 *Separate Incoming and Outgoing ESA Roles*

Separate incoming and outgoing roles are a popular ESA deployment architecture because it allows you to dedicate the right amount of resources to each task. Incoming email can be unpredictable due to the collective behavior of all Internet email senders. Outgoing mail traffic, although it varies over the course of the day, is much more predictable in terms of volume, connections, and message sizes. Separating the ESAs means that during periods of high-traffic incoming mail, outgoing ESAs don't have to cope with the additional burden.

If you want to deploy separate inbound and outbound ESAs, there are a few recommendations:

- Anti-spam filtering of outgoing mail is usually unnecessary and ineffective, but I recommend applying antivirus filtering, with notifications to an administrator about outgoing viral messages. You need to be aware when an internal host is sending virus infected messages.
- Even if specific ESAs are intended for an incoming or outgoing role, you should configure all the ESAs identically so that they can be used for either. You may decide to collapse incoming and outgoing into a single role at some point. More importantly, when all ESAs are prepared for either role, you can change the role of any ESA to deal with changing traffic volumes. If the outgoing ESAs are handling all traffic with plenty of headroom, you may decide to move an ESA to the incoming role. Centralized Management features make this configuration simple.
- Don't restrict the access of the incoming layer to send outgoing SMTP messages. Even though they might be dedicated to incoming messages, they will still have the need to deliver delivery status notifications (bounces), notifications, or reports. Restricting them also makes it harder to redeploy as outgoing servers.

Aside from separate incoming and outgoing groups, some other examples of ESA grouping by functional roles include

- **Dedicated DLP layer:** Message scanning for sensitive content or regulatory compliance can be performed using the DLP Policy features on the ESA. Segmenting this filtering on a separate layer allows for delegated administration, tracking, and storage of DLP violation messages.
- **Segmenting bulk and normal traffic types:** The traffic from individual users to remote, typically passing through the ESAs from the groupware servers, is handled by one set of ESAs, while bulk, machine-generated messages are handled through another set. Separating traffic onto separate servers can provide the appropriate horsepower for each task, and prevents high-volume bulk mailings from interrupting important person-to-person traffic. Using separate ESAs, with their own IPs and hostnames, also restricts any damage from blacklisting. If your organization does marketing, order updates, account statements, or other automated messaging, you should consider segmenting.
- **Dedicated "private mail" layer:** Many organizations send and receive mail over private links when dealing with subsidiaries or partners, for security purposes. These links may be dedicated circuits or VPNs, and may be used for other traffic besides SMTP. Although this trend is on the decline thanks to the use of TLS for secure message transmission, it's still common to find these private links in use. A dedicated ESA can direct traffic as needed over these private links for any mail sender in the organization.

Large Message Handling

One last example of ESA grouping is large message handling. During the course of the day, SMTP traffic volumes fluctuate in both number and message sizes. When you size an ESA environment correctly, you have enough horsepower to handle even peak message volumes at average message sizes. One factor that makes performance difficult to predict is large messages: They drive up average message size and take significantly more resources to process, even though they typically make up a very small number of the total message count.

The result is that a system that is comfortable handling thousands of messages per minute with little latency can become temporarily backed up while it processes a few large messages. What we want to do is to make the impact of large messages more predictable and avoid backing up hundreds or thousands of small or moderate messages just because a couple of large messages are being scanned.

Take this example of an organization's message size and volume spread in Table 13-1.

Table 13-1 *Message Size and Volume Distribution in an Enterprise*

Size Range	Total Data, in MB	Message Count	Average KB	% of Total Bytes	% of Total Messages
0–5 KB	7.06	2847	2.54	0.53	28.38
5–10 KB	11.87	1637	7.43	0.90	16.32
10–15 KB	14.50	1203	12.34	1.09	11.99
15–20 KB	12.50	732	17.48	0.94	7.30
20–32 KB	30.82	1248	25.29	2.32	12.44
32–64 KB	44.01	1028	43.84	3.32	10.25
64–96 KB	23.87	312	78.35	1.80	3.11
96–128 KB	19.18	180	109.16	1.45	1.79
128–256 KB	49.59	286	177.57	3.74	2.85
256–512 KB	65.11	187	356.55	4.91	1.86
512 KB–1 MB	87.70	124	724.29	6.61	1.24
1–5 MB	372.97	174	2194.96	28.10	1.73
5–10 MB	378.20	56	6915.73	28.50	0.56
Over 10 MB	209.69	17	12630.85	15.80	0.17

Table 13-1 shows an enterprise count and volume spread that is very typical. The two rightmost columns, percentages by total bytes and percentage by message count, show that most of the messages (by count) are very small in size; but, most of the bytes come from a very small number of large messages. If we can do something about these large messages, we can make average throughput much higher, and much more predictable.

I make the assumption that you're not allowed to set your message size limits very low! Instead, my suggestion is to move these large messages to a different server. Once they're accepted at the perimeter, don't do any kind of filtering on them whatsoever, but send them to another host and move them immediately to delivery. The only overhead incurred is the transport of bytes, which is trivial compared to the scanning effort. A simple message filter can perform the redirection:

```
large_message_offload:
if (body-size > 64KB) {
    alt-mailhost ("largemessage.domain.com");
    skip-spamcheck();
    skip-viruscheck();
    skip-vofcheck();
    skip-filters();
}
```

Of course, also take care with content filters in the web user interface (WUI), where you should create similar logic to bypass all the filters there. Remember that the message filter action skip-filters does not affect the content filters engine later in the pipeline. Where should you send your large messages? To another group of ESAs dedicated to large message handling. A conceptual diagram of an ESA architecture segmented by size is shown in Figure 13-5.

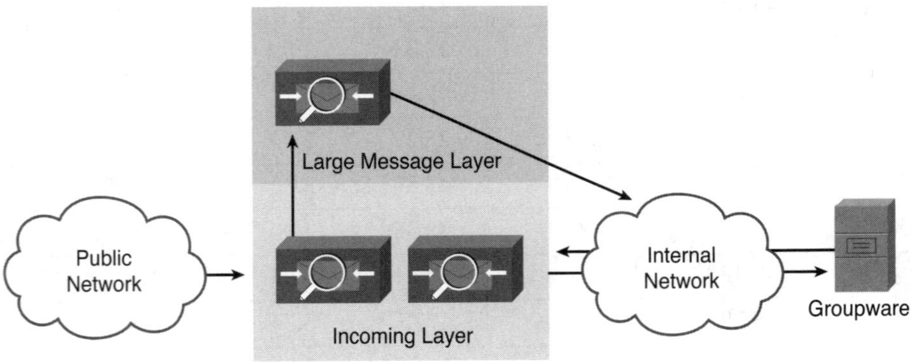

Figure 13-5 *Large Message-Handling Architecture*

This message segmenting results in message latencies that generally match user expectations: Small messages are delivered quickly no matter what, so rapid back-and-forth email discussions aren't interrupted. Large messages are handled as quickly as they can be, with a minor addition to latency, but users typically don't have the same expectation for quick email delivery on messages over 1 MB. It's akin to moving heavily laden tractor trailers to a slow lane on the expressway; the tractor trailers still get there in about the same amount of time, but the passenger cars can breeze right by.

The message size redirection point is up to you, but it should be somewhere so that you are still processing most of your messages on the primary ESA layer. I've seen good results in practice in places where we've processed 50–90% on the perimeter ESA layer, sending the remaining to the large message farm. I picked 64 KB in this example, because that covers 85% of the total message count. Using 32 KB would still cover 75% of the total message count and improve performance on the perimeter layer further.

Architectures with Mixed MTA Products

The modern architecture separation between perimeter email security and internal email groupware and message store means that most organizations will have more than one vendor's products handling SMTP. Some organizations have multiple products from different suppliers in the email architecture, typically for specialized function at each step in the processing chain.

Some environments have a temporary need for multiple products. If you're evaluating ESA to replace another MTA server, you will likely be running both in parallel for some time.

If you need to incorporate third-party products for encryption, archiving, or DLP, this section will describe some deployment strategies and the ESA configuration required to support them.

Integration with External Systems

The primary challenge with integration of disparate SMTP systems is that they typically only have SMTP in common. There is no clearly established practice for sharing data across MTAs, and no standard protocol for transporting message data other than SMTP itself. Even with those limitations, though, you can build a reliable environment that incorporates other types of SMTP servers with the ESA.

As discussed in Chapter 11, when describing filters and routing to incorporate external SMTP servers into an ESA environment, there are two primary approaches:

- **Inline:** All messages are delivered from one server to the next, in order. For incoming traffic, this usually means ESA to external server and then to groupware. For outgoing traffic, the path is usually groupware to external server to ESA for final delivery.
- **Cul-de-sac or "out and back":** ESA handles all incoming and outgoing messages, but redirects some or all to the external server for handling. The external server redelivers any resulting messages back to the ESA for final delivery.

Of the two, I typically recommend using the cul-de-sac model, because the external server is often not designed for high volumes and high throughput, and in most cases, typically doesn't need to act on all messages. The ESA can act as the traffic cop, directing messages to the external server as appropriate.

External Email Encryption

Email encryption refers to encrypting the SMTP transport, or encrypting email message content, attachments, or providing a secure means of retrieving message content. The ESA has supported Transport Layer Security (TLS) for SMTP since its inception. Because TLS is not uniformly available and does not provide encryption all the way to the end user's MUA, Cisco has offered an email message encryption feature called envelope encryption.

If you're using envelope encryption features on the ESA directly, this section isn't for you. If you're using envelope encryption or other message encryption features on the IronPort Encryption Appliance (IEA) or other external encryption server, the architectures here apply to your environment.

We categorize encryption solutions into a few main types:

- **Secure "pull" solutions:** These encryption solutions generally accept messages and store their contents in an encrypted database or filesystem, and allow end users to access their secure messages through a secure web (HTTPS) connection. When messages are stored, the encryption server generates a notification to the original recipient, informing them of the secure message and providing an HTTPS link. The encryption solution may also include authentication via web-based form login. The advantage of this model is the simplicity for the end recipient, although it does require that you provide storage, redundancy, and public availability to the encryption server.
- **Secure "push" solutions:** The message content and all of its attachments are encrypted using well-known ciphers, like AES, and the resulting encrypted data is packaged up and sent to the original recipient. The challenge these solutions have is packaging the data so that the end user can open it. Many solutions require the recipient to have or install some software for this; the Cisco Envelope Solution uses the recipient's web browser as the decryption platform, so the user doesn't have to download or install other software. For the user, this model is convenient and easy to open provided he has a web browser. For you, the sender, the advantage is that it doesn't require local storage at all; once the message is encrypted, the encrypted package is sent to the recipient.
- **Public/private key pair encryption:** These solutions use private/public key pairs to encrypt the content, usually based on knowing the recipient's public key. As with all PKI systems, the challenge is in the key management. These solutions also typically require software on the client to encrypt and decrypt messages.

Regardless of the encryption method and recipient access model, using an external encryption server generally works like any other external server. Policy dictates when messages should be sent for encryption:

- **User initiated:** The user indicates in the message that it should be encrypted before delivery. This can be a subject-line string, a marker such as message sensitivity recorded in a header, or even text contained in the body of the message.

- **Sender/recipient based:** Your organization may have requirements that all email to specific third parties be encrypted or that all messages from certain groups, such as legal or accounting, be encrypted. This could be based on static address or domain lists or tied to LDAP grouping queries.
- **Content scanning initiated:** Encryption can be an action taken based on DLP policy or other message-body and attachment content scanning. For example, a DLP policy for payment-card industry data security standards (PCI-DSS) might encrypt messages based on the presence of a credit card number with an expiration date, whether the sender wanted the message encrypted or not.

Deciding on the policy is the hard part; the ESA can implement filters to enforce the policy or even to establish a workflow forcing users to follow the encryption guidelines. Of course, the ESA can also enforce multiple policies, and it is typical to provide both "user initiated" and "content initiated" encryption.

Here's an example of a filter configuration for an external encryption server, based on the subject starting with the string [ENCRYPT]. We begin with a short circuit, bypassing any further processing of messages that come from the encryption server. Message traffic from the encryption server could be encrypted content, or notifications to recipients about encrypted messages. If the contents are encrypted, there's not much the ESA could do with them, anyway. Then, we redirect messages based on the subject test:

```
encryption_short_circuit:
if (sendergroup == "ENCRYPTION") {
    skip-filters();
}

encryption_redirect:
if (subject == "(?i)^\[ENCRYPT\]") {
    alt-mailhost ("encryption.domain.com");
}
```

External Data Loss Prevention (DLP) Servers

Scanning email messages and attachments for the purpose of identifying confidential, sensitive, or regulated content is an established and growing need in most organizations. Cisco introduced Data Loss Prevention (DLP) filtering for email on the ESA with AsyncOS 7.0 in 2010, but many customers have deployed a dedicated DLP solution, one that handles SMTP email but also web, instant messaging (IM), databases, and document file servers.

The subject, for this section, is how to integrate an external SMTP DLP server with an ESA environment. We discuss the built-in DLP solution in Chapter 15. The ESA only supports SMTP transport of message data, so you cannot use other protocols, such as ICAP for DLP integration.

Like all the other third-party server integration we've seen, DLP servers can be incorporated through SMTP in two fundamental ways: inline, where messages pass from one server to another in the delivery path, and cul-de-sac, where the ESA controls the messages "out and back" to the DLP server.

External DLP starts with a message or content filter redirect that looks a lot like the encryption solution from the last section. In fact, we can start from basically the same message filters. In this case, I assume that you want to send all content to DLP:

```
dlp_short_circuit:
if (sendergroup == "DLP") {
    skip-filters();
}

dlp_redirect:
if (true) {
    alt-mailhost ("dlp.domain.com");
}
```

In encryption, we're not expected to do much on the ESA with the traffic returned from the DLP solution, because the messages are either encrypted content or notifications to recipients about encrypted content. DLP, however, could be different, because the ESA can act as the point of enforcement when the external DLP solution discovers a violation.

If you want the ESA to act as the enforcement point for DLP violations, the DLP server has to have some means of indicating which messages violate policy. A common technique is to use a message header added to messages that contain a violation. ESA acts on the presence or value in a header:

```
dlp_short_circuit:
if (sendergroup == "DLP") {
    if (header ("X-content-scan") == "(?i)violation") {
          quarantine ("Policy");
          notify ("dlp-managers@domain.com", "DLP Policy Violation",
  "$EnvelopeFrom", "dlp.notify");
    }
    skip-filters();
}

dlp_redirect:
if (true) {
    alt-mailhost ("dlp.domain.com");
}
```

The header name is arbitrary, as are the values. ESA is only looking for a string match. If the DLP engine is scoring a message with a numeric score, the ESA can't directly make comparisons on the numeric value. However, we can play some tricks with regular expressions to do numeric matches. Suppose the DLP solution will score a message from 0 to 100, writing the value into a header called X-policy-severity, and you're interested in stopping messages that score 70 or higher. This filter condition finds all the two-digit severities above 70, or 100:

```
if (header ("X-policy-severity") == "([789]\d|100)")
```

Email Archiving Servers

Another common integration point is with email archiving solutions that store a copy of all messages to meet records retention requirements. There tend to be two approaches to archiving: direct integration with the groupware and a standalone solution. Email archiving solutions that are directly integrated with your groupware servers storing copies of messages sent and received by users—anything that passes through the groupware. For messages that don't pass through the groupware, such as application-generated messages, other arrangements must be made. Standalone systems typically require that copies of email messages be sent to the archiver by all servers that transport or store enterprise email.

Whether standalone or groupware integrated, you likely will have a need to direct copies of messages passing through the ESA to an archiver. There are a couple of approaches, depending on your need. The first approach is archiving inline or cul-de-sac, treating the archive SMTP server as we would treat an external DLP or encryption solution. The other approach is to simply send message copies, using a BCC or notify filter action, to the archiver, allowing the original message to pass through unchanged.

Archiving Inline or Cul-de-Sac

It's a common approach to treat the archiver as just another third-party server in the ESA architecture. The same filter rules that were discussed earlier can be used to route messages to and receive messages back from the archiver. An inline model is simple: The incoming email path is ESA to archiver to groupware. Outgoing is the exact reverse: Groupware to archiver to ESA. The inline model is less than ideal, however, because most archivers have limited MTA capabilities (if any) and are not designed for the high throughput that the ESA delivers.

The cul-de-sac or "out and back" model is more appropriate for archiving, because the ESA controls the message path. The ESA in this model gives you some flexibility in determining whether messages should be sent to the archiver.

It makes little sense to send messages to the archiver if the message has already passed through it. In those cases, some HAT sender group and filter magic can save us the work. These filters show an ESA redirecting messages to the archiver, only if they did not come from one of the groupware servers. The assumption is that the archiver is integrated with the groupware servers and already has a copy of those messages:

```
archive_short_circuit:
if (sendergroup == "ARCHIVE") {
```

```
   skip-filters();
}
archive_non_groupware_messages:
if (sendergroup != "GROUPWARE") {
   alt-mailhost ("archive.cisco.com");
   skip-filters();
}
```

These actions don't have to be done in message filters, and can be done in content filters. In fact, doing so after spam filtering can avoid the archiving of junk messages. The filter can also be applied to specific sender groups, email addresses, or LDAP groups. Any filter logic available on the ESA can be used in deciding what is and what should not archive. My experience with enterprise email environments tells me to err on the side of caution: It's better to archive too much and have duplicate copies of some messages than to miss any messages.

Archiving Through BCC

Archiving is not like DLP or encryption, where we expect that the message contents returned to the ESA will be different than what was sent. We expect to see exactly the same message contents back from the archiver in any kind of inline or cul-de-sac model. So, why bother sending the message there for delivery? Why not just send a copy of the message?

Most archivers support receiving messages addresses to a specific email address at a hostname. Given this, we can write a simple archiving message or content filter:

```
archive_all:
if (true) {
   bcc ("archiver@domain.com", "$Subject");
}
```

When it encounters the BCC action, ESA creates a new message with the BCC address as the sole envelope recipient. The new message is identical to the original in other respects.

This is an ideal solution except for one problem: Because the BCC copy only includes the archiver address as envelope recipient, the original envelope recipient list is lost. This is fine if all the envelope recipients are also listed in the To and CC headers. To and From headers are preserved in the BCC copy, as all other message headers are. But, if the original message already had one or more BCC recipients (that is, envelope recipients NOT represented in the To and CC headers), they will be lost in the BCC copy.

If you must archive the message with all the original envelope recipients—whether or not they also appear in To or CC, you must add the original envelope recipients to another header, like this:

```
archive_bcc_all:
if true {
```

```
    insert-header("X-rcpt-to", "$EnvelopeRecipients");
    bcc ("archiver@domain.com", "$Subject");
}
```

Now, listing the envelope recipients in a message header defeats the point of a blind carbon copy, because any recipient smart enough to look in the headers will see the original recipient. You can strip this off the original message without affecting the bcc with a simple addition:

```
archive_bcc_all:
if true {
    insert-header("X-rcpt-to", "$EnvelopeRecipients");
    bcc ("archiver@domain.com", "$Subject");
    strip-header("X-rcpt-to");
}
```

Because the BCC exits the filter processing at the point of the action, the message copy sent to the archive will still have the X-rcpt-to header intact. The original message will have the header removed by the last strip-header action.

Other Archiving Ideas

The normal enterprise requirement for archiving is, obviously, that messages are permanently stored for compliance. What drives product selection in this area, though, is typically the other side of archiving, that of management and discovery. The entire point of most compliance-driven archiving requirements is that the archived messages be easily searched for and retrieved when necessary.

On the other hand, in some environments, there's really little need for discovery. Sometimes, message archiving is just for disaster recovery or troubleshooting. If you'd like to keep a copy of messages on-hand, there's a way to do so with the ESA's message filters. The archive action writes a plain-text copy of the message data verbatim. For example, if you want to keep a copy of all messages sent to a particular recipient, this filter accomplishes that:

```
archive_rcpt:
if (rcpt-to == "chriport@cisco\\.com") {
   archive ("rcpt");
}
```

How does the ESA store these messages, and where? By creating such a filter, the ESA automatically creates a log subscription where the files are created. Unlike other log subscriptions, this one is not managed through the WUI page or the CLI **logconfig** command; rather, it's managed in a new menu option in the **filters** command called **logconfig:**

```
esa02.cisco.com> filters

Choose the operation you want to perform:
```

```
- NEW - Create a new filter.
- DELETE - Remove a filter.
- IMPORT - Import a filter script from a file.
- EXPORT - Export filters to a file
- MOVE - Move a filter to a different position.
- SET - Set a filter attribute.
- LIST - List the filters.
- DETAIL - Get detailed information on the filters.
- LOGCONFIG - Configure log subscriptions used by filters.
- ROLLOVERNOW - Roll over a filter log file.
[]> logconfig

Currently configured logs:
1. "rcpt" Type: "Filter Archive Logs" Retrieval: "Manual Download" Retrieval
  Interval: "None"

Choose the operation you want to perform:
- EDIT - Modify a log setting.
[]>
```

You have the same options for this log subscription that you would for any other log: file size, file count, rollover schedule and various file transfer options to automatically move logs to another server. You can use CLI log commands like **rollovernow**, **tail**, and **grep** on these archive files. Because the ESA has limited storage space for logs, if you want to keep a permanent archive, you must move the logs to another server.

When a message is written to disk, it uses a plain-text format for message data usually called mbox format, after the name used by a number of UNIX MUAs and transports to store a user's mailbox. It's essentially the exact same text as was injected in the SMTP data command, but with the SMTP MAIL FROM written as the first line of the archive:

```
From cporter@chrisporter.com Wed May 18 16:11:16 2011
Received: from host101.domain.com (HELO [192.168.1.5]) ([192.168.1.5])
  by mail.chrisporter.com with ESMTP/TLS/DHE-RSA-CAMELLIA256-SHA; 18 May 2011
  16:11:16 -0400
Message-ID: <4DD427E4.2030705@chrisporter.com>
Date: Wed, 18 May 2011 16:11:16 -0400
From: Chris Porter <cporter@chrisporter.com>
User-Agent: Mozilla/5.0 (Macintosh; U; Intel Mac OS X 10.6; en-US; rv:1.9.2.17)
  Gecko/20110414 Thunderbird/3.1.10
MIME-Version: 1.0
To: Chris Porter <chriport@cisco.com>
Subject: Cisco IronPort ESA
Content-Type: text/plain; charset=ISO-8859-1; format=flowed
Content-Transfer-Encoding: 7bit

Simple message text.
```

A blank line is used as the delimiter between messages. All attachments are written in their plain-text encoded MIME format.

Introducing, Replacing, or Upgrading ESA in Production

Whether you're introducing ESA into your environment for the first time, or upgrading or replacing an existing ESA, you will find yourself occasionally facing the task of bringing a new ESA online and putting it into production.

Adding the First ESA to the Environment

For the first ESA that you're installing, you've hopefully read through the earlier parts of this book, including basic system setup and establishing security filtering and directory integration. I assume that, at this point, you have a running ESA with a tested configuration. The ESA is either on a publicly routable IP with a world-resolvable hostname or an internal IP with NAT to such a public IP.

There are a few options for introducing an ESA into an environment where other products are already running:

- Adding the ESA's external hostname to your current MX record as a lower-priority host. By adding the ESA as a secondary MX, you can introduce a bit of production traffic without interrupting normal mail flow. As secondary, the ESA will only get a bit of junk traffic, but you can see how the ESA runs in production. This will allow you time to gain familiarity with the product, use the reporting, tracking, and troubleshooting tools with live traffic, and verify the initial ESA configuration.
- Adding the ESA's external hostname to your current MX record as a primary host. This can be done either as a first step or as the second step after Step 1. Remember that changing MX records is not an immediate change; you have to wait for SMTP clients to expire their cached DNS entries and lookup the new record.
- Adding the ESA into a load-balanced pool. If you are using a load balancer, adding the ESA into the pool will give you precise control over how much traffic is initially sent to the ESA.
- Direct replacement of an existing server. This approach is fast and quick, but requires some juggling. If you intend to replace an existing host by giving the ESA its IP address and hostname, you'll have to do some cable-swapping or switch port manipulation in the DC, because both hosts cannot be online with the same IP at the same time. I generally recommend configuring and testing ESA with another IP until you're ready for the swap. It's a good idea to suspend the ESA listeners until network connectivity is confirmed. Some switches can take a while before they notice the change and update MAC address tables. Any kind of switch port MAC security can cause a port to be disabled if the connected device is changed.

- Inline with the existing solution. ESAs can be run in a tiered fashion in front of or behind the existing solution. This approach has a number of drawbacks, not least of which is the complexity of a two-tiered solution of different products. If you need this "belt and suspenders" approach during a transition period, I recommend putting the ESAs on the Internet-facing side, because the security filters are severely hobbled when receiving messages from another internal host.

Whichever method you choose, remember that the change affects not only the email administrators, but also all the end users. To avoid surprise, it's a good idea to provide plenty of notification about the change.

Replacing an ESA for Upgrade

At some point, an individual appliance in your environment will likely require replacing. Reliable as ESA is, computer hardware can experience failures. Or you may be upgrading your appliances to handle more message capacity, or running advanced applications like encryption or DLP. Whatever the reason, replacing an ESA with a new unit is straightforward if you follow a few simple steps. I assume that you want to remove an existing ESA and replace it with another that has the exact same configuration.

> **Note** Cisco ships ESAs running an AsyncOS release known as the MR (Manufacturing Release) version to customer on new orders. The MR version changes over time as Cisco updates AsyncOS. This MR version is usually somewhat behind the current available GA (General Availability) or FCS (First Customer Ship) versions that you can install using the ESA upgrade features. In all likelihood, you will need to upgrade any newly shipped appliance to match your existing ESA environment. It's a good idea to run ESAs at the same software version; it's a hard requirement for ESAs in a centralized management cluster.
>
> If you are normally conservative about upgrading the ESAs, and your production servers are running a release more than a year old, the MR version on new appliances may actually be newer than the release you're running. If you want to avoid upgrading all of your production appliances to a later release, you can request that Cisco ship an older version of software on the appliances. It is not possible to downgrade a newly shipped ESA. Be aware, however, that if hardware models have changed, the new hardware will have minimum software level requirements. You can't run AsyncOS 6.5 on a new C670 model, for example. The C670 hardware is first supported in AsyncOS 7.0 software.

Any ESA hardware faults, alerts, or outright failures should start with a call to Cisco's IronPort support; you cannot return ESA hardware without a Returned Materials Authorization (RMA). Assuming you have an RMA or are just going to take the system out for other reasons, the next step is to remove the ESA from the production traffic flow:

1. Suspend the listeners on the ESA using the CLI command **suspendlistener**, or the WUI page at System Administration → Shutdown/Suspend. Do not suspend delivery. The ESA will gracefully close existing connections after they have finished and

not accept any new ones. Run the **delivernow** command to force the ESA to make another attempt to deliver all messages. You can use the commands **hoststatus** and **status detail** to determine when all the messages have been delivered.

2. Export a configuration file using the CLI command **mailconfig** or the WUI page at System Administration → Configuration File. You must deselect the option to mask passwords, or answer N to password masking. Configuration files with masked passwords cannot be used to restore an ESA configuration. If you're using the end-user quarantine Safelist/Blocklist feature, you must export this table separately.

3. Release or delete any important messages from the system quarantines using the WUI page at Monitor → Quarantines. If the messages are unimportant, you can leave them, but you may want to delete them before returning or disposing of the appliance. For messages stored in the spam quarantine, you can release them to end users or delete them. I suggest browsing through the recent additions to the quarantine to release any false positives, and then delete all the messages.

4. Retrieve any other important data from the ESA: reports, logs, or older configuration data. We will restore the configuration values from all the tables in the ESA, but log files and other data stored on the appliance filesystem are not part of configuration.

Note that I didn't list a step of removing the ESA from MX records or load balancer pools or anything else; if you are using either of these recommended methods to balance SMTP connections, you won't need to. SMTP MX rules will allow clients to connect to other hosts listed in the MX record, and load balancers will recognize the unavailability of the ESA and stop directing connections to it. The ESA will not accept new connections after the **suspendlistener** command has been issued.

After the system has been "draining" for some time, there may still be messages in the delivery queues. You have a few options here: examine the messages in the queue and then either bounce them, delete them, or redirect them to another SMTP server, including another ESA. Typically, the messages in queue after more than a few hours are probably never going to be delivered at all. It's often misdirected bounces, mistyped recipients, or other unimportant messages.

To examine the messages in queue, you'll have to switch to the CLI and use commands like **tophosts, hoststatus, showrecipients,** and **showmessage** to examine the queues and messages in them. To delete individual messages by MID, you can use **removemessage;** to delete messages by sender address or recipient domain, you can use **deleterecipients.**

If there are a lot of NDRs (non-delivery records or bounces) and other less important messages, you can just use **deleterecipients** to remove all of them. Obviously, this is dangerous. **bouncerecipients** is slightly less dangerous; bouncing NDRs causes a "double bounce" and drops them, but any other messages are returned to the sender.

If there are a lot of messages in queue that you want to preserve, you can send them to another system, including another ESA, using the **redirectrecipients** command or by changing the default route in the SMTPRoutes table. Remember that the other ESA must list the ESA you're replacing as a RELAYLIST host so that it accepts the messages.

At this point in the process, you have an ESA that is not accepting new connections and has no active messages in any queue, including the quarantine. Any sensitive data, like logs or old configuration files, are deleted. You are in possession of an up-to-date configuration file. You can shut the old ESA down using the **shutdown** command in the CLI or using the System Administration → Shutdown/Suspend page in the WUI.

You're ready to install the new appliance. Following the guidelines for setup in Chapter 2 (WUI) or Chapter 5 (CLI), run the System Setup Wizard to get the configuration basics on the new ESA. You don't need to provide complete data for all the tables and settings, as we are next going to restore the configuration from the old ESA. What's important here is getting the network configuration right and enabling the security filters and accepting their license agreements.

Warning Before you put the new ESA on the network, suspend the listeners using the WUI or CLI. A new appliance with even a basic configuration will have an active listener and begin accepting connections.

Once you have the new ESA up and functioning on the network, here are the steps to restore the configuration:

1. To make the configuration restore easier, the new ESA should be on the same version as the old ESA. Often, importing an older configuration into a new AsyncOS version will work fine, but newer configurations won't import into older versions. It's best not to take a chance; if the old ESA was running 7.1.1-101, you should match that in the new version.

2. If the new ESA has an identical network configuration to the old, including IP address and hostname, continue to Step 3. If not, you have two choices: Edit the XML configuration file and change these values prior to import. Or, when you get to Step 3, change the IP address and hostname *after* the import, but *before* you commit the change.

3. Import the configuration file using the WUI's System Administration → Configuration File page. If you get an error on the import, the error message will include the line number and element name where the first import error occurred. This should only happen if you modified the configuration file and made an editing mistake or you're trying to import a configuration from a newer or older AsyncOS version. You can try to correct the mistake and import again.

Once you import the configuration, but before you commit the change, examine the settings in the WUI to be certain the settings are accurate, especially the network settings. Commit the change to finalize the configuration.

To resume the operation of the system, run the CLI **resume** or **resumelistener** command, or use the Shutdown/Suspend page in the WUI.

Management of Multiple Appliances

In all the discussion of deploying multiple appliances, I skipped over the assumption that they will all need to be managed. In most cases, I'm in favor of deploying ESAs in a flat, single-layer architecture with all appliances configured identically. Regardless of the deployment model, you will have two or more ESAs to manage.

The Cisco IronPort Centralized Management (CM) feature is ideal for managing multiple appliances in clusters as large as 20 ESAs. For four or more appliances, it's imperative that you use this feature, not just because it's tedious to make the same configuration on multiple machines, but that it's impossible to be 100% consistent in making those changes on every ESA, every time; eventually, you will end up with configurations out of synch.

The only alternative to using centralized management would be a process of exporting and importing configurations across multiple ESAs. In practice, this isn't terribly time consuming, but it is more effort than using centralized management (CM). Because an ESA configuration file contains host-specific network information, such as IP address and hostname, the configuration files need to be edited for each target machine. These settings are grouped near the beginning of the XML configuration. This process of export, edit, and import can even be automated using configuration scripts on an external system in a scripting language, like Perl or Python.

Centralized Management Overview

The centralized management (CM) feature synchronizes configurations across multiple peer ESAs organized into a "cluster." No single device in the cluster is considered a master configuration; changes made on any system in the cluster are communicated in a peer-to-peer fashion to all the other systems. It provides robust error handling, allowing for the update of machines that have been temporarily disconnected from the cluster.

In addition to keeping configurations synchronized across multiple ESAs, CM makes adding and removing ESAs from the environment easy. To add a new ESA, simply configure it for the network, and add it to the cluster. It automatically picks up configuration settings from the other machines.

Note Cisco uses the term *cluster* to define a group of ESAs linked through the CM feature; it's the top-level taxon in a CM hierarchy. I refer to clusters and clustering throughout this section and everywhere else where CM is discussed in this book.

It is important to understand that this term does not refer to any kind of load balancing or failover features. In the industry, clustering usually refers to multiple physical servers sharing IP address information, combined with monitoring and failover capabilities. This is not what ESA clustering refers to; it is purely a configuration synchronization feature.

CM doesn't provide centralized reporting, tracking, or quarantines; no form of data or logging is centralized. Per its name, CM is strictly limited to configuration data.

To use CM, all the ESAs must be able to communicate with all the others, typically via SSH. For systems on the same subnet or neighboring subnets connected only by a router, this should not represent much of a problem. For ESAs separated by network equipment, like firewalls, you may have to account for the SSH traffic by opening firewall rules.

Creating a CM Cluster

Creating a cluster must be done from the CLI command **clusterconfig.** This command is only available if you have a valid, active CM feature key installed on the ESA. When you run it for the first time, you're given a short list of options:

```
esa02.cisco.com> clusterconfig
Do you want to join or create a cluster?
1. No, configure as standalone.
2. Create a new cluster.
3. Join an existing cluster over SSH.
4. Join an existing cluster over CCS.
```

Choose 2, "create a new cluster," to start the configuration process. You are prompted for a name for this cluster, which is a friendly name that identifies the entire environment. Use a name that's appropriate, like Perimeter or Inbound. If you have more than one cluster planned, appropriate naming is important.

Next, you have the choice of communicating by IP addresses or by hostnames. If you have proper DNS A records for the interfaces you want to use CM on, go ahead and choose the hostname option. If you'd rather not have a dependency on DNS, or DNS for the ESA's IPs is not available, choose IP.

At this point, the ESA creates the cluster and add the machine to it. That's all there is; you don't need to commit this change. From now on, whenever you commit configuration changes, notification is sent to all machines in the cluster about the changes. Each machine is responsible for applying the appropriate configuration changes.

Joining an Existing CM Cluster

Once you have a cluster created using the previous steps on a single ESA, you need to add additional machines to the cluster. Clusters of single ESAs aren't interesting. On the ESA to be added, you need to run **clusterconfig** and choose option 3 or 4 to join the cluster:

```
esa03.cisco.com> clusterconfig

Do you want to join or create a cluster?
1. No, configure as standalone.
2. Create a new cluster.
3. Join an existing cluster over SSH.
```

```
4. Join an existing cluster over CCS.
[1]> 3

While joining a cluster, you will need to validate the SSH host key of the remote
  machine to which you are joining.  To get the public host key fingerprint of
  the remote host, connect to the cluster and run: logconfig -> hostkeyconfig ->
  fingerprint.

WARNING: All non-network settings will be lost. System will inherit the values
  set at the group or cluster mode for the non-network settings.  Ensure that the
  cluster settings are compatible with your network settings (e.g. dnsconfig
  settings)

Do you want to enable the Cluster Communication Service on esa03.cisco.com? [N]> n
```

Option 3 tells the system to join using SSH, which defaults to using the same standard port 22 SSH that you're probably logged into the CLI with. Option 4 uses the Cluster Communication Service, CCS, which is still SSH under the hood, but uses a nonstandard port for SSH that doesn't allow interactive (username and password) configurations. Unless you plan to completely disallow remote logins with SSH to your ESAs, the extra flexibility of CCS is usually not necessary. Because it requires another port to be opened between all of your ESAs, I recommend against using CCS.

The process continues by prompting you for the IP address and port of a machine in the cluster. It doesn't matter which other machine, as long as it's a cluster member. You're prompted for the "admin password of the cluster," which is the password of the admin account on the other machine, and which is a one-time event. Joining a cluster involves establishing SSH keys between systems for secure connections without passwords:

```
Enter the admin password for the cluster.

Please verify the SSH host key for 10.92.152.28:
Public host key fingerprint: b9:c3:8d:bc:3f:91:2e:d7:3b:3e:88:75:0e:2f:1c:7d
Is this a valid key for this host? [Y]>
```

If there is more than one group in the cluster, you are prompted to choose a group to join:

```
Choose the group to place this machine in.
1. PHL
2. SFO
[1]> 1
```

After that, the ESA finalizes the process and applies the CM configuration. There's no need to commit this change.

Creating and Managing CM Groups

Within a cluster, you can configure one or more CM groups. A group is a subset of cluster members that have some settings that differ from other groups or from the cluster. All ESA machines in a cluster are members of a group. Even in a new cluster where no groups have been configured, the default group called **Main_Group** is created for you.

Every configuration setting on the entire ESA exists at machine, group, or cluster mode. In a new cluster, there are sensible defaults for what mode the settings exist at. Listeners default to cluster mode. IP interfaces default to machine mode. When you're using the CLI or WUI to manage the ESA, your administration interface changes to reflect the mode you're currently working in. We saw the effect on the WUI in Chapter 4, "ESA Web User Interface." The CLI prompt changes to include the mode—for example, the prompt

```
(Cluster Mail)>
```

Indicates that you're configuring at the cluster mode. To change modes, use the **clustermode** command:

```
(Cluster IronPort)> clustermode machine

Choose a machine.
1. esa02.cisco.com (group Main_Group)
[1]> 1

(Machine esa02.cisco.com)>
```

The CLI prompt changes to reflect the new settings. Another way of changing the current mode is to let the system prompt you. When you change to a page in the WUI or run a CLI command for a configuration setting that uses a different mode, you are prompted to change modes.

Initially, no configuration settings are performed at the group mode—all settings are either machine-specific, like IP interfaces and routing, or cluster-wide, like listeners and filters. You can move the settings from cluster mode to group or machine mode, creating a three-tier configuration structure. You cannot move machine mode settings to group or cluster mode. That wouldn't make sense, anyway: Two ESAs cannot share the same IP address, for example.

Let's look at an example. Suppose you have an architecture with two locations—Philadelphia and San Francisco—and each location has two ESAs. You want to use CM for managing configurations. Such an environment is shown in Figure 13-6.

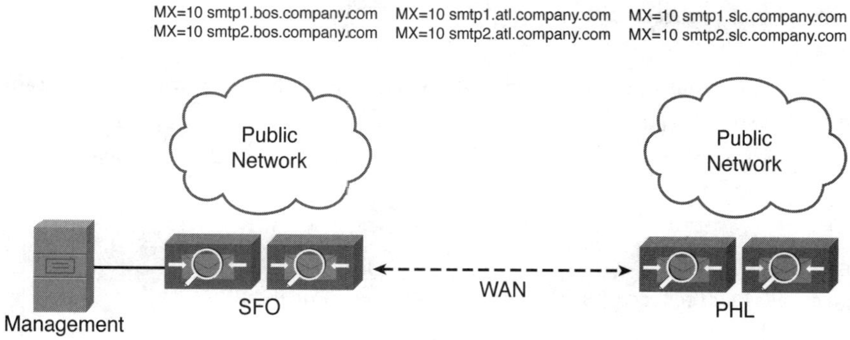

Figure 13-6 *ESA Environment for Cluster Configuration with Two Groups*

Each ESA has its own IP address, hostname, and default gateway, and in the CM hierarchy, these are machine-mode settings. You want most policies, like anti-spam, filters, and DLP, to be identical across all appliances. But, some settings are location-specific, such as DNS server settings. Other common location-specific settings are NTP and SMTPRoutes for delivering to different groupware servers. DNS servers are probably the most common, so let's look at how group configuration of DNS works.

First, you should create the two groups. You can even do this right after you create the cluster, with only one machine. Groups can be created and settings can be managed, even if the group currently has no members. Creating or renaming a group is done through the **clusterconfig** command. I already renamed the default Main_Group to SFO; here's how we add PHL:

```
(Cluster Mail)> clusterconfig

Choose the operation you want to perform:
- ADDGROUP - Add a cluster group.
- SETGROUP - Set the group that machines are a member of.
- RENAMEGROUP - Rename a cluster group.
- DELETEGROUP - Remove a cluster group.
- REMOVEMACHINE - Remove a machine from the cluster.
- SETNAME - Set the cluster name.
- LIST - List the machines in the cluster.
- CONNSTATUS - Show the status of connections between machines in the cluster.
- COMMUNICATION - Configure how machines communicate within the cluster.
- DISCONNECT - Temporarily detach machines from the cluster.
- RECONNECT - Restore connections with machines that were previously detached.
- PREPJOIN - Prepare the addition of a new machine over CCS.
[]> addgroup

Enter the name of the new cluster group to create.
[]> PHL
```

```
Cluster group PHL created.
Cluster Mail
```

Now, we have two groups in our cluster, and you can check the setup with the **list** command within **clusterconfig**:

```
Cluster Mail
============
  Group PHL:
  Group SFO:
    Machine esa02.cisco.com (Serial #: 002218D49A91-7YPLHH1)
```

There's still only one machine in the cluster, and it's in the SFO group. No matter—we will configure both SFO and PHL before adding any others. To start that process, let's change into group SFO at the CLI:

```
(Cluster Mail)> clustermode group SFO
```

Now, run **dnsconfig**, where you get a warning message:

```
(Group SFO)> dnsconfig

NOTICE: This configuration command has not yet been configured for the current
cluster mode (Group SFO).

What would you like to do?
1. Switch modes to edit at mode "Cluster Mail".
2. Start a new, empty configuration at the current mode (Group SFO).
3. Copy settings from another cluster mode to the current mode (Group SFO).
[1]> 3
```

To configure settings at the group level, we choose option 3 and copy the settings from the cluster:

```
Choose the mode from which to copy settings:
1. Cluster IronPort
[1]> 1
```

Now, you have the familiar DNS server settings that are part of this command. Go ahead and configure the DNS server settings for the SFO location:

```
Currently using the Internet root DNS servers.
Choose the operation you want to perform:
- NEW - Add a new server.
- SETUP - Configure general settings.
- CLUSTERSET - Set how DNS settings are configured in a cluster.
- CLUSTERSHOW - Display how DNS settings are configured in a cluster.
[]> setup
```

```
Do you want the Gateway to use the Internet's root DNS servers or would you like
  it to use your own DNS servers?
1. Use Internet root DNS servers
2. Use own DNS cache servers
[1]> 2

Please enter the IP address of your DNS server.
Separate multiple IPs with commas.
[]> 10.1.17.3

Please enter the priority for 10.1.17.3.
A value of 0 has the highest priority.
The IP will be chosen at random if they have the same priority.

[0]>

Choose the IP interface for DNS traffic.
1. Auto
2. mgmt
3. primary
[1]>

Enter the number of seconds to wait before timing out reverse DNS lookups.
[20]>

Enter the minimum TTL in seconds for DNS cache.
[60]>
```

For Philadelphia, repeat the same steps, but start with

```
Group SFO)> clustermode group PHL
```

And enter the DNS server settings for that location using **dnsconfig.** Once you're done, running the **clustershow** command in **dnsconfig** should list this:

```
dnsconfig Settings
==================

Configured at mode:
Cluster: Yes
Group PHL: Yes
Group SFO: Yes
Machine esa02.cisco.com: No

Machine Usage:
Machine esa02.cisco.com: Group SFO
```

This output shows that we have settings at the cluster and group mode. The only machine in the cluster, esa02.cisco.com, is getting its DNS server settings from the group that it's a member of, SFO. When more than one setting applies because a configuration exists at more than one cluster mode (in this case, both cluster and group), the **most specific** wins. If we add a machine mode DNS configuration, for example, that would override the DNS settings from both the group and the cluster.

With two groups created, and DNS server settings configured appropriately for each group, it's time to add additional hosts to the cluster, choosing PHL or SFO as appropriate:

```
Choose the group to place this machine in.
1. PHL
2. SFO
[1]> 1
```

There's another approach to modifying the mode at which a particular command is set, which is to do it from the command or WUI page itself. This gives you a few more options, including moving (versus copying) configurations to another mode. We examine these as part of the next sections.

Using CM in the WUI

Once CM is configured in the CLI, you can configure ESAs and manage CM settings in the CLI or WUI. An ESA that is a member of a CM cluster has a slightly different WUI page compared to a standalone ESA. For example, the standalone SMTPRoutes page in the WUI shown in Figure 13-7 is compared with the same page in a clustered system in Figure 13-8.

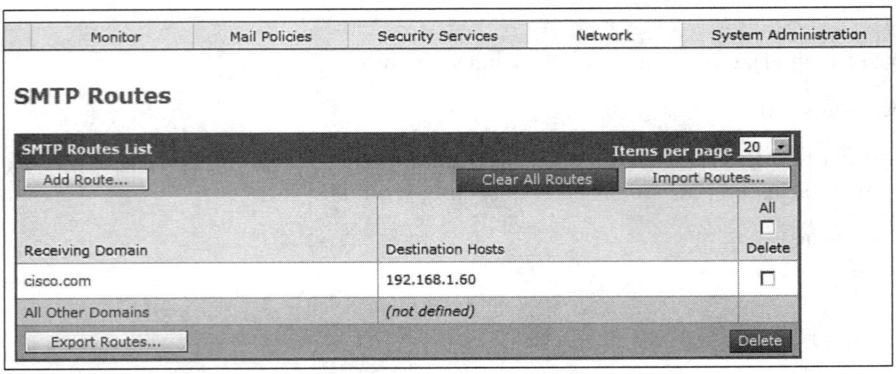

Figure 13-7 *SMTPRoutes Page on a Standalone ESA*

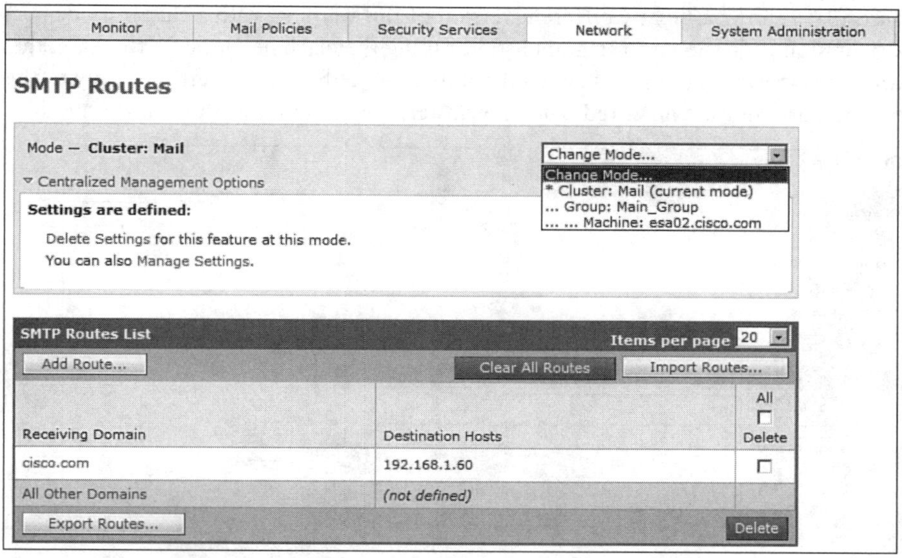

Figure 13-8 *SMTPRoutes Page on a Clustered ESA*

The extra WUI elements in Figure 13-8 are

- **Mode indicator:** Tells you which mode you are currently in. In Figure 13-8, we're at cluster mode in the cluster called Mail.
- **Mode selector box:** The drop-down on the right indicates we're currently at cluster mode and gives us an option to select group or machine mode. With multiple machines in the cluster, you can actually select machine mode for another ESA in the cluster.
- **Centralized Management Options:** When you expand the options window, you're given links to manage the settings for this particular configuration page. You can delete, copy, or move the current settings to another cluster mode.

Whenever you reach a page for a setting that's configured at a different cluster mode than your current setting, you receive a warning about the mode. You won't be able to make any changes to the configuration unless you change modes or modify the CM settings for this page. Figure 13-9 shows the warning.

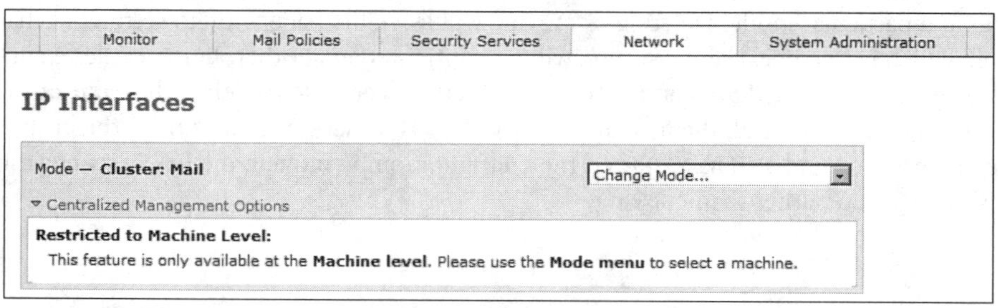

Figure 13-9 *CM Mode Warning*

Figure 13-10 shows a slightly different version of this warning, with a cluster mode configuration page shown to an administrator using the machine mode. In this case, the settings are shown on the screen, grayed out, because although the settings apply to this mode because they are inherited from the cluster, they cannot be edited at this mode.

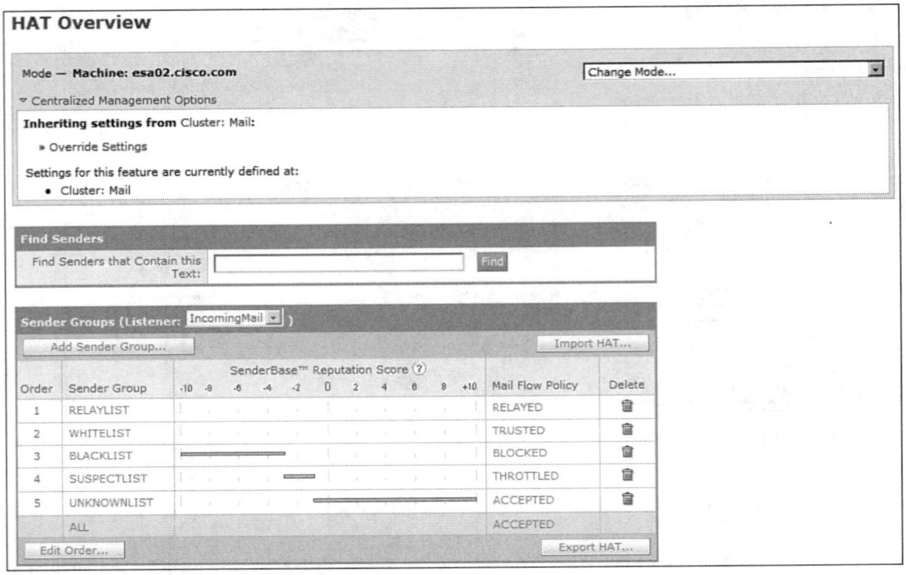

Figure 13-10 *HAT Overview, a Cluster Setting, in Machine Mode*

In general practice, you'll probably be setting up your CM settings for configuration once, when you establish the cluster. From then on, any administrative work you're doing will apply to one of the cluster modes. You'll quickly get into the habit of using the drop-down box to select the right mode, and the WUI itself will clearly tell you your current mode and the mode that the page is configured in.

If you want to change how a particular table or setting is handled in the cluster, you can do that by clicking the Manage Settings link in the Centralized Management Options section of the configuration page you want to modify. Figure 13-11 shows this for DNS settings.

To establish new settings at another layer of the cluster, you have the choice of copying or moving the setting from somewhere else. There's also a delete option, to remove settings at a particular mode. Deleting or moving will leave the page with no settings at that level, which is fine because the setting will be configured at another. In the earlier example using groups named SFO and PHL, it's perfectly acceptable to delete the value at the Cluster mode, because all the machines derive their DNS server settings from the group they're in. We could also have started the configuration by moving the DNS setting from cluster to group, rather than copying.

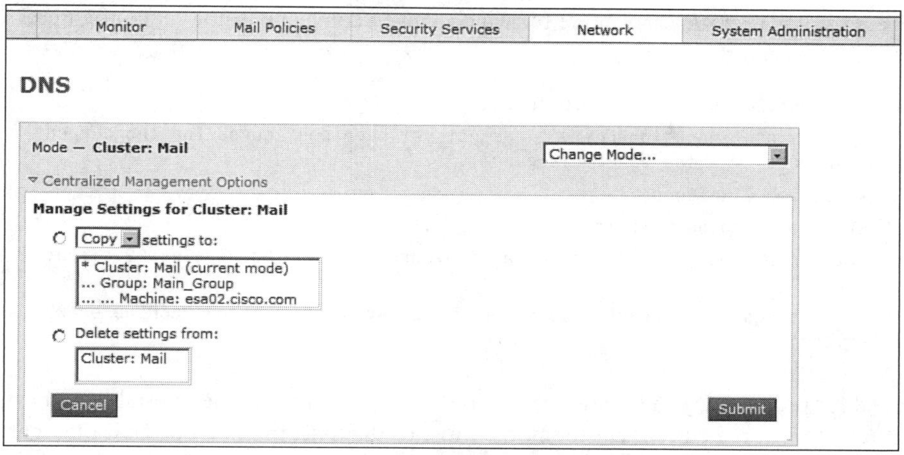

Figure 13-11 *Managing CM Settings in the WUI*

Using CM in the CLI

When using the CLI on a clustered machine, there are a few changes to the normal CLI interface. First, the command prompt changes to indicate the mode you're currently operating in, whether Machine, Group, or Cluster:

```
(Cluster Mail)>
```

Further, every configuration command in the CLI has two new menu options: **clusterset** and **clustershow**. Here's an example of **dnsconfig** in a cluster:

```
(Cluster Mail)> dnsconfig

Currently using the Internet root DNS servers.

No alternate authoritative servers configured.

Choose the operation you want to perform:
- NEW - Add a new server.
- SETUP - Configure general settings.
- CLUSTERSET - Set how DNS settings are configured in a cluster.
- CLUSTERSHOW - Display how DNS settings are configured in a cluster.
[]>
```

Clustershow is used to list where this command is configured: cluster, group, or machine mode. Some settings can be configured at more than one level, and the most specific match for this ESA "wins." Clusterset allows you to change the level at which the command is configured, and copy or move the configuration setting to another level.

Whenever you're in a cluster mode for which a given command is not yet configured, the CLI gives you this warning:

```
(Machine esa02.cisco.com)> smtproutes
NOTICE: This configuration command has not yet been configured for the current
  cluster mode (Machine esa02.cisco.com).
What would you like to do?
1. Switch modes to edit at mode "Cluster Mail".
2. Start a new, empty configuration at the current mode (Machine esa02.cisco.
  com).
3. Copy settings from another cluster mode to the current mode (Machine esa02.
  cisco.com).
```

The CLI is prompting you to either move to the proper cluster mode or establish a new configuration at the current cluster mode. Most of the time, the first option is the right one, which is why it's the default. Pressing Enter moves you to the right cluster mode.

Some commands, like monitoring, status, and log searching, are limited to machine level on the machine you're currently logged into. No, you can't search logs of other ESAs in the cluster from one SSH login. When you run a command that requires you to be in login machine mode, you are presented with this warning:

```
(Group PHL)> w
This command is restricted to run in machine mode of the machine you are logged
  in to.  Do you want to switch to "Machine esa02.cisco.com" mode? [Y]>
```

Again, the default is what you want, provided you really want to run the command that you typed. Commands that apply to the management and monitoring of clusters, like **clusterconfig** and **clustercheck**, are restricted to cluster mode. No commands are restricted to group mode.

The commands limited to machine mode are listed in Table 13-2. Most of these commands can be run on any machine in the cluster from a single login. In other words, you can log in to host A, change mode to machine on host B, and run a command like **delivernow**. That command will affect mail queued on host B.

Table 13-2 also lists commands that are limited to machine mode on the host you're logged into. If you run these commands in any other mode, or in machine mode for another host, you'll be prompted to change to machine mode of the login host. For more detail on any of these commands, refer to Chapter 5.

Table 13-2 *CLI Commands Restricted to Machine Mode*

Command	Machine Mode Limitation
antivirusstatus	Machine mode on any host
antivirusupdate	Machine mode on any host
archivemessage	Machine mode on login host only
bouncerecipients	Machine mode on any host

Command	Machine Mode Limitation
deleterecipients	Machine mode on any host
delivernow	Machine mode on any host
diagnostic	Machine mode on login host only
dnsflush	Machine mode on any host
dnslisttest	Machine mode on any host
dnsstatus	Machine mode on any host
etherconfig	Machine mode on any host
featurekey	Machine mode on any host
findevent	Machine mode on login host only
grep	Machine mode on login host only
hostrate	Machine mode on any host
hoststatus	Machine mode on any host
interfaceconfig	Machine mode on any host
last	Machine mode on login host only
ldapflush	Machine mode on any host
ldaptest	Machine mode on any host
netstat	Machine mode on login host only
nslookup	Machine mode on any host
oldmessage	Machine mode on login host only
outbreakflush	Machine mode on any host
outbreakstatus	Machine mode on any host
outbreakupdate	Machine mode on any host
packetcapture	Machine mode on login host only
ping	Machine mode on login host only
quarantineconfig	Machine mode on any host
rate	Machine mode on any host
reboot	Machine mode on any host
redirectrecipients	Machine mode on any host
removemessage	Machine mode on login host only
resetconfig	Machine mode on login host only
resetcounters	Machine mode on any host
resume	Machine mode on any host

Command	Machine Mode Limitation
resumedel	Machine mode on any host
resumelistener	Machine mode on any host
revert	Machine mode on login host only
rollovernow	Machine mode on any host
routeconfig	Machine mode on any host
sbstatus	Machine mode on any host
setgateway	Machine mode on any host
sethostname	Machine mode on any host
settime	Machine mode on any host
showmessage	Machine mode on login host only
showrecipients	Machine mode on any host
shutdown	Machine mode on any host
slblconfig	Machine mode on any host
status	Machine mode on any host
supportrequest	Machine mode on login host only
suspend	Machine mode on any host
suspenddel	Machine mode on any host
suspendlistener	Machine mode on any host
tail	Machine mode on login host only
techsupport	Machine mode on login host only
telnet	Machine mode on login host only
tlsverify	Machine mode on any host
tophosts	Machine mode on any host
topin	Machine mode on any host
trace	Machine mode on any host
traceroute	Machine mode on login host only
tzupdate	Machine mode on any host
upgrade	Machine mode on login host only
version	Machine mode on any host
who	Machine mode on login host only
workqueue	Machine mode on any host

All the other commands not listed in Table 13-2 are available at any CM mode.

Centralized Management Limitations and Recommendations

The ESA CM model is extremely flexible and makes synchronization of configuration a breeze. Frankly, I wouldn't run multiple ESAs without it. However, it has some limitations, and there are some recommendations to mitigate those limitations.

An important recommendation is for you to not be afraid of adding and removing machines from a cluster. Nothing is lost, and the cluster settings, including all the group settings, are preserved, as long as one machine is still in the cluster. There are plenty of occasions that call for removing a machine temporarily to perform some work and reconnecting later. Even if an ESA is intended to run independently, it can be useful to connect it to a cluster to receive common configuration items like policy, filters, and administrative settings, and then disconnect it for its specific configuration.

Size of CM Clusters

The first limitation is the number of ESAs that can practically be included in a single cluster. Cisco designed the feature to support 20 ESAs in a single cluster, but due to the peer-to-peer nature, practical considerations should limit a single cluster to 15–18 systems. An environment this large is not typical: ESA deployments of more than 8 systems probably represent less than 5% of Cisco ESA customers. Most environments of this size, with multiple physical locations and ESAs configured in layers, are anyway likely to find more benefit in running multiple clusters based on location or function.

Configuration Files in Clusters

Configuration file management becomes more difficult in an ESA cluster mode. You can still export a configuration file in XML format, but this exported file cannot be used to restore the cluster or an individual machine. The good news here is that you usually don't have to: Replacing a machine is as easy as putting it on the network and joining the cluster. The machine gets its settings from the other ESAs.

If you require the ability to backup and restore configurations of individual machines, you can remove a machine from the cluster, export, and then join the cluster again. This process isn't harmful: The configuration is "flattened" for the individual machine and the resulting file can be used to restore the configuration.

Upgrading Clustered Machines

Upgrades present a special challenge with CM clusters, because all appliances in the cluster must be running exactly the same version and build. In fact, the upgrade process disconnects all machines from the cluster as the first step when you run the upgrade command on a clustered ESA. This can create some headaches when you're not upgrading all the appliances in a cluster at once.

First, if you plan to upgrade a single machine, disconnect it from the cluster first to avoid the disconnection of all machines. After the upgrade and reboot, the ESA maintains the cluster identity, and you can even reconnect the machine. However, because it's running a newer version of AsyncOS, you essentially have a new cluster at the new AsyncOS level.

Let's illustrate this process with an example. Suppose you have four ESA hosts called A, B, C, and D, in a cluster called Mail. Each ESA is running 7.5.0, and you want to upgrade each to the 7.5.1 point release. Here are the steps to upgrade all four ESAs:

1. Remove the first ESA, machine A, from production by suspending the listeners and drain the queues as previously discussed . This step is optional, but highly recommended.

2. Connect to the CLI and run **clusterconfig.** Choose the **DISCONNECT** option in the menu and disconnect the ESA you're currently logged into. Your CLI prompt now changes to `(Cluster Mail) [Disconnected]>`.

3. Run the **upgrade** command in the CLI or connect to the WUI and use the System Upgrade page on the System Administration menu. I prefer the WUI for upgrades. You can ignore the message that says *You must disconnect all machines in the cluster in order to upgrade them*. It's not accurate in this case, if you've already disconnected the machine you're logged into. Answer **Y** to the query *Do you wish to disconnect all machines in the cluster now?* The disconnect will not be sent to other machines provided you've already disconnected the machine you're logged into.

4. Allow the upgrade to proceed and reboot at the end of the process. Confirm that the ESA has the new version installed. Connect to the CLI command and run **clusterconfig.** The CLI should ask you if you want to reconnect to the cluster. Answer **Y** to have the machine reconnected to the cluster. Once you're satisfied, don't forget to **resume** services if you suspended them in Step 1.

At this point, having upgraded only machine A, you now effectively have two clusters: one at version 7.5.1 with only machine A as a member, and one at 7.5.0 with machines B, C, and D. Cluster communications will not synchronize between the two versions. To complete the upgrade, repeat all four of the steps with machines B, C, and D.

You can certainly perform some of the machine upgrades simultaneously, if you have capacity to shift email traffic to the others. In the example, if two ESAs can handle the whole traffic load for your environment, you can upgrade A and B first and then when they are restarted and reconnected, repeat the process with C and D.

Summary

Almost every environment based on ESA will include more than one appliance, because of throughput or redundancy requirements. There a number of ways to scale your environment to meet those requirements, and you should be able to confidently choose a model that works for your organization. This chapter covered the topics of deploying groups of ESAs using MX records and load balancers, mixing ESA with other SMTP servers, and adding or replacing ESAs.

Once deployed, you need to manage all of your ESAs, and we covered the use of the CM service and protocol and discussed how it differs from administering a standalone ESA. We covered replacing and upgrading machines that are part of a CM cluster.

The next chapter combines everything we've learned so far about Internet email security and ESA and looks at the big picture of architectures and policies for maintaining a highly available and highly secure SMTP edge.

Chapter 14

Recommended Configuration

In this chapter, you will learn the following:

- Ideal configurations for common and uncommon scenarios
- Recommendations on policy, filtering, and actions
- Architectures to suit a variety of different organizations

Best Practices

This single book cannot provide recommendations for all possible challenges sent down to the messaging team. I do hope to provide enough guidance to build a reliable and resilient gateway security architecture that requires low administration day-to-day, but is flexible enough to deal with the changes in tactics by the bad guys and the changes in business requirements that affect email.

Ultimately, the goal of your ESA environment should be to have 100% uptime for gateway email services. This is definitely achievable. Appropriate redundancy and disaster-recovery strategies are a critical component. The ESA is widely known for its resilience and reliability, with individual appliances experiencing zero unplanned downtime, but for email to be reliable end-to-end, other components also have to be in place.

Redundancy and Capacity

For a mission-critical application like email, redundancy is a chief requirement. I covered the topics of multi-ESA deployments in Chapter 13, "Multiple Device Deployments." The generic architecture that I recommend includes multiple ESAs equally sharing the combined email traffic, either through equally weighted MX records or via external load balancing.

In addition to redundancy of the ESAs themselves, you must plan for redundancy in the services that the ESAs rely on.

Domain Name System (DNS) is the most important dependency of the ESA. In a typical configuration, the ESA makes 6–8 DNS queries for each incoming connection, and several more for delivery of every recipient. Certain features, like external DNSBLs, Envelope Sender Verification, and Sender Authentication with SPF and DKIM, can add even more queries. The total count of DNS queries from the ESAs can be 10–20 times the total SMTP connection count. Although most of these DNS-dependent features timeout quickly, without successful lookups their intended effect can be blunted.

There are three approaches to DNS reliability: Use the built-in caching DNS resolver on the ESAs, use multiple local DNS caching servers, or a mix of the two. By using the Internet Root Servers setting, the ESA's own resolver can use the redundancy of the global DNS hierarchy. For local servers, you can specify a priority associated with each DNS server and so create a load balanced or failover relationship. You should always provide two or more local DNS caching servers. If you're using the hybrid approach, it's still a good idea to use multiple local caching servers even though the ESA will query most to its own resolver.

Once configured, any connectivity issues affecting DNS will result in email alerts, but you should also consider monitoring via other paths, like SNMP. The ESA exposes an outstandingDNSRequests object that will increase dramatically during an outage. DNS servers should also be independently monitored.

Lightweight Directory Access Protocol (LDAP) is another important dependency for ESAs when it's being used. As with DNS, redundancy is critical for reliability: The only way to protect against failure of an individual LDAP server is to provide two or more. The ESA can load balance or fail over connections between LDAP servers.

The ESA does have resiliency in its LDAP-related features. LDAP Accept queries, because they operate at SMTP conversation, are more time critical, and you have two options when LDAP is unavailable: temporarily reject all messages or let the messages in without an LDAP check. Of the two, I recommend allowing messages in. Despite the additional volume of mail, it's preferable to rejection, which effectively creates an email outage if LDAP is unavailable.

The other LDAP query types are performed after message acceptance, immediately before the work queue, and will be held there if queries fail. This will impact message delivery, but not acceptance. Like with DNS, LDAP connectivity failures will generate email alerts.

Securing the Appliance

Of course, reliability isn't possible if the ESAs are compromised by an unauthorized entity, whether it's a remote intruder or a local user poking around the network. It's possible to make configuration changes on the ESA in a few seconds that would turn it into an open relay or disable security filtering. The ESA itself is designed to prevent unauthorized access, but it's easy for an administrator to loosen restrictions and anyone with appropriate credentials and network access to an appliance can log in.

Standard security best-practices safeguards should be taken with the ESA:

- **Limit access to the management interfaces using a network security device, like a firewall or with network ACLs:** If the ESA has multiple IP interfaces, don't enable the management protocols on outside interfaces at all.
- **Establish a change control process for making configuration changes:** At a minimum, this should include the file export process described in Chapter 10, "Configuration Files."
- **Use lowest privilege accounts:** For day-to-day configuration, you only need Operator level privilege, not Administrator. Using a separate account with appropriate privileges for each authorized user not only helps prevent accidents but also assigns a name to every change, for auditing purposes.
- **Don't use insecure access methods:** In the case of the ESA, this means don't use Telnet, FTP, or HTTP. Use SSH for CLI and SCP for file transfer. Web-based access should use HTTPS only, with HTTP redirecting the connecting browser to HTTPS.
- **Don't use the default password:** The ESA System Setup Wizard prompts you to change the admin password, but doesn't prevent you from reusing the default—ironport.
- **External logging:** You should configure copies of important log subscriptions to be sent off-ESA via syslog or via FTP/SCP file transfer. The most important logs are the system logs, text mail logs, configuration history logs, and GUI/CLI access logs. You don't have to stop logging locally, because you can just create an additional log subscription.

In addition to the standard safeguards, you should restrict access to the ESA by enabling these features:

- **WUI inactivity timeout:** The ESA defaults to 30 minute inactivity logout, which may seem inconvenient, but be wary of making this longer. Leaving yourself logged in to the WUI lowers the barrier to unauthorized access. This value is controlled in the Network Access page in the System Administration menu.
- **Administrative access control lists:** Limit the source IP ranges that are allowed to access the management interfaces through the **adminaccessconfig** command or the Network Access page in the System Administration menu.
- **Strong password controls and login restrictions:** If you're using local administration accounts, limit the number of unsuccessful login attempts, and enforce some or all of the password complexity options. You can find these options under the Users page in the System Administration menu.

Security Filtering

The ESA's default policies are designed to be effective right out of the box. If you set up your ESA using the System Setup Wizard, and the ESA can connect and download rule and engine updates, you will have an effective security policy immediately.

Of course, there may be room for improvement depending on your organization's preferences. For one, you may prefer a more aggressive stance on spam than the default to catch more junk at the expense of a higher false positive rate, or conversely, a less aggressive stance to reduce false positives.

The settings for anti-spam, antivirus, and zero-hour outbreak filters are covered thoroughly in Chapter 8, "Security Filtering," so I want to focus on connection and rate controls in this section, chiefly via the tools in the Host Access Table (HAT).

HAT Policy Settings

Earlier chapters covered the ESA pipeline and its security filtering. As stated, the ESA defaults are very good: They are restrictive enough to prevent overwhelming from external Internet senders and allow wide-open access to specified internal hosts.

If you want to move to more aggressive settings, my general guidelines on HAT policies are as follows:

- Rate limits should be as restrictive as possible for both internal and external senders. Very few legitimate senders will use more than a couple of simultaneous connections. If your clients connect directly to the ESA for delivery, and not through a groupware server, you can also limit total recipient counts to 100 recipients per hour or less.
- Internal hosts other than designated groupware and application servers should not be allowed to connect to the ESA to send email. Allowing SMTP relaying directly from internal user workstations will result in compromised hosts having a direct path to send spam and malware messages to Internet recipients.
- Set the listener global limits on connection timeouts. The ESA can disconnect senders that have been inactive for a while. There are two limits: a limit for unproductive connections that have resulted in no message data sent and a total connection timeout. Setting these to 1 and 5 minutes, respectively, prevents abusive or broken SMTP clients from monopolizing your bandwidth with idle connections.
- Set the listener global limits on connections. Each ESA model has its sweet spot for simultaneous SMTP connection handling, from around 100 on the 1U models up to 300–400 and 600–800 for the larger enterprise models. This will change with each hardware generation. It's tempting to set this as high as possible, but handling large numbers of simultaneous connections, especially with TLS, can actually result in lower total throughput.

My recommended defaults for a restrictive ACCEPTED mail flow policy are detailed in Table 14-1. Defaults for other mail flow policies follow from this: THROTTLED should be more restrictive, and TRUSTED should be less so. The motivation here is not to completely stop messages by policy, but to make the sending of high-volume messages more time consuming. Legitimate senders, even large ones, do not consume massive resources in their attempts to deliver messages in bulk and will retry when you push back with restrictive HAT policies.

Table 14-1 *Recommended HAT Settings*

HAT Policy Setting	Value
Maximum messages per connection	No more than 10. Limiting this forces high-volume senders to reconnect to deliver. This does not prevent senders from delivering all of their mail, but simply requires that they reestablish a connection to do so. If this is too large, a single sender can monopolize connections.
Maximum recipients per message	No more than 20, but ideally less. Large numbers of BCC recipients is a junk sender tactic to try to deliver to more people in a short period of time. Limiting this does not prevent senders from sending these messages, but forces them to retry and break up their recipient lists.
Max. concurrent connections from a single IP	One or two. Most legitimate senders do not make multiple simultaneous connections from a single IP.

In some environments, you might find my recommendations too restrictive. Service providers, higher education, and retail environments may find that they need to support high volumes of mail from other similar organizations. It's common to need to allow higher connection and message rates from the big four of webmail providers: Microsoft (Hotmail and MSN), AOL, Google (Gmail), and Yahoo!.

For those cases, I recommend a "pseudo-whitelist" HAT sendergroup and policy that allows more connections and higher recipient rates, but still applies security filtering. It's not wise to disable anti-spam filtering from these senders, because compromised accounts in those environments are a big source of junk.

I don't recommend these settings for cable, fiber, or wireless ISPs. Those types of service providers host residential and business customers with their own equipment. Because of the potential for spam-sending malware infections in those networks, even a pseudo-whitelist allows more spam in. I prefer to let the HAT defaults and SBRS sort these senders.

Table 14-2 describes the modified settings for such a HAT mail flow policy. Be certain to keep anti-spam and antivirus enabled on this policy.

Table 14-2 *Sample HAT Mail Flow Policy for Large SPs*

HAT Policy Setting	Value
Max. Messages Per Connection	Up to 100. If you're accustomed to large volumes of mail from big SPs, allowing more messages is more efficient.
Max. Recipients Per Message	Up to 100. Most legitimate messages do not use large numbers of recipients.
Max. Concurrent Connections From a Single IP	Up to 10. Most big SPs use many source IPs to deliver mail, so the per-IP limit doesn't need to be high.
Max. Recipients Per Hour	Unlimited.
Directory Harvest Attack Prevention (DHAP)	Either unlimited, or a fairly high number, 100 or 250 or so. Major webmail SPs are not typically sources of DHAP, as they limit the volume a subscriber can send.
TLS	Off or Preferred. These SPs don't use TLS for deliveries.
Spam Detection	On.
Virus Detection	On.

Once you have your pseudo-whitelist sender group, you need to add the senders to it, and the best way to do that is by domain names. Domain names in DNS are double verified by the ESA, meaning that each connecting IP is queried by PTR and the result A queried; to be considered part of a domain, the hostname returned by the PTR must have an A record that includes the same IP.

Table 14-3 gives some of the entry syntax for the major webmail service providers. Note that this information can change at any time.

Table 14-3 *Webmail Service Provider Sender Group Entries*

Provider	Sender Group Entries
Yahoo!	mail.yahoo.com, .mail.yahoo.com
Microsoft Hotmail and MSN	hotmail.com, .hotmail.com
AOL	mx.aol.com, .mx.aol.com
Google Gmail	google.com, .google.com

Whitelisting and Blacklisting

Security filtering, especially anti-spam filtering, is often subject to corporate policies or even personal whims. The common policy of manually *whitelisting*, or excluding some domains or senders from spam filtering, is one of these. Whitelisting is justified by the need to eliminate false positives in business critical communications, a laudable goal. There are several problems with the practice, however:

- The definition of sender varies. Users typically mean the visible From address, which, like all other SMTP data, can be forged. ESA normally uses the sending IP or its attributes, like SBRS and hostname, when referring to senders.
- Whitelists of senders are often imported from other solutions, where they've been added onto over many years. Any static list suffers from becoming outdated. Any two filtering solutions are unlikely to have the same false positive problem with the same senders, making imported whitelists fairly useless.
- Excluding some sources from filtering is a security risk. Even whitelisting based on source IP or verified hostname can result in threat messages being accepted and bypassing scanning. Even good senders can have their environments compromised and become a source of spam and viruses.

The last of these is especially important, because the landscape of threat messages has changed. It is no longer possible to simply describe spam as unwanted advertising. The anti-spam engine on the appliance defends against phishing, fraud, advertising, spyware, and malware spread through URLs in messages, and bypassing it lowers your security stance.

As a result, I take the position that whitelisting any incoming messages, by any criteria and for any reason, is a potential security risk. If you are requested to institute such a policy, you should be aware of the risk/reward that that policy entails.

Similarly, adding IP addresses or email addresses to a manual *blacklist* to reject or drop spam messages is counter-productive. It adds administrative and processing burden and is actually unlikely to make a dent in spam volumes because of the constantly shifting sources that spam senders use. However, there are some cases where it may make sense to manually block some senders:

- Senders that are harassing employees. HR may require that communication from some external email addresses must be stopped in order to maintain a harassment-free workplace.
- Senders involved in any kind of targeted security exploits or industrial espionage. Email is a popular means of contacting employees for soliciting insider information.
- Dedicated letter-writing campaigns. Organized senders of mass email, often through web-based forms. These campaigns are often political or policy focused, but if your organization decides it shouldn't be allowed, you need to use policy tools to stop it.
- Policies that prohibit use or communication with major webmail or other service providers. If your organization has no need to communicate with senders on particular networks, or from other countries, you can use a HAT sender group to block these networks by IP range or domain name.

Of course, recommendations aside, you may find other reasons that you must have a policy to manually allow, or block, certain senders. The default ESA HAT includes a WHITELIST and BLACKLIST sender group that you can list IP addresses, CIDR ranges, domains, and network owners. The HAT is for invoking policy at connection time, although it does have the ability to block SMTP MAIL FROM addresses at connection time using the Exception Table. That HAT is not the place for blocking email addresses.

Once a message is accepted by the ESA, you can create policies for sender and recipient email addresses in Incoming Mail Policies. I find it convenient to pre-create a policy for blocked and allowed senders. Keep the Allow policy at the top so that it takes precedence over your other policies.

Figure 14-1 shows the incoming mail policies table with an allowed and blocked sender policy.

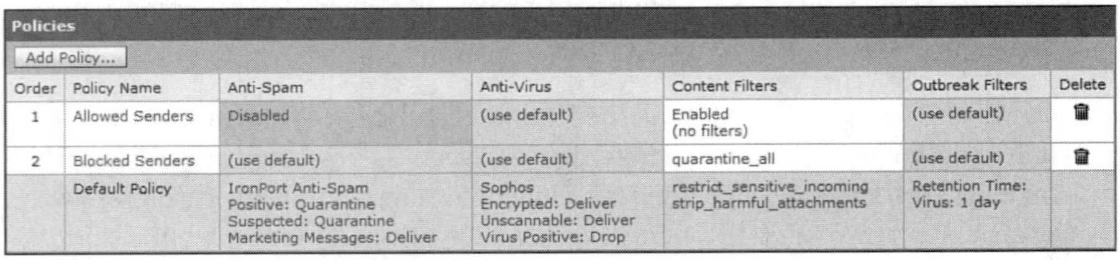

Policies

Add Policy...

Order	Policy Name	Anti-Spam	Anti-Virus	Content Filters	Outbreak Filters	Delete
1	Allowed Senders	Disabled	(use default)	Enabled (no filters)	(use default)	
2	Blocked Senders	(use default)	(use default)	quarantine_all	(use default)	
	Default Policy	IronPort Anti-Spam Positive: Quarantine Suspected: Quarantine Marketing Messages: Deliver	Sophos Encrypted: Deliver Unscannable: Deliver Virus Positive: Drop	restrict_sensitive_incoming strip_harmful_attachments	Retention Time: Virus: 1 day	

Figure 14-1 *Incoming Mail Policies with Allowed and Blocked Sender Policies*

Spam Quarantining

The anti-spam filtering features on the ESA have as an option to quarantine spam or suspected spam messages and store them for manual sorting later. You, as the administrator, can decide whether to quarantine or not. If you are quarantining, you can decide whether the stored messages are accessible to the end users or only to administrators.

Deciding to Quarantine or Not

The decision to quarantine messages is a business policy decision, not a technical decision. The primary reason for using quarantine is to protect against false positives—that is, messages marked as spam but that are legitimate. Because an anti-spam engine could potentially drop a legitimate business message, the choice is made to save the messages so that the recipient can sort it out for themselves. Many anti-spam products on the market focus on this capability, making up for inaccurate spam filters with generous end-user control.

Obviously, having an accurate anti-spam filter helps enormously to reduce the risk that false positives affect business, but there's no such thing as absolutely and completely zero false positive rates. There are still several arguments against using a quarantine, and especially against end-user access to the quarantine:

- **Overhead of storage and end-user access:** Quarantines occupy disk space, either on the ESA or centralized on the SMA. End-user authentication can use standard enterprise credentials, but requires LDAP or POP/IMAP configuration.

- **Judgment of end users:** The ESA does not allow actual virus-positive messages to be easily sent to the quarantine, but it's still possible for spam-positive messages to be dangerous. Phishing and other fraud, and malware distributed via URLs, come in email messages that are cleverly crafted and difficult to distinguish from legitimate sources. Giving users access to release these messages means the potential for those end users to gain access to fraudulent or malicious software that the ESA was designed to prevent them from reaching. Even with warnings, the additional step of using the quarantine UI won't be enough to make all users sufficiently wary of releasing messages.
- **Time and effort:** Quarantining spam moves part of the work from the spam filter to the end users, requiring each user to dedicate time to sorting through messages. A major reason for implementing the ESA and its spam-filtering technology is to reduce the time and effort impact of spam on your environment.

End-User Quarantine Access

If you intend to allow end-users access to the spam quarantine web interface, you have a choice of access methods: via the URLs in the digest only, via the WUI directly with authentication, or both. Authentication of end users is via LDAP or via POP or IMAP login authentication against a mailbox server.

Digests are summary messages that display sender and subject of stored messages, along with Release and Delete links. There's also a link to the WUI for that user's spam folder. The user can always reach their quarantine space through the URLs in the digest, so as long as they have at least one digest message in their inbox, they can reach their messages. The administrator determines the frequency of digests from several times a day to once weekly or once monthly.

Because the digests provide all the information, control, and access that the spam quarantine offers, it's not necessary to require direct authentication. A digest is generated for every email address recipient that has new spam in quarantine since the last digest. If users have more than one email address, use the alias consolidation feature so that the quarantine produces a single digest for all the messages for a given user, regardless of the address the messages were sent to.

Administrative-Only Quarantine Access

Another approach to the spam quarantine is just to use it as *storage of last-resort* before messages are deleted, restricting access to administrative users who can retrieve messages upon request. This increases the load on the helpdesk or messaging team, but eliminates the need for end users to be trained or to support their continued access to the quarantine. By eliminating that end-user exposure, you eliminate the risk that users will release messages that are cleverly crafted phishing messages. Assuming that administrative users are better trained, they can make a decision about a message's threat potential before releasing.

Administrative access is the default for the spam quarantine unless you specifically enable end-user access.

Automated Notifications

In general, notification to end users, either senders or recipients, is counter-productive in security-filtering policies. Notifying users about viruses, spam, or dangerous attachments is likely to result in confusion and helpdesk calls.

You should take care that your policies never result in notifications to an outside organization. That is, you should never set a policy where notifications are sent to the sender of incoming messages or to the recipients of outgoing messages. This also includes bounces—you should never bounce incoming messages because of security filtering.

Ideally, your ESA configuration will never produce an automated reply, bounce, or notification to an Internet sender. In the case of spam, phishing, or other fraud, it's likely that the sender address is forged, resulting in your environment being a source of junk bounces sent to other domains, sometimes called *blowback* or *backscatter*. A configuration that allows this will result in having your email servers blacklisted, a topic we discuss later in this chapter. The following recommendations for ESA configuration can prevent this from happening:

- Use LDAP or SMTP call-ahead recipient validation to reject non-existent recipients at SMTP conversation time. Do not use the options to bounce these messages in the work queue.
- Do not use the Bounce action in anti-spam verdict settings or content filters for incoming mail policies.
- Make sure that the destination hosts for the domains you accept mail for are reliably accepting that mail. The ESA can queue messages for hosts that are temporarily unavailable, but will eventually start bouncing undelivered messages depending on your settings. The default maximum queue life for a message is three days. This can be set higher, but three days is a long period of time for a destination system to be unavailable.

There are a number of cases where notifications or bounces make sense, of course:

- Notifying your internal senders about modifications or dropping of messages that violate policy: attachment rules, DLP, or other acceptable use. This can be useful if your policy expects that users will understand their mistake and correct it.
- Notifying your internal senders about undeliverable or delayed delivery of messages. ESA does not, by default, notify about delayed deliveries; you can enable this in Bounce Profiles.
- Alerts to administrators or security officers about spam, virus, or outbreak messages that trigger on outgoing messages. Alerting the sender rarely makes sense, because in most cases, they are unaware of the use of their credentials in these messages.

Being a Good Sender

The reception that your Internet email messages meet at a remote server has a lot to do with the battle being fought against junk senders. Recipient MTAs vary considerably in their policies and often don't explain how or why messages are rejected or discarded. It's easy to get caught in the net of some service-provider's filtering rules. For most environments that send only user-to-user mail, sent by employees to other real people in modest volumes, you'll rarely encounter these issues.

For larger environments with different kinds of email, both user- and machine-generated, trouble with delivery is an inevitable part of Internet email. Ultimately, the best thing that you can do is establish and enforce good sending policies. This ensured that your environment doesn't get lumped into a "bad senders" group.

Being Rate Limited

Most organizations have MTA software or appliances in place that, like the ESA, can control SMTP connections and rate limit messages, and that can slow your deliveries to them. The ESA, as SMTP client, responds to this easily, using what is called the "good neighbor" algorithm. For every destination domain the ESA delivers to, it opens connections incrementally, one at a time, to deliver messages as quickly as the destination allows. If the volume of messages in the queue for that destination is small, it may use only a single connection. It attempts to reuse the connection to deliver multiple messages. If the remote side rejects or closes the connections, the ESA backs off and waits before opening any more.

You can override this behavior by setting maximum connection and rate limits in the Destination Controls Table, but there's little you have to do to deal with being rate limited. The ESA delivers as much mail as possible without being too aggressive about it.

If you want to be preemptive about connection limiting to certain domains, or to all domains, change the Concurrent Connections setting in the Destination Controls table. The default on the ESA is 500 concurrent connections, which for all intents and purposes is unlimited. In SMTP terms, that connection volume is staggeringly high. Even a limit of just a few connections, 3–5 per destination, is enough to deliver thousands of messages per hour.

You can also put absolute limits on the rates of recipients being delivered to a given destination. For example, you might limit the ESA to delivering 1000 recipients per hour to an external domain. There's not much call for this setting, however, unless you know specifically that a destination's policies prohibit rates above a certain amount. This setting can be useful in controlling inbound delivery rates to servers within your network, like application or groupware servers, if you want to protect these systems from high fluctuating volumes. For example, most automated list servers handle bounces and unsubscribe requests, but may not be able to process more than a few per minute. Setting a rate limit using the destination controls table will allow the ESA to act as a shock absorber in the case of a high volume of bounces or replies. Messages will queue on ESA and trickle out as the rate limits allow.

Outbound Sending Practices

Most email administrators oversee environments that send many more kinds of messages than they realize. Email is treated by users as a sort of utility, always there, always reliable, and so they find ways to use it for many different purposes. Email is extremely popular for marketing, notifications, and customer communications. Application developers send alerts and updates. Ecommerce applications send statements, order receipts, and updates via email. Your IT organization may be expected to support this kind of traffic without question, but out-of-control applications and unsolicited messages can impact all email delivery in your organization, even messages unassociated with automated applications. For this reason, consider establishing policies for automated messages and ESA configurations to enforce them.

If your organization handles any kind of automated messages, special planning is warranted. Any message not specifically created and sent by a user (but by an application) creates additional risk because of the lack of human oversight. The ESA, as yet another application, can't provide that oversight, but you can use the features to enforce policies.

In general, for any kind of bulk or automated email messages sent to external recipients:

- Prefer double or confirmed opt-in subscription services. For any kind of new subscription request, the new subscriber should be sent a message asking her to confirm her opt-in. Without confirmation, the address is not added to the subscription. Single opt-in, where the address is added to a subscription list once it is submitted, is subject to abuse.
- Prominently include an unsubscribe link or unsubscribe by reply—or both. In some jurisdictions, automated messages are required to have this by law.
- Use proper reply-able return addresses. In particular, the MAIL FROM sending domain must have an MX and be configured to receive replies or bounces.
- Manage your subscriber list and remove unsubscribed or unavailable mailboxes promptly. Keeping a clean mailing list is critical to being well received.
- Don't use automatic reply software. Autoreply systems can be abused unless they have enough logic to prevent it. Out-of-office replies fall into this category, but are typically well tolerated.
- Rate limit your delivery of automated messages. In most cases, the ESA's "good neighbor" delivery prevents overwhelming a destination host, but you can forcibly limit connection and deliver rates.
- Segment your traffic. Use the ESA VG feature, or separate appliances altogether, to deliver different types of mail from different source IPs. This shields you from a single blacklist stopping all of your outgoing traffic. If you segment your delivery using VGs, blacklisting of one IP because of a runaway application or mailing list won't stop your user-to-user email while you work to fix the problem.

Traffic segmentation is somewhat arbitrary: You can divide your mail by source (application versus user mail) or by business division or sending domain. I like to roughly organize mail traffic into three categories with varying levels of confidence:

- **High confidence:** User-to-user mail or user-to-many mail, but generated and sent by a real person.
- **Medium confidence:** Automated, but high-quality messages, like order receipts, order status, paid subscription deliveries, and account statements. Generated by machine, but expected by the recipients and unlikely to be complained about. In general, these messages are individually composed to each recipient and sent in response to an action by the recipient.
- **Low confidence:** Other automated messages, from alerts and news articles to catalogs, coupons, and alerts. Almost anything generated by machine, and composed based on a schedule. Sent proactively, not in response to a particular action by the recipient.

Obviously, you should, at a minimum, consider a separate VG for each confidence category, but if you can spare the IP addresses, creating a separate outgoing VG for each application or source in your environment is ideal.

Handling Bounces

Maintaining a clean list of subscribers for automated mail means handling cases where recipient addresses being emailed by the application isn't valid. There are a lot of reasons for invalid recipients: subscribers make typing mistakes, accounts get suspended, and sometimes messages get rejected for mysterious reasons. When the original sender is a user, he can read the text of the bounce message, correct his typo, and all is well. Application-generated messages are another matter—they have to interpret bounces and decide what to do with them.

I described DSNs in detail earlier in this book, but in summary, there are two kinds of bounces: conversational and nonconversational. By default, the ESA generates a DSN for the message that was rejected at SMTP conversation time during its delivery attempt. Nonconversational are the ones that are generated by the remote side, sometime after the original SMTP connection. To the ESA, the original message is recorded as successfully delivered; the bounces come later.

The DSNs generated by the ESA are predictable in format, while the nonconversational are not. The software that manages the mailing list must be able to accept and parse these bounce messages and take the appropriate action. If the software in your environment requires a specific format, you can use the ESA's bounce templates, available in the Text Resources page of the Mail Policies menu, to compose custom bounce messages.

In most cases, a bounce means an unreachable recipient who should be removed from the address list. What that entails depends on the software.

If your application or mailing list software can't or won't remove a particular subscriber, you can use the ESA's policy and filters, or the dedicated Global Unsubscribe table, as a last resort. Global Unsubscribe is available only in the CLI **unsubscribe** command. I describe it as a last resort because applications really do need to manage their subscribers properly, but in some cases, it's not possible to act quickly on that. In some environments, it's not even clear who owns or administers a particular offending application. ESA is another tool in your pocket for those cases.

Variable Envelope Return Path

If any part of your business sends bulk, automated email, handling bounces can be the single most challenging part of your email infrastructure. When a bounce is generated on a remote site, you have no control over the contents and format and, in fact, it doesn't even need to be in the same language as the original. These bounces can be hours or days after the fact. The bounce your application receives may have no reference whatsoever to the original message, leaving a mystery as to which recipient you need to act on.

Variable Envelope Return Path (VERP) is an approach to message addressing that can eliminate this mystery. VERP is not a feature of the ESA itself, but an approach that many mailing list software packages support, and a technique you can use with in-house applications.

The approach is simple: The only attribute of a bounce that can be relied on is the recipient address. That recipient address is, in turn, created from the envelope sender address that you used in the original message. The VERP approach is to modify that sender address so that it contains information about the original message.

For example, if I'm accustomed to sending out order receipts with a return address of

```
orders@example.com
```

When one of these receipts is undeliverable, the bounce ends up going back to that mailbox. The remote site composes a bounce that looks like this:

```
From: MAILER-DAEMON <mailer-daemon@isp>
To: orders@example.com
Subject: Undeliverable
I'm sorry, I couldn't deliver your message. Remote server said:
550 - No such user
```

Well, that's not helpful, is it? There's no reference whatsoever to the earlier message—none of the original headers or body, or even a record of the original recipient. You can tell that this had something to do with the "orders" mailing list because of the To: address. That's a fact that we can exploit. Instead of a static sending address, a VERP scheme might use a return address of

```
orders+chris=chrisporter.com@example.com
```

For a message whose recipient address is chris@chrisporter.com. The original recipient is encoded into the sender address, with the delimiter + separating the list from the subscriber and = replacing the @ sign. Now if this message bounces, that encoded address is the recipient, and you can easily see the list member in question. You can go further with VERP, encoding other information, such as the list name or a subscriber ID. Because VERP is created and consumed only by your organization, you can use it as you see fit, subject to the limits of email address lengths.

VERP has its limitations. Because you're encoding a single recipient in the envelope sender address, and there's only one per message, your messages must be single recipient or be split into single recipients. Some security filters that act on sender addresses, like graylisting or challenge-response schemes, don't deal well with variable email addresses, although those two particular anti-spam techniques have mostly disappeared.

DNS and Sender Authentication

Any host sending mail on the Internet should have forward-and-reverse DNS matching. Before you deploy a new ESA host, make sure that all the routable IPs it uses, or the outside NATted IPs it uses, have PTR records in DNS that provide a proper hostname, and that hostname's A record matches the IP. You should also go one step further to match the hostname in the ESA IP interface so that the banner hostname in SMTP matches again.

Sender Policy Framework (SPF) and Domain Keys Identified Mail (DKIM) are recently introduced protocols that attempt to add a layer of authentication to email messages for the purposes of reducing fraud. I discuss these thoroughly in Chapter 15, "Advanced Topics." You should strongly consider using these authentication methods in your environment.

Dealing with Blacklisting

If your organization has never found one of its email-sending IPs on a public DNS blacklist (DNSBL), or been on a list of banned IPs by a major ISP, you've been extremely lucky.

How do you know if you've had an IP added to a blacklist? Typically, you receive no notification or alert about blacklisting as the only indication is in the SMTP 5yz response code to connections or commands, which is recorded in the bounce message that the ESA generates back to the sender. On the ESA, a backup of messages in the delivery queue or a high number of attempted messages for a particular host can indicate a blacklisting. If you suspect a blacklisting, there are a few places you can look for confirmation:

- **hoststatus** command or the delivery status page for a given domain. The "Last 5XX error" displays the most recent rejection and the human-language reason.
- Text mail logs, SMTP conversation logs, or domain debug logs. These log types record the SMTP response code and text verbatim.
- Telnet to one of the hosts for the destination domain in question. Most hosts reject the connection with a 552 or other 5yz SMTP response code at the banner level and immediately close the connection.

Here are a couple of examples of the messages you might see that indicate a blacklisting. The first is specific to the ISP recipient domain:

```
550 mx1.isp.example.com
ERROR: Mail Refused - <1.2.3.4> - See http://security.isp.example.com/cgi-bin/
  block-lookup?1.2.3.4
```

The second example is one where the recipient domain is using a third-party DNSBL that has your IP listed:

```
554 Service unavailable; Client host [1.2.3.4] blocked using SpamCop; see http://
  www.spamcop.net/
```

Blacklisting of your IPs happens for one or more reasons:

- Complaints from end users. Any service provider that allows end users to report spam or fraud messages will block IPs that are a consistent source of complaints.
- Sending from IPs in ranges considered part of residential broadband networks. Most cable, wireless, and fiber-optic broadband providers maintain separate networks for business versus home use. Many of the residential networks aren't authorized to send email or host websites, and other ISPs will often reject connections from residential IP ranges.
- Incorrect or missing DNS information. Sending IPs with no PTR are almost certain to be rejected. Hosts that have DNS mismatches may be heavily rate limited or rejected.
- Too many delivery attempts to nonexistent accounts. These attempts look like "dictionary attacks" that attempt to find valid accounts.
- Activity on other ports and protocols. IPs being used as the source of malware, worms, DoS attacks, or even network probes are often blacklisted. In short, SMTP blacklisting might be rooted in a cause other than SMTP behavior.

Each blacklisting service or ISP offers its own methods of investigation and remediation. Most use a web-based form, where you can query the database and request an immediate removal or reevaluation. Your process for resolving a blacklisting should be

1. Examine the report from the blacklist or ISP and understand the source of the issue. If it's the IP address of one of your external gateways, look at the message data to determine the original sender. Use the ESA logs to find the original injection source.
2. Resolve the root cause. Was the message injected by an infected system? Clear the infection, but also revise your relaying policies to prevent infected systems using corporate mail services. Was it due to a runaway application? Make sure the owner is aware, and revoke the application's privileges until the issue is corrected.
3. Request the delisting. Most of the blacklist services and ISPs have a simple form for requesting a delisting. What happens next depends on the service: Some are automated systems that will remove the IP immediately, but reserve the right to re-list

if the issue occurs again. Some have a provisional removal process, which lasts for 24–48 hours, where the IP will not be relisted, even if new reports are provided.

If you request a delisting without investigating or resolving the root cause, you'll likely be relisted in short order. If the root cause appears to have simply disappeared, by clearing an infected workstation, it's likely that at some point another infection will cause you to be relisted. It's worthwhile to investigate the source and put an obstacle in the path.

Compromised Internal Sources

In many email environments, the challenges presented by user behavior are as acute as those presented by public Internet senders. Two chief user behaviors can result in trouble for your entire email environment: infection of workstation operating systems with spam-sending malware, and user account credentials being compromised. Either one of these can result in an insider becoming a spam or virus source that uses SMTP to further the spam cause.

I'd love to have a silver bullet for client desktop infections, but that's certainly out of the scope of this book. Instead, we must deal with the possibility of infections using SMTP.

To prevent infected machines that have their own SMTP client from delivering junk mail directly to the Internet using your environment, you have to take two steps: denying ordinary desktops from making direct port 25 connections to Internet destinations, and denying them from using your ESAs as a relay host. The first must be done with a network security device like a firewall. It may be possible to do this on the desktop operating system with a "personal firewall," but many malware systems are capable of disabling such protections.

Denying relay access to local hosts on the ESA is fairly straightforward with HAT policies. To allow relaying in the first place, the HAT must have a mail flow policy with a relay behavior. A default ESA configuration has a sender group called RELAYLIST and a policy called RELAY specifically for this purpose. This sender group is empty by default, and you should limit your entries to the short list of authorized sending hosts: specific groupware and application servers that you know are a source of mail. Add senders by individual IPs or hostnames, provide a good description in the comments field, and remove old entries as they become dated. Adding large network blocks for internal hosts to RELAYLIST is a recipe for disaster.

If you're using a single listener for incoming and outgoing mail, your default HAT will have the RELAYLIST at the top and the WHITELIST, BLACKLIST, and other groups afterwards. At the bottom is ALL, where unclassified senders end up. The ALL group has an ACCEPTED policy by default. Figure 14-2 shows this default configuration.

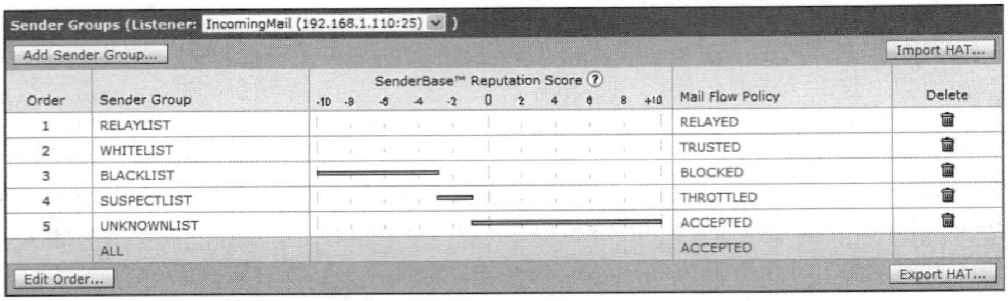

Figure 14-2 *Default Public Listener HAT Policy*

Let's suppose an internal client machine, infected with spam-sending malware, connects to this listener. It won't fall into the RELAYLIST, because you've smartly limited that group to a small set of hosts. It's unlikely they'll fall into the other groups, especially if you're using RFC 1918 private address space, because those IPs won't have SBRS scores. They'll fall into the ALL/ACCEPTED bucket. This infected machine will be able to connect, but because of the RAT, will only be able to send to local domains. That's pretty good, because it prevents the infected machine from turning your environment into a spam source for the entire Internet, but it does let an internal machine send to other local users. We can do better by manually classifying your internal networks and creating a sender group and policy. This is easy to do if your internal network space can be easily summarized, as with RFC 1918 networks.

Figure 14-3 shows such a HAT configuration.

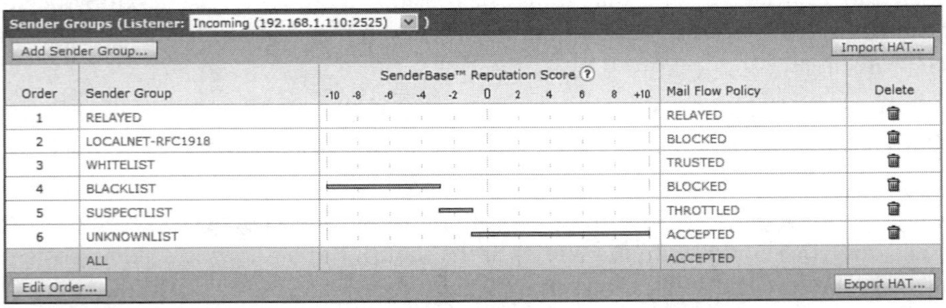

Figure 14-3 *HAT with Specific Handling of Internal Address Space*

If you have two or more listeners, with a private listener for outgoing mail, your task is simpler. You still have a RELAYLIST, which should still be kept to a bare minimum of entries. The only other group is ALL, and in this case, the policy should be BLOCKED. In other words, any client that connects either has specific relay privileges or is not allowed to send mail at all. That HAT configuration, which is the default for new private listeners, is shown in Figure 14-4.

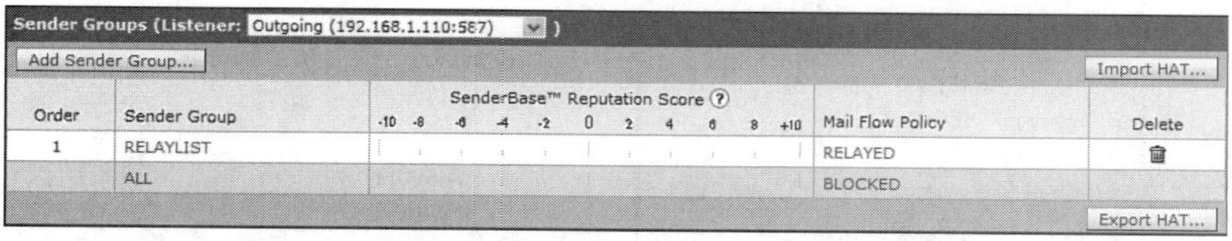

Figure 14-4 *HAT Exclusively for Outgoing Mail*

When you have an "outgoing only" listener like this, you're not limited to relay-or-nothing policy. You can provide multiple relay behavior policies, each with its own appropriate connection controls and rate limits. This approach is ideal for controlling runaway applications before it happens; just because a server needs to send Internet email doesn't mean it needs massive concurrency to do so.

Figure 14-5 shows an example. There are policies for application mail and a generic throttled relay policy for other uses.

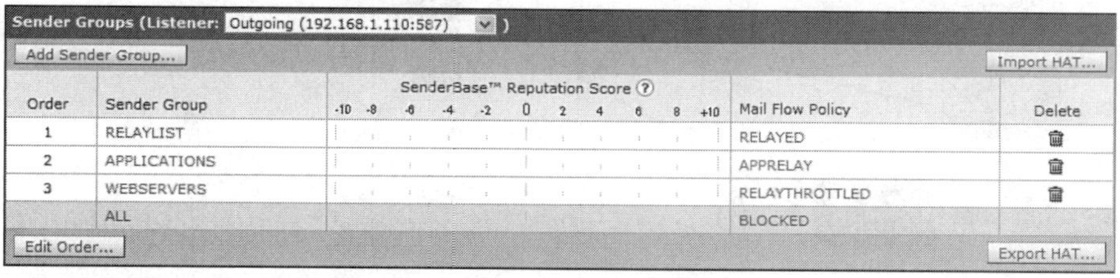

Figure 14-5 *HAT for Multiple Relay Privilege Levels*

Bounce Verification

Earlier, I described problems with sending bounce messages, notifications, or any kind of automated reply message. So many sender addresses are forged that automatic replies go to unassociated third parties, making legitimate organizations become a nuisance. This can go on in your environment without being obvious. One of the most important things you can do, for your own environment, and for others, is not to be a source of this "backscatter."

Figure 14-6 shows in concept how this works. In most cases, the backscatter is unintentional, the result of automated messaging and bad policy, but the bad guys have figured out that they can also use it deliberately. Either way, it's not their problem, as the messages get bounced to someone else.

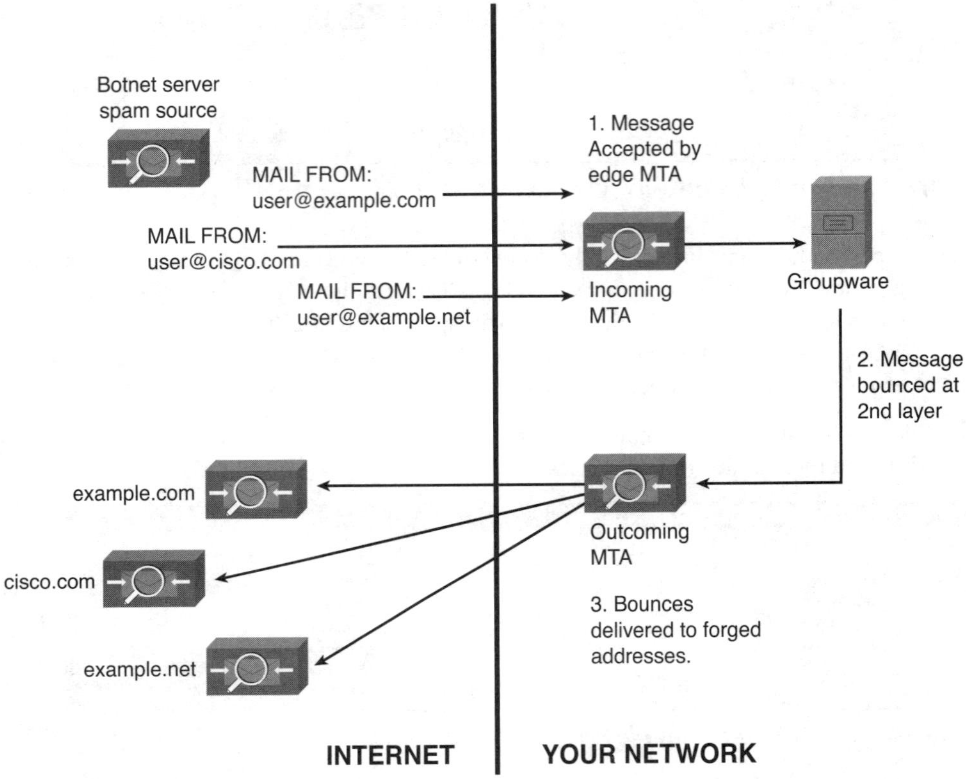

Figure 14-6 *Email Backscatter Problem*

What if you're the victim of this sort of attack? Consider a situation where the perpetrators of a fraudulent email message send millions of copies of that message to as many recipients as possible. They use an email address at **your** domain as the sender address. Most of the messages will be filtered and dropped by the various recipient hosts across the Internet. Some of the messages will be rejected. But, some sites have the problem described earlier: They will accept the message at first and bounce or reply to it later. If the volume is low, the resulting automated messages can be just an aggravation, but in higher volumes, the message traffic can become a DoS attack.

HAT policies that rate limit or reject based on SBRS can mitigate the issue. Legitimate senders that are routinely used for backscatter attacks will find their reputation scores dropping or have their IPs listed on DNSBLs, allowing your ESA to automatically move them into an appropriate policy. This will not necessarily stop all these messages, and your own local policy may override the SBRS settings for some senders.

Another option is to simply drop DSN messages, as indicated by a blank envelope from address, with a message filter like this:

```
drop_dsn:
if (mail-from == "^$") {
   drop();
}
```

Using a simple filter like this is a pretty blunt instrument, dropping any bounce regardless of source. The ESA has a feature specifically designed to prevent backscatter from becoming a denial of service (DoS) attack, without dropping legitimate bounce messages: bounce verification.

The concept behind bounce verification is simple: First, mark up messages leaving your environment through the ESAs. Look for that markup on any bounce messages, where a bounce is indicated by an email with a null return address. If the original markup is present, it means that this is a bounce of a message that originated in your environment. If the markup is missing, the bounce is fraudulent and can be rejected or dropped.

The markup that the ESA uses is in the envelope sender address. It actually modifies the address stated in the SMTP MAIL FROM command with a hash of a secret key and some timestamp information. For example:

```
chris@example.com
```

This is altered to

```
prvs=3158b5fc3=chris@example.com
```

prvs stands for private signature. This method, and the acronym PRVS, come from the Bounce Address Tag Validation (BATV) Internet draft specification. The visible From: header and other SMTP headers are not modified.

Because the envelope sender address is intended for MTA-to-MTA use when sending status messages, normal mail traffic will not be affected. When a recipient receives the marked-up message in his inbox, the envelope information is discarded, and the user sees only the normal From: header. Replies and forwards work as normal. It's only when a message bounces, and a DSN is created, that the difference emerges. In that case, the remote MTA composes the bounce with a blank sender address (<>) and the tagged recipient address. The ESA receives the bounce, verifies the tag, and removes it before delivering it as normal. Features that act on recipients, like LDAP accept and RAT, are checked after the tag has been removed.

Before you deploy bounce verification, there are a couple of architectural recommendations:

- You should tag *all* outgoing mail. This is easy to do if you adopt the "last hop out" architecture with ESAs. Share the tagging key across all of your ESAs. Untagged bounces look fraudulent and will be rejected.
- ESA should be the "first hop in." The prvs tags are specific to the ESA and only an ESA with the same tagging key will be able to verify and strip it. Centralized management (CM) ensures that bounce verification settings are identical on all ESAs. Tagged recipients will likely be rejected or bounced if they get delivered through another MTA or directly to your mail store servers.

Enabling it on the ESA is simple. First, create a tagging key on the Bounce Verification page in the Mail Policies menu. Decide on the action to take with invalid bounces: Either reject them outright or accept them and add a custom header. Rejection is higher performance, but adding a header allows you to act on them in content filters with nondestructive actions.

Once enabled, you must invoke the tagging and the verification in the Destination Controls and HAT mail flow policies, respectively. These are simple Yes/No settings.

I hesitate to recommend bounce verification unilaterally for all environments, because of a few problems with the way some recipients handle addresses and bounces. Once the message is delivered, the envelope sender address really shouldn't be visible to the end user, but some systems insist on using it in place of From, making it visible to the recipient. That can lead to confusion, and replies to that address end up going to the wrong place.

Any scheme that modifies sender addresses, like bounce verification or VERP, runs the risk of interfering with systems that key on the envelope address.

Bounce verification may be overkill for everyday preventative use, but during a DoS attack that brings email to a halt, it easily and quickly remedies the issue and restores service.

Recommendations for Specific Environments

Throughout this book, I used the term *architecture* to refer to the complete email environment for an organization. In some cases, I use the term to refer to just the ESA (and any SMAs) and, in other cases, to all the servers in the path of email flow or that depend on email.

Chapter 13 described the planning, deployment, and administration of environments with multiple ESAs, which as it turns out, is nearly all of them. I made recommendations for load balancing and centralized management. In this section, I give specific examples of the challenges faced by different organizations and some possible architectures to meet those challenges.

Obviously, email environments have been around longer than the ESA, longer even than the World Wide Web, and it's unlikely that you'll find yourself building a completely new environment from scratch. But, if you're planning an ESA deployment, or just contemplating some changes with an existing one, these templates will hopefully provide a good starting point. Of course, the recommendations on security settings, policies, administration, and multidevice deployments from other chapters apply here, too.

I break down the recommendations first by size of organization, because email volume tends to follow user count: more users, more email, both legitimate and otherwise. Larger organizations tend to have more network egress points, more email groupware, and client locations, and more servers for supporting protocols, like DNS and LDAP. Complexity often follows from size.

It also makes sense to break down the recommendations by type of end user. Higher education, which typically favors less centralized control and strong aversion to policy, presents some challenges that no other organization will see. Service providers and higher education often have one major handicap: little or no direct control over the sending client.

Small and Medium Organizations

Small and medium-sized organizations, with up to about 5000 users, tend to have their email gateway environment hosted in one physical location, with all users in a few locations. These environments aren't without their challenges, but because volumes are typically modest, the count of ESAs is lower. It's not always true but small organizations tend to have more uniform policies and fewer sources of email to start with.

Throughout this book, my recommendations have already been mostly focused on this type of environment, with special exemptions for special cases like automated messages. The ESA's default settings are an ideal place to start for deployment:

- Multiple ESAs should all be configured identically for handling both inbound and outbound. ESAs that are handling all traffic are better utilized, sharing load evenly rather than overwhelming one or two while others are idle. It's also easy to remove an ESA for maintenance, administration, or replacement.
- Load balance using equal-weighted MX records for all ESAs. Hardware load balancing is overkill for four or fewer ESAs, but certainly useful if you have them.
- Take care with public webmail interfaces to groupware servers. Webmail is convenient for employee use outside of the office without requiring a VPN, but the single-factor authentication of corporate webmail interfaces make it a prime target for attackers. Phishing users for their account credentials is widespread and, once compromised, provides an open avenue for sending. Webmail servers rarely provide rate limits or other outbound controls.

Large or Complex Organizations

The criteria for being a large organization isn't just numbers of users, but complexity and higher message volumes that tend to follow high user counts. If you have multiple physical email egress points, with users and groupware servers in many different locations, your environment falls into this category regardless of user count.

Automated messaging from databases, web servers, and in-house applications are also a common feature of larger organizations. Throughout this book, I stressed the importance of controlling and segmenting this traffic to maintain the reliability of email as a whole. In large organizations, email administrators are less likely to know about or be informed of automated applications, and there's a tendency to treat email as a general always-on utility.

In addition to those recommendations, I can add the following:

- I prefer identical configurations across all ESAs, even if they will be deployed in separate roles, such as primary/DR or inbound/outbound. Identical configurations are easier on administrators and makes replacements easier when necessary.

- Load balance via equal-weighted MX records or using external load balancing. Load balancers with client stickiness have some advantages in larger email deployments, by sending the same client IP to the same ESA, making rate limiting and DHAP more effective.
- Segmenting of traffic is a must. At a minimum, separate email delivery over different outbound VGs based on confidence categories.
- Consider a multitier architecture if you have significant internal-to-internal traffic or routing between divisions.
- Consider a "large message" architecture if your policy allows for large attachment sizes. This approach can improve average throughput and reduces worst-case performance, making performance more predictable.

Service Providers

Service providers (SP) that handle email for clients tend to handle lots of it, and that distinction—volume—is what separates service providers from other kinds of email environments. These environments are challenging to design reliably because of high and often wildly fluctuating email volume, and the possibility of abuse resulting from client activity itself or responses or retaliation against clients.

Certainly, SP environments based on ESA have a large number of appliances, often in multiple locations. The recommendations for other large environments hold true here, too:

- External load balancing via hardware or DNS, or multiple IPs per A record, is almost always a requirement. Publishing dozens of hosts in MX records can result in very large DNS query results that exceed UDP payload limits. This forces the connecting client to shift to TCP, something a lot of environments can't handle. In short, very large MX records can cause SMTP clients to break.
- For multiple physical locations, combine ESAs with centralized management, reporting, and tracking on a per-location basis. Each location pod requires separate configuration and reporting, but you avoid sending high volumes of data and configuration information over WAN links.
- Make use of LDAP or SMTP call-ahead for as many features as possible. Many SP environments have domain lists and aliases that exceed the ESA's static table capacities.
- Aggressive connection rejection and rate limiting helps to keep message volumes down. If you plan to reject senders based on their DNS lookups or blacklist membership, it's helpful to senders if you explain the rejection reason in the SMTP banner that you can customize in each HAT policy. That way, if aggressive controls affect a legitimate sender they can correct their mistake.

Higher Education

Higher-education organizations encounter the same planning and policy challenges in email security that other environments do, plus an ever-present battle between privacy and academic freedom on one hand and security on the other. Filtering email messages for text content, attachments, and other policy reasons may seem intrusive, but administrators are responsible for keeping an environment running properly and in compliance with regulation and organizational policies.

Often, the opposition to any kind of filtering even extends to spam and virus filtering. Some departments may prefer to manage and maintain their own email infrastructure for this purpose. If that's the case, it's a good idea to treat those mail environments as separate organizations altogether.

In addition to the usual email architecture recommendations, I can add the following:

- Use LDAP group policies to allow departments and offices to define their own restrictions and filters. Predefine policies for aggressive, conservative, or moderate spam filters and allow users a means of setting their preferences in the LDAP directory.
- Segment delivery traffic. The usual recommendations on user-to-user versus automated mail apply, but also consider separate delivery of student, faculty, and staff-originated messages.
- Provide SMTP AUTH services for clients directly on the ESA, preferably on a separate submission host and port.

This last item warrants more thorough treatment. The most unique aspect of higher-ed environments is the common need to support many roaming user mail clients without requiring VPN or other network connections. For inbound mail, POP or IMAP services are provided to clients, and these protocols don't directly impact the ESA. For sending mail, however, SMTP AUTH is used to authenticate connections over the public Internet, and messages that are submitted are granted relay behavior when authentication is verified. ESA can provide this capability and offer some policy control.

It seems simple to allow for SMTP AUTH directly on your MX hosts on port 25, as all other messages are. However, there are distinct advantages to separating this submission traffic from your regular messages, and in fact, TCP port 587 is reserved specifically for this purpose. You can provide this submission port on the same IPs as your port 25 MX hosts or on separate VGs. The advantages of keeping submission separate are as follows:

- You can allow any source IP to connect. Students and faculty are fond of delivering mail from broadband, DHCP, and wireless IP source ranges, all of which may score very low in SBRS. A default ESA configuration will reject these senders at connection time.
- You can enforce TLS and SMTP AUTH for all connections. This excludes some botnet clients and prevents disclosure of plain-text SMTP AUTH credentials.

- You can severely rate limit all connecting clients, so that when a user account is compromised, the damage is limited. A heavily rate limited connection is not much use to junk senders, and having these limits can deter further attempts.

If you're not already using this configuration, client MUAs need to be modified to reflect the host, port, and TLS settings.

The HAT and RAT configuration to support SMTP submission is fairly simple:

1. Add the listener to one of your IP listeners on port 587. Choose the public listener type.
2. Modify the HAT and delete all the included sender groups, leaving only the ALL group.
3. Modify the ACCEPTED policy, turning on TLS and SMTP AUTH and making them both Required. Lower connection and rate limits to 1 connection per client IP, one message per connection, and no more than 25–100 recipients per hour.
4. Configure the RAT to be empty (that is, the only entry is "All Other Recipients" with a value of Reject). This means that any connecting sender that fails to SMTP AUTH has no sending privileges whatsoever.

In this private submission listener, when a client connection is made to port 587, the client will be required to use TLS for encryption of credentials, and must authenticate to send any messages. A client that does not authenticate will have an **accept** mail flow behavior applied, but the RAT check will prevent them from sending to any recipient. A client that authenticates properly will skip the RAT check because it gets elevated from **accept** to **relay** behavior. This works without a RELAY group because of the privilege elevation of SMTP AUTH. The rate limits in Step 3 will limit the abuse of malicious senders who steal valid credentials.

Email "Front End" to Complex Internal Organizations

Another class of email architecture one finds is the front-end service provider. In these environments, the focus is on email hygiene and local message delivery, not the mailbox storage directly. For some organizations, that's all there is to it: message acceptance, security scanning, and delivery; the end users are part of another organization or part of a separate division of an organization.

Many state and local governments use this architecture to provide a consistent front-end email service across the many different government divisions. Some large multinational and conglomerate commercial companies use this architecture, with global email gateway services providing a veneer of single-brand identity to many different divisions. Some business-email service providers and domain registrars also fall into this category, where clean messages are delivered to each client's specified mail host.

These environments often have to deal with every single challenge that could affect an email environment: external threats, internal threats, bad sender policies, uncertain reliability of next-hop hosts, and extreme variations in message volumes.

- Keep restrictive policies for both incoming and outgoing mail connection and rate limits.
- Use LDAP group policies to allow divisions or clients to define their own restrictions and filters. Predefine policies for aggressive, conservative, or moderate spam filters and allow users a means of setting their preferences in the LDAP directory.
- Segment traffic. It's often not possible to provide every client or division with a separate VG for delivery, but if you have a modest number, it's recommended. This prevents a single group's email traffic behavior from impacting others.
- If you handle a lot of domains that are continually updated, the RAT may present capacity or administrative limits. The solution is to use an open RAT, combined with LDAP accept queries on the domain portion of the address, or LDAP or SMTP call-ahead on the entire address.

The last of these warrants more attention, and certainly needs to come with very strong warnings about the configuration. An open RAT is one where the default policy is ALL ACCEPT, meaning that the ESA will allow sending to any destination domain. This creates an open relay configuration, which by itself is extremely bad: It allows your MTA to be used by anyone to send mail anywhere.

To prevent the open relaying, the domain verification can be done via LDAP. Test and enable an LDAP accept query. When an SMTP client connects to deliver mail, the destination domain passes the RAT and then must go to LDAP for verification. As new domains are provisioned and added to LDAP, the ESA automatically accepts those messages. When you assign LDAP accept queries to the listener, make sure that you choose the option to temporarily reject mail by issuing a 451 SMTP response code. Allowing mail in creates an open relay if LDAP were unavailable.

Warning If you use this open RAT configuration, you *must* use LDAP accept or SMTP call-ahead to validate recipients, and you *must* use the option to temporarily reject messages if LDAP is unavailable or SMTP call-ahead fails.

I made the opposite recommendation elsewhere in this book, that of choosing "allow mail in" and thus relying on the RAT to prevent relaying. In this configuration, the RAT provides no protection.

Summary

This chapter discussed the best way to run a secure, reliable gateway email environment with the ESA. Starting with the first line of defense, the HAT, we discussed connection controls and rate limits. I advocate strong rate limits, but I hopefully gave you enough information to judge the risks and rewards of a lock-down configuration. Because tight controls often require exceptions, we discussed creating specific groups for legitimate large senders, like major webmail providers.

Email security encompasses the sending of outgoing mail, and you need to take into account your policies for filtering and delivering messages. Nothing can affect the reception of your messages at other organizations more than your outgoing configuration. We also discussed the problem of bounce backscatter and how to avoid being affected by it, but we also discussed how to avoid being part of the problem.

Architecture has been a focus of this book, and this chapter discussed recommendations for different kinds of environments and the challenges each can face.

In the next chapter, we close with a few advanced topics: new trends in email authentication and filtering concepts.

Chapter 15

Advanced Topics

In this chapter, you will learn the following:

- New protocols for authentication of email senders
- New challenges in regulatory compliance that place pressure on messaging directors
- How to protect an organization's intellectual property in email

Recent Developments

Recent industry noise might convince you that email as a communications medium is on its way out. However, the raw statistics don't bear this out; although daily Internet email volumes fluctuate day to day, it's apparent that volumes of Internet and internal email are on the rise. As of this writing, the Cisco statistics on spam and other threat messages shows a change in approach from high volume, less sophisticated, advertising junk to lower volumes of sophisticated fraud, but the numbers of both continue to be high.

Although other communication technologies arise and gain popularity with consumers and businesses, none are about to replace email in business, government, or education. New technologies with value usually complement existing ones, not replace them. Most companies still use telephone, email, and instant messaging (IM) to conduct business; social networking and dedicated collaboration tools will find a home alongside them in most environments. The future is naturally difficult to predict, and technology futures are legendary for authors that dare to make predictions. But, there are a few developments in the venerable world of SMTP email in the last few years that are worth mentioning, and new technology standards are emerging. Email has also become the subject of legislation in many countries and in most U.S. states, either directly through laws regarding electronic communication or indirectly through restrictions on the transmission of private information, regardless of form. Regulatory compliance in your jurisdiction may impose obligations on how you handle email communication with outside organizations, and the future inevitably means more of this type of legislation. Industry or organizational requirements may also dictate how and whether email is used to handle proprietary or confidential information. Detecting and controlling the information contained in email messages is the stated goal of Data Loss Prevention (DLP) features on the Email Security Appliance (ESA), so I examine those capabilities.

Authentication Standards

One of the major sources of headaches with Internet email is the lack of sender authentication in SMTP. SMTP provides no mechanism to verify that the sender address, specified in the SMTP MAIL FROM command or in the visible From header, is being legitimately used. In fact, SMTP specifically provides for a number of cases where these addresses can be "spoofed" for legitimate purposes. The reality is that you cannot always trust, or always mistrust, the sender address.

With the wide adoption of email and SMTP to transfer it, it's extremely unlikely that a change in the protocol itself would be welcomed. It would be difficult to justify—despite its problems, SMTP has been scaling to meet the global Internet email volumes for almost 30 years.

So, as with many other IP problems in the past, the proposed solution takes the form of optional, but recommended, add-on protocols to provide proof that you are who you say you are when sending Internet email. Today, there are two fundamental approaches: path verification, which proves that the IP addresses of hosts sending messages are authorized to send for a particular domain; and message authentication, which uses public-key cryptography to digitally sign messages. The two approaches are complementary and can be used together. Either way, the goal is to allow legitimate senders at a particular domain to prove that they are authorized to use it and to make it easier for recipients to recognize fraudulent use of that domain.

It's also important to define what these authentication standards are not. They are designed to reduce or eliminate the fraudulent use of domains in sender addresses, as is often the case in fraud, phishing, or other social-engineering email messages. They are not designed as an anti-spam mechanism, and messages that pass the authentication check should not necessarily be construed as good messages. In reality, the spam, virus, or fraud senders can, and do, use these authentication mechanisms. All the better for us—authentication means more information we can identify these bad senders with.

Adoption of these authentication standards is ongoing, with SPF the most widely adopted as of this writing. Adoption is the challenge here: Many organizations won't see definitive benefits to sender authentication until more senders sign or publish and more recipients verify. There are some immediate tangible benefits to using these standards, however.

Verification has the benefit of being able to clearly identify some fraudulent senders, and eliminate their messages before it reaches their user base. For commonly phished domains in the financial and retail industry, you're protecting your users' personal information by allowing their Internet service providers (ISP) to eliminate clearly fraudulent messages. Publishing and signing has benefits for your organization in terms of brand protection: Recipients can more confidently trust messages, and service providers are less likely to send messages to spam folders.

Path-Authentication Standards: SPF and SIDF

The first attempts at establishing a protocol for sender authentication were based on the idea of a "reverse MX" record in Domain Name System (DNS). Since early in the history of SMTP, DNS MX records have provided the means of identifying where messages for a given domain should be sent. Unfortunately, MXs do not constrain where messages sent from a particular domain should originate. If a DNS record offered the reverse of an MX, we could easily determine where email messages with a particular sender address should originate. Domain owners could control the use of their domains, and fraudulent senders would be easily discovered.

Two authentication proposals—Sender Policy Framework (SPF) and Sender ID Framework (SIDF)—attempt to provide this information. The idea is, in summary, to list the IP addresses that are authorized to send mail for a specific domain and to make this list available via DNS. The DNS record is a TXT query for the sending domain. When the receiving Message Transfer Agent (MTA) accepts a message, it looks up the appropriate domain via DNS TXT query and compares the lookup results to the IP of the connecting host. You can do the lookup manually using **nslookup** on most operating systems (OS):

```
nslookup -q=txt example.com
```

I think of SPF as being an acronym for "Sender Permitted From," because that perfectly illustrates the idea. Here's an example SPF DNS TXT record:

```
example.com IN  TXT    "v=spf1 ip4:204.15.82.0/24 ~all"
```

SPF is evaluated from left to right. All SPF records must start with the version tag v=spf1. SIDF uses the same format, but with version v=spf2.0, and there's some difference in how the sender is computed, which I cover later in this chapter. After the version tag, the record consists of a series of SPF parameters called *mechanisms*. This simple example uses one host mechanism, **ip4**, which specifies an IP address or range. The last entry in the record is the **all** mechanism, which matches all other hosts and IPs. There are a few others, which are listed in Table 15-1. For the mechanisms that operate on domain names, you can either specify a domain for the test or let the client use the domain of the sender of the message in question.

Table 15-1 *SPF Mechanisms*

Mechanism	Description
ip4	Matches on a 32-bit IPv4 address or a CIDR style range of IPv4 addresses.
ip6	Matches on a 128-bit IPv6 address or range.

mx mx:<domain>	Matches any of the IPs obtained from A records of hosts in the MX record for this domain, or for any other domain if specified.
a a:<domain>	Matches on any of the IPs obtained from the A record for the domain. By itself, this mechanism refers to the current domain being looked up. If a domain is supplied, that domain is used for the A lookups.
ptr ptr:<domain>	Matches if the client IP has a forward-and-reverse DNS match to the sending domain or to the specified domain.
exists exists:<domain>	Matches if an A record exists for the current or specified domain. It doesn't matter what the result is; any successful lookup passes.
include:<domain>	Doesn't specify a host, but forces the recipient to look up the specified domain's SPF record and treat it as part of the current SPF record. The sender is considered authenticated if it passes either the current SPF record or any of the included SPF records.
all (expressed as ?all, ~all, or –all)	Matches everything; by using it at the end of the SPF record, it tells the recipient what to do with all other hosts on the Internet. The qualifier specifies whether these other hosts should be treated as valid, neutral, or failures.

Each mechanism can be prefixed by one of four qualifiers (+, -, ?, and ~) that tell the receiving side how to treat hosts that match that mechanism. The + character tells the recipient that IPs that match that mechanism pass the SPF test. It's the default and so it isn't necessary to explicitly include it. That is,

```
"v=spf1 +a +ip4:192.168.6.0/24 -all"
```

is the same as

```
"v=spf1 a ip4:192.168.6.0/24 -all"
```

The other three qualifiers are typically only used with the **all** mechanism, which specifies what to do with all other hosts and IPs (meaning the rest of the Internet). It should be last in the SPF record. The – (dash) character indicates a failure; any connecting IP that matches that mechanism is treated as an SPF failure. It's a certain verdict: You're telling the reader of your SPF record that hosts that match this are not authorized and should not be trusted. The ? (question mark) prefix indicates that the receiver should treat matching hosts neutrally; that is, don't consider them to actually be a match or a mismatch. The ~ (tilde) prefix indicates a soft failure—that the host isn't explicitly allowed, but that the receiver still shouldn't act on the message. These last two can be thought of as "testing" modes, asking recipients to perform the SPF check but not to act on the verdicts.

To be really effective, SPF records should be published with **-all** at the end to allow receiving MTAs to treat failures as fraud. The goal is to allow the recipients to act on the messages that didn't really come from your hosts. If you're just starting with SPF, and you're not sure that your SPF record is complete and final, use **?all** or **~all** to indicate that. For example:

```
"v=spf1 ip4:192.168.6.0/24 ~all"
```

This tells recipients that hosts outside of that network range are not known valid IPs for the domain, but that they shouldn't drop the messages. It's a good way to start using SPF, but your final goal should be to move to **–all** whenever possible.

Determining the Identity of the Sender

I described SPF and SIDF as tests against the domain of the message sender, derived from the SMTP MAIL FROM command. There's actually more to it than that. Both SPF and SIDF specify how to calculate the domain of the sender, although the protocols differ on what the sender of a message is determined to be.

For SPF, either the domain from the SMTP MAIL FROM or the domain of the host in the SMTP HELO banner can be used. For messages with an empty MAIL FROM, like bounces and system-generated messages, the HELO check is used. If the two are different, the sending host should be checked against SPF records for both domains. A successful result for either implies an SPF pass verdict for the message. For example, this partial SMTP conversation:

```
220 mail.example.com ESMTP
EHLO esa02.cisco.com
250-mail.example.com
250-8BITMIME
250-SIZE 20971520
250 STARTTLS
MAIL FROM: cporter@ironport.com
250 sender <cporter@ironport.com> ok
```

should check both the cisco.com and ironport.com DNS TXT records for SPF. If either one matches the connecting host, the SPF check passes.

SIDF goes further, providing a means of calculating the identity depending on what's specified in the DNS record. It can use the same MAIL FROM identity that SPF does, but SIDF also provides other means of defining the sender identity, controlled by the SIDF DNS text record. Table 15-2 lists the possible values.

Table 15-2 *SIDF Identity Values*

Version String	Description
v=spf2.0/mfrom	Use the MAIL FROM address as the sending domain.
v=spf2.0/mfrom,pra	Use either the MAIL FROM address or the Purported Responsible Address (PRA), calculated according to the SIDF standard.
V=spf2.0/pra	Use only the PRA as the sending domain.

SIDF defines the notion of a Purported Responsible Address (PRA) to use in the DNS queries to the sender domain. The PRA is determined by looking for the headers **Resent-Sender**, **Resent-From**, **Sender**, and **From** in that order. The header must have a single value that contains a domain name. In most messages, the PRA ends up being the visible **From** header that users see.

Another part of the SIDF protocol states that the recipient should accept and evaluate "v=spf1" records, but calculate the sender address according to the "v=spf2.0/mfrom,pra" method.

Unfortunately, the PRA of a message may differ from the MAIL FROM or HELO sender, so SPF and SIDF can have a conflicting opinion on the true sender of the message. It means that if we apply the SIDF rules to an SPF record, we can reach a failure verdict when it would pass under the original SPF specification. SIDF effectively overrides existing SPF records and forces them to be interpreted in a way that the original SPF record creator didn't intend.

Because of this unresolved incompatibility, SIDF is not currently widely adopted, and its future as a proper Internet specification is in doubt. I recommend that you consider SPF and DKIM first and foremost when considering using sender-authentication specifications.

Deploying SPF

The process of deploying SPF for your domains is fairly straightforward. Note that this process doesn't require configuration on the ESA. Because messages and addresses aren't modified by SPF, you don't need to do anything other than publish an SPF record to have your outbound mail flow be SPF verified. I'll return to ESA configuration when discussing SPF verification of senders. Publishing SPF for your domains requires these steps:

1. **Identify the legitimate sources of mail:** For any given domain, you must determine the IP addresses that are sending mail to the Internet. When in doubt, be generous in what you include. For example, if your organization owns a large network block, it's better to include the entire CIDR range for your organization if you're not sure which specific IPs do the sending. If you have third-party senders that send using your domain, you should include their IP ranges or reference their SPF record with the include mechanism.

2. **Construct the SPF record:** Use a wizard or manually build the SPF record. All records must include the SPF version in the **v** tag and at least one mechanism.

3. **Publish the SPF record:** SPF records must be in DNS as TXT records for the sending domain. For each domain, you must publish a separate record.

To help you with this task, there are several SPF wizards on the web that will create an appropriate record based on your answers to a few questions about your email environment. If you're not certain that your list of sending servers is authoritative, use the **~all** mechanism, but your ultimate goal should be a complete record and the **–all** mechanism.

Here's one last important recommendation about SPF records. If your organization owns domains that are not used for sending mail whatsoever, you can preempt their use in fraudulent messages by publishing a blank SPF record like this:

```
example.com IN  TXT     "v=spf1 -all"
```

This allows email recipients to block all messages using that sender domain.

SPF Challenges

One of the chief complaints about SPF is that the specification does not account for mail forwarders—that is, legitimate senders that resend mail on behalf of other domains. For example, a user that has a university alumnus email address, like this:

```
user@alum.example.edu
```

Email sent to this address is accepted and redelivered to another address, based on the user's preferences. If the message is delivered intact with the original envelope and body sender, the forwarding service's IPs will not pass an SPF check for those domains. Any such service that redelivers messages intact is in the position of spoofing legitimate domains as it forwards the message. Other examples of mail forwarders include mailing lists and discussion groups that forward messages intact from one sender to many recipients. If you publish SPF records, be aware that any forwarder accepting messages from one of your users won't be included and will fail the SPF check. For the forwarding services themselves, there are solutions to this problem, the simplest of which is just using a new, local, envelope sender address.

A bigger issue may just be a conflict between your organization's policies and the intent of SPF. The goal of SPF is to provide a small list of valid sending hosts for a given domain, and this may conflict with your organization's preferences for use of the domain. You may want to allow roaming senders to use their email addresses from a variety of locations, without requiring VPN or authentication. For some environments, it may simply be impossible to narrow down the possible source IPs for all senders in the domain.

Another subtle challenge with SPF is an issue with DNS in many environments. DNS is a protocol that primarily uses UDP/53 for resolving records. However, many administrators are not aware that DNS also requires TCP/53, and as a result, many email MTAs on the Internet have firewall rules preventing TCP connections on port 53, preventing DNS from using TCP. Why is this an issue with SPF? DNS clients shift from UDP to TCP when the resulting record is larger than 512 bytes, too large for UDP. Some SPF records are too large for DNS via UDP, forcing the client to switch to TCP. If your SPF record requires DNS via TCP, many sites will not be able to resolve the record due to their misconfiguration, and may reach an error or failure verdict when receiving messages. Many organizations do not realize that DNS uses TCP, so they do not allow port 53 TCP connections for DNS resolution. The results of tests in your environment, or via independent DNS testers, may show that SPF resolves correctly, but you can still have issues with some SMTP servers. The best way to avoid this is to keep your SPF records as short as possible—make use of CIDR ranges where possible.

Using SPF and SIDF Verification on ESA

With SPF and SIDF, publishing records is all in DNS, and there's nothing to configure on the ESA. However, if you want to take action on SPF results from Internet senders, you need to configure the ESA to perform the lookups and verification, and then use content filters to act on the SPF verdicts.

Start by enabling SPF/SIDF verification in the HAT for each mail flow policy in which you want to perform the tests. This setting simply performs the appropriate DNS lookups and if an SPF record is found, evaluates the conditions based on the computed sender address of the message. The verdict is stored for later use.

The option for SIDF conformance level deals with the conflict between the SPF and SIDF specifications. Remember that SIDF specifies that SPFv1 records should be treated as spf2.0/mfrom,pra, which for many domains conflicts with the SPF MAIL FROM and HELO identities. The ESA provides you with a choice of handling this. Table 15-3 describes the conformance settings. Unless you have a specific reason to change it, I recommend using the default: SIDF Compatible.

Table 15-3 *SIDF Conformance Levels on ESA*

Conformance Setting	Description
SPF Only	Forces ESA to behave according to the SPF rules only, as specified in RFC 4408. This means that the sender test uses either the MAIL FROM or the HELO domain.
SIDF Strict	Forces ESA to behave according to the SIDF rules only, as specified in RFC 4406. SPFv1 records are treated as SPF2.0/mfrom,pra. This is almost certainly not what you want, as it may result in an SPF test against a PRA.
SIDF Compatible	Behavior is according to SIDF rules specified in RFC 4406, except that SPFv1 records are treated as SPF2.0/mfrom.

Now that you have your basic SPF verification options in place in the HAT, the ESA is performing the tests and recording the verdicts. To make use of these verdicts, you must create a content filter to act on them. Table 15-4 describes the possible SPF verdicts.

Table 15-4 *SPF Verdicts*

Verdict	Description
None	The domain doesn't have an SPF record. You should not act on these messages—let them be delivered normally.
Pass	The SPF record for this domain includes this sending IP. These messages should be delivered normally.
Neutral	The sending IP matches a host mechanism with the ? prefix. These messages should be delivered normally.

Fail	The SPF record for this domain does not allow this sending IP. This is because the IP matches the -all mechanism at the end. You should drop or quarantine these messages.
SoftFail	The SPF record for this domain does not allow this sending IP, but the record specifies a soft failure for disallowed IPs. This verdict results from the IP matching a ~all mechanism at the end. You shouldn't drop these messages, but you might want to quarantine them or deliver them with a subject-line markup.
TempError	A temporary error during DNS lookup. You shouldn't act on these messages.
PermError	An unrecoverable error, like a badly formatted SPF record. You shouldn't act on these messages.

Of these, the most definitive, and the one you can freely act on to change message processing, is Fail. A failure verdict indicates that the IP is not listed among the authorized hosts for this domain, and the domain has specified that you should treat mismatches as a hard failure; in other words, it's a spoofing attempt. For example, suppose your ESA receives an inbound SMTP connection from 192.168.10.20, and the client uses a MAIL FROM of user@example.com. The SPF record looks like this:

```
example.com IN  TXT    "v=spf1 ip4:192.168.6.0/24 -all"
```

It does not include 192.168.10.20—and thus, the client fails the test. You can drop or quarantine any messages from this client that uses MAIL FROM example.com.

Figure 15-1 shows a content filter that drops messages based on the SPF failure verdict.

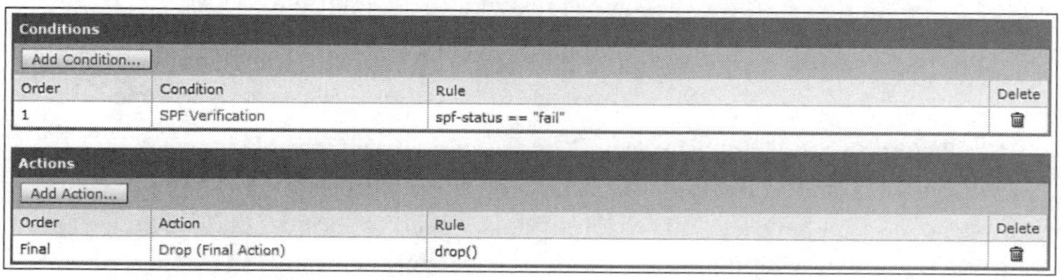

Figure 15-1 *SPF Fail Content Filter*

Figure 15-2 shows a content filter that quarantines SPF soft-failure verdicts. This is more aggressive and could potentially result in false positives, but it may stop more fraud messages.

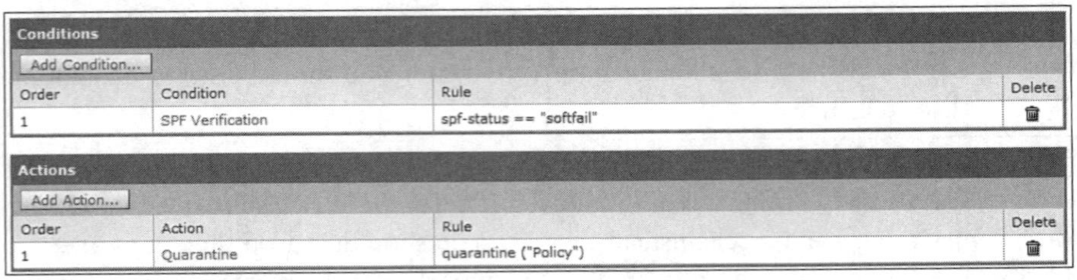

Figure 15-2 *SPF SoftFail Content Filter*

Message Authentication: DKIM

DomainKeys Identified Mail evolved from two similar standards: DomainKeys from Yahoo! and Internet Identified Mail from Cisco. The goal is to provide authentication for individual messages originating from a domain, rather than authentication for the IP source of such messages. To accomplish this, DKIM uses public-key cryptography. The sender hashes the message body and some headers and signs it with the private key known only to the sender. The signature is added to the message in the DKIM-signature header. To verify the message, the recipient performs the same hash with the same data. The recipient must retrieve the sender's public key via DNS and validates the message signature.

Because it uses public-key technology to sign a hash of message headers and body, the signature also provides proof of nonmodification—that is, a valid signature not only proves the authenticity of the source, it proves that the message hasn't been modified in transit. DKIM signatures operate on message headers and bodies, and so the signature is expected to be valid even if the message is relayed across multiple MTAs.

Unlike SPF, there's work involved on the ESA for both DKIM signing and verification.

> **Note** ESA still supports the earlier Domain Keys specification in addition to DKIM. Because Domain Keys is effectively deprecated, you should prefer DKIM over Domain Keys unless you have a good reason to do so, such as support for a legacy configuration. You can also sign messages with both technologies, but there's not any good reason to do so.
>
> If you're planning a new message authentication deployment, the choice is easy: Use DKIM and don't bother with Domain Keys.

Enabling DKIM Signing on ESA

To start DKIM signing messages on the ESA, you have to perform several steps for every local domain that you want to sign messages for. Luckily, the ESA makes this easy:

1. Create a signing key. Go to the Signing Keys page under the Mail Policies menu and add a signing key. You can either import a key or generate one directly by choosing the key size.

2. Create a domain profile. On the Domain Profiles page under the Mail Policies menu, click the Add Profile button to get started. You need to provide the domain name you're signing and the signing key. There are many other options here that are discussed later; the defaults are sensible.

3. Generate and publish the DNS TXT record. The ESA generates the appropriate record from the DKIM domain profiles page. For any valid profile, the link labeled Generate gives you the string value that should be published as a DNS TXT record for the appropriate domain. As with SPF, be careful with the size of this record, because some recipients may have problems retrieving DNS records over 512 bytes.

Of course, ensure that the DNS text record is published before signing any messages, or recipients will be unable to verify the validity of signed messages. The ESA even has a test for DKIM profiles that performs the same DNS lookup that recipients will, and you should make sure that this test passes before you start signing messages.

The DKIM-Signature Header

Before I get further into configuration of DKIM signing on the ESA, it makes sense to describe what a DKIM signature is. All the authentication information that DKIM adds is written to a single header in the message called DKIM-Signature. It includes information about the sender, DKIM version, the headers that are hashed and signed, the body length that's hashed and signed, signature and hash algorithms, and the resulting signature itself.

Here's an example signature added to a message:

```
DKIM-Signature: v=1; a=rsa-sha256; c=simple/simple; d=example.com; i=@
  example.com; q=dns/txt; s=usermail; t=1322839742; x=1354375742; h=message-
  id:from:to:subject:date:mime-version; bh=6Q3o7H71IqtCMyICTU5zF3l4XSUpTvSG6dWMW
  D71BSo=; b=lCxegm/RWwetbp3IkHsGU8kw14SDaHkmegCC6GCFaRbkyS4TwIlr2Lapajk1++bzVX9+
  pkmdSNwtIsWIFA8eZ5Gf4bWJPsGVQpHkxoUoHhl/qKkuKA/6da8qOAXHeI876oBf+/haZhimQwPEC
  3wbdSgj3aRT2fu39pjtLDOFXo8=;
```

This SMTP header includes the signature and other data in *tag=value* pairs. The tags contain enough information for the recipient to perform the same hash operation and verify the signature.

This particular signature indicates that it's signed for the domain example.com, has a selector of "usermail," and the headers message-id, from, to, subject, date, and mime-version have been included in the hash. It specified DKIM version 1, the only version supported as of this writing, and a signature algorithm of RSA and hash algorithm of 256-bit SHA.

DKIM Selectors and DNS

To validate a received message, the recipient needs three things: the message, the DKIM signature header, and the sending domain's public DKIM record. The first two—the message and the signature header—should already be present in the email message body. In fact, the trigger for DKIM verification is the presence of the DKIM-signature header itself, so the recipient won't start verifying unless that header is present. The recipient gets the public DKIM record from DNS by querying for a TXT record for a hostname of the form:

```
selector._domainkey.example.com
```

The *selector* is written into the DKIM signature by the ESA, and it's one of the options you're required to specify when creating a DKIM profile. A selector is an arbitrary string label that the recipient will retrieve from the message's DKIM signature. The recipient uses that string, prepended to the domain's DKIM namespace, when constructing the hostname for DNS lookup. Essentially, selectors allow you to use multiple DKIM profiles and key pairs for a single domain and specify which one you're using for that message.

Other DKIM Signing Options

The DKIM-signature header must include enough information for the recipient to look up the sender's public key, perform the message hash, and make the cryptographic verification, and so the ESA always includes those required pairs in the signature. You can add a number of optional tags to the signature, too. The available optional DKIM tags and their use are described in Table 15-5. ESA, by default, includes i, q, t, and x tags.

Table 15-5 *DKIM Signature Tags*

Tag	Description
i	Identity of the individual user or software sending this message. This is a standard email address, although the user part can be omitted. The domain part of this address must be the same as, or a subdomain of, the value in the d tag.
q	Query method that the recipient should use to retrieve the public key. For the current specification, only dns/txt is supported.
t	Timestamp when the signature was created. Specified in a standard UNIX format of number of seconds since Jan 1, 1970 UTC.
x	Signature expiration timestamp. This is an absolute timestamp, not relative, in the same format as the t tag.
z	Header names and values in a list separate by vertical bar (|) character. The purpose is to record the original values of the signed headers. Typically used for troubleshooting signatures and verification.

Other tags that you see in the DKIM signature, like v, c, s, h, b, and bh, are not optional and so are always added by the ESA if the message is signed. You do have some control over what is used for some of the tag values in the DKIM profile. Those other options are:

- **Canonicalization:** Controls how the recipient should treat minor message modifications that some MTAs perform, like combining whitespace or changing capitalization of headers. Simple means that the sender signed the headers as-is without modification. Relaxed means that whitespace has been folded together per the DKIM spec.

- **Headers to sign:** DKIM hashes and signs the value of a standard set of headers that includes Date, Subject, From, To, Message-ID, and MIME-version. You can add additional headers to sign, but be careful about what headers you choose; you should not pick headers, like Received, that are typically modified by MTAs as a message goes to final delivery. If you sign a header whose value changes, the recipient will reach a DKIM failure verdict.
- **Body length to sign:** There are three options in the DKIM profile: Whole Body Implied, Whole Body Auto-Determined, or Sign First *n* Bytes. The first two, obviously, hash the entire message body; the difference is whether or not later additions to the body are tolerated or not. The last option allows you to specify how much of the body to sign. The sensible default is Whole Body Implied, which makes it possible to detect modifications to any part of the message body.

In most environments, the profile defaults are adequate. Signing the entire message body has performance implications, as discussed in the next section.

DKIM Signing Performance

Because of the cryptography involved in signing messages, DKIM affects the performance of the ESA, reducing peak throughput compared to an unburdened configuration. If you're already doing heavy work on outbound mail traffic, such as antivirus, content filtering, or DLP filtering, the additional overhead for DKIM is lower by comparison, and you likely won't see any change in CPU utilization or in your peak throughput. Performance in those burdened configurations is dictated by the throughput of the scanning engines, not by DKIM signing.

You can do several things to keep DKIM signing performance high. First, shorter signing keys means higher performance. Shorter keys also mean weaker cryptography but because the purpose of DKIM is sender authentication and message hashing, and not encryption of the contents, shorter keys don't pose much of a security risk. As of this writing, 768-bit keys are still not trivial to brute force, and obtaining the key only means that the attacker can fraudulently sign messages. Aside from that, it's simple to generate new key pairs in the unlikely result of a compromised key.

Another way to keep DKIM performance high is to sign less of the message body. To do this, choose the option to sign the first *n* bytes instead of the "whole body" options, and use an appropriate value. A small value, like 1 K (1024) reduces the performance hit and makes it more predictable. You can even set this to zero, causing the ESA to sign only the headers. The tradeoff of signing only a portion of the message is in detecting message modifications; unhashed portions of the message could be modified after signature without being detectable.

DKIM Verification on ESA

Using the DKIM verification features on ESA is similar to that for SPF: Turn on the DKIM verification tests in the HAT mail flow policies and act on the verdicts in content filters.

Table 15-6 lists the available verdicts and their descriptions.

Table 15-6 *DKIM Verdicts*

Verdict	Description
Neutral	The message was not signed with DKIM so verification was not performed.
Pass	The message was signed with DKIM and the verification was successful.
TempError	Reached an error that temporarily prevented DKIM verification, like a DNS timeout.
PermError	An unrecoverable error in verifying, like a missing or malformed public key, or an unsupported value for a supplied option.
HardFail	The message contains a DKIM-signature, the ESA was able to retrieve a public key, but the verification process failed because the signature is not valid for this message.
None	DKIM verification wasn't attempted, because the HAT policy this message was accepted on has DKIM verification disabled.

DKIM Challenges

DKIM is a sophisticated specification that requires some thought both for signing and verification. Adoption is uneven but slowly growing, with many prominent webmail and broadband service providers supporting verification. There are a couple of known limitations that you should be aware of as you plan to start using it.

DKIM verification at the recipient side is triggered by the presence of the DKIM-signature header, so unsigned messages won't be verified. This means that although you may sign 100% of your outgoing mail, a fraud perpetrator can send out unsigned messages that won't go through the DKIM process at all. In other words, there's no way for you as a sender to tell recipients that all unsigned mail for the domain is fraudulent. An extension to DKIM called Author Domain Signing Practices (ADSP) is a proposal documented in RFC 5617 to allow senders to specify such rules, but as of this writing, it has not been widely adopted. More recently, a draft proposal called Domain-based Message Authentication, Reporting & Conformance (DMARC) has been created with the intention of standardizing how recipients treat both SPF and DKIM authentication and authentication failures.

Updating or changing DKIM signing keys over time can create a situation in verification of older signatures. When you change keys and alter the DNS records, messages signed with older keys can't be verified any longer. This could create a problem if you "flash cutover" to new keys with the same selector because, for a short period of time, you can have messages in the wild with the old signature but only new keys in DNS. The expiration (x) tag in the signature is designed to provide a time limit on verification. Even if expiration is ignored, it's extremely unlikely a recipient will be verifying older, stored messages, as there's no value to doing so. You can avoid this problem by changing keys and selectors so that the older signatures can still be verified. After a short period, certainly within a week, you can retire the old keys and selectors. That allows enough time for any message stuck in queues anywhere to be delivered and verified or dropped.

DKIM and SPF Recommendations

When deciding to go ahead with either one or both authentication standards, the best place to start is examining and documenting your email environment. For SPF especially, you need to know all the valid IP sources of mail for your domain. If you use the recommended "First hop in, last hop out" architecture with the ESAs, preventing any other internal hosts from being an SMTP source, you're in great shape. Be aware, however, that many organizations use external providers to send mail "on behalf of," and you may not even be aware of this traffic. It's easy enough to allow an external sender to use your domain, as long as you know about it. For SPF, your DNS TXT record needs to cover all the valid source hosts. For DKIM, that's less important because you can use selectors, and not necessarily have to sign all your outgoing mail, but it's still important to be aware of the valid sources.

For the path authentication standards, SPF enjoys much wider adoption than SIDF. At the time of this writing, it seems unlikely that the SIDF standard will ever reach a critical mass. You should focus solely on SPF instead.

SPF host mechanism rules other than the IP address ranges require the receiver to perform additional DNS queries. In the case of **ptr** and **mx** mechanisms, multiple DNS queries are required. Each DNS lookup increases the time and effort for the recipient to validate, and increases the chance of encountering a DNS timeout or lookup error. You should prefer **ip4** and **ip6** mechanisms as a rule, then, or at least you should order your SPF record to put IP ranges first so that clients can optimize their lookups—remember that, with SPF, first match wins. In other words, this record:

```
"v=spf1 a mx ip4:192.168.6.0/24 -all"
```

is slightly better expressed as:

```
"v=spf1 ip4:192.168.6.0/24 a mx -all"
```

But even better is eliminating the a and mx mechanisms in favor of IP:

```
"v=spf1 ip4:192.168.6.0/24 ip4:172.19.0.0/16 -all"
```

This, of course, may have its drawbacks in terms of maintenance should your IP ranges change.

Signing with DKIM comes with a number of recommendations. First, if you're signing on multiple ESAs for the same domain and selector, make sure all the outbound gateways have the same signing keys and profile configuration. Create the keys on one and import them into the other. You can use the same key for different profiles, and hence for different domains, but you still need to publish the DNS TXT record once for each selector/domain combination.

DKIM selectors are flexible enough to be used for a variety of purposes. You can create separate selectors for different classes of email: user-to-user versus application generated, for example. You can also use them to sign a portion of traffic, allowing you to adopt DKIM on a step-by-step basis.

Regulatory Compliance

Regulatory compliance that affects IT organizations is a large and involved topic that encompasses many different protocols and processes. Some compliance rules are specified and enforced by private parties or industry groups through contracts and others by public legislation. Some email compliance rules are defined by your own organization. Some are precise in their requirements for prevention and remediation, and some are maddeningly nebulous. Organizations must have a complete strategy for regulatory compliance that involves access control, secure storage, and leak detection. Such a complete strategy is beyond the scope of this book. It would be incorrect to suggest that a single policy engine on the ESA would suddenly make an organization compliant, or even that email should be your sole area of concern. However, the ESA can be a key component in a compliance strategy, because of the prominence of email as a communication medium.

The ESA provides features to help customers meet regulatory compliance and intellectual property protection through the integration of a scanning and policy engine from RSA Data Security. Like other third-party products on the platform, the engine is thoroughly integrated into the ESA pipeline and its configuration is through the familiar ESA WUI and CLI. DLP is a separately licensed feature that requires an active license key.

I examine the DLP policies and features on the appliance later in this chapter. Before that, I want to cover some of the concepts and terms that will be used throughout.

General Concepts

Many different kinds of regulatory and industry compliance operate on common information entities that can be encountered in email messages and their attachments. Some of these are not precisely defined by legislation or industry, while others have specific definitions. The ESA's DLP policies are specifically designed to search for these entities, using matching rules called *classifiers*. There are built-in classifiers for a large number of information entities, and you can create your own. Classifiers are grouped together in policies.

The requirements that affect email boil down to two components: identify information that should not be transmitted in email by persons not authorized to do so, and taking action on non-compliant messages to stop their transmission or to make it compliant.

Personally Identifiable Information (PII)

PII is one of the more nebulous terms in regulatory compliance. It can be interpreted as any set of data that can be used to identify a particular individual.

The focus of most PII discussions tends to be identifying numbers: unique identification numbers on government documentation like driver's licenses, passports, and social insurance cards. In the U.S., the familiar nine-digit Social Security Number (SSN) is of chief concern. But, other data falls into this category: unique patient identifiers in healthcare, banking account numbers, even phone numbers and street addresses. In essence, if I can read an email and identify an individual person from its contents, it contains personally identifiable information. To be personally identifiable, a number must somehow be associated with other data—a passport number by itself doesn't identify a person, but in conjunction with a personal name, phone number, and a street address, it does.

The ESA's data classification includes honoring the rules for particular identifying numbers. Passport numbers in most countries have a fixed number of digits. Not all area and group digits in U.S. SSNs are valid. Many ID numbers have a checksum or check digit to confirm their validity.

Payment Card Data

Payment card refers to credit, debit, prepaid, and ATM cards used by consumers and businesses. The data is not necessarily just card numbers, but also related cardholder information.

Protecting this information to reduce fraud is the purpose of the Payment Card Industry Data Security Standard (PCI-DSS), and discussion of payment card data is usually under the context of compliance with this standard. Organizations that store, process, and transmit this data are required to take steps to secure the data. If the path of transmission is the ESA, you can use it to recognize and act on messages that contain payment card information.

Finding payment card numbers in email messages requires more depth than can be accomplished with regular expression searches. Most payment card numbers have a fixed length of digits and may or may not have delimiters, but they also require some additional verification such as a checksum. The ESA DLP features perform the appropriate checksum for all the classifiers it uses, whenever appropriate.

Personal Financial Information

Regulations and legislation focusing on financial transactions define the entities that are used in banking and investment accounts. These identification numbers may have an industry standard format or be dictated by legislation, depending on jurisdiction, or may be defined only by an individual organization. If your organization handles personal financial information specific to your organization, you have to define your own classifiers in addition to the industry-standard ones.

Common entities in this category include American Bankers Association (ABA) routing numbers, used to identify individual banking organizations in the U.S., Society for Worldwide Interbank Financial Telecommunication (SWIFT) codes for similar purpose in other countries, and Committee on Uniform Security Identification Procedures (CUSIP) codes, which identify financial securities in North America.

Mitigation

Most regulations and industry standards have rules for handling sensitive data. Some information cannot be transmitted at all. The ESA allows you to send the message back to the user, notify someone else in the organization, or hold it in quarantine for manual review.

Most regulations allow for the transmission of data between business entities or between business and consumers if that information is encrypted in transit. The ESA allows you to choose encryption actions for DLP violations, namely TLS encryption for SMTP connections and Envelope encryption for message bodies, or both.

Data Loss Prevention (DLP)

The topics of Regulatory Compliance and Data Loss Prevention (DLP) often go hand-in-hand, but your organization may have the need to examine email messages for reasons other than compliance. DLP is often used to enforce business confidentiality and protect intellectual property. Sometimes, DLP is as simple as enforcing encryption or preventing email traffic between certain individuals.

The ESA's DLP technology is licensed from RSA, the security division of EMC, a recognized leader in the market. The RSA DLP engine provides both the scanning technology that examines the messages, and the predefined matching rules and policies that define violations. You can use the built-in policies with or without customizations, or you can build your own custom policies that make use of the predefined data entities that RSA defines.

As a strategy, DLP excels at helping organizations discover business processes that routinely violate regulations or company policy. For example, DLP can easily detect an ecommerce application that sends automated receipts to purchasers that includes their payment card information. It can uncover users that are mishandling data due to lack of training or simple carelessness. It's less suited to discover deliberate information breaches by determined individuals, but it can still trip up users' intent on distributing sensitive data.

Enabling Data Loss Prevention Policies

Creating and applying DLP policies to email messages requires the same steps that the other ESA filtering engines require:

1. **Enable DLP globally:** The engine and global options are controlled on the RSA Email DLP page of the Security Service menu. You must have a valid license key to enable the engine.

2. **Add and customize DLP policies:** The RSA Email DLP engine ships with more than 100 predefined policies for regulatory and industry compliance, and you can create your own custom policies. This "library" of policies can be managed in the DLP Policy Manager page of the Mail Policies menu.

3. **Apply one or more DLP policies to the outgoing mail policies:** DLP policies aren't active until you add them to one or more of your outgoing mail policies, just as you do with content filters. By tying policies to LDAP in outgoing mail policies, you can achieve per-user or per-group DLP.

Note that DLP is only part of the outgoing mail policies as of AsyncOS 7.5 and can only be applied to outgoing mail.

Adding a DLP Policy

All DLP policies start by clicking the Add DLP Policy... button in the WUI DLP Policy Manager page on the Mail Policies Menu. All new policies start from one of the predefined templates. If you want to start from scratch with a blank policy, choose Custom Policy at the bottom of the list. Custom policies are targeted for users who know the kind of data they're searching for.

How should you choose which of the other policy templates to start from? If you're configuring the ESA because of a particular regulation or industry security standard, clearly you should start with the relevant predefined template. Even if you're not subject to a particular regulation, or in a jurisdiction not governed by specific rules, these policies cover common data entities and make a good start. For jurisdictions and industries that haven't yet adopted such rules, it's likely that when they do, they will follow the established pattern of existing regulations. If you have a general need to identify a particular entity—like U.S. SSNs or credit card numbers—independent of any particular regulation, start with one of the policies in the Privacy Protection category. As a last resort, if you need to match multiple IDs, or data that's not otherwise covered, or if you want the most flexibility in tuning, choose the Custom Policy option.

Once you choose a policy template, the customization and actions page comes up. At a minimum, you must define the action to take on critical violations to submit the page, although you can simply accept the default action of Deliver, which records the violation but does not act on the messages.

Taking Action on Matching Messages

The policy actions for messages that trigger a match are grouped under the heading Severity Settings in the WUI page for each policy. This marks a major difference between DLP and ESA content filters: A DLP policy match always includes a severity score that represents the likelihood that this message violates the rules. The severity takes into account the type of content that matches as well as the number of matches. A standalone nine-digit number may receive a low severity score in a HIPAA policy, while a list of U.S. SSNs and street addresses receive a higher severity. Some individual entities score a higher severity than others: An individual credit card number might score 10 points while an expiration date only scores 2.

After the message is examined by a policy, its total numeric score is compared against the severity scale for that policy to determine the severity category. Each category then defines an action that can be taken on the messages. The severity categories are critical, high, medium, and low, and the score ranges for each category are set at the bottom of the page. Every severity category "inherits" the action of the category above it, unless you override that inheritance by configuring a different action at other levels. Using this, you can, for example, specify that medium, high, and critical violations be quarantined while low violations be delivered with encryption.

The actions that you can use for DLP violations are similar to those of content filters:

- **Deliver:** The message continues to delivery, with or without modifications. The match and the severity are recorded for reporting and tracking. You can choose to encrypt the message, either with TLS or envelope encryption.
- **Quarantine:** This stops processing of the message and sends it to the specified local system quarantine. Administrative users or designated guest accounts can review, release, or delete the message per the available quarantine controls. No access is provided to end users; this option is intended to allow an administrator or policy officer the chance to review a message for violations.
- **Drop:** The message is immediately discarded. There are no configurable options, but you can use notifications under the advanced options.

In addition to the three basic verdicts, there are three advanced options under each of the main verdicts:

- **Modify the message:** Change the subject, add a header, or add disclaimer text above or below the message body. Messages using the Drop action cannot be modified.
- **Modify the delivery:** Alter the destination host or send a blind carbon-copy (BCC) to another email address. If you use BCC, the original message continues delivery to the original recipients. Messages using the Drop action cannot be modified.
- **Send a notification:** Sends a new message to sender or specified recipients, notifying them of the violation. You can either use the predefined standard notification or create your own in the Text Resources page of the Mail Policies menu. You can also include the original message as an attachment. Notifications are good for training users on appropriate content by sending them their messages back. Notifications can be used in conjunction with the Drop action.

There is an important difference between content filter and DLP actions. When any DLP action is taken because of a match on that policy, the message does not continue to further DLP policies; that is, there can be at most only one matching DLP policy for a given message. Messages are scanned by DLP in a top-down order, but exit that scanning on the first match. For example, suppose a configuration that applies both PCI-DSS and a PII policy, in that order. A message that contains both credit card information and U.S. SSNs will be flagged by the PCI policy and will not be examined by the PII policy, even if your action is set to Deliver.

In the category score ranges, you'll see a category called Ignore that by default covers score ranges of 0–9. This isn't really a severity category at all; messages that fall into this score range are not considered a match, do not have any action applied, and continue to the next DLP policy in the list.

Classifiers and Entities

It's worth reviewing the concept of classifiers before we see examples on how to use them. Classifiers are the bits of logic that attempt to identify a specific piece of data. There are a large number of built-in classifiers supplied with the DLP engine, and you can create your own. The built-in classifiers are each given a fairly self-explanatory name and can be categorized by the methods they use:

- **Numeric calculations:** These classifiers recognize patterns of digits and can perform an arithmetic operation, like a checksum. The classifier may only define particular ranges of numbers as valid. Payment card numbers, some national identification numbers, health insurance numbers, and bank account numbers are defined in this way.
- **Dictionaries:** Lists of words, phrases, and regular expressions that define the entity in question. Predefined dictionaries include those for corporate financials, academic degrees, disease and injury terms, and drug and compound names. You can define custom dictionaries to be used exclusively for DLP policies.
- **Proximity matches:** Multiple simple terms can be considered a match if they occur "close" to each other in the message. For example, the word "expiration" might not trigger a match, but if it's near the word "card," the message may refer to the expiration date of a credit card.
- **Weighting and scoring:** Each individual term or classifier can have a numeric score associated with it, and a total score calculated from all of the terms encountered. The total score is compared to a threshold value to determine a match, in the same way that the ESA weighted dictionaries and thresholds work.

The predefined policies are built by combining one or more of the supplied classifiers, and you can see the classifiers in use by a particular policy in its customization page. For example, the policy for Sarbanes-Oxley (SOX) uses the classifier "Corporate Financials" and PCI-DSS uses "Credit Card Track Data" or "Credit Card Number" classifiers.

Custom Classifiers

You can only create and use your own classifiers by starting with a custom DLP policy. The Settings page for a custom policy allows you to select one or more classifiers to include in the policy. You have access to all the built-in classifiers that RSA provides. In the drop-down box, select either a built-in classifier or Create a Classifier and click the Add... button. Continue to select and add classifiers as needed.

When you add multiple classifiers, you combine them with Boolean operators AND (all classifiers must match) or OR (any classifier can match), with the Boolean NOT available to invert a given classifier. You can use the NOT rule to negate matches in order to reduce false positives.

If you choose the Create a Classifier option, the ESA displays the custom classifier page. To create a custom classifier, you need to give it a name and define the rules for the classifier. You can only use the custom classifier in the DLP policy where you created it. An example of a custom classifier is shown in Figure 15-3.

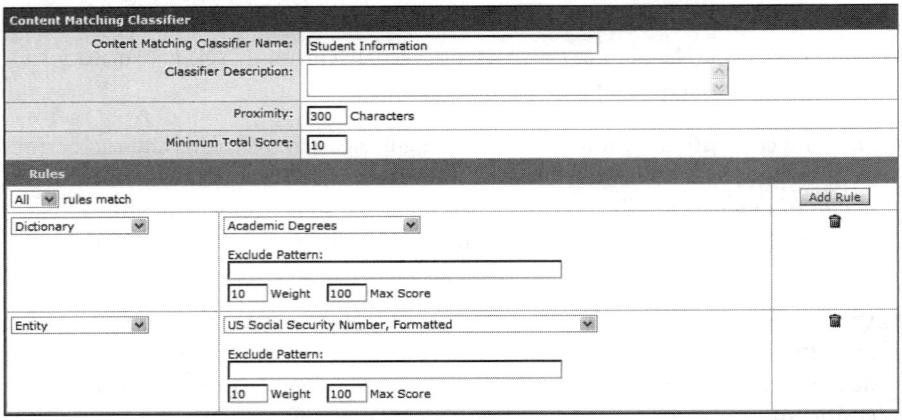

Figure 15-3 *Custom Classifier Based on a Predefined Dictionary and Entity*

To use a dictionary in a custom classifier, that dictionary needs to exist before you create the classifier. Local custom dictionaries are created in the main page of the DLP policy manager, and not in the ESA dictionaries page. These dictionaries are strictly for DLP use only and aren't stored or managed like the ones used in content filters.

Let's look at an example for an organization that needs to protect sensitive payment data when processing orders. We could use the PCI-DSS policy for detecting payment card information, but that policy can't be customized with specific order-related terms. Starting with a custom policy, we can use the built-in credit card classifiers and combine them with a custom classifier for order information.

Let's start with that custom classifier for order information. The organization uses a specific alphanumeric format for order numbers, with four digits for the year of the order, a two-letter code for the country the order was placed in, and a 6-digit ID number, all separated with dashes. As an example, the string "2010-AU-001454" might be an order number.

Creating classifiers to match specific data can be more art than science. A regular expression can easily match our order string format, and we can certainly create a classifier that matches just that regex. To avoid false positives, it makes sense to combine that regular expression with words or phrases that tie it to orders. Matching alphanumeric strings in a vacuum without other corroborating data often ends up with too many violations, forcing manual review of messages.

Here are a few recommendations when creating custom classifiers:

- **Be as specific as possible:** Regular expressions should include length and format qualifiers, if possible. Prefer phrases like "Purchase Order" or "Place an Order" over individual generic words like "order."
- **Don't reinvent the wheel:** Use the built-in classifiers and entities wherever possible. These are tuned from the factory to match without false positives.
- **Don't put too many rules in a single classifier:** All the scores from all the rule matches add up to a single total score for the classifier. Lots of rules mean lots of matches, making it difficult to troubleshoot which rules are causing false positives.

In this case, we combine a few phrases with the regex for order numbers. Because the regex for order numbers is specific, it's weighted at 10, while the phrases have a weight of just 2. We'll leave the proximity settings to 300 characters.

The final custom classifier rules are shown in Figure 15-4.

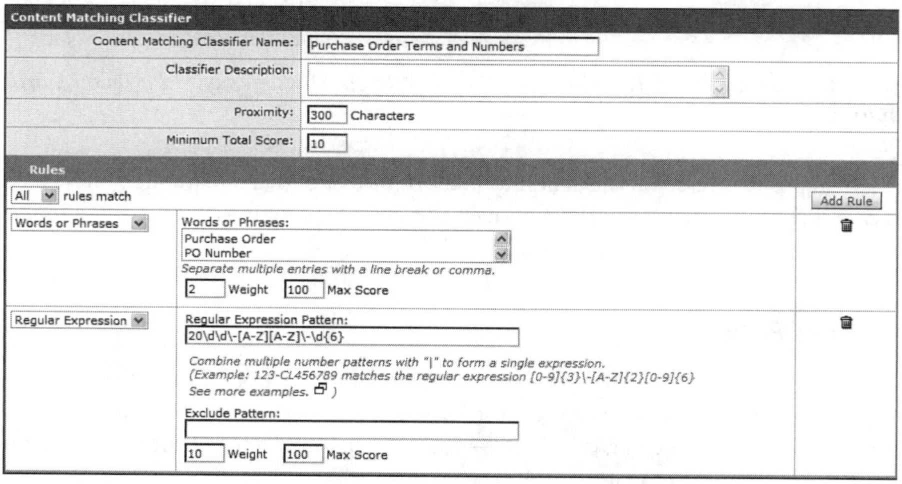

Figure 15-4 *Custom Classifier for Order Information*

Finally, we'll add a built-in classifier for credit card numbers to the policy, and require that both match before considering the message to be a violation. Using the built-in classifier for credit cards is preferable because it matches the number pattern and the digit checksum that defines payment card numbers; using a custom regular expression will not compute the checksum.

The final classifier configuration for this policy is shown in Figure 15-5.

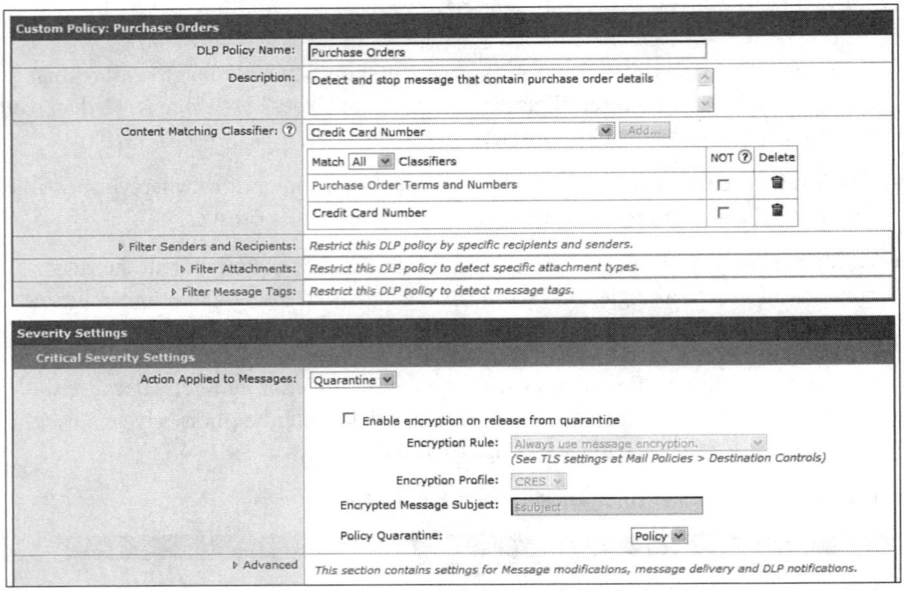

Figure 15-5 *Custom Policy for Matching Order-Related Messages with Payment Card Information*

The last step is to decide on the action to take for messages that violate the policy. In this case, I chose to quarantine the messages, but any of the actions previously described are available.

Customizing Policies

Some of the built-in policies recommend or require customization of matching rules before you use them, and are marked Customization Recommended. Truly custom policies have no content matching rules at all—you must define them and the combinatorial logic that contributes to a match.

Customizing Content Matching on Predefined Policies

The policies that require or recommend additional matching rules accept regular expression matches. The regular expressions define other identifiers that you want to consider part of a DLP match. For example, in healthcare environments covered by the HIPAA regulation, patients are often identified by a number or string that varies depending on the treatment facility or the patient's insurer. Because such an identifier is specific to an organization but critical to accurate matches, you must define these or risk a very high number of false positives.

If you want to use your custom classifiers, you must start from a blank Custom Policy. You cannot add built-in or custom classifiers to any of the other standard predefined policies.

Customizing User and Attachment Rules

Every policy allows you to restrict which senders, recipients, and attachment types that it applies to. Sender and recipient restrictions are pretty straightforward: Just add the email addresses to the relevant text box and choose whether it's an inclusion or exclusion.

For example, if you know that Alice and Bob in Human Resources are authorized to transmit PII outside of your organization, add their email addresses to the sender list and choose Is Not from the drop-down. You're restricted to full or partial email addresses; LDAP lookups are not supported. Figure 15-6 shows an example.

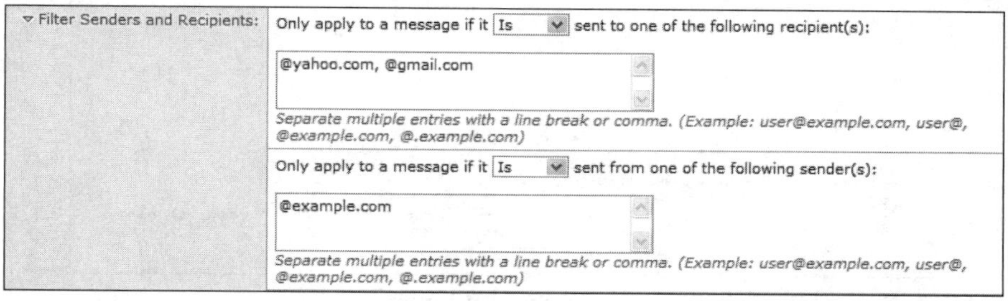

Figure 15-6 *Exclusions Based on Sender or Recipient Address*

Applying restrictions to senders or recipients in this way somewhat duplicates the capabilities of outgoing mail policies. Normally, if you have a need to apply DLP policies to particular groups of senders and recipients, you would do so by creating an outgoing mail policy with the appropriate membership, and then select the right DLP policies. I prefer this approach because it's consistent with all the other policy configurations, and it's easy to see everything in one place on the outgoing mail policies page.

Further, if your DLP policies are tied to LDAP group information, you must use outgoing mail policies to define your group because the DLP sender or recipient restrictions can't use LDAP lookups.

So, why is this feature here? For cases where you need to apply or exclude a policy based on both sender and recipient. For example, suppose you need to examine all messages coming from your HR department for PII, except when being transmitted to your company's health insurance provider. You can certainly create an outgoing mail policy for your HR department by tying it to LDAP group membership. To meet the second requirement, you need to use the DLP recipient exclusion for the health insurance company's email domain.

For attachments, you can specify individual attachment types or categories from a built-in list in the drop-down box. These are file types covered by the ESA's attachment fingerprinting and can be recognized even if the attachment extension is changed or the file is archived or compressed. For any file types that aren't defined by fingerprint, you can enter additional file extensions.

The other two options aren't often called for, but they can be useful in eliminating false positives if the DLP engine is incorrectly classifying some messages. Attachments that don't meet the minimum size that you enter aren't examined. The other option excludes encrypted or password protected attachment types.

Figure 15-7 shows an example of attachment exclusions using both built-in and custom defined types.

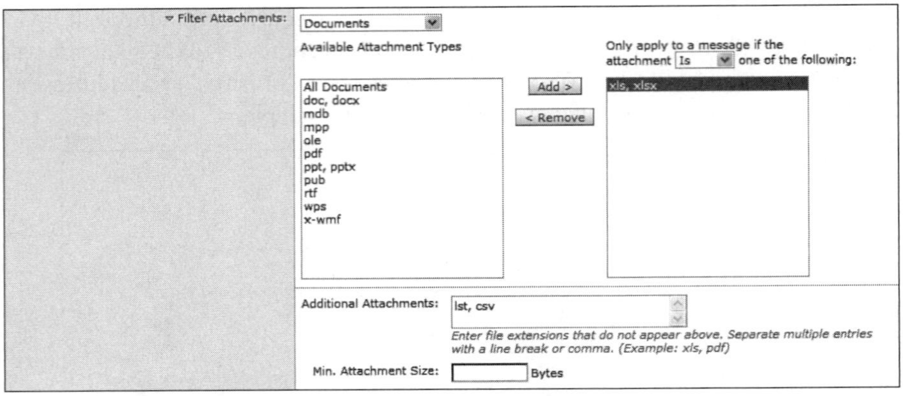

Figure 15-7 *Exclusions Based on File Types and Extensions*

You cannot restrict attachments by other conditions, like any of their text content, MIME type, or even by complete filenames. For more advanced attachment rules, you may need to use a content filter with your DLP policy, discussed in the next section.

Integration with Content Filters

If the built-in DLP policy restrictions don't meet all of your filtering requirements on their own, you can use the results of content filters with *message tags*. A message tag is a markup on the message that can be acted on in DLP policies to include or exclude messages based on the result of a content filter. The markup is internal to the ESA and invisible to the end users; it's just a variable added to the ESA data structure that stores the message.

Message tags are flexible because content filters are flexible and the Add Message Tag action can be added to any filter. The value for a message tag is an arbitrary string. Once added, you can configure the DLP policy to act on its presence or absence.

Some examples of requirements that can be met with message tags are

- **Excluding particular filenames from DLP policies:** If your policy is consistently flagging a spreadsheet named PriceQuote.xls or a document named PressRelease.pdf, but it's clear they don't violate policy, create a content filter to match the filename and add a message tag.
- **Providing a means of bypassing DLP restrictions:** If your organization's rules allow it, a filter can be used to look for text in the message that triggers the bypass. For example, messages that include a text disclaimer from the sender, like "contains confidential account information," might bypass your policy on disclosing account information.

- **Multicondition bypass rules:** Because content filters can combine multiple conditions, you can easily bypass DLP for messages with a particular subject and attachment, for example. For example, if your rules allow the message with "Account Statement" and attachment "statement.pdf" to be exempt from confidential information scanning, create a content filter to act on those two conditions and create a message tag.
- **LDAP-based lookup:** Content filters can use recipient and sender LDAP group checks that aren't available in DLP. These results can be written into message tags for exclusions from DLP scanning.
- **Include or exclude messages based on Subject or other header:** If particular subject keywords should be used to force a scan, or skip the scan, you must create a content filter to add a message tag for this. The DLP engine does examine the Subject in making its determination, but only in the larger message context, not as a means of bypassing the policy.

Figure 15-8 shows an example of a content filter using the message tag action.

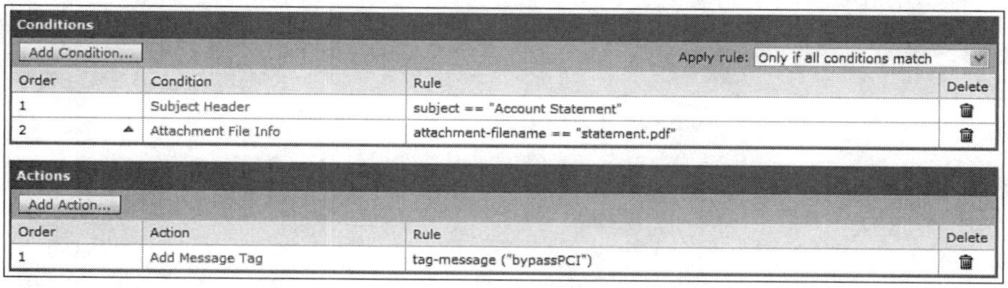

Figure 15-8 *Content Filter with Message Tag Action*

Summary

Email is one of the oldest protocols on the Internet, but being old doesn't mean that it can't learn new tricks. Because of its popularity as a communication medium, it's popular for fraudulent abusers who stand to gain from exploiting individual's trust of domains and websites they know. SMTP doesn't specifically address the authenticity of senders, but recent proposals, like SPF and DKIM, attempt to rectify that. We discussed how SPF and DKIM works, what you need to do to use the standards, and how the ESA fits into an authentication strategy.

Another challenge with email that stems from its ease is that it's easy to mistakenly or deliberately expose confidential information. Good business practice dictates keeping intellectual property and confidential data from being disclosed. Industry groups have created standards for handling financial information. Legislators and regulators in many jurisdictions have crafted laws to prevent the disclosure of private personal and financial data. This chapter showed how to configure DLP policies on the ESA to detect and act on potential regulatory and disclosure policy violations and how to enforce the use of encryption when sensitive information must be sent outside of your organization.

Index

Symbols

A

B

C

D

E

F

G

H

I

J-K-L

M

N

S

T

U

V

W

X-Y-Z

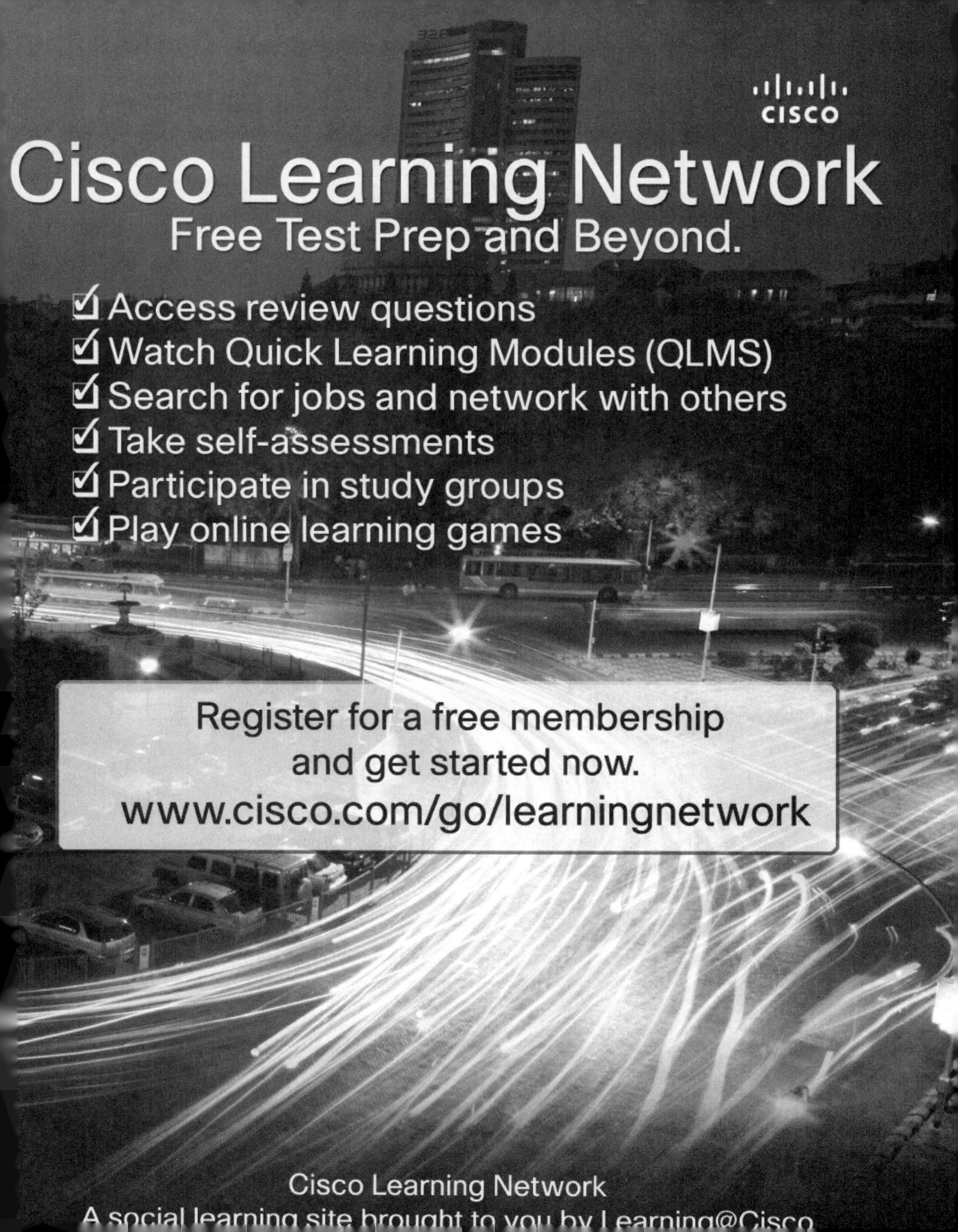
cisco
Cisco Learning Network
Free Test Prep and Beyond.
Access review questions
Watch Quick Learning Modules (QLMS)
Search for jobs and network with others
Take self-assessments
Participate in study groups
Play online learning games
Register for a free membership
and get started now.
www.cisco.com/go/learningnetwork
Cisco Learning Network
A social learning site brought to you by Learning@Cisco